With Love, Edith

Also by Edith Schaeffer

AFFLICTION

CHRISTIANITY IS JEWISH

COMMONSENSE CHRISTIAN LIVING

EVERYBODY CAN KNOW

FOREVER MUSIC

HIDDEN ART

L'ABRI

LIFELINES

THE TAPESTRY

A WAY OF SEEING

WHAT IS A FAMILY?

With Love, Edith

THE L'ABRI FAMILY LETTERS
1948–1960

Edith Schaeffer

A Ruth Graham Dienert Book

1817

HARPER & ROW, PUBLISHERS, SAN FRANCISCO

Cambridge, Hagerstown, New York, Philadelphia, Washington
London, Mexico City, São Paulo, Singapore, Sydney

Library of Congress Cataloging-in-Publication Data
Schaeffer, Edith.
  With Love, Edith.

  "A Ruth Graham Dienert book."
  Contents: v. 1. 1948-1960.
  1. Schaeffer, Edith—Correspondence. 2. Schaeffer, Edith—Family. 3. L'Abri (Organization) 4. Christian life. 5. Christian biography. 6. Schaeffer family.
I. Title.
BR1725.S354A4   1988   267'.13'0924 [B]   87-45722
ISBN 0-06-067092-4 (v. 1)

FIRST EDITION

88   89   90   91   92   HC   10   9   8   7   6   5   4   3   2   1

TO THE ONES I LOVE,

and to whom I wrote these letters—
my mother and father, for whom I wrote in the first place,
my sisters Elsa and Janet, my cousin Marion, and cousin Vida . . .
and so many dear friends who faithfully read and actively prayed—
in New Wilmington, Chester, St. Louis, Grove City. . . .

Letters are a link,
a continuity in life that help to hold together
the writer and the ones on the receiving end.

My loving dedication
is to all those who responded eagerly
and inspired my eager desire to close the gap
made my oceans and mountains—
bringing a "togetherness" with a reality greater
than that which can exist in the midst
of geographic closeness.

Thank you mother
for writing to tell me that I was not to feel bad
about being so far away for so long,
as these letters made you feel as if you were with me,
"seeing" things as we lived through them.
That was my greatest comfort when you died—
after not seeing you for six years.

CONTENTS

FOREWORD

A Letter to You from the Author

Dear Reader:

It's 1987 now, though the first letter in this book was written in 1948. Add thirty-nine years to your life—and what do *you* get? History is fascinating in so many ways, but when you overlap personal history with what is going on in the world at the same time, and keep some record of your feelings and ideas, your worldview and spiritual growth, your reactions and hopes, your longings and desires, your expectations and disappointments, your happy surprises and tragic shocks, your illnesses and glorious energy, your sunshine and storms, your surprises of joy and tears of sorrow, your love of some *one* . . . and your frustration and dislike of someone, your overflowing love for family and your uncomfortable dislike and unhappiness about the same people at another time—then what you come up with is *life* recorded as it is being lived, moment by moment, and *not* after you have had time to think about it and sort things out.

This is a book full of letters—letters written to my personal family, then copied for a few friends by my mother, then later multiplied for a few more. As time went on, and life and changes continued, the letters became known as "the L'Abri Family Letters."

To put *all* of *all* these letters into books would bring forth about 4,000 pages! Understandably, the publishers didn't want that many pages, and you would find it hard to have time to read that much!

If you were in Switzerland or Holland or England during some of the time covered in the letters, and you were in our home, or with us somewhere in Cambridge or London, or Leiden in Holland, or Huemoz or Lausanne, or Milan in Italy, or Norway and Sweden, and your name is *not* mentioned, *please* consider what has taken place. The problem is that *more than three-fourths* of the letters have been cut, as Elsa Van Buskirk (my sister) and Mary Lou Sather (a friend here in Rochester) read with a pencil poised to slash out paragraphs and pages, amputating letter after letter with surgical precision; they had to cut out more than three-quarters of the history of what was going on, and of the stories of people, as well as much of the flow of history and the incredible diversity of individuals in that history. As all three of us have talked over what has been covered in these letters (which with the second volume will cover thirty-eight years), we have felt frustrated and even saddened by what has had to be "cut" or "omitted." However, that which has been included is not just a jumble of isolated sentences, mathematically stuck together—but is that which gives the flavor of life, the flavor of family life, births, deaths, the kind of change and growth that take place during the years a two-year-old becomes a thirty-two-year-old, or an eleven-year-old approaches fifty.

When I started to write, I myself was thirty-four years old, a young mother with three little girls, not to have her son for another four years! I have recorded the months and happenings—not only the "birth of L'Abri" and all that preceded it, but the growth of a family and the overlapping of generations that takes place as life goes on. The children were to become aunts and an uncle, then parents themselves. I have been writing as a mother of a growing family—then as a grandmother, and in the last two years as a great-grandmother!

Time—and *space*—what a mystery! Personality, individual creativity, significance of human beings in a significant history—how important to realize how precious these facts are, in time.

What is a good length for life? When do creative ideas stop coming? When is there nothing left to discover? When is there no new thing to do? How long is "long enough"? When is a person a person? The "dignity of human life" is not a subject to discuss; it is an understanding to be *lived*— it is a life to be understood.

The difference between reading these letters and theorizing about life or discussing life is that there is a plunging into a bit of history itself to which you can relate, a flowing, changing history down-to-earth in detail. What is expressed in the letters was written to members of my personal family—across thousands of miles of ocean and land. The letters went to be pounced upon and read as if the writer were in the room talking. The sentences have been left *as they were written*. The older me has not edited the younger me; I have not changed things to express them as I would now. There is growth evident not only in children, but in Fran and myself as years went on. People are not pieces of sculpture that do not change with study, and with spiritual and intellectual growth and understanding. What has been written shows a family growing, changing, being real and not plastic at different periods of history. Although much (pages and pages) has been cut out, what is here are paragraphs that are untouched.

The fascinating thing to me is that what is contained here was written over a period of all the years—but each letter was written in the context of the moment during which it was written, without the knowledge of what was coming next. They were not written as a biography, with reference to what happened later, but written with the reactions, the feelings, the responses of people, places, events as they were at the time, with the future covered in fog! You may turn a page and read the next letter, but when I signed one "with love, Edith" it was without any knowledge of what would be in the next letter, because the content of the next one had not been *lived* yet. True future is always in a fog— yours, and mine. It is why God has told us clearly that if we state an expectation of what we will do tomorrow, or next week, or next month, we should always say, "God willing, I will do thus and so, or go to this place or that."

God alone is able to write precisely what He wants us to know about the future; the rest He keeps behind the fog. He has condensed His verbalized truth to us, giving as much as He means us to have in prophecy as well as in history. Our condensation of the many pages of letters is not perfect, simply because perfection is not a part of the possibility of human judgment. However, it will give you a possibility of forgetting the hubbub of your city, or the crickets' noise after dark in the country, and perhaps it will even help you forget the wave of problems that threaten to engulf you at this time—as you walk through the years with me, beginning as we arrive in Holland in 1948!

With much love,

EDITH

1948

August 5, 1948   Scheveningen, Netherlands

Dearest Family:

It doesn't seem possible we have been here 5 nights already. I've lost all track of time. I hope the cable arrived safely and that Mrs. S. telephoned you. I mailed a letter on the boat in the nick of time to go with the Southampton mail—it was the only letter I wrote on the boat. The "hours of leisure" were not quite as I imagined them. With three children there is always something. However they were (the children) *very good*—the whole second class were remarking on their good behavior at meals, etc. Even Deborah was *quite* independent, knew her way around all those complicated halls, and knew the various decks and how to get elevator rides, etc. Susan's illness really was the thing that ate up time— meant one of us needed to be in the cabin all the time. Harlee Bordeaux stayed with her at mealtime (he had second sitting) and the last dinner our Steward brought two meals and *he* stayed and ate with her!!

In spite of everything I enjoyed every minute of the boat trip and felt I'd be quite content to go on for a month. *Plenty* of everything one needed, either sick or well—*hot* water, Kleenex, ginger ale, oranges, broth— fabulous meals—all wonderful. To try to go on where I left off—we finally docked in the Southampton Harbor about 1 A.M. Fran and Harlee and I were on deck (no class distinction, from that night on everyone had the run of the boat—so first-class deck was perfect place to *see* from)—from about 10:30 P.M. on. It was *most* interesting to see the big boats and tugs and watch all the maneuvers of being pulled and pushed in. Our only sight of England was the harbor and the dock and a few English Bobbies and a variety of men standing around. We meant to be up in the morning to see it all by daylight—but our awakening moments brought the realization we had missed it—our boat was moving. Fran of course was in the next cabin. The girls awakened me with, "Oh there's a boat." "Of course," I said, "we're in Southampton Harbor, you'll see lots

Here we are just before leaving St. Louis.
Front row: Edith, Debby; Back: Susan, Priscilla, Fran.

of boats." "Oh *no* mother—we're way far away—see?" I drew myself up to a standing position on my bunk and peered out of the porthole. We were on our way—green shores were swiftly moving by—*and*—"Why there's a *castle*," grey stone with turrets and green lawns down to the water's edge. That was my last sight of England—wherever it was!! A quick shower, everyone dressed for breakfast, an order for Susan— breakfast over—and we were out of sight of land!!

This was Friday—Susan's temp. 101°—and our bags to be repacked by 5 P.M.—also lines to be stood in to receive landing cards, to have passports checked on, and to "fill in" customs declaration papers. "No cigarettes! No tobacco?" Great amazement. At 3:30 I dashed up on the "upper prom deck" for a quick look at "Le Havre" harbor and the "oil painting" view of the cliff-like coast of France—all white, cream, and buff colored, dipping into the blue water. Fran wrapped up Susan and let her see it for a few minutes and I went on to finish that which only I could do—repacking. By 5 o'clock it was all ready for the Steward. Our last dinner on the boat—what should we choose—the roast beef or goose—the lamb chops or pork? The Steward ate with Susan and she went to sleep in the middle of her dessert! Debby was soon in bed too. Priscilla went off on a last "roundup" of wandering all over the softly lighted lounges of 1st, 2nd, and tourist class—the strictness and scheduled "boat life" was all over. Clusters of people stood discussing how much the tips should be. There was nothing to stay up late for—not being due in Rotterdam till morning. We took *both* ½ grapefruit *and* orange juice for our last breakfast—when again? Susan's temperature was normal. Now—last-minute things stuck in the suitcases which we were to carry ourselves—last look around our cabin—a deserted look fell over most of the ship—lounges closed up—lights out at the bars, rooms empty—beds bare, dining rooms closed and dark, deck chairs piled up, baggage piled on decks, the hold open and all the freight piled high on upper deck—could it be the same luxurious boat?

By 10 A.M. we had all joined the rest at the deck rails to thrill at our first view of Holland. A *long* inlet from the channel to Rotterdam Harbor took us through miles of Dutch countryside. We saw our first windmills and green fields dotted with black and white cows. We passed several towns and villages—houses built in rows (like Philadelphia) and canals full of little boats. We passed a huge ship-building place and a factory for Lux toilet soap!! It was so exciting because we were so close to it all—just like going up the Mississippi in an ocean liner. Every town we passed was full of excitement at the passing of the *Nieuw Amsterdam*—people running to the end of the street to wave—others hanging out of their windows. Small boats full of excursioners blew little blasts on their horns and the people waved and cheered—our majestic boat answered the blasts with the deep-throated whistle and we dipped our flag in answering salute.

As we came to the huge rounded-out piece of water that is Rotterdam Harbor, five tugboats came up to push and pull us into the *right spot.* Hollanders in wooden shoes on the tugboats throwing lines and shouting orders in Dutch made us sure of where we were. As we approached the pier we saw hundreds of people on both the first and second floors of the building. As we came close we could see their faces and bouquets of flowers clutched in their hands, little flags with family names to guide the eyes of those coming home to wave to the right ones, and many colored handkerchiefs—the waving was frantic both by passengers and those on shore, and their emotion caught us up in it and made us choky, not for ourselves but for all those who know separation in this world and especially those who have no hope—what a terrible thing *permanent* separation from loved ones is. It spurred us on in the desire to make truth known.

We watched this scene for some time and then went down to be sure our bags were safe and ready at the right gangplank, etc. We perched on seats near our bags about noon—sure of going off in a few moments when suddenly a call went up, "No one off—not yet." Tongues buzzed—mostly in Dutch—and Fran went off to see what he could find out. "Man died last night"—"Someone sick"—"Health doctors coming"—"Police on board"—"Jewel robbery." Finally our head waiter told us a woman who got off in Southampton had smallpox—cable had just

Almost there! Debby, Susan, Priscilla, and me on the deck of
the Niew Amsterdam.

reached us, "We are quarantined." "Well, let's pull out deck chairs in the sun and be comfortable." The crew had almost all gone ashore—no food in sight nor anything to drink. About 3 P.M. Priscilla came excitedly back from a tour of inspection to announce that coffee and sandwiches were being served in the lounge. We hastened to get in on it and found tables and seats enough for us all. The sandwiches kept disappearing before they reached us. I *was* able to get a little milk for the girls in a strange assortment of glasses. The waiters were elevator boys, the librarian, and a few others—robbed of their usual trim look by the ordinary land clothes they were dressed in, robbed of their joy as the hands of the clock tossed away their precious hours at home. Finally we got some of the open-faced sandwiches and a little coffee just as a call went up, "Everyone off"; we ate our food and were the last ones down the gangplank. We'll never know the whole story of what happened.

We entered a large warehouse-like building smelling like fresh cement—white and clean-looking. Tables placed end to end formed a large square and on these tables were piled suitcases under the letters of the alphabet. As we scanned the room and hurried over to table S, I thought, "How convenient that all the passengers chose names beginning with different letters!!!—wouldn't it be awful if they all started with the same letter?" Our 17 pieces were piled high on the table and out in the center of the room our crated things stood among others. There were Janet's and Elsa's trunks, the China trunk (none the worse for the trip), the boxes of books, the refrigerator, the old toy box with its cotton covering still tacked on and a band of steel over that, the barrel of dishes, etc.—yes, everything was there safe, and all together. Meantime the children had found a little "playhouse" of a grouping of crates and were happily settling down to play with their dolls. Fran went off to find out about storing our things in the warehouse until we are ready to send them *all* on *together*—also to find out about uncrating our bikes to use here in Holland.

I stood behind our suitcases—wondering how I'd ever get them shut again if the contents were ruffled up!! A pair of very blue Dutch eyes in a tan face were soon scanning our "stack" of stuff. "All this?" "Yes," I said and explained a bit. "How much tobacco—cigarettes—liquor?" "None." "What will you smoke?" "We don't smoke." Fran came over, then. Questions repeated—answers repeated—then out came a piece of white chalk and in less time than it takes to write it, all our things were cleared through the customs without so much as *one* case opened. "The Lord *is* with us," we breathed. Then Fran went on with the other arrangements—soon hammers and chisels were opening our crates and out rolled our 4 bikes. The warehouse was emptying itself of people and baggage. Although the *Vierdam* was to dock in 2 days, all the tables were being cleared out—soon we were a little island in an almost-empty place. 4 bikes, 7 pieces, plus Elsa's trunk to get to Scheveningen. Debby was going to sleep on my lap, when Fran came back with a beaming face—for 10 guilders ($3.80) the red truck which belongs to the warehouse would take *all* our stuff, right down to the hat box—to 8 Haarlemasche Straat, Scheveningen *right* away!!! (Since then we have found that that is an unheard of thing—they *never* use that truck for such a purpose.) So the Lord had smoothed out the way—and all your prayers were answered.

It turned out to be a special holiday (The Hague's 700th birthday), trams were crowded—and ours would have been an impossible task. We were however free of baggage and settled down in a rickety old cab by 5:30 P.M.—The cab driver told us he would drive us all the way to our destination for 12 guilders—train fare would be more than half of that and would mean a long wait and perhaps standing all the way. We had a *lovely* ride—first through Rotterdam—along busy canals and market districts—then out a highway—clipped hedges bordering it all the way. The most exciting thing about the drive was a little side trip through Delft, where "Delft pottery" comes from. It is a very quaint place with the narrow streets at their narrowest—people and bicycles swarming over them. We turned into one quiet street after another—over a little bridge and beside a most breathtaking little canal. The water level was way below street level and the brick walls bordering the canal became a thing of beauty because of the window boxes full of geraniums and ageratum placed *on* the walls halfway between street level and water level, on *both* walls. It was hard to believe that it was real. The houses

Priscilla, Susan, and Debby playing house among our crates on the Rotterdam dock.

that bordered the canal were *banked* with flowers that spilled over the edges of the wall and were reflected in the water below. I want to go back there some day and just *sit* a while.

Scheveningen is truly an "Atlantic City," though much smaller. The beach is very crowded—the "free" beaches rather dirty (full of papers, etc.). The road along the beach is lined by hotels, about eight large ones—two of which are closed and looking out with staring eyes made blank by bombings. The pier is no more (bombed)—but bright lights, rows of fish stands, ice-cream stores, and outdoor restaurants make a rather gaudy sight at night. Our taxi swept along the beach road, turned up a street in the very center of the cluster of hotels, post office, eating places, etc.—jutted over to the left and—"There it is"—6–8—big as life on a cream-colored plastered house with mammoth windows (we'd call them studio windows) downstairs and up. It seems almost like a glass house—all tiny leaded panes. Fran ran up to ring the bell—Debby was sound asleep on my lap (she had missed all the sights) and in no time at all a young man was carrying the sleeping Debby "oop to her bad"—and we were being greeted with "Velcom Velcom" by Mrs. Mager and daughters Annie and Gene (Dutch "G" so you gargle it!). Mrs. Mager added a stream of Dutch to her "Velcom"—and beamed along with it—Gene translated, "Tea in room—now?—dinner ready zoon."

We found our rooms to be at the end of the long hall—the side of the house—windows on 2 sides. The rooms are joined by large glass doors (crinkled glass—light goes through—but opaque). The windows reach from the ceiling to 18" from the floor and are not provided with shades—hence the sunlight streams in all day. Heavy woolen curtains—moth-eaten and a faded brown in color—hang from big rings ready to be pulled across the windows for the night.

The first room you enter is sort of a "living room"—it has a mantelpiece from which hangs the inevitable piece of tapestry (seemingly a *must* in Dutch interior decoration), a table covered with plush, 5 heavy dining room chairs, a large hanging light—a single bed and a cot. *All* the floors of the house are covered with a straw matting—corner to corner—and all walls are light cream color. The next room has 2 single beds pushed together and made up as *one*—*one* sheet and one blanket across them. At the foot of this arrangement is a low crib—mattresses about 6" from the floor—sides as high as ours but solid wood—hard to make—A washbasin at one side with "Kaud" running water completes the furniture!! The beds are hard and bumpy. The pillows, gunnysacks stuffed with now-lumpy and matted cotton—but the blankets are *beautiful* and pure woolen!! On the table stood that which *really* warmed my heart and made up for the lumpy beds—one dozen *long*-stemmed red roses and eight huge, long-stemmed white carnations just to welcome us!! *No* drawers—*no* dressing tables. How glad I am for Elsa's trunk. It and the suitcases are constantly in use. It took some *time* to rearrange and re-pack—I fortunately brought that thing I bought that can be hung on a door—to hang clothes on—remember? It is really doing a good job!! Our windows look out on the end of the trolley line to Scheveningen. People *pour* in day and night (and out again), for some time at this seashore resort. We also see backs of hotels and a few bright red neon signs—nothing "quaint" in this view except the pushcart milk and bread deliveries in the A.M. and the *variety* of bicycle riders who go by.

Deborah's sleepiness proved to be a forerunner of an illness. Her temperature was 102° several hours after we arrived. Sunday we decided to have Sunday School in the midst of the open luggage—even though Debby was not well. We invited Dick (twelve-year-old son of Annie Mager, I don't know her married name) and Hanz his brother (seven), and Dick beamingly accepted. We felt it was an "earnest" of the Lord for our work in Europe—to have this Dutch lad in a S.S., improvised though it was, only 17 hours after landing in Rotterdam. Fran told the story of Jonah—I drew illustrations in colored chalk—Annie and Gene left their bedmaking to listen—we used our hands and sometimes the dictionary—but got the story across—also the black hearts and white hearts illustration of the way of salvation. Dick has had one year of English in school so he tried singing with us and we sang several choruses. They all appreciated it and it was good for our children.

Deborah seemed fairly well—about 100° temp. but happy all day—that night 103° and headache and backache which worried me. Fran had to be in Amsterdam next morning (Monday), hence left early. Susan and Priscilla went off to the "Kinderstrang"—children's beach—with Dick and Hanz and an older boy (young man who lives here and plays in dance band at night!—speaks Dutch, French, and English and seems clean-cut and fond of children). The Kinderstrang is 30 cents (Dutch money, about 12 cents our money) and you can enter any time 9 A.M. to 6 P.M.—leave when you like. They have swings, a bumpy slide and big rocking horses, and a push merry-go-around—and two nurses in attendance. It's right on the sand and not as crowded as free beaches.

I spent Monday, Tuesday, Wednesday nights in our rooms with Debby. She seemed fine each A.M.—runny nose but low fever—often up to 103½°—then down by 6 P.M.—then up in the middle of the night to 104°. I gave enemas, sponge baths—prayed—and hoped it wasn't polio!! Tuesday I got a doctor—one who was attending a little girl in this house—he went over Debby—chest, etc. "It is nossing—far from America—changes of climate." But Wednesday the temperature did the same thing. Fran came home Thursday afternoon and by that time Deb's temperature was normal and it has been ever since. It is now Friday. She is white and wan-looking—I hope she improves steadily. She and I have seen little of Scheveningen but Janet Priscilla and Susan have explored much of it and surrounding countryside on their bikes.

Annie Mager speaks very little English and Gene not much more—hence I have quite a time explaining my smallest wants—such as "a tray" or "hot water to wash clothes." I've taken to looking words up in the Dutch-English dictionary, and taking a stab at it—we mutually roar at each other as we try to communicate. They are *so* nice and so good-natured. "Ash du blief" (if you please), "dank u vell" (thank you very much), and a few other phrases are quite a fixed part of our speech now. I can buy tomatoes from the vendor now—and utter all the necessary Dutch answers (which isn't much).

Fran took the children out yesterday afternoon. After supper Priscilla sat with sleeping Debby and I went for a bike ride with Susan and Fran. Then Fran stayed with Debby while I took the girls to the end of our street to watch the fireworks on the beach in honor of the 7-year-old Princess's Birthday. A young 6'4" man put Susan on his shoulders to see, and an older white-haired man lifted Janet Priscilla up. Janet Priscilla was so anxious for me to see a "set piece" that before I knew it she had been put down and the old man had *me* hoisted up above the crowd to my startled amazement!

Fran not only covered an amazing amount of ground last summer but he *remembers* his way around. He is able to say, "Now left—now right—2 more blocks—and this is the house," for *all* the places he has been!! He knows how to get around Amsterdam and The Hague, etc., as well as Philadelphia and Wilmington. He also knows the men in the various countries and has a grasp of their church situations which exceeds the knowledge of even Kok* (not in Holland—but the other places)—hence the pressure is borne upon him to do the International work. The two Chinese delegates are supposed to arrive today—and so is Miss Lee. But I'm away from all that. I hope to get to Amsterdam for at least one day of the meetings. It depends on the children's health.

Our food is quite a contrast to the boat. *Breakfast* = bread, butter and jam, milk. *Lunch* = bread, butter, and milk, *sometimes* a thin piece of cheese, *or* a thin slice of baloney—*once, raw* herring!! *once* slices of tomato, that's *all!!! Dinner* = a small amount of some sort of soup—*lots* of potatoes, 1 other vegetable (so far either cauliflower or string beans), either fish or cheese or a *thin* 2"-square piece of meat. Dessert either sour cream or a cornstarch pudding (not very sweet). As you can see it's almost all starch. The bread is rather wet and heavy brown bread. Tastes good. But so much starch makes you feel stuffed but not satisfied. We're glad milk is an "open market." They give us 3 bottles a day—at our door—we keep in our bedroom!! Iceboxes and refrigerators are not the usual thing. Butter is always soft—they *have* no ice in the house here. I'm giving us all 2 vitamin capsules a day. A fruit vendor comes each day and from him I can buy tomatoes for 50¢ a kilo (about 2½ lbs.). 1 Guilder = 38¢ American money = 100 cents Dutch money so tomatoes are cheap. They are nice small ones with green stems—smooth and even, and taste like *right* out of the garden. So that settles my vitamin problem. We add tomatoes to both breakfast and lunch. He also has peaches, pears, and grapes but they are expensive—1 peach = 40¢ or 50¢ = 15¢ or 19¢ apiece American—so I'm not indulging much—but we will get *some* fruit. I splurged and got 2 small grapefruit yesterday for 1 guilder, 20¢ (for the 2), which was cheap—usually 1 guilder apiece *when* they have them. I have not seen any oranges.

Your letter was waiting here for me, mother, and *very* welcome—so glad I called from the ship—it was worth it—they *got* you 3 minutes after I put in the call on a written form. There is only *one* circuit to America and all the ships on the Atlantic use it, so it was very fine that we got it through so quickly. Elsa's letter was delivered to me among others on the ship after we sailed. Miss Drummond's package *never* arrived—please check with her. It was to contain books, games, and puzzles. The children were quite disappointed. I would have stocked up at the "5 and 10" if I hadn't expected that—I didn't even get new crayons!! I had a letter from Elsa the Tuesday after we arrived here—good to have it. Could this please be shared with Elsa and others? I'll never get all this repeated. Maybe Janet could copy some of it.—By the way, psychologically the food situation is making the children appreciate food more

*Dutch Ambassador Arie Kok, who served in Peking, China.

than this length of time would be expected to. I think Priscilla is eating more than usual! After a month of it they should really enjoy the variety Switzerland has to offer even though it will not be like America. There wasn't a drop of the grapefruit left when I got them—and our 1 egg apiece (1 in 2 weeks) was eaten to the last crumb without any urging—by all 3 of them!! You'd think they hadn't seen an egg in years! Yet on the boat where they could have had 1 dozen eggs if they wanted them—*any* meal—they *never* wanted one!!

Give my love to David and Jonathan—we'll be sending cards to them—love to each of you—how is Ralph? *Please* tell Miss Richards, Sarah Bruce, and "the three" that the sweaters are *wonderful*—and I *will* be writing them though I don't seem to accomplish much at a time. Maybe some of this can be shared by them. This is now Saturday. I shall go out to mail this. Fran is due tonight and tomorrow we plan to go to The Hague, to church in a Christian Reformed Church which is cooperating with our Council. We pray for you all each day.

Much, much love,

EDITH

August 12, 1948   Scheveningen, Netherlands

Dearest Family—Mother and Dad, Janet and Ralph, Elsa and Roger:

I have written you one letter from Southampton, one from here, and now this is the third. I have done so *little* letter writing that this must not be long—I must get some others done also. Then I need to spend time on typing and shorthand this afternoon. I am going to try to go to Amsterdam every other day to attend some of the Congress, hence I have only the in-between days to wash, iron, tidy, study, and write. As you know, washing in a basin in one's bedroom with running cold water (a little hot brought up in a pitcher) takes more time—I did 12 dresses and a few other things today—Tuesday I washed underwear, slips, and pajamas. Saturday I will iron on the table in our room (padded with blankets from Debby's crib). Strange how no matter where you are in the world—no matter how lovely the outdoors (such as Cape Cod) nor how important the things are (such as Amsterdam), a woman with children must needs spend much time slushing around in water in some container!!! Seems sort of silly—yet there's no getting around it. The wind and rain and cold weather have made it impossible for the children to spend much time out-of-doors. When a nice bit of dry weather (I mean a few *hours* of such) does come—I send them out—and spend my time doing whatever they have hindered while they were in. It has rained several times today but now I hope the sun will stay out for the rest of the afternoon (2½ hours), while I get some writing done—and while my clothes dry on the line.

I mailed my letter to you on Saturday I believe, and Deborah's temperature had gone down to normal. It has stayed normal ever since and she has steadily improved and is now quite well again. What really caused the high temperature I'll never know.

Sunday we tried all day to get to a church service—Fran was home over the weekend—and Sunday morning we finally got a telephone call through to a minister or "Dominie" as the Dutch call them—in The Hague—he was out of town but his brother-in-law's wife answered and said church had already begun but would we come for coffee at twelve, dinner at two, and stay for afternoon church (Fran understood at four). So off we went at the correct time (this is a church in the Bible B. group) in a taxi because of a rain which was blown almost horizontal with a heavy wind. We arrived at a very typical brick Dutch home—built in a row with the front door right on the sidewalk. We were ushered in by a flow of "Holland" (*they* don't call it "Dutch"—they "sprecht Holland") and we gathered that the Dominie was not yet home. The lady spoke *no* English—so the conversation was limited!

We sat and enjoyed the very typical Dutch home—the hangings of tapestry, the *real oil* paintings, the large bouquet of fresh pink carnations, and the beautiful big windows. The dining rooms *always* seem to have huge French doors—with windows on either side, opening into the little walled-in back garden. The walls are covered with ivy, the garden *intensely* planted and "landscaped"—tiny but complete with little gravel walk—tiny patch of grass—black black earth with perfect little beds of flowers, a bush or two, and a small tree. All in a pocket handkerchief space. I am very impressed with the number and the size of them. The front and back of even fishermen's cottages are practically out-of-doors—they are almost all glass. Apartment houses seem to be *all* windows—I've seen some actually solid with windows—just the frames in between. I've seen some like this—very ultra-modern looking (must have steel frames) in both The Hague and here in Scheveningen.

The Dominie, another brother (studying for the ministry), and *his* wife and several children came home after a time and we all had a cup of coffee (with milk for the children—hot—which Susan nearly choked on trying to drink "without swallowing—, cause it tasted awful"!!) Conversation picked up a bit. The Dominie spoke some English and although it was a *strain* to understand and be understood, we found he was one with us in our stand for the Faith. He smoked black cigars as he talked—but he had just walked several miles from the church because they do not use the trams on Sunday!! Yet on essentials we were in accord. He had been in prison during the war for a few months because he prayed (in Church) for their members who had been taken away to Labor camps by the Germans. He is in the Christian Reformed Church (the Holland one) and will be attending the Amsterdam meetings.

Dinner was served on a long table in the dining room. The meat had been put on each plate—and I felt like weeping as I saw it. They had shared with us their meager ration for the week (300 grams apiece for 2 weeks). On each plate was about a square inch of meat—*some smaller* (½" x 1")—and *Fran's* and *mine* a bit larger. I hated to eat it, yet anything else would have been impolite. They made no apologies. It was about ¼ of an inch thick. There were large plates of potatoes and string beans and a gravy made of a "substitute" for meat flavor. The dessert was a cornstarch pudding with very little sweetening, and a jar of home-canned cherries poured over it to give flavor. The Dutch all eat such *mountains* of potatoes and whatever other vegetable there is—I guess it makes up for the lack of meats and sweet things. I helped with the dishes—and tried a few Dutch words—the ladies tried to say a few things to me. We didn't succeed very well but we laughed a great deal. They knew no English at all—but I resorted to my little word book and that helped a little. The kitchen was all-white tile with blue and white checked material in a ruffle all around an open shelf which went clear around the room. It looked just as you'd expect a Dutch kitchen to look!!

As soon as the last dish was dried, it was time for tea—a huge pot was made and the cups filled and passed around in the living room. It was hopeless to try to explain that the children didn't drink it—but the "payoff" came when Priscilla took her cup and Susan's out of the kitchen and they were promptly returned, *full* again!! When I said, "That's enough thank you," *my* cup was filled again—with a beaming smile!! It seems they drink 3 cups! The Dominie said, "One makes afternoon calls—drinks 20 cups of tea—in America what do they give you?" When Fran said, "Nothing"—he could hardly believe it!!

As time wore on we found that church did not begin until 5 o'clock—½ hour service and 1 hour of preaching could make it 6:30—and then ½ hour to get home. Our supper would be served at 6 and Debby had just been ill and was getting *very* restless. One and a half hours of a service in Dutch seemed like too much to expect of her just at bedtime. So when Dominie explained that he also had a preaching service in a Christian School house in Scheveningen at 7 o'clock we decided to go home—put Debby to bed, let Janet Priscilla stay with her, and take Susan to the evening service. (By the way—we gave them some Ivory Soap and I hope we can see that a can of meat gets to them from Bordeaux's supply to give away.) Fran and Susan and I walked miles through the fishing village section of Scheveningen looking for the address we had been given. When we finally found it we found he had given us the *wrong* address. The school was closed up and no *sign* of a service. So we walked on in the driving wind—got turned around a bit—but saw very interesting things—antiaircraft gun placements, etc., all down by the shore in the fishermen's section. Finally we found a bus that brought us back home and we had our own service after a futile attempt to worship in a believing church. *Next* Sunday they can hear their own daddy preach in the Beginjhof—English Reformed church in Amsterdam.

Monday Fran went back to Amsterdam about 9 A.M. and I went with him to learn the way. It takes two hours from our door to his door. We spent some time in the office (Kok's) and then had lunch with Mrs. Kok and a Dutch Dominie—later Mr. Kok and Chia Ju Ming joined us. The latter came all the way by air from China in his black Chinese gown and his rather *thin* but *long* white beard and *radiant* face!! We then walked along a very quiet canal and through the grounds around the Rijksmuseum and stood watching the golden figures of men who ring the half-hours (and hours) with a golden mallet—we watched as they rang 2:30—up in a tower of the museum—and then went back to Kok's office where Fran was to meet some men for a committee meeting.

I had a half-hour with Miss Lee of India—and then came on home "on my own"—the tram in Amsterdam, train for The Hague (Den Haag), then a tram from Den Haag to Scheveningen. I know my way now and can ask for a ticket 2nd or 3rd class and can read the "way-in" ("eengang") and "way-out" signs and the "2nd person" or "platform" signs, etc. The view from the train windows is very interesting. You see a quiet and peaceful-looking landscape scene most of the way. Near Leiden I saw several sailboats in among the fields of cows!! (They were on canals of course but green fields and cows were on either side of them.)

The children had gotten along all right. Priscilla was in charge. Of course I was home in time for dinner, etc. That evening I took paper downstairs to write—but Gene Mager sat by me and we talked about our International Council. I showed her our program and told her my plan to attend every other day. She said they'd be glad to see that the children had their meals, etc. I planned to go at noon in time for the opening of the Congress at 2:30—on Wednesday. It turned out that Wednesday was Dick's birthday (Dick 13, Hans 7, sons of Annie, another of Mrs. Mager's daughters). The "Kur House" (a part of a Hotel—an auditorium where concerts and operas, etc., are held) was having a children's program (Kinderen's Poppen)—which I figured out from her talking with her hands was to be a puppet show and a magician. I bought tickets as our treat to Dick—and our three and their two went. I had an early lunch and dressed the girls and gave them a roll of Lifesavers—and then I went off (with a smoked herring sandwich as a treat for Fran) on the 12:30 train. I found the famed and ancient Beginjhof by myself and slipped in to a back pew. The ancient building which had seen the Pilgrims kneel in prayer before they left for America was now half full of men from many countries. They sat on the narrow seats with their faces turned up to watch Ambassador Kok as he welcomed them from the high preaching place. Mr. Kok made an excellent speech—thrilling us again with the purpose of our stand for the Lord as a Gideon band set against the host of Midian. Only two-thirds of the delegates were there.

Dr. Lambie hasn't arrived yet nor have some others from other countries. Fritz Larson of Denmark had a heart attack and cabled his regrets—but I shook hands with Hedegard of Sweden and he said to me, "I was so happy to see your husband. God sent him to us, that was the *only* day last year that those men of three countries were all together at once!!" (Denmark, Norway, and Sweden)—his wife is here with him. The Mexican Delegate "Perez" was at the last minute prevented from coming—by his government. The NBC and Columbia Broadcasting are giving time to us on August 23 when Otis Fuller will be back in the U.S.A. to report on our meeting.

After the meeting, Fran walked with me to the station and ate his "herring sandwich" as he walked—I also had brought him a piece of gingerbread (bread is scarce in restaurants and we get plenty of it here in the pension) and a chocolate bar from our small store (Chardy's gift)—so he had a fair supper and would stop for milk, etc., after he left me. We had about an hour together walking through the "tougher" section—narrow streets and warehouses lining canals; I left him with two minutes to get my train. Sat next to an American college boy all the way to The Hague, son of the American Ambassador to Sweden. As a boy, he went from American schools to French school in Paris and after the first month got along fine. This encouraged me for Priscilla.

I got home at 9 P.M. to find Priscilla had put Debby to bed at seven and Susan at eight and both were sound asleep. They had eaten well at dinnertime and all seemed happy about it today. Atmosphere is more like a home than a hotel. Priscilla quite proud of herself! So I guess I can go again with a free mind.

Our rooms have convenient place to wash hands, etc. Toilet is down the hall and one carries the paper along!! Meals are brought up to the room—dishes carried down by Annie—when other two are in bed Priscilla goes down to play a game of Monopoly with Dick (who talks of guilders instead of dollars as they buy and sell—for 13 he is more a little boy than an American boy of that age would be in spite of living through the Rotterdam bombings). Down the hall each room has at least one if not three children deposited in the beds at 8 P.M.—then parents go out to the "boulevard" (like our boardwalk only made of brick) to walk or to the Kur House Concerts or to theaters. The children all seem to go to sleep promptly. So Annie and Gene are used to having children left alone sleeping in the evening—and we have the added protection of Priscilla. Hence I think it's quite all right to go every *other* day. I'll go again tomorrow, then Sunday I'll take all three with me and not leave them alone till Tuesday.

The big order we sent Magers finally arrived today: 200 lbs. of sugar, lots of puddings (Knox), a case of lunch meat (like Spam), a case of beef and gravy, a case of dried beef, a case of Crisco, a case of Mazola salad oil, a case of Ivory, a case of Lux, a case of another soap. They are very pleased and Priscilla just dashed upstairs to say that they have made us butterscotch pudding for dessert—in a "fish mold"—so pretty! Also some stewed pears!! So the food is looking up. Priscilla wisely remarked, "We'd better keep on eating up here because they wouldn't want to give us extras in the dining room." It's easier for me with three youngsters to be alone rather than in a big dining room and it's more like having a home. We may not be able to do it, after we leave here, for a long time. So I think we'll stay up here.

They have stopped bringing me tea and bring three-liter bottles of milk each A.M., one for each meal. They have no ice or refrigeration so I keep them here in our room. I discovered we can have a nice warm bath in a bathroom tacked on the back of the house. It contains a bathtub, also potatoes, vegetables, butter, pickles, and big jars of pickled fish with peering eyes!!—and our four bicycles! However, the water is warm and it's wonderful to bathe! We hang our clothes on the bicycles while we bathe. We don't do it too often as it means marching through the kitchen.

Mother and Janet, your letters mailed August 9, 10:30 P.M., arrived today, August 12, just as I was getting to the end of this. That's good time. Elsa, yours took five days, too, the last time. It's so wonderful to hear from you all.

Please could you each take this letter as an answer? I have spent much too long on it—so it should count for several letters. Also it would be nice if some others could share it because I'll never go into this much detail again.

The children are still talking about Cape Cod—and this beach is compared unfavorably to it. Priscilla was sighing for the Cape Cod library today—she misses books—no place to get English books. Our own books are stored in Rotterdam and we won't be having them unpacked until we find a house, whenever that will be!!

So we are *all* house-hunting for October! We will pray for your hunt as you pray for ours. Deborah also seems to think that growing up is a magic thing. She thinks her size will determine our return to America. "I wish I would get big so that I can go back to see Grandmother and Johnny," etc. She thinks, fondly, that *she* will be the oldest of all when we go back—and the other girls will be younger! She and Jonathan certainly think alike. The children enjoyed hearing your letters and loved the bits about the cousins—they pray for them all every night. So sorry Barney couldn't be a part of their memory—but they always include him and think of him. Raining *again*—the whole world seems to have lost summer!! People here wear knitted things and coats—I've worn my tweed almost constantly for going out. You will be weary reading this but I so long to have you "see" it all with me—then you seem nearer.

Much love,

EDITH

August 24, 1948   Scheveningen, Netherlands

Dearest Family:

Here I've gone five days over my weekly "deadline" for the letter home. There seems to have been no time I could properly use for writing. Right now it is 10:30 P.M. and I am perched out in the hall so as not to disturb the children. Fran is coming home from Amsterdam tonight *sometime*—so I'll spend the "in between" with you. I have worked steadily today. In the morning after breakfast and tidying, etc., I typed for 2 hours (practice typing—I'm on lesson 26); then I threw off the role of student and became a secretary for the next hour (plus some time this afternoon) and typed two letters from my shorthand notes taken from dictation yesterday. Then I did a big ironing until dinnertime, just finished it. I'm doing two letters a day for awhile. Fran thinks it is better to to go on completing most of the course of study to increase my speed, rather than spending all my time on his letters now. We'll gradually get caught up on the correspondence. I still have to finish my speedwriting course too—but I'm taking dictation right along. I hope I can soon finish the studies because we're going to start French and German as soon as possible after reaching Lausanne.

Now to try to get caught up on the past week. I mailed your letter with the outside P.S. on a Friday. The night before I wakened at midnight to see an adult form in the dim light of the street lamp—standing near the bed. Before I could get awake enough to freeze with horror, Fran said, "I came home because I'm sick"—relief that it wasn't my turn to find out how I'd react to a thief!!! He got into bed and I gave him an aspirin and tried to keep him warm—he was having a chill. He ached all over, especially his back, and was quite miserable Friday. He concluded Susan and Debby and he must all have had "flu." By Saturday afternoon he had no temperature and felt he *must* go back to Amsterdam in order to preach on Sunday—couldn't take a two-hour trip *before* preaching. So off he went—though rather wobblingly.

Sunday I had the three girls, all neat in their navy coats, and myself, through breakfast and on the tram by 8 A.M. After buying tickets for "tway and a hel-of" (spelled as you pronounce it), two and a half (it's so much fun to say "hel-ef ell-ef"—which is half past ten; they say "half of eleven"), we boarded the 3rd-class coach and the children were thrilled with the scenery from The Hague to Amsterdam—their first trip out of Scheveningen. Susan and Deborah kept their noses plastered against the window and Susan verbally pointed out every windmill, canal, cow, sheep, pig, flower garden and all else she deemed important for us to "look at"—we got through the Amsterdam station without losing a child—and boarded the #2 trolley. I had practiced saying "Spui"

(Spowi, only don't think you have it right—it's a very difficult sound and they always tell you, you have it wrong!!)—so the conductor would *know* where we wanted to get off—and he *understood* me!! The children were amazed as we entered a small door seemingly in the side of a house, and walked into a courtyard, enclosed by five-story houses, to find the little old church tucked away from the sight of anyone on the street. The church was full (holds about 300 I should guess) and we had to sit in chairs facing the sides of the pews. I wondered how I'd manage three of them in *chairs* right in full view of everyone. However they all seemed on their best behavior and made not a sound through the service. The two older ones were really thrilled to be worshiping where the Pilgrims had been. Fran gave an excellent message with vigor that would not indicate he was ill. However after it was over he felt "all in" so went back to his room to lie down for a few hours. Dr. Holdcroft took the children and me to dinner and we had a pleasant time. The children were delighted to have some *real* pieces of beef and gravy. One can get nice portions of meat in restaurants here. The prices vary according to the "swankiness" of the place—but on the whole they are cheaper than in the U.S.A. However, in a pension like ours, you get just the regular fare of the Hollander, which is very regulated by ration stamps. After that we walked back to see Fran and took a "family walk" through a park (depleted of trees by the Germans) and along a canal, ending up at the same restaurant, where Fran ate a dinner while the children and I shared two orders of "fruit compote" (consisted of apples, pears, and grapes—we haven't seen an orange or a banana in Holland).

Here it is Sunday 29th and I am no further than *this!* Fran has taken the three girls up to Amsterdam to hear Dr. Holdcroft speak at the four P.M. service. I begged off because I didn't know *when* else I would write letters. We have only eight more days here (we leave the morning of the 7th) and we want to spend *one* day (or part of day) at the Rijksmuseum and one day in Rotterdam with the Missars (the family Fran stayed all night with last year—remember? They met him on a train—and took him home with them. We sent them a food parcel as a "thank you"— they have attempted several times to see us—waited 3 hours on the dock the day we arrived, came here a day we were gone, etc., so we *must* see them *once*). We *must* go one evening to see the lights of Amsterdam (I'll explain later) and I have to repack and send ahead some things to Switzerland—repack other stuff for Paris.

And I *have* to study speedwriting and practice typing each day—and take 2 letters from Fran in shorthand and type them each day—and I have two more washings and ironings to do—one tomorrow and one on Saturday so as to be "caught up," sooooooo—my writing time will be scarce. Living in two rooms gives you no place to retreat to!!!

Monday the 16th—I did a huge washing in the morning—a clear day fortunately—children spent the afternoon on the beach—I typed and studied all afternoon. Put the children to bed with stories—went to bed early myself. *Tuesday the 17th*—Priscilla took care of the girls while I went to Amsterdam—left about 10 A.M. and got there in time for lunch with Fran, Harlee B., and Stonehouse. Tuesday and Friday are "no-meat" days at the restaurants so I had to eat fish!! However the cooking was a change. We then walked to the church for the afternoon business session, preceded by a devotional message from Mr. Carrel. I had a few minutes to talk to Miss Lee, also to some missionaries from Italy and some others Fran met last summer. It was so interesting to have the *names* come to life. Guiton invited us for tea when we are in Paris. He is fine—so strong in his stand and very keen in his thinking, which showed up in his help on the wording of the constitution. The man from Austria lived formerly in Czechoslovakia—but was put out after the war because he was German originally. When he went back to see if he could get some of his furniture or belongings they threw him into prison and beat him with oak sticks because they found a picture postcard collection of his children's with cards showing Hitler's picture on them among the other cards. He was kept in prison a year without being allowed to tell his family where he was. Another delegate from Austria was a refugee minister from Yugoslavia who also lost *everything* he owned—has five children. They both have pastorates now—Methodist. It was a very interesting dinner conversation though not exactly cheerful! Fran walked with me to the station afterwards and I took the train back. As the meals are brought right up to the room, Priscilla can manage very nicely.

Wednesday the 18th Susan awakened with a fever and a sore throat so I kept her in bed all day. It was grey and chilly out so Janet Priscilla and Debby were in and out. Janet Priscilla played Monopoly most of the afternoon with three Dutch boys—Dick 13, Manos 16 (who can speak English), and Manos' brother 13. I typed beside Susan's bed and didn't accomplish too much. *Thursday the 19th* was the last day of the Council meetings and Fran was expecting me. I stayed home till noon to feed Susan her lunch and kept taking her temperature. I left doses of aspirin (every four hours) and two pieces of sulfa gum for her throat and decided to go at 12:30 o'clock—telling Janet Priscilla I'd call at suppertime to see if I was needed or could stay for the farewell meeting. I missed being there for the official pictures so you won't see me in any of them!! I got there in time for most of the afternoon session and then called Janet Priscilla while they had an executive committee meeting. She reported temperature coming down and all O.K. so I went with Fran for dinner at a place he had discovered where you could really get good cold water to drink with your meal!!—most unusual. The evening meeting was one of testimonies and prayers by delegates. Testimonies as to what the council meetings had meant to them. Pastor Guiton was quite witty and among other things he mentioned the fact that he had made many mistakes in English. He said he had written down, "I wish to thank the two charming typewriters in the office for their help," and the girls hastened to point out his grave mistake!! The Dutchmen presented Garman, Carl M., Kok, and Poole with engravings, for their work on the council meetings—and gave plates to some of the ladies and a tile to others. I was given a tile commemorating the Queen's 50-year Jubilee! Fran decided to come on home with me so we made a dash for the 11:05 train. The Hollanders are very long-winded!!

I ironed some and typed and studied. In the evening I went downstairs to put in a phone call—and Manos (the 16-year-old boy) began a conversation in English with me. I discovered his father is an atheist and his mother, "she believes nothing." His father is the leading psychiatrist in Holland. His mother is Jewish, his father 50 percent Jewish. He himself knew a fair amount of Liberal theology and accepted it. So I had a *long* talk to him about Jesus—who is either God and Savior—or *not* worthy of being used as an example at all. He was intensely interested—has a brilliant mind—you could talk to him so much more intelligently about philosophy, theology, and world events and history than most schoolboys in America. Pray for him. I want Fran to talk to him before we go. Fran came back about midnight.

Saturday 21st Susan seemed quite fine again and in the afternoon we took a trolley to The Hague and a sightseeing boat down the canal to Delft. The boat is glass-covered and built like a big flat rowboat with a center aisle and seats wide enough for 3 people on each side of the aisle covered with red Fabrikoid. Very comfortable and not a draft for Susan. We went slowly down the canal and had plenty of time to view back gardens, fields and cows, factories, etc., as well as opportunity to peek into the open doors of the little house-like cabins on huge canal barges. Big dirty-looking barges carrying coal surprise you with such neat-looking little cabins with shiny sink and stove and checked tablecloths. Always there was evidence of a baby or children, also there was always a pot of geraniums—a pen put on the deck, diapers on a line, or a little fat face peering out over a doorstep. Often the woman of the "house" would be sitting with her feet out the doorway in a spot of sunshine, knitting. Susan and Priscilla thought it would be fun to live on a barge!! Glad they can't choose where we are to live!!! When we arrived in Delft a guide walked with the boatload of people all through the town, pointing out famous spots—such as the place William of Orange was killed— the "old church"—1300 and something—the "new church"—built in the 1400s!!! Everything was built of brick—streets, bridges, churches, houses. The old church leans over about 6' and gives you a weird feeling as you look up. The narrowness of the streets and the way houses and churches and buildings are built all jammed up gives you a feeling of informality—that's not exactly the word either—but it's very *different* from anything I've ever experienced. We had another chance to see the canals with flower boxes—which weren't quite so charming when you could see the dirty scum on the water!!

Sunday the 22nd—we all went up to Amsterdam.—Fran preached at

*Fran and me at the International Council of Christian Churches
reception in Amsterdam.*

the 4 P.M. service and the Koks took us out for dinner. World Council
people seemed to *be everywhere* with their name tags and labels setting
them apart. Amsterdam was full of people of all nations in native costumes and it made you a little sick to your stomach to realize what they
were there for. *Monday the 23rd* Harlee Bordeaux came and had lunch
with us—we stretched the bread—and opened a can of Spam. He rode
my bike and Fran and Susan and Janet Priscilla rode theirs and they all
went off for the afternoon. I stayed and typed to keep Debby company
because *she* had a fever and sore throat!!! *Tuesday the 24th* Fran went to
Amsterdam for an executive committee meeting. Fran said Kok and
Shields and others tried to railroad them a proposition to keep Fran in
Amsterdam to help Kok for six months. Fran made a speech in which he
said nine months ago he had decided definitely against working for the
International Council and was sure the Lord had led him into the other
work for the Independent Board. He said we must start languages, etc.,
and a delay would not be fair to our work or to the Board. Then he left
the meeting and came home!!! He feels he did the right thing in leaving
and making it final. I'm so glad he did.

Wednesday the 25th Holdcroft came in the late morning. We opened
another can of Spam and stretched the bread again. It was nice to have
him in our "home"!! He went with us into The Hague to the art muse-

um—when we arrived we found three-year-olds were not permitted to go in—seven years and older just let Susan in!! Deborah was quite insulted—but Fran took her off for a walk and some "milk ice" and Holdcroft went up with us to see the Rembrandts, Vandykes, etc. They really are *lovely*—one picture 450 years old had such exquisite hands—and beautiful coloring—an apple and piece of cheese that looked real—it seemed to melt the years away and bring back the model to life. The museum itself is dark, with red plush walls—a *very* poor place to display such paintings. Holdcroft went down after one-half hour to sit with Debby on a bench while Fran came up. Debby had quite a conversation!! She is so in a fog about time and space, etc. She said once, "After this war we are going home aren't we?" and another time, "When we get through with all these countries we'll go home." Another time, "Why didn't you leave me with Aunt Janet and Jonny while you two came to Europe?" "But Debby, wouldn't you be lonely for mother and daddy?" "Well yes, but Aunt Janet could bring me to Europe when *she* came. Say—how did we get to Europe anyway?" "Don't you remember Debby, we came on a big boat." "Oh *yes*—and we walked too." The boat was a place where we *lived* but as for covering any *space*—it made no more impression than walking from the trolley.

Dr. Holdcroft stayed with us for dinner too. We divided the meat a little smaller and there are always plenty of potatoes and carrots (or string beans)—never any other vegetable! I'll never want to *see* a string bean or a carrot again. How I'd love peas or corn or broccoli or any variety of vegetable!! However, the children actually *eat* up all their vegetables without fussing—they don't expect any variety and they act starved and eat quantities of potatoes and carrots—especially Susan. Priscilla has learned to eat raw fish and pickled herring! It's amazing how only 5 weeks of this has made them appreciate food—also lack of space and comfort does not make them *less* able to sleep—but they go to sleep even with a light on if I *have* to do something in the room. I think this is all very good for their training—better than their darling individual rooms, desks, closets, toys, etc., in our St. Louis 12-room home. Not that I'd *plan* to deprive them—but it's working out for their good. Priscilla is always so careful to say, "No thank you," if someone offers her *rationed* food because she doesn't want to deprive them. They'll be different girls than they would have been.

Thursday 26th—Deborah finally had a ride on a bicycle, Fran had the seat put on his for her—a little leather seat with an iron back and railing round the sides. She was proud as punch and they all rode off for awhile. I kept at my typing and shorthand—Fran figured out accounts which are horribly complicated—divided this month between "Ind. B." and "Am. C."* and everything was paid in guilders and exchange must be figured in—and you know how he checks and double-checks!! Fran

*Ind. B.=Independent Board
  Am. C.=American Council

and I went to the Kur House for an orchestra concert 8 P.M. to 10 P.M. — just one and a half blocks away. The music was lovely—the violins seemed *perfect*—and the conductor very tall and thin in *long* swallow-tail coat was very fascinating to watch. Sometimes I thought he was going to take off and fly—his tails swooped up and feet almost left the floor. You could see *any* kind of clothes, from very formal to cotton dresses—and *styles* from seven or eight years ago to the very *ultra*-latest styles. There's more contrast than in America. He ended with "The Sorcerer's Apprentice."

Friday 27th we went to the Isle of Markham and Volendam with Dr. Holdcroft and Harlee B. via tram for half an hour—a long wait in a funny little fishing town—then boat for 15 minutes to the Isle of Markham. 1,400 inhabitants. Settled 900 years ago by Norwegians. They intermarry but never marry folks from the mainland, all wear native costume. They *rent* costumes for pictures—so we dressed up the girls and snapped them—a tourist also took their picture and paid them 5¢ (Dutch) for their trouble—thought they were natives!! Wonder where *that* picture will go? Not much to the town, so full of tourists you stepped on each other's toes!! Then we took a boat to Volendam—where within the first half-hour we lost each other (that is, Fran, I, Sue, and Janet Priscilla were together—Dr. H., Harlee, and Debby were somewhere else) and spent the next hour looking for each other!! Volendam is a *very* quaint fishing town—every way you turn you want to take a picture. I like their costumes—the men's especially. They wear the big balloon (black) shaped pants and black knitted scarves tied tight and flowing out behind. We wandered all through the back streets and a little girl took us to see her home (we paid her)—*one* room—bed built in the wall with a space *below* it for the children and a niche at the foot—in the wall—for the baby. All very compact for a five-person family. Tram back to Amsterdam where we all ate together and then home and bed.

Saturday the 28th—I had neuritis pains for first time in months—I guess that's what it was—hence did very little except type. *Sunday the 29th* is today so here I am!!! I must not let it pile up again. But I may not be able to write such full accounts. Of course once we are in Switzerland maybe there won't be so much to tell!! I could spend *pages* telling you about the street decorations in The Hague and Amsterdam—but maybe the papers will give it. Every day since we've been here more decorations have gone up—lights, lights, lights strung all *over*—the windows of many buildings are outlined with bulbs, trees have clusters of orange lights, strings festoon some streets, castles are built and outlined with lights—posts have false bottoms of light wood, built like huge boxes, filled with flowers and decorated with the coat of arms and the house of Orange—*flowers* (geraniums, ageratums, petunias)—growing in boxes on lamp posts—on street corners—*everywhere*. Some streets are more elaborate with gilt crowns and huge lanterns of every shape and description. One street is hung with fishing nets festooned over pillars

Debby, Susan, Priscilla, and me on our first hike in Europe.

formed by fish barrels—all strung with lights. They will be all lighted on the 31st (Queen's birthday) and every night for a week. Last week they tested them on one night while Fran was in Amsterdam and he said it was like fairyland. The canals are strung with lights—it's breathtaking. So he's anxious for us all to see it sometime. As you look down each street, it has a canopy formed by decorations. My wrist is cramped and I have other letters. There are a few things else I should say. Our sheets have not been changed since we arrived and won't be till we go I guess! Wish I had time to tell you about Magers' war experience.

Thank you Janet for typing a copy for Mother Schaeffer; she and her neighbors and friends have enjoyed it and have written to say so. Please tell me who else you send it to. *Please* send anything you do to Mildred Kern, 7815 Grove Ave., Webster Groves 19, MO. She writes me faithfully every Sunday and has done more for us in expenditure of time and energy as well as money—I'd like her to have letters that equal this in length—but just *can't*—so—if when you all have read it you'd send it on—you wouldn't have to copy it. Or when you copy excerpts be sure to include her. She has taken on the support of Susan—so has special part in the work that way too.

We had a nice note this week from a lady who lives in our Swiss Pension (Madame Turrian* does *not* speak or write English) to tell us she has a nice little pink baby bed for Deborah and that she is sure we will like the place and that Madame Turrian is very charming and kind!! It is wonderful the way the Lord prepares a nice welcome for us at these pensions—even when folks can't speak your language a welcome smile and a *prepared* room and an "expecting you" attitude mean *so* much. We never would have *had* that except for the Lord working things out. Pray for a good tutor for French—and for our ability to learn it quickly—and for the children in School. We leave here the 7th for 10 days of vacation—

*The Swiss proprietor.

(American Express, 11 Rue Scribe—Paris till the 17th). We have reservations in Paris for three rooms and a bath!! Paris prices are cheap this year. We'll take baths all the time—and revel in the space—*if* it is clean!!

Much love to you all—the children *love* to hear about the cousins—

EDITH

P.S. It's quite all right to send it on to Mildred because she will be silent about bracketed parts. Have her send it back to you.

September 25, 1948   Lausanne, Switzerland

Dearest Mother and Dad, Janet and Elsa, and families:

Our last week in Holland was full to the brim with packing and sightseeing and business correspondence (which meant typing for me). A day at the Missars' home gave us a real picture of Dutch life as well as an opportunity to see the festive lights of Rotterdam under expert guidance. When we arrived Mrs. Missar and the two boys greeted us warmly with the one English word they had learned for the occasion—"Goodbye, goodbye." It was rather startling! Mr. Missar speaks English and he told us of their war experiences—how they lost everything, and lived on tulip bulbs, etc. The human frame is amazing, the way it can go through such things and yet come back to normal. Rotterdam harbor was like fairyland, with huge pictures and buildings outlined in myriad lights, floating about.

We also saw the decorations of Amsterdam and The Hague, but as for the actual processions in which the Queen rode, we did not try to see those. People take seats or blankets and sit or stand for *hours,* even all night, to save a spot on the route, and we were not inclined to do that! Buses, trains, trolleys, etc., were jammed all that week. The day of the coronation, I was washing one last batch of clothes and the sound of the solemn ceremony filtered up through the floor from the Magers', below—where their family (plus our Priscilla) were gathered around the radio. As they sang their impressive hymns and Juliana became queen, the rinse water dripped off my elbows and the tears filled my eyes as I was filled with emotion for so Christian a ceremony in a nation which has stood so fast in History, and yet is even now moving away from true faith. You can imagine Priscilla's excited reports as she dashed up every few minutes to be sure we knew what was going on! The hotel at the end of our street, the front of which could be seen from our front window, housed the Queen Mother of Belgium and an Indonesian Prince and a few other such, during the festivities. Each time they went out or came in, a long line of grey limousines, accompanied by motorcycle police, paraded past our door, much to the enjoyment of the children. Two

Riding bikes in Holland.

guards in full dress marched up and down in front of the hotel all day and all night. The exaggerated clicking of their heels and precise "quarter turns" made them look like part of a pageant. Priscilla and Susan and some Dutch children went up and sat not 2 feet away from them for an hour one day and just stared! Then Priscilla and Dick marched up and down in front of our house for about a half an hour! "Playing guards" is now a new "pretend" added to the collection of things to play.

We bought "klompers" or wooden shoes for each of the children. The wooden shoes were bought at a "klompen winkle" (wooden shoe store) where the fishermen get theirs. We were taken through the store to the fitting room, which was on the other side of a crooked little stone courtyard and in a sort of shed. There they had shoes in all stages of making and one could make a selection, trying them on while balancing on the other foot! The children must wear heavy socks, 2 or 3 pairs, and in the winter the Dutch children stuff them with straw. The shoes are *only* worn outdoors, left on the doorstep when coming in.

I wish you could have seen us riding the bikes. Susan and Priscilla knew their way around town and rode each day. I went a few times with them, and Fran took Debby on the back of his in a little seat. We rode, too, on brick-paved bike paths through sand dunes, like a wilderness.

We had several good opportunities that week to talk to Mrs. Box. She and her husband and the children may come to Switzerland for Christmas. At any rate we will keep in touch with them. They lived 4 years of their short lives in a Japanese prison camp amidst untold horrors, sleeping on a stone floor, eating unspeakable food, and their bodies swollen with "beriberi." The children never speak of that time; the mother told me all about it. An experience like that sweeps away the belief in "man" as a "good" creature. There's just no answer except the Scriptural one. The little girl, almost 6 years old, didn't walk till she was 3. Mrs. Box was pregnant when she was captured. Mr. Box was not with them, never knew what went on till 4 years later! He didn't know of Patsy's existence till then. As our taxi glided through the early-morning quiet of the holiday-decked streets of The Hague, we felt a real sadness at leaving Holland, much as we looked forward to the vacation and even more to the beginning of our days of preparation for the work.

We had reserved seats in a *Wagon Lits* car, 2nd class, and so there was space for our bags, and all went surprisingly smoothly. The trip to Brussels would take much less time if it were not for going through customs. At a border station the entire trainload of people get off with all their luggage and go through customs, first Dutch, then Belgian. About a half-dozen officers from each country scrutinize your passport and then they select a bag to open and poke at, first in Holland, then as you go out on the platform to await the signal to return to the train.

We arrived in Brussels about 4:30 P.M. and were greeted by a flow of French from the porter. It gave us a queer feeling to realize that here was not just another language, but one that must soon be *ours*. We arrived at the hotel bag and baggage, all in one taxi!!, by 5 o'clock. Our rooms were on opposite sides of a court, Priscilla and Susan in one, Deborah and Fran and I in the other. Miles of halls between us, but we could wave across the court. We all had 3 desires: to take a deep, hot bath; to eat something different; to sleep in soft beds. We had all 3 wishes fulfilled in that day and a half in Belgium! We took several baths apiece. We also ordered eggs and canned peas, but discovered that the only milk one could get was a very *tiny* glass of *canned* milk and the cost was terrific, 25 francs a glass. (45 Belgian francs to one American dollar made that 50¢ a glass!) We drank it that time, but ordered water after that.

This was the beginning of our ten-day vacation. The next day we walked all over the city of Brussels, Fran carrying Debby on his shoulders most of the time. It is rather hilly and the streets are paved in cobblestones or rough bricks. The main street is wide and lined with restaurants, theaters, stores, etc., with lighted signs which help it to really look like its nickname, "little New York," but as you go back in the town, it is quite different. The streets are narrow and crooked and the buildings old and crumbly-looking. Geraniums grow in the most surprising spots—on window ledges high up in a grey plastered wall, or in a doorway that leads into dark and musty halls. The cathedral is amazing because of its tremendous size, piles of stone that have stood there for centuries. We went inside for a few cents. It is *huge* inside. Parts are not used at all. Piles of broken benches, etc., are stacked in most deserted-looking sections, yet other parts have burning candles, confession boxes, etc. We went through two museums, the one of Ancient Art, and the Contemporary Art. The former was the better, of course. It is most awe-inspiring actually to gaze upon the originals of the masters. Rubens' works are most prominent there. We were dead tired by dinnertime, but we had covered the prominent spots of the city plus a lot of in-between streets, all by foot!! Brussels really has *everything* (but milk), such a contrast to Holland, Oranges (Sunkist) for sale, bananas, soap, candy, *everything*. But most of it much too high for the average person to buy.

The children were so delighted to have an orange. Afterwards I was sorry I hadn't bought a dozen to take to Paris where there are *none*. We did fix a lunch to eat on the train, but should have brought more.

The next day we left for Paris, after 2 nights, one full day in Brussels. Things had gone so well when we boarded the train in Holland that we anticipated an easy time. When we arrived at the station and showed our tickets to the porters, they began shaking their heads, gesticulating wildly, and shouting French. At first all we understood was that there were too many bags. More wild gesticulating. Fran waved his arms and talked English. The men grew more exasperated. "Well, here we stay, I guess, right on the sidewalk." Finally a man came up who spoke some English. "They say your tickets are not for Pullman; you have to put your baggage in a baggage car." "O.K. then, how do we do it?" The translating bystander pointed in the direction of a counter where bags were being checked, and then walked off. The porters picked up our bags, herded us and the children over in that direction, and then began more explanations in very loud French. Fran must buy some sort of tickets. We *had* tickets. Well, with a heave of satisfaction, the now-perspiring porter got Fran lined up in a ticket line. Fran stood for about 2 minutes, then after looking over his tickets, decided he had one for each of us for reserved seats for the trip itself—what was he waiting for?—the train would leave in 5 minutes. Out of the line he popped, pointed to the clock, pointed to our bags, pointed in general direction of the train.

Now the porter became exasperated as though dealing with a stubborn child. He pushed Fran back in the line, shoved him near the window, shouted orders for tickets. Finally Fran emerged with a ticket for each of our *bags* in the baggage car. "Hurry now—up we go—this way?—no *this* way." Debby, "My dolly's panties fell off." Fran, "I've got them, go ahead." The porters have our bags, they herd us along like chickens—"Who can tell what these crazy foreigners will do next?" they seem to think. They indicate that Fran must go up to the baggage car. Off he runs with money, papers, keys to our bags, and dolly's panties all in his hand together. They push us in to our car. Susan wails, "We'll go without Daddy now." Deborah takes up the cry, "Where's

Daddy? We're going without him!" I reassure them and get them on the proper seats, hang up their coats. My own pockets are bulging with the lunch (string had broken).

A whistle blows. One of our perspiring porters sticks his head in the window and shouts, "Stay on the train" (in French)—"Monsieur est —." The train starts. Where "monsieur est" we are not sure. The children begin to cry. Suddenly Fran appears and sinks into his seat with a sigh. "What happened at the baggage car?" "Oh, I was supposed to open my bags for the customs official. I had so many keys, I could not find the right ones. Then it was time for the train to go and the official picked just *one* bag to open. When I got the key for it, only *one* end would open, the other end stuck. The whistle blew. 'One end is enough, go ahead,' the official said, then threw the bag in the baggage car." Fran jumped on after it, and the train started! It really was awfully funny, but it made us realize how wonderfully the Lord undertakes when things do go smoothly, and how amazing last summer's trips were through 13 countries with no serious holdups in time.

Our Paris hotel had been selected for us by the American Express, a family hotel, not expensive. It turned out to be Hotel de France et Chaisel. When we drove up, there was no impressive front, only a huge pair of doors on the sidewalk. There are hundreds of these doors in Paris, which lead in to courtyards of various descriptions. At night one walks

We took a ride in Paris in what the girls called
"the golden chariot."

*Fran snapped this picture of the girls on the hand-powered
merry-go-round.*

along street after street without seeing a light or a sign of life. Windows
on the street side of most buildings are shuttered or heavily curtained.
When one of these huge doors swings open, you get a glimpse of light
and life from the windows bordering the courtyard. As we entered the
doorway, went through a corridor, and stepped into the courtyard, we
formed (the children and I) our first impressions of Paris. The courtyard
was paved in bricks, a narrow porch with wooden pillars circled it, here
and there more potted trees in green wooden buckets, and to complete
the picture, a live turtle made his way slowly across the bricks. We were
shown to our rooms, up a winding staircase, on the second floor. The
light fixtures, plumbing, etc., were all very old-fashioned, beds were
high and narrow, Deborah's crib narrow, made of curlicues of iron—
nothing modern or luxurious about it, but it had one wonderful feature
for a vacation: we had an extra room, with a table, 5 chairs, a small couch,
and 3 large mirrors! Here for a short time we could have a living room
again, and the children were overjoyed. We had powdered milk with us
(no milk in Paris) and so we ate our breakfasts in our "room"—powdered milk shaken up in a Thermos and dark tough bread provided by
the Hotel. Except in extra-fancy restaurants, the only bread you get in
France is dark and tougher than usual because of a lack of ingredients.
The only place we had "French dinner rolls" was on the SS *Nieuw Amsterdam* coming over!

The children loved the flowers and all the beauty of the views from the Gardens, but most of all they loved the merry-go-round and donkey rides. A small merry-go-round is pushed by a little old woman and a little old man (like a storybook). They push until it picks up speed, then he grinds a crank to finish the ride. For all this you pay 5 fr. (about 1 2/3 *cents* American) a ride. The donkey rides are 10 francs, and there were just 3 donkeys, so the girls were able to ride at the same time. Fran said if he had let them, the girls would have been content to stay there all week!

You mustn't imagine the Paris vacation as one long dreamy week of perfection. You see, one after another we had tummy aches and intestinal upsets, which meant someone was always not well and several mornings and evenings were consumed in caring for the sick.* The last night we were there, Susan awakened and had a long spell of vomiting which, plus packing again, plus getting up at 5:30 A.M. to get our train, made kind of a siege out of the last night there. We were a half-hour early for our train thinking we might have difficulty again. However, in spite of 2nd-class coach tickets, we were allowed to pile all our bags into our own space and we had a half-hour to sit and watch the station come to life in the light of the rising sun. This train trip was the most interesting one of all. It was intensely interesting to see that section of France and to see the little villages and rolling hillsides and finally mountains piled upon mountains as we neared Switzerland. It was also the dirtiest train trip I've ever taken. We were all black with soot before we arrived. Food was covered with soot as you ate it! But we all thrilled and exclaimed as we rushed from one side of the car to the other to see the varying views.

We were all excited as we pulled into Lausanne, to be stepping in to our new Home Town. This ceased to be "sightseeing" and became "getting acquainted" with what will be home. The very first thing that struck us as we stepped off of the train was the *air*. The clean, pure *feel* of it is hard to describe. Things *look* different, as they do when you have just freshly washed your windows. You know how you think, "Why, I didn't know they were *that* dirty!" Well that's how you feel as you just look around you here when you first arrive. Once again we went through customs with our bags, and found a taxi.

The taxi climbed and climbed and climbed. In Lausanne you are either going up or down in any of four directions. It is all built on hills, *large* hills (small mountains!); no place is level at all. Back yards are straight up or straight down, depending on which side of the street you live, but you'll hear lots more about this later. Finally we saw "Rosiaz" and then "Blvd de le Foret"—and at last "Riant Mont." Out we tumbled, bags and children, pay the driver—"Bonjour, madame; bonjour, monsieur; bon-

---

*The "powdered milk" had been mixed with water! I was too naive to know about buying bottled water.

*Our first picture on arrival at Madame
Turrian's pension in La Rosiaz.*

jour, les enfants; bonjour, bonjour." We are greeted by Madame Ochsenbein, Mademoiselle Ochsenbein, and Monsieur Tecoz, who have
come from Belmont (2 miles away) just to greet us! In a moment Madame Turian and the two German-Swiss girls who help her came down
to help us up the steps. A large stone retaining wall keeps the front
yard from falling into the street (all along this side of the road the front
yards get higher and higher). An arched opening in this wall allows
you to start up the steps, up, up, up, to the level of the house. Here we
are in the house, up, up stone stairs winding to 3rd floor (have to watch
out going up and down, children, careful to step on the wide part)—
these two rooms (all talk in French, no one in the house except one
guest speaks any English at all, and she leaves for Africa next
week!). . . .

We have two rather small bedrooms. In one there are 3 beds: a single
bed, a daybed, and a medium-sized wooden crib freshly painted
pink—for the children. This room also has a table and chair, a chest of
drawers, a wash basin, and two closets. Not much space left over! The
other room has twin beds pushed together, a table and chair, wash basin, a "chifforobe" affair to hang clothes in, a closet with shelves in it (2
for Fran and 2 for me), another small closet—no chests of drawers or
dressing tables. It also has a small built-in book case, which was immediately pounced upon for office supplies and the most necessary com-
mentaries and books.

Upon first glance it seemed impossible to find space for the contents of the suitcases, the typewriters, the projector, etc., let alone the contents of the boxes and trunks to come. However, it was a challenge to one's ingenuity and we find it can be done, like a jigsaw puzzle. One room is strictly the children's for toys and books, clothes and *living!* The other is ours, a combination bedroom and office. I'm not sure if I'll work all night or sleep all day! It's a very compact way of living; no unnecessary space.

If the inside feels a bit cramped after dwelling in a whole house, the *outside* makes up for it. The vast stretch of the view takes one miles away without moving from the bedroom or the office, as the case may be. We each have a tiny balcony. The window is not a window but French doors, inner glass doors with curtains shutting out the view—they can be opened, inward of course. Next come a pair of doors with glass that you can see through; then, for cold weather, a pair of solid wood doors, to keep out the very cold wind for which this section is famous. Of course when the wooden doors are shut, the room is as black as your hat. On warm days the doors can all be open and the sun streams in, which is very pleasant and is like pushing out a wall to enlarge the house. Since we are so high, the view is very special, for which we praise God. It would be tantalizing to look out on walls when the mountains are surrounding you! We praise God many times for His wonderful leading in bringing Mr. Ochsenbein into the place where he could help so much. Mr. Ochsenbein couldn't have selected a better place in which to reserve 2 rooms. The price is cheaper than in other pensions, and the house is scrupulously clean. Madame Turrian is very kind and pleasant, and the view is a gift of the Lord! We are up in the highest part of Lausanne, just out of the town limits. The train line ends two houses away, so transportation is close. Yet we have country sounds and smells around us, the smell of hay and pine trees, and the constant sound of musical, tinkling cowbells. There is a farmer right behind us, a small farm with a meadow and an orchard and about 20 cows who wander about making music. In the afternoon they go higher up on the hill to graze. Priscilla and Susan and Debby have very little indoor space, but Madame Turrian's front garden, which goes downhill from house to wall, has a few pine trees with lovely spots underneath them for pretend houses, etc. The back yard, which goes straight up for about 30 ft., has a small vegetable garden and a rabbit and chicken house. The children watch the rabbits and chickens get fed each night, and Priscilla is allowed to gather 2 or 3 eggs which appear each day! This makes up a great deal for living in one room. The Lord is so good to His children in filling their needs in one way if not in another.

I must hasten along if you are ever to get this. Now it is the 30th. We arrived Friday, unpacked Saturday, and Sunday continued the custom which we started in Holland—having our own Sunday school and church service in our bedroom. I teach Sunday school, Fran conducts

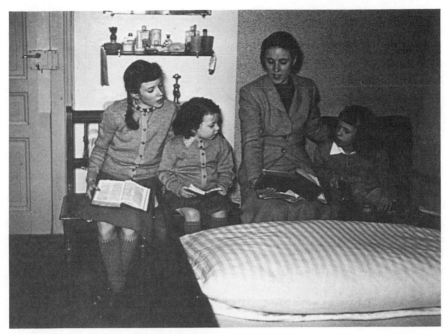

Fran's congregation!

regular church service and preaches. We remember all of you in our special prayer time and all the B.P. churches, especially those who have part in our work here. It is a very precious time to us. We have prayed that the Lord will give us some others to join us at that time.

We found next-door neighbors, introduced by Madame Turrian, Mr. and Mrs. Wildermuth (Vildermoo), who are linguists. He is a language professor. She has also taught some. He speaks French, German, Italian, English, and teaches each of these. They have been most helpful in translating for us, to help us discuss arrangements with Mrs. Turrian, the police, customs men, etc. We have engaged Madame Wildermuth as our tutor. She comes each A.M., 10 to 11, for a French lesson, 6 days a week. We get enough in a lesson to take all day studying! But of course there are other things to do. Fran carries vocabulary on cards and we do vocabulary incessantly, riding trains, waiting for police, eating meals, etc. Professor Wildermuth will begin tutoring us in German after we have French really under way.

They also helped us find a school for the children. They have 4 children themselves. Their Suzanne is the age of our Susan. Madame Vodoz's school has only about 20 pupils and is a 15-minute walk way from here. She was skeptical of taking Debby as she has 4-, 5-, 6-year-olds in same room, and 6-year-olds are learning to read. But after 2 days she reported Debby o.k., quiet and works away at puzzles and drawings and blocks just like 4-year-olds! So all 3 go off together now, as last year. In bad weather they can take the tram. Susan is going along all right in the work of the 2nd grade. She is learning to write French words in the French handwriting which looks so neat and pretty I'm amazed! Arithmetic is confusing—7, 0—and of course all numbers must be *said* in French.* Susan writes numbers backwards anyway sometimes, so she gets very mixed up, but I think she'll do all right. Priscilla is learning French, French, French, verbs, verbs! All sorts of grammar exercises and phrases and vocabulary. They won't be giving her anything else till she can really talk and understand, because 6th-grade work would be too hard. We *couldn't* put her in a public school—children her age have *had* 1 year of German and are doing Latin! Anyway public school for this district is a mile and a half straight down, so steep there are railings partway! No trolley that way, and the climb up too exhausting for a child. Children around here all go to one or another of these small private schools (very inexpensive). Priscilla is very hungry for English books as she is running out of reading materials. Secondhand ones would be very acceptable for Christmas.

We spent many hours these first days at customs offices, police, etc. So much red tape to go through for every time you turn around! Our boxes and trunks arrived and we have signed many papers saying we will not sell or give away any of this stuff for 5 years! Poor Madame Turrian was upset when she saw all the stuff. However Fran worked like a beaver, lifting heavy boxes of books and breaking up crates, etc., and now her cellar is in perfect order again. The crates are reduced to a pile of boards, which will be useful when we get a house. We had to store some things at a storage place—they won't *let* you store a refrigerator and beds *here* or anywhere except under the eye of a customs officer, afraid you'll sell them! The bikes are tagged with metal tags, to be spotted if sold. The 2 tiny chests of drawers we have squeezed into the rooms and the tall thin one, to Fran's delight, has drawers just the size of a sheet of typing paper, so will do to hold his files. We are glad we brought it. Wish I'd brought a typing table; they are *so* expensive here. Everything is. Switzerland has everything, but you need to be rich to benefit by that fact. Prices are higher than in America, including rents. The wooden box, which used to be Fran's toy chest, traveled the ocean and now fits perfectly under the children's wash basin, to hold toys, serve as a stool for Debby to wash her hands, and as a bed for Susan's doll at night! The nail keg (covered with leather) fits under our table and provides a seat, still as good as ever! And so we have a few of our old home touches.

Now I must draw to a close, but first I must give you a picture of our days (of course there are exceptions) so you can think of us accurately! We feel getting the language is the first requisite. You can't imagine (or of course *you* can!) how it feels to be reduced to a moron, with only the

---

*The seven they learned to write in St. Louis was 7, without the crossbar.

ability to speak in a few short sentences using a very limited vocabulary. We can't even get to know people, let alone tell them anything, till we know French. However, one good thing, the very strong desire makes the work go faster, and my high school French *does* help; I find, as I study, that I really have a foundation. Thank you, whoever made me take French.

We arise at 7 A.M. or slightly before, and try to whisper the children through their dressing. The house contains 5 elderly ladies, 1 elderly man, Madame T. and her husband, 1 college boy, and the Schaeffers. Six elderly people require much quiet (a disadvantage in raising children!). Spurts of laughter or protest always seem to burst through the quiet! We then eat breakfast, which first consisted of bread and tea, but now (after discussion) is of 1 small dish oatmeal each, cup hot milk apiece, toast (very hard to chew, oval loaves of dark bread made by M. Turrian, healthy, but hard on tooth fillings!). Then a period of preparation and last-minute things and the children go off to school. Priscilla *has* to be there by 8:30, the other two not until nine. Fran and I then either study French or he dictates to me. At ten Madame Wildermuth arrives and we have our French lesson. She usually gives us extra time and the lesson does not close before 11:30. We then return to our room for more dictation until our 12:30 lunch. The children have until 2 P.M. for lunch hour and return to school 3 days a week from 2 to 4 P.M. No afternoon school other 3 days. School on Saturday also. In the afternoon I type and take dictation. Of course so far there've been filing and sorting and unpacking also. Fran studies French while I type (my "foundation" carries me along right now). We have family prayers right after lunch, the long noon hour gives us plenty of time for it. (Stores and offices here have 12 to 2 noon hour, close shop, but work until 6 and 6:30 P.M.) Dinner is at 6 P.M. for the girls (special favor by Madame T.) and is always soup and macaroni, or eggs, and some sort of dessert and hot milk again. I get Debby in bed right after that, the other 2 *ready* for bed, then we eat at 7 P.M., and Priscilla and Susan read or study or play a game in our bedroom until we come up. In the evening we study French (except tonight I'm writing this).

We feel after various inquiries that getting a house now would be almost impossible and also foolish. Prices are sky high for rent, for food, etc. And we know so little and could get easily cheated. Coal would need to be bought, etc., etc. Then our minds would be filled with material problems. This place is crowded and restricted (for children and home life) but has many advantages. The children love Madame T. and the bunnies and chickens and cows tinkling their bells over our back fence. They are happy here. We feel God led us here. Hence since the cost is close to what an apartment plus food, etc., would be, we plan to stay here for at least the next 6 months. We will then have: 1) Freedom to study and get work under way unhampered by daily things that come with starting with a new home; 2) Time to gain wisdom and knowledge before making a selection; 3) Time to live here awhile before the police start to search out our motives, etc., for moving, which they do *much* more in connection with house or apartment than with pension; 4) A place to practice daily in conversation that French which we know. Oh, there are lots of other reasons, too. So, unless something intervenes, D.V.* we will be here for some time. There is a pile of correspondence to catch up on and the Lord is going to open things up *a day at a time,* I know.

Now I must not use another sheet. Please forgive delay. I'll try to write short letters each week now.

Packages take about 7 weeks to get here. Any *warm* things are welcome for Christmas, books for the children, or games that can be played in small space, or Sunday materials. Wool knee socks for youngsters or short- or long-sleeved sweaters. Wool socks for Fran. We'll feel the cold, I know.

Much love to all,

EDITH

October 28, 1948

Lausanne, Switzerland

Dearest Family:

When I last wrote, Susan had just had an attack of swollen glands. Dr. Decker pronounced her well for school the 12th. Friday the 15th she ate very little supper, almost went to sleep in her chair, and presto, the glands on the other side were up. Dr. Decker prescribed a heavy black ointment and sulfa. She wasn't sick enough to rest but wanted something to do every minute. That can be very trying in the midst of office work or French. When she was well again, the doctor ordered a single dose of vitamin D, 600,000 units in a tiny vial, to be dumped into ½ glass of milk, called Vi-do. "Il est tres fort!" Smelled like ether and was *strong* all right! Susan had to take it before a meal, hence all the interested eyes of the elderly ladies were upon her, helping to stiffen her willpower. We all waited for something to blow up, but we've seen no effects except a very normal Susan. This was followed by daily doses of iron and multiple vitamins.

Priscilla has been very well, eating better than ever before and really gaining weight. Fran, however, was sick in bed Friday and Saturday.

Since the bedroom is also our office, he can dictate as well there, and since the study is also the bedroom, he can read and study with all materials at hand. It's very convenient, living in one room!

Deo Volente, or "God willing."

Now for Deborah, the healthiest-looking one of the family. She has been rosy and very gay. Last week the children had a holiday from school. "The Grape Holiday," harvest time for the quantities of grapes grown on the steep hillsides. It was a lovely week of sunshine, perfect fall weather, and the children enjoyed outdoor play and walks in the warm part of the day. Sunday we had our usual church and Sunday school service in the sun-flooded children's bedroom with the flower-decked pulpit and chairs in a row turning it into church. It was such a beautiful day that I decided to take the children for a walk alone since Fran wasn't well enough to go. The countryside is all so fascinating that I guess we went too far and perhaps Debby was too tired (no Daddy to carry her on the stretch home!). It was suppertime when we returned. The next day I kept Debby in bed for the day. She was not at all sick or feverish and had a lovely time sitting in on our French lesson and coloring while I typed. Tuesday we almost sent her back to school, but decided against it since the skies were grey. By afternoon she had a fever and I called Dr. Decker again. "Bronchitis." Have you ever tried to discuss symptoms and treatment with a language barrier to hamper every phrase? Dr. Decker's English is no better than our French. Our little red dictionary is in constant use as he tries to find the word for "cup," "pill," etc. It's quite painful.

We moved Deborah's crib into our room. How?—by moving our one armchair out, then angling the crib in that place so that there is a foot of space on either side to squeeze by our bed and the wash basin. We wanted her where we could care for her at night and also not disturb the other two. The sulfa, etc., did not seem to improve her condition. The next day she was about the same, fever of 38° (100.6° as closely as I can figure it), with intestinal trouble added. I called the doctor through our tutor, but he said not to be alarmed. That evening her temperature started to climb and was over 39° (102.6°) by morning. Madame Turrian, our landlady, who is fond of all the girls but especially of Deborah, was quite distressed and asked Decker to come again. He came about 10 A.M. and said pneumonia could start through the day. If by 5 o'clock her temperature was not down, he would take her to the "clinic" to determine the extent of the infection by looking at her lungs and then keep her in the hospital for a few days to administer penicillin. After he left, Deborah looked whiter and whiter and began to complain of her chest hurting when she moved. We really had an anxious time. We couldn't feel right about taking her out on a cold, grey day, and then leaving her in a French-speaking hospital, alone and frightened, to say nothing of our own feelings at being separated from her and not fully able to discuss anything with nurses or doctors.

We prayed. Debby's temperature went up. Just as we were feeling we ought not to wait for 5 P.M., Madame Wildermuth came for our French lesson. She took our problem as though it were her own. Her own doctor, specialist in "malades des enfants," *would* have been called in the first place, but she *said* she couldn't speak English. However, Madame Wildermuth decided to call and ask her advice. Result, Dr. Decker was told we had called a specialist and the "doctoress" as they call her came in a half-hour's time—Dr. Meyer Kousmine came in *so* efficiently, a dark-haired, dark-eyed, slim, and strong-looking woman, in her forties. She spoke *much* better English than we expected, a strange choice of words but no hesitation. Her verdict, "She wishes to have pneumonia—she has been receiving only half enough sulfa—I will prescript for to-day—I think we have time yet." She also ordered packs on her chest of "decongesting," which comes in an aluminum can, is heated on the stove, spread on linen, and placed on the chest, with changes every 6 hours. It is a clay, but smells like Anaphlogestine. She also ordered a process to be done to her back (it has a French name), little tiny glass bottles, with a mouth the size of an orange juice glass—which are filled with vacuums! That is, one places a piece of burning cotton in the glass, quickly inverts the glass on the back (upper section), the flame goes out instantly and the flesh is drawn up in the glass. Madame Wildermuth knew how to do this and came over with her little basket of glasses and a candle, which seem to be a part of all household equipment. 10 glasses were inverted on Debby's back while she lay without moving (much to our amazement). It was rather a strain on our nerves, all so new and different. Debby cried after they were all on, but a story kept her quiet for the required 15 minutes. After all this she slept, but her fever kept climbing. It was almost 40° (104°) by 6:30 and so the doctor (who asked for a report) decided to come back in the evening. "It is still bronchitis, but she wishes to have pneumonia. It is not *necessary*, but it is intelligent to give a penicillin this evening." It seems they give penicillin with 2 different bases here, with oil or with blood. She calls the second method a milder one and more effective. Hence Fran was called upon to sit in a chair and bare his arm, while I held Deborah over my lap. A spot was prepared on Debby's thigh, then an ounce or more of Fran's blood taken, mixed with penicillin with a quick shake, and plunged into Debby within a few seconds. By midnight her breathing was better and the fever began to drop. When the doctor returned this morning, she said we were in time and the pneumonia danger has been averted.

October 29, 1948

It is now a regular case of bronchitis, no more shots, but we continue with sulfa, the packs, nose drops, vitamin C, and bed of course. No more cups! We do praise the Lord for answered prayer, because according to this doctor, the small doses of sulfa would *not* have averted it and we would have had no alternative than the hospital because the first doctor wouldn't treat pneumonia here at the house. It has been a strain, but we have had a new opportunity to see how the Lord works. It has given us an opportunity to discuss basic things with Madame Wildermuth, also to become closer to Madame Turrian, who has been *so* kind and helpful, and also an opportunity to meet this doctor who will be good for the children as well as another contact.

October 31, 1948

I worked until 4 P.M. on letters, then Fran and I rode to the Post Office on our bikes while Priscilla stayed with Deborah for awhile. It was my first time out of our room for a week, except to telephone. I even ate meals there.

The descent (to Pulley) is steep, but so interesting. No rows of houses here, no two alike. Steep, narrow streets are bordered by thick stone walls, many of which are covered with ivy or moss; gates in these walls open into steep steps which lead up to the house or a lane of houses. Vineyards and vegetable gardens, square pastures, and orchards appear in between clusters of houses, like the pictures in a child's storybook. Many houses look centuries old, with red-and-white or green-and-white striped shutters, and geraniums bordering balconies. Some of the oldest houses have a barn built in, as a 1st floor, with a watering trough for cows out front. Yet the hillside is dotted with the loveliest of modern cottages and Swiss chalets and villas. Some of them are concrete (many in fact), pale pink, or yellow, with concrete walled-in gardens, and the loveliest of windows, terraces, balconies, perched to get just the view they want. Houses face the best view, rather than the streets! And the *gardens!* I wish Ralph could see them. What an inspiration they would be to a gardener. Flowers of all descriptions are blooming even now. Dahlias and chrysanthemums vie with each other for attention. White daisies still fill the fields and many rosebushes are still alive with roses. Fruit trees are not kept in orchards but they join the flowers to decorate a front garden. *These* apple and pear trees are pruned carefully so that they grow branches only from 2 sides, flat-looking. They are grown right up against a wall or fence, or a row of them hold each other's branches and form a fence! Trees of this sort, only 3' or 4' high, have 8 or 10 or even more large apples or pears hanging on their diminutive branches. They look as though they were tied on for decoration. There is such an air of unreality about these little houses and gardens anyway, such prolific flower plants, with gay colors, tiny vegetable patches so full of lettuce and spinach, and colorful urns of pink or blue, often a wee fountain beside a stone bench, all with a breathtaking view when the air is clear.

Our permit has finally come through to live here, but—"No evangelization in Suisse." Do pray the Lord may overcome this in His own time and in His own way.

Two weeks ago today Fran and I were out for our Sunday walk, the last we've had together but we'll hope all well next week! As we were descending a steep but paved road, I slipped on some little gravel-like stones, went down on my left knee, then because it was so steep, slid for a few feet! My poor stocking was hopelessly torn to shreds and little stones were ground into my knee. Fran bandaged it with his handkerchief, and I sat on a conveniently placed little stone wall and admired the scenery and picturesque hillside (below Belmont) while I ohed and ahed over my knee. A little old lady and a little old man offered assistance down the road, so with Fran on one arm and the couple on the other side, I hobbled to a tram stop and came a roundabout way home. It was very painful for a week but is healing nicely. We've made good use of our 1st-aid kit.

Now about the weather and the heating system. We have had some of the loveliest autumn weather, though always cold after sundown. Then we have also had days when the Brise Noire rattles the windows and makes us feel cold all day. Right now the air is rather icy, the beautiful fall leaves are turning brown, and the end of fall seems near, though the flowers still bloom where they are sheltered. A week ago it snowed up in the mountains and I should think that would chill the air. However Lausanne has milder winters than some other parts of Switzerland. Houses are not kept as warm as ours in America but some do have furnaces. This Pension does have a furnace and hot-water heat. Fire has *not* been kept in all day (they have piles of wood to make fresh fires) but when we keep doors and shutters closed, it's quite nice for Debby, though I keep sweater and socks as well as shirts under her pajamas. The people, especially children, all dress more warmly. You *can* buy anything you need to wear *here*, in the warm line especially. Prices are high. I haven't priced woolen stockings yet, but the woolen socks I bought the girls were $2 a pair, one pair for each child. The stairs and hallways are all stone and there is not heat out there. Unless shutters are shut, the place where my typing is done gets breezes through the cracks. We are fortunate to have radiators though. Next door, the apartment house has wood and coal stoves in each room. We must dress warmly as protection from cold.

One can buy great varieties of food in Switzerland. There are wonderful-looking bakery shops, meat, etc., but prices are *higher* than in America. Canned foods and frozen are so expensive as to be prohibitive and appear in limited quantities on the shelves. We, of course, must eat what is served us here, so have not had opportunity to see how it would be to "choose" food here. We have better fare than in Holland, but of course seasoning and cooking changes flavors and makes things strange to us. The food follows a regular pattern week by week. Friday, fish; Wednesday, cheese; Sunday, one of the rabbits, etc. Breakfast is always the same—slices of dark bread, hot milk, and oatmeal (they have just tea and bread themselves). Dinner comes at noon—potatoes, fish or meat or cheese, and a vegetable—spinach, Swiss chard, carrots, or onions (you can see Fran passing it by!). Dessert at noon is always choice of an apple or a pear. Sundays we have a salad added to this, and French-fried potatoes. Supper starts with a soup made of a cereal base, sometimes just a gruel, other times with vegetables added. The base is

*Priscilla, Susan, and Debby in Susan's improvised
Halloween costumes.*

one of these: oatmeal, Cream of Wheat, barley, ground wheat, rice, or ground-up rice. After that comes either rice with grated cheese (put on just before it is served, not cooked with it) or macaroni, spaghetti, or noodles ditto, or one night a week a toasted cheese on bread and one night a week an egg. We have a dish of lettuce with this and some cooked dish of garden stuff (strange to us) that looks like celery but tastes like licorice. I imagine when the gardens are all finished, the diet will change. Lettuce and greens are still growing here.

On Sunday we get 2 rolls apiece. The rest of the week it is the same bread. The bakeries are full of lovely cookies, breads of all descriptions, fancy *patisseries*, etc., but one doesn't see them *here.* On Sunday night we have crumbled chestnuts with whipped cream. It is rather sickening to us because we're not used to cream except on top of something that cuts the richness. The cream here is stronger than at home, almost tastes sour—not quite but *almost*—and without vanilla flavoring, it isn't like our whipped cream. The milk is very rich, thick cream on top, and no refrigeration. Debby complains so much about pain in her tummy, Susan has frequent stomach upsets, and Fran also, and we wonder if the unpasteurized, unrefrigerated rich milk is at the bottom of the trouble. Maybe not, but something is!

November 2, 1948

Do pray for the children. It is especially hard for Janet Priscilla and Susan. After supper and before breakfast they are always "sh-sh-sh-ed"—it is really an old folks' home here. Madame Turrian tries to do nice things for the children, but lack of space and need of quiet all the time is hard to get around. Lights are very poor, 20-watt bulbs, and they are shocked if you turn 2 lights on, so *that* is a problem. Susan has been more homesick for a home, mother in kitchen, and English-speaking friends. All this comes in periods, you understand, not constantly, but do pray for them in these things.

I must tell you about Susan and Halloween. Sad about no celebration, she shut herself off for 2 hours. We came up from dinner to find all 3 with masks on of Susan's creation (Deb in crib of course). Our room was "decorated" and "games" (pin nose on pumpkin) had been crookedly made on backs of old form letters. She had even gone into the orchard and picked up some hard little green apples (like walnuts) to "bob for"! We contributed 100 gms. of cookies and the party (½ hour) was a success.

We would appreciate your prayers for us in these weeks and months of preparation and groundwork. The devil has many ways of hindering, both from outside in government difficulties, opposition of other Christians to our stand, etc., and from inside our own minds and hearts from time to time. Of course I'm sure you can shut your eyes and imagine what a terrific contrast our present life is to that so packed with variety and activities which we have lived for the past ten years.

Now here we are in our little two rooms and the very slow-moving job of tedious study of French, office work, and "going home at end of day" means no change of scenery! Even though we are getting stacks of letters out, even though the French teacher is pleased with our progress, at times it seems we are doing *nothing* and working *harder* to do it!

We have sweet fellowship as we try to make our "bedroom-church" seem *real* for the children's sake, having added "Young People's" and Wednesday Prayer meetings. The children are so sweet about singing, leading meetings, and enthusiastically announcing "Empire Builders" (which is what Fran's Saturday walks have turned into) that it sort of hurts, and our minds turn back and *wonder*. Ah, but the Lord is so *good* in having led us so *clearly*; as we go back over the steps one at a time, *where* could we have changed the succession of events? Surely *He* has led us here, and we must go on as He leads, though the French, then German, then the tremendous need of Europe, seem *far* too great a task for us even to begin!

Please uphold us in prayer, that we may not look down, like Peter,* and start to sink.

Much love,

EDITH

*See Matthew 14:22–31

November 29, 1948   Lausanne, Switzerland

Dearest Family:

Deborah recovered very nicely from her illness. She looked pale and had little energy at first, but we were amazed how completely her cough disappeared. Gradually she has regained her appetite, color, and energy though she still tires more easily than before. That is to say, she tires out on a walk which would tire many grown folks too! We are not sending her back to school for the present and maybe not until after the cold weather is over. It is a long walk for such a little thing in the early-morning cold. Her playmates are the ladies of the pension, one 78-, four 80-, and two 90-year-olds! I think she is having an unusual experience, don't you? One 90-year-old lady made her a paper hat the other day and the others all came to admire it. Another time she had all the ladies singing Christmas carols with her. One 80-year-old, Mme. Bartrei, is her favorite. She gives her a crochet hook and Debby thinks she is really crocheting as she sits in the circle of ladies. They all love her and call her "the little ray of sunshine." Hence her being home is not the hindrance that you might expect it would be to our work. It is wonderful the way the Lord works out the little details, isn't it? On nice days Mme. Bartrei even takes her out for a little walk in the sunshine. All these things make us realize how impossible it would have been to have kept at the office work so steadily with a house to care for, and how wonderfully the Lord has planned our being here.

You know I told you how hard the language has been for Susan and how impatient she is about trying to understand or speak, and had several very homesick spells. Last week she didn't complain so much about going to school and we were very pleased to notice quite a difference in her general spirits. How to account for this? One day I discovered to my amazement that each morning she was removing her shoes in the vestibule, shoving them under the umbrella rack, donning her Dutch wooden shoes, and "klomping" off in them like a regular Hollander. These are just as much of a curiosity here as they would be in America. She said that the first day a crowd followed her down the street, "but now they are used to seeing me." You see the children here must wear bedroom slippers in school. It is the rule. The floors are a beautiful parquet, laid in patterns. Each week all the wax is removed (there is no other finish on the floors) and a fresh coat of wax put on. This is done by a maid or housewife putting a wad of steel wool on the bottom of her shoe and vigorously scrubbing with it in line with the grain of the wood, turning and twisting the foot to follow the pattern. After all the wax is removed in this fashion, a coat of wax is applied and then it is polished with a heavy polisher. Not exactly an easy job. During the week each worn spot is refinished each day, so that the floors always look new. It is no wonder that they require bedroom slippers in school and like to have you wear them at home, too. You see, then, Susan is accustomed to leaving her shoes at the door of the school and no one cared about the wooden ones outdoors. Why she got so much satisfaction and comfort from wearing them, we cannot figure out, unless the noise made up for the need of quiet here at the pension. She said proudly, "I can run and jump in them, too, and I can even jump and kick my heels together in the air without losing a shoe."

Priscilla is doing very well with her French, though she gets extremely tired of studying nothing else at school, except arithmetic. Her vocabulary will have to be a good bit larger before she can go into her own age group and listen to lectures in History, Geography, and German, all in French, even though she is anxious for a change. She has finished the scarf she was knitting for Fran and has started on another one for herself. They are given about 20 minutes to knit in school. Both she and Susan are starting stamp collections and Fran is becoming very interested in stamps again, though he has collected for years without ever having time to catalogue them. They plan to spend some time each week sorting them under Fran's supervision. The ladies help to supply them with stamps.

I can't go on to tell of all the letters and opportunities that loom on the horizon, but we feel it is an earnest of the busy life that lies ahead. Do pray that we can keep on the study of French without getting too busy before a good grasp of the language is ours. We had also just made a new resolution, to take a little exercise every day. We feel being cooped up in one room for 6 days at a time is not healthy for body or dispositions! Pray that we can keep it up. In 3/4ths of an hour Fran and I can leave here, bike up the road a ½ mile over the beginning of the beautiful road to Belmont, turn to the left, and get down from our bikes to push them up a steep, bumpy, stony dirt road, through a forest of straight, tall cathedral pines. Part of the way the ground beneath the trees is red-brown with a blanket of needles; then we come to a section where a green, green ivy covers the ground and creeps up the tree trunks. We often stop to admire the cathedral quietness as well as grandeur of these magnificent trees. At the top the road, still dirt and a bit muddy now, winds around a field and past a Swiss farm house of crumbling old stone, which is barn, chicken house, and dwelling all under one sweeping roof.

On we go, riding again as we hit a comparatively level spot, past 2 more of these house-barns, children and chickens hiding from our approach. Always there is the covered cement trough for cows to drink out of fed by a stream of water continuously flowing from a pipe as though connected with a spring, which probably *is* the case. Much of the time you see a big tub of clothes standing under the stream of water, being rinsed for hours at a time. When or where they are washed, I haven't yet discovered. Suddenly we come out of this dirt road on to a paved highway (though not wide) and then we have the reward for all the up-push! Woosh, we go—whee, the wind whistles past our ears—past little houses, around a curve—ooooh, what a sunset—there is a modern castle of a place named "la Florida" (every newly built place has a name), don't look too closely, though, watch this next curve, it is a steep one and ooooh, cliff-like rocks loom up on the right—a deep drop on the left—that valley is between us and home—on around, why this is like a miniature Storm King Highway—"Fran, I never knew there was anything like this around here"—better not talk, whish around again, and now we are coming to the city, that is, apartments and houses—put out your hand, turn a corner—put on the brakes, it's too steep here—there's the Chailly Church with its towering steeple on the left—watch out for the old man crossing the street—that's our post office—we have come at least 2½ miles without pumping once, all downhill! What a ride! On up the street we pump, cheeks red and hands stinging with the cold. Riant Mont, pick up the bikes, lug them up a flight of steps, put them away, dash up the stairs—the clock says we have been gone only a short 45 minutes. If only we can keep our resolutions, this exercise can do us a world of good to say nothing of what the beauty does to push out the walls of our room as it flashes through our minds through the day.

Now I must tell you about Thanksgiving. Last Sunday I was explaining to Madame Turrian as much as I could about our American Thanksgiving just as a matter of interest. We ourselves hadn't talked much about it and I couldn't think of any way to celebrate except to take a walk in the woods and stop somewhere for "tea." However, on Wednesday morning Madame Turrian came to me and asked if I would like to prepare a meal on Thursday for our "American Fete." Excitedly, I decided that a meal at 5 o'clock would not interfere with anybody since supper is a light meal not served until 7 P.M. She agreed that I could have the kitchen from 3 P.M. on. After our French lesson on Thursday, Fran and I rushed to get our bikes and whiz down to Pont Chailly to shop (stores all close Thursday afternoon). We discovered a can of Armour's tomato juice in one store, too high in price but the first we had seen for months so a real treat. Brussels sprouts, tiny tangerines the size of walnuts, a bar of chocolate, and then the discovery that a bottle of vanilla was not to be had. Vanilla beans to soak in your own syrup, or vanilla "sucre" was all. We tied our purchases on to the bike and returned feeling very festive. Madame Turrian had ordered a chicken for us, but it seems that chickens in Switzerland are very tiny. The largest to be had weighed a little over 1½ lbs. in our weight. Chickens imported from France are larger, 3 lbs. to 4 lbs., but are far too expensive, $1.50 a lb. Our 2 little ones looked like birds. A search through the trunk revealed my cookbook and a measuring cup. After typing until 3:20, we closed up the office. Fran took the girls out on their bikes, and I donned an apron and descended the stairs for my fun in the kitchen.

I made plain cookies, fixed a bowl of Jello made from a package Mother Schaeffer had put in our trunk, stuffed the tiny chickens, and cooked the Brussels sprouts so that they were bright green and tender (vegetables are so overcooked here and often cooked with meat or fat, very different). I put the cloth you made us, Mother (with the grapes embroidered), on our table. Fran and the girls came in with some greens. With those, a little American Flag, 2 white candles stuck in apples for holders, we almost thought we were back home again. (The only colored candles we could find were the small ones used on the Christmas trees here.) The only thing we missed was the cranberry jelly, which is strictly American! The ohs and ahs that greeted the meal could not have been more appreciated if we had had a turkey and pumpkin pie. Before we finished, the ladies came in for their supper and they seemed to enjoy our festivity as much as though they were sharing it. We shared our cookies with all the folks—and then came up to our bedroom for a Thanksgiving service. We took turns giving our reasons for thankfulness, verses of Scripture, and prayer, just as we did in our service in St. Louis, going around twice since we are so few. The girls' stories were full of praise and thanksgiving to the Lord for all He has done for us. We prayed not only for Europe and the great need here, but for all of you at home. It was a most satisfactory day in every way. We sang, "Great Is Thy Faithfulness" to end our time.

Much, much love to you all,

EDITH

1949

January 9, 1949   Lausanne, Switzerland

Dearest Family:

In a Christmas letter, I had told how Fran had narrowly escaped serious physical trouble. He had been carrying on his very full schedule while trying to work out solutions to a number of difficult problems. On one particularly difficult day, he developed a pain in his left shoulder and chest and very suddenly drooped into someone who looked about a hundred. After fighting the feeling for a couple of days with no success, he went to the lady doctor we had for Debby. She is the right one for us all, I think. She, in her broken English, bawled him out for trying to work too hard for too long without adequate rest, etc., and said it is *not* his heart, but neuralgia caused by a liver which is not functioning properly, caused in turn by fatigue. A long vacation would be the best cure, but she said she could give him injections which would help, if he would also rest and promise to regulate his life more sensibly from now on. She gave him the first injection then and there, a large one of several small bottles of various vitamins and one of calcium. They are very powerful. She said that when a person is just ordinarily fatigued, one shot will make him feel fine. Fran has had four shots two days apart and is beginning to feel better, but still has no energy. The pain still is there but much better. Even if he had wanted to, Fran couldn't have done much this last week. I praise the Lord for this doctor's understanding diagnosis for I feel Fran was on the verge of some kind of a break, after accumulating fatigue for years, and the threatened break has now been prevented from being serious.

The date looks unreal, both year and day. How time does fly. If this present life were all that we had, the quick passage of time would be most depressing. How glad I am that we are getting closer to the "beginning of eternity with Him" rather than to the "end of life." Since I last wrote, Christmas has come and gone again, and we are already hard at work with the work of a new year.

We had a great deal of correspondence to get out before going away, so my typewriter was clacking away up to the last shopping hours before Christmas. The children had been reporting each day the contents of the *Patisserie* windows. "Now they have the cutest things made out of candy—cabbages, carrots, heads of lettuce, cauliflower, fruits, *all* made of candy," etc., so I wasn't allowed to forget the approaching date. One afternoon Susan and Deborah came excitedly upstairs with each hand full of the thinnest cookies you can imagine, as thin as potato chips. Madame Turrian had rented the special equipment for making the Vaudois Christmas cookies. It was due back at the store for the next person to rent it by suppertime, so she had to work fast. For generations in the Canton of Vaud the recipe has been handed down from mother to daughter. The thin batter is poured into a contraption that looks something like our waffle iron. It makes four square cookies at a time, with a little pattern in the center of each one. People sign up at the store for the hours they wish to rent a cookie maker, and they are continuously exchanged the last two weeks before Christmas.

Our tutor went away with her husband and children to spend 3 weeks at their chalet in the mountains enjoying winter sports during holidays. We have plenty to do studying verbs until she comes back, and we also have engaged someone to read with us and give us oral work. We have had some really good talks with our regular teacher about the Bible. I wish you would be praying about her. She certainly has been lovely to us.

The day before Christmas I finally put away my typewriter. With the then-impatient children, we set out for the shopping tour. The children wanted to buy something for each other and we needed their feet to try on the gifts we had decided to buy them—ski boots, which are heavy and practical for walking in the snow to school as well as for any snow sport. We let them window shop as we priced boots, looking for the cheapest, of course! Although there are no elaborate decorations as in our big-city department stores, each window is decorated in some way. The candy shops have real works of art in their windows; whole scenes made of candy make you feel as though you had stepped into "Hansel and Gretel."

Finally we found a shop which had the cheapest ski boots and we led the girls in one at a time. We explained to the clerk that this was to be a Christmas surprise, and she was delighted to try the boots on the blindfolded children! Fran tied his scarf around the eyes of Susan while Priscilla and Debby stayed outside, etc. They may have guessed, but at least they didn't see them and it was lots of fun. I wish you could have seen Deborah's face as the heavy boots replaced her shoes.

After this we took them to make their own purchases at a store that is more like our 5 & 10 than anything we have seen over here. It was jam-packed, people with arms full of packages, branches of pine, and even Christmas trees. Susan and Priscilla did very well buying with francs and centimes and figuring out what they could afford. Deborah needed help, but was quite satisfied as I held her up to hand over her money for the lead pencils she had selected for her sisters. After they were through, Fran marshaled them on to a LA ROSIAZ tram, giving Priscilla full charge. We are only 3 houses from the end of the line, so they were safe enough. They were anxious to wrap their presents and decorate them with the Christmas stickers which had been so thoughtfully sent to them by "Uncle George" Gilchrist. We continued shopping, and found, to our pleasure, that our French had improved to the place where we could make ourselves understood by the clerks at least, though it doesn't exactly flow yet! We climbed on the back of the crowded tram, glad to be able to get in at all. Fran had our Christmas tree, with its neat little stand made out of small branches and twigs so that it looked as though it grew that way, and a plant for Madame Turrian. I don't know if the conductor punched an extra hole for the tree or not! They do charge half fare for each suitcase and whole fare for a dog! Children ride half fare on trains and trams until they are 16.

After untangling our old strings of lights, screwing in the same bulbs we have used for many years, plugging them into our transformer, we found to our delight that they still worked, bringing into the room the colorful glow of past Christmases. That helped so much to make us all feel at home. We put the little tree on the raised step in front of the French doors, a perfect place for it we all agreed. Next came the trimming, first with the lights, then with silver and gold foil-wrapped candy which they sell there for trimming trees. Each piece represents something. One has a watch face painted on it. Another is shaped like a pair of scissors. Another has cardboard points around it to look like the sun. We finished the trimming with silver tinsel also brought in the trunk with memories.

For supper that night we "treated" the ladies to some red and green American Jello, which they gingerly tasted for the first time! After the children were asleep, Fran and I went to observe the service in the big church at Saint Francois. It is a huge stone affair taken over by the Protestants at the Reformation. The ancient walls filled with the music of French Christmas carols, interspersed with short Bible readings by the pastor. As we sat there I prayed for our work over here, not only among unsaved, but among those who believe but are blinded to what modernism is doing in taking away the very Gospel which would save their children. The church was cold, but people dress expecting that.

Home again, we found Madame Turrian and Bluette and Trudy decorating the dining room and fixing their little tree in there. They had a service on the radio from Saint Peter's in Geneva, Calvin's old church, and we all joined in singing "Silent Night" in French. We brought down our gifts for the Turrians and the two girls, and they gave us some things to put upstairs for the children, which touched our hearts. Next came the filling of the stockings, topped with a colored balloon from a street stand. Each had tangerines from Spain in the toe and foot. I wakened at 5 o'clock to hear the voices of the children as they discovered the stockings on the bottom of their beds—"Shhh, it isn't time yet." Later I wakened again to discover Priscilla had read them back to sleep.

Our little room was almost too small for the exuberance of children on Christmas morning. Having everybody close to the tree was a problem. However, Fran was glad to help out by reclining on the bed to make room for the others! It was worth the customs trouble to see the joy of the girls (and to feel the same way ourselves) as they opened things that had actually come from America such a short time ago, even though I had had to repair the wrappings. The customs did not bother to open a package which contained food and candy. We had a happy morning and then went for lunch to the home of a young man and his family who are studying French here. There we met another university student from America, studying engineering.

When we came home, there was just time to dress up in our best finery for the special Christmas dinner Madame Turrian and the girls had been preparing. All the ladies were dressed up to eat in the dining room. Even the 90-year-old man, who always eats in his room, was at a table. Our table had been enlarged and the Turrians and the 2 girls were ready to eat with us. The window sills and open shelves were all decorated with pine branches with tiny candles fastened to them. In one corner there was a Christmas tree with 50 little candles on its boughs. We brought down the can of cranberry jelly Mrs. Schaeffer had sent us and shared it with everyone. It tasted like home! We had a real treat—turkey. We didn't get to see the bird as it was served cut up. Madame Turrian said it weighed about 3 kilos (about 6 lbs. our weight) and she seemed to think that was a good-sized one, so they must be a good bit smaller than our American turkeys. Of course with 15 people eating it, the portions were not large but the taste was *good.* When dessert was served, Madame Turrian lighted the tree. The blazing candles warmed up the room amazingly and were really a pretty sight. Susan inched away from her dessert so that she would be closer to the door; she didn't trust the candles and was preparing to leave in case of fire! When the candles had burned for a while, the final touch was put on the tree as the sparklers were lighted. A Christmas tree with 50 candles and a dozen sparklers showering down a rain of golden stars is quite breathtaking. (Sparklers are like the kind we used to have on July 4th.) Deborah was entranced, but Susan whispered that she liked looking at it but didn't like being there while it was going on.

At this point, our 3 girls were asked to sing. I wish you could have seen them with their faces glowing in the candlelight as they sang a French Christmas carol they had been taught. Then Priscilla spoke, and the surprise she had been bursting to tell us for weeks came forth as, with great expression and many gestures, she gave a poem about Christmas, in French! Bluette had been helping her to practice it in the kitchen so that we should not know about it. The ladies all seemed to be so pleased with the celebration that it seemed too bad as the candles went out to have them go back to the solitude of their own rooms, so Fran and I hurriedly arranged to bring down the projector and pictures to show them our country! We had quite a trip. Through the colored slides, we went to Philadelphia, Wilmington, St. Louis, and many other parts of America. It was fun to see you all again: Mother Schaeffer on the front steps, all her neighbors; the Sevilles and Bragdons in the back yard; Dr. Holdcroft and Mr. Armes in front of 151; the whole Friday night Bible class in St. Louis at Heists; as well as many other groups we took pictures of out there. Now you have been introduced over here for the first time, but not for the last as we expect to use these pictures for many different things. Several of the 80-year-old ladies were quite worried about the 90-year-old man staying up so late, but he wouldn't budge until the last picture was shown. Then he beamed his thanks, with a hearty handshake to emphasize it.

On Sunday we had our usual services, with an extra one in the afternoon to give the Solmans an opportunity to see and hear the Christmas story with flannelboard. They brought with them a little German boy whose parents were in business in China, and his Austrian nurse. These 2 did not understand English, but we hope the pictures gave them some message. If only our police restrictions were lifted, we could have some people from the University for a Bible class perhaps, but as it is we must wait. You know, a retired Swiss minister and his Christian friend on the police force have talked to us and said the restriction that has been placed against us is against the Swiss constitution. They are working on it, and we must have patience until we can do something further about it. . . .

Some Christmas gifts we had received made it possible for us to take a trip as a family, a combination of business and pleasure. A young man who is a converted German Jew, formerly of Berlin, now a British citizen, at present working in a mission to the Jews in Italy, had for a time been having correspondence with us. He was going to be in Adelboden, Switzerland, for 2 weeks at Christmas time, but he could not get here to see us. We had prayed about it and written concerning arrangements. Madame Turrian had said she would take off a certain part of our expenses here while we were gone; then gifts came in time to buy the tickets. Fran has not been at all well for a few weeks, as a result of the overwork of the last three years. We felt this trip could be a real help to him as well as an opportunity for the children to see something of the mountains in the snow. So we decided it was the thing to do.

After fog and grey sunless days, we were more eager to see the sun than anything else as we boarded the train Monday noon. In an hour we stepped off at Bern, where a 20-minute wait gave us time to dash up a block and peer at the tower of the capitol. En route we were able to help a little old lady across two streets. The poor old soul must have had a fright at some time, for she stood screaming for help. Back we dashed just in time to hop up in the third-class coach of the train for Speiz. It was packed with people and skis. Most people travel at this time of year with ski suits and boots on, a knapsack hung over shoulders with necessary clothes in it, skis and sticks variously carried, all headed for the mountains—young people, old people, babies, whole families with all sizes of skis. Baby carriages on sled runners travel in the baggage car. . . .

At last the bus arrived in a little village, enlarged now by many years of catering to skiers. The main street is lined with shops housed in the Swiss-chalet type of building you see in pictures, with designs painted along the line where the roof meets the front wall. Out we piled to find porters from various pensions and hotels waiting, each with a sledge to drag the baggage. After the crowd had melted away, a nice, homey-looking man came up to us and announced that he was Mr. Hari of the Pension Hari, where we were going. He put our suitcases on the sledge, and Deborah perched on top of them. He walked with us, pulling the sledge by the two big curved pieces of wood which are an extension of the runners and almost shoulder high. We went through the village, making our way through children on sleds, people on skis, others swinging skates as they hurried to the rink.

Adelboden is in German-speaking Switzerland, so German is predominant, but we heard Italian, French, Spanish, and a fair amount of English. You hardly knew how to greet people, for "bonjour" would be as foreign to some as "hello" would be to others. On we went around a curve and out of the center of things. "Oh, look!" the children exclaimed. There was a sledge with a load of milk cans on it being pulled by a huge St. Bernard dog. We passed chalets built several hundred years ago, most of them with Scripture texts written around the top of the front wall in beautiful German printing. There is no doubt that in those days the Bible was really loved in Switzerland, and that that gave this country the foundation for the liberty and prosperity she still enjoys. Mr. Hari told us his father opened the first guest house in Adelboden for Christians to come for a rest. Each evening a service was held after supper. This is still a requirement of the place, though other pensions and hotels are not patterned after it. As we went to our rooms, the children were reminded of Harvey Cedars.* It is the same general type of building, though much smaller, and the high beds with foot-high featherbed covers are in no way similar! Outside each room is a wooden, tray-like affair on which to leave boots while snow drips off! . . .

We rented skis for two days for the entire family. Mr. Hari's brother was giving skiing lessons to some English boys that week and said our family could be included for the first three lessons—perfect for us and

---

*Harvey Cedars is a summer campground.

*Our first time on skis—at the mountain top. At the bottom
we were in different positions!*

cost practically nothing. The Lord used even this as an opportunity for contact. As I stood poised on top of the hill, getting my feet in position for a try at "stemming" down, the Englishman who seemed to be in charge of the boys made his way over to me. "Oh, I say, do you happen to know Shields of Toronto?" !!!! He said that he was a toy merchant, but his main business was as superintendent of a mission in downtown London for children. And so we came to know another of those Christian laymen the Lord has scattered over this world who are earnestly giving their lives to the Lord's work. He had brought these boys on his own money, piled into his little English car, for a week of vacation and getting close to the Lord. They were from various circumstances of life and various church playgrounds. As we sailed down the hills and toiled up again, as each took a spill from time to time, we had opportunity to get to talk with these boys and their leader, who is a member of a church in London, where we have wanted further contacts!

It was good to see Fran with a bunch of boys around him again, listening intently as he told them of many things, lastly of modernism and why they did not hear the Gospel preached in some of their churches. I wish I could take you all there in the brilliant sunshine to see the trees covered with what looked like boiled icing, and to talk in the powdery snow which didn't seem real with faces feeling sunburned. I wish you could have seen Deborah as she watched each one go down the 2 long slopes and then took off herself when no one was near her. Down she flew, sticks held up properly until she reached the end in a heap of sticks and skis. Up she came with the help of the daughter of Mr. Hari. After that it was a continuous process, not a bit of fear in her. The other two girls really followed instructions, learned to step sideways up the hill; to lift first one foot and then the other to gain balance and confidence going down; to jump a little bit for the same reasons; to "stem," which is the first way you learn to slow down on a hill, etc. Fran really distinguished himself. The instructor said he could hardly believe it was his first time on skis. He pointed him out to the boys as he went down— "That gentleman has just the proper ease and suppleness; try to do it as he does"!! Needless to say, Fran likes the sport so I hope he gets some more time to practice as it should be good for him. Real Swiss skiers don't think of it as an afternoon's recreation however. They go, with packs on their backs, for "tours," up one mountain, down and up another, staying all night in huts along the way. I don't think we'll ever be that advanced. . . .

We left again for home Monday morning, pushing our way through another new layer of snow. Deborah rode down to the station on a sled, the advantage of being three years old. Our ride back to Lausanne was again an interesting one as we had come in a circle and this was new to us. There were many little tunnels and "horseshoe" curves that our toy-like train swished around as it brought us down from the mountains to the level of the lake at Montreux, where we stayed at lake level until we reached Lausanne. It was the first time we had left a place and *returned* again, so it was a real "homecoming" and a very nice sensation for us all. We were warmly greeted by the folks here, our rooms looked home-like, and most exciting of all—our remaining packages had arrived that day. After unpacking and getting a bit settled, we lighted our Christmas tree lights and had our second Christmas. With the sun setting outside the window and the glow of lights within, it was as nice as the first one! . . .

Lots of love,

EDITH

January 30, 1949 Lausanne, Switzerland

Dearest Mother and Dad:

Yesterday afternoon was lost as far as my plans for letter writing were concerned! A puffing Bluette delivered a telegram saying, "Plane delayed" [Fran's], which I translated into French for her and three-year-old English for Debby. The letdown feeling didn't make for zeal to write; when Priscilla asked me to please mark her work books, I gave in easily. Miss Walker kindly sent here her 6th-grade books from Stevens School (Philadelphia), and she is reading History, Geography, Science, English, and Democracy regularly. With several there is an accompanying "Work Book" in which she can write answers to questions on the material in the text. Thus she can keep up with the American course of

*Priscilla, Debby, and Susan inside the tram in Lausanne.
Priceless!*

study while attending the regular Swiss school—balanced education. She finds a lot of the history corresponds with what she is getting here in French, but it is easier to read it in English! She is getting along very well in French grammar and Dictee. Dictee is like our spelling, except that the teacher dictates several paragraphs and the girls must write them with no mistakes in spelling or punctuation—or accent marks! One day she had a perfect Dictee, which has given her a more respected position in the eyes of her classmates, who used to make fun of her pronunciation. They each had several mistakes! Subjects which require much reading in French are still very hard for her because of insufficient vocabulary.

After finishing with Priscilla, I offered my services in the kitchen. Madame Turrian has a bad case of grippe with quite a high fever; Monsieur Turrian should likewise be in bed but is working around with a fever; Bluette is coughing and looks as though she should be in bed; Trudy has almost lost her voice but feels all right. Hence I felt I could help out a bit. I made an apple pudding for the dessert under the watchful eyes of the girls. I was a bit fearful lest it be a failure. The children were anxious for my reputation and even more anxious about the reputation of American cooking, which they felt was on trial. When each of the ladies took a second piece and murmured approval, Trudy looked over at me with a pleased twinkle in her eye, so our reputation is safe!

Thick fog was evidently the cause of the delayed plane. Since there are only three trains a week from Amsterdam to Lausanne, a trip of 25 hours, I wondered when we'd see Fran. Just as I was insisting Susan was *not* to wait longer but get tucked in this minute, I heard Fran's voice on the stairs. Susan threw herself at him, joyful that her feeling he would be there to say good night had been right! His plane had taken off after a six-hour delay and had landed at Basel to avoid the mountains in the fog. Passengers were sent on by train from there. The small

Basel airport was full of planes from many countries, unable to proceed. Needless to say, Fran was thankful to be home the same day.

This letter is going backwards. You will wonder why and when Fran left for Holland. There was a meeting of the Holland branch of the Executive Committee of the International Council on January 27th. The week before, Fran had a telegram from Mr. Kok asking him to come for that week to discuss important things. Hence he left Monday for Amsterdam. The Koks had arranged to have him stay in a room above their place; he ate with them at a nearby restaurant. His time was full with interviews morning, noon, and night with Professors and Dominies. . . .

Backwards again! After the New Year, Banque Galland & Co., who have a real-estate department, told Fran of the first two renting possibilities since the end of September. One was an apartment, "very small, with two beds for three persons"—hardly a description fitting our five! The other was "a villa, seven rooms furnished, all comfort." The rent sounded too much, but we thought, let's see what fits that description and we *might* get the price down. Up a gravel path we walked between huge rhododendrons and hedges toward a stone house full of turrets, jutting-out windows, and balconies overlooking a garden of mammoth pine trees, with a view beyond of the lake and the jagged peaks of the Savoy Alps. We breathed a deep sigh of unbelief—could this be a seven-room house? Surely they don't count all the rooms. The agent turned the key. The door opened into a huge entry hall, next into a hall that looked like the corridor of a school—here is the bath, large enough for a bedroom, with twin wash basins, a huge tub, and shower—across the echoing hall he hurried to open shutters so that the sun could stream into the living room—a beautiful parquet floor, but—"Where is the furniture?" we chorused with the man from Galland's. A slight error! No, this was not furnished. This fact certainly allowed no argument as we inspected empty room after empty room, twice seven of them! Down tiny winding stairs to a restaurant-sized kitchen and two rooms that were waved at as "the dining room." Although the front door was level with the walk leading to the house, here on the floor below we found doors opened out of each room on to the terrace of the back garden. The second floor revealed enough rooms to start an orphan asylum! We discovered the house had to be leased for a year at a time, and had no regrets that this was not possible. We were reassured that we are living in the only possible place for the present. God is able; if He wanted us settled in a house, that's where we would be. It is so comforting that *He knows the next step and is making no mistake in the preparation for it.*

Lausanne, in fact all Switzerland, has been short on electricity for the last month. There hasn't been enough snow to keep up the level of the water behind the dams to make hydraulic electricity. This means we have hot water only certain hours during the week; you have to be careful to conserve even then. Our weekly bath must be a smaller one; I launder (in our face basin) when I discover the water is on. The electric inspector comes frequently to make sure the heater is turned off. Electric heaters are not permitted for warming rooms unless there is a very young baby. Fortunately this house is heated with a coal furnace. The fire is allowed to go out every night, and is built anew each morning. A great deal of wood is used in the morning and they get by on four tons of coal a winter, not keeping it as warm as Americans are used to. You can't blame anyone for saving coal bought at about $50 a ton. Naturally people wear warmer clothing. Most houses and apartments are heated by stoves in each of several rooms. Bedrooms go without heat.

Our Christmas tree met with a glorious end. We put it out on our balcony, its branches brushing against the glass doors. Though dead and brown, 5 minutes after I filled the branches with crumbs it was alive with twittering sparrows. We have counted 20 birds in it at once. They make easy-to-care-for pets, and fun to watch.

Do be praying about the police restriction against our "evangelizing" in "territory Swiss." A retired Bible-believing Swiss minister to whom Pastor Guiton introduced us became agitated about this as he felt it denied the religious freedom which Switzerland is supposed to have. He talked with a Christian lawyer friend of his, who wrote a letter to the police pointing out that this restriction is against Swiss traditional freedom. He pointed out that he himself had enjoyed the freedom to preach in Italy both during the fascist regime and after. No results yet; *keep praying. . . .*

I wish you could see Susan as she starts out for school these days, not in Dutch wooden shoes now but proudly carrying a Swiss school bag. These bags are distinctively Swiss. They fit on the back like a knapsack; instead of soft leather, they are hard and box-like in shape. Hers is imitation leather and is made firm with something stiff so that when she runs, everything in it rattles around at a great rate. Some are covered with fur, and they tell us in mountain villages they are made of wood. The Swiss bag is a wonderful invention for Susan as it can't possibly be lost! Susan can be so good it hurts you, and so bad you have to hurt her! She has been teaching Debby verses from the Bible, all on her own, and teaching her to answer questions on Bible facts. One afternoon she invited us all in to miniature "closing exercises" of the miniature Bible school.

However, another day Larry was here playing with Susan and Debby when a loud howl took me running to the scene. Larry was sprawled on the floor where he fell from "walking tightrope" on the rail of Debby's crib. Uneven crayon printing announced lemonade for sale (water in glasses). Deb had a book on her head which she was being "trained" to carry ("So she can live where the ladies carry water that way," explained Susan later). The whole idea had been Susan's, who had goaded Larry on to his "feat" by announcing, "Pooh, that's nothing. Soon as you get through, I'll jump rope there." The lecture that followed didn't seem to cover sufficient possibilities of danger, because today the latest episode was an attempt to ski on the floor of the little room. It ended in a purple egg which formed on Susan's forehead when she contacted the face basin at the finish of the "ski run"! . . .

The grippe or flu has spread all over several countries. There is a heavy epidemic in France, Holland, and right now in Switzerland. We have really had a lot here in the pension. As one person after another has gone down with it, I have tried to guard the children as well as I could, but of course the germs are everywhere. The girls had one day of an intestinal upset two weeks ago, but have kept very well, until today Deb started a temperature. She says, "My feet (points to ankles) hurt, and my elbows hurt, and my head hurts" so I guess it is the grippe. She has slept all afternoon. I hope it isn't going to be a bad case, and that the rest of us escape it. This morning two of the ladies on our hall have started grippe. One has the intestinal variety, and the other has a heavy cough and bronchitis, and a high fever. Madame Turrian is better today, but Mr. Turrian still has a high fever.

Deb just woke up with a fever of about 102.5°, so I have called the doctor. She ordered the pills the doctors are all giving for this grippe epidemic, a combination of vitamin C and quinine. And will come to see her tomorrow morning to be sure there are no complications. Wonder if the rest of us can escape? I'm afraid you will have to wait until my next letter to find out.

With much love,

EDITH

February 28, 1949 Lausanne, Switzerland

Dearest Family:

It has been a month since my last long letter, a month of many ups and downs in weather and health, encouragements and discouragements. You remember the grippe had just caught up with us at the end of January. Deborah was first. Susan followed with a bronchial variety. February was ushered in with a fierce wind that tried to blow the house down; that night Priscilla started a high fever. Deb was already in our room so that I could care for her more easily in the night. Now Priscilla came in to join her since the little study was like an icebox on the north side of the house. Fran moved into the study to sleep away from our germs. I say "our" because the next day I started the grippe myself, and our room became a ward. Fran was nurse! Susan was lonely in her private room and often wished the wall could be removed. The doctor ordered vitamin C and quinine for us all; sulfa for Priscilla because her ears became affected, for Susan because of her bronchial cough, for Deb because one of her ears was a bit inflamed. Temperatures three times a day kept Fran busy, as well as doling out the various medicine doses with water to wash them down. Fran kept a chart of all these very methodically. He feels quite sympathetic with nurses now, as the care of four patients seemed to eat heavily into the waking hours of each day. There wasn't much "in-between time." Our "nurse" became our "chaplain" on Sunday and we had a happy service in the "ward" with the "private" patient visiting us. Each patient was allowed to pick out a hymn, a Bible story, and each lead in prayer. Priscilla chose the book of Jeremiah, Susan wanted to hear the story of Jericho, and Debby wanted the Christmas story again. We had time for prayer together and much conversation during these days, which the children enjoyed since mother is usually too busy with office work to stop and answer all the questions.

At the same time everyone in the pension was ill except for one lady and Fran. Madame Turrian recovered from flu, but worked again too soon and came down with pneumonia. This was an object lesson for the rest of us. Two others had pneumonia. Monsieur Turrian had bad heart complications. "Guards" (nurses) came and went, giving penicillin to those who needed it. The whole place had the atmosphere of a hospital. Bluette and Trudy had the cooking and entire work of the pension. Here in Switzerland 17- and 18-year-old girls (especially from the German-speaking part) all go to a home or a pension to do at least one year of housework, both to learn French and to learn to do housework. They certainly work hard.

The Lord showed us once more how tenderly He cares for the little details of our lives. First of all, in this time of illness we received practically no mail for several days, a very unusual thing. This meant that we were not being constantly aware of office work piling up. Then, the first day we were all in bed, a package arrived from a friend in Philadelphia. Out came an assortment of used puzzle books, coloring books, crayons, picture sewing cards, and some bouillon cubes. This had been sent two months before, but the Lord had brought it just at the time when most needed. The children were very much impressed by the care of their Heavenly Father. A short time before a carton of two dozen cans of fruit juices had arrived from Wilmington. This meant that we had just the proper liquids for our time of illness. For a few days we opened two cans of juice a day, and had a cup of bouillon apiece, which was so good after the months without these things that we almost enjoyed the grippe! I'm sure these juices also helped us to recover without complications. The doctor was especially pleased that Deborah did not develop pneumonia. Then last, but most wonderful of all, Fran did not get the grippe at all. This kind of grippe left people feeling so weak and fatigued, that we praised the Lord that he escaped altogether. Humanly speaking, we feel the vitamin shots were a real protection against the germs.

Fran and I had planned to go on a short trip up to Champéry, a mountain village not far from here. Madame Wildermuth, our French teacher, was born and brought up in Champéry, where her parents owned and operated the hotel. Now her parents are dead, and her brother and sister operate the hotel. Monsieur W. teaches at the Hotel School in Lausanne, which has its summer vacation in July and August. Therefore the whole family goes to Champéry for these two months. They have a very old chalet there. (A chalet, by the way, though it sounds fancy, is just any house built entirely of wood. It always has wooden balconies on the south, and an overhanging roof. Inside are wooden walls, not plastered or papered.) Madame W. had frequently remarked how fine the mountain air would be for the children, etc. After praying about summer plans, we talked to Madame Turrian and found that she has plenty of offers for her rooms so that she could rent ours for the summer, then have them for us in September. The next problem was the storage of our things, but Madame W. offered us a room in their apartment next door for the two months, to store anything we wanted. We felt we should keep up our French study through these months; if possible to follow our tutor, we could continue without a break. As for office work, typewriter and supplies can go along wherever we go. Part of the time will be our vacation, but there can't be even a month's break in office work and language study at this point, or we would get hopelessly behind. We felt the Lord was working things out in His own wonderful way to give us a change of air, food, etc., and a vacation without too much time lost.

Of course, the final step was to find a place to stay within our means. Madame W. was at Champéry and carefully looked over all the available places. Most places are rented by the same people each year, but she found two for us to look at. This saved us the time and difficulty of trying to find a place by ourselves.

Fran: "I don't want to pick a house. *You* go. I'll take care of Deb today." Thus I was sent on my first trip alone in Switzerland. The snow was falling in the grey of the early-morning light as I ran to catch the tram. At the end of that ride, I ran down the steep hill to the station, hoping I wouldn't go headfirst into the crowds coming up from the station to work. Breathlessly I announced my destination to the ticket man, but my accent was not quite right and he sold me a ticket for the wrong place! I discovered the mistake before dashing off, and made myself understood the second time. Hoping it was the right train, I settled myself in one of the hot compartments. Finally I screwed up courage to ask a couple if this train stopped at Aigle, where I was to change. He assured me it did and got out a timetable to show me the exact time. You buy a timetable here! He and his wife spoke German, but knew some French, so we got along on our small amount of French. I was sorry it was not a clear day so that I could see the mountains as we rode along the lake to Montreux. At Aigle, I found the next stage was to be made in a trolley-like affair with two cars, one for baggage, one for passengers. The next change was made shortly. This time there was only one car divided in half, one-half for baggage, one-half for passengers. Now began our ascent from the "lowlands and foothills" (comparative) at the end of the lake, up into the Alps. Slowly the car moved up, my nose plastered against the window so as not to miss anything. So quickly the little village became a toy below us, it seemed impossible that we were moving slowly. The mountainside dropped so sharply below that I wondered how the little chalets stuck on in a heavy wind. Streams, now frozen, made frozen waterfalls in spots. As we went through the tunnel, icicles plopped on our roof, brushed off by our passing. One of the stops on this line is a hospital on a mountain slope, balconies around every side where in the summer patients must enjoy recuperating. I wonder if those who have always lived here see the beauty with eyes of appreciation. It is the same with Christians. We should never allow the wonder of God to become commonplace, even if we have known Him since childhood.

Champéry! Last stop! Madame Wildermuth and two of the children were waiting to greet me as I jumped from the train step into snow, thankful I had my ski boots. It was almost 11 A.M., with only a few hours to complete arrangements and see everything. First we went up a path which winds up from the village street to the towering heights above. Partway up the mountainside we came to two chalets built close together. One is the *one* available chalet for summer rent. A Hungarian family lives there in the winter but go to Austria for the summer. The owner lives next door. The place is furnished, clean, small rooms but enough to have even an extra bed for a visitor! Kitchen, clean and sunny in mornings, with a little electric stove. There is a bathroom; even though there will be only 30 liters of warm water a day, we could have more baths than here. There are dishes, cooking utensils. The man is very fond of flowers and takes care of both gardens, which have fences around them (to keep the flowers from falling down the mountain, it looks to me!). We went over the cost of the rent, electricity, tax (which each person pays for staying in the village), etc. After lunch we looked at the other place, an apartment in heart of village, larger rooms but not nearly as clean or attractive, and with a wood stove for cooking. (Both have wood stoves for heating the rooms.) Since the price was almost the same, I decided on the chalet, and we went back to get the necessary papers drawn up. Madame W.'s chalet is just a little farther up the path from "ours" so that we will be near our teacher, as well as have her advice on daily problems.

We went on to visit the meat market, the grocery store, and the electric store, to look over Mme. W.'s old bills and figure out whether we could meet the bills within our budget, before signing the agreement for the house. Then we discovered that before train time I would have time to go up on the *telepherique*, a hanging box-like affair that swings its way up a cable to a high ledge above. The "station" for this ride is just one minute's walk away from the village street. Some young girls from a nearby school were the only others. They had hung their skis on a place made for that on the outside of the "box." Out we swung over the trees; in seven minutes we had ascended 2,800 feet. In some places we were 400 feet above the tree tops. Did I ever tell you high places make my knees feel funny? When we arrived, at 6,000 feet (the village is about 3,000 feet), I found we were just at a good place to "begin a nice climb"! The "Dents du Midi" still towered over our heads. In the winter there is a ski lift starting at the point to take skiers on up, but in the summer they say the walking is delightful—real mountain climbing is necessary for any-one who wants to go to the top of the "Dents." No wonder when you are down in the village, or in the chalet, you feel as though you were at the bottom of a mixing bowl, sides formed by mountains and the horizon so high that the sky looks like a ceiling.

In the 15 minutes which we spent at the top of the *telepherique* ride, we went into the tearoom to get out of the biting snow. I called Fran back in Lausanne to see how Deb was (for only 20 cents), ordered tea, and had three minutes to swallow it before we slid down the cable again.

It was dark as the little trolley-train made its way back to the level of the lake. In spite of dark, the view was thrilling to me. Little lights twin-kled at a hundred different heights; thick clusters of lights indicated where the villages were. The waiting between trains was rather dreary and cold. On the second train, I had a little conversation in French with a girl from Italian-speaking Switzerland who spoke Italian, German, and French but no English. Though it was inadequate, yet I tried to give her some answers to life in my limited French. I do know one Bible verse in French—"Believe on the Lord Jesus Christ, and thou shalt be saved." We are reading some of the Bible with our teacher now.

On the train from Montreux to Lausanne, a tall dark-haired girl got on and sat in the seat opposite mine. She spoke French to the conductor to explain that she had become separated from her friends and they would meet her in L. with a ticket, etc. Then she turned her face to the window and tears trickled down. I sat and prayed for the words to say to her. Finally she looked up and I said, "Parlez vous Anglais?" To my delight she answered, "Yes, I do." She never did tell me why she was crying but the way opened up amazingly for a talk about the hopeless condition of the world and the fact that the only thing that could help anyone was the simple message of God's Word, that Jesus had died for the sins of those who would just accept Him as their Savior. I told her what we had come to Europe for. "Thank you for coming," she said. "Your work is so needed, but will be so hard because people don't know when their souls are sick and in need. It is easier to be a nurse, like I am, because they do want help for their bodies, but your work is more important." She is Greek, graduate of the American College in Athens, comes from a wealthy family who now live in Lausanne, but is giving her time to Red Cross work among her own people. At present is in L. studying sociology and psychology in French to get a different viewpoint, as she has completed these in the American College. She gave me her name and address on the back of an envelope and said she would be interested in talking further. She is Greek Orthodox. *Do pray for her* that another contact may really be used of the Holy Spirit to convince her of her personal need of Christ.

News Flash—Your prayers and ours have been answered in relation to the police restrictions. In answer to the letter written to them by the Christian lawyer, they said they had thought the matter over and had decided to give us permission to speak anywhere we were invited and to hold small meetings. Any public meetings widely advertised must first of all meet their approval. That gives us all the freedom we can use at present, for which we praise the Lord. . . .

Fran went several times to the Brethren meetings. Mr. Andre invited him to come with him to observe his Saturday afternoon work in a little village on the other side of Lausanne. There he gathers children from the streets and has something similar to Sunday school for them. He also has a home for children out in the country, where he brings children from Brethren families in Germany and France to live for three months and get built up physically. Fran went this last Saturday, and we all went afterwards to Andres' house for "supper-tea." It was the first time we had eaten in a real Swiss home. . . .

I had a talk with one of the girls who works for the Andres. She said she'd love to visit, but wasn't sure she could *this* Sunday. "Just come ahead if you can; if not, come next week," I said, and gave directions. At that point she had to go to the kitchen and I didn't see her again. The next morning we got ready for church, hoping our congregation would be swelled by *one* but assuring each other that we really didn't expect her. "We'll wait for one more tram," said Fran, "then must start." As we heard the peculiar hum of the wheels that announce its approach, we all crowded out on the balcony to watch the tram pour forth its passengers. Then we spied a dark head tilting uncertainly as its owner scanned the houses—"There she is! Priscilla, run down and meet her." I don't think anyone can know the happiness that swelled up within us, unless they have had part in the beginning of similar work. She asked if she could come back again next week and bring a Dutch girl with her who is also working here and understands English! You can imagine our answer! . . .

The spring weather of the last half of February disappeared today as a real blizzard is ushering in March. When there is room sometime, I want to describe some of the sunsets we see from our front doors (we have glass doors instead of windows). At sunset time each night, some member of the family is always calling, "Oh, come quick—you haven't *ever* seen one like this before," and we usually rush out on the balcony because we *haven't*—it is always different. Only a few days have really crystal-clear moments when all the mountains can be seen and when the shores of France seem so very close, but after the fogs are over, each day brings some new type of beauty, especially at sunset time. Today was the most unusual of all. It has snowed all day, but about a half-hour before sunset it stopped. At one moment we looked out, there was a black cloud hanging over the lake like a huge balloon. Under this cloud the lake was sparkling with sunlight. Gradually the cloud lifted until we could see the shores of France, the thick buildings of the city, with hills of fields behind all, brilliant in the sunshine. Suddenly the air here was white with snow again; the cloud had lifted and was over us as though it had been pulled by a string. Fran got his camera and snapped a picture of the sun-washed shores of France through the snow (I'm typing by the door and told him about it). Now all is solid grey and you wouldn't believe a lake was even in existence. The mountains took no part in this play today. It was as if they were in the wings. . . .

Much love to you all,

EDITH

March 27, 1949   Lausanne, Switzerland

Dearest Family:

March was coming in like a lion when I ended my last letter to you, and the lion stayed with us most of the month in the form of snow storms and that very penetrating "brise noire." Yesterday and today March seems to have been making preparations to go out like a lamb. The temperature has made a sudden rise, the sun is bright and warm, and all fields are covered with tiny wildflowers as though by magic. Yesterday Madam Turrian took Susan and Deborah to a field at the top of the hill behind our house to gather flowers for the tables. They came home with a basket full of lovely little yellow flowers, roots and all. They are only about two inches above the ground. The Swiss pick thousands of them by the roots each spring, yet the fields are always covered with them. Today the house has blossomed forth with bowls of these yellow flowers, which make winter seem a thing of the past. Spring is always such a wonderful picture of the hope that is ahead in the resurrection of our bodies "like unto His glorious body."

Did I tell you how much the children missed putting in the "offering"? We didn't discover this at first. When we did, we decided to have an offering at the Young People's service even though just our own family attends. The children put in a generous share of their tiny allowance (Deb usually gives 100%) and talk about it through the week. Priscilla is Treasurer. When she announced that there was enough to send away, we had a business meeting to decide where it should go.

The discussion was very full, then a vote was taken. The result was that this first gift was sent to Pastor Guiton of Paris to help send out the "Cry of Alarm" to more people. Now the second amount has been gathered, and they have voted to "give it to Mother to buy materials for starting Children for Christ classes in Holland." Thus with prayers and gifts the children are having a real part in the beginning of the work here.

The first Sunday of March not only gave us some English-speaking companionship but also brought a wonderful *prayer answer*. I'm sure many have been praying for the opening of doors for Children for Christ in Holland, and in my last letter the answer seemed far away! However, that Sunday brought a telegram saying that the decision had been made. The answer was —*yes*, and they wanted Mr. and Mrs. Schaeffer to come in April to teach them how to commence the work! You can imagine how thrilled we were to realize that Children for Christ would be a reality in one country of Europe.

Of course this news contained more than a message of happiness for us. It meant that we must plunge into more work than ever for the month of March. We had already planned a full office-work and study schedule which we felt must still be done. Now there would be much to do for preparation of materials and plans, which meant shopping trips, correspondence, pasting and cutting flannelgraph figures, etc. For awhile I typed from early morning till bedtime, not even going downstairs for dinner. There is only a little more typing that has to be done before we leave, though of course the typewriter will go along to Holland. I also discovered that all the children's clothes from last spring needed hems let down. Hence I have ripped hems and sewed on buttons, etc., during our verbal French classes. All that was necessary for the French was my ears and tongue; that left my hands and eyes free for the sewing.

Priscilla has been helping a lot with office work. Fran taught her how to file. She has been spending some time each week filing all the carbons and the incoming mail. She also has mailed all the letters on her way to school, keeping a written record of the postage for each letter— and settling accounts with her Daddy each night. This is good training for her as well as a real help to the work. She often has a conversation with Bluette, one of the serving girls in the pension, about the Bible (all in French, of course). The other day she got stuck in one place as she was talking to Bluette and asked for my help. As a result Bluette is now reading the Gospel of John each day, and coming to me with questions!

The French is coming along. We never seem to have the time to study properly, but your prayers are helping and real progress is being made. Fran had quite a talk to the folk downstairs the other night about the modernism in the World Council, all in French. He reads the daily paper fairly easily now. When you think that before he came, he had never had any French, that is quite remarkable considering our age. We read a passage in the Bible with Madame Wildermuth every day now. She feels our accent in reading aloud is almost perfect in those passages we know well, except for that French "R" which still needs a lot more practice and will always mark us as foreigners, I'm afraid. As far as the French goes we are sorry that we will have to be away for three weeks hearing nothing but Dutch all around us again. The last few nights Deb has been saying, "Good night, sleep well," in French and Dutch just to keep in practice.

The children are thinking of Dutch phrases again not only because of our coming trip. We have had a lady from Holland here at the house for the last few weeks. I told you about the 90-year-old lady. Well, she seemed near the end of her life and the doctor said to call her daughter in Holland to come. When the daughter arrived, and the son from England, they were greeted at the front door by their pleased mother, who was supposed to be on her death bed! She has been better, then worse, then better again, and is now in a nursing home where she can have more care when she needs it. The daughter from Holland is still here in the house, spending her days visiting her mother. We were delighted to find that the daughter is a real Bible-believing Christian who works among ladies in Holland. We feel this is another of the Lord's wonderful providences in bringing together those who have a need for each other's help. . . .

In the midst of all this rush of work, Fran met and talked with our Brethren friend, Mr. Andre. In the course of the conversation he invited Mr. Andre and his wife to "come—bring some friends if you want to—and spend an evening seeing my pictures of Europe and various leaders, etc." So it was that Friday night, March 18th, we entertained again. This time there were 14 people from the Brethren group, our Dutch lady here at the house, and the English girl and a Dutch girl who work for the Andres. . . . The result of this evening was that we were invited to come to the Andres' home the following Wednesday and bring materials with us to talk about and demonstrate Children for Christ. Thus, after all, Lausanne is the first place in Europe where we have had an opportunity to talk about Children for Christ.

This unexpected opportunity meant that I had to hurry to shop for black flannel, flannel for background, etc. Holland still is on rationing for materials and we are taking enough material with us to "back" the pictures and cover the flannelboards, etc. Since I needed it for Holland anyway, I bought the entire amount at once. Shopping for this flannel— "the cheapest stuff you have, it doesn't have to be any good, to paste on the backs of pictures . . . some blue for water and sky"—needed some explanation to the curious salesman. In fact I had the head of a department asking questions about the Bible for over an hour as a result of buying this material. Then at home, as I spread flannel out over the dining room tables, pasted figures for the whole book of Luke, made backgrounds, everyone in the pension became interested in what I was doing and in the stories the pictures were to illustrate. So the whole time of preparation became one of opportunity to witness. The interest also resulted in help offered. Madame Turrian said, "You have so much to do, I will wash the children's wool skirts and press them for you." Bluette knitted some new feet in Susan's wool stockings, which were full of holes. The lady from Holland took several sheets of the "figures" with her as she went to sit with her mother, and brought them back all cut out!! So you see how wonderfully the Lord works all things together.

Finally by 8 o'clock Wednesday night we were ready to go to the Andres', with a suitcase full of materials, our "crate-lid" flannelboard, and 4 maps. I hadn't had time to eat supper and Fran just swallowed a few mouthfuls, but one good thing was the fact that we were this much farther on in our preparations for Holland. When we arrived there, we found that there were about 40 Christian men and women waiting to hear the message. There were doctors, businessmen, an art teacher, and various others who lived in widely separated parts of Lausanne. Fran gave a message, first using the map of the world, then a map of Europe, then a map of Switzerland, then a map of Lausanne, showing that though we all accept the fact that we should be interested in mission projects somewhere else in the world, it becomes a different thing when we come to our own country, town, and neighborhood. He stressed our responsibility to reach those in our own neighborhoods with the truth, because after all that is where the Lord has put us. Then he showed how Children for Christ was the best method of doing this, telling a bit of the seven-point program of C. for C. Then I spoke, showing the teaching methods and illustrations, etc. Afterwards we had time for questions and conversation. Several spoke of how deeply touched they were by the fact that they had never before felt their responsibility right here. Everyone seemed genuinely interested. Of course we will be away right now, and so cannot go on with anything here. However, two families invited us to come to their homes as soon as we get back to talk further about the practical side of C. for C. here in Lausanne. Do *pray about this.*

The English girl has continued to come to our meetings on Sundays. Yesterday she came over for a Saturday afternoon outing. Since I had so much sewing, mending, etc., to do, I let her take my bicycle for a ride with the rest of the family. Then she had "tea" with us. It was good to have a chance to know her better. She has graduated from the school where so many of the C.I.M. children go, is the only Christian in her family, and is going into nurse's training in London in August but will leave Lausanne in May. She wants to take literature and materials back to England with her. You never can tell what the results will be in an interest like that. This morning when she came to church, she said that Mrs. Andre wants to begin translating the Scripture memory packets which we have in a series of six boxes for Children for Christ. Hence this afternoon the first bit of translation work for our children's work has begun! French will mean that they can be used in France as well as here, and will be ready for the first opening there. After dinner today, the lady from Holland asked for more "cutting" to do. This I did not have for her, "but I have an idea—would you like to translate a few Bible choruses into Dutch for me?" She graduated from a conservatory of music here in Lausanne years ago and is a fine musician, so I felt this would be just her "talent." And so in another part of town this afternoon, "The B-I-B-L-E" is being translated into Dutch, and maybe the "Assurance March"—that is, if the translation will fit the music. By the way, the lady from Holland lives in Amsterdam and hopes to be home before we leave and can be a great help to the work there. . . .

Now only three days are left before we leave, three days brimful of work which we hope will be finished in that time. Suitcases must be packed with clothes for various weather changes; C. for C. material will fill one alone. The screen, projector, etc., must all go as well as office supplies and typewriter. So we may look like gypsies again! We leave on the morning of March 31, going to Basel, where we will change for the International Train to Amsterdam. There will be no further changes before arriving in Amsterdam the next morning, but we go through four countries (France, Belgium, Luxembourg, Holland), which means that during the night we will go through customs four times! What that will be like you'll have to wait until the next letter to find out. The children are going with us since there is no one here to care for them. We will use them to help out as a "demonstration" class in Holland. Our first meeting will be with the "Dominies" from five churches to explain the children's work and demonstrate the methods. Then we will have a public meeting with people from these churches invited. After that we will meet with those who respond to the call for ones actually interested in starting classes. We will need several teachers' meetings, and time spent in translation of various things. Then the men in Holland are anxious to see Fran's pictures and have arranged three meetings for his pictures and message. One is for the young people of the churches, one for a Christian Reformed Students' League, and one for a seamen's meeting. We will be in Holland just three weeks, leaving on April 21, so *please be praying especially for Holland* in April, that the Lord may open hearts and homes for the salvation of children. Pray too for physical strength and lots of energy for whatever work there is for us to do in those three weeks.

The next letter will come to you from Amsterdam, or at least it may be started there. I don't know how much extra time there will be. We are all well, for which we praise the Lord. Isn't it good that the sicknesses didn't come at this time? The children have a vacation from school from March 31 to April 19, so they will only lose a few days of school. It is wonderful to see the details work out.

Much love to you all,

EDITH

May 2, 1949   Lausanne, Switzerland

Dearest Family:
  When the last letter ended, we had just three days left before leaving
Lausanne for Holland. We had been praying about the matter of finances for the trip, and also that our rooms might be rented in our absence to save money. On the last day before we left, Madame Turrian
had several inquiries about rooms for the Easter vacation; and the last
thing in the afternoon she found that a schoolteacher wanted a room for
three weeks' vacation, starting the day we left, and that a man and his
wife from Basel also wanted a room for the same amount of time! It was
with thankful hearts, though tired bodies, that we began to "move" late
that night after the packing had been completed. All closets, drawers,
etc., in the children's room and ours had to be emptied, and our own
chests containing files, sewing machine, toy box, etc., all had to be transported to the little office (the smallest and least desirable of the rooms
without a view of the lake and mountains). Since our storage space is so
small, this meant the emptying process was quite a task and required
many cardboard boxes. What a jammed-up mess the office was when we
got through! I groaned inside when I thought what it would mean to
sort all this out again. It was a packing for a journey, a spring housecleaning, and a moving all rolled up into one. However, though it meant
a lot of work, we were glad we were in a pension where the expenses of
our time away could be cut to the rent of one small room, instead of in a
house where expenses would continue to be the same.
  The five Schaeffers and their even dozen of things to carry and
count — "Do we have everything?" — were all ready to pile into
the taxi at 6:30 A.M. in a drizzling rain which we fervently hoped
wouldn't ruin our things draped on the outside of the taxi. We careened down the empty streets at a terrific rate, down steep hills which
seemed like a toboggan slide, and arrived at the station in plenty of
time to get our things into the third-class car before it was too crowded.
This through-train to Basel took us through the Jura Mountains, not as
rugged and high as the Alps, but with a beauty all their own. We have
come to love the Swiss scenery in all its variety. I think the most striking thing about it is the fact that we can see so much at any one spot, as
though we were viewing a tiny model of a town with the landscaped
countryside around it.
  We thrilled at seeing tiny toy-like towns with their small neat watch
factories, houses, and churches clustered together, a cemetery on the
outskirts, and cultivated fields beyond that. Both in Switzerland and
France, people seem to live in villages rather than on separated farms
such as farmers live on in America. As we chugged through mountain
passes, which the Swiss have heavily guarded, the children excitedly
discovered doors in the sides of huge boulders indicating the places

where there are great caves and rooms holding ammunition and guns, with space enough for hundreds of Swiss soldiers, and supplies enough to keep them for months if it is ever necessary. We also saw cannon openings in the rocks where the soldiers could fire down on the railroad, if it became captured by another country. Switzerland has kept out of wars, but is certainly heavily defended. As you can imagine, it became quite a game to try to spot these places in the rocky sides of the mountains.

At Basel we had a four-hour wait for the train to Amsterdam; so we hurried to spend the time at the famous Basel Zoo, our first chance to see a European Zoo. The children thanked the Lord in their prayers that night that although the rain had splashed against the train windows all the way, when we got to Basel the sun came out! The crocuses were in bloom all over the lawns of the Zoo, as though scattered there by some flower girls. How we all enjoyed the well-displayed animals in their natural-like rock settings. We discovered that many of the animals are accustomed to being fed by the visitors, so that when they saw us coming, they hurried to the fence to greet us—it made them seem so friendly! Then to the sheer delight of us all, when we went to leave the cage of an owl, it said "Whooooooo" in a deep bass voice. "What did you say?" we all chimed forth, and the answer came right back, "Whooooooo." We had quite a conversation with this loquacious owl, though his answer was always the same. None of us had ever heard a real owl in a zoo say "Whooooooo" before, have you? The baby chimpanzees were to be fed at eleven, so we arrived just in time to watch. Imagine our amused surprise when the keeper brought out a small table, two tiny chairs, sat the chimps in their places, and put bibs on their chests! He then gave them each a bowl of soup and a spoon. For quite a time the chimps politely ate with their spoons; then, just as I had said to the children, "After this, I'll have to tell you to eat like a monkey," they both decided that a spoon was too slow, and throwing the spoons on the floor, drank the rest of the soup. The rest of the meal was eaten in regular monkey fashion.

Because we had brought along a cold lunch for our supper on the train to save going to the diner, we reluctantly left the Zoo in time to eat a hot dinner. Then we went to the station to go through customs for entering France. The children were excited to hear two men standing near us speaking English with a good, familiar American accent. Later, on the train, Priscilla became acquainted with these men and discovered that they were from Wilmington, Delaware, and that one of them owned the drug store where their grandfather buys some of his things. You can imagine the urgency with which she urged her Daddy to "come on and talk to these men." Fran found a real opening to talk of the things of the Lord and of Faith Seminary. It seems other Faith Seminary men also trade at one of his drug stores. The world seemed suddenly a very small place!

The girls loved feeding the animals at the zoo.

The next part of our trip was through French countryside very near the German border, where we could see smoke rising from German smokestacks in the distance. In this section some of the heaviest fighting went on during the war. We could see many houses and buildings which had been bombed into wrecks still standing in that condition, while all around life was going on as usual with the spring planting occupying the peasants. We didn't see any tractors. Most of the work was being done by hand planting and ploughing, or with an animal at the most. Near each big town we saw hundreds of tiny garden patches, each with a shed on it to keep garden tools, etc. Women and men and children were planting and weeding these patches, which supplement their food supplies, while other members of the families were sitting on old chairs knitting or mending. Each patch is no bigger than a small back yard, yet they are grouped together here a couple of miles from the city "flats" where they live.

We enjoyed our supper. It included salty crackers and chipped beef from a welcome package from America which had arrived just before we left, as well as bread and an orange from Switzerland. We went through Belgium and Luxembourg after dark so have nothing to report from there. The conductor took our passports and the customs officers did not bother us in these two countries, for which we were thankful. The children slept pretty well, except that at 3:30 A.M. the Dutch customs officials came in to go through our things and to check up on what money we were bringing into the country, and after that Susan stayed awake a long time whispering reports of things she saw (or imagined) as she peered out into the dark countryside from her upper berth. How we appreciate

America, where we can travel so far without a constant stream of questionnaires to be filled out and papers to show.

We arrived at 8:30 A.M. in Amsterdam to find a cold, damp spell had just commenced. As we shivered into a taxi, I was thankful the suitcases held the children's winter woolens. The familiar canals and streets of Amsterdam gave us all a homecoming feeling as we drove through the thick stream of bicycles carrying their owners to offices or stores. Amsterdam has 300,000 bicycles, so, as you can guess, the automobiles are in a minority as bicycles jam the streets at rush hours.

Pension Museum is more like a small hotel in size. Our rooms were on the third and fourth floors, up flights of steep, narrow Dutch stairs. "Watch out, Debby, if you ever start to fall, nothing will stop you before you hit the bottom!" Priscilla and Susan had a tiny room on the fourth floor, and Susan's bed folded into the wall by day. This suited her perfectly; she discovered it was great fun to have Priscilla shut her up in the bed! Our room was perfectly huge, big enough to hold all three of our rooms in Lausanne, with five big windows on three of the six sides (a corner room). It had three beds, a large dining table, a big desk, and heavy chairs, typically Dutch. The Dutch go in for big rooms, heavy furniture, many large windows. From our windows, we could see the canal in front and parts of at least six streets, and a bridge. So the children had much to look out at on the many rainy and some snowy days during that unusually cold April. All our meals were served in our room, which would have seemed quite homelike if it hadn't been for the cranky man who lived underneath us banging on the radiator every time we walked across the room! However, that only made me appreciate the 90-year-old man who lives under the children's room here; he never complains.

Mother, you asked about the beds. Yes, they were not comfortable, and Priscilla's had a ridge in the middle where half of the mattress rose to a higher level! The only uniform thing I have found about mattresses in Holland is that they all seem to be made in two or more pieces to facilitate their being aired and turned. The food was a good object lesson in appreciating what we have here in Switzerland. We found that we needed to supplement what we were given by buying a bunch of carrots to eat raw, or some lettuce and radishes, to make the meals satisfying. Of course we could have bought good meals in a restaurant, but we did not feel this a right expenditure of the Lord's money when our meals were so much cheaper at the pension. . . .

Our first interview concerning our work in Holland was with Dominie Bikker, with whom we spent several hours explaining Children for Christ and also our entire purpose in coming to Europe for the Independent Board. Our first meeting was with the interested Dominies. There were seven there, representing three denominations. This was a morning meeting in the study of Dominie Prins. Even the children felt tense with the importance of this meeting, because if the Dominies did not approve of the program of Children for Christ, of the flannelgraph, the choruses, etc., it would mean much delay in trying to make changes to conform. Naturally we know there will be necessary changes in various countries, but the overall ideas need to be the same.

Fran spoke first, giving a picture of the need of evangelization among the children of the world, narrowing it down to Holland and then Amsterdam. . . . I went through an actual class meeting and Priscilla, Susan, and Deborah became the class. They sang a half-dozen of the choruses, such as "The B-I-B-L-E," "In the Sweet Bye and Bye," and "I Will Make You Fishers of Men," etc. One we illustrated on the flannelboard, others were "motion songs," and for "Watch Your Eyes, What They See" we used the poster illustrations. After the first song, Dominie Prins went out and brought in his own two little girls to see and hear the rest. (How our hearts jumped within us at that—"He must like the song!") Before the last verse of "Fishers of Men" several of the men were nodding their heads or tapping their feet in time with the music. Of course I told them how we explain the meaning of these songs from the various Scripture passages from which they are taken and how they are sung by the children in their homes, in some of which the Gospel has never entered before. Then I gave a flannelgraph of the story of Daniel in the Lions' Den, and showed how a study, such as of the Book of Luke, can be reviewed each week by the children on the "review board." The men were like boys in their interest in the flannelboard, the Gospel walnut, etc. After we were through they took turns putting figures on the board and watching them stick there, pleased as punch with the results. You can't imagine what a thrill this was to us, not unless you have realized the differences in Dutch worship services and church programs, because we knew the Dominies not only approved of these, which were new methods to them, but actually liked them for their own use. We went back to our pension with our ears still ringing with the last words of the ministers, that they would urge their people to come to hear about this work, would advertise it in their Christian newspapers. We had a thanksgiving prayer meeting back in our rooms by ourselves, for answered prayer thus far in the work. I think our girls were almost as happy as we at that moment, in the answer that had come to their earnest prayers for C. for C. in Holland. . . .

The first public meeting for Children for Christ was advertised in "Trouw" and we found to our amazement that some had come as far as 150 miles to hear about it. It was held in the evening in Dominie Biesma's church. We presented about the same things as we had to the ministers, and the children were with us to sing. They did so well. Deborah charmed her audience with her hands folded in prayer for "Read Your Bible and Pray Every Day." Again the songs were *liked* and the Dominies joined in on "Fishers of Men." After my demonstration of the materials, Dominie Bikker told the flannelgraph story, using Daniel. He told it with much gusto, seemed to enjoy using the pictures, and the audience was much impressed. I had made 100 white hearts, each with a Scripture verse copied out of a Dutch Bible, during that afternoon, as samples of the sort of thing we give the children. These along with many leaflets describing the work were all given out that evening. A constant stream of interested folk stepped up afterwards to talk to us. Again we felt prayers were answered and doors were opening wide.

As you can imagine, it is a strain to speak one sentence at a time for translation; then the children found it hard to sit still over and over again for meetings in cold, unheated churches. We feel their going was a tremendous help in breaking the ice in the matter of the songs. One time when we had an illustration on the board, Debby called out, "Oh, that's Zacchaeus! I remember that story." The Dominies were impressed that three-year-olds could have so much to interest them in a Bible class.

Our Sundays were spent visiting churches in Amsterdam which are working with us. Messages were all in Dutch, but it was good to sit in fellowship with Christian friends. The Dutch have long services, no special music, and only the singing of Psalms. The sermon is divided into three distinct sections. After a half-hour of preaching, a Psalm is announced, and you think you are singing the closing Psalm, but when it is finished, everyone settles back in his seat, the children are passed a new square peppermint, and the sermon goes on to the second point. The same thing happens 20 minutes later. There are also three offerings taken, in little velvet bags on a long pole. This was wonderful in the eyes of our children, three chances to drop money in fascinating bags! The men of the congregation stand during the prayers, both long and short, but the women never stand, and all the singing is done sitting down. There are many children at the services; all keep wonderfully still (with the help of peppermints) for the one and a half- to two-hour service.

The children found once more that Dutch children on the sidewalks, in the parks, and in the yard of the pension are much more friendly and ready to play than Swiss children. Even without the language, they were able to play ball, hide-and-go-seek, tag, and were made to feel a part of the group. Here, even in their own school, children are not so friendly to anyone who is not Swiss, though that is gradually changing as the girls learn French and are staying on.

We went for two "expeditions" with the Koks while in Holland, feeling the children needed some outings to make up for the many meetings where they had to sit still! One was a trip to the famous tulip fields. Cold weather held back the flowers this year; they were much later than usual. The day we went was pleasant and sunny, but the flowers needed more such days. First we took a train to Haarlem. Then, as we approached Hillegom, we began to see flowers. Hyacinths were in full bloom, daffodils and narcissus were just finishing up, and the first tulips were out. The fields are planted to raise bulbs for sale, so they are a crop to these farmers just as wheat is to others. Imagine riding on a bus through very flat farm lands; instead of fields waving green or yellow, imagine a huge checkerboard of squares methodically planted with flowers. One huge square is of pink hyacinths; the next, of deep, deep blue; next, of scarlet tulips; beyond that, pure white hyacinths. Quickly look in the other direction: there is a square of narcissus, with deep yellow daffodils in the next. Is it a gigantic patchwork quilt? No, just the flower fields of Holland. After leaving the bus in Hillegom, we walked to the edge of one of the little canals which form lines separating these fields. There was a little barge-like boat with a flat, rough board surface, a rail around the sides, and a few chairs on it. For a few cents, we had a ride, poled along the canal by two men walking along the side of the canal. As they pass a crossing canal they vault with the pole, land on the boat, and vault off again on the other side. I was a little afraid Susan was going to try a vault, she was so engrossed in finding out how it was done! The men led us by foot along a narrow path bordering the flowers. As we admired them, a man (through interpretation of Mr. Kok) pointed out to us the spots where Dutch boys hid from the Germans during the war right in these flower fields. Many had been killed here; others, captured for labor camps in Germany. Our guide had himself hid safely for over two weeks in one of the little huts used for storing farm implements. The Germans found these fields hard to "clean up" because the crisscrossing canals prevented tanks from pushing through. . . .

At Dominie Floor's home, where we were invited for coffee after a morning church service, the children sang the songs for all his assembled family. He has eight children; the eldest three are married and there were grandchildren there, too. One of his sons-in-law is a musician who also writes some poetry. He volunteered to translate some of the songs into Dutch equivalents. Dutch language uses two or three words to one English word, so it is impossible to make a word-for-word translation. Before we left, I made a notebook for him of our favorite songs and he is working on them.

So we came to our last day in Holland. As the day approached, we knew we had not had enough time to finish the job we had come to do. We had counted on less widespread interest and time to instruct a few women to teach. I did have the opportunity of instructing quite fully two young girls, one of them Dominie Bikker's daughter, in the use of the flannelboard and the making of materials. To my delight they asked permission to use my Easter story for their Sunday school on Easter. It was given before the entire Sunday school. The little object lesson of the bulb and the lily was the first object lesson they had ever seen or used. All were so pleased because it made spiritual truths of the resurrection so clear for children. . . .

We were "farewelled" at the train by the Koks, the Pols, and a young couple from one of the churches who spent an evening with us talking about "Kinderen voor Christus." As the train pulled out in the dark of night, we felt a deep satisfaction in knowing that a great step forward had been made in one definite purpose for which the Independent Board had sent us to Europe, "to strengthen the things that remain"; and at the same time, a second purpose, "to do all we can for the children of Europe," had also made real progress. Surely the Lord has done exceedingly more than we had expected in these few months of what we had thought would be a time of language study and the making of contacts. Of course this trip meant more contacts which will also help in other parts of Europe for the work of the Board.

The trip home was very like the one going except that we started at night and arrived at Basel in the afternoon. Priscilla became acquainted with a college girl who had just come from New England for a short business trip with her parents. The girl said she did not believe in a personal God, but thought God was in nature and in love, etc.—"Each flower is a part of God." Priscilla really knew how to answer her with Scripture. After talking to her about "what the Bible says" for over an hour, she came to me to get a Bible and to have some more passages marked for her. Fortified with the 5th of John and some other chapters, she went back and spent the entire morning with the girl. Priscilla was very thrilled to have such an attentive listener as she "expounded the Scriptures," and the girl was amazed to find an "eleven, going on twelve" who knew so much more about the Bible than she. It ended with the girl promising to read the New Testament through to find out just what it did say, as she looked for the things Priscilla had told her. "I've never heard of these things before *as actual truths.* I'll read it from that slant." So do *pray for this girl* that the Word of God may work as she reads. Priscilla was pink-cheeked in her delight at finding that explaining truths in this way is really a thrilling experience. We do pray that all our girls may grow up so close to the Lord that they will always have their greatest joy in such things. . . .

It was bedtime when we got in the pension, but Madame Turrian had some hot milk and bread for us before we went upstairs. We found she had arranged our rooms as well as she could with our things so stored. A spring housecleaning had taken place in our absence; the clean sheets and clean rooms with a bunch of lilacs for a welcome made us feel at home indeed. As you can imagine, unpacking, moving back all the things, getting caught up on office work, starting French again, attending to many details at the bank, etc., absorbed all our days for a time. Now the children are well started on the new year at school (the school year commences here in the spring) and we are deep in the work of study and the office again. Priscilla is now starting the study of German from French. . . .

Now I must stop, though there is more to tell. It will have to wait for the next chapter! *Please pray* in May especially for Children for Christ in French-speaking Europe (which includes Switzerland, Belgium, and France). We hope to take a short trip, without the children, for three days, to Paris, to talk with Pastor Guiton, show him our materials, etc., and plan something for fall to introduce "Les Enfants pour Christ" in France. Pray also for the work in Lausanne. Plans are being made now to open home classes here in Lausanne in the fall. Materials are now being ordered and some printing is being arranged in French for memory verses, tokens, etc.

Do keep praying for us, for physical strength, for wisdom in making decisions, and for the funds to keep moving forward as the opportunities come.

With much love,

EDITH

June 13, 1949   Lausanne, Switzerland

Dearest Folks:

. . . The weather this spring has been upside down, according to all the nationals of each country we have been in. May in Switzerland was as cold, rainy, and miserable as was April in Holland. Our time in Paris was spent darting between the showers of rain and hail. However, this last week we have begun to have some sun and mild weather. Saturday afternoon we took a bicycle ride for quite a long distance. It is hard to imagine how the earth in the millennium can be much more beautiful than Switzerland on such a day. The wildflowers literally grow like weeds! Fields are full of gently waving, colorful tops, inviting you to come and gather. Everyone is allowed to stop and pick where he will. In a country full of rules and restrictions, here is one thing no one hinders you from doing. There are daisies with lovely long stems; shiny yellow buttercups; clover, pink, purple, and white, so tall and with such large flowers that they look artificial; and a multitude of flowers I can't name. Some look like small asters on a long stem; others, like wild snapdragons, striped pink and white, red and white, others red or lavender. In between them all are long, spiky, deep purple flowers closely resembling our delphinium. You see motorcycles with huge bouquets tied on the side, bicyclers with great bouquets tied on their backs, children with their arms full—yet the fields never seem to have less. Up higher in the mountains there are fields full of narcissus, free to the public. Hundreds of people have been picking narcissus for weeks now, yet they tell us the fields still look as though covered with snow. . . .

The Swiss have a knack of building their houses to look as if they just grew here. They do not face the road, but perch on hilltop or little curve to get the best view. Then trees, shrubs, rock gardens, and flowers are so lush that houses are sheltered in privacy from the road. Things must grow more easily here—why, I don't know—either the earth or the air or something. Roses are so tall, blossoms so huge, gardens so crammed with flowers, fruit trees so close together and yet so heavy with fruit, that every square inch seems productive. A row of roses where we could see nothing but concrete walk and wall made us stop, and we found only an inch strip of earth next to the wall! We are constantly amazed. Now the vegetables are beginning to make neat rows in everyone's garden. The farmers are cutting hay. Striking to us is the way the women work beside the men doing equally hard work in the fields. Sometimes you see whole families, even little tots, with hay forks. In between all this the vineyards cover space, terraced so that no hill is too steep for them. How can so much "cover" all the space! Flowers, grape vineyards, lush fields of hay, vegetables—all seem to cover the ground at one time. How wonderful the earth will be in the millennium when all the curse is removed from nature and Messiah reigns as King. The fertility of Switzerland, meaning much labor on the part of hard-working people, seems to give us a little glimpse of how the whole earth will be at that time.

One day we came in to find that Priscilla had been translator for Madame Turrian and a lady who wished to rent a room. The lady spoke German and English, Hebrew and Arabic, but no French. She spoke English to Priscilla, who put it into French for Madam Turrian; everybody was happy as the room was rented! That evening I discovered this lady was a citizen of Israel and found much to thrill me as well as to make my heart ache as we talked together. She has lived in Jerusalem for 20 years; was originally a German Jewess. She said the changes in the last year have been miraculous. "Everyone in Jerusalem says it is the doing of God—people are just drawn back to Palestine as though a magnet were drawing them," she said. She went on, "Never was I taught the Old Testament, but now our children in Israel are not only taught the pure Hebrew, they are taught the Old Testament and there is only one ideal in their lives and that is to build Israel into the nation it should be." She works in the diplomatic office in Jerusalem and seems to really know what is going on. As she talked about their determination not to have Judaism divided, not Orthodox and Reformed, but simply *one,* I wondered how soon the prophecy will all be fulfilled. Certainly it seems like the time of the end. Even she is amazed by the rush with which all this has come. She showed me the stamps, the money, etc., and said, "It is like rapidly growing grass, the progress that is being made in our nation."

My plan for the evening became unimportant as she showed not only desire to talk, but willingness to listen. I cannot record all that conversation, but slowly I led her from the reality of what was happening to the prophecies of Scripture relating to these things. Then we went from the hopes of the people today in Israel to *what God has said* concerning those who go back in unbelief, how *if* the New Testament is correct and the Messiah has truly come, then how terrible a thing it has been for these who are His own to have rejected Him through the years. "He came unto

His own and His own received Him not, but to as many as received Him to them gave He the power to become the sons of God."* Then I pointed out to her that not *all* "His own" rejected Him, giving the conversion of Saul of Tarsus, etc., then on to Romans 11, where I showed her that this is not a Gentile religion but we Gentiles have been "grafted in" to the true olive tree through faith in Christ (though we are "wild branches") while so many of the "natural branches" have been cut off because of their rejection of Christ in Whom *alone* is there any salvation. She listened carefully and in conclusion shrugged her shoulders and said, "Maybe." She has now left here, but before going gave us a map of Palestine in Hebrew, a few stamps, etc. This made an opportunity for us to give something to her.

After she has been here a few days, I had wished I had a Prophecy edition of the New Testament with the quotations from the Old marked in darker ink. I prayed about this, but felt quite sure there was nothing to do about it since it would take too long to send to America for one. Then one day, we received an invitation to attend a conference at Emmaus Bible School at Venne. The closing message of the afternoon was made by Davis of the Million Testament campaign. Afterwards I spoke to him and asked if he had a Prophecy edition with him. He reached in his pocket and handed me one!! Therefore, on the day our Jewish friend was to leave, Fran went down to ask her a few questions about Palestine, to thank her for the map, and to give her the New Testament. We praise God that she took it thankfully and promised to read it. *Pray for her.* We are going to send her name and address to our Mission in Palestine so that Dr. Lambie or some of the others may contact her.

May contained two birthdays: Deborah was four on the third and Susan eight on the 28th. Each time we had a family party, which Madame Turrian kindly let me prepare and serve at 5 o'clock, giving us two hours before suppertime. These meals were prepared out of the American food boxes we have received. The tomato soup was heralded with whoops of joy, as were the dried-beef sandwiches, the Jello, and the cake (made from cake mix and topped with boiled icing. As I cook, I must explain what I am doing in French to the very interested audience, Madame Turrian and the girls. Our girls were as excited about these family parties with their wildflower decorations, as though they were having a dozen youngsters and an elaborate meal. It is really fun to do without certain flavors for a long time and then rediscover the taste as a treat. Priscilla's birthday is Saturday (18th), when she will be 12; another celebration.

When we came home from Holland the new school term had started; the year begins after Easter vacation, all final exams taken before. We went to talk to M. and Mme. Vodoz about the educational system here, which has been so confusing to us. It seems they have four years in the primary school. What follows depends on whether the child expects to go on to University. Classical education is continued in "Ecole Super-

*John 1:11&12

83

ieur" (for girls—boys have another), where the 10-year-old goes in April to enter the "6 classe" (then 5, 4, 3, 2, and finally 1 classe). These six years offer only two choices of courses: one requires Latin and German with a choice of Greek or English; the other gives some art courses and sewing instead of Latin (called the more feminine course) and will not admit the graduate to University. Both courses include History, Mathematics, French grammar and composition and literature, and other usual subjects. Entrance exams have to be taken for admission. Once admitted, the pupil must work hard to complete the six years, then go on to a three-year course called the "Gymnasium," which ends in what they call "the Baccalauréat." Then the student is ready for any European University, which is more like our graduate school. The Gymnasium is comparable to the American College. However, no one here is sure of comparable standards. We feel we have a little idea of what the children are aiming for, though we still want to study the situation more to see what corresponds with what, where!

The little school the children attend is really for ones six to ten years, with kindergarten for younger. However, M. Vodoz has a group of older girls who for some reason need special help before taking exams to enter the Ecole Superieur. Priscilla is in with this group. M. Vodoz is trying to prepare her for the exams next April which will admit her to classe 5 instead of 6. She would then be only one year behind her age. *Please pray* especially for Priscilla this next year. It is all very well to say a child learns a language quickly. True, and all three of ours can chatter in French and understand a great deal. Deb has "no English accent." However, this is very different from being experienced to do advanced schoolwork *in* that language. Not only must Priscilla study German through "new vocabulary" words (words others her own age are just learning) by defining their meaning in French, but sometimes it all seems hopeless as the perfection that is required in getting every accent mark exact, etc., seems impossible to attain in just another year's time, with *new* work coming each day. If she *is* able to do it, it will be a real victory that will mean a splendid foundation for a true bilingual ability. On the other hand, there is a real question as to whether it will be possible or not. So, please pray about it. . . .

As the end of May drew near, we began preparations for Paris. . . . With only two of us, one bag with our clothes, another full of Children for Christ material, we didn't need a taxi; we started out on the tram with lots of time to catch a bus to the railroad station, early enough to find a seat in the often-crowded third-class coach. We found to our content that very few people had decided to go anywhere on that train and we had a whole compartment for eight people all to ourselves the whole way! The nine-hour trip was peaceful and we both were able to catch up on a lot of back reading matter, which often piles up on the desk. This one train a day to Paris gets in about 11 P.M., so we were glad to go straight to our reserved hotel room. At breakfast we discovered that the flour in France has improved somewhat since we were there before. We ate all our meals at the same restaurant, so had a basis for comparison. The rising value of the French franc seems to have helped practically, especially in food. This time we found fruit more plentiful and varied. Oranges were in the grocery stores; crackers could be bought without ration points; bread was less dark, heavy, and coarse. There is still no white flour in France.

That first afternoon we went out on the Metro to the suburb where Pastor Guiton lives. A long walk over a bridge of the Seine River, past many little cobblestone streets, and finally we see, a block away, Pastor Guiton's familiar beard and mustache and his beaming smile, which no beard could hide, moving rapidly toward us. He had feared we would miss the house as the entrance is rather complicated and the number not on this street. We were led down a steep alley, turned sharply to the left into an entrance hall—a child looked shyly at us from a door-way—up a flight of steps—"And this is my study." Picture a room in which the smell of old books is like a library—books, books, books line walls where what can be seen of the wallpaper is very, very old. There are tables full of pamphlets, booklets; chairs full of papers, pamphlets. "That is where the stove belongs," he said apologetically, pointing to a spot completely filled with piles of books, "but I don't need a fire in winter—you know books are very warm—they keep out the cold. It's very remarkable."

But now we must have tea and we go up another flight of stairs where their remaining rooms are. Very humble quarters, but with a wonderful view over the city of Paris, the Eiffel Tower making a clear landmark, the clouds tumbled together forming an artificial ceiling to the city which was spread out before us like a map. The walls of their rooms are filled with pictures which their artist son has painted, along with some fine pen-and-ink drawings by Pastor Guiton, There is a pi-ano here, near the tea table, on which Pastor Guiton plays each even-ing. He composes all his sermons, many of his articles and books (of which he has written a great many), while he is playing the piano. . . .

When we finally hurried down toward the Metro stop, I thought to myself, "It must be very late, perhaps after 7. Wonder what time the restaurant stops serving dinner—we have a half-hour on the Metro—it's still very light though. What a lovely sunset light in the sky." Then, out loud, "Fran, what time is it?" "Let me look at my watch–why, Edith, it is 20 minutes of *10*." Our conversation had driven all thought of time away. The interesting thing was the *light*. Paris does not need daylight saving time. In the summer it stays light until past 10:30 with-out it. Each evening we found it hard to judge the hour.

Another afternoon we went to see Mme. Blocher. She is pastor of a church and head of a Bible School which have made a fine stand for separation in the past and are in no way connected with compromise now. Fran first contacted her in 1947. She attended the International

Council in Amsterdam for a day. Now we have had this visit, a time of real fellowship with opportunity to discuss some of the issues of the day, modernism, compromise, etc. She also invited us to speak there on Children for Christ when we go in the fall or winter. The church was badly damaged by bombs, but is now being rebuilt. Workmen were there that afternoon; the auditorium seems almost completed. Other buildings nearby have been torn down, or are still standing as they were damaged. It is a great testimony to the Lord's faithfulness that they have been able to rebuild when others cannot.

The next day we met Pastor Guiton and his wife in Paris for lunch. Mme. Guiton does not speak English, but I found that she understood my French. Though I must have made many mistakes, yet we had quite a conversation while the men were discussing the spiritual condition of France, liberalism in the Protestant churches of France, etc. France has 40 million people; of those, only one million are Protestant and, of those, only a small minority are true Bible-believing Christians and, of *those*, only a very tiny minority are willing to take a stand against compromise with modernism and unbelief. The need there is tremendous in that largely Roman Catholic nation.

After our lunch, Pastor Guiton asked us to walk with him that he might show us "the old city." The original city was built on the island in the Seine River. As we walked we were given a history lesson, very valuable to our understanding of France, on the very spots where the events took place. The Huguenots seemed to come alive again as we viewed the place, in front of Notre Dame, where thousands of them had been killed. Here in the courtyard of the Louvre we can almost hear the gay sounds of the wedding feast which had brought together all the fine leaders of the Christian Huguenots, only to be dragged from the party by the Roman Catholic soldiers and slain or thrown into the Seine. From an upper window in the Louvre, then the Castle, the ones who tried to escape by swimming were shot like animals. As we hurried by the Palace of Justice, moving among the lawyers in their picturesque black robes and white dickeys, Pastor Guiton made us see it in an earlier day when the very pavement our feet trod on was running with the blood of the Huguenots. Then we mounted the steps to the chapel—La Sainte Chapelle—which has the most beautiful stained glass windows in the world—it is really breathtaking. Each tiny section of the hundreds of panes (the walls are just solid windows) was taken out during the war to be preserved against the bombings; now almost *all* are back in again. We see the point of the island back of Notre Dame and find that from this spot many little boats carried hundreds of Huguenots each Sunday morning to worship at a place down the river since they were not permitted to worship in the city. As they rowed off, they sang hymns of praise to the Lord for Whom they were willing to be persecuted even unto death. What separation and a stand against compromise cost these faithful Christians! . . .

We had a daily card from Priscilla, but nevertheless were glad to be headed back to the children after five days. Susan had faithfully waited at the tram stop for us for two hours with a bunch of flowers she had picked. She threw herself at us with the warmest welcome, but declared that she had loved it at the Vodoz'—"It was just like *Little Men;* I want you to read that story to me again now." Tongues ran on as Priscilla and Deb joined the welcoming committee. "Oh, Mother, it was fun taking care of Deborah. Here is a chart with all the things she did, checked. She was good *all* the time. Mother, she was asleep before my supper every night, so that I had all evening to study." Your prayers for them in our absence were answered "exceedingly above." Each had learned the Bible verse I had sent on a card, so that even without family prayers or another Christian to care for them, they had spent time with the Lord. Thank you for praying.

We returned to find much mail needed answering and some appointments immediately necessary. There was a note from Bob Schaefer (an American G.I. studying in Zürich, fine Christian fellow) saying he would be visiting us on Sunday. Sunday afternoon he arrived; we served him tea (such an easy way of entertaining, nice custom you in America should copy!) with some cookies out of a box that had arrived from America while we were away. He appreciated a taste of something from home as much as we! Just as he was discussing with us about a man with whom we had had correspondence (in Zürich) and was telling us something of this man's past history, the doorbell rang—and there stood the man himself! Mr. K.'s story is unique in this day of compromise and lethargy. The Lord certainly worked out the two visits. Mr. K. speaks German, Italian, some English, some French, but the latter two with an accent. Hence with Bob translating from the German, it was much easier to carry on the conversation. Mr. K. was formerly a pastor in the state church in Zürich; however, various sorts of pressure were brought to bear upon him because he preached clearly that salvation was through Grace and not of works. One time he was told that he must not mention the devil by name in his sermons; another time he was asked to preach on good works rather than the grace of God so continuously. He says that most ministers heed these warnings to tone down the fundamentalist type of preaching, but he would not stop preaching what he knew was right. Each canton has different procedures.

In the canton of Zürich the pastors are voted on each six years. Those who pay their taxes are eligible to vote—it being a state church. And so it was that our friend, his wife, and children (a small one soon to arrive) were on the outside, without a charge, without a home, and without money. At first Mr. K. went into secular work, but later he felt the Lord sent one hard thing after another to speak to his heart and to show him that he should be back in Christian work. So it was that he began again to teach the Bible in homes, to make trips to Italy, all on his own, just to preach the Gospel. The Lord has cared for their needs in that they have a house now, a small portion of which they live in; the other rooms are rented to students at the University. He has taken a stand of separation all alone. Surely there are not many who have the courage of their convictions or who even have such strong convictions. He slept on the couch in the living room downstairs for the night and Monday Bob Schaefer came back to continue his help in translation. They even both accompanied us to the dentist, so as not to waste time, and while one of us was being drilled by the dentist, the other drilled Mr. K! *Please pray very definitely for Mr. K. and his leading for future work.* Please *pray, too, for Bob,* as he is in a time of making his own decisions for the future. We feel the talk may have been a help in clarifying his outlook too.

The day after they left, we went to Neuchâtel. We took Deborah as she rides free on the train. It was a fast, clean Swiss electric train and the trip took only a little more than an hour. Mr. G. was at the station to meet us and to help with the heavy Children for Christ suitcase. We walked beside the lake from the station to his apartment. Neuchâtel, built along Lake Neuchâtel, is much smaller than Lausanne but very charming and with even steeper streets, it seems. We left the suitcase in his rooms, with their makeshift furniture (he lost all his own when they escaped from Belgium a few days before the war) and walked with him to see the panels in the Neuchâtel Art Museum. There we saw three huge panels which cover the walls of the upper part of the broad stairway with scenes of the second coming of Christ. Undoubtedly painted by a Christian painter,* many years ago, these depict Biblically the events of the end times. In the booklet describing these pictures, sold by the museum, the way of salvation is made very clear to all who may read. The people of Neuchâtel certainly have no excuse for not accepting Christ as Savior, as they see in one portion of one picture an Angel of Justice weighing the works of men on a scale with the other side of the scale dipping down with the weight of a slain lamb which outweighs the works. The booklet would make a good tract. The paintings are magnificent. We left the Art Museum to see the little house where Farel* lived, then to the Cathedral. It gives a tingling feeling to walk through doors built in 1200-something, into an enclosed building that has looked down on many priests, an enclosed garden that has echoed steps of many monks—then to consider that these same stones saw the Reformation, this same pulpit felt the pound of the Reformer's fist as he preached salvation through grace alone, through faith in Christ, not through good works. As we sat looking quietly at the beautiful windows, the deep-blue ceiling studded with hundreds of gold stars (these European churches are full of color), saw the changes in the

*Paul Robert, Sr.
*The Reformer Guillaume (William) Farel.

building brought about by the Reformation, we realized anew that only the power of the Holy Spirit could have made possible the great sweeping reform from the evils of the Roman Church at that time, to the extent that great sections in a country like this became Protestant. Today modernists preach from these pulpits! Reform is just as badly needed now; what if Farel could speak again? However, the Bible is the same, the Holy Spirit is the same; if the Lord willed it, we could see just such power today. . . .

And opportunities increase in correspondence. Mr. Kok has sent us a number of new contacts in Scandinavia as he is there speaking on behalf of the I.C.C.C. Names come from Finland, Norway, Sweden, Denmark, interested as he has mentioned Children for Christ to them. *Be praying* for these countries, that if the Lord wills, children's work may commence there.

Love,

EDITH

August 13, 1949   Lausanne, Switzerland

Dear Family:

. . . I left you in the middle of June. We had a busy half-month, with appointments, office work, and sorting and packing all our belongings. All three rooms had to be emptied this time. Winter clothing had to be aired and put into trunks in the cellar. Innumerable trips had to be made to the attic by Fran with armloads of stuff. He did the ladder climbing and I sorted and handed things to him. We are constantly reminded that "here we have no continuing city" *or* home. Toward the end of June Fran made a very worthwhile trip to La Chaux-de-Fonds, a Swiss town, where he spoke to a Free Church group about Children for Christ and also about the International Council. Quite a number of contacts have come as a result and a number of Free Church groups may start Children for Christ work. That same day we had an invitation to the annual Sunday school outing of the Brethren group of Lausanne. I took the children. It not only proved a treat for the children to play with others their age, but was a time of renewing contacts and making new ones. Among others I had an interesting conversation with an Egyptian girl who is starting to teach in a Presbyterian mission school in Egypt. I regretted that I did not have more time with her to talk of the issues of the day concerning modernism and unbelief and prayed another opportunity might come to talk before she went back to Egypt. (Watch for answer.) Sprinkled in this period were dentist appointments for us all. When the dentist came to Susan, she cried several times and he dismissed her in the middle of a filling. A second time, with courage screwed up, Susan sat through a redrilling of the tooth, only to twist herself into knots at the wrong time and hump her tongue so that saliva went into the tooth on top of the cavity lining. She must come back was the dentist's grim verdict. The third time, the tooth was so tender that the dentist's drill caused Susan to shriek in no gentle tone, at which point the dentist ordered her out of the chair and refused to work on her ever again—all this in French accompanied by what he thought of Susan in French also! A crestfallen Susan and a pair of exasperated parents took the advice of helpful neighbors and Bluette to try the Chailly Village dentist, "who certainly has patience because he works on the inmates of the asylum" (feebleminded, etc.). The whole family felt quite homesick for our Doctor Moore in St. Louis for his patience and lively conversation! Much to our relief, the village dentist took Susan by storm. She said, "I *love* him— he sits down as if it were *easy* to fill a tooth and he keeps his doors open so you feel the fresh air—I *love* it there." Just like Mary's little lamb, the dentist likes Susan, too, and said he couldn't imagine why anyone would have trouble with such a good girl! This seems a small incident, but it gives one a different feeling to have such difficulties in a strange country.

Because of dentistry, schoolwork, other appointments, office work, and packing, we put off our needed booster shots for typhoid until the last possible moment. July 2nd, Saturday, we all trooped to the doctor's office to get our shots, or "piqure" as they are called here. Susan had been practicing all day, picking at her arm to gather courage, so we thought we would let her be first. As she sat on the stool and stuck out her *arm*, the doctor prepared a place on her *chest*. A howl and a kicking of feet was Susan's uncourageous reaction to that surprise—"Do they have to think of a different place in every country?" she wailed. Priscilla was next, then Deborah, who saved the family reputation by watching with mild interest as the needle plunged in and not crying until she got out into the other room. We all gaily walked home through a park, glad to have it over with. Ahhh—how mistaken we were! Our carefree walk under the trees was only a prelude. As soon as we reached home, I began packing suitcases with much fervor. Gradually it began to be harder and harder to lift my head as I leaned over. Wheee, is my head going to burst in six directions? "Mother," said Priscilla, "you are turning yellow and your hands are *blue*." By this time my teeth were chattering and soon even blankets and hot-water bottles couldn't keep me warm. "If this is what typhoid is like," I thought, "I suppose it is a good thing to have shots; or maybe this is just as bad." Then vomiting began and I was as sick for the next few hours as I have ever been in my life. By midnight my temperature was over 103°. Meantime the children each commenced fever and sickness of varying degrees. Priscilla went off to sleep and slept hers off, but Susan and Deborah began to talk to each other and talked half the night. Fran had a very sore chest; the place where the "piqure" had gone in was swollen like an egg, but he had no sickness or fever. We are wondering if the dosage was stronger than that given in America, or whether our reactions were fairly normal. If any of you know, we'd be glad to know before next year comes around. The next day I was almost as sick, but by Monday morning I was able to get up and slowly finish the packing so that the truck we had hired to take us to Champéry could be loaded. You see, all our office files were going along and many suitcases and boxes, so we thought a truck could do the whole job and provide transportation for us at the same time for less money than all by train.

Deborah and I sat in the cab of the truck with the driver. Outside perched on various pieces of baggage sat Fran and the other two girls. The clatter was louder than it might have been because the Wildermuths had asked the truckman to add a wooden bedstead of theirs to our load. None of us felt too well yet, but nevertheless we enjoyed this change to look at Switzerland from a new angle. Things look different from a train and we had never gone this far on our bikes. Leaving Lausanne we went along the lake to Montreux and then drove through the Rhône River valley, one of the few flat spots I've seen in Switzerland, full of well-farmed fields, bordered by mountains all around. The Rhône itself is the color of putty at this place and *looks* as thick! Of course, it couldn't be. Suddenly we started up a steep mountain road which from the first moment never stops going up! Not only are these mountain roads steep; they are narrow. Two cars, especially a truck or bus, could not pass each other. What happens then? At intervals there is a widening of the road where a car may pull over and stop if it hears or sees an oncoming car. We always seemed able to find one of these when needed, or the other car did. Even parked in one of these wider spots, it takes maneuvering for a bus to pass. One side of the road is often a cliff-like drop—all in all not too comfortable a feeling, but a beautiful ride if you can get your mind off the road problems which might arise! Champéry is really not far from Lausanne, only about two hours of driving, but feeling as we were, it seemed quite a long time before the truck stopped going up and we drove down the village street of Champéry, about 3,000 feet in altitude. The next stage of our trip was on foot. Our baggage came up on a horse-drawn cart as our path is too narrow for a car. Fran and Susan helped to push the cart as the horse pulled. Every so often the horse decided he needed a rest and stopped, at which point the driver (who was walking) hurried to put wedges under the wheels to keep the wagon from dragging the horse back down. The horse seemed to rest more than walk and only he could decide when and how long he would go! However, we reached our chalet at last and it was a wonderful feeling to walk into a house that would be all our own for two months.

The first few days were spent in unpacking, settling, marketing in French (good practice for our language), getting back into housekeeping again, and catching up on office work. Besides this, first Susan and then

Deborah was sick with fever, restless nights, etc. Perhaps the change or perhaps still reaction. After a few days we settled into a schedule, not inflexible however. The mornings are definitely for study and work. At least two (if possible, more) hours in the afternoon are for outdoor exercise; the evenings are for study or office work. Saturdays we try to take a longer time out-of-doors for a hike and a picnic lunch. Sundays are different, of course, with our family services and a hymn-sing together. Fran decided that if we are ever to learn to speak French, we must use it in our family. Hence a rule was made that French is to be spoken from the moment breakfast begins until supper begins. With what a sigh of relief we all sit down for supper, everyone wanting to talk English at once. The hardest thing to do is to scold the children in French. I must confess that I often break the rule at this point! It is a distinct disadvantage to have to search around for a word in the midst of a scolding. Our French teacher lives only a short distance up the path—and really *up*— which is very convenient. She comes in the morning, sometimes at night. We have been reading the book of Revelation with her. The other day she asked Fran to explain it to her as we interpret it, which gave another good opportunity to witness to her of the wonder of salvation through grace, which makes us *all* "saints" and heirs of God, not through merit of ours but because of the death of Christ in our stead. Do continue to pray for her. She has a keen interest in spiritual things.

You may be interested to know that Fran still uses the little vocabulary cards that he began making when we first came to Switzerland, tiny pieces of cardboard with French on one side and English on the other. Now he has hundreds of them. Believe it or not, he is never without several bunches of these cards held together with elastic bands. As we go down the path to play tennis, he is going over a pack of verbs and we must wait to start until that one is finished. As he walks around the swimming pool keeping an eye on Priscilla as she crosses back and forth at the deep end of the pool practicing her various strokes, he keeps his other eye on a pack of cards, unless he is in a spot where hands are needed as well as feet. If he goes with me to market, he sits on a bench (always a bench in front of these Swiss village stores) and studies these cards while waiting for me to come out with packages to fill the pack on his back. The pack for the back is the most convenient way to carry a load up mountain paths; the Swiss use them for everything. Tiny children have little packs. There are huge packs that would carry a week's supply plus shoes and blankets. Farmers carry baskets on their backs with sticks for firewood and as they bring the hay down which they have cut on the steep, steep slopes; it makes them look like walking haystacks.

The children complain about study during vacation, but we feel the hour a day won't hurt them this summer and will help them in the fall. I can't say the whole hour is spent in concentrated study; every five minutes Susan shouts out, "Quelle heure est-il? Mama, papa, combien de

The wonderful walk uphill! This is the view as we bring our milk home to Chalet Bon Accueil.

temps maintenant?" (What time is it—how long now?) The end of that hour is a relief. The children also help with bed-making, table-setting, dish-drying, and cooking, which helps their education since they live so much in a pension. The best-liked job is going for the milk, which consists of carrying a milk pail down the path to the village *laiterie* and getting three liters of milk dipped into it before breakfast each morning. Priscilla has taken over the job since the morning Susan fell flat on her face hurrying back up the path and landed at home with very little milk in the pail plus an assortment of dirt, sticks, and even a good-sized stone!

Housekeeping is a bit more complicated than in an American city, where milk appears on the front steps and the refrigerator keeps things in good condition for days. Here we put our things down in the "cave," *a cold room in the cellar where the floor is unfinished dirt* and there are stepping-stones to keep our feet out of the cool wet mud. No frozen vegetables; each vegetable and fruit is only seen in its season. Of course, the summer sees quite a variety. When we first came, strawberries were ripe, then for a few days there were raspberries, but now they are finished and we have the first small apples and peaches. It is a very dry summer and unusually hot for the mountains, which has been hard on the growth of vegetable gardens. I'm enjoying every minute of cooking and treated myself to making a few jars of jams and jellies, though Fran continually warned me to remember we weren't living here all year!

As you know from my letter last winter, this little chalet is perched on the side of a mountain right above the village. Each side of the house is on a slightly different level, so that on one side you walk out on a bal-

Chalet des Frênes.

cony which is a story above the ground, while on the other side you walk out on the sidepath. Never do I tire of looking out at the mountains. In Lausanne it is wonderful to look at the mountains in the distance on the other side of the lake, but this living right in them is a very different experience. Not only are the mountains different each day and each part of the day as the light and clouds vary, but as days go on and you become familiar with the various trails, you feel that you actually *know* the mountains. You can gaze across at the rushing waterfalls on the lower part of the Dents du Midi (the 10,000-foot peaks across from us) and you can at the same time remember the spot high up above these waterfalls where you crossed that same stream. You can look way up at the highest chalet, where the Swiss go for the summer as they take their goats and cows up high to graze on the top slopes, and as the morning sun hits the speck of a roof, you can remember what it is like to sit under the shadow of that very roof, with the smell of the barn in your nostrils, gazing down on Champéry and your own speck of a chalet from there. Gradually as you take all the walks, the mountains become very familiar to you and their beauty becomes something you feel is sort of "in the family." As you sit in a room, you can't see the peaks because they are too high and too near you. It is necessary to go out on the balcony to see the rocky cliffs, which form the last 3,000 feet of the mountains, suddenly change from grey to a warm terra cotta as the setting sun paints them each evening. And again in the morning after a night which has been rainy down here, it is necessary to go out on the balcony to discover that the clouds which are drifting up the mountainside are uncovering the rocks to reveal the fact that they have been dusted with snow in the night, like a huge cake with powdered sugar.

We had been here about a week when Bob Schaefer came to be our house guest for a few days. As you remember, he is the American student at Zürich whom we have contacted several times before. He is now through school and will be working in Germany this summer in Christian youth work, after which he is undecided. He was happy to get some American cooking after a year of mediocre fare and it was fun to cook for another American who had missed the same things we had. Unfortunately for him it rained most of the time he was here, but the last day he and Fran took an all-day hike together and talked over the Christian issues of the day in relation to Bob's life work. Do be praying for this boy. He had studied French too, so was very good in keeping to French through the day. The children enjoyed having him here and Susan made decorations and games for a breakfast farewell party the day he was to go. All the decorations announced, "Welcome 1949"—a little late, but Susan meant well. She is always original in her parties!

One evening when it was warm enough to go out without even a sweater, Fran and I walked to the village tearoom for a cup of tea. There were no other customers that night because, the hostess said, "The weather is too good, all people go for a walk and get too tired." She pulled up a chair to chat with us after she waited on us and talked of many things—the war, her part in it in Belgium, her native land, the inevitability of another war, her desire to go to America, and finally she said, "I am a Catholic—tell me, what is the difference between the Catholic and Protestant?" Whereupon Fran told her of salvation through faith alone, of the possibility of assurance of eternal life because of the finished work of Christ on the cross. She seemed intensely interested and has said she would like to come to the chalet and talk to us again. She hasn't come yet, but do please pray for her.

Priscilla and Susan hurried through their lessons several mornings in order to finish in time to take a swim before lunch. In those mornings Priscilla became acquainted with a group of English schoolgirls who had come to Champéry on a chaperoned excursion from their school in Bournemouth, England. One morning as Priscilla was helping me with the marketing, we met four of these girls and stopped to talk to them. They wanted to know why we were in Europe and in explaining to them, it was necessary to tell a good bit about Children for Christ as well as to give a general picture of the church conditions throughout the world today. The girls seemed interested and asked if they could see the kind of things we used to teach children, whereupon I invited them to our house for tea and a demonstration of a Children for Christ class the next afternoon. I made a nice cake and biscuits and honey to go with the tea because they had told me a bit about the stringent food conditions in England and how they were enjoying the abundance of food here in Switzerland. They were thrilled with the chocolate-iced white cake and all of them declared that it was the first big, iced cake they had ever seen outside of pictures in magazines. They range in age from 14 to 18 and have lived under strict rationing for 10 years now. That afternoon a teacher came with them, so I had four girls and the teacher listening as I demonstrated the Children for Christ work with a flannelgraph story, the Gospel walnut, the wordless book, and four ladders made out of various colors of paper, all too short and broken to reach heaven except the one red one which represents the blood of Jesus. In the afternoon they heard the way of salvation carefully explained several times. They were interested in America and we invited them to come another evening to see the Kodachrome slides Fran had of the photos taken as he traveled speaking all over the U.S.A. in 1948. I made another cake for that evening. Though they enjoyed the pictures, they almost didn't get a piece of cake and a glass of lemonade because two teachers called for them at 9:30. To my query, "Can't you give them a few more moments and join us for refreshments?" the answer was, "No, the girls must come immediately; they have a hard day's traveling ahead of them tomorrow," and the "no" was very emphatic. I shivered in my boots for all English schoolgirls under such unbendingness! Then while they were donning their identical navy blue coats, I hurried to fix a plate of cake for the girls to carry back to their pension with them. The next morning they came back to deliver the plate. They were really lovely girls and I felt constrained to speak more personally to them about the Gospel message and their own salvation. Of course, I did not press them for any decision as it would have embarrassed them in front of each other, but they promised to write, and I have already had a card from one of them with a promise on it of a letter to follow. Do pray for them and pray that the contact with them may later lead to other opportunities. . . .

We miss Fran these days, but aren't a bit afraid to be in the chalet alone. The town lights twinkle down below us and the stars twinkle above the silhouettes of the mountains and it all seems very protected and safe. One afternoon the children and I were invited for tea by an American girl who has a chalet with another American girl here in Champéry. Priscilla, again, had got acquainted with them! This American—Ann—is daughter of a man in the Treasury Department in Washington. She came over here for a government job and after the job ended, didn't want to leave! The other girl is daughter of a Naval officer. As we entered their chalet, we discovered that they had about a dozen house guests. People are coming and going all the time. There was an elderly lady, German, who lived in Egypt 40 years and lost everything in the war. There was a Swedish girl and a French girl and a Norwegian girl and a German girl who lives in Lausanne. Several Canadian girls and an American mother of one of our diplomats in Belgium completed the picture at the tea table—all but us four lived in the house! It was all very interesting, but the most worthwhile part of the afternoon came when I had a chance to talk alone with the German girl. She listened with intense interest as I told her what we believe and why we have come, and she said, "Oh, but that is what Germany needs." She said that her sister, a Countess, is now a widow with four little girls; her husband was hanged after the war. "And my sister has nothing to live for but religion. I want you to talk to her. She will be in Lausanne for a month soon to visit me." She went on to say that she knew of fifteen friends in Germany to whom she would like us to talk. Pray about this—the Lord could use it. This girl is to be married to an Austrian in October and they want to live in Britain. So much more I want to say, but I'm going to try to keep to six pages! I promise it will be a month next time or less.

Love,

EDITH

September 18, 1949   Lausanne, Switzerland

Dear Family:

Yesterday was the anniversary of the day on which we arrived in Lausanne a year ago. We can remember how impossible it all seemed then that there would be anything of much interest to write home about in the year ahead, which we thought would be all taken up with language study and correspondence. How wonderfully, above all that we hoped for this year, has the Lord opened up doors where at first there seemed to be a solid wall! . . .

One day after Fran came back from Amsterdam, he took Priscilla, Susan, and an English boy (he has both Swiss and English nationality) for a hike to the pass in the mountains between Switzerland and France near Champéry. They used the wide, well-used path on the way, but decided to try a different route back. The path was well marked with orange paint splashed on stones—at the beginning. Suddenly it ended in a precipice. Each way they tried from that point on ended also at the edge of a precipice. It began to get grey as evening approached and Fran wondered if they would have to spend the night there. They stopped to have a prayer meeting, asking the Lord to show them a way back to Champéry. Immediately after that they discovered a dry streambed, steep but a possible way down the mountain. Sliding and crawling, they helped each other down, Fran leading the way. It was pitch dark and raining hard when a well-soaked, muddy three returned, a full three hours after I had expected them. Hot baths, clean pajamas, and a hot dinner soon had them feeling comfortable. As I put Susan to bed, we discussed the object lesson of that hike. Those orange splashes looked like the markings of a fine path, but they only led to a precipice. Just so many people are following what looks like well-marked paths to heaven, only to find that they end on the brink of hell. It well behooves us to follow only the paths we know about from the maps, etc., as we climb the mountains; as for heaven, the Bible says there is only one path—through faith in Jesus Christ and His death for us. "Why, Mother, I see it," says Susan. "Some people are *being* the orange markings on the wrong paths, making people get mixed up like we were." Susan's prayer that night was sweet with new understanding.

One afternoon we met the two American girls (Ann and Mary of my last letter) as they were walking along toward the *laiterie* swinging milk pails. We chatted a minute and ended up inviting them to the chalet to see Fran's European pictures. The evening gave us a real opportunity to talk of the things of the Lord; I'm sure they went home with lots to think about. They are typical of the young Americans who are wandering around here in Europe, doing a bit of study and some sightseeing but with no desire to work now or ever, and with no purpose in life except to see how they can stretch their money a little longer before settling down to a dreaded job. Pray for these two girls; in all probability we will be seeing them again and we would be happy to see them find the Lord. That night they mentioned that the elderly German lady wanted us to visit her as she had many problems and thought we could help her. We only had a few days left in Champéry but we promised we would be there before we left.

As the time drew near for our departure from Champéry, the children became very unhappy. They love the simple village life where a walk down the village street (only one real street) brings a greeting from each shopkeeper and where they now know the names of the children playing about. We began to see many summer visitors go and the return of goats, sheep, and cows from the mountains, and chalets changed hands, from summer visitors back to village folk who had spent the summer high on the Alps with the cows and goats. Fields nearby grew noisier with bells of all sizes and the noise of bawling cows reached our ears in the mornings as some were being sent by the little train down to the markets in the valley below. A broken tooth took me down to Monthey to the dentist several mornings and I had a fine trip each time watching pigs, sheep, and cows come on board at the tiny villages all the way down. The trip down takes only one hour and each trip meant a time to witness. Twice I had good conversations with English tourists; once, with a Jewish girl who is working in a home where displaced Jewish children are sent for three months at a time, three months of Swiss mountain air and better food to make up a bit for their lives in the German camps as they wait their chance to be sent to either America or Palestine. Each conversation gave me a chance to witness to the wonder of our Lord and of His Word, the Bible, which has the answer for all of their problems. English folk are so pathetic under their unhappy socialism, which has brought them less and less liberty and so little food.

Our landlady, Madame Marclay, began to talk to me while Fran was still in Amsterdam, about renting the same chalet for the year around. She said she had grown so fond of the children she hated to see them go. As I talked with her about the possibility and explained to her our work and our need for my freedom to type, etc., and of our various trips which necessitated having someone care for the children, or an inexpensive place to store our things if we all went—she answered each with ideas which started a whole new train of thought to me. First of all, she informed me that they expect to pay all their taxes, etc., and gain most of their profit with their summer's rent. The month of January also gives them the opportunity to rent to people who want winter sport vacations, but as for the rest of the year, the demand for a place in the mountains is so small that the rent is only a fraction more than the rent for the two or three vacation months. The first thing my mind did when she gave me the figure for the year-round monthly rent was to jump to the thought of the cost of our "extra room"—was it right to pay so much for one extra room for an office when a whole house could be had for about the same price? Why, we are so pleased when making a trip to be able to store all our things in one room; but if we lived in a chalet for the year around, the things could be kept in their places in a whole house and not cost more. Then there is the matter of the storage we pay on the things we have no room for—the dishes, refrigerator, etc. If we had a house, all these things could be in it too. Hmmmmmm—my mind zoomed, doing multitudinous arithmetic problems, and came to the happy conclusion that it would cost *less* to live in the mountains in a chalet, employ a woman to do the housework, pay railfare to Lausanne for all small trips, eat better food, have opportunities for entertaining others for meals—than it would cost to remain in a pension with three rooms. Could it be?! My mind and emotions were in a whirl from that moment on. Is the Lord sending this idea or is it wishful thinking? We had inquired and looked at houses in Lausanne and after a year we had found that even a small apartment of three or four rooms would cost far too much to enable us to have help for the housework and free me for the office work. As you know, we had come to the conclusion that we would remain living in a pension for the sake of the work. But here I was discovering that a mountain village could give us a very different rent, thereby freeing the money for help, thus putting the whole idea in a new light.

Fran returned to a flood of information! However, as we talked to the Marclays, they said their chalet is not free for a year and two months. The folk from Yugoslavia are returning for the winter and it is already rented for next summer; in fact it is very much sought-after for the summer months and only the Lord enabled us to get it this year.

"If it is a saving in money, if it is workable for our work, if the children can get schooling here, and if it will be better for their health—*if* we find all this to be true," said Fran, "then I think we should think about doing this thing *this* fall. Why wait a year, especially since our fund for the extra room is almost exhausted."

We began to pray about it. "Dear Heavenly Father: if it is Thy will for us to be here *this* year, the Marclays could easily get word changing the plans and freeing this chalet; or perhaps there is another chalet suitable for us. Please show us Thy will." Then we proceeded to inquire about schools for the children. Switzerland has State Churches—and in some cantons the State Church is Protestant, in others it is Roman Catholic. Champéry is in a Roman Catholic canton; hence the schools are taught by Sisters of the Church, just as religion is a school subject in the Protestant cantons. Therefore, we did not want our children in the village school. We went to Ecole Alpina to discuss Priscilla's school needs. This is a boys' boarding school which prepares boys for the difficult state "College Classique" and is prepared to teach all the subjects she would have had in Ecole Superieur—Latin, German, French, History, Mathematics, etc. There are five men professors, but the classes differ each year; that is to say, they do not always have boys of every age since boys are often sent for just one year to improve their general health. The school has classes in the morning and again from 5 to 7 in the evening, leaving the afternoon for outdoor sports. Other schools in Switzerland have school from 8:30 A.M. until 5:15 P.M., 6 days a week, leaving the child ten years old upward no time in the sun. The director said he would be glad to make an exception and take a girl student *externe* (day student). However, when there are no boys her age, she will have to be tutored privately by the various professors. In spite of the fact that that would be expensive, we feel we could manage it *within* the budget allowed for the pension. Then we went to "Home Eden," a children's combination pension and boarding school, where younger children come for various lengths of time freeing their parents for trips, or to stay for their own health. This "Home Eden" is run by two Protestant ladies. They very sweetly told us that they never never take day pupils as they have too much responsibility for the health of their children to allow village germs to be carried in! However, as we told them of our work in Europe and of our need for leaving the children at times (perhaps sometimes with them), they agreed to make an exception of Susan and, if we came to Champéry, would allow her to come as a day pupil—at a very low cost. There are only twelve children there for the winter, and the schoolmistress seems very capable. Hence, it seemed that for both the children, the problem of a nerve-racking school program would become a much happier situation in these small schools which put emphasis on building health. Of course they would continue to be taught in French as the teachers do not speak English!

With that problem out of the way, we turned our thoughts and prayers in the next few hours and days to the opening up of a chalet for possession this year. One place came to our attention, a place built by a Geneva watchmaker for his summer vacations and for rent now since his wife had had a stroke and could not return again. This place was lovely to look at but we were not sure how warm it would be for winter living. However, our minds were settled when we were told that the watchmaker was going to "hold" the place for a friend. We were now very near to the day of our departure; we had asked the Lord to show us by Friday of that week so that we could let Madame Turrian have a long notice before the contemplated move. The children were trying to keep cheerful as Friday morning had arrived and no place had turned up—the decision was almost made, wasn't it? they asked.

Then Friday morning Fran and I were walking alone along the village street, feeling a bit dejected ourselves as we realized that we had let ourselves dwell on the nearness of having a home again, when we suddenly looked up to see Madame Wildermuth's sister standing on the steps of their hotel. "Are you renting Blanche Neige" (the Geneva man's chalet)? "No, it is being held for a friend—I'm afraid we won't be living here after all." "Well," she said, "I have been wondering if you would be interested in our chalet—that is, the one we rent." She went on to tell us of the Chalet des Frênes, which had been built by an English woman twenty years ago for her *winter* vacations in Champéry. She told us how well built it was and how no expense had been spared to make it exactly as this wealthy woman wanted it, even down to the imported English bricks in the fireplace. "You know," she said, "I have hesitated promising it to those who are in it for the summer, for next year, and I'm glad I have, because if you want to live in it the year around, we would much prefer it. It is always a headache to me to have to prepare it for the visitors." We excitedly agreed that we did want to look at it and to hear the price—if too high, we couldn't do it. As she came out with the price her brother quoted, she said he was asking *less* than it would rent for the two summer months plus the winter sports time, less for the entire year than for the four months, if we wanted it for the whole year. (Later Madame Wildermuth said to me, "I think the Lord must have put that into his heart, or he would never have asked less, *losing* money on renting it by the year.") As the price was divided into monthly rent, it became apparent that we could afford it and still manage.

Now to see it—! As our steps hurried along to the opposite end of the village where we had been living all summer, I looked at everything with new eyes, trying to imagine returning from trips pulling our suitcases along in a cart from the station along this very way, to find a house, a home, with belongings in their own places, instead of facing a moving problem after a long trip! Wouldn't it be wonderful? Now we began to climb a bit, but not too steep a path and quite wide enough for a truck to bring our things. "Here we are," and the wide gate swung between two trees admitting us into the garden of Chalet des Frênes. Enough place for a vegetable garden with plenty of space for the children to play—big trees, gravel path, a stone terrace where outdoor meals could be eaten, even a little summerhouse on the highest spot whose three sides and a bench would make a lovely playhouse for the children. How wonderful is our God, our Heavenly Father Who had made it possible for us to find such a place. As we inspected the inside, finding central heat (furnace and radiators almost unheard of for a mountain chalet), finding ample space not only for our family and office needs but also for guests—we wondered if the Lord were not preparing to take us into a new stage of the work.

Among other things we had hoped to do when we came to Europe was to keep some possible workers with us for some length of time to teach them our methods of children's work, or to train them in Bible Presbyterian doctrines that they might be ready to carry on as national workers for the Independent Board. Here was a place where such things could take place—perhaps the Lord was preparing the way for what He knows is ahead of us. We found the house, although built along the lines of a Swiss chalet, was finished off inside with wood paneling painted white throughout, and with good floors covered with rugs. The living room, dining room, and kitchen make up the first floor; five bedrooms on the second give the children each a room and us a bedroom and an office. The third floor provides us with two guest rooms and a good bit of storage space besides. The house is completely furnished with electric stove for kitchen as well as a wood stove, and even sheets, etc. The only problems are those connected with washing clothes, as the English woman provided no place for that since she sent all her things out and it was built exactly for her own convenience! There is a fine bathroom with tiled walls in my favorite turquoise, and I couldn't help but thrill as I thought of the house being built twenty years ago while I was entering a high school in Canada and yet containing so many of my "favorite things." Does the Lord care about the little things? Yes, I believe He does. He knows the little desires of our hearts as well as the important big things. He Who is able to do all things is building mansions for us in Heaven. If it has not been His will to fulfill your small wishes here, someday in Heaven I verily believe you are going to be amazed at what your mansion contains. I really had thought this past year that home life for our family, which we all missed so much, was going to be put off for several years, maybe until we reached that mansion. We had all said we were willing to remain in two or three rooms if that proved best for the work. But the Lord, Who brought us here, had used this English woman to build a house for our needs 20 years ago!

Maybe you would like to hear some of the little things this house contains that are among my favorites: A big picture window in the living room which reminds me of the one we left behind in Chester, except this looks out at the majestic Dents du Midi; a fireplace which looks so inviting to sit by after a year of living in bedrooms without a comfortable chair; the corner cupboard which is so like the one in St. Louis that I hated to part with; a tea wagon which makes transportation of food into the dining room a rapid affair; and the dining room itself, with its two sides of windows making it like an outdoor room.

When you asked the Lord to open or close a door by Friday and such a place was found on Friday afternoon, would you not have felt that you had the answer you sought? We did and signed the contract the next day. We felt it would not be fair to Madame Turrian to leave her without adequate notice, hence signed for November 1st, with a clause that if Madame Turrian found people for our rooms before that, we would come earlier. Then you know what happened? Right after our contract was signed and sealed, the lady who has been in it this summer asked for it for next year. When she found we had rented it, she tried to buy it. The owner* is in South America and does not expect to live in it, but does not intend to sell it either. In the next two days several tried to rent it for summer or winter sport months, but the Lord held back these inquiries until we had the matter settled.

Several people said that it would be impossible to find a woman who would come each day to work, that the only available help would be a young girl from German-speaking Switzerland who wanted to learn French! Such a girl (we have observed at the pension) must be constantly supervised and would not be the kind of help I need. We prayed that a village woman could be found, one with experience. Only one day after that, Mademoiselle De Fago (Mme. Wildermuth's sister) came to us with a beaming face and said that she had found the woman who had worked for several years in that same chalet. This woman loves to work in Chalet des Frênes, understands the furnace, the stove, etc., and could come in the morning returning to her own home in the evening since she lives not far away on the same path. Hence, she has already been signed up to come the day we move in to do all types of housework to free me for the office work. Isn't it wonderful to have a Sovereign God planning your life? We found that villagers (which means us) can buy trip tickets for the little mountain train, making the trip to Monthey very little more than the expensive tram fares here in Lausanne. Also this little train connects with the express train to Milan and Rome, Italy, as well as with one to Paris. Of course other trips will require connections at Lausanne or Geneva, but the connections are good.

As for language study, we can have the French professor at the Ecole Alpina. There is no doctor in the village, no dentist, but Monthey, one hour away, provides both, and the doctor will drive to Champéry on call as well as having office hours in Champéry one or two afternoons a week. We hope we will be so well we won't need him.

The children were happy beyond anything you can imagine. They declared they would never be homesick living in a real home in a friendly little village. . . .

The next day, packing finished in the nick of time with some things stored in Champéry to await our return, we left our little village. . . .

Coming back to the pension would have been unhappy, I'm afraid, if we had not known it would only be for a short time. After the summer of American cooking again, of food available for in-between meals if anyone wanted it, of fruit for breakfast, etc., it was hard to come back to boarding-house diet. However, we continually satisfy our temporary hunger with thoughts of our home-in-November!

Priscilla and Susan are back in school. Again Priscilla is tense and ner

---

*The De Fagos cared for it in her absence.

vous about it, making us happy for her that a change is on the horizon. . . .

We have been impressed by the opportunities given to us on train trips to reach Americans with the Gospel, Americans of a group it is hard to touch in America. For instance, one time this summer as I was on the train going from Monthey to Lausanne, an American businessman and his wife sat down beside me. After an inquiry as to what language I spoke (he thought I was French or Swiss—I am never taken for an American) and a hearty laugh over the fact that we were fellow Americans, the couple asked what I was doing in Europe—"Having fun?" So I gave an explanation of our work. The man then began to talk quite eagerly. "I am a student of the Bible and a seeker of truth"; the words just flowed out, but what a jumbled mixture of error. He feels all mankind is essentially good if they could just bring out the good in themselves, etc. The time was short and it was hard to get a word in edgewise, but as I scrambled my belongings together at Lausanne, he gave me their address on Riverside Drive in New York and asked that "either your husband or you send us a line because I want to talk further to one of you and we'll be coming abroad again soon." His heavily jeweled wife showed very little interest. Do pray for this man and the many others like him whom we meet, having much of this world's goods but poor in the knowledge of eternal things.

The time has rolled around again for the application for renewal of our police permit. We went down to the headquarters a few days ago, but this time accompanied by a man from Monsieur Andre's office. We feel that with his help the application will bring a result which will give us more liberty and will find such a statement printed on our permit. Nevertheless, it still is a matter for your prayers. When we move to Champéry we will need to apply again, since it is a different canton. However, we find that all our official dealings will be with the one village policeman whom we have already met, and that Monsieur Marclay, our landlord of the summer and a very helpful friend, as an honored postman has a good bit of influence in the town. Hence, although it is a Roman Catholic canton, we may find it easier to get our desired permit than it was here. Please pray about that also.

Forgive me for going over the six pages this time. I was anxious that you understand completely how wonderfully the Lord gave us this new place.

Much love to all of you,

EDITH

October 26, 1949   Lausanne, Switzerland

Dear Family:

In the midst of the last final rush, a large mail arrived. I accompanied Fran on the train to Geneva in a double capacity, therefore—as a wife to say goodbye at the airport, and as a secretary to read the mail and take dictation on the train, using the hours to good advantage. When we arrived at the airport, Fran was herded with the rest of the London passengers into a pen to go through customs; I went along with observers into an aisle which led me on to the field. Outside, I found myself in a "sheep pen" arrangement with a number of others there to wave goodbye and still more who were just watching planes take off and land. The Geneva airport is a cosmopolitan place, planes coming in every few moments from distant spots. I hung over the fence watching a plane from America unload—a little crippled fellow walking with his nurse, elderly couples, young businessmen, crotchety-looking older men, a Negro couple—just think, 24 hours ago they were all in New York. Next my eyes turned to a group going up the ladder to a plane marked "Air India"—several colorfully dressed Hindu women pulled their robes out of the way of the steps as they made their way up, a turbaned man followed them in, others crowded behind to disappear through the dark opening—slam, whirrr, and their plane moves slowly down the field. Wonder if Frank Fiol will see those wings in his sky in a few hours. What a strange world we live in these days when on a strip of dirt walk many feet which will soon be oceans apart. It means an ever-increasing possibility of contacting people from all over the world as they travel in parts far removed from their homelands, ever-increasing possibilities for witness to those who live in lands you will never see.

Suddenly I head, "Hey." I look over to find that Fran and his fellow passengers for the London plane have been put in the pen next to ours, about 20 feet away. "Won't they let you out?" "Don't know, guess this is where we say goodbye." "Hope you find a hotel room waiting for you and Mr. Kok." "They said I'd get a message about it at the Kensington air station." "How much longer before your plane goes?" "Oh, about 15 minutes. By the way, I forgot to give you any money—here, I'm coming over." At which point Fran lifted the chain, opened the gate, came over, and handed me the francs he had for me and had forgotten in the rush. Within a few seconds a uniformed man came up to Fran and demanded to know, in French, what Fran had given that woman—why had he left his pen? Fran tried to explain that the woman was his wife and he had merely given her some money he had forgotten to leave for her. Our grim-faced Swiss customs officer put his hand under Fran's elbow and ushered him back into the building. A shiver of dismay went up my spine. "Oh well," I thought, "surely they will understand and I have the francs here to prove it." I thought how terrible it would be to be behind the iron curtain where on the slightest provocation you can be marched off without ever a chance to explain. One moment before we entered that customs building, we had been perfectly free creatures, but now we were under strict regulations for the time being—what a terrible thing to live where *all* the simple freedoms of life were forever snatched away. To my relief Fran's smiling face soon reappeared among the London-bound crowd. He called over that after explaining to the head man that it was only his wife and only some francs (in French) and evidently being measured up as honest, he was released. After you are once through customs, you are not allowed to exchange, give away, or receive anything. Soon the London crowd boarded their silver plane, a last wave from the steps, and Fran was out of sight. The motors throbbed a long while before it was their turn to take off. I waited until the plane roared over the field and became simply a bright spot on the distant horizon. Praying that the Lord would take him safely there and would work out each step of the mission for which he was going, I turned away to find a place on a bus going back to the Geneva railroad station. It was full of people who had just arrived from Barcelona. Some were speaking Spanish and some Portuguese. It sounded so much like gibberish that I realized again we had made *some* progress with French—it now sounds like a language even when we don't understand completely! . . .

Fran had left me plenty of work and the rest of the time while he was gone was spent typing, except for the hours for the children.

Before Fran reached home again a week later, I had already read a carbon of his report, in which he told of the gracious reception Mr. Kok and he were given in the Colonial office by the head of the West Africa division and of his careful listening as they went over with him the particular case in Kenya and as they told him of the difference between the World Council and the International Council. He promised to see that the matter received proper attention and seemed to understand just what we believe and why we take the position we do. However, he said a decision could not be given until the papers arrived from their office in Kenya. The matter would take about a month. After this there did not seem to be any use trying to see the Honorable Arthur Creech Jones, with whom they had at first tried to make an appointment—at least not until further word from them. It may be necessary to go back once again; at the very least, it is most important for you to pray about this matter this month, and perhaps much longer, that the Lord may work the thing out to keep the door open in Kenya for our mission, also to establish a precedent for future negotiations on the part of the International Council in behalf of believing, separated missions.

After Mr. Kok and Fran had finished their business and written the full reports necessary, Fran called the London mission from which the children came to whom we had spoken in Ballaigue in the Jura Mountains here in Switzerland and went out to be with them for a meeting. Some of the children came as far as seven miles to see him again, which was a heartwarming welcome indeed! The mission superintendent is really quite serious about starting Children for Christ. It is a very humble little mission in a poor section where the Gospel is badly needed. Pray about this opening for reaching more children with the Gospel.

Fran also fulfilled his promise to Baroness von Dumreicher and called the home of her relatives, the de Courcys. Mr. de Courcy was most cordial and invited Fran to come out to their country home for dinner that night; in fact, he said they'd like him to stay for a few days since the Baroness had written so much about us. Fran zipped back to the hotel, had his suit pressed, donned a clean shirt, and made his way out to the outskirts of London. As I have always read is the custom of proper Englishmen, everyone was formally attired for dinner. However, Fran and his clean shirt were quite at home in spite of that! Mr. de Courcy is editor of a prominent private news magazine, an interesting person and seemingly a real Christian. His elderly mother is a most understanding and spiritual Christian. Guests for tea were just leaving as Fran arrived and among others he met the Greek Ambassador to Britain. At dinner and after, he had some wonderful opportunities to speak of things of the Lord to a French count who lectures in the U.S. and also to an English lecturer. Both these men were interested. One of them has just recently gone into the Roman Catholic Church. Both expressed a desire to talk further about world conditions, philosophy, etc., in the light of the Word of God. We have written to each of them to invite them to spend a few days at our chalet for further talk. Do pray for them.

Mr. de Courcy also talked with Fran in his office another day, with time for the things in which we are most interested—the Bible Presbyterian Church, the Independent Board, and the International Council. We feel the Lord has a definite purpose for all these contacts in England. The more we know of England, the more we feel the need for a truly separated church there. . . .

When I went back to Mme. Depersinge's home in Lausanne for a second afternoon of the Luke course and explaining teaching methods, the children and I were met at the door by a rather agitated lady. It seems the little six-year-old Depersinge had decided all this preparation had gone far enough and had invited all his friends to come to the first Children for Christ class that afternoon!! The friends were going to arrive in a few minutes and the roly-poly six-year-old boy was most contentedly standing on his head in anticipation! His mother was full of little worry frowns, but did not like to dampen his ardor in reaching his friends for the Lord, nor did she like to turn away the little folk the first day they had come. Could we get ready in a few minutes? I had the English copy of the first lesson with me—she had the figures ready. We went over the lesson together and she decided she could give it. The boy soon proudly conducted six friends into the room; with the other three Depersinges and the three Schaeffer girls, the first Lausanne Children for Christ class got off to a good, though informal, start!

Since that day things have progressed rapidly. There are now four classes each week in Lausanne; one in Morges (a few miles away); one in Lyon, France (conducted by the Closed Brethren there who were in Ballaigue this summer and heard about the children's work there); and one in Ballaigue itself. At present there are little German children at Ballaigue who will be there for three months. They are having a lesson each day! Meantime the writing and translating of the lessons in Luke are going ahead and tokens have been mimeographed in French with the memory verses for each lesson. We praise the Lord for this translation work as it will be a great help in France when we make a trip for the work there. I spent a part of one morning singing choruses to Mme. Andre to help her pick out some which might be good for translation to use for the classes. . . .

Yesterday afternoon as we returned from doing errands downtown, we found three excited little girls, dancing around a box beautifully sewed up in cloth, singing out, "A box came from America, a box came from America!" As soon as they could be quieted enough to put some end to the confusion, I got a piece of paper and a pencil to write down the contents of the box as they were removed, knowing that we were not the first ones to undo it—because you see, the customs men go through it very thoroughly before we ever see it. Then we sat down and took out the things . . . as I will list them now . . . to be sure you know it all arrived safely . . . along with the comments you would have heard if you had been listening at the keyhole!

1-lb. package of regular beans—"Oh boy, we can have pork and beans."

1 cloth bag of baby limas—"Mmmm, I love those . . . look, recipes too . . . soup and everything! Wasn't that nice, putting those in?"

1 cloth bag of large dried limas—"Now we can taste baked limas with bacon." "Debby, you don't remember that taste, do you?"

1 large cloth bag of red kidney beans—"Oh mother, now at last we can have chili con carne." "Yes, can't you imagine it—some cold night when the wind and snow are beating against our chalet and you come in from school all shivering . . . you will sit down to a big plate of chili and mashed potatoes." "We can't wait!"

1 can of pumpkin—"*Pumpkin pie!* We'll have that on Thanksgiving like we did in America." "How many pies will that make, mother?" "Debby, you don't remember pumpkin pie do you? I can't remember the taste either." (This is Susan speaking.)

1 can of pumpkin pie spices—"Now wasn't that thoughtful of them; they have thought of everything—it really will taste right now."

1 can of Crisco—"That means cakes, biscuits, cookies, and all sorts of things that mother can make for you." "Oh goodie, goodie . . . I'm so glad we are going to have a home again." "Only six more days now isn't it, mother? . . . Oh it is so exciting my tummy keeps turning over." "So does mine." "So does mine." (All three girls.)

1 hot-water bottle—"Now two of us can have a hot-water bottle at the same time—that's good."

2 pair of bed socks—"Aren't they pretty?" "Feel how soft they are."

1 apron made of hankies—"Isn't that darling?" "What a cute idea." "I think that is for mother when she is all dressed up."

1 barrette—"Look at the sweet little doggie on it." "That is just right for Debby."

3 notebooks with picture of Jesus on front—"One for each of us, that's nice."

2 pocket combs, 2 combs for fixing curls—"How pretty." "Can I have one for my pocketbook?" "It will be easier to fix curls."

1 tin box of hard candies—"Mmmm, can we have one right now?" "Aren't they nice ladies?" "Yes, I think they know all about children."

1 red pencil case for Priscilla—"Oh mother, I needed a pencil case—it was my secret wish!"

1 pencil box with crayons, pencils, ruler, and tiny books in each for Debby and—

1 pencil box just the same for Susan. These three from Mrs. Rynearson.

It was just like Christmas to the girls and they really needed pencils, not only for schoolwork, but for all the drawing they all do.

Please thank everyone in the Sunday School class for this lovely box and for all the pleasure and good food they have given each one of us. We will think of you many times in the coming weeks as we enjoy the contents. You know it couldn't have been better *timed* in arriving. It came just in time to go with the things as the movers take them from here this Saturday and deliver them at Champéry on Monday, the 30th. It means that we will start our housekeeping in our new home with a lovely supply from America. My birthday is the third of November and we should be enough settled so that I can use the Crisco for a birthday cake which the whole family will enjoy.

Thank you for all the trouble you went to to pack it so nicely and to make the firm cloth covering and the cloth bags for the beans. We will make use of the cloth too. We also appreciate the love and prayers which we are sure came along with the box. We need your prayers constantly. The Lord is blessing and opening doors, but the way is at times perplexing and there are many problems that face us.

A slow walk to Belmont one Sunday afternoon gave us an opportunity to get a bit of exercise and also talk to Mr. Ochsenbein. You remember he was the one who was in the Swiss Consulate office in Philadelphia and did so much to help us get our visa and chose this pension for us. He is now back in Switzerland to work for a year at Bern after which time he will be sent to another country. He expressed much interest in our work, said he would do anything he could to help us, and we look forward to more conversations with him before the year is over. Incidentally, we didn't need any more help on the police permit for Canton de Vaud—it came through *with all the former restrictions removed, with permission to evangelize in this canton!* Complete reversal, *which God can give.* Thank you for praying—and remember we need a *new permit* for our new canton, Canton de Valais.

Speaking of our new home—you can imagine that all through this busy month we have been happy to see the days checked off and the time draw close for our move. The children are as excited as though every day were Christmas Eve, and complain that "my tummy keeps turning over when I think of it, Mother." We are never allowed to forget how many days are left. Each morning Deborah says, "Now one more finger is gone." She has kept count on her fingers! Susan has worked harder than ever before at school so that she will be sure to be as advanced as possible in the new school. They all have been praying for people to rent the rooms, as I know you have, too, and Susan even tried to do a little soliciting herself. She met an elderly lady on the street and said to her, "It is a very good pension—with wonderful soup—for ladies like you." (Susan has hated the soup ever since we have been here and when she fusses, the ladies tell her how good it is!)

Prayers have been answered in regard to these rooms. Madame Turrian came to me one day and said, "I believe that the Lord wants me to be willing not to rent them, to stop saying they must be rented." We had a nice talk together and she said she would stop worrying about it. The very next morning two elderly sisters, who had several days before said "no," called up to say that they had changed their minds and would like to take the "middle room"—the one the children have been in—starting November 1st! You can imagine how Mme. Turrian felt this was a real answer to prayer and that God had dealt with her. A few days later our room became rented too, by an old lady who will live here the rest of her life. One bed will be removed, giving her more space and though she will eat up here and not get out much, she will have all those wonderful sunsets on the lake and the ever-changing view to make it less lonely. Now—only one room remains to be rented. Madame Turrian was very touched by the fact that folk in America were praying for her. She is quite happy now, except for the fact that she will miss the children. However, Debby will be back for a few days in November as Madame Turrian will care for her while we are in Paris.

Only space left to squeeze in my love to you all.

EDITH

November 30, 1949   Champéry, Switzerland

Dearest Family:

By the time you get this, Christmas will be in the air. Our greetings will arrive in the midst of preparations for special church services, hurried shopping trips, and rustling tissue paper, and so—*Merry Christmas to you all.* May the Lord give you each a special blessing at this wonderful season when to each Christian the thrill of the angel's message to the shepherds on the hills comes with new wonder in singing of carols and retelling of the old, old story. How sad it is to think of millions celebrating the birthday of the One Whom they in reality have rejected.

As I left you in Lausanne in the midst of a rush, I must turn from thoughts of Christmas and go back a month so that you can get up here to Champéry with us! Things didn't get any less busy as November 1st rolled around. Days were not long enough to hold all that needed to be done, it seemed. Packing was almost entirely crowded out by office work, calls to be made, etc. Toward the end, as certain people suddenly became aware of the fact that they had "been meaning to have you in our home," invitations came for meals, evenings, etc. Several urged us to be sure to stop for a meal when we came back to Lausanne on business. One family offered us "a bed any time you need one for the night." We really felt more at home than we had all year! We know from experience, and any stranger who lived in Switzerland for a length of time will tell you, that the Swiss are not easy to get to know. Many strangers feel lonely here. We praised the Lord as we realized in our going from Lausanne that in a year's time we had been given some real friends. Of course packing was inevitable at the end. The day before the movers arrived found us once more making trips to attic and cellar, trunks, packing all night, but it went with amazing rapidity, due partly to much practice and partly to the fact that it is easier when everything goes than when you are sorting and storing some things and packing others.

Late that afternoon, when my hair was spilling out its pins and I felt as dusty as the trunks themselves, the doorbell rang. Approaching footsteps announced the fact that it had been for us. Madame Turrian herself stood at our doorway, holding out two white-swathed packages, quite obviously plants. A careful separating of the paper revealed a cyclamen plant full of scarlet buds which a stiff, white card proclaimed was to welcome us into our new home—with love from the family which was first to have a Children for Christ class in Lausanne in their home. This loving gesture and the thought of the rapidly approaching moment when our home would be a reality sent me back to the packing with renewed vigor, filled with a warm and happy glow! Much to our surprise, packing was finished by 7 P.M. After a rapid change of clothes, a quick supper, we were able to catch a tram to keep our appointment for the evening without having to face packing after we returned.

Next morning, bright and early, the moving men were hoisting heavy boxes and trunks on their shoulders and walking down flights of stairs inside and flights again on the outside until they reached street level, where our belongings disappeared into the yawning black mouth of the truck. I stayed upstairs to see that they didn't carry off any of Madame Turrian's things by mistake, while Fran supervised in the cellar. Then as they pulled away in the truck, we ran for a tram to follow them down to the customs house, where they were to pick up our things which had been held there until we could produce a year's lease on a house or apartment. These included our refrigerator, a barrel of dishes, a box of kitchen utensils, a few lamps, a box of pictures and knickknacks, and the children's double-decker bed. All these things had been packed in St. Louis before we left and, along with the boxes of books, had not been opened for nearly two years! As we saw the familiar boxes rolled out onto the truck, with their black crayon markings which had been so carefully put on before their final destination was thought of, and realized that at last they were completing the journey they had started on, the feeling of being in transit began to leave us. No matter how long or short a time we will be here, we began to feel really at home.

The brother of Madame Turrian's brother-in-law works in this branch of the *Douane* (Customs) and his "word" made the process easier and much less expensive than it would have been a year earlier. We had to sign another paper declaring that we would not sell or give away any of these articles until after we had lived in Suisse for five years—from that moment. If we have to leave in a hurry before that, we wonder what we are to do—make a bonfire?

That afternoon we were free to finish up many details, such as having Priscilla's eyes tested and getting the new prescription for her glasses, measuring the children at the sporting goods store in case we could get them skis for Christmas, buying some new woolens for the children to take the place of the much-mended ones from last year. Wool from the skin out is a necessity here where houses cannot be kept as warm and where schools expect all children to be so dressed as to be comfortable in cooler temperature. Swiss people keep warm in winter, both indoors and out, by dressing warmly. Most women wear woolen stockings with heavy-soled, laced boots in the mountains and warmly lined high shoes in the cities. Galoshes and rubbers are not worn so much here since shoes are made to be warm and protective.

We could not leave Lausanne without calling again on Baroness von Dumreicher, so that evening found us in chairs drawn close to her bed talking into her ear trumpet, which she fondly calls "my teapot" ever since a waiter in a restaurant carried it away and placed it with the teapots! We were glad we had come as she had been ill again with her heart and felt heavily burdened with her troubles. It is lonely to be in a pension in a strange country, without friends, at the end of your life. Circumstances make it impossible to return to her home city in Germany. Our time of Bible reading and prayer with her brought her a comfort which was evident on her face. As she embraced me when we left, I felt as though we were saying goodbye to one of our own congregation. She begged us to look out for her grandson Peter if anything should happen to her. She meant spiritually. She is worried concerning his salvation, especially since she feels she has not taught him as she should have when he was a boy in her care. Do continue to pray for them.

The movers had informed us that they would arrive in Champéry very early Monday morning. Not being through with our business until late Saturday afternoon, plus the fact that we could not get provisions late Saturday night in Champéry, made us decide to do everything in Lausanne on Saturday, have our "farewell service" in our little room Sunday morning, and, with our one remaining suitcase, take the afternoon train to Champéry, arriving in time to get the children in bed early. The Andres invited us to have dinner with them in their home after our church service, so things worked out perfectly. Our last service in that little room was attended by the elderly Irish lady, who has attended quite frequently. The whole pension family lined up to bid us goodbye. We found a bit of tug at our heartstrings, even though we could hardly contain our excitement at this moment of our "homegoing." Debby assured Mme. Turrian that she would come often to visit her. Amid a rain of "au revoirs" we walked away from Boulevard de la Foret, full of thoughts of what the last year had contained and of thankfulness to the Lord for having brought us to the very sort of place we needed for the first year.

We had a delightful time of fellowship and prayer at dinner with the Andre family, but even though the children enjoyed being with children their own age, I found Susan spent most of her time watching the clock and counting the minutes until "we can go home." Having left so many cold station platforms in the last year with none to wave us off, it was a warm farewell indeed to have the folk drive us to the station and wait until our train pulled away—to wave with one hand, that is, while the other hand pulled their children back from the train where they were giving it an unnecessary push! Debby had her face against the window saying, "Goodbye lake, goodbye lake, we're going to live in the mountains." As we changed at Monthey for our little mountain train, we found our car full of boys who had taken an afternoon walk and were riding back up. We later found they were from the school where Priscilla is going. At last—"*Here* we are, Mother"—"Daddy, here we *are*." We climbed down to find that a cloud was enveloping the village and everything was dripping with dampness. The view was completely closed out. Night had settled down. But—here is a reception committee! One of the Wildermuth children, spending a week with her aunt, is here to greet us, along with a man her aunt has sent to carry whatever bags we might have, and a most enthusiastic black cocker spaniel. We make our way down the deserted village street, the dog jumping up to lick our hands and running back and forth wagging his stub of a tail to make sure we know we are welcome. How different the village is now than in "the seasons." Now it is so quiet you can almost hear the silence! Hotels are closed. Hotel Champéry, the largest, boasting 70 beds, is now occupied by Mademoiselle DeFago and her brother and the cocker spaniel, Poosey. We are guided to the empty hotel and taken into one room heated by an electric heater, where Mlle. DeFago has prepared hot milk, coffee, and bread for us. Mlle. DeFago is to be our French teacher here, giving continuity to our study as our first teacher was her sister. We are praying that our contact with her may also be a means of opening the Word of God to her.

Susan leads the trio in their excitement at turning into our own gate. This is their first glimpse of the inside of the house. After the first squeals of excitement over finding their rooms—"Oh, look at this"— had died down, we had a prayer time of thanksgiving for what the Lord had given us, thanking Him that we were now able to appreciate more full the privacy and spaciousness of a home, after living in two, and then three, rooms of a boarding house for over a year. It was wonderful to walk in and go to bed without even having to make beds—the place was clean and prepared for us.

The movers soon fixed the orderliness of the house! As all our trunks, boxes, etc., were dumped into the place, the halls became knee-deep with shredded paper. St. Louis barrels and boxes were sort of like a treasure hunt, for we had forgotten what we had packed. The shrieks of delight at finding old book friends filled the house for a whole afternoon. The older girls plunked themselves down every two minutes as the books came out of waterproof wrappings to read snatches to each other or Deborah. "I remember this one, oh you'll love it." "I can't wait to read this one again. Aren't books wonderful?" The furnishings do not include bookcase space for our books. We decided to get one made from our packing boxes. Confusion reigned for a week. The Mayflower Movers in St. Louis did a good job of packing the dishes—not a one was broken after all this time. We put the double-decker bed in Debby's room, releasing another single bed for Priscilla's room, which of course gives us more space for guests. We found a wonderful big closet on the landing of the attic stairs, which holds all the Children for Christ supplies. What a pleasure it is to see it all stacked in little piles and easy to find. We were full of joy that week getting settled, even though little Deborah questioned one night as I tucked her in bed, "When are we going to begin to *live*, Mother?" I must confess we had to pinch ourselves at times to be sure that it was *real* that we actually had places *to* put everything and an actual office, typing desk and all. The Lord has surely given over and above all that we have asked for in this place.

On the fifth of November a premature snow started and continued for three days, finally 18 inches deep. It was a wet, clinging snow and transformed the entire landscape into white marble. Thick, lumpy white trees, telephone lines two inches in diameter, white fences with blobs of white hats topping the posts, rounded white roofs on all the chalets, mountainsides around us sporting a herringbone pattern as the snow outlined the regular branches of the pine trees. Then the sun came out— plop, down fell all the white sculpturing, including the snowmen and snow lamb our three had made in our garden. The jagged peaks of the Dents du Midi (Teeth of the South), the range directly opposite from us, glittered in the sun like diamond-studded white castles floating in a brilliant blue sky. But the weather changed again and we had rain for days, rain at our level (3,000 ft.), snow up a few thousand feet higher. We could see it doing both at once. Here weather is stretched out before you and you can actually see the changing of the seasons in various stages at one time.

You'll be wondering about the children's schools. Priscilla found that in the interim, while we were at Lausanne, two 12-year-old boys had entered Ecole Alpina, so that instead of having to be tutored in her work, she has regular classes with them. This makes a big difference in price, so we feel it is a real answer to prayer. One boy is Turkish and the other Belgian. The professors are Swiss, French, Belgian, quite a League of Nations! She has classes from 9 to 11:30 and from 4:30 to 6, with a great deal of homework. Though she is working hard at her studies, she likes it much better than in Lausanne and is most happy. Susan goes each morning to school at Home Eden. Since you will be hearing a lot about our leaving the girls at Home Eden, I'll take time now to describe it. The house itself is a large, rambling chalet in the village. Some of its numerous bedrooms are single, some double, and some for four children. As do all pensions for children, it takes children for periods of time as parents take vacations or business trips. Switzerland is full of such places, boarding houses for children. Some are only open during summer and winter sport months, but others, such as this, are open all year around. In year-around ones, downstairs contain not only a dining room and a play room, but a school room and a mistress. Home Eden has a fine schoolmistress who teaches all the children who stay there, "country school" style of teaching. This winter it happens that they also have only boys, though they take both boys and girls. They have seven boys, between the ages of seven and ten. Susan makes the eighth pupil. She loves the teacher and that is half the battle with Susan! She is working hard at her work and we hear no more complaints about school. She is going ahead more rapidly, not only in arithmetic and French, but in history and geography (European history and geography studied in French). She gets a bit of music and drawing, too, which makes it more fun for her. "The teacher and I sing a funny tune while the boys are singing the regular tune—oh, it's lots of fun." Home Eden also has a sort of housemother who takes care of the children who live there. Susan calls her the "puffy one"—describing her stout appearance! Neither of these ladies speaks English, but Susan doesn't mind that now, since she speaks French with equal breathless rapidity as she does English and sounds like any of the other children. Quite a difference from this time last year! Deborah is staying home with us all day. It will take her time to get adjusted to not having the old ladies to call on as she had in the pension. Living in a home with nobody but the family seems a very new thing to her. She is doing 1st-grade work with the teaching help of myself and Priscilla. Miss Walker sent all the 1st-grade books from Stevens School. Though she is only four, we think it is important that she reads English before she starts school here where all her work will be in French. She puts her dollies in a row in front of her little table; they are her classmates!

Another confirmation of the fact that the Lord chose this place is the suitability of the "bonne" (houseworker) who is working for us to free me for office work. It is not only difficult to find one for such work, but more difficult to find someone industrious who does not need constant supervision. This woman has worked hard all her life. She is in such poor circumstances, she really appreciates the job and is anxious to please. A poor Swiss peasant, she lives in a rough chalet on a steep slope, right in the woods, off the path about a half-hour's walk from here. Their only means of livelihood is the bit of land they own, the 18 sheep, three goats, a few ducks, and rabbits they have. In the summer they cut hay on the mountainsides, so steep you could hardly climb them, let alone cut hay and carry it down on your back. They haven't sold the wool the sheep yielded last year yet and the bit of wood her husband cuts brings in the only cash. The chalet has no electricity or water; the heat for warmth and cooking is produced with wood stoves and they go to bed so early that they don't use much oil for their lamps. Water is brought in from their spring. No wonder she thinks my washing machine is able to produce clothes "more agreeable to touch than those rinsed in the icy spring." She has two children, Michel 17 and Lucy 11. Michel has finished all the school the village offers and is waiting to find a job somewhere, meanwhile helping his father to cut wood, feed the animals, and, now that mother is here, to do some housework! The Swiss peasants have a very limited diet consisting mainly of black bread, potatoes, and cheese, frequently goat's milk cheese. Their soup is mainly an oatmeal soup and for meat they kill an animal once in a long while. These folk have killed a goat and smoked the meat for this winter; she says the goat meat is rather tough. We praise the Lord for her helpfulness to us and are glad that the money is such a help to her. We do hope that we will be able to help her know the Lord as her Savior and to help the family a bit. We hope to fix a nice Christmas surprise box with something for each of the family as a project for our little "Young People's Society." Lucy has never had a pencil case, a pocketbook, or some of the other things which the village children make fun of her for lacking. She looks so shabby trudging past, I long to dress her up. . . .

Fourteen days after arriving here found us packing again, but only necessities for the trip. That meant a suitcase for each of the children, one for our clothes, one for Children for Christ material, the typewriter, screen, projector, pictures, and transformer. We really need more hands! Susan was anxious to get rid of us—"Now when the puffy one says lunch is ready, I can go in with the *other* boys instead of going home." She wanted to really belong. Priscilla was not so glad to have us go; she was dubious about staying at Home Eden with "all those little kids." Deborah was very happy to be going on a visit to "Mama Turrian's" and I praised the Lord that I knew Mme. Turrian was just as anxious to have her and would give her most careful attention. Mme. Turrian knew just how to feed her and all about her needs, so I felt quite comfortable about leaving her—that is, as comfortable as possible. It's not fun to leave a four-year-old and I'd *never* do it if it wasn't for the work. The day we left, the sun came out after the long rain. We walked down to the station, our baggage in our little Swiss cart; butcher, baker, fruitstore keeper, and others waved goodbye as we passed. The two girls ran along with us to see us off, having special permission to leave classes, and we were content to be leaving them in such a safe informal village rather than in a city where they would be boarding trams to go to school and where there would be more opportunity of "something happening" to them. As the little cog railway carried us away from our mountain spot, Fran took a couple of pictures of the Dents, just in case they would never be quite as dazzlingly white again. Our eyes watered as we looked up at them shining in the sun, not a dark streak on them. Usually there are streaks where the cliffs are too straight for snow to stick.

We ate our lunch on the train between Montreux and Lausanne and arrived in Lausanne ready for a busy afternoon. We had a few necessary short calls to make; checked our baggage; went to the bank; shopped for Christmas presents for our immediate family in America and wrapped them up in a store; delivered Deborah to La Rosiaz where she happily embraced her friends, unpacked, and waved us off—without a tear; rushed back downtown to the post office to fill out the multitudinous forms needed for sending a package off to America and got the packages into the hands of the clerk just as the place was closing; hurried off to the home of the family which is working with us in children's work, where we have been invited for supper and to spend the night. They had a number of things they wanted to discuss in the evening. . . .

Next morning we stuck some things in my typewriter case, left the other baggage checked and some things at this Christian home, attended to some more business, and caught a train to Geneva. . . .

Our time in Lausanne was very short—a bit of lunch, a quick scramble into old clothes for the very dirty trip to Paris, repack, and off again for the train. That train swishes up to Vallorbe in an hour, then stands for another hour, long after everyone is through customs. In this waiting time I called Mme. Turrian to find how Debby was. Debby talked to me, but all in French, being used to it there. She seemed perfectly happy. We were in the third-class coach which had come from Italy and was full of assorted people and odors! Many bring a knuckle of meat with them, a knife, a loaf of bread, and a bottle of wine. Someone is always eating. All these trains are divided into compartments seating eight; four ride backwards and four frontwards. The compartments were very full this time. We had a most interesting conversation with a French woman and her daughter. When they discovered we were Americans, they were most friendly and began telling us of the wonderful things the Americans had done for their little village during the war. A surgeon who lives on the West Coast was especially kind to their family and to all in the village and he still writes to them. They were the first family in Europe whom we have met who liked us *because* we were American. It was heartwarming to see the tears of appreciation in their eyes as they described what Americans had done for them and their people. We talked a bit about our work, the children's work especially, and as they left the train at their village, we gave them a tract in French and our name. In return they gave us their name and address. The name revealed the mother is a Countess. This conversation opened up a contact with another woman in the same compartment, a Parisian. We also gave her a tract.

When we pulled into Paris it was raining and never stopped all the time we were there. Our grandly marked "room and bath" turned out to be the same room we had stayed in last year. The "bath" is across a cold and drafty hall, in a cold room, dingy, water barely lukewarm! At least it was familiar! The next morning Fran made some necessary calls. I stayed in in case anyone called us at the hotel, and the rain poured down! . . .

Back at the hotel again, we barely had time to eat dinner—but were confronted with a line of maid, bellboy, and manager waiting to get us out. It seems a misunderstanding had arisen. They thought we were leaving and had rented our room to another couple! Upon being convinced that we had asked for reservations *through* that night, they allowed us to have two funny tiny little rooms up in the attic where the sloping roof made the faded wallpaper and stiff little beds look like my childhood idea of an artist's "garret," where artists starved to death before they knew they were going to be famous! Oh well, we saved money up there! We had very little time to eat after this move, before we were due at the home of a Christian man who is leader of another group in the Paris area. We didn't have long to stay in the beds before the alarm went off at 6 A.M. and soon after that we left to take our train back to Lausanne. It was a tiring but very successful stay in Paris and we pray now that the Lord will cause that time to bear much fruit.

Rain splashed against the windows of the train in such torrents that the view was completely shut out by a grey curtain; again the third-class coach was full. This time we had little opportunity to talk and caught up on reading. Fran hadn't felt well for a couple weeks and we decided to see the doctor as we stopped in Lausanne. The doctor said the prickles in his hand and foot were from nerves—fatigue over long years—try to sleep longer hours—take an hour of exercise each day—etc.! We'll try to put that into practice here in Champéry in between trips or any other specially pressing work.

Deborah greeted us with great excitement and much affection, glad to have us back. Mme. Turrian said she had been as good as gold and hadn't even cried once while we were gone. The ladies enjoyed her presence so much, she said, and Debby had a fine time "knitting" with them! She sang all day long, they said, just like having a songbird in the house. You can imagine my relief. We stayed in the pension that night in our old office and took care of our visiting over the telephone. The morning gave us time enough to gather up our things left behind, separating for our various errands and meeting at the station platform. Each of us felt the other would never make it, so we were glad to meet just a minute before the train left.

After all the rain, it was good to have sunshine welcome us back to Champéry and to find our girls running down the street full of excitement, both talking at once. Susan had knitting in her hand—"Look, I can knit, look, I can knit." They had a lovely time at Home Eden. A puppy who lives there, too, had won Priscilla's heart and she also had enjoyed reading the boys a bedtime story. Her heart was touched by the fact that some boys had lived there for over three years "and never have their mothers to read to them." Their life had been regular, but not too stiffly regimented and they both had been happy and looked rosy and well. Another praise note.

We got back to our house to find men putting in a new boiler, so our house was cluttered up with smoking men for a week! Nevertheless we had our Thanksgiving day on the right day (the next day) and even had a turkey. The peasants next door to us started to raise turkeys last spring and ours was the first they had sold. Susan said various village children asked her what the turkey tasted like as she walked to school the next day. You can't exactly live a private life here! We certainly had much to praise the Lord for and thank Him for as we gathered around our crackling fire for our Thanksgiving service after dinner. Now we have office work, the Gospel of Luke lessons to write, French lessons daily again, and house guests coming at various times in the near future. Fran is sawing logs for our fireplace for his exercise and the fireplace in the living room is conducive to quiet reading as the office is cold at night, so we hope he will continue to feel much better. The Lord has given us a home for this reason, too, we believe. It is so much more restful.

Please pray about finances for trips. The Scandinavian trip in March or April will take about 600 dollars—of course we go third-class railroad and by boat across the water. This is about a third of the cost of plane fare. We are not sure of the length of trips in the various countries—so an exact estimate is not possible. We have been invited officially by the Free Lutheran Church of Norway and have other invitations in each Scandinavian country which we feel are very important and would be the means of seeing Children for Christ started up there. Please pray as we write to these folk that we may soon be able to give them definite word about dates and other details. We are asking the Lord to send in what is needed ahead of time, if that is His will. He is able.

May the Lord give you a rich blessing at this Christmas time and all through the coming year.

Lovingly,

EDITH

1950

           Champéry, Switzerland

Dear Family:

The New Year has already started. Though this should be dated December and be the letter in which I wish you "Happy New Year," the necessity of writing it a few days late does not spoil the opportunity of being able to tell you, at the beginning of this 1950, that we will be praying for each of you who receive this. Our prayer for you, and for us, is that it may be a year of drawing closer to the Lord than ever before, of being used by Him day by day as a witness to others, a year in which we keep our lamp wicks trimmed and the smoke polished off of the lamp chimneys, a year in which all we say and do may be to the glory of God....

Right here I want to give you an outline of our *usual* days—though many *unusual* ones knock this schedule to pieces. As you know by this time, my work is that of being secretary to Fran, for which I prepared during the last six months we were in America by a correspondence course in typing and speedwriting. Before we ever came to Europe we realized our work would require a full-time secretary; since a secretary would be an impossible expense for this new work, the only answer seemed to be for me to prepare to do it. At first my work was painstakingly slow, but the speed has increased with the increase of work; now Fran says I can turn out the work any regular stenographer could do. However, this means that on a normal day my hours in the office must match that of a regular stenographer. The day begins, then, with my preparation of breakfast, getting the children off to school, and then my disappearance into the office while "Vic" does dishes, makes beds, does the general housework, and answers doorbells, etc. An hour before the noon meal, I dash downstairs to prepare dinner in time for the reappearance of hungry schoolgirls. Dinner and family prayers over, back I come to this typewriter until time for our French lesson. The French lesson is held in front of the fireplace—with no fire in it. We try to save coal and wood as much as possible, lighting the wood fire only at night. The central heating is supposed to be enough in daytime—brrrr! That depends on whether you call 60 degrees warm enough. Nevertheless it can't be very harmful; so far the children have kept very well this winter. French lesson over, back I run for another period of concentrated typing—sometimes stopping in the kitchen on the way up to stir up a dessert for supper. After this time, the day's work is ended. Evening's work begins with cooking supper. Supper ends with a hymn, a reading of "Daily Light," and I put Deb in bed with a "bednight story" as she calls it, while Fran reads to Susan for a precious 20 minutes. After this the evenings differ. Some evenings Fran dictates letters or articles to me until midnight. Other evenings we work on Luke lessons, spreading out the flannelgraph illustrations and discussing them together as we collaborate on the writing. One evening a week we do the week's washing and hang it in the attic where Vic can find it dry and ready for her ironing and mending. Sometimes we both type during the evening. Other times we have the luxury of a night of reading before the fire. This is an outline of our daily work, into which schedule must be injected our marketing trips (we pull the cart, with its sides made of spokes set at an angle, into the village to buy food supplies), Fran's daily stint of woodcutting, the occasional trips to Lausanne, the coming of visitors, the longer trips for the work—and the lovely surprises the Lord is continually sending by way of increased opportunities (read on to learn about one of the most exciting of these surprises that came on Christmas Eve). Of course, the children need attention through the day—a bloody nose, an "impossible" arithmetic problem, a page of American schoolwork to be corrected; any bits of time that spill over the cupful of day's work get quickly lapped up by the needs of the children! Sundays are different, with our family church services, Sunday school, etc. And now—but wait, you must hear in order! We also hope to inject some hours of exercise, such as skiing, to help us keep fit according to doctor's orders, but in spite of the doctor, these cannot be daily. I mustn't forget to tell you that Fran has the fire to keep going, which means a trip outdoors since the house is built without any entrance to the furnace room from inside. The lady who built it never wanted to go down to the furnace so why should there be a pair of inside steps? As the heavy shutters on all the windows are pulled shut after sundown, the last trip at night to the furnace gives us a chance to see what the weather is doing; what at first seemed to be a nuisance has turned into a pleasure.

Now to go on with the month's news. Before Christmas we needed to go to Lausanne. We had two more Luke lessons ready to deliver for translation, business at the bank, flannelboard to deliver with some supplies, and our Christmas shopping to do. This last was made very thrilling by the arrival of money designated by a Missionary society for a phonograph record player for the children. Since we have neither a radio nor a record player, the prospect of hearing some music in the home was as exciting to us as the opening of the gift would be for the children on Christmas morning.

Such a day! Debby begged to go along to "see Mama Turrian" and after assuring us that she would go along to La Rosiaz, not taking a minute of Daddy and Mommy's time, we gave in and took her along. She travels free on Swiss trains until she is six, though now she is four she must pay on trams in the cities. Six A.M. found us hurrying along through the dark, with the flannelboard, a suitcase of supplies, and a typewriter to be repaired, the wagon creaking and bumping along beside us, to catch the first train. Two huge pigs were stubbornly refusing to head down the village street toward the train and kept agitating their master by turning into every little sidepath. How can anyone think that village life is dull? It is so much more fun to race for a train with pigs than with ordinary folk—adds variety, you know! We watched the daylight gradually change the midnight blue of the sky and blot out the stars as we moved down beside the lake to Lausanne. We joined the others rushing for the bus to the center of the city after we arrived at the station. Deborah by this time was all smiles, and, when at the end of the short bus ride we put her on the tram for La Rosiaz, she was radiant— "I'll say, 'La Rosiaz, s'il vous plait' and if there aren't enough punches in my card, I'll ask for another card," she said as she patted the money we had buttoned in the pocket of her snow suit. I hurried over to a phone in the post office to let Madame Turrian know Deb was on her way, but I needn't have worried. We found out later that Debby proudly rang the doorbell, pleased as punch with herself to have arrived before anyone had had time to meet her! "People probably thought I was silly, traveling all alone at my age, but I thought it was fun."

We zipped into action after Deborah had departed and gradually checked off the things on our long list. Some conversations took longer than we had anticipated and some of our calls had to be made by phone, but by skipping supper, we were able to finish all our business and shopping, including the gifts for Vic's Christmas from our Young People's Society and the wind-up phonograph. Our purchase of records was limited to Beethoven's Fifth Symphony and the "Hallelujah Chorus" from Handel's *Messiah*, but I'm sure our contemplation of hearing this music was as exciting as the feeling folk had when the Victrola was first invented. Deborah alighted from the 7 P.M. tram (all trams run on an exact schedule) quite a seasoned traveler and chattered all the way down the steep hill to the station. During the day we had encountered several problems connected with Children for Christ in Switzerland and had also talked to Baroness von Dumreicher again. Please pray for both of these.

You can imagine that as we alighted from the tiny mountain train here in Champéry, our arms full of packages, Deborah draped over her father's shoulder, fast asleep, it was a happy surprise to find Vic had, all of her own accord, decided to stay until the train arrived and meet us with a sled to pull home the packages with Deborah perched on top. When I told her she should have gone home as soon as Susan and Priscilla had eaten, she answered that *anyway* she couldn't have rested tonight. Her uncle had died early that morning in the tiny mountain chalet near hers; if she hadn't waited for us, she would have had to spend the evening on her knees praying over his dead body. She felt that there would be enough relatives praying for him and she was glad to give this evening to us since we had been so kind to her! Later in the week she took a couple of hours off to go to the mass at the church for this uncle, whose body had been drawn down the mountainside on a sled. Do pray that our testimony to her in many small things and the Christian storybook we included in the Christmas box may gradually bring the knowledge of salvation by grace to her mind and heart. . . .

Our Christmas tree was a gift from Vic, cut near her house and borne down the mountainside by her boy. Fran brought it in to measure, found it not only too tall for the room but too big to be backed out again! The sawing off from the bottom took place in the kitchen. Soon the whole house was filled with the festive odor of pine. The extra branches made a dark green forest of the cornice above the fireplace. This was Friday afternoon. By twilight the tree was decked with twinkling American lights, the children were carefully tying ornaments on it, my last batch of cookies was in the oven browning—when suddenly the doorbell rang. A dark, young French-speaking minister was ushered into the scene of a family Christmas Eve.

I stayed out of sight of the visitor since I had to manage the cookies, supper preparations, and another marketing trip to the village for vegetables. It wasn't long before an excited Susan swished into the kitchen to report the visitor's errand and then swished out again. It sounded like a daydream come true. It seemed he had come to visit the few Protestants in town. While visiting, a director of a girls' school here for the winter holidays asked if there would be a Christmas service in English for Protestants. Well, he couldn't speak English and anyway there isn't a Protestant service of any kind here except in the summer. Ah—but another person in the room spoke and said, "There is a Protestant pastor in Chalet des Frênes, maybe he would conduct a Christmas service in English for the girls"!! There were no strings attached. The service could be in the French Protestant church if some wood could be found to heat it and if someone would pay a woman to clean it. The hairdresser's wife, who is Protestant, would come about 3 P.M. the next day to discuss the hymn tunes, etc., as she was the only one who could play the organ. Now, would he? The next day was to be our Christmas; do you think this appointment for the afternoon would intrude? You know the answer. We couldn't have had a more wonderful gift than this opportunity to have our first public service for preaching the Gospel on a Sunday morning here in Switzerland. I don't know who in the family was the happiest.

Debby stood on her head on the couch and sang happily, "Daddy is going to preach in a really, truly church with lots of people there. I can't 'member a really, truly church with Daddy preaching." Daddy himself studied over the notes of the sermon he had thought he was preparing for our little family service. I felt as though I floated down to the store a few minutes later!

There was a warm, joyous glow within us as we gathered in the living room the next morning to read the Christmas story from Matthew and Luke and to give thanks to the Lord for His unspeakable gift,* for the joy of the opportunity ahead of us, and for the gifts we were about to open. Of course, personal letters will be coming to each of you who sent those charmingly mysterious brown-paper parcels so full of love and thoughtfulness, which brought America right into our living room that day! I wish I could include the rapt delight on the faces of the girls as things tumbled out of their wrappings. What a time they had tasting, seeing, feeling, then *hearing* their presents. In addition to Beethoven's Fifth, which Deborah feels she must lead right through (keeps amazingly perfect time, too), the set of six nursery rhymes and Christmas carol Little Golden Records from America completes our repertoire. We managed to have our dinner eaten and the wrappings cleaned up by the time the organist arrived to compare music and hum tunes of the most familiar carols. She has been most unhappy living in this Roman Catholic town and wept as she told us of her troubles. She seemed to appreciate our time of prayer with her and promised to come with her husband some evening. Pray for this little family. Not many minutes after she had wheeled her baby down the road, the children spotted the Pols' car. Debby remarked, "Oh look, now we have a car." They had had no trouble coming up the mountain as heavy rains had washed away all signs of snow here and on up another thousand feet or so. The five children's tongues clacked fast and furiously for awhile as they compared notes on life and school in Holland and Switzerland. I had prepared the meals for that day before going to bed the night before, so without too much time out, we nine Americans were gathered around the two tables (the dining room table can't be enlarged, so an extra one was lifted in) with their centerpieces of holly leaves without berries (from our yard) and fat white candles adorned with mistletoe the Pols had brought.

It was icy cold as we hurried down the street Christmas Sunday, though there was no snow and the sun was gilding the snow about us as it hit the peaks preparatory to pushing above them far enough to bathe the village in its warmth for a few short hours. Debby stamped her feet to warm up her toes in between the skipping little steps. "Who will come to the church to hear Daddy preach?" Fran had gone ahead to make sure all was in order. We couldn't help an expectant shiver as we wondered whether after all *anyone* would come. A moment's glance as

* II Corinthians 9:15 KJV

we stepped inside the church showed us that our cup was truly full and running over. Filling whole pews in methodical rows were schools and schools! There was one group of identically dressed girls from a London school, here for two weeks of skiing. Other groups hemmed in by teachers were also obviously here on vacation trips from England. Right at the front was a small school of girls, and another of kilt-clad Scottish boys. There were also some from Swiss schools, and individuals from hotels. Altogether, there must have been about a hundred and fifty people. A silent prayer went up that we might have opportunity to talk to some of these people personally, rather than just having them drift out and away, without our knowing whether they had particular problems.

After the service was over, Susan bounded out happily to where I was standing, and whispered loudly to me, "There's a man and lady talking to Daddy about could we have another service next week."

Face beaming, Susan bounded in again, not wanting to miss anything. Permission had to be sought from the committee, and rather than giving permission for "one more service" they replied that they would be glad to have us use the church for anything we would like to use it for, "as long as you live in Champéry."

Regular Sunday morning services were added to our schedule, and I had the fun of sketching, and printing by hand, twenty-two posters to put in the various hotels and pensions, announcing a church service in English, at the "Temple Protestant" near the railroad station. The hotelkeepers were pleased to have one more "provision" for the tourists, especially at no cost to the village! We were thanked by the pensions too, where school groups would be staying, and we were told of various ones coming for winter sports. When we spoke to a Christian businessman in Lausanne about the commencement of these regular services he was amazed. "And I thought you'd be burying yourselves in Champéry . . . and now this! It really is a remarkable opportunity."

We soon discovered that among the English-speaking people at the services were girls who came regularly week by week, and who said they were in a finishing school which had rented a hotel, and would be staying in Champéry until March. Most Swiss schools which have an international group of young people in them—and all the "finishing school" type of schools—go to a ski resort and rent a large chalet or hotel for the winter season. The whole staff goes along, and school lessons are done in the morning, while ski lessons are given on the sunny slopes in the afternoon (or vice versa!).

An invitation was given to some of the girls as they stood talking at the back of the church to "come to our chalet this Thursday night for an informal evening of conversation and tea. Bring any questions you might have concerning religion, or the Bible, or just anything that troubles you."

They accepted enthusiastically, but later in the week we were disappointed by a call from the Director, Monsieur Fonjallaz, who said rather coolly that the girls had come for the purpose of skiing and studying . . . that's *all* . . . and could not come. This seemed final.

That same week we had a splendid talk with the doctor from Monthey who came to visit Susan, who had complained of an ache in her knee. He evidently liked us as much as we liked him, because we found later that he had talked enthusiastically about us to the Director of the girls' school—Monsieur Fonjallaz. We soon received an invitation to have dinner at the school (Fran and I), and to show colored slides of European countries to the girls. That evening Monsieur Fonjallaz was delighted with the slides, and kept saying, "The girls ought to see more of these. . . ." To which we replied that we'd be glad to have them come to the chalet any time! The result was that a *general* invitation was given, and rather than the half-dozen who would have come from the first invitation, thirty-two turned up! There were Zoroastrians from India, Buddhists from Siam, and girls of various backgrounds of religious or antireligious views from England, Canada, Argentina, Haiti, Denmark, Scotland, America, and Czechoslovakia. We had a most stimulating evening, which started with slides being shown, tea and cakes served, and ended with more serious questions.

That was the first of many such nights—the only changes being that we soon dropped the custom of starting with slides, because everyone wanted more time for questions. Pray for us as we have more opportunities to talk to these dear girls.

With love,

EDITH

January 31, 1950   Champéry, Switzerland

Dear Family:

In my last letter the main news was our services in the French Protestant chapel for the English schools and visitors who come to Champéry. I know you have prayed that this opportunity would continue and you will praise the Lord that it has. We wondered how soon someone from the State Church, which we supposed controlled this chapel after we were told it was controlled from Geneva, would investigate and perhaps remove permission for services after they found out the stand we took against modernism and the World Council. One day as we worked in the office, the doorbell rang, a man's voice floated up, and Fran was summoned—someone from "Le Temple Protestant." As I typed, I prayed. The conversation came through the floor in a mumble. Fran dashed in for pen and paper "to take notes on the history of the chapel"—and out again before I could discover how things were going. At last the voices went to the door, it opened and closed, and my curiosity was satisfied with this thrilling story. As you read it, remember the letter which told how the Lord prepared this unusual home for us and how we felt He was leading us here, in spite of the fact that the canton was Roman Catholic and some felt we would be burying ourselves as far as local opportunities went.

Many years ago, before the woman came who built Chalet des Frênes, an English woman came to Champéry every summer for her vacation. She grew to love this little corner of the world with its magnificent mountains viewed from the quiet village, its many winding paths through forests and flower-strewn fields, but she felt deeply the lack of any Protestant testimony. Though only a handful of Protestants lived in the village, she felt they should have a place of worship. Hence she bought a piece of land on the main street near the railroad station, a spot where everyone would pass, and gave the money for the erection of a church. Some interested friends gave toward it, but most of it was paid for by this one person. As you will see from the picture, it is a lovely little building and if you could walk in and sit on one of the wooden pews, you could read the many fine Scripture verses printed in graceful brown and dark-green letters on cream-colored walls. Your eyes might wander up to the high pitched ceiling with its fine dark beams, to where the wall meets these beams with a flourish of painted ivy vines, but they would soon come back to the messages of salvation given so clearly in French. Your feeling would be, "Whoever planned this building really loved the Lord."

As the church building was completed in 1912, it was put in the hands of a *private committee,* some pastors and friends from the Neuchâtel region making up the majority. The lady's only stipulation was that a member of her family should always be on the committee and that the building should always be under this committee, not the State Church. Hence, the man concluded, "I, a nephew of this woman, am on the committee to carry out her wishes." To date, the building has only been used in summer for regular Sunday services at 3 P.M. each Sunday. The rest of the year, the pastor comes one Sunday afternoon a month from Monthey; there are so very few Protestants. "Therefore, Mr. Schaeffer, the building is very seldom in use, and as you have told me of your use of it for the English visitors, I want to tell you that I know my Aunt would have been very happy to have it so used." He went on to say (oh how our Lord prepares and plans for us even beyond all our imagination, doesn't He?), "I speak for the committee and you may have complete use of this little building for services on Sunday or *any other time just as long as you live in Champéry"!!* Not only has He prepared a home for us and a building which is so charming for our church services—and if the way opens up, for conferences, etc. Here are chalets for rent for the summer all around us; if the need arose, we could rent them for a young people's conference, with a building complete for the meetings. Of course all that is just a dream so far, but can't you see the limitless possibilities? The charge for this building is simply wood to heat it and pay for a woman to clean it. That's all.

After the exodus of the holiday groups of students, attendance settled down to girls from Madame Juo's school and a larger group from a girls' school quartered just since Christmas in the Hotel du Parc (used by Jewish refugee children last summer). To keep things straight I'll call them the Lutry School because that is where they are the rest of the year. The first Sunday these new girls were there, we felt so encouraged; after the service, I enthusiastically invited them to come to our home Thursday evening for an informal gathering—"Bring your questions on the Bible—religion—anything that troubles you, and we'll sit around the fireplace to discuss these things." A girl from Florida, one from Virginia, another from Scotland, a fair-haired one from Argentina, a blue-eyed one from Denmark, all chorused, "Thank you, we'll come." The teacher with them was sure it would be permitted. Hence with new joy we walked back to the Hotel du Parc with the teacher to visit a girl who had been hurt skiing. This little blond (about 4'10" though 18 years old) had begged the teacher to bring the American minister back to call on her. She is from Washington, D.C., expects to be an actress, is studying French and traveling "abroad" for a year before entering a theatrical school. She was so glad to see someone from America, delighted with her five callers, from Fran to Deb! We talked a bit about "home," then Fran read a bit and prayed. Thanking him, she promised to come to church "as soon as they let me walk." If you want to remember her especially, just pray for "D.," her nickname. . . .

Madame Wildermuth, our old French teacher from Lausanne, came for an afternoon. We had a wonderful talk with her about things of the Lord. She seemed just as eager in her interest as ever. She says she believes all that we tell her, but she believes that these things are also believed by the Roman Catholic church. She evidently had some very sweet "sisters" in the convent when she went to school and has seen a different side of the Roman Catholic church than the usual. Keep praying for her. She took a devotional book and some Grace Livingston Hill novels to read. You see the Christmas books will be used more widely than just in our family. Books are so expensive here; anyone who can read English is glad to borrow a book.

Madame Wildermuth told us of the appeal that has been sent out over Radio Geneva concerning the Greek children who were carried off from Greece by the communists at the end of the guerrilla warfare, in revenge because the communists lost. *Twenty-eight thousand children* were kidnapped from Greek villages and are being trained to be communists somewhere in Soviet Russian-controlled territory. A move is being made by Radio Geneva to get these children brought into Switzerland and gradually to return them to their homes. The appeal was asking

Swiss people to open their homes to the children. That evening we held a family confab at the supper table. "What would you think about our taking care of one of these poor children?" we asked after explaining about the 28,000. These were their answers, in order: Deborah (four years), "We couldn't take *all* 28,000, but we could take *one*. I'll give it one of my coloring books, one of my dolls, and one box of crayons." Susan (eight), "We could teach it about Jesus, couldn't we? If you want, I'll give it my room; it might be afraid up on the third floor alone and I can sleep on the top bunk in Debby's room." Priscilla (12), "I hope we can keep it forever because if we get attached to it, it would be awfully hard to let it go back." The feeling was unanimous and we decided to send a letter to the radio station the next day. This has been done now and we wait, along with all the Swiss who have responded, to get further news. Prospects are not very good however, as we hear the communists are not holding them so much as hostages, but to indoctrinate them in communism for a future thrust into Greece. It is horrifying to think of these little children dragged away from their mothers and fathers and even their country, terrified in their hearts, now being trained some few hundred miles from here to overthrow their country's leaders. Yet there is so little to do about it! We do pray that Switzerland may be successful and that we may have our small part in helping.

Late in the week Fran decided to call on the director of the Lutry school. The conversation resulted in an invitation for us to come there for supper and bring along the colored slides to show the girls! The first snow since November arrived the day we were to go. It arrived after all the vacationers had left, which seemed too bad for them since it had meant a trip up the mountain on the *telepherique* for those who would a-skiing go! But it was gleefully welcomed by all who will continue to be here and for our family—it means skiing in the front yard. This has certainly been a winter of mixed-up weather! As we waded out through the snow, the projector and screen, etc., came along on a sled pulled by the gardener of the Lutry school. We sat at a table with the director and his secretary and were making polite conversation when the doctor arrived and the director excused himself to make the rounds with him (several small skiing accidents to be attended to).

Now it happened that we had had a splendid conversation with that doctor just a few days before when he came to see Susan, whose knee hurt a good bit. We had found that he was the only Protestant doctor in these parts and has a huge territory covering miles of mountain roads. We talked with him of many things including the Bible. Evidently he had liked us as we had liked him, because when the director came back he had a much-changed attitude toward us. He said heartily, "Well, I found that the doctor knows you folks and thinks a lot of you. We think that doctor is a splendid fellow." Fran showed his pictures of Switzerland, which have increased through the year into a breathtaking set of winter and summer scenes; a series of sunsets from our balcony in Lausanne never fail to bring out the "ohs" and "ahs." The girls made a most enthusiastic audience—about 35 in all. There are 40 in that school. Monsieur Fonjallaz sat next to me and kept saying, "My, these are wonderful. Really I've never seen anything like them." By the time pictures ended he was saying to me, "Now, you and your husband go ahead and just say anything you want to the girls." I said, "I'd like to invite them for an evening at our chalet, to see more pictures and have a time for questions on the Bible. Do you think that could be arranged?" "Just go ahead," he answered. "Ask them for Sunday night, if that would suit you." So after Fran talked to them a bit about Sunday morning services, I got up and gave the invitation to any who would like to see more pictures and then have a time of discussion together, or a study from the Bible, to come to Chalet des Frênes next Sunday night. As the girls filed out shaking hands and thanking us for coming, we discovered they represented many countries: England, Canada, America, Argentina, Haiti, Denmark, Scotland, India, Czechoslovakia, Switzerland— most of them here for just a year. The Lord can use this brief opportunity to touch so many lives from so many places, as He will.

Next came our trip to Lausanne. Again Deb came along to visit pension friends and again we took the 6:17 A.M. train. We were lugging a crate back with us, as well as our things packed in a suitcase, so Fran and Deb sat astride the crate on the sled and careened down to the station, arriving several minutes before I could walk there. I hadn't wanted to endanger my good stockings! Crates, various sorts of tin cans, all bottles must be returned to the store to get the rebate—you pay heavily for the container to assure its return. This time we decided to go to La Rosiaz with Deb after we got rid of our crate. We were warmly welcomed. After having a talk with Madame Turrian and some of the others, we were about to leave the house when in walked a missionary friend of Madame Turrian. Of course she was anxious that we meet each other. Finding she spoke English well, we began to talk of many things. She had been in Africa for a number of years but at present is doing some nursing. When she found that we live in Champéry, she pulled out pad and pencil to write out for us the names of several hospitals and nursing homes in Leysin—a town at a higher altitude in another direction from Aigle, but not too far from us. She then told us how many English people are in these hospitals for TB and how there is not a pastor or a service for them. "Oh if you could only go there sometime and talk to these whose names I'm giving you, I know they would let you hold services for these poor discouraged folk. That would be such a fine work, even if you went only once a month." Of course we took the names and have promised to go there to see what can be done. There is not much extra *time*, yet it sounds like a need and untouched mission field all in itself. Pray about this. It was the first time in months that she had called on Mme. Turrian, yet we met her by a margin of several minutes. Again it seemed the timing of the Lord.

Back in the city for a day or so always means multitudinous errands and small things to attend to. Our day was full of such errands without pause until everything shut down tight for the lunch hour. Have I told you before that all stores, banks, places of business, schools, etc., close from 12 until 2 each day? We used our time in eating, then in planning the rest of our time and in calling Baroness von Dumreicher. "Where haff you bean?" her voice came reproachfully over the phone. "I haff so moch to talk to you about. You will come to see me now?" We assured her that was our intention. She invited us to have supper with her at her pension. At afternoon's end, we had just time to rush to the Andre's where we were to stay overnight, leave our bulky parcels (groceries are cheaper in the city and vegetables fresher, so we take the chance to stock up), dash out again to the tram stop, buy a bunch of yellow daisies (breath of spring for Baroness von Dumreicher), and catch the Number Nine for her end of Lausanne. She welcomed us as though we were her own people and began to tell us all her troubles of the past month. As we ate we heard of how she had not been out of the house since before Christmas, of various illnesses, of how Peter has been away in Germany on business leaving her quite alone, of how she dreads going into a nursing home (which she fears she must soon do), of news from her family in Germany and her English relatives now in Morocco—then suddenly her face brightened. "But I must tell you about the dear boy who has been so kind to me . . . " and the next few hours of conversation were interspersed with descriptions of Christian—a great tall Norwegian lad who, she said, comes almost daily to call on her.

It seems that Christian is studying medicine in Lausanne, has been there over two years now working very hard. He came not knowing a word of French, but began to take his medical course in French and has studied so hard that he is making a fine success of it. He lives in a little room, cooks his own breakfast, makes a bit of lunch, then eats one meal a day in a very cheap, poor restaurant. He mends his own socks, washes and irons for himself, and helps his landlady in part payment for the room. She went on to tell us of how little money he has, never goes out with girls or seeks entertainment, spends only what is necessary to live and study. "He comes when I'm sick and fixes my pillows for me, fixes a cup of tea, but he talks very slowly and never talks unless he thinks he has something to say! Are you beginning to be interested in him?" We were. "Do you suppose," said Fran, "that Christian would like to come up to Champéry for a weekend?" "Oh that would do him so much good. If only he would do it—ah, but how much would it cost?" Fran answered, "Here is the money for the carfare. Tell him that it is in part payment for all the Norwegians did for me when I was sick in the hospital in Oslo and ask him to come this weekend." With her eyes twinkling in anticipation, she promised to see if she could persuade him to take it and come to the home of strangers. He had spent Christmas alone and she was anxious to see him have this to make up for that.

The next morning was spent talking over Luke lessons with Mme. Andre's sister, who is to do the translating, and praying with her about it. The afternoon was spent in various conversations about the work. Just before train time, Fran met Deb at the tram stop while I packed our stuff. Ten minutes before we were to leave, the phone rang—it was Christian! He would be glad to come—what would be a convenient time—could he bring anything! I assured him we only wanted him to bring himself. We were looking forward to meeting him as we would so soon be traveling to his home town. "Oh, are you going to Oslo? My mother and father would be so happy to have you stay with them. You see I am an only and they like news of me." You can imagine that our train trip home was full of happy review of Lausanne happenings.

I wish I could describe that weekend in detail to you. We arrived home to find Champéry decorated with flags again as on the 1st of August—this time for the sports "fete" taking place that weekend. Freshly fallen snow added to the beauty and festivity. The next morning Christian arrived. The children met him down the road and brought him to the kitchen door in their haste to get him in the house. Six-foot-six, Norwegian blue eyes, and a thatch of light hair had made him easy to recognize. He was so appreciative of everything—"Oh it is just like home—you don't know"—that it was a pleasure to have him. He was a most thoughtful house guest, seeing little things to be done and doing them. He shoveled snow from the driveway, "so that all those girls coming Sunday night won't track in too much snow." The children were enthralled with Norwegian fairy tales by the fireplace. He seemed to have a knack of doing most helpful things. Fran and he had several good tramps together in the snow watching sports events on Saturday. He grew very interested in "your way of presenting Christianity—so much simpler than anything I've heard before." He asked many questions concerning the present and future in relation to the Bible. We felt surely the Lord was working with him. Although he is not a confessed Christian in spite of his name, he seemed so happy in the atmosphere of family prayers, church services, and conversation dwelling on the things of the Lord.

He went with us to the chapel for Sunday morning service although most of the town was moving in the direction of the climax of the ski events. We had only four girls that morning, among them the little actress one! A tiny minority, yet we felt glad for these four since the big sport event was set for the same hour as the service. We weren't sure what to expect for that evening. I had made dozens of cookies and arranged things for a tea at the end of the evening, not sure who would eat them! However at 8:15 they began to pour in, a chattering bunch of girls, snowy boots and mountainous coats. Soon the hall was full of boots, stocking-footed girls were spreading themselves on the furniture and floor in the living room, and Christian was mounting the stairs, his long arms piled high with coats.

Fran showed more pictures, ending with Mars Hill, which of course gives the perfect setting for giving Paul's speech, Acts 17:22–31. After that we had refreshments, which rapidly disappeared. We announced that every Sunday night Chalet des Frênes would be open for any who cared to come. "Bring your questions on the Bible and religion next week and we will have a box ready for you. The questions will be answered the following week." The girls left with many expressions of appreciation. The English and Scotch girls especially were glad for tea and a real fireplace. Won't you pray about the following weeks? The ice is broken now and we hope to get into more personal and definite things. The Holy Spirit can prepare their hearts and can bring just the right ones back again. You can imagine what it meant to have our home full to overflowing with young people again. Christian discovered that the Danish girl and he could speak together in a common tongue, so as the girls called back "goodbye," one call was utterly foreign to us. We must learn to say hello and goodbye, please and thank you in each of the four countries this spring—you feel so tongue-tied without at least that much to add to your smile.

The next morning was Fran's birthday. Christian brought down a package hastily fixed up for the occasion—quite obviously a pair of mittens sent to him from Norway, super-large size. However, such a gift cannot be refused, nor could the piece of cheese from Norway (which we happened to know from Baroness Dumreicher makes up the largest part of his diet, sent by his mother). He proceeded to teach us how to each this dark brown cheese, cut into paper-like slices between slices of bread. It is too rich and full of flavor to be eaten in larger pieces. The whole family wished he could be persuaded to cut the afternoon laboratory. ("What will he do there?" asked Deb later. "Oh, he must learn how to cut people, to study the body, you know, so he will learn how to operate." "*Live* people?" "No, dead people." "Hoh! I thought you *buried* dead people and here they cut them up in little pieces!" Christian was sure he should *not* cut lab, much as he hated to leave the mountains. So he left, his thanks written in our guest book in three languages, and saying we had given him much to think about. . . .

Now we have a family in Oslo! Monsieur Andre is looking up information from his Scandinavian offices as to the cheapest way to travel there. We need to take projector, slides, Children for Christ materials, typewriter, and transformer as well as a few clothes. Wish we could take Debby along! Meantime we have February ahead of us, with two girls coming for this weekend to learn how to teach C. for C., from La Chaux-de-Fonds, Peter next weekend, and Pastor Guiton for a week after that.

Thank you for your faithful interest and prayers, so evident in the answers that come. The results belong to you in a real way.

Lovingly,

EDITH

February 28, 1950   Champéry, Switzerland

Dear Family:

February brought us visitors, Luke lessons, office work, arrangements for the Scandinavian trip—and mumps.

The first weekend, two girls from La Chaux-de-Fonds arrived. Although Swiss living at the same altitude as we do, they had never been in Champéry and found our mountains different from their home in a comparatively big city. They enjoyed the view while our tongues wagged incessantly in French and English. One, the schoolteacher, did not speak or understand English; her sister, who works in their father's watch factory, has some English. We discovered from the schoolteacher that not only is Susan doing all the work others her own age *born* here are doing in the Swiss schools, but she is doing work ahead of her age in that she has started German (in French), which is not begun until children are ten years old. She is also doing her American schoolwork at home and is progressing so rapidly in her reading of English that Daddy is almost out of a job at bedtime—she feels she gets a longer story when she reads her own! The weekend seemed all too short for properly finishing the variety of conversation; as Fran pulled their suitcase on the sled to the station, tongues wagged on!

Saturday morning the telephone rang. It was Christian, the Norwegian medical student, to say that Peter couldn't come for his expected weekend visit. It was a beautiful day with a bright sun and lots of snow and I had a feeling he would like to get out of the city himself. "Would *you* like to come in his place?" "Oh, could I?" "Yes, that is, if you have had the mumps." "The what?" I described the mumps in French, then in English. Finally he understood, said he remembered having them and would come on the first train he could get. He arrived in the midst of my regular Saturday afternoon baking spree, the time I make cookies and cakes for the Sunday night Bible class. After first visiting "mumpy" Debby and entertaining her with a few Norwegian stories, he took Priscilla and Susan off with the sled way, way up on the little road that winds up the mountain behind us. Swiss sleds have immovable runners and are higher from the ground, steered by the feet of the person riding (who always rides sitting up). Going left? Let your left heel drag a bit and vice versa. Some time later the trip arrived back with shining eyes and scarlet cheeks. "Oh, Mother, Mother, come and look." Both girls talked at once. "Christian took us sledding the Norwegian way." It seems he had scorned the Swiss way of steering as hard on ski boots. So stepping into the woods, he showed them how to select a long, long pole from a tree branch. It must be 15 or 18 feet long. "Now we have a proper method for steering a sled," he said. All three hopped on the little sled, all three pairs of feet were held up, and down they *flew*, no dragging to cut the speed, the long pole trailing behind acting like a ship rudder in the expert hands of Christian. Around curves, around piles of logs which line the roads waiting to be transported by their owners, around sledges of hay, on they flew, keeping exactly on the course he chose to take. "Oh, Mother, it is wonderful! Don't let anyone cut the stick up for firewood; we want to try it again."

You remember the wife of the town hairdresser who played the organ for us each Sunday morning? The service Christian attended was the last one she was to play for, since she and her husband were to move to another town. What would we do for an organist after that? Sitting over on one side of the chapel that morning was a fine-looking woman whom I had never seen. "Who is that?" whispered Susan. I shook my head. As we stepped outside afterwards, I went over to greet the unknown one. "Do you live here?" "Yes, I do," she replied with a German accent. As we began walking up the street together, she told me of her life. She was a German; a number of years before the war, she married a Swiss who lived in Zürich. Her mother came to live with her at that time. Now her husband had died and she has very little money since she spent a good deal of it helping displaced persons to find their families. She found it too expensive to continue an apartment in Zürich and came to Champéry where she has a tiny "doll house" of a chalet. The chalet has only two rooms and a kitchen and the steps upstairs look like a little ladder. She went on describing the place with—"My one downstairs room is almost completely filled up with the grand piano, but I could not think of living without my piano." "Ooohh, do you play?" "Yes, but I have lost much of my skill because I play very little now for some years." You know the next question, don't you? And she said, "Yes, I would be glad to play for the church services always. I did not know about your services or I would have come before." The music cared for before the other organist has left town—and this in a village of only a couple of hundred people with fewer Protestants than the fingers of your two hands!

Later in the week, when she came to talk over the music, I discovered her mother is 90 years old and quite childish now so that she cannot leave her for any length of time. She supplements her meager income by making dolls to sell, which are purchased by village folk for Christmas and paid for with wood, potatoes, milk, or butter! Now a new idea popped into my mind. "Have you ever taught music?" "Of course. That is what I did for years before marrying. I even continued in Zürich." "Do you teach here?" "Ah yes, if I had any pupils, but peasants do not give their children piano lessons." She agreed to give music lessons to Susan and Priscilla for a very small price—"I have little to do and it will make me happy. The extra money will provide a little meat for us which we so seldom have." Now twice a week the girls go for a lesson, taught in English, explained again in French, then given in German—she thinks that will help the girls in their language study. In between she has told them they can come to practice; while they do so, she sits and knits, telling them their mistakes. What a wonderful opportunity for the children. They had to stop their music when we left St. Louis and we thought that opportunity might never come again. Now—in this tiny village the Lord has given them a splendid teacher, at a price so much lower than city teachers ask. So many times I have been reminded that we do not give anything up for the Lord, not really, because He repays us a hundredfold in *this* life; in the life to come, we cannot even imagine the surprises He has in store for us.

It is now March, but since the next letter will be one of travel, I want to finish in this the time almost up to our leaving.

Our last guest came as a surprise. On March 3rd we received a card from Doctor K.—the woman who had been our doctor in Lausanne. Before we left Lausanne we said, "Do come and visit us if it is ever possible." This card proved she had taken our invitation seriously. "We are coming to see you. *We* are my son and I and my maid, who will soon leave Switzerland and has never seen Champéry." They arrived early Saturday afternoon with skis, packs on their backs, and a desire to spend the weekend outdoors. Fran, Priscilla, and Susan went off with them to ski for the afternoon, while I stayed home to get that night's dinner and to cook the refreshments for the Bible class. It is much easier to do all that in an empty house (though Debby was around to "help"!). Dr. K. was astonished at the "miracle" of our getting this house. Swiss visitors are always amazed because they know all too well the cost of a small apartment. To see this furnished house in the mountains at such a price seems to them a miracle and makes a good place to begin in telling of what a wonderful Heavenly Father we have.

Dr. K.'s son is Priscilla's age. He and our girls had a table to themselves where they held forth in French. Dr. K. is anxious to improve her English so was glad of the opportunity to use that language with us. As she followed me around while I put Debby to bed and helped me to wash dishes (insisting she would not sit by the fire unless I let her help) I gradually learned something of her life history. Born in Russia of Russian nobility, she was brought up in an atmosphere of wealth, spending several months a year in Russia, more in St. Moritz, and the rest in Biarritz. Her father had inherited his great wealth and did not know any life except that of sports and society. Then came the revolution! They lost all their possessions and money and were able to escape to Switzerland with very little else except their lives! Her next years were those of extreme poverty and struggle as the parents tried to provide a home and education for the two girls. Her mother learned how to sew and did dressmaking, while the father did the housekeeping. The girls must have been brilliant. Not only did they finish university, but Dr. K. finished medical school and began to practice in Lausanne. Now her sister is a professor of physics in Lausanne University and Dr. K. is a well-known doctor with a splendid practice in Lausanne.

But the interesting part of the story is the present, even more than the past. Dr. K. is now supporting her son and her mother with her practice, besides paying the wages of four people who work for her—nurses, a secretary, and someone to work full-time in her laboratory. But she says the practice is only to provide enough money to care for her responsibilities; what she is *really* interested in is cancer research. She has been doing research in her especially equipped lab for years now and feels she really is on the track of a new discovery. She works at being a doctor from 8 A.M. until 7 P.M. with only time out for dinner at noon. She eats a light tea in her office in between patients at 5 P.M., skips supper, and goes straight upstairs to her lab of 400 white mice, etc., at 7 P.M. when her office hours close. Then begins what she calls her "real work." Without any backing of a "foundation" or any funds from outside at all, she has continued this way to make her research.

If she has found what she thinks she has, if she is on the right trail— then someday the world will be beating a path to her doorstep. This summer she will present her findings in a speech at the Cancer Congress in Paris. Because of her intensive work, she feels she must keep fit by taking the weekends to ski (or climb in the summer) with her boy. So she told us she would be leaving our chalet early Sunday morning to go on a "course" for a day of skiing through the mountains with packs on their backs, a course which would finally bring them to a village quite a long distance from here where they would board the train for Lausanne. Naturally we were disappointed that they would not be with us for church, etc., on Sunday but made the most of our time on Saturday night. She is definitely an unbeliever, a person with no religion whatsoever. However, she was most interested in our faith and our explanation of what the Bible had to say. We discovered that her parents were Russian Orthodox. Her first experience with "religion" was when at an early age she went to church. The priest told her to kiss a cross at the same spot where all the other villagers kissed it. When she refused, he forced her mouth against it so violently that her teeth cut through her lips and she returned home with a bleeding mouth. "That finished it for me! I vowed I'd have nothing to do with religion." She is anti-Catholic, both the Roman brand and the Russian or Greek Orthodox, but she has nothing to take its place. We felt a real interest on her part as we gave her a verbal picture of the Love of God. Do put her on your prayer list. She has said she will be back again to see us.

All through this month in which I have only touched high spots concerning visitors, we were continuing our regular work. Luke lessons have been coming along slowly but surely. Not only is the translation work going on in French, but we have heard from Holland that the actual translation work is beginning there with one home class beginning to use the lessons in Dutch. We feel that when they are all finished, they will also be useful in English in America.

There is so much more I would like to tell you—about the monkey that Priscilla's school has added to its family, about our mailman going back to school for three weeks (the custom here for boys until they reach the age of 20; they must "brush up" on their studies though they stop school at 14 in the villages), about the avalanches that are booming down the mountainsides like thunder in the night because of the recent sunny days, about the birds that come to our birdfeeding house each day, about the daffodil plants pushing up through the snow—but I must stop both for your sakes and for mine. I really feel I must say "goodbye" this time, because leaving here seems like going farther away from you. However, distance is nothing to the mail planes, so—until next month—the Lord bless you.

Lovingly,

EDITH

March 25, 1950

Stockholm, Sweden

Dear Family:

Before I can bring you here to Stockholm with us, I must take you back to Champéry to the last days before our departure. We had to spend one day in Lausanne for last-minute details—making sure our tickets were in order, getting our month's money in Swiss francs to pay bills before leaving, getting other money changed into the amounts officially allowed to be taken into the various countries, Sweden, Finland, Norway, Denmark (finding out it was impossible to get any Finnish money after all), getting some American Express traveler's checks and doing all sorts of arithmetic! That took a *chunk* of time! Taking the typewriter to be cleaned before the journey, shopping, telephone calls, took up the rest of the morning. Lunchtime found us meeting the appointment we had made with Baroness von Dumreicher to eat with her at her pension. Tears filled her eyes as she told us she was afraid she would not be there when we returned from our trip. Poor soul, she feels constantly worse in health; although she has peace now concerning her own self, she feels burdened about her grandson. Peter came while we were there, but as always we felt his interest was only skin-deep politeness. As before, Baroness von Dumreicher brightened up as she spoke of Christian. "That boy has changed so since he went to see you. Before he would always shrug his shoulders when I talked about religion, *but now*—why he is a different boy, *really*. His face, it is so *happy*." She went on to tell us how wonderful she thought the change was and how she would like us to invite some other young folk up to the chalet, naming an American nurse especially. Our time ended with prayer and an invitation to her to come to Champéry when we returned.

We had to hurry off to an appointment with M. and Mme. Andre. There we talked about the Luke lessons, various problems, our trip, and the invitation they had extended to Debby to come to visit them part of the time while we are away. Their youngest is a little girl, Ninette, almost Debby's age. Mme. Andre felt that if Debby could come to them for the last two weeks of April, it would help the time to pass more quickly for her. She showed me the twin bed in pink where Debby would sleep as she "roomed" with Ninette, the lovely pink doll furniture and toys they would share, and the park where they would walk afternoons, thinking it would make it easier for "mother" too if she could picture her little girl. These folk are so thoughtful. She also said she would call up Home Eden to see how the girls are getting along and would drive up for Debby in the car. It certainly gives us a more comfortable feeling to know there are Christian friends personally interested in our girls.

Next, Fran went to look for Christian while I went to finish up the shopping, agreeing to meet at a certain tearoom at 5 P.M. As I pushed in the revolving door of the tearoom, my eye caught sight of two heads bent together in earnest conversation at one of the tables. There sat Christian and Fran. After the preliminaries, Fran turned to tell me the wonderful news. "Edith, Christian has just told me that he has accepted Christ as his Savior." I immediately thought of all of you in America who have been praying for this young man and how you would join in the thrill of answered prayer, sharing our happiness just as you shared the work. Fran said he felt led to ask directly, "Christian, are you God's child? Have you accepted Christ as your personal Savior?" and the answer came, "I came back from Champéry and I looked in the Bible for all you tell me, and I find it is all there! I thought it all over and I see that you have to come as a little child, and I say, why not?" This explained the change Baroness von Dumreicher had seen in him; he was "born again." This basic happiness now colored everything for him. First of all he had written his girl in Paris (also Norwegian) and had told her and had sent her a testament to read. (We have since written to Lorraine Woodson and given her this girls name and address.) Then came a blow—which before would have crushed him, but which now he can see as one of the mysteries of God's plan for him. His money for study has come to an end. That is, he has not enough, when changed from Norwegian money into Swiss, to continue in Lausanne. He would have to leave as soon as exams were over, which meant he could neither spend his vacation in Champéry nor finish his course of study. To get into a Norwegian medical school he would have to take much work over; whether it will be possible is a question. "I will be so sorry not to be able to be in Champéry and to have Sunday school for the girls, but if I go back to Norway, I want to tell all my friends about the Bible and those things I have learned from you."

We not only prayed with him about this but tried to find some way out. However, our ideas fell through. Unless anything further has turned up since we left, we will next see him in his own home town of Oslo next week. Our last glimpse of him was as he ran along beside our train telling us just when he would be leaving and assuring us that he would spend as much time as possible with us in Oslo. The Lord's ways are not our ways and we have yet to see what He will do with Christian. He has been saved not just to go to Heaven, but to be used of the Lord. Pray now that Christian may do in each step ahead of him, just what the Lord wants him to do. . . .

The final moment of leaving Champéry meant a terrible tug in leaving the children. We had planned something to take their attention from the emptiness of the house the morning they were to awaken with us gone. They wanted to stay at home that last night, but since our train left at 6, we would have to leave them in Vic's hands. You can imagine the day of work that preceded this night! At 4 P.M. the children's suitcases, etc., had been pulled down to Home Eden in the cart. From then on came the task of packing our things, last-minute tidying, defrosting the refrigerator, boiling a dozen eggs, etc. Then at a "wee hour" just before tumbling into bed, we put the "surprises" on the foot of each sleeping child's bed: two new doll dresses for Debby, a jump rope and drawing pencils for Susan, some writing paper and badminton shuttlecocks for Priscilla. These wrapped up the gay paper would help to bridge the gap from the moment of awakening to that of going over to Home Eden and settling down in the life there.

It was still dark as we tiptoed around, but just as we left the house a sleepy Priscilla and Susan crept down the stairs for a final kiss, then back to bed. Vic was there to get their breakfast later. Our wagon made a dreadful clatter through the silent village, but the baker was ready with his first batch of rolls to give us our dozen ordered ones to take along for breakfast. As we boarded the train we began counting the luggage—one to nine—which we will continue to do until we finally get off that same train again. Nine pieces to carry, with screen, projector, transformer, and a suitcase of literature. As we said goodbye to our mountains, the early-morning light streaked them with fresh beauty. I discovered at Monthey that if I carried the transformer with two fingers, I could add the flannelboard to the other two and take the typewriter in the other hand, thereby saving some steps. Fran managed the heavy bags. There are three very heavy bags, one fairly heavy, and five light things, so it works out quite well and we have it down to a fine system. Between Monthey and Aigle we munched our fresh rolls, our breakfast that morning; it started us off right in our determination to make this trip cost as little as possible. At Aigle came our second change—"Nine?" "Yes, all here"—and I hurriedly wrote some cards using one of the station carts for a desk! "Now the children will be *sure* to have something tomorrow." Between Aigle and Lausanne a cranky conductor wanted us to put all our baggage in the baggage car at so much a pound, or kilo rather. However, we were in Lausanne before anything so drastic could be done! . . .

At 8 o'clock the next morning we were ready to pull up our blind and discovered we were in Hamburg. We saw a double-decker train standing near ours, evidently filled with people going to work. This was my first glimpse of real bomb damage. It's startling to see great apartment houses with a section blasted away leaving jagged walls and inside walls exposed while curtained windows and life going on as usual showed the buildings quite obviously occupied. These buildings are no different from ones you see every day—squint your eyes and pretend only part of them remains. Whole blocks of the city were nothing but loose bricks in forlorn-looking, unkempt piles, while other blocks remained untouched. As we passed a park we saw women wheeling baby carriages and little tots in bright sweaters and hats playing under the big trees. At Flensburg we went over an amazing bridge which goes in a complete circle like a twist in a piece of rope, twisting out at a lower level. This gave an interesting view of the red-roofed houses, the Kiel Canal, and the industrial plants of this town. It seems strange that so much remains after a war. A thing like this bridge, for instance. Next we came to Eckernförde—all out to go through customs—passports please! This takes us out of Germany and officially into Denmark— what are these? Pink food tickets for meals in Denmark. Rationing is still in effect there and one needs meal tickets. They allow you five meals a day, so that should be plenty. How many would they expect you to eat without tickets? At Padborg a new man came on as porter. He advised us to get off for the night at Copenhagen. He said we would arrive at Nässjö at 3 A.M. and before that there would be many disturbances. It would bring us in to Jönköping sometime after 4 A.M., most inconvenient for whoever was supposed to meet us. We took his advice since our ticket was good for any number of stopovers. . . .

At Malmö, after crossing the stretch of water about 20 miles wide, we had to go through Swedish customs. Here they really gave us a workout. Every bag had to be opened, all things thoroughly poked, and the Thermos of Champéry water was smelled a couple of times! However, they did not charge us any duty and were very courteous and smiling. A bus took us with our nine pieces from the boat docks to a train station, where we boarded a train for Nässjö. And if you think you can make a train conductor understand where you are going just by pronouncing this, just try it once (unless you are Swedish). Nässjö is *something* like this—"Nayshur." And Jönköping is *something* like this— "Yinshipping," the accent on the Yin. But it took us awhile to find this out! No one had ever heard of the places we wanted to go!!! . . .

That evening we walked out to buy some provisions at a grocery store. Found that bread must be purchased at a special store, milk at another. Although we couldn't speak, we pointed; people seemed to mumble nonsense at us! Nevertheless we returned with purchases bought at very low prices. Milk here is pasteurized and sold in bottles as cold and lovely as any in America—for only six American cents a quart! Bread is of many different and lovely varieties, close-grained and soft of crust with a rather sweet flavor, like the Swedish rye you buy in your grocery. These purchases we planned to keep for breakfast and eat supper in the hotel restaurant. We found this to be a most unusual place down in the basement with thick curved pillars like those in cellars of ancient monasteries. In the center stood a large table with many dishes upon it. (Ah, thinks I, our first Smörgåsbord; we'll find more of this in Stockholm. But since being here, I have discovered they *ended* this custom here during the war and no Stockholm restaurant serves in this old manner!) We couldn't read a word of the menu, but our waitress pointed to the table and motioned us to help ourselves. Smörgåsbord consists of a variety of cold meats, jellied meats, fish, jellied fish, pickled fish, creamed fish, cheeses, eggs done in various ways, meat loaves, meat balls in sauce—pickles and pickled beets being the only vegetables in sight! You take a plate, some bread and butter, and pass around this table filling up your plate with all you can eat. What a place for anyone who likes meats and cheeses and isn't keen about vegetables! The Swedes are excellent cooks, certainly know how to flavor such dishes. After we had stuffed ourselves on these things, anxious to taste the varieties, we discovered that that was only the first part of the dinner; a hot fried fish and boiled potatoes were served along with an enormous glass of milk. The price of all this was less than 65 cents. You really ought to visit Jönköping. If you are hungry, Sweden is the place to come.

Next morning, the bottle of milk and loaf of bread provided us with an early breakfast in our room before we went off to catch a train for the Bible School where we were to speak on Children for Christ. We were told by Mr. Simeonsson on the way out that the entire group we would be meeting with in Jönköping were of the Swedish Alliance Mission. This school is theirs. This mission is about 100 years old, formed in order to send missionaries to various foreign fields. However, through the years they have built buildings and have had their own church services apart from the State Church. Sweden has a very strong State Protestant Church. When you are born in Sweden, your name is entered on the Church roll just as you would be registered in the courthouse in America. So, in a way, everyone is called a member of the State Church, even atheists. . . .

We got our bags, checked out of the hotel, walked around a bit to look at Jönköping, which is a medium-sized town at one end of Sweden's second-largest lake, 20 miles long. My poor, long suffering shoulder bag gave out under the strain of holding tracts, pencils and paper, postcards to send in odd moments, scissors, pins, needles, extra film, etc.; the strap broke. So my system for carrying things broke down at this point! The Simeonsson family came to the train to see us off and we felt as though we were saying goodbye to old friends. Fran finished the Champéry eggs on the station platform at Mjölby as we waited between trains. That dozen did a good job!

As we peered out at the dark platform at Motala, we saw Dr. Hedegard's familiar face topped with a high black fur hat, so common here in Sweden. "Velcome, velcome, velcome to Motala!" We piled into a car, which a friend was driving, and drove about eight miles through the darkness to Tuddårp, the farm upon which the Hedegards live. What a treat, to stay in an old Swedish farm house! As the car turned into a tree-lined driveway, the wheels crunched on the gravel and we slowly curved around a circle of garden guarded by two enormous evergreen trees. The open door let a square of yellow light fall on the porch; we stepped out of the car onto pine boughs, making a soft mat at the foot of the steps. This is an old Swedish custom, very pretty and practical as a foot wiper too. Dear Mrs. Hedegard met us at the open door with "velcome"—and as she had been studying English by means of a course on the phonograph—she proudly added, "How—are—you?" Then as we counted our luggage she counted to ten in English to show her accomplishment and we laughed heartily together! I couldn't keep my eyes away from the corner of the room where the wonderful old Swedish stove stood. It reached from ceiling to floor, a dazzling white tile, with hand-painted flourishes of flowers in three different bands. In the living room stood another of these corner stoves, perfectly cylindrical in shape, large white tiles with an oak-leaf border painted in three places, shiny brass doors where the fire was held. It looked like a storybook come to life.

Our bedroom had another of these stoves in it; most practical, as a few pieces of wood will heat up the bricks inside and keep the room warm for a long time. We washed at a little ancient washstand with clear cold water poured out of a pink and white pitcher into a pink and white bowl and went to sleep feeling truly this was the Sweden few people now see. . . .

That night we packed for an early-morning departure, sorry to be leaving the Hedegards, of whom we had grown so fond. Although she couldn't understand English nor I, her flow of Swedish, we had a fine time together motioning with our hands and laughing hilariously. At mealtimes Dr. Hedegard translated for us. Before we left, some mail arrived which we were happy to get. The most exciting piece was an invitation from a chaplain in Munich to come to Germany this summer and conduct a summer Bible school for the American Army children. He also wants Fran to give a series of evening messages during it. Since knowing Molly in Champéry, I had often thought about these children and had hoped we could in some way do something to reach them. Please be praying about this opportunity that has opened to do this.

As we left, Mrs. Hedegard broke off a piece of a plant to pin on my coat, a Swedish custom when someone is leaving your home. He and she stood together on the steps waving to us until we were out of sight. . . .

The next day was a big holiday. The Swedish people celebrate the angel's announcement to Mary that she will have a Son whose name is to be Jesus. Like so many holidays, it has lost its *raison d'être* in the customs that grew up around it and is now chiefly a day to eat waffles. We discovered that in the Swedish language the word "Our Lady" sounds somewhat likes "waffles," and through mispronunciation the custom began. This explained why we saw such quantities of waffle irons and pictures of waffles in department store windows and so many waffles on tables in the restaurants. . . .

We were fortunate to have the opportunity of seeing so much real home life in Sweden. The most striking thing about the decoration in Swedish homes is the universal use of many green plants which grow up the walls. Vines which grow in dark corners and climb up forming frames around pictures and covering whole walls with their bright green leaves are present everywhere from country to city, from tiny apartment to great houses.

We left Sweden hopeful of good results, but it is better not to speak of what is "hoped for," but to wait awhile to see what the Lord does. We will have one more day and night in Stockholm on our way from Finland to Norway and expect to see two more of the Christian leaders who were out of town last week.

We found when reached Stockholm that, although Dr. Hedegard had tried to reserve places on the boat for us, a place had not been reserved because the ticket must be *bought* first! The boat we expected to take on the 28th was full. We could only reach Åbo on time by taking the boat leaving at 4 P.M. on the 27th, which had *one* vacant cabin on it. So 3 P.M on the 27th found us going through Swedish customs, after which we boarded the little boat. When our nine pieces were stored in our tiny cabin, taking all the space except the double-decker bunks themselves, we went on a tour of inspection. This revealed the source of the strong onion smell, as great bags of onions were being lowered into the hold, going from Sweden to Finland. We have since discovered onions are as expensive as oranges in Finland, that the only other vegetables on the market are potatoes, carrots, beets, and turnips. . . .

And here I shall have to leave you until the next letter. We are now in Åbo, Finland, and it is March 29th. Remember while you wait in the Baltic Sea to keep praying for us and for those to whom we speak. May the Lord bless you for your part in this.

Much love,

EDITH

April 28, 1950   Copenhagen, Denmark

Dear Family:

We must cover a lot of space in this letter, so get a comfortable chair and be sure you have enough time to go through Finland without jumping up in the middle of it!

When the boat was rolling sickeningly in that open stretch of the Baltic Sea, we stayed on deck until we were chilled to the bone, then decided to leave the beauty of the star-studded sky and the white-cap-studded water, and try to get some sleep. We soon should be in the Finnish Archipelago and, we assured each other, that would be nice and quiet like the Swedish Archipelago. Light out, we had been trying to sleep for some time when—boom—crash—cr-a-a-a-ack—c-r-e-e-a-k—what on earth could that be? Sounded like the boat breaking up! I scrambled out of my bunk and fixed my feet on a suitcase, leaning over to peer out of the tiny porthole. "Fran, *come* and *look*," I called in the direction of the upper bunk. "*You* look and tell me about it," came the lazy reply! "Well, we are going through ice. *Imagine!* I had fondly believed we were to cross the *water* between Sweden and Finland—no one told me it would be *solid* water." Huge sheets of ice as big as a tennis court were divided from each other by streaks of black water and we were pushing through them. The ice seemed to be six and eight inches thick. What a sight—I felt as though I were dreaming. After that, the night was spent in trying to sleep—and in scrambling curiously to the porthole to discover the reason for some new kind of noise! The boat jerked and the ice thundered against its sides; sometimes the ice was in smaller chunks about the size you would put in an icebox, and other times it was solid between us and the shore. Then all of a sudden we came to a full stop. This time curiosity got the better of Fran and he came tumbling out of the upper bunk to get to the porthole first. "Edith, there are *people walking around on the ice.*" It sounded unbelievable, but when I found my place at the porthole I saw it for myself—there was a man with a lantern in his hand slowly approaching the boat over the uneven ice. The shore was off in the distance! After him came another man wheeling a wheelbarrow full of canvas bags, and then, stepping gingerly as though he expected to go through at any moment, came a dignified man with a topcoat, felt hat, and suitcase—just as though he were in Union Station! Just at that moment a ladder swung down across our porthole, and the man who was all dressed up ascended the ladder from the middle of the ice to the boat.

"How do you buy a ticket from the middle of the ice to Åbo?" questioned Fran. It all seemed so very unreal. Two men got off the boat in the same way—the mail bags were lifted on with great hooks, and another bag of mail was lowered down to the ice. Four men now walked slowly away, placing their feet with great caution before trusting a new spot, and our boat moved away at the same time—with much creaking and cracking of ice. We were so glad that it was spring, and not winter, when the ice would be a *hindrance!* This was a mere nothing and the boat was right on schedule!!!

Morning came with a blue sky and sunshine to complete the picture of the glistening white ice and the snow-covered islands. Up on deck it was really cold, but we stayed as long as we could to watch the path of our boat through the ice. We neared the harbor of Åbo where a channel is kept clear but where boats are still frozen in the ice at the two sides.

As we stepped off the boat in Åbo, Finland, we knew it was no use to wave a white handkerchief because we were a day early and, therefore, no one would be meeting us. Fran did not even have the name of the pastor we were to be with, only the name of the church—the Free Church of Finland. Wonder of wonders—we found the porter who was lugging our bags could speak some English and he found the address of the church for us. The taxi, an ancient Chevrolet, drove us through the bleak landscape—dirty snow, low wooden buildings box-like in structure—to a wooden church building set in a muddy courtyard where a woman was hanging up clothes. Fran got out to speak to an elderly woman who appeared from somewhere inside the church building. There was no use speaking, however—she understood nothing; and the taxi driver and she held a conversation in this language which was so utterly foreign to our ears, having *no* connection with any languages we had heard before. Finnish is closer to Hungarian and has no tie with the other three Scandinavian languages.

Next we were driven to a grey concrete apartment house, where the taxi driver found a woman who indicated that we were to bring our bags upstairs! Not knowing where we were going, we go out and dragged all our things up to the third floor where we were greeted by a flow of Finnish and were shown, by the waving of arms, that our things must come in! Soon we were left alone in a dining room, rather crowded with nice dining room furniture, a piano, and a daybed. A book on Hudson Taylor among the books in the bookcase made us feel that we were probably in the right place. After about half an hour another lady appeared and spoke to us in halting English; she had learned to speak only in school and that many years before. This lady—Miss Anderson—explained that we were expected the next day (explanations given) and told us that we were to stay with them in this apartment. They are members of the Free Church and glad to have us with them, she said. We were given the room next to the dining room, also with a daybed crowded in it, bookcases, a desk, etc. Later we found that these two women have a three-room-and kitchen apartment. Each had her own bedroom but, since the Russians have taken so much Finnish land, well over 450,000 Finns were made homeless, and everyone has to share. Each person's house or apartment was measured and only a certain amount of space allowed to each person. Hence one of their bedrooms is occupied by a woman who rents it from them and they must double up! In spite of this crowding, they welcomed us to share the space with them. We were given the daybed for one of us and the piano bench for the other!! Now how can you sleep on a piano bench? Well, at night the furniture is pushed aside and the piano bench *unfolded*. As the top is lifted you discover that inside pieces of wood are hinged together which, when unfolded, make the framework of a bed. Now a piece of canvas is unrolled from one end (where it has been stored within the bench) and is stretched out full length, making a canvas cot. Next a mattress-like quilt is placed over the canvas, covers added to it, and presto—you have another bed in the room!

If you will find on your map the section of Finland called Karjala, you will see that it is in the south and is a large section right by Russia. It is full of lakes and we are told it is very beautiful. Many of the Russian nobility had summer homes in this area and fled there to live during and after the Russian Revolution. In the winter of 1940 the Russians advanced against the Finns. This war started November 30, 1939, actually, and is call the "winter war"—it lasted until March 13, 1940. It is an amazing thing, attributed by the Finns to answered prayer and the care of God, that this little nation was able to fight against that mighty and terrible neighboring nation and win a victory. In 1941 the Finns were faced with a terrible decision. The Germans were advancing and the Russians were coming against the Germans. Russia has been the enemy of Finland for a long time—Finns know and hate its communism, they know the Russian determination for conquering the world, they know and have experienced the ruthlessness of the Russian soldiers. Finland has only the number of inhabitants of the city of Philadelphia—how easily they could be swallowed up by Russia! They were faced with this decision—should they join Russia against the Germans?

In spite of the fact that the Russians at that time were allies of America, the Finns knew they were still *their* enemies and that if they allowed the Russians to come in as friends they would never again leave their country, even after the war. So *many* said to us, "We knew the Russians too well—we had only one choice." They joined the Germans against the Russians on June 24, 1941. Actually, they told us, the Germans went to the north of Finland where there are few Finns and fought on that front, and the Finns themselves were fighting the Russians on the southern border! This lasted until August, 1944. Picture the years of war for a people only as numerous as the population of Philadelphia at war with Russia for that length of time. You know what happened on that day in August—the war was over, America had won, but for these people Russia was the victor. However, by the grace of God they were given their freedom again, that for which they had been fighting. Karjala was kept by the Russians, Hangö was given back—but in its place Russia "rented" a piece of land for 50 years, a piece of land

60 × 60 kilometers, right on the shore between Hangö and Helsinki—just like a bite taken out of a sandwich.

Now, you know the Russians have Estonia and you will see on the map that, with Estonia on one side and this piece of land taken out of Finland on the other, they have control of that whole big bay—and of the port of Helsinki! Now to go to Helsinki by train, you have to go through the Russian-held territory. What can you see?—not a thing! Why? Well, believe it or not, there are thick *iron curtains* on the trains. When the train approaches this territory, the iron curtains are pushed up along the grooves made for them until they completely cover all the windows and the train is as black as a coal mine. These remain in place until you are well on the other side of the Russian territory. The Finns laughingly joke about this and call it "the longest tunnel in the world." The Finns know all too well that the Russians are building heavy coastal defenses in this section. As for the people in this section, they were given from two weeks to two days to pack up what they could and leave their homes and land—for 50 years or forever—with only what they could carry with them on buses or trains. But the rest of the Finns have provided space in their homes or in new housing projects for these homeless ones, and most of them now have work too. Russia also has imposed heavy "war taxes" upon the Finns—to be paid in five years. Russia has changed the type of things the payment may be made with, several times, each time choosing something harder for the Finns to do, but in spite of that, the Finns are up to date with their payments and you have the feeling that they are all working unitedly to pay off the war fines. Individuals don't grumble, they feel their part in it all. When you speak of courage, remember these people.

Estonia is only three hours away by boat, but no one may even write to his friends in Estonia, let alone visit them. Finns who have formerly lived in the now-Russian-controlled territory and carry the passport of these countries, such as Estonia, are disappearing from Finland, carried off in the night! Though Russia controls their land and sea borders on two sides, and even occupies territory within their country, yet defiantly in the last election the Finns chose as their president the very man Russia told them they must not choose—the general who had led their troops against Russia! English is taught in all the schools as the first foreign language. America is well spoken of and as you talk with person after person, you feel ashamed of whatever fear has been in your own heart concerning the future. Here they sit—within a stone's throw of the enemy—with courage and, among the Christians, with complete faith and dependence on an all-powerful God. Pray for these people, but take courage from them too; our God is the God of Gideon, of Moses, of Daniel, of the young men in the fiery furnace—He has not changed and we are *His* people through faith in Christ.

As we were a day early, of course no meeting was planned for us that night, but we were asked to come to the missionary sewing circle meeting at one of the homes. Here about 35 young people and young married couples with little children were packed into a small room as they knit and sewed and sang hymns. Many of their hymns are in the minor key and the singing is very different as syllables are given equal force and r's are rolled and other consonants emphasized. The singing had a Slavic sound and the strong clear voices throbbed with feeling. We were warmly welcomed and each of us was asked to speak, with a little woman translating for us who had formerly been Russian Orthodox, was in America several years, and had been saved in a church in Cleveland, Ohio. She went to China as a missionary and now is back in Finland working. She told us that when she returned to Finland and asked the Russian Orthodox priest to take her name from the roll because she had accepted Christ as her Savior and was now a Protestant, he gave her a slip of paper saying on it that because of her action she would be sent to hell forever—by the authority of the priest!! . . .

We were then told of the various bombings that spoiled much of Åbo. Miss Anderson was at work in her factory when bomb warnings came and, with others, she rushed to the bomb shelter just in time, as their factory was hit and burned to the ground. She said she never expected to leave the shelter alive but a few hours later found herself going back to the apartment, all right except for a headache! There she found two bombs had struck in the street beside the building, making huge craters but only breaking all the windows in the apartment house! As we came back to eat dinner, she apologized for the fact that since the war most Finns eat only two meals a day—breakfast which consists of porridge and milk, bread with cheese or a berry sauce (something like our jam but with not much sugar in it), and coffee; and dinner at about 4 P.M. with potatoes, meat or sausage or fish, and some pudding. There are no vegetables in winter as they are too scarce and expensive for ordinary people. Fruit is also scarce and expensive and in most homes these berries, found in the woods in the summer, are preserved and used for both fruit and vegetable. Between these two meals people drink coffee and eat little cookies or cakes which can now be bought again. Up until a year ago they had only black flour and no nice things which can be made only of white flour—so the sweet breads and cookies are much appreciated. . . .

The next day I stayed in and typed while Fran went out to do some picture taking in the sunshine and to try to get a cabin on the boat going back (no success), to get stamps, etc. Several people had been invited in to meet us at "afternoon coffee," and all too soon evening had arrived and it was time for our meeting on Children for Christ. This time even more people had crowded into the building, so that chairs had been placed down the aisles and the back was full right to the doors with people standing. Later in this letter I want to give you an outline of our Children for Christ meetings as we have planned them for this trip. People swarmed up afterward and looked over the materials at the front, like ants swarming over a pile of sugar. Many wanted to buy the "Heart of Salvation," others asked for the flannelboard lessons to begin using them right away. People wrung our hands and thanked us over and over again for coming to Finland. One old lady with a deeply wrinkled face and a scarf tied around her head in peasant fashion, smiling widely showing her one remaining tooth, kept hanging on to my hand and patting my face and saying over and over, "You come again, you come again" (in Finnish of course). In between other people she would keep coming back. She is one of those poor souls who lost her home in the section where the Russians now are, and who also lost her two sons in the war. After the people finally went away, we were taken into a back room where tea and sandwiches had been fixed in a festive manner on a plain table in the center of this rather bleak room. Here the Sunday School teachers were gathered to have a "reception" for us. They sang some of their songs for us and asked us to sing some of ours for them!!! Here they further discussed Children for Christ and said they really wanted to begin. We said we would let them know details after we had been in other churches of their denomination and had found someone to do translating work. The minister's 15-year-old daughter asked for a picture of our children and asked if she might write to Priscilla and practice her English that way. Back at the apartment again we packed our things, wrote in the guest book, made up our piano-stool bed, and tumbled in.

The morning found us up early to get the first train for a spot near Hankö, where the Free Church has their Bible School. The pastor came with a taxi and insisted on carrying most of the things out himself. The two ladies produced a bunch of bright pink azaleas they had bought and pinned two in Fran's buttonhole and the rest on my shoulder as we left the house. They came along to the station and so we had plenty of help putting our bags on the train. The pastor stopped Fran from going for tickets as he placed two tickets in his hand saying, "Our church bought these for you to take you to the next place." They were second-class tickets, so we traveled that morning on upholstered seats! The train was a rusty-looking affair with an old-type engine. We noticed the slots beside the windows and the iron curtains ready to be pushed in place when we approached the Russian section. The landscape was dotted with box-like farm houses, no porches, nothing to relieve the matchbox look, and badly in need of paint. The most striking thing about the view was the mile after mile of birch and pine woods. At a small town we got off and were met by the director of the Bible School, dressed in riding jodhpurs, high laced boots, and a shabby tweed jacket. A high black fur hat topped his smiling, round face. He pointed out to us the battlefield of war between Russia and Finland. "There are the tank traps"—long lines of large, sharp, natural rocks placed in methodical rows—"and there is where our men stood holding them back for five months. Only God gave the victory to our little nation—it was miraculous." We passed on, over the blackened tree stumps of no-man's land, and on through the section

A familiar sight—Fran preparing to show our slides.

where the Russians had stood.

Finally we came to a spot in the woods where the train jolted to a stop. "Hurry up, we get off—not a regular stop." Out we tumbled, dragging our bags, shoving them to each other—whew!! The train started almost before we got the last foot off the step and we looked around to find ourselves in an apparent wilderness. Then a sleigh came bouncing up toward us, as a young lad tried without much success to stop a half-broken horse. *"Brrrrr,"* he said to the horse, *"Brrrrr,"* with a rolling of the r's. This is equivalent to our "Whoa." As our bags were piled in, the horse reared up and started off. *"Brrrrr,"* he quieted down again for a second. All the bags in, I stepped gingerly into the place offered me and—swish!—off we went before Fran and the other man could get in! This time the horse had no intention of paying attention to any of the *"Brrrrr's,"* and he kept right on galloping home. The boy, standing on the runners behind me, had all he could do to guide the horse and keep him on the road. What a wild ride that was—with me hanging on to the projector for all I was worth to keep it from sliding into the road when the horse decided to go up little hills on one side and dump the contents of the sleigh out, if he could! I won, though! The baggage and I arrived intact, though Fran and the director didn't arrive until after a half-hour's walk. At the school I was met with a flow of Finnish and given a chair near a big corner tile stove where I warmed up a bit. When Fran arrived, we were taken around to see the school. It is a Christian High School and a Theological Seminary. The High School students live there for one or two years and have a practical course. They are country boys and girls living where there are no high schools and they are trained in woodwork, farming; the girls have cooking and housekeeping and weaving. After a lunch prepared by the cooking pupils, Fran went to speak to the 14 theological students while I found a quiet corner to type.

The cooking class prepared and served our supper too, a really very fine meal, and then we had our evening meeting on Children for Christ. We met with the same enthusiasm. After a few songs in the minor key by the school chorus, Fran showed his slides and talked a little bit about the I.C. We had just this one evening, so tried to get everything into one day. Although we thought it was too late and we ought to be finishing, people stayed afterwards to ask questions, to look at materials, etc., and so it was *very* late when we finally got our things packed up again for an early-morning start, and went to bed in another building a short walk away. A small pitcher of cold water and a little basin were all the accommodations there were for shaving. Fran has shaved in cold water now for almost the whole trip. His face is still in one piece, though. We took a bus after an early breakfast and the students accompanied us to the back road where the bus stops. Some loosely wrapped sandwiches were placed in our hand "for a little lunch," and the students sang to us as our bus started off, waving and singing until we rounded a bend in the road. The bus skirted around the Russian-held land, so we missed the iron-curtained section of the railroad. We were met at Helsinki by a young man almost the same build as Fran, with wavy blond hair, blue eyes, and a most engaging smile, who told us he was to be our interpreter as long as we were there. With him was an older man, Professor Saarisalo, who is Professor of Archaeology at the University of Helsinki. It didn't take five minutes for us to find out where this professor stands—and that is right on the Word of God. He told us he is not allowed to teach the theological students at the University—"They are afraid I might contaminate them with the Bible." He told us how strong the Barthian-type theology is in Finland in the State Church. He told us he would rather have the old-fashioned kind of modernism back again: "It would be easier to fight the Devil with horns and hoofs than in his present form." We had lunch with Professor Saarisalo and had two hours to talk with him; then take him to his bus where he had to leave for the north of Finland for a few weeks. He certainly is one with us and, if it is financially possible, he will be in Geneva. . . .

At the end of his message Fran said, "We in America admire your country in its courageous stand. We admire the Finnish soldiers for their bravery. This is a greater war—between the Devil and God. We urge you Finnish Christians who are one with us in Christ to stand by our sides in this warfare." The response to this message was real and from the hearts. . . .

In the morning Fran had more appointments while I typed and packed. At noon we ate a hurried lunch, writing cards to the children as we ate and then went off to the station to catch the train for Tampere. . . . The train was very crowded—no place even to move our feet, let alone shift our position—but at least we were sitting down. We arrived in

Tampere with only an hour before meeting time to get to our hotel, change, etc. We were taken to Emmaus Hospice and—surprise—found we had a room with a bath, the first since Stockholm. The water was actually hot (though brown with rust), but a quick bath meant more than a dinner, and we managed to have a glass of milk before leaving for the church. A 15-minute fast walk brought us to the church after the people had already filled it, and as they sang the first song Fran started unpacking the suitcase while I screwed the various parts of the easel together and fixed the flannelboard. Then as he spoke I arranged my things.

During these meetings Fran speaks about 35 minutes on the world as a mission field, not only the places far from you but right around your own doorstep, the need of reaching children, and the plan of Children for Christ for reaching these children and grounding them in the Word of God and bringing them to the Bible-believing churches. He explains the Seven-Point Program, showing some of the materials for each point, and then turns the meeting over to me to explain the Home Class and demonstrate a sample class and the materials for such classes. . . . Then I go through a sample class period, starting with songs (which I sing to demonstrate, each time wishing the children were along to help sing), going through a flannelboard story, giving an object lesson, and finally showing them the plan and materials for our Luke lessons. In ending, I sing that chorus, "Lord send me, here am I, send me. I want to be greatly used of Thee. Across the street or across the sea, here am I—Oh, Lord, send me," and I say, "We have cross the *sea*—to ask you to cross the *street*—to reach the children whom we could never reach." The Lord has used this ending to touch people, and in many places people have come up front to say, "I want to cross the street, like you said." Several of the pastors have mentioned it in their closing words to the people and I am sure the Lord gave that thought alone which would stick in people's minds and hearts. The people in this church in Tampere were just as enthused as the other Finns had been and want to begin the children's classes as soon as possible. . . .

Back at the hotel we made use of the hot water to wash out some clothing and then sank into bed ready for sleep, as you can imagine! The next morning we wakened a bit late and had our pictures taken for their Christian newspaper. . . . We walked, then (I *ran* because this Kalerea's* idea of walking is a trot for me), across to the other side of the town. . . . Here we were welcomed into the home of the city's leading architect for breakfast. . . . There we sat to look at the folders of photographs which had been taken by the architect and for which he had won awards. The most striking of these were the ones he took during the Russian bombing of Tampere. He was permitted to go anywhere taking pictures and he has amazing shots which gave us a feeling of what it would have been like to be there—shots taken as fires were blazing in a dozen build-

* Director of Youth Work for the Free Church of Finland, he was in his 20's at this time.

The Finnish newspaper caption for this read, "Rev. Francis Schaeffer is 100% Finnish. Mrs. Edith Schaeffer claims to be American, but we know that she's Italian."

ings at once—shots of half-burned homes hanging with icicles—one of the inside of a home with the piano, dining room furniture, pictures on the walls, all hung with thick icicles—a shot of the department store in rubble with the manikins standing ludicrously upright in the jagged broken glass, still wearing their painted smiles and stylish clothes. The main buildings burned, broken, crashed, but people doggedly walking through it all to their daily work—a shot of a refugee family gathered in the home that had opened its doors to it, having a little Christmas celebration for the children. Tampere was a discouraging ruin of a town, but now it looks as built-up and well cared for as the town in which you live. The Finns are a remarkable, strong-willed people. As we left this house, we walked up a hill in the woods behind it, to climb up a lookout tower. Here we saw the city, with its many smokestacks telling of its industrial works, stretched out between two lakes. . . .

The Bishop whom we had met in the Helsinki station had called our hotel that morning and invited us to "coffee at one o'clock." . . . The Bishop began telling us of the fact that he was going to be in Canada this summer as a member of the Executive Committee of the World Council. Fran didn't waste any time telling him what we believed concerning the Word of God and why we could not conscientiously have anything to do with the modernism, Barthianism, and Greek Orthodoxy found in the World Council. He told him that we believed the Bible-believing Christian has the only tenable position both religiously and intellectually, that the only other logical position would be agnosticism. Fran also spoke to him concerning the Communism of the World Council, especially of Dr. Chao, World Council president in China. Being Finnish, the Bishop is not happy about this, as the Finns are strong against Communism. As the conversation ended Fran emphasized the responsibility men have before God when they are in the position of "undershepherd." Do pray for this man. The Lord can use whom He will and I'm sure He had some real reason for bringing us this contact. . . . Communism has practically no friends in Finland.

Back at the hotel we packed again for an early leave, slept an exhausted sleep, and at 8 A.M. were crowded together on a train again. After an hour we changed trains to branch off for Åbo, while Kalerea went back to Helsinki. Only three minutes to change trains meant a very hurried swish of our bags across the platform and, "Goodbye—come back soon."—"Hope you can come to Switzerland to see us. Thank you and the Lord bless you." "Thank you for coming—God bless you." The last we saw of him was his smile as he leaned from the train and then it disappeared around a curve.

We had no seats but were perched on our bags in the cold vestibule of the rackety old train when suddenly Fran said, "My camera!" In the rush it had been forgotten and now it was speeding away in one direction and we in the other. We might send a telegram to the Helsinki station, but as we search the train we found not one person who could speak English. Nothing we could do, but one thing, and after all that was the most effective, better than a telegram—we prayed. "Oh, Heavenly Father if it be thy will, cause Kalerea to notice that camera under the ladies' coats on that hanger." And then we sped on. It was a miserable ride: the train lurched from side to side and we were cold. Five hours brought us to Åbo, where as we descended the steps, we were met by the smiling 15-year-old daughter of the pastor there and as her father helped us to carry our bags down the platform the loud-speaker boomed out—"Pastor Schaeffer—gibberish—gibberish—Pastor Schaeffer—gibberish." "Fran," I called, "did you hear that?" "No, I never listen to those things—can't ever understand them anyway." "Well, it must be about your camera—they are calling you." A visit to the station office produced this telegram, "Don't worry your camera it comes five o'clock bus Kalerea." Good old Kalerea, he really is on his toes and praise God for answering prayer and drawing his attention to it. . . .

The boat was supposed to sail at 7 P.M., but when we got to the dock at 5:30 to go through customs, etc., we found that it had not yet even come in—fog had held it up! We still had no cabin and spent some time trying to see if one had become available—no results! Four of the young people from the church arrived with a bouquet of flowers and stood around the dock with us. Finally the boat arrived a little after 8. We waited in line for passport control, money control, etc. As we came to get the bags through customs, we found that the same porter who was so helpful when we landed had taken charge of our things. He told the officer that we were here on Church work and not to open our things, hence the chalk mark was quickly put of all bags! Meantime, two of the girls rushed off home to get a Thermos of coffee to fortify us! We boarded the boat to get our bags on and to ask again for a cabin. "Nothing, all full." "Such a little boat, and everyone is going away on Easter vacation." It was Good Friday evening. We came back on the dock again to be served coffee by the excited girls who had brought cups, sugar lumps, and cookies to complete it. There we stood on the dimly lighted wharf drinking our farewell coffee, after which a general handshaking and "farewelling" took place. Miss Anderson, tall, dark, and dignified, embraced me like one of the family, and we parted from Finland with our hearts very full and the tears close! We stood by the rail waving intermittently for half an hour.

Steel was unloaded but much remained to be put on the boat. We called to Miss Anderson, "You'd better go home—you'll get so cold." She came over the ropes to the side of the boat, saying, "We wanted to sing as you sailed out." "Do it now, then—it may still be very long." And so the group came to the side of the boat and sang eight verses of a Finnish hymn. Their sweet voices rang out a clear message as the huge crane swung steel from boat to dock—the mumble of voices was hushed as everyone stopped to listen, and then it was over. "Goodbye, come back again—we will never forget you." "Goodbye, the Lord bless you—we will pray for you." They moved away backward, waving all the time; Fran waved his hat and I waved Nalee (Debby's teddy bear). As they reached the trolley car and got on, the motorman left the door open so they could continue to wave until they were out of sight. Such a farewell from a country where we had come as strangers only ten days before—such is the depth of our oneness in Christ. Won't heaven be a wonderful place as those from every tribe and nation gather together as citizens of one country speaking one language! Meantime, pray for these in their especially difficult place, in their new efforts to reach the children for Christ, and for the children that they may become firmly fixed on the Rock, which is Jesus Christ.

We ate dinner with the "first sitting" at 10 P.M. I don't know when the third sitting finished eating! After this we bothered the Purser again— "Anything yet of a cabin for the Schaeffers?" "Nothing, unless you want a single cabin back in the crew's quarters." "Sure, we'll take it. We want a quiet spot to work and someplace to get some sleep tonight." So we were led back through a door marked "Personnel—No Admittance" in Finnish, and shown our cabin. It had one small porthole, a mirror, a couple of hooks to hang clothes on, and a locked cupboard full of officers' clothes. That was all, except a *very narrow* bunk. There was no room for our baggage, so we left it all outside except for one suitcase to serve as a table for me to type on as I sat on the bunk! However, it looked good to us after seeing the people without cabins scrambling for a spot on a camp stool, or on some piled luggage, trying to get comfortable for the night. We were supposed to be in Stockholm at 8 A.M. The bunk was hard as a board, as well as narrow, but we managed to lie down with our heads at opposite ends. The ice was much thinner than it had been ten days before and so there wasn't much noise. Now for some sleep—at least this won't last long.

This time the foghorn blasted out to waken us. It sounded as though it should gargle before continuing its insistent blasts. The little ship gave a shudder and then came to a stop, a clanking, grating noise informed us that the anchors were being let down. Then all was quiet again except for the lap-lapping of water against the boat's sides. Might as well sleep— wonder how late we'll be? "We have an appointment in Stockholm at 2 P.M., but of course we'll be in plenty of time for that." Once through the night the anchors clanked back up again and we moved ahead slowly, the foghorn intermittently announcing that its throat was no better, but in a half-hour we were anchored again. Morning light showed us that we were standing in a thick fog—still in the Finnish Archipelago but not able to see even ten feet away. The Purser came importantly to tell us that *Borevann*, another one of these boats, had something go wrong with its radar and had struck a rock last night; 213 passengers were taken off in the lifeboats in two hours—no one hurt but the boat! *We* don't even have radar, so of course the captain was taking no chances. Nothing to do but wait for the fog to lift. How glad we were for the cabin. Fran dictated letters and we went ahead in our temporary office! Fran found it possible to call Stockholm from the ship's radio office for very little money. Hence, a call was made to break our appointment for 2 P.M. and to explain that they gave us no hope of reaching Stockholm before about 5 P.M.. . . . Noon came and the fog lifted a little. We moved ahead slowly for a couple of hours and then it all came down again and we were closed in by the thick grey walls. Clunk went the anchors and there we sat. As night drew on people looked so glum; some poor ones had only four days of vacation and here was the second night being spent out there. We tried to find a way to show the Kodachrome slides in the dining room. The Purser was happy at the thought but there was nothing but direct current and no converter on board, so that ended that possibility. People in the corridors ceased trying to look dignified and sprawled out on the floors, covered by their coats or blankets they had with them. It was hard to find a place to step without treading on someone's outstretched hand or foot. We stepped into the cramped little cabin to spend a second night on the narrow shelf-like bed, thankful not to be on the drafty floor outside.

As we were dressing in the morning a throb went through the boat; the engines had started. A cheer went up from the passengers in the halls! Going up on deck we found the sun had broken through, the fog had disappeared altogether, and the murky waters were changed into liquid floating with a million diamonds in the sparkling sun, framed by the rocky islands. As we came to the port at the mouth of the Baltic proper, we saw dozens of boats of assorted sizes nosing into the dock as though to compare notes on where they had spent the night.

Now nothing hindered us and we steamed ahead, all passengers looking happy in spite of lost time. It reminded me of a very wonderful truth—though perhaps it was a poor picture of anything so wonderful—how inconsequential will seem the hardships of this life, how short a time after all the waiting will have been, when we hear the glad shout, "Christ returneth, hallelujah—the night of waiting and fog is over!"

With much love,

EDITH

May 1, 1950   Aboard the Scandinavian Express,
                                                Copenhagen to Basel

Dear Family:

This follows right on the heels of the last letter because it is an extra one. I found that I couldn't possibly get all that there was to tell about Finland and Norway into one letter—thus you will get some extra reading this month!

As I left you, we were steaming into Stockholm in the beautiful sunshine the day before Easter. Our boat finally came in 30 hours late—taking 42 hours for the 12-hour trip. It was about 4:00 P.M. when we stood by the rail watching the boat unload, and soon after we were inching along with the other passengers awaiting our turn to go through the passport control. Through customs, we started to look around for a porter to help us with our things, when we discovered the young professor, at whose home we had visited two weeks before, who had come to meet us. As he helped us into the taxi with our baggage he said that this was the fourth time he had tried to meet us. He first came when the boat was scheduled to arrive and had since tried to be there each time the reports came through that it "will not be long now." He said there had been much excitement about *Borevann* getting its bottom torn out, and they were thankful we were not on that boat. He took us to the "Christian Hostel" where they had arranged a room for us, and insisted that we use it for a few hours even though we could not stay overnight. There were 37 letters waiting for us as well as other mail, so it was nice to have a quiet place to sit and read it all. The mail occupied us until time to catch the train to Oslo. . . .

Mr. Svensen of the Free Evangelical Lutheran Church was waiting at the steps of the train as we stepped down. This fine Christian businessman is one of the leading elders and is also head of the Sunday School committee for their whole denomination. His kindly smile and firm handshake welcomed us to Norway quite as much as his "Velcome." . . . This Easter morning Fran was to preach in the East Church. The square auditorium with a balcony around three sides was well filled—I should guess about 500 people. . . . In Finland, Sweden, and Norway the church platforms are built with some shallow steps at the back and the choir comes up to the front when it is time to sing and fills up these steps. The director stands with his back to the pulpit. In Norway the choir sings unaccompanied usually, while in Finland most of the choir members also play the guitar or another stringed instrument *while* they are singing. . . . It was a joy to Fran to be preaching on Easter in such a splendid Bible-believing church. After the service we drove out into the suburbs with the Svensens to their home. The road took us up, up, up above the city where we could see the fjord stretching out below—with islands and ships in it, bordered by rocks and pine trees. . . .

The folks in the car were reminiscing over the years as they remembered that just *ten years ago that day*—April 9, 1940—they had awakened to find that the Germans were entering Norway. As we looked through the trees, over the rocky gardens, down to the fjord below at the shining waters, they said, "The warships entered right through there. One of them was attacked by our soldiers from a fort, over there, and it was sunk—taking down with it 2,000 Germans including the officers who were going to rule Norway. That hindered their progress enough for our King to make his plans and escape." They shook their heads as they remembered it vividly—the planes roaring overhead, the boats filling their harbors, and the occupation that followed for five years. Some of their ministers had been imprisoned in Norway, others sent to concentration camps, or work camps in Germany. Friends had been killed or had died because of severe changes in living conditions. In the north of Norway many whole towns were burned to the ground, not a single building left standing. The Germans did this as they left the north, thinking the Russians were coming and determined to leave nothing standing for them. In these burned-down towns the Free Church lost some church buildings, a school, and an old folks' home. These they are now in the process of rebuilding. The people in these sections were all evacuated before the buildings were set on fire. . . .

That day I typed until it was time to take the afternoon train for Halden. As we rode farther south Mr. Svensen pointed out the historic spots to us and the foamy white waterfalls which make electricity so cheap in Norway. Wood is also one of Norway's chief resources—and we passed many pulp and paper mills. Halden is a small town built at the foot of a hill upon which an old fortress sits, dominating the town even though it now stands empty and idle. This fortress is full of history and has figured largely in the various wars the Norwegians have fought against the Swedes. The last time it was of practical use was in 1905, when it was re-fortified at the time the Norwegians separated from Sweden. The fort has never been taken during the history of Norway, until during the last war the Germans walked into Norway and used this fort for a garrison. . . .

Sunday the white frame church was crowded for the morning service, at which Fran preached, and the Sunday School, to which I spoke, had about 210 children in it. European Sunday Schools have only children under 14 in them—so these were all children. Fran took a picture of the children afterwards which should be full of color as almost 75 percent of them had either red jackets or caps on. Red seems to be the favorite color! After Sunday School the pastor's little blond-haired, five-year-old daughter came up and put her hand in mine and led us to her home! There we had dinner—but the conversation had to be translated in both directions through Mr. Svensen, as none of the others spoke English. Churches in several nearby towns had been invited to the late-afternoon Children for Christ meeting so the building was crowded with a wing opened up for the overflow, and the balcony filled. When it came my turn to speak they found that the flannelboard and blackboard could not be seen by most of the people—and so someone brightly put it up on a table—there that's fine, except that I can't even reach the bottom of the board! Someone else helpfully handed up a straight chair and so with the audience waiting expectantly—there was only thing to do—go ahead and do the drawing, give the flannelboard story, etc., and speak, all while standing on a chair. That should be included in a public speaking course! At first I was constantly fearful that I might step off into space, but I got through without mishap. The people seemed most receptive, but had no time to shake hands as Mr. Svensen rushed us off to get a ride with a member who was driving to Moss after the service.

We drove straight into the sunset, which lingers so long in these north countries as the summer approaches. The far north of Norway has no night in the summer—and around Oslo there is only about an hour of dark. The longest day of the year is celebrated by everyone with night picnics on the hills and the building of huge bonfires. "You ought to be here in May and June," everyone said. The most interesting thing we passed on the drive was a large circle of tall, pointed rocks—"That is a council circle from before Christian times." Such centuries ago—if only the stones could speak, what a story they could tell. From Moss we took the train to Oslo—and finally a taxi to Sandvika, arriving at midnight, tired and glad to get back to our temporary home. However, there was to be no time for rest! . . .

The Norwegians say thank you for more things than you can imagine. After you have completed a meal you turn to first the hostess and then the host and say, "Takk for maten" (thanks for the meal); when you have been any length of time with a person you say when leaving him, "Takk for i dag" (thanks for the day). A pastor always says, "Takk for i dag" to the congregation when the last hymn is finished and they are ready to go out the church door. He also says, "Takk for kollektion" (thanks for the collection). The first time you see a person after spending an evening with him or an afternoon the previous day, you say, "Takk for i går" (thanks for yesterday)—and after a few days or even weeks you say, upon meeting a friend, "Takk for sist" (thanks for the last time I saw you!). We had lots of fun learning these various "takks" and trying to say them at the proper time. "Tusen takk" (thousand thanks) or "mange takk" (many thanks) is the way you say thank you for other things. On the other hand, they never use a title in speaking to or of a person—not even Mr. or Mrs. very often, they just say Jonson or Engeset or Svensen. Politeness differs so in different countries. . . .

We had so much to do in Norway that we stayed until Tuesday the 25th and if we had had time we could have spent several months there. As we sailed off down the fjord there were 12 people waving goodbye to us—Pastor Engeset, Miss Brynhildsen, Mr. Svensen, and others— "Come back soon—you are welcome in all of our churches." "Takk for alt." In spite of a pouring rain they stood there waving their hats and handkerchiefs until the grey mist blotted them out. The boat from Oslo to Copenhagen is more than twice as big as the boats from Stockholm to Åbo and is very modern with small, but comfortable, cabins. It was too bad it was raining, as otherwise it would have been a beautiful trip. Eight o'clock in the morning found us dressed and on deck watching the boat nose into the dock at Copenhagen. Our hotel was only a short walk from the boat, so after going through customs, and arranging for a porter to bring our baggage on a pushcart, we walked up through the square on which the king's palace and other government buildings face. The guards with their two-foot-high black fur hats and their colorful uniforms were pacing up and down on the four sides of the square. Usually guards look so stiff and wooden, but these merry-faced guards looked like little boys hugely enjoying a parade! Later one day we saw them changing guards and as they mumbled whatever it is they say as they change places—they smiled as though it were a game! . . .

One of the things Fran enjoyed most on this trip was the opportunity to talk to leading conservative theologians in Finland, Norway, and Sweden—and to find that he has understood Barthianism exactly as they have. Men in each of these three countries have a different approach to the problem of Barthianism and the related theologies in their Universities, which gave Fran a wonderful opportunity to add to his knowledge. He was pleased to find that these men expressed strong appreciation for that which he has worked out for himself in this field. . . .

When we boarded the train for Basel we had no "space" for our 36-hour trip—but again in finishing our trip—as in beginning it—the Lord had prepared a place, and we found a compartment had been vacated in Copenhagen—hence we had quiet and room enough to work. We had left Norway before spring had arrived, but as we rode south through Denmark, back over the Isle of Fyn, all the brown had been covered with a coat of varying shades of green. The blossoming trees in Germany on the first of May looked like giant bridal bouquets spread out in methodical rows on green velvet. As the train passed through the German woods it went so slowly that we felt as though we were having an afternoon walk in the woods—there was a group of German children playing tag—and another playing ring-around-a-rosy—children and neat little spring gardens—flowers and tender green lettuce—and ugly war clouds threatening the world! As long as the way remains open, surely we should do all we can to reach the children of the world with the message they should hear—that of eternal salvation and joy in Christ.

Now I will leave you, with the journey away from Switzerland over. Thank you for your gifts and prayers which have made it all possible and for your thoughtfulness in writing to the children.

Much love,

EDITH

May, June, Middle of July, 1950   Dachau, Munich, Germany

Dearest Family:

As we crossed the river into Basel we found ourselves full of excitement to be once more approaching home. The train slid along the tracks bordering Lake Neuchâtel. The perfectly clear day gave us a wonderful view of the Alps, the sail-dotted lake, and the beautiful gardens. We had passed from the earliest signs of spring in Norway to the advanced flower gardens of Switzerland in just two days or so—the speediest spring I've ever experienced. We opened our window that we might see better and breathe the freshness of the air, and assured each other that there isn't anything else quite like Switzerland! We longed to go straight through to Champéry that same evening, but because of business stayed in Lausanne overnight. We had talked with Madame Andre on the phone and so knew that Debby had been sick in bed with a bad cold, but when we saw two little girls, identical straw hats tied under their chins, racing to meet us, we scarcely recognized Debby. Her face looked so white and her hair was arranged quite differently. Soon after a little pair of arms had given us a strangling welcome hug, she was perched on her Daddy's shoulders hugging the new Teddy Bear and we were hurrying down to the station with Ninette leading the way and Madame Andre telling me all about Debby's illness.

It seems that when she came down from the mountains her old bronchial trouble flared up again. However, the Andres' doctor lives in the same apartment house and had come in daily to keep a close check on both girls as Ninette was in bed in the same room with a cold. The children had evidently had quite a good time amusing each other, but

Debby had not been without homesick moments. After we got home she was unnaturally quiet for several days, but we later found that she had forgotten quite a bit of her English after speaking nothing but French for seven weeks. It didn't take long for the English to come back and while we were away all three girls have greatly improved in their French.

Waiting for us at the Champéry Station were two beaming jumping-jacks with "le petit char" (the little cart) and Vic waiting behind them. Unlike Debby, Susan and Priscilla were not troubled by silence! Both of them tried to talk at once and continuously all the way home and for the next few days! Everything that had happened in the seven weeks—both happy and sad—came tumbling out. Life at Home Eden was described minutely, with imitations of the various teachers and the mothers of the children who had come to visit. Hence amid much hilarity we were soon caught up on the happenings of the seven weeks. The house was a bower of daffodils as a surprise for us. The girls had picked them in the fields and had filled every vase and pitcher in the house. Although mail had followed us around through the seven weeks, there was much piled up on the desk to greet us! Not only mail from many other parts of the world, but a goodly amount from the four countries where we had just been. Most of it was thanking us for having come and giving orders for Children for Christ material—but among them was the letter from Bishop Bergrav which you have probably read in the *Beacon*! It is difficult to "get going" immediately after you return from such a trip—in fact you feel more like relaxing. Added to this lazy feeling we were slowed up by the fact that all three girls came down with a touch of grippe which seemed to be epidemic in the village, perhaps caused by the cold rainy weather. Fran had brought back a bad cold with him from Norway and it didn't improve for over a week. With all this we pushed ahead very slowly it seemed, gradually picking up speed as the days progressed. Our office became a packing room as I struggled to pack the various sizes and shapes of Children for Christ material into neat packages for Norway, Finland, and Sweden. The discouraging moment came when Fran dragged back the little cart from the Post Office—still half full of packages! These were being returned to me for repacking—since they did not meet the postal specifications!

One of the excitements of our homecoming was the opening of a seed order which had arrived from Burpee's Seed Company, sent by a thoughtful missionary society. What a thrill it was to plant radishes, lettuce, peas, and especially the things we cannot buy here such as broccoli, sweet corn, lima beans, etc. Little by little through the month of May we planted row upon row in the garden which has been dug up in our front yard and in the little plot we rented across the road. There seem to be more stones than dirt in the garden; in spite of that the little green shoots came popping up, filling us once more with the wonder of God's creation, each thing bringing forth after its own kind. How many of these things will actually mature and "bring forth fruit" at this altitude, amid the stones and in spite of the bugs, I will report at a later date!

One Sunday afternoon as Fran, Debby, and I were walking on a winding, climbing little path that leads through the woods and on up to chalets above us, we stopped to speak to our "milk lady" who invited us in to see two small kids she was sending to the butcher the next morning. The meat of a very young kid is considered better than lamb in these parts. The boy kid was rambunctious, but the little girl kid bleated so sweetly and then cuddled down in our arms so trustingly that we hated to think of her being anyone's dinner that week! A family confab resulted in a vote to waylay the procession to the butcher and to add a kid to our family for a time. Tuesday found us with a big box in our cellar and a pure white kid living in it.

My passport, having been issued two years before, needed renewing before May 28th. Since it is required that you come in person, it meant my going to the American consulate in Geneva. Fran's was renewed last year so is all right until next spring. Priscilla needed new shoes badly so it was decided that she should go with me. It was the first time she had been out of Champéry for seven months and guess what was the most amazing thing to her as we got down into the valley? The *sky!* "Oh, mother, look how much *sky* there is, I had forgotten the sky could be so big." We have such a small ceiling of sky above us here. . . .

Finally before we left for France we did get to the place where we could put other things aside and go ahead on the lessons. We chose the guest room on the third floor as a workshop. There we could spread out the flannelgraph pictures on the beds, put up our board, open up our Bibles, and get to work. We do the writing together, you know. After first individually studying, I sit at the typewriter and Fran dictates—but before he has gone very far, I suggest a change in a sentence or give an idea for the next phrase or paragraph. And so we go on, first one and then the other, until we are both satisfied with the results. We pray very much that the Lord will make these lessons helpful to children of many nations and backgrounds. We write them keeping in mind the fact that they are to be used by people of different Bible-believing denominations in many parts of the world and it is our attempt to make them not American or French, but such that will be easily adapted to any country. Do pray for us in this particular work. The first 12 lessons are finished. They have already been translated into Norwegian, Finnish, French, and Dutch. Pray that we may be able to do the next 12 or 14 and have them ready by early fall.

We resumed the services in the French chapel as we returned. Each Sunday brought a few visitors. However we wondered what we would do when summer came, because French services are held there in the summer, and Church of England services have always been held for English visitors in a tiny brown wooden chapel built for this purpose behind the Roman Catholic School. Will we be able to have our services in the height of the summer season? The time passed swiftly by and it scarcely seemed possible that we had been home six weeks and that the time had come to leave again.

Each of the girls had had a birthday. Debby was five on the very next day after our arrival. It took her several days to get used to being five, and in spite of a birthday cake and family party marking the occasion she kept saying "four" when asked how old she was. "I don't look any older than I was when I was four," she remarked after gazing in the mirror! Susan became nine a few weeks later and she almost burst with excitement. "All my life I have been waiting to be nine. When you are nine you aren't really little any longer." We had to sing "Happy Birthday" many times to mark the importance of this tremendous milestone! Ninette was with us to help celebrate and so our happy birthday song had to be sung in French too. Susan cut the chocolate cake decorated with yellow roses pressed into shape between mother's well-washed fingers, but her celebrating spirit did not end with the last crumb of the cake—for days she kept saying with excitement, "Just think, I'm nine now." Mary N. had breezed in three days before our going to France and said she would love to stay with Susan and Priscilla and the goat in our absence. It would only be four days and Debby was to visit Madame Turrian. Susan and Priscilla were delighted at the prospect. Mary couldn't have chosen a busier and more hectic time to be with us. Between typing, last-minute "musts," packing, gardening, etc., some preparations also had to be made for our trip to Germany, which would so soon follow. Yet in the midst of all this came Priscilla's birthday! She was thirteen on the 18th—but since we had to leave the 18th, we celebrated the day before with a birthday dinner complete with cake—so you can imagine the rush of that day—with the baking sandwiched in between packing, mending, and ironing. . . .

After our return from France, we had the evening to get caught up on reading the mail, to dash off a few imperative business notes, and to begin sorting out Bible School material. What a day the next one was! Fran, Mary, and the children worked on getting the garden weeded and cultivated in order to leave it in good condition for the following two weeks, while I sorted, ironed, mended, and packed for the family. We were to leave at six o'clock the next morning and it seemed impossible to get everything done in that one day. Ten o'clock at night found us with the children bathed, hair washed, clothes laid out ready to jump into, and their clothes packed, but with all the Bible School things yet to pack. When you have to carry everything with you, from report cards and stars to study books and flannelgraph stories, it takes a good bit of maneuvering, and that takes time. There wasn't much time spent in bed. By five-thirty the household was awake again. Soon the procession started down the street. All three girls had their rucksacks on their backs. (We bought those in Norway and Denmark—blue, green, and red in varying sizes according to age.) These held the rolls, hardboiled eggs, etc., for

A rare picture Fran took of the girls in Zürich as we traveled.

our food along the way, as well as things they had individually stuck in to amuse themselves on the train. There were altogether 17 pieces of baggage to be accounted for at each change! It was a hot day and everyone seemed to be going to Zürich so that as we changed at Lausanne we were not able to find seats together in third class. However, Swiss trains are always pleasant enough. At Zürich we took a hurried walk for the girls, and my first look at this city, thereby nearly missing our train.

As we puffed into one of the many second-class coaches (it is a very long train and crowded, the travel agency had advised second class through Germany with all our baggage), we began trying to fit all our luggage in around those of the other occupant of the compartment, which had five reservation tickets fluttering on the backs of the seats. "Hum, too bad Kuoni didn't reserve seats for us." Inspecting the tickets I discovered that they *were* reserved by Kuoni—two whole and three half tickets—why, they *are ours*—"Hey Fran, look at this." Fran said he knew all the time we were supposed to have reservations but he thought it was hopeless to try to find them at that late moment. And so we moved, the extra space making the effort worthwhile. Finally as we settled down for the long afternoon, we began to look at the countryside. This is a portion of Switzerland we had not seen before. As we rounded the end of Lake Constance we found ourselves stopped for passport control. Is this the border of Germany? No, surprise, it is a little corner of Austria. We hadn't realized we would be in Austria. This beautiful lake and mountain region is certainly a good ad for Austria. After a few miles we were out again and went through German customs, passport control, and now we are in Southern Germany or Bavaria. Lush-looking, green, rolling hills with rich farms and well-painted farm houses; villages of bright white houses, red roofs, and gay window boxes interspersed with thick, tall, quiet pine forests. Could war ever have raged here? It looks too peaceful and prosperous. It is dark as we pull into the Munich station so the contrast of the city and the beautiful farm lands is saved until a later time. Chaplain Myers is on the platform to meet us and to help us out to the waiting Army Staff car with our things. Debby has been fast asleep for some time so is hard to awaken. Susan had been rudely awakened about an hour before when a trainman playfully flashed his lantern into her face! Now we and our baggage are stuffed into the car and we are driving through the city and on out through a bit of country to Dachau. American guards stand at the gates of this huge section and pass on the credentials of those entering. How many thousands passed only *one* way through these same gates just four or five years ago! . . .

We are welcomed by the whole family and shown our rooms in this Army Officer's house where we are to live with the Myerses during the Bible school time. Chaplain Myers and his family have been here just one year. . . .

We divided the school into five classes—threes and fours, fives, sixes and sevens, eights and nines, and tens or older. To plunge right in to such a school with such a very short time (we think a two-week school is much too short), and with no time to find teachers, was a seemingly impossible hurdle at first. . . . "Afraid you'll never hold these children without handwork" was what we heard, but we held an average of forty and the children weren't *made* to come. The only class that fluctuated at all was the three-and four-year-old group and most of them were absent for illness. One fell off her little chair and broke her collarbone—right in Bible School! We had the hottest weather on record, but *still* they came! Before the two weeks were up each had said that he or she wanted to be sure they had been born again, and said he or she believed on the Lord Jesus. My class was so interested in hearing about Heaven and about the time when the Lord would come that as a treat for good drilling I would turn to Revelation and explain a bit each day. . . . Then on Friday night came the closing night and the children carried home invitations clutched in their hot hands. All afternoon we had had thundershowers, would this ruin the evening? The little chapel, situated inside the stockade, reached by crossing over a stream of water that had been electrified during the war to keep people in the concentration camp, had been built by prisoners during the war out of scraps of wood and material. Music floating out of its open windows reached the ears of American soldiers held in the stockade prison for some misdemeanor, and on the side reached into the D.P.* camp, from which we were separated by only a high barbed-wire fence. Here hundreds of D.P.'s live in tiny two-room apartments (if such a name can be applied to these drab wooden shacks)

*Displaced Persons

which during the war were occupied by thousands of the Dachau Concentration Camp inhabitants.

This was that Friday night. Officers of various ranks, wives and little tots, and proud students of the Bible School with their Bibles under their arms appeared, and even some G.I.'s came out of curiosity. "We haven't had this many people in this chapel since Christmas," the chaplain exclaimed excitedly. As well as people from this Post there were a few visitors from other posts who had come to see what kind of a Bible School this had been. . . . Two weeks—none of the children in Bible School previously—yet what a testimony it was to the worthwhileness of Bible School. The parents were impressed, "flabbergasted" would be a better word, with what their children had learned in just nine short mornings. The Air Force Major got up at the end and asked for an offering to pay for the materials. In this he spoke of the fact that he imagined that many parents and friends had tonight realized how far short they had fallen in teaching their children the things they should know—"If this much can be taught our children in nine days of school—we who have had them in our homes all our lives ought to be ashamed of the little we have taught them—most of us leave them with German maids all day long and never even take them to church on Sunday. . . ."

I could spend pages on Munich itself and the Concentration Camp. Let me try to squeeze it into a small space. We went to the P.X. one afternoon in the center of Munich. Each block of driving is a fresh shock to one who is new to it. People living here get hardened. One whole block will be nothing but rubble—one wall standing, a radiator hanging on at about the third story but the rest of the building merely an enormous pile of brick and dirt. Bodies have never been dug out of places like this. There are too many such places; it is too discouraging. Here are four walls and the inside all gone, but no—out of that broken and jagged window a wash is blowing—one room must still be occupied. On we go—now we are in the center. I can't go inside—no P.X. card—I wait for the Myerses. What is there for my eyes to see? There are the remains of an enormous department store, fancy trimming still remains on the front wall, mounds of dirt, bricks, twisted iron, and blades of grass are what you see through the windows. One small place has been cleaned out on one side and there are plate-glass windows, orange awnings keeping the sun from fading the furniture on display. How fantastic this seems—this one tiny dug-out portion of the bombed-out store. There is a square with a broken statue and useless fountain in the middle. It is surrounded by ornamental street lamps, the black metal twisted in ugliness like broken scenery for Christmas train sets; almost unbelievably the lamp shades are still on some of them with twisted wires and filaments sticking out at all angles. What is man? Is he "essentially good"—as the novelists tell us? Is he getting better and better? Five years since the war—yet this destruction. And what of the future? What misery it would be if our only hope was in mankind!!

Now let's jump away from the center of Munich to the center of the old Concentration Camp at Dachau. Here we approach the old Crematory. We walk up a path where many hopeless feet have trod. This was the last walk that over 250,000 people took before their death. Here the men, women, and children who were Jews or political prisoners were killed for an "offense" or for being too ill or old to work. We stop before a huge mound covered with grass now, and bordered with flowers; the sign tells us that the ashes of "thousands" are in this place. And there stands the same grey wall where a multitude were shot to death and there, the little stone says, "Here lie many thousands." On a bit farther as we walk on the gravel walk and the soft breeze flutters the leaves, we come to a tree with a heavy branch that looks just fine for a child's swing. Here, the sign informs us, many were hanged. A bleeding-heart plant is growing under the tree now. We see the portion, closed in by walls, upon which are built dog kennels—at one end is a building with hole-like windows. Here vicious dogs were kept and let out to devour certain prisoners before the eyes of their relatives—to "teach them a lesson." There are some empty buildings with strange cement tubs in them but we have no guide to explain them—spider webs and dust cover the strangely gay wallpaper.

Now we enter the biggest building. Here a sunken-eyed man is ready to explain in halting English. He is a Polish survivor of this very camp of Dachau. His body must have been strong as he continued in hard work through the entire five years of his stay. "I was just like a skeleton when the Americans came in to free us. I don't go back to Poland—I am no Communist." He shows us the cement corridors through which people walked. Their clothes were sprayed with disinfectant, so the clothes could be used again by the living. Then he took us to the heavy iron doors marked "Showers" (in German, of course). Here people were disrobed, given a cake of soap and towel, and told to go in to take a mass shower. We stepped inside this "shower room"—it had no windows—no lights—only a tiny opening where a guard could peer in. Cement walls, cement ceiling with spray attachments on it— and then when they were all inside and the doors were bolted—the spray was turned on—the spray of gas! So we were inside the famous gas chamber of Dachau. The time charts are still on the doors telling just how long it should take! Now we go into the furnace room. Four or five big furnaces have openings just large enough for the steel stretchers which still remain there, stretchers upon which the bodies were put before they were shoved into the white-hot fire, murdered bodies of those too weak to work any longer and therefore useless. There are some dried-up wreaths which were placed upon these furnaces a few weeks before by a group of survivors who came to celebrate the fifth anniversary of their liberation.

"Yes, five years ago we were liberated," says the Polish guide as he toys with a torture rack. "Five years ago—our civilized university men—inventors—scientists—men of an advanced civilization—what do we find?" "The heart is deceitful above all things and desperately wicked, who can know it?"* Jeremiah said that before Cancer Research was dreamed of, before airplanes and air conditioning, television and refrigerators were ever considered—but is it true yet? Is man essentially good? If he is, would there be a Dachau—not only in our lifetime but during our children's lifetime? As I stood there surrounded by the horror of so recent past, watching an old woman tend the bleeding hearts over the mounds of ashes, the only thing that gave my heart any peace was the though of the Lord Jesus Christ who died that we might have our desperately wicked hearts washed clean, who gave us His righteousness that we might stand before God clothed not in our filthy rags but in His Goodness—and the remembrance that it was for anyone who would take Him as Savior that He died. There is the only hope for mankind—the only hope we can give to the hopeless. And the future? What can we promise our children as we return from a place like that and the radios are all on at the Post blaring forth the news of war in Korea and the Air Force in Munich is immediately put on a six-hour alert—what comfort can we honestly give them? It is only the comfort with which the Lord told us to comfort one another. He is coming again, this very same Jesus is coming again. When we shall see Him we shall be like Him for we shall see Him as He is. With Him we shall be forever happy—there will be no more death, no more crying, no more wars—one day all things will be perfect for the children of God. And until that happy day? If we are His, He will care for us and all things will work together for our good. The day of Christ's return seems near and how we long for Him to come before another Dachau—but until He comes, are we making use of the short time we may have among those with whom the Lord gives us opportunity? It is important that people know of the one way, the one door to heaven through belief on Jesus.

The evening meetings ended on Sunday night, the 9th of July. One young Army wife from Atlanta, Georgia, sobbed her thanks for the message as she came out. "I came over from another Post when Mrs. Myers invited me—and I'm so glad I came. We don't live right, over here, and we need messages like that but we don't get them." She promised to begin family prayers, as I talked with her afterwards, to grow in the Lord through feeding on His Word and to come over to hear Captain Myers sometimes. The next morning at six A.M. found us on our way out of Dachau going to the station in a Staff car. The trip as far as Zürich was strenuous in that we had both a woman technician from Munich and an American Roman Catholic Priest to talk to. We were stopped at the border because of a carton of groceries which Mr. Myers had helped us

*Jeremiah 17:9.

get at Munich, things we can't find in Switzerland. Since the train was about to depart before they had figured out the duty on these things, we had to leave the package behind and were told we must pick it up in Lausanne. Because of this and other things I needed to tend to in Lausanne, I stayed at Madame Turrian's overnight while the rest of the family went on up to Champéry. The groceries took a couple of hours the next day: to find just where they were, to go through customs with them, etc. Such red tape! Fortunately the man who had to figure out the customs duty was a friend of Madame Turrian's and was very kind to me, but I did find out how duty is figured. It is *always* by *weight* under certain classifications—candy so much a pound, meat so much, cookies with sugar so much, and crackers without sugar so much. What you have paid doesn't mean a thing but any information as to what is actually inside the packages helps them to classify it. Leather shoes so much a pound, cotton clothing so much, etc. Everything is treated in the same way—for Switzerland that is, of course. . . .

Now to tell you about the chapel services here. Fran started out last Saturday (the 15th) to find the French pastor to find out what hour we could have for our service. On his way down the village street he was stopped by our organist, who said, "They are waiting for you to begin the English services—the English chaplain went home." What is this? I joined Fran after that and we went together to the pension where the English chaplain has lived each summer for years. The little white-haired lady informed us that there are so many Italians and so few English here this year that the chaplain of the Anglican Church got discouraged and left. "He told me to send for him if more English people arrive and he will return, but you know, I *won't* send for him at all. Why should I, when we have an English-speaking pastor right in our village?" "Who owns the little wooden English Church building?" "Oh, the town—it was built by the hotels for the benefit of the tourists—the English Church just sends a Chaplain each summer." We found that in the Temple Protestant, where we have our winter services, the French services are held at ten o'clock and Sunday School at 11 A.M. making afternoon the only possible time for us there—so it was decided that once more the Lord had done a marvelous thing for us and had arranged for no interruption to our services. We are now having Sunday School at 10 A.M., Church services at 11 A.M. and at 6 P.M. The keys are in our possession, the building is ours for the summer, and there is no other service we are "rivaling"—hence the town hotelkeepers feel we are doing them a service!! Notices are up all over—and we have been thanked for taking over when the Englishman gave up! We feel the Lord continues to show us that it was He who led us to Champéry.

Oh yes—the garden. We have had two meals of delicious sweet peas; one of tiny beets; three of cabbage; and two of cauliflower. Such excitement! The string beans should be long enough to pick soon, the squash is in flower, the corn is tasseling, and I even have hopes for the lima beans—though the bugs tried to turn them into lace instead of plants. We expect to share our garden with missionaries visiting from Arabia and Africa who will appreciate the taste treats as much as we ourselves. We are gaining respect from villagers who scoffed at the idea of planting corn up here. They actually expect us to get corn from it now—though they are puzzled as to how we will eat it. "Will you grind it up and make cornmeal for porridge?" the *Douane* (the border patrol man) asked us quite seriously. "No we eat it fresh with salt and butter, like you eat peas." "Tiens, tiens"—"Hold, hold" or "Can you imagine that?" as we would say. Wonders never cease! I am determined to see that he tastes corn.

In spite of the work connected with the Congress and the influx of company from the four corners of the earth, the next weeks must also see some long hours of work on the Luke lessons. Please pray for us in this as it is so hard to find consecutive hours to do creative work when there are so many details to attend to. Yet in some ways these lessons are the most important part of our work at present.

Much love,

EDITH

August, September, October, 1950   Champéry, Switzerland

Dearest Family:

Hope, based on our own good intentions, is not always fulfilled! Remember (if you can remember that far back) that as I ended my last letter I hoped it would be the last time that there would be a long lapse between letters! That was an honest hope but you see its basis was not sure. What a sure hope the Lord gives us when He tells us in His infallible Word that we may look forward to His coming again, that we may know He is preparing a place for us, and that we will spend all eternity with Him there, if we have believed in Jesus as our Savior. How wonderful it is that as we give others the promises in His Word, the hope in His Word, that we need not add any "ifs" such as the kind of physical "ifs" which bind our own desires—"If I have time," "If I am not ill," "If no accident befalls me."

I left you just on the eve of the arrival of three women delegates to the conference As the rain poured down the next day, the chief interest of our missionaries from Africa was not that the mountains had been blotted out, but that a regular waterfall was coming down from our roof just outside the dining room windows, and we had no tank to catch it in! "Look at all that good water going to waste." And they continued to be astonished at the plenteousness of water for bathing, for washing dishes, for watering the garden. . . .

We heard all sorts of things about India, Arabia, and Africa—of who has the largest scorpions, of mosquito nettings and malaria attacks. We were transported to Africa one night as we were shown the Kodachrome slides. How much more vivid becomes their need for more water tanks as we see the one lone tank which catches the water as it cascades down the parched rock during the infrequent rains. We hope that when they go back there will be enough tanks to catch all the overflow and hold it for use during the long dry seasons. Isn't it wonderful that the One Who says, "I will give you of the water of life freely," does not indicate any special seasons—the water of life is always there for those who will come and drink.

We tore ourselves away from this fascinating fellowship to get down to a division of labor. Edna Barter became schoolteacher and supervised our three girls in their English summer schoolwork. We try to keep them in touch with the American schoolwork by having them go over all the books each year during vacations or sick-in-bed times. They do the regular French Swiss studies in their schools here, so this is "extra" and sometimes not much appreciated! Miss Barter added swimming and diving lessons to the curriculum and the girls tore down the hill to the swimming pool with great enthusiasm each clear day, coming back to dinner a bit late with bedraggled wet hair and great stories of the progress made. . . .

The first of August is like our American Fourth of July—or I should say like the old-fashioned Fourths we have heard so much about. The celebration of this national holiday was most interesting in a small mountain village. As the darkness finally enveloped the mountains and village alike, the people thronged the paths as they moved toward the already crowded village street. The children made spots of light along the paths as they swished sparklers in energetic circles in front of them. The parade formed here on the steep side path which was full of people with their various shaped lanterns which were being carefully lighted. We saw that the banker and the butcher's daughter and other neighbors were setting off fireworks which sprayed right over the moving crowd. All of a sudden the band burst forth and people stepped back to make way for the parade. The band leader came, right back of the town idiot who was carrying the flag. And the band leader?—he was the enormously fat butcher who spends all his time in a cafe drinking, in between customers. He smiled and nodded at us, bobbing the tassel on his elaborate headdress. The rest of the parade consisted of schoolchildren and townspeople all carrying candle-lit lanterns which bobbed up and down precariously close together. We fell in behind the parade to follow it to the football field where the patriotic speech was made. It was fantastic to be moving with a crowd which was setting off fireworks as it went, but it seemed incredible to

Priscilla was a great help to her dad at the International Council of Christian Churches conference in Geneva.

see friends from America mixed in with all the others. . . .

The evening church service is at six o'clock and we had invited people to come for tea before church. Again we had to pinch ourselves to make sure it was real. Over 25 people who are today thousands of miles apart again met for tea in Chalet des Frênes! Transportation in our day melts away the great distances of the world.

The next day the chalet was practically empty—that is, only Edna B. and Muriel H. had stayed while all the rest left for Geneva. However, it was no day in which to sink into a chair and take a deep breath. Washing, ironing, packing had to be done to prepare myself and the children for Geneva, and then there was that sewing!! Muriel felt quite ill after the two sleepless nights caused by long delays on the plane trip and so she spent most of the day in bed. That meant there was no entertainment, hikes, or picnics, or even cooking! A solid day and almost a solid night of working brought us to the moment of departure a bit the worse for wear. The little cart made several trips to the station that day, but in spite of the rush we missed the early train and had to wait for a later one—a breathing spell in which to walk slowly up the street and get a bit to eat. Vic went with us for her first trip in 20 years! She has only been in a big city once—and that was also Geneva—20 years ago. Such excitement! Her main impression was the *noise* both on the train and in the city.

Here we were—actually at the Congress of the I.C.C.C.! We tumbled out of the taxi with children, bags, etc., and immediately began to meet old friends—"Hello, Stan Allen" (California), and, "How are you, Mr. Straub?" (Missouri)—and so it continued throughout not only that evening but the ten days to follow. . . .

Morning—and the first session of the Congress was about to begin in a short time. Everyone hurried to get the bus going in the direction of the Grand Theatre. . . . I had to spend hours behind a table of Children for Christ material—answering questions. The questions poured in and I gradually felt like a phonograph record! "Is this a Sunday School work?"—"What is the difference between this and Child Evangelism?"—"Will you explain the seven points of your program that the poster tells about?"—"Please explain this sketch on the blackboard—are those houses meant to represent different parts of the world?"—"Do you send out missionaries? We would like one in Brazil to help us get started."—"Is your material translated into our language?" . . . And in between these came requests from people I had to refuse—"We want to buy some of your material for our Sunday School." . . . Then there were little personal questions from those troubled and confused by being in a foreign land. "Do you happen to have pills for indigestion, or can you tell me where to buy something that will help?"—"What bus should I take to get back to the hotel?"—"Where can I get my watch repaired?"—"Do you know of a drug store where they speak English?"—"Where could we go for a sightseeing trip before that first plane leaves?"—"Please tell me what all these pieces of money are worth."

Meantime, where was the rest of the family? Well, Fran was deeply engrossed in taking the Minutes of the meetings during all the business sessions since has was Recording Secretary for the Conference. That meant sitting on the platform and writing away through it all. . . . As for the children? Someone overheard Susan seriously complaining the second day, "I think I should be allowed to stay for the whole thing. Why, I'm getting so much out of it. This morning I listened to it all, every word of it—all in Portuguese!" . . . The little portable boxes with earphones were like a radio, and you could tune in on the meeting in French, Spanish, Dutch, and Portuguese. Priscilla thought it was a fine thing to be able to help out with translation and errands at the Information Desk and listen to the meetings at the same time. She also helped many hours in the Press Room and Mrs. Belz (Iowa) taught her how to put in the stencils and run the mimeograph machine. As for Deborah, she went independently into the meetings, often sitting beside people she didn't even know, and usually listening to it all with her earphones tuned to French. Long after it was all over, we discovered that she had voted during one morning session, both by raising her hand and saying "aye" every time the Chairman called for a vote! . . .

Saturday morning there were no regular session of the Congress and Sunday there were to be the regular Worship Services. We had our own services to care for in Champéry and so we planned to be home for the weekend. . . . Before the last train was due that evening, Fran came wearily in. His train had made very poor connections and he was left with a three-hour wait at Aigle, so he decided to *walk* up the mountain, not realizing how many miles it was. Finally, however, he had found a ride up with a relative of one of the villagers. He ate a warmed-up dinner by the fireplace as he told us of the interview with Barth. One thing encouraged him in the interview—after working so hard on his paper to give at the Congress on the New Modernism, he found that the conversation with Barth only emphasized more clearly his findings and conclusions on Barthianism and that his paper would give a true picture of this school of thought. . . .

After the weekend we went back for the second lap of the Congress. Early in the week Fran's paper was given and that is one time I listened inside the auditorium, not because I hadn't heard it before, but I wanted to be praying *as* he was giving it—the wife's part. . . .

We were the last ones out of the building that night—Rudy Schmidt and Fran working on last-minute things—I packing up the Children for Christ materials after the last inquiry had been cared for. After we reached the hotel there was more packing to do and the next morning found us once more on the outgoing train. Fran and Dr. MacRae were on their way to Morges to speak to the leaders of a French Christian organization who were gathered there. Fran would be coming on to Champéry in the evening. All the baggage and materials, Dr. Laird Harris, Mr. and Mrs. Salmensaari and Mr. Salaronta from Finland, the three girls, and myself were to go straight up to Champéry. . . .

Laird Harris had to leave the next morning, but Edna Barter arrived to take his place. She had agreed to take a place on the last plane so that others who were particularly rushed could have her place on an earlier plane. It is lovely to be "on the way" between many missions fields and America: it means that Chalet des Frênes can be a sort of Missionary Rest Home! After the folks from Finland started on their way, we were ready for the next batch of company! (And incidentally if we had not had them here they would have seen none of Switzerland except Geneva because they didn't have the money to go sightseeing.) They carried a lunch that would satisfy their hunger for at least part of their long journey. (Not only did they not eat in the diners on the trains, but Kalerea sat up through two long nights on the train from here to Stockholm, and then again a third night on the boat on the Baltic, which meant he spent the night on one of those camp stools in the corridor—this is to let you know how *careful* some people were to cut down expenses paid by gifts from America.) [This is followed by two paragraphs listing the names of guests we entertained following the Congress.] . . .

Now a fatigue overtook us, and we felt inclined to obey the doctor's instructions and take a 10-day rest, away from everyone, even the children. Ten days of sunshine and repose, without needing to talk or even think! However, there was some tremendously pressing office work and we felt it must be done before we could leave. So the next week was spent in feverishly trying to get this important work out of the way so that we could leave with a good conscience. I also discovered that plums and tomatoes were cheap and did some more canning and jam-making in the evenings! Winter offers such a small variety of fruits and vegetables—and at such a high price—that I felt the need of capturing some of this food while it was still possible! Vic said she would stay with the girls while we were away. The weather was still nice, though cold, the garden still had plenty of corn, broccoli, carrots, and beets in it so that meals would be easy for her, and since the children had had such a fine summer they were anxious to have us take a vacation.

At last we were ready—no typewriter and suitcases of materials this time: just a few clothes, and for Fran a great backlog of reading material which he hoped to finish on the vacation. I was wishing we could add the lima bean plants to our luggage! The warm climate would have helped them!! . . .

The next ten days were truly a gift of the Lord to our tired bodies. It was past the "season" and so the hotel and beach were almost empty there in Alassio. We spent long hours in the warm sunshine—Fran reading his accumulation of papers, clippings, books, and religious periodicals, while I mostly sat with my eyes shut. The sea water was warm even this late in September and so salty one could lie floating as though one were in bed! We took some walks through the picturesque town with its clean stone streets, narrow between the yellow plaster buildings, the walls of which were alive with twittering canaries who sang to each other from their tiny cages hung outside on hooks near the windows; and we were impressed by the antiquity of the place as we walked up above the town one afternoon, following a road built in Caesar's time. . . .

After dinner one night (and by the way, meals always began with spaghetti or macaroni in some form) we lingered to talk with the woman who runs this hotel. We were the last of the guests, we and some German-Swiss folks also making use of "after-season" reduced rates, and she was closing the place for the winter as soon as we would leave. She gave us a vivid description of life during Mussolini's time, of the newspapers, radios, schools all saying the same thing—"How wonderful is Mussolini—Il Duce has great display of troops in Florence, in Rome, in Naples—a display of the tanks given to each place." Later they found out it was always the same troops, always the same tanks being carried around from place to place. She shrugged her shoulders, "How could we know? We had no other news except that which he want us to have." She told us how Communists try to frighten the workers into striking, how they promise them they shall live like kings when the Communist regime comes in. "The people are stupid, they believe them." Now it seems to be somewhat better—Communism is losing popularity. This young woman lost some of her family during the war; the hotel was ruined inside, but she worked tremendously hard to restore it enough to run, and now is supporting her aged father with the income.

We left Alassio several shades darker in color and feeling quite rested. The trip home was rather a letdown because not only were the Italian trains crowded as usual, but the first one was an hour late, causing us to miss our connection in Milan. That meant that we missed connections all along the line, and ended up reaching Monthey after the last train had gone up the mountain. So we took a room for the night with a cracked pitcher of cold water with which to remove the train dirt and called the girls to tell them we would be up in the morning.

As we reached home we began to make our plans for October, but the Lord had other plans. . . . October was for us a month of physical trouble and personal spiritual blessing. We had been looking forward to the coming of a new little one to love and enjoy and bring up for the Lord to use, but on October 4th the loss of that hope was a keen disappointment to us. That it is a part of His plan, we do not question; and we know His purpose for us is not only for a momentary reason but has bearing on our entire future closeness to Him and our service for Him. We could see the Lord's careful planning as the doctor arrived, from a territory that covers miles of mountain roads, just at the moment when he was most needed to save my life (according to his own judgment of the seriousness of my condition). The next few days in bed gave me much time for Bible reading and prayer, and as I grew anxious about the office work, the Lord taught me a new lesson. I have always had the feeling that if work piles up higher and higher, the thing to pray for is more strength to work longer hours and accomplish what needs to be done. That day "my God shall supply all your need" became vivid to me in a new way. If that need is money, strength, time—He can supply it but if the need is not to follow the usual pattern of your past life, if it is to supply someone else to take your place for awhile, or even forever, He can supply that too. I prayed that particular day that the Lord would, before the day ended, send some sign from both America and right here that would indicate that the office work could go on in spite of my being temporarily put aside. That afternoon in the mail the first answer came in a letter from Dr. Holdcroft in which he said that he felt we must have additional stenographic help. In the evening the second answer came in a telephone call from Madame Andre in Lausanne during which she offered Fran the help of her husband's secretary for a couple of days, if he would come to Lausanne early the next morning. What a load was lifted from our hearts as Fran was able to dictate for two days and dozens of letters were on their way within a week and all without my doing it. I had learned one new lesson!

When the doctor came he decided that he was not satisfied with my progress and ordered me to go to the hospital at the end of that week. So, at 8:00 A.M. on the 27th of October I found myself on the way to that pretty little hospital perched halfway down the mountain between here and Monthey. . . . Late in the afternoon of the following day the doctor stopped to see me; since my progress was good, he felt that it would be all right to take me home, that is if I promised to go right to bed and stay there through another couple of days. Fran was to leave for Rome the next day, so I was anxious to get home—in fact, it was necessary to be there with the children. . . .

Fran then went to Rome to observe the official defining of the dogma of the Assumption of Mary. It was a tiring trip—many hours of standing in crowds to be where he could take pictures and observe the whole thing. How his heart ached for all those thousands upon thousands of earnest, seeking pilgrims doing all they were supposed to do to gain an indulgence—when salvation is a free gift of God, if they only knew it. . . .

We have had some fine letters from Holland concerning Children for Christ. You know there was much interest during our time in Holland a year and a half ago; a committee was formed and translation work was begun, but the people were very slow to actually begin any classes. However, one young Art Critic* and his wife began a children's Home Class in their own home, and to their own amazement, the Lord wonderfully blessed this class. They have been using our Luke lessons which he is translating. Now we hear that to their own great astonishment the children have all returned this fall bringing new ones with them, so that the class which started with two now has over 16 in it. They tell us that four new classes will be started in Amsterdam, and one in Haarlem, and they speak of much interest in other places. They urge us to come again to Holland. We feel this is an answer to prayer. We also have constant letters from France as a result of our short trip there last spring. They also are hoping to start classes in three villages and have sent for the lessons and pictures. Other countries are also on our hearts, such as Spain, Portugal, Italy, etc.

Then we hear from the Army Camp in Dachau that an Empire Builders work has started there—and we pray for those boys and girls with whom we worked this summer. So, we stand on the brink of the winter with much encouragement as we see these tiny shoots of green coming from the seed already planted, and we long to be everywhere at once, watering the plants, and planting in new gardens!! Pray that the funds for travel will come in, and that the Lord will very definitely guide as to the places He wants us to go. In the immediate future we will be completing the book of Luke lessons and sending out material to get all these classes under way. Please pray with us that during this time the Lord will lay it on the hearts of those who can, to give so that lack of finances will not hinder the putting out of new material, the travel to these various places, and the office help necessary to our moving forward.

Thanksgiving will be close when you get this and I want to end by telling you that one of the things we are most thankful for is the knowledge of the love and prayers of each of you "back home."

Lovingly,

EDITH

---

* Dr. Hans Rookmaaker, much later to be Professor of History of Art at the Free University of Amsterdam and collaborator with Francis Schaeffer in the work of L'Abri and in the production of *How Should We Then Live?*

December 16, 1950   Champéry, Switzerland

Dear Family:

How quickly the year has passed this time, a year that has brought increasingly "wars and rumors of wars." What can the words of the Christmas story mean to those who are looking only for peace in this world? What discouragement must be theirs!

Going back to the beginning of November brings me to my birthday. Fran got home from Rome in time to help celebrate around the sponge cake (made in memory of Mother's sponge birthday cakes of the past!), which we cut in front of the fire, the most comfortable spot in the house. The girls had bought gifts with money saved up for many weeks and planned for with many whispered secret conferrings, usually in my presence, so it was a real party in several ways. . . .

During this time we were having heavy snows which coated roofs, bushes, and trees with great fat cushions of snow. After typing late one evening we went upstairs and entered the bedroom, to feel water splashing in our faces. Splash, plop—we looked up to see great yellow spots of moisture on the ceiling and counted five places where a steady drop was splashing down on the rug below. Fortunately all five missed the bed. We dashed around and found five bowls and pails to put under the spots and then ran up to the third floor to see what was going on. On the left side of the attic we found a leak almost the entire length of the roof which was soaking the stored possessions before it went through to the room below. Going back downstairs I thought I heard another plop from the direction of Debby's room and soon discovered a steady drip right beside her bed. Poor Debby had been unjustly accused of playing with water before bedtime as I discovered the wet place on the floor without discovering its source. I must apologize tomorrow, I thought as I placed a pail beside the soundly sleeping cherub! What a night that was, as we continually awakened to hear new drips and to scurry around trying to catch the water in new sorts of containers. We learned the next day that the snow had melted on the roof above the house proper, but had remained a solid frozen mass on the overhanging part of the roof— therefore a lake had formed and had found its way under the tiles. The next week was one of terrific rain and storm. The rain came down in such amounts that the peasants were afraid of avalanches. Streams were formed where none had been before, and ran directly through people's chalets. It really was amazing, and the children were full of stories to tell of men and boys standing watch with picks and shovels trying to direct the rushing torrents of water away from the houses in the village. It finally ended with the rain changing into snow—and we have had snow ever since. . . .

Jean Faye arrived with Fran on Saturday afternoon. He was tall and black enough to cause a real stir as he walked up the street. Windows opened and boys followed to get a better look at this Senegal African who is a typical example of the men used by the French to frighten the Germans in the first World War. It was not long before Debby was seated on his lap learning to count in Senegalese. . . . As we ate dinner the children asked all sorts of questions about African food and we were given recipes for rice mixed with peanut butter, red pepper, and meat! When asked what sort of implements the Africans eat with, Faye replied, "The fingers," and told of the custom of all eating from one bowl. His family uses knives and forks but when his father (a government official) entertains, many of the men don't know how to handle them and resort to their fingers. He was certainly exposed to Bible teaching that weekend. As walked to church Sunday morning half the village was out to see us go by, and we heard that many were cross with the priest because he kept them in longer than usual at the mass and they "missed it." Vic brought a question to us that had been troubling her—"Is his blood black, too?" Sunday afternoon around the fire gave time for the showing of the gospel walnut and the Heart of Salvation, and as we gave some of these children's materials to Faye he promised to show them, with the accompanying stories, to his younger sisters. . . .

On Monday afternoon a phone call came from a neighbor asking Fran to go immediately to the home of Mme. Fleishmann. He found, when he arrived, that the little 90-year-old mother had slipped quietly away from her frail body as she rested in the arms of her daughter. It seemed to come as an answer to prayer, as we felt sure she belonged to the Lord, and to be absent from the body is to be present immediately with the Lord. She had no memory for a long time, and recently scarcely knew her daughter. It relieved Mme. Fleishmann of all need for decision for care for her mother and will give her the opportunity to have the rest she so badly needs. Mme. Fleishmann felt that the Lord might have sent us to Champéry *especially* for her. . . . I was surprised to find that there was no such thing as an undertaker or embalming here in Switzerland; *no* one then takes charge of the arrangements. We called the young pastor in Monthey to take the service on Thursday (it would take all that time to get the proper papers in order!), and meantime Mme. Fleishmann could not leave the little house (so small that her own bed was partly under the piano), and a steady succession of village women came to keep her company—which was a trying ordeal for her. Poor Mme. Fleishmann declared she would not bury her mother before Dr. Otten declared her really dead! After complicated searching I located the doctor, who agreed to come at *six A.M.!!!* and then to take us down the mountain after breakfast.

At seven the next morning we were sitting down to a hot bowl of porridge when the doctor came in and joined us—"Hot porridge in Champéry—what a break!" Whizzing down the mountain in the doctor's car is quite a contrast to jerking down on the cog railway. Fran had for his companion on the back seat a peasant who had missed the early train for market and was overjoyed to have a lift with the doctor. We passed everything on the road, including a bus with a rear platform on which two calves were taking their last ride before turning into veal! . . .

Now for a speedy walk through the market section of Geneva to reach the Bible Store where we were to be met and taken out to Alexander's Bible School. Fran practically had to drag me past the stalls. "Oh, *look* at those oranges, about a third less than the ones in Champéry!" (Hurry, hurry—no time for that—we're late.) "Dates—*look*, dates—only a franc a package. Why that's half price!" (We didn't come to buy dates—we have to be there five minutes ago.) Fran won, and of course he was right as we had little enough time as it was for all the necessary conversations of the day. But the bargains were very tempting! . . . We were warmly welcomed by Mr. Alexander, his wife and family, and several of his workers, and ushered in to dinner immediately. After dinner we all went through the park-like grounds to the apartment. . . . They told us of the history of their Bible School and "Action Biblique." Mr. Alexander is a Scotsman who came to Switzerland many years ago with his aunt. He was an evangelist and his meetings in Neuchâtel and other parts of Switzerland resulted in the salvation of many souls. Soon he started Bible classes for those saved in his meetings and gave them the vision of being soul winners. . . . In miraculous ways the property and money came in for the beginning of L'Ecole Biblique de Genève, the first Bible School in Switzerland. Other schools followed later, but none took the position his did.

His students must all know a trade *before* they enter—hence he has nurses, stenographers, watchmakers, mechanics, technicians, etc. After they have had one year of Bible training, they go out as colporteurs and evangelists for a year of practical work, then return for another year of training. During the middle year constant reports are made to the school. When his students graduate, they go to towns in French-speaking Africa, Syria, France, South America, and Switzerland and begin their own work (as watchmaker, etc.), using all opportunities of contact to spread the gospel. They give out tracts and sell testaments. In some places a Bible Bookstore is opened; where there are fairs and markets, bookstalls are set up to sell the Bible and speak to people. Bible classes and Sunday services are started in the home of the worker. All this he calls "Action Biblique." One great advantage is that the passports of his workers are marked "mechanic," "nurse," etc., and each one has his or her daily job, so visas are not questioned. It is a most interesting work and there is no doubt the Lord has blessed it. . . .

The next morning Fran met Priscilla and Susan at the station where they had come with Mme. Fleishmann, and then Debby at the tram stop, where she had come from Mme. Turrian's (her destination of the day before—traveling that far alone!), and we all went together to do some Christmas shopping, and to the oculist where Priscilla was given a prescription for stronger glasses and Susan was told her habit of squinting and practically diving through the piano to look at the notes was simply a mannerism and not due to her eyes, "which are perfect"! We went to lunch at Mme. Turrian's, where we were warmly welcomed. It really seemed like home. . . . Susan was coming back to spend the night, fulfilling an oft-expressed desire to visit there, and Debby would be with us at Andres'. The big excitement of the trip for the girls was our visit to the sporting goods store to get ice skates as *this* year's Christmas present from "Mother and Daddy." The happy moment over, we were slowly going out the door looking back at the shining array skates and skis, when suddenly Fran bumped into a man and we heard them exchanging friendly greetings—"Hello, hello"— Who could it be? Why, it was the headmaster of the girls' school which stayed for three months last year in Champéry. "Are you coming again?" "I should say so—we'll be arriving early in January. Say, have you time to come with me now for a spot of tea?" "No, we will be busy right up to the moment when we put Priscilla on the train at 7:20. She has to return tonight for school tomorrow." "Fine, I'll meet you at the station at 7:20 and take you to the school to have dinner with me. Have some things I want to talk to you about." "Now," we said to each other, "isn't *that* of the Lord, bringing us in contact with him at that particular moment." The afternoon errands finished, the girls had supper with the Andre children and then separated—Debby to go to bed with Ninette, Susan to go to La Rosiaz, Priscilla to meet Mme. Fleishmann and go home.

We were met by the headmaster M. Fonjallaz and his dog Trix—a huge Airedale the size of a Great Dane—and then taken to his school at Lutry. Le Grand Verger is a boarding and finishing school divided into two types of school. The one at Lutry is more serious and prepares girls of various countries for entrance into the universities of their own country. The other one at Duchy (a couple of miles away) is a finishing school, and in case you don't know what that includes, it is: "French, Cookery, Housekeeping, Dressmaking, Mending, Ironing, Sports, Music, and Physical Training." It is attended mostly by English girls who are promised "a year in Switzerland" for a graduation present. The cost prevents all but the wealthy from sending their girls. We were served dinner in the private office and living room of the headmaster with his secretary acting as hostess. He told us much about the school, his various problems, his personal interest in the development of the girls' characters, his discipline problems and how he handles them, etc. He said his aim was not just to run a sort of fancy hotel and vacation place for girls, as some finishing schools do, but to give them something worthwhile that would affect their whole attitude toward life. "You know, most of these girls will be in fairly influential positions during their lifetime, and I feel I can do a real work by giving them something solid in the way of ideals, etc." Then we talked to him of Bible-believing Christianity, starting with a bit of Church history and ending with the departure of the Church as a whole from the Word of God. We then went on to say what a privilege we felt it to be to give the Word of God to his girls last year, both in the Church services and in the Bible classes around our fireplace. We told him that, believing as we do, we felt the greatest thing that could be done for the girls, and for those whom their lives would touch, was to have them "born again." We were thrilled to have him declare—"I want to cooperate with you in working with the girls, and when we come to Champéry I want to do everything I can to have the girls attend the services and come to your home for the Sunday evenings. I certainly appreciate what you did for them last year. I'm not capable of doing anything along those lines myself." Soooo, we are given a free hand and will feel more freedom this year than before.

As for the girls? During the evening he brought some of them in for an hour or so to talk with us. Molly (American Army Colonel's daughter of last year) bounced in first with her usual noisy enthusiasm (she certainly isn't *finished* yet!)—"Hi, Mr. and Mrs. Schaeffer—boy, I can't wait to get to Champéry. I've been telling all these girls about it." Then came about eight more American girls—all daughters of the Occupation Troops in Germany. None of them has seen a Swiss village yet, nor the mountains "close up like that," nor have they ever been on skis. "No movies?—what on earth do you do up there?" They all promised to come to our home. There were 14 American girls this year preparing for college and a number of English girls in the finishing school. As a final thing before we left, the headmaster said, "I'd like to offer you the opportunity of having your eldest daughter attend the school classes with the American girls while we are in Champéry—American History and Geography, etc., and also the ski lessons if she wants to—at no cost of *course*. It is little enough to do in return for the work you have done for my girls." Pray about this opportunity; we are not sure that it will fit in with Priscilla's other schoolwork. It would be so nice for her to be with girls for a change. . . .

A quiet Lord's Day was appreciated after this busy week, and as well as a good service, we had a lovely afternoon reading out loud a true Christian story of Czechoslovakia to the family. This has been *another* busy week. It is now Saturday night. One thing, the folks who were at the hotel that night all came to our chalet last night to see Fran's pictures. All were thrilled with their beauty and interested in his talk, which took the form of a message. Almost all promised to be at church for the Christmas service. Pray for us with these opportunities. We've no idea how many English schools will come this year, if any. As war reports come to us, we wonder what the next few weeks will bring. The American Consul in Geneva has told us all Americans will be sent back to America if general war begins. No matter where we are in the world, it seems to me we should be working and witnessing in the light and the possibility of the soon coming of the "night." While it is "yet day" we should continue with the urgency of those whose time may be short. We should each pray that our time, day by day and moment by moment, will be spent as the Lord would have it spent, since He alone knows what the future holds.

Lovingly in Him,

EDITH

1951

Dearest Family:

One-twelfth of the New Year has already passed! Our life measured by months and years goes so quickly—I am so glad we have eternal life, which, when we have passed the first 10,000 years, will have just begun!

The Christmas season was still in the future when I left you last time, and people were wondering whether war would break out before Christmas. The Korean situation was so bad that we wondered ourselves whether we would ever get a chance to open the parcels from America, or whether we would have to be following the instruction of the American Consul in Geneva to leave everything and come to Geneva awaiting evacuation. During these rather tense days, Susan presented her old Bible to Debby—she had just received a new one from the St. Louis Sunday school—and said, "This is the most important thing to take with you if we have to leave in a hurry." Debby obediently kept it near her at all times! (for a few days). Our Swiss friends urged us to stock up on a supply of fat, oil, sugar, flour, macaroni, rice, etc.—enough for a month—as they have been instructed to do. Mme. Andre explained, "All our stores close for a month as soon as war is declared—they did last time too—and one needs a good food supply." . . .

The Swiss are well prepared and heavily fortified, and have figured out just how long they can hold out against Russian invasion—they will never give in without a stiff fight. We think they will be like the Finns in this. The real Christians here feel a new burden in teaching their own children as much of the Bible as possible—"We don't know what our children will face if the Russians come." We feel too that the threat of war makes Children for Christ more important than ever in all of these European countries. One stormy night a knock came on the door and it was Mme. Marclay, our landlady of the first summer we lived in Champéry, owner of the little Chalet Bon Accueil. She said her husband wanted her to tell us that if we needed to leave suddenly because of war, they had an extra room they would give us to store our things until it was all over. Then she went on to tell us of the help they had given to Jews (utter strangers to them) who were escaping by foot from Holland during the last war. Imagine walking all the way from Holland—through France and over the mountain pass at Col de Cou, an hour's walk from here, and into Champéry!

Happily the holidays arrived, with fresh snow, sunny days, and an influx of tourists, and our minds turned to the opportunities of the moment. Posters were put up in all the hotels and pensions, announcing the services; decorations were planned for the church; cookies were baked and packaged and delivered to teachers, some old folks, and sick ones. The season came and went in a peace which gave once more the opportunity of preaching the Christmas message in this village. The sister of the Englishman from Kenya undertook to make candlesticks for the church from bark-covered logs and did a fine job of it with just a saw and a knife. Michel, Vic's son, cut some pine boughs and little trees for us and with part of the forest indoors and candles snapped on the boughs, the little chapel smelled like a pine woods and looked as twinkling as the starry sky. After the morning service, we hurried home to eat a bite and then prepare for the first Children for Christ class in Champéry. Yes, in French! Susan invited some children and Priscilla is teaching it. They enjoyed the Christmas story and all promised to come each week. So you see, prayers are beginning to be answered as to a testimony in the village. We followed the children out the door and down through the softly falling snow into the village where voices and sleighbells were muffled by the thick snow. Up the steep hill we climbed until we reached the tiny chalet of Mme. Fleishmann, where we were greeted and ushered in to have hot chocolate and cake around her grand piano, which looks as though it had been placed there first and then the house built around it. She had invited us to sing carols—French, German, English, and American carols. It was a lovely hour, but we couldn't linger because we all had to be at the church on time. We had planned our candlelight service for 5:30 so that people in the hotels would be more apt to come. Dinner is served so late it makes an evening service difficult.

Christmas day was a family day especially appreciated because we had felt so uncertain about being here. We had a cozy time around our warm, crackling fire opening gifts so carefully prepared weeks before by loved ones in America. . . . We lunched on sandwiches and a "Frostee" milkshake—straight from someone's grocery back in the States! Late in the afternoon, Mme. Fleishmann came to admire things with the children and to eat dinner with us, a dinner complete with cranberry sauce and pumpkin pie from America. Folks here are always so interested in American food. As dusk grew to dark, we put the sparklers on the tree in good Swiss fashion and lit them with the flame of a candle. For a few moments the sturdy pine tree was transformed into something that looked like a falling star with its shower of sparks. You really ought to see it someday. . . .

We had a well-attended service that last Sunday morning of 1950, and a sober congregation as Fran gave them a picture of the blackness of the world's hopes in this year of chaos ahead and the need of each individual of Christ. . . .

The day after that was one of those rare, warm sunny days, like nothing we have ever seen elsewhere. We decided at noon to drop everything else and take a picnic up to Planachaux to introduce Carl Steinhauser to skiing. A scramble to make sandwiches, stuff in a few cookies and tangerines. "Everybody have their skis?—put in an extra sweater—right here in your sack, Susan—OK? let's go"—swish we go off down our road, which is downhill from here to the *telepherique* station, just in time for the last "tele" before dinner. Up, up, we swing—over the jagged rocks, over the sharp snow-covered slopes, over the tree tops, on up to the last bit—an angled pile of rock that tops the cliff. We find a table in the outdoor "tearoom"—just a wooden platform built out on props to give a flat spot—brush the snow off it, and spread out our meal, having left our skis and *batons* (poles) standing in a row as they were stuck upright in a snowdrift. We order hot chocolate, and the waitress in a short-sleeved dress, tiny white apron, and heavy ski boots, wades through the snow with her tray held aloft! The sun is like summer, and skiers rest as they eat with their jackets thrown off. We have a glorious afternoon as we practice stem turns and try to work toward getting the "Christiania"—Fran being several steps ahead of me! We end up by going up on the ski lift and coming down once, though my courage fails each time the going gets too fast and I plunge headfirst into the powdery snow. Even that is fun when the snow is like it was that day—just a fine spray in your face. The beauty is so intense it almost hurts—the dazzling white snow, dark pine trees, and jagged mountaintop against an unbelievably blue sky. Ahh—I thought—how could heaven be more beautiful; yet it is, because the Bible tells us that eye hath not seen anything like that which the Lord is preparing for those who love Him. We took one more afternoon to ski with Carl and with the children before school started again, and how glad I am that we did, because since then I have not had a minute for even a walk outside—let alone skiing! Perhaps there will be another opportunity before winter is over, but I am not at all sure—work piles up so high!! . . .

The next day Mme. Wildermuth came for tea, I had a long talk with her alone. I asked her definitely whether she had accepted Christ as her Savior, and she said, "Yes, didn't Mr. Schaeffer tell you in Lausanne the evening he stayed at our home so late, that he was sure that I had then?" We had a time of discussing many things from the Bible, and I feel there is growth in her life. Pray especially that she will study the Bible for herself. . . .

Saturday afternoon Vic and Debby went down on the sled to get a few things at the store. Not long afterwards they returned, both talking at once almost incoherently. *"Telepherique"*—"terrible thing"—"avalanche"—"Alphonse Vieux and two other men"—"not down yet." . . . The street was full of people, as though it were Sunday, and shocked groups were standing and discussing it all. The two men who take tickets in the two *telepherique* cars, and the man who works the controls at the top station, had been told to remove the snow from the top, just at the edge of the precipice, because the cars could not swing into the station since the snow was so high. They took shovels and left their ropes lying on the snow beside them, so familiar was the job to them that they were careless of danger. Suddenly a small avalanche started and they were swept out away from the rock and dropped through 250 feet of space, only to land on the sharp, rocky side of the mountain below, to roll over and over for a thousand feet and then to slide with the snow for another 2,500 feet. One of them had only broken ribs, as well as bruises and shock, of course. He made a great effort to get the other two out of the snow and then ran through the deep snow to the nearest chalet for help. He was a green color when he arrived there, but was able to tell where the other men were and to take a sled and sled down the rest of the mountain right into the village himself!! Meantime, the one girl who was alone at the top station called the village for help and worked the controls to bring some men, including Dr. Otten, up *halfway* on the *telepherique*. There they stopped by the second tower and climbed out on top and down the tower to search in the snow for the remaining two men. One was mentally upset by the shock and had the skin torn and loosened from half of his body, but the other had a broken neck and was already dead. "Who is dead? Oh I hope it's not my favorite man who let me ride up on the roof of the *telepherique* cabin last summer," said Fran.

Just then Priscilla burst in the front door. "Oh, have you heard the terrible thing? Oh, mother, one of the men was killed—and he is our favorite man, the one who loaned Susan the raincoat that day, the one who has those four cute little girls. They live right down the road here past us—" And here she burst into tears. "Are you *sure* it is he?" "It's Alphonse Vieux and that's the one." We were plunged into sorrow because of the striking by sudden death of the one whom we had thought so kind and nice. And was he saved?—Was he saved? What a heaviness of heart was ours that night. "But I don't want that man to be dead," sobbed Debby. "I don't want that man to be dead. He was our favorite man in the village. . . .

The body was brought down on a sled and the priest came up the little path behind our house to meet the procession. The stunned wife waited at the *douane*, finding it difficult to believe that this broken body was that of her cheerful husband who had so gaily waved to her such a short time before.

We took flowers to the little chalet on Monday, stepping out of the way as the paper-wrapped coffin went sliding by on a sled as it was being delivered by the young man who rode astride and guided it all with his heel. There is no embalming and no undertaker, so the body is always placed on a bed or couch by the family. Life is such a personal thing in this small village. We put a card in with the flowers, on which I had written a number of Scripture verses in French. The vegetable man who was arranging all the bouquets stopped to read the card out loud as I slipped it in among the blossoms. "That's nice—good words—*oui, oui.*" We found that we could help out by taking the three-year-old girl home for the night, and so the little bereaved child became a part of our family for a few days, tugging at our hearts with her happy chatter—"My papa has flowers, lots of them. My papa is asleep."

The entire village went to the funeral, as well as number from nearby places and from high in the mountains. As the time came to go, we walked down the path to find that the coffin was being carried along the street, with everyone walking two by two behind it, men first and then the women. As it passed various stores and homes, people fell in line, until finally the church was reached and all filed inside. . . . The mass took a long time, as there were several hundred people there. As we stood at the back and watched so many of those familiar faces—the ski teachers, the postmen, the border patrol men, the electrician, the banker, most of them with trembling lips and tear-filled eyes, my own eyes overflowed, not just for Alphonse, not just for all those families bereaved by avalanches, but for these people themselves. Death, whether sudden or not, is always sure. . . .

And now to tell you about the Sunday nights with the girls. Mr. Fonjallaz asks at tea each Sunday that those who expect to go to the Schaeffers' will please raise their hands—that is all there is to the announcement. They come entirely out of choice. The first night there were about 12; that was the average for a few weeks, until it dropped to seven one night because of several cases of grippe, a broken ankle, two phone calls from America being waited for anxiously, etc. Then came last week—a record Sunday with 17!! The girls are so full of questions that they pop right out with them. The groups change from night to night, but some come regularly, among them a pair of twins (English), two East Indians who are Zoroastrians, another Indian of Hindu background, and American Army officers' daughters—all significant individuals with diverse lives ahead. . . .

February 7, 1951

As you see, it is now February 7th and the letter has had to be put aside for over a week. It has been an eventful week in many ways, hence I am going to add another couple of pages. I want you to be right up to date, because of your prayers and also because I don't like to save news that is so wonderful.

The first event was that Susan swelled up on one cheek—not unlike mumps—but the source turned out to be an abscessed gum. At the same time Priscilla had such a cough and cold that I kept her in bed too, and Dr. Otten stopped in to see them both. Priscilla had been taking a few classes at Mr. Fonjallaz's school—American History, English Literature, and English Grammar—and as she was in bed we had time to discuss the contrast between the two schools. Things came out which she had never told before, and coupled with some other things we had not liked, we felt the Lord was clearly showing us she should leave Ecole Alpina. She has a wonderful record there—came out second from the top on exams this winter—and educationally she was soaring ahead. However, as we heard some of the language that had been used in class, we realized that no education at all would be better than going on in this school. When the doctor stopped in, we had not yet arrived at this decision, but I said casually to him, "Priscilla finds Mr. Fonjallaz's school such a fine place and the people at the other school are quite cross about her going there." "*Voila, voila,* she should *always* go to Mr. Fonjallaz's school." "But, Dr. Otten, you know quite well that is for rich people, and they will so soon be returning to Lausanne where it would be *impossible* for Priscilla to go." "Hmmmm—I talk to Mr. Fonjallaz—goodbye." That was Thursday. Friday Vic didn't show up, and Lucy later stopped to say that her mother was sick in bed with a fever. So I plunged into housework for the day. We had prayed and thought and discussed Priscilla's future, and decided that she should not go back to that school, even one more day, although we could not see a solution unless we would send for the Calvert Course. Hence Fran and I went to tell this to the director, and we hope that is a closed chapter.

Saturday Fran went down to Lausanne to dictate, the German student from Geneva arrived for the weekend, Mme. G. sent people to sort her things in the attic preparatory to selling the chalet, and Michel came to tell me that his mother (Vic) was worse and wouldn't have a doctor but that his father knew that Mme. Schaeffer would know what to do if she would come and see her and would I please come. I was buried in preparations for Sunday. What a day that was! With everyone helping, the house finally got cleaned, cookies were made, 53 cream-puff shells puffed up gloriously and stood waiting to be filled for Sunday night, a rabbit stew simmered for Sunday dinner, Saturday's supper simmered on another burner, and the student dried dishes for me, while Susan and Debby followed the procession up and down from the attic as things were carried out, wearing by turns a tall silk hat that had been unearthed up there! . . . When Fran returned, he and our student climbed up to Vic's chalet with me. It is quite a climb in the winter with ice and snow making the steep path something like a toboggan slide! The light was dim inside and the flickering oil lamp didn't make much impression on the darkness. They waited outside as I passed through the tiny, dark kitchen into the other room where Lucy was studying her lessons by the lamp and Vic was lying on the bed (there were four beds in the room). They assured me that the thermometer was broken because it had stuck at 36.2 degrees C. all day, but after I tested it in warm water (much to their wondering admiration), I discovered that this was her actual temperature. I had had a talk with Dr. Otten by phone before coming and he had told me of the medicine needed and helped me give them an idea of what she should eat. After praying with her, my first "doctor" visit ended! Since that I have gone once more to see my patient, getting an idea of what it is to be a mountain doctor, slipping and sliding and puffing up an icy ascent, but enjoying the quiet beauty of the cathedral pines shutting out even the view of the mountains. The family is more cordial than they have ever been and most appreciative of the care given to Vic. She is improving, but weak, so it will be some days yet until I can stop doing double duty. However, I am sure the Lord is using it to incline their hearts even more to the gospel. . . .

Sunday was another busy day, with a guest for breakfast, church service, dinner, dishes, the Children for Christ class in the afternoon, the preparation for the girls, and 17 girls plus a teacher plus Mr. Irmer and our family for the evening! The questions again came spontaneously and centered mostly around, "Do you think that people of other religions cannot go to heaven?" In spite of the Indian girls, we answered as firmly and strongly as God's Word does—there is *only one way*—giving passage after passage and illustration after illustration. "But if you believe that your sins are all forgiven, then you would just do lots more bad things." On and on we talked, but over and over the same truths must be presented, because you see these girls are the product of the modern teaching of toleration of all religions being the only kind thing; the matter of *truth*, the desire to *find* that truth, does not seem important to so many of them. Miss B., the English English-teacher, had a hard time getting them to put on their coats and go home that night.

Mr. Fonjallaz and his secretary came for dinner on Monday night. The day was a sort of a race, to get through the various types of work that had to be done and have a company dinner ready, with the children out of sight for the night, but I reached the finish line just in time! We had a most interesting time together, and when we were telling Mr. F. about the chalet being for sale he looked most concerned. "If I had the money, I would certainly buy it for you and give it to you." He meant it, too. You know, Mme. G. is anxious to sell it before March, but as yet the man has not come to set the "fair price." Please pray with us that if the Lord will have us remain in our beloved home, He will put it on someone's heart to buy it for the Mission, or that someone will buy it who will rent it to us. The place seems so perfect for our needs and has been so used of the Lord that, humanly looking at it, it does seem that it would be a great hindrance to the work to have to move. It would also be impossible to find another similar place anywhere in Switzerland for the price we have been paying. The Lord is able. . . .

We talked for hours around the fire, of many, many things. Both Mr. F. and Mlle. Y. seemed interested in the things of the Bible and in our work. He was shown the various Children for Christ materials, ending with the Door of Salvation, and he made no objection to the Bible teaching which we told him his girls were getting. His school is one of the best of its kind in Switzerland and is on approved lists all over the world. He has received the permission to give American College entrance exams for any college, and has now added American subjects to the curriculum. We like his personal interest in the girls and their problems and his desire to see them helped in every way by their time in the school. But if he were personally a man assured of his salvation and growing in the Lord, the resulting influence would reach many parts of the earth through the girls. As the evening approached the end, we mentioned Priscilla. Dr. Otten had *already* talked to Mr. Fonjallaz, and his first remark was, "And what subjects do you want Priscilla to have? She will go into the most advanced class in French and French Literature, and I suppose you want her to keep up her German as well as American History, English Literature and American Literature, English Grammar, and Algebra. And do you want Latin this year or later?" "But, Mr. Fonjallaz, what about the money? We can't afford your prices at all, you know." "Now Mlle. Y., what room shall we put her in?" "Well, that one girl has left, which makes a vacancy in Happy and Shirley's room—with the English girl, that would make four in there." (Happy and Shirley are already Priscilla's favorites!) "But," I butted in, "what about the *money?*" "You know," Mlle. Y. said, "in a school like ours there is always enough left over from each meal to feed five more—*really*, and you see that bed is vacant, and the teachers are there anyway." I began to feel as if we were in a fairy tale— could it be *true?* "But what will it *be?*" Finally he named a sum that took our breath away, it was so little. "This is just a little arrangement among friends, and after all you are doing so much for our girls, for us—" They seem to feel that Priscilla will be a help to have in the school, both in the classes and with the girls in everyday life. Do pray for her in a special way now, that she may be kept from temptation and that she may be used as a real witness among the others. She is to remain at home until they go back down to Lutry in March, and then she will go with them. Meantime she will go daily to the school, staying for meals whenever it is convenient, and skiing, etc., with the girls. She is so happy she is absolutely walking on air. "Oh, mother, it's just like being back at Stevens School in Philadelphia. The teachers are the same sort and everyone is so friendly and nice." It is a dream come true for her and now the only trouble will be that she will be ready for college too soon! What amazing things God does for His children. Since that marvelous working out of our problem we have been filled with songs of praise. Debby and I have gone about the housework singing through the hymn book together! There remains the problem of the house, as well as many shadows on the future—but our God is able to do all things and He has gently reminded us of this again in giving us this surprise. So we look to the future with renewed confidence and thanksgiving in the knowledge that He works all things together for our good and His glory and will make His plan for us clear, step by step, if we stay close to Him.

Lovingly yours,

EDITH

March 29, 1951   Champéry, Switzerland

Dearest Family:

It has snowed in Champéry for the last three days; the roofs, trees, and fences are topped with puffy coverings and the ground is fine for skiing. However, snow loses a little of its romance when it has remained for over five months!! . . .

Instead of the small spring birds, I see the colorful jackets of skiers swooping down the path just on the other side of the bedroom window. However, yesterday Susan went to a spot where the first daffodils appear and scraped away the snow to find green shoots and even buds pushing up, in spite of their chilly blanket. She cut some of them and the buds are beginning to burst already. So we know the ground is prepared to blossom as soon as the snow stops coming down and the sun warms it up. The thought of all those flowers now hidden from view, yet preparing for spring, reminds me of the preparations going on in Heaven, hidden from our sight now but which shall be ready for that moment when He has planned to reveal it all to us.

By the way, two Indian girls, Dinoo and Keeta, begged me to allow several of them to come each Saturday morning "to watch you make the wonderful cakes and things we eat on Sunday nights. We want so much to learn to cook such things." So my Saturday mornings turned into a "cooking class" and, rather than getting all my baking done in the mornings, I aimed at their really learning. They copied recipes, donned aprons from my drawer, and took turns breaking eggs, stirring, folding, etc. Such fun they had! The Indian girls had never been allowed in a kitchen before, having been accustomed to servants galore. Dinoo said, "Our cook even made my mud pies for me when I was little and iced them with some kind of plaster mixture." We tried to think of ingredients which could be used in India or purchased in England with its rationing, and made in all sorts of weather. The mixtures were sampled in all stages—"Mmmm, this is good *raw*"—and before 56 cookies could be dropped on sheets, the amount would dwindle into only enough for 36!

The last morning they each made a pie shell, and we made orange chiffon filling for one of them. (In the afternoon I made four more shells and filled all eight of them before bedtime.) Such a time they had, picking out their own peculiar edges and proudly passing them around the next evening. Our constant prayer was that in some way these Saturday mornings would be used of the Lord with each of them to bring them closer to Himself. Interestingly enough, the school director was pleased too. All these things work together, we feel sure.

Dinoo came over one afternoon, alone, bringing a box of chocolate as a gift, and staying to talk over teacups. "We have only French Roman Catholic missionaries in our part of India. I went to one of their schools. French and Irish sisters were my teachers. We wanted to come Sunday nights to see if it was the same religion. We have found that it has absolutely no resemblance to the Roman Catholic." We spoke further about the Bible. She told me that their main point in *their religion* was never to change—her father's only stipulation to their going abroad for study was that they never change their religion. Asking the Holy Spirit to guide me, I did not feel it was time to ask her for an unfolding of her present thoughts, or of pressing her to a decision. I said, "Dinoo, I want you to know we love you, and you know what we believe. Believing as we do, and loving you, we will never forget you as long as we live. We will pray for you, for Kit, for Keeta, and also for your parents, that you will find Christ as your Savior, and we will all be in Heaven together one day. Kit used to speak angrily of a God who would have only *one way* to Heaven—but God has brought you all the way to Switzerland, way up to this little chalet in the mountains, and here you have studied His Word. Through you, India—your people—*may* hear. *This* is how God has sent the message throughout the years." She thanked me—took several things to read, and said she wanted to study the Bible further. Then last night, I wish you could have seen Kit's face when she asked, "When Jesus changes us in a twinkling of an eye—oh, I mean when He changes *the believers*—will our faces be the same?" Such a soft look in her face and eyes—she who sneered so openly. Keep praying!!! . . .

The ski meets came on two separate days. I went to one of them and Fran to the other. Girls from various of the same type of Swiss schools took part, with huge numbers importantly tied across their chests and backs. The races—slaloms, etc.—are clocked, individually run, and no one knows the scores until the prizes are given out. Each must do her best—if she falls, she must get up and go on—her time may still be ahead of another's. It reminded me so much of our Christian life as I stood shivering in the fog at the top of the run.

My disappointment in the first meet was the Priscilla couldn't enter. She disqualified for the "Beginners' Class" because she had skied last year. The morning of the second meet Mr. Fonjallaz called up and asked me if he could enter Priscilla's name. "We have one place vacant for our school." "Go ahead," I said. Fran stood at the finish line that day and reported that a graceful Priscilla swooped through the last few zigzag posts without a waver. That night we were busy and Priscilla insisted that no one need go to the Berra Tea Room. "I didn't win anything and I don't think prizes are given for this one anyway." Susan insisted on tagging along. Hours later the front door burst open—*"Mother!! Daddy!!"* Two voices shrieking—"I was third"—"She was third." Everything got told twice that night! "See my cup?" "See her cup?" It was a wee little silver one, but it was a sure-enough thrill. And the plant? "I got that for being the youngest one in the meet." "She got that for being the youngest one in it, see?" We were sorry we hadn't been there to hear the cheers. Her time was one minute seven seconds—first place, one minute—second place, one minute six and a half seconds.

You are waiting to know about the house. Madame G., the owner, came one Saturday afternoon and swept through the house selecting things from the walls, the cupboards, the drawers. "I want this tablecloth and this teaset today." (It happened to be the only teaset and had 15 cups, badly needed for the next evening with the girls.) "I don't think I'll take these dishes." (No, I didn't think so either. Granny Fisher gave us those plates long, long ago—the idea!) She was most unpleasant about every conceivable thing. "You must let me know immediately when you hear the price if you want to buy it." We lived in comparative peace for a couple of weeks, borrowing teacups and later buying some new ones. Next an appraiser came to appraise the value of the house. Meantime, more things were snatched out from under us. Finally the price came through. Fran and I opened up the papers quietly before the fireplace. About $19,000 empty—over $22,000 with furniture. Two days to inform her before it would be advertised—or 1,000 francs for an option! Our hearts fell. Goodbye, dear fireplace—goodbye, house of dreams-come-true! Susan burst in the front door. "Mother, Dad—" "Susan, the price came—it is much too much. We will have to leave it. Even the A.'s won't buy it at that price." "Will we? Oh, I have the most exciting news, Mother and Dad. I have been visiting at the Vieux home every day, and now Mme. Vieux says the little girls *can come* to our Sunday Children for Christ class!" What difference did it make about a house? Susan's heart was filled with joy over her fishing for men. We looked at each other—"Seek ye first . . . and all these things shall be added unto you." Susan was surely putting the things of the Lord first. In a few minutes the front doorbell rang. Susan and Debby raced each other there to let Priscilla in. "Priscilla—guess what?" (What would come first?) "The Vieux children can come on Sundays—their mother said so. And our house is gone—we have to move."

Phone calls were made. "No, we can't think of it at that price. Sorry, we would have liked to help you stay there." . . . We began our search the next day. Then followed a few days of discouragement and blues. . . . "Chalet Bijou," so typically Swiss peasant chalet on the outside—no hot-water boiler, shabby in many ways, down in the hollow, hard to get lug-

gage to the train, but it has a furnace and an electric cooking stove. . . .
The Obers, who own Chalet Bijou, spent two evenings with us. We discussed the need of a water boiler for our washer. These two brothers and one sister are hardworking. One brother is an electrician, who also works in the fields during haying time. The other takes care of their cows, etc., and the sister works as hard as both of them. Bijou is their pride and joy. An Irish man and his wife lived in it for 17 years. There are some shelves and built-in cupboards, a built-in couch around the stone stove in the living room—these are the work of his hands. Americans rented it for another long period—artists—summer folks. Finally, you know we first met Mary, Anne, Madame Dumreicher, and a long string of contacts there, and the Andres have come for Christmases. It has memories for us already. They obviously want us, and as for us, it is the only possible place in Champéry. They have not enough money to put in the boiler all alone. We promise to help them with that and to make some other improvements. You see, the rent is less than here and we intend to use the difference to help make it more livable and to provide some of the things already provided in this house. We came to an agreement and our moving day is the 30th of April! Fran measured the steps from the station—exactly the same number as from here, but not a road—a bumpier path and uphill *going*—steeper, that's all. We decided we like the seclusion, pines all around us, no near houses, no path past the windows, just trees and mountains and a little rushing stream and a lovely place for our own garden.

The chalet has two delightful Swiss balcony-porches. The second-floor one is like a room—open on the side which gets the afternoon sun. It has a big table and shelves built around it—all ready for children to "live on." The walls are all wooden—big cracked slabs of wood, except for the living room which had paper—a wild yellow, orange, and silver. We have now covered it with a plain woodsy beige. The worn rugs are a problem, but we will bare the wide boards of the floors and wax them hoping to get rag rugs from America if shipping is not too much. The dining room stovepipes look ridiculously like a musical instrument. Perhaps we can make notes come out of it! The kitchen has a stone floor and the walls have once been painted so it won't take too much paint to give it a new coat, and some decals will make it gay. Oh yes, the dining room walls were covered with "jute" (like burlap) 50 years ago—just a bit worn now!!! We have ordered new jute where the peasants get theirs for haying time! We hope to really make a charming room out of the living room with plaid drapes, some lamps, and a few little tables if we can find bargains. I have an old pair of curtains—bought the stuff the first year we were married and Fran was at Seminary. They will cover a worn, old couch and make it look quite fresh. The dining room has a door opening into another room—just right for our office. So we will have a first-floor office. Upstairs is sort of summer-campy—unpainted wooden beds in unpainted wooden-walled and -ceilinged rooms. Gay bedspreads, gay gingham or chintz curtains, and lamps will eventually make them charming. Meantime they are very livable. We will have as many beds as in this house, and room, therefore, for just as many guests. Of course, if we had unlimited time, we could paint, hammer, sew, and fix up this place, but time is difficult to find. Pray that the Lord will show us just how much time we should spend on "things" to make an attractive place to be used in His work. . . .

We will be nearer some of the children and a bit farther from others who come to our Sunday class, so we are hoping it will make no difference. Priscilla, by the way, is coming home each weekend to teach it. She travels half fare in Switzerland until she is 16, so combined with a special trip ticket the cost won't be much. We like the idea of having time each week to talk over any problems. . . . One girl, divided home, has a real mother and a stepfather here, a real father and a stepmother in Montreux; she has never seen a Bible in her home. She too bought a Testament and we have promised her a Bible when she learns a box of Scripture verses. She is 10 years old. Another Testament was bought by a boy in Home Eden who is sharing the stories with two Roman Catholic brothers who are not allowed to come! The whole pension is singing the songs and hearing the stories retold, even though they are not allowed to come. Five-year-old Miriam, the child of the Border Patrol man, says her mother is reading the Gospel of Luke she took home, reading it out loud to her father and herself. Pray for the Scripture portions going into a number of village homes now. . . .

Fran and I are to start on a tour of some Swiss towns next Monday, being driven around by our interpreter provided by the Ecole Biblique in Geneva. Pray about this tour. Later we will need to go to France, not only for these folks, but to visit another church which has been writing to Fran, sending a pathetic plea for him to lecture. They so long to stand against apostasy, yet their denomination wishes to remain in a middle position.

It will take several pages to tell of our important days speaking in Geneva at the Easter Conference of Action Biblique. Fran and I and the girls went for an amazing time of real results. Not only were our messages used to start *many* children's classes, but Mr. Alexander's messages and the new hymns he had composed had a very special effect as a refreshment to the whole family and as a beginning of further relationship.

Here we are in April. Susan now has the flu, too. Fran went down with Priscilla so the three patients are caring for one another! His call from Monthey this afternoon ends my letter with a special request for prayer. Mr. Fonjallaz of Priscilla's school does not know whether to say "yes" to our coming for Bible classes or not. The girls of India are "too obviously interested—what will happen to my school if girls come and then change their religion?" We can see *his* predicament: if it becomes known that some had changed from Zoroastrianism to believing Christianity there, it would ruin his reputation as a secular finishing school. Only the Lord knows the solution. Please have special prayer about it.

How wonderful it is to know that you are back there praying! We pray for you too—individually, your churches, your testimony, and all that concerns you. May the Lord bless you everyone in whatever special need you have.

Much love,

EDITH

June 4, 1951   Champéry, Switzerland

Dearest Family:

. . . Skimming through Lausanne, the car turned toward Lake Neuchâtel. Signs of spring were definitely present in these valleys, but as we sped along the lake, a cold wind whipped against the car and churned the lake up so that the waves resembled those of the ocean. I was beginning to wonder how I could ever speak that night—the wobbliness of the after-flu weakness had not left me, and my head was beginning to ache with stabbing little darts. However, the lovely European afternoon tea custom came to my rescue and a cup of tea and an aspirin helped a lot. Tea over, we left Neuchâtel to go up into the Jura Mountain section of Switzerland. These mountains are very different from the jagged, towering Alps. Among them a great percentage of the world's watches are made. The neat little factories dot the landscape and fill the cities and villages. Here is one that looks like an ordinary house, and another that looks like an apartment house. That one looks like a miniature model factory and another could pass for a schoolhouse. Watches, clocks, barometers, chronometers, go out over all the world from these peaceful-looking little towns. How interesting that the watchmaking industry of the world developed from this particular plot of the world's surface!

How we have stopped in La Chaux-de-Fonds, almost American-looking with its wide main street. We are warmly welcomed by M. and Mme. Vuilleumier, at whose home we are to have supper. "Yes, I am a watchmaker. My father was a watchmaker and my grandfather was a watchmaker." As we eat supper we learn a few things about watchmaking and also something of the Action Biblique group in that place. Together we hurry into the parlor for prayer before leaving for the meeting. As we enter the warmth of the meeting room, we find it already filling up with those who need more than an April snow storm to discourage them from coming to hear of a way to reach children with the Gospel. As she had done night after night, Debby sweetly and seriously sang to demonstrate the various types of songs we use. We found her a great asset to the meetings as she sang in English and in French and sat so quietly alone while Mother and Daddy were on the platform speaking. We marveled at how she could sit that way so many evenings through the same messages without making a sound! Three people signed up to start classes in La Chaux-de-Fonds that night.

After this meeting we were driven for about 15 minutes to the next town, Le Locle, to sleep at the home of the Goulets. Debby was soon tucked in a crib behind which a musical alarm clock had been set to mystify her in the morning! Mr. Goulet is the director of the Angelus Watch and Clock Factory and the house is full of various kinds of clocks and watches. Twenty-seven of these were displayed to us—clocks which tell the time, day, month, and position of the moon; a clock which tells the time all over the world (designed by their son who is now a missionary); a tiny stop-clock built into the telephone; clocks with various types of chimes and musical alarms—and, most interesting of all, the watches that the father and sons had made completely by hand when they were in watchmaking college. Each student must make a watch with only metal and tools to begin with—all the parts must be painstakingly made by hand. Of course, in these days watch parts are made by machine, but each graduate of the school must have made one watch by hand in spite of not needing to do so later. The father told us that his watch, made about 30 years ago, had never lost more than a minute a month in all that time. In this home also, the grandfather had been a watchmaker as well as the sons. The designer son is one of the Action Biblique workers in Portugal, with a watch store and a Bible House combined, and the second son is soon leaving the Longine factory, where he has an excellent position, to go to India as a missionary. In the morning we went through the Angelus factory to be fascinated by the process of watchmaking. Several of the men turned from their work being assembled under a magnifying glass, and assured us that they would be at the meeting we would have later in Le Locle. You would be surprised to see the number of girls and older women who have their part in sorting, counting, and putting together some of the microscopic parts of your watch. . . .

Debby found it hard to tear herself away from the 20 puppets and several dolls she had been given to play with by the kindergarten-teacher-daughter of our hostess, but we could not linger after breakfast. We drove off in the direction of Orvin, a village not far from Bienne but a long distance from where we were. There our destination was a remote spot several miles outside of the village where Paul Robert, the great Swiss painter, built a most fascinating house and studio away from everything except the rolling hills and valleys he so loved to paint. Here gardens and trees, vines and rose bushes, songbirds and little fish pools seem to ramble where they will, unrestricted by any formality, and the great vine-covered house with its flagstone terrace looks as if it had been there for centuries! We were welcomed by Mrs. Robert, Jr., and one of the daughters, and ushered in to an enormous room with high raftered ceiling and many windows. A stove *and* a fireplace made of blue and white picture tiles made one cozy corner, but since a chimney fire had started a few days before, they could not be used, and we shivered through our dinner on the other side of the room, warming ourselves with the beauty of the paintings hung on every available space on the walls, something like an art museum. These are paintings by the now-living Paul Robert, son of the man who built the house and who painted the wonderful murals in Neuchâtel. The son is also a splendid painter and does many portraits for the well-to-do as well as lovely scenes which are exhibited each summer and viewed by the hundreds of visitors who seek out this place. After dinner we went up to the artist's room, where he was recovering from the grippe, and he and Fran discussed art, Christian things, and Children for Christ while I warmed my feet on a hot stone! He is going to take the initiative in starting some classes for children in that area. We saw his studio before we left, but changed our minds about buying one of his pictures when we saw the prices, and bought postcard copies instead!

Going back to Orvin we visited the unusual State Church pastor there, who not only truly believes in the whole Word of God but also in speaking out against apostasy in the church. We had a most interesting talk at tea with him and enjoyed visiting the lovely church building in which is a wonderful picture of the Second Coming by the older Robert, and beside which building both the artist and his wife are buried. This old pastor, who is unique in his stand in that whole Jura Mountain area, has preached and fought for the Gospel for over 30 years in that one place. We should pray that the message of such a one will not die out with the death of the man. . . .

The next days were a whirl of packing, writing lessons, carting books down to the other house, cutting out a slipcover, deciding to finish some dressmaking before moving, sorting, and throwing out. There was correspondence and visitors from Geneva again to go over some more materials together. There was Debby's suitcase to pack to go to Geneva, and Susan's for Home Eden, and ours for Belgium and Paris as the moving day approached.

The 30th of April! It had been snowing steadily for several days, and so we wakened once more to a blanket of snow, but oh, joy—there was a glittering of *sun* on it. "The Lord has given us a clear day." "Are they coming with the jeep or the horse and wagon?" "I left it indefinite and told them to decide whichever would be best." "Let's hurry—start carrying down things to the front hall. They should soon be here." "It's almost 10:00 and no one has come yet. Susan, go up and try to get Vic's husband to come. At least he could take a *petit char* with some of the things in it." "Oh, Susan, there's Vic's husband passing by on the little path above. Hurry—catch him!"

Susan hastens to leave and soon comes back—alone. "*Susan*, did you speak to him." "Yes." "Susan, what did you say?" "Bonjour." "What did

Our moving van!

he say?" "Bonjour." "But didn't you say anything else?" "No—nooo—
you see, I didn't know if it was Vic's husband or not. It had the *face* of
Vic's husband, but I wasn't *sure* it was Vic's husband, so-o-o—so I was
afraid to ask"!!!! Fran hurried off to the village to catch him and to get
the cart belonging to the Bazaar. Soon he returned with both, and close
behind him came our "moving van"—not the horse, not the jeep—but
Herman! Herman, the slightly "slow," but very good-natured Ober, am-
bling slowly along the road, pulling a great sled mounted on wheels.
How thankful we were that Vic's husband was already with us. Then
started the process of "packing" the sled. Vic's husband hoisted a trunk
on his back and Herman followed him down from the attic carefully
bearing the straps! Vic's husband put our mattress out of the window
and Herman stood with hands uplifted under the window as if he were
catching a bridal bouquet ("Hurry up, Fran, go out there before it is completely ruined"). The two of them decided to take the double-decker bed
downstairs without taking it apart, ignoring my pleas and insistence
that it was *not* possible. Then it got stuck in the hall between two door-
ways and they decided to go on and do something else for the moment!
We crawled over and under until Fran came with his tools to take it
apart. As the first "load" was being tied on the sled, Vic's husband remarked that the rope looked as if it would break at any moment, and that
Vic had better get Lucy to bring their rope. Whereupon Herman replied,
"No need to do that—I have a very good rope—at home!"

I wish you could have seen the procession as it started down the path.
First came the bulky sled with its top-heavy load swaying from side to
side, as Vic's husband steered and held it back with his feet. Then came
Herman with one hand on the side of the load. Then Fran with a very
full cart, and finally Susan and Debby with our little cart jogging along

crookedly in the rear. Fran stayed down at Bijou to unload and supervise the placing of things, while I stayed at des Frênes to get things ready for the next load and to wash sheets, etc., making use of our last chance to have hot water. We kept the washing machine working right up until the moment *it* had to leave for Bijou! Evening found us down at Bijou with half of our things still at the other house. Herman promised to come back with the "luge" as soon as he had finished the milking in the morning. You can imagine that we welcomed sleep that night after we had found food, eaten some sort of a supper, made beds, found night-clothes, built a fire in Debby's bedroom tile stove, etc. The next morning found the same procession making several trips down the steep paths until afternoon brought a sudden change.

Now it was time for the refrigerator and washing machine to make the trip. Herman's electrician brother and a plumber arrived importantly on the scene, and as I hung out of the window to view the preparations I nearly fell out on my head. *What have they there?* Why, it is Debby's mat-tress, which I left safely on her bed with sheets tucked in around it. What can it be doing back here?? "That mattress went down to Bijou yes-terday. What—" "Yes, yes"—they knew that—hadn't they just had all the trouble of lugging it back? "But we took special care that it wouldn't get dirty, and look at all the mud—" "Yes, yes—that will brush off." They needed an old mattress and—"But this isn't an old mattress. That is, we brought it all the way from America and it is full of little springs—" "Yes, yes," they knew that—they thought all those little springs would assure the refrigerator and the washing machine of a soft ride!!! After I rescued the mattress from the disappointed movers they secured the refrigerator to the sled with thick ropes, under which we tucked soft cloths, and started off with it. I must say that it was a tremendous relief when both trips were finished and the report came back that both ma-chines had reached their destination without toppling over on the steepest part of the path. As we made our final trip with a basket of freshly ironed sheets, clean clothes, the ironing board, etc., we realized that our life and work at Chalet des Frênes was a closed chapter. The next day I had to go back up with Vic to see that everything was clean and in order, and that the number of sheets, pillowcases, towels, knives, silverware, etc., all corresponded with the inventory. This took much of the day and seemed an anti-climax to the moving.

The *next day* was Debby's birthday, so in the midst of putting the kitchen things away and finding a place for foodstuffs, I stopped to make a cake (with a cake mix one of you sent from America) and ice it, to make biscuits cut with a chicken cookie cutter, Jello also from America, and to invite some of the village children and Home Eden children for a "party." Susan managed the games and, since the children were youn-ger than herself, got along fairly well until one little girl refused to play musical chairs unless there were enough chairs for *everyone* to sit on, and the rest joined in on the strike! It turned out to be a rather satisfactory sixth birthday with cards and gifts to open in spite of unpacked boxes and general confusion. And the *next* morning we were on our way to Brussels by 6:17, having left Susan's bag at Home Eden and Susan herself waving on the platform. Debby went as far as Lausanne with us, where Priscilla met us, and after a lunch together we took our separate trains. . . .

In Basel we shopped for rolls, fruit, cheese, and cookies so that we could eat without going to the diner that night. Once we were through customs (Swiss and French, as Basel is a border town) and settled on the train, Fran brought out a stack of reading to "catch up on" and I finished some last-minute stitches in my dressmaking! . . . We arrived in Brussels at 7:00 in the morning and found, to our relief, that our hotel room was ready for immediate occupancy! We had taken a room and bath that first day and night, not only because of the train trip but because there had been no hot water in Bijou before we left and the tub and wash basin were standing on end in the hall—disconnected! The hot water splashing into the tub certainly was music in our ears that morning! We had been invited to the wedding of Lorraine Woodson to John Winston, Jr., at the Belgium Gospel Mission at 11:00 that morning, so we had time to rest a bit and get ready in a leisurely fashion. As we walked to the Hotel de Ville (city hall) we began to wonder just how we would find the right room. There was a wedding out front having its picture taken as we arrived; and after peering into several doors, we suddenly discovered Lorraine coming out looking radiant in her beautiful satin wedding gown. . . . We soon discovered that the ceremony had been a civil one and was early because the brides and grooms must line up and take their turn! Wednesdays and Saturdays are wedding days at the city hall and the ceremonies follow one another as quickly as possible so that all may have their turn! Anyone wanting a Christian ceremony must have it afterwards. As the bride didn't consider herself properly married yet, she was not accompanied by the groom; and thus it was that I found myself in the back of the car going back to the Mission with the bride and the wee flower girl. Taxis in Brussels, which are ordered for a wedding, come beautifully decked with a floral piece arranged on the back of the back seat; so, with the sparkling white bride beside me, I truly felt as though I were riding "in state." Fran rode up front with the taxi driver. . . .

You'll be interested in a custom that is Belgian. People send flowers to a wedding as we would send flowers to a funeral! Lorraine and John had bought a few things to decorate the front of the chapel and then the day of the wedding the bouquets began to arrive. Soon the front was filled with plants, roses, white iris, white lilacs, etc., and they continued to arrive, even with the guests—some being presented to the bride as she was standing in a receiving line after the wedding was over! These were placed at her feet as she couldn't very well shake hands and hold flowers too! There was a very lovely dinner at noon at a restaurant attended by out-of-town guests. The wedding itself took place at 3:00 in the chapel. The ceremony was in three languages—French, Flemish, and English—and the bride and groom sat on special chairs at the front during the hour that it took. This is the custom in several of the European countries, where weddings are much longer than at home and the pastor preaches a regular sermon. . . . However, they say that in some parts of France weddings take as much as three days, so I suppose a full day is not so bad by comparison. . . .

Remember Mme. Marclay, our landlady the first summer we were here? She has been coming quite frequently to see me and help out with sewing. She is reading the Bible which we gave her, regularly ("I'm on page 197 now," she said), and has a real hunger to talk of the things of the Lord. "I love to hear you tell about things in the Bible; your religion has such joy in here," and she pounded herself on the chest. She was German-speaking originally, so I want to buy her another Bible in German. "Then I'll give the French one to Norbert to take to Service Militaire," she said. (Norbert is her son who speaks French more than German.) We continue to have many opportunities to witness in the village. Another new child is coming to the Sunday children's class. . . .

And May didn't close without another cause for rejoicing. A lyrically happy letter arrived from Priscilla telling of her time with "Ush." "Ush" is her new roommate from Germany. The room has four beds, you know, and the English twins occupy the other two. As lights go out at 10:30 and the girls study or talk up to the last minute, Priscilla usually retires to the doorway of the connecting bath to read her Bible. The twins have for a long time said, "Read it out loud to us." So it has become a regular procedure. When Ush came, she listened too. Ush is a 16-year-old from Düsseldorf and has come to Le Grand Verger for a year to perfect her French and to "really" learn English. She understands and speaks English surprisingly well for having had it only as a subject in school. One night as Priscilla was reading the Bible, she stopped and said, "Ush, how do you get to heaven?" "Well, I don't know really—some people say you must be good, others that you must keep all the ten commandments—but really I can't do either of those things." Then Priscilla explained carefully the way and looked up verses for her in the Bible. After the twins had gone to sleep and time was forgotten, Ush came to the moment when she said in her characteristically abrupt way, "Stop talking—I want to do somethings." She bowed her head and a few moments later she said, "All right—it is done—I did it. I accepted Christ as my Savior and told Him." What a thrill it was for Priscilla to have been used to lead this girl to the Lord! . . .

We look forward to writing you soon to give you an account of the many visitors who will be in our home during the month of June—among whom will be Ush.

Till then, much love,

EDITH

July 7, 1951   Champéry, Switzerland

Dearest Family:

Yes, it is actually time for me to pop in with the month's news. . . .

At the present moment we are having sun, which has continued for almost a week now. If you could look out past this typewriter, you would see the fields around Bijou being cut by Herman, raked, tossed into piles, raked into great piles (by Robert and Rachel), and finally loaded into great haystacks which Herman deftly ropes and groaningly hoists onto his back to stagger with up to the little hay shed by our house. Lift your eyes a bit and you would see all the steep slopes peopled by children, men, and women with all varieties of headgear for protection from the sun, cutting, raking, tossing, and becoming walking haystacks. The gay flowers, almost three feet high, are now lying in sweet-smelling stacks, drying in the sun; the lofts above the chalets are becoming full for the winter; the untouchable fields ("Don't walk there—stay on the path—that is hay, remember"!) have suddenly become great pale-green stretches of stubble, giving the whole area a park-like appearance and inviting youngsters to two weeks of freedom for running and rolling. After that, the late crop of grass begins to grow and the taboo is on again. Everyone is working for himself—even the 70-year-old women are raking their own fields with their enormous rakes stretched out ahead of their long black dresses; but there is a community spirit brought about by the sharing of long hours. The rising hour now is 3:30 A.M.—after a breakfast of bread and coffee, the families are already in the fields taking advantage of the first streaks of light. By 7:00 they are hungry again and stop for potatoes and cheese. Hot and dusty, the next "refreshment" comes during a half-hour stop for bread and cheese, and perhaps a bowl of soup, at 11:30. At 4:00 comes the "tea time" or "quatre heures," and then the work goes on until there is no longer enough light, or until the individual is entirely too tired to go on! Supper comes after that—supper and bed! It's a picturesque scene to watch, but grueling work for the people doing it. . . .

Coming home from Vevey one afternoon the man who owns the village electrical shop, who is head of the Champéry Electric Company and at the same time the head of the Champéry Swiss Ski School, moved into the vacant seat by Fran and began asking him questions about the Bible and about the Protestant belief. He stated that he would enjoy coming for an evening of conversation about these things as he had many questions. Since he is in the same class as the hotelkeeper, likes drinking too much, and is one of the village "upper-class fast set," his interest was most surprising to us. . . .

Friday brought Priscilla, accompanied by Ush. How can I make you *know* German Ush? Ush, with her determination to work no matter what the other girls at the school do—"I got up at 5:00, but of course, I have much studies done while those lazy girls sleep until the sun is growing big in the sky!" Ush, with her scorn of foods strange to her— "Jam, jam—and white bread—what breakfast! I am having my grand-modder send grey bread and sausage (a sort of salami)—then I shall eat proper breakfast at that school." Ush, with her background of no play—"At home I work in my papa's store (he has three clothing stores) before school each morning and after school each day. We do nothing but work and we even have store stock in our one room—yes, we four sleep and eat in one room—is not more place in Düsseldorf." Ush, with her utter disregard of proprieties—"So I said to Mademoiselle (a teacher), 'That dress is not for you—it makes you look terrible—you are too fat *here!*' " Ush, with her desire to learn more of God's Word—"Wait before you read—where is it in my German Testament you give me?" Ush, with her appreciation expressed so often sentimentally—"I eat one more biscuit which you made with so much love in them." Ush, with her slightly dictatorial manner—"Give me a tray. I spread out those strawberries; you must not leave them in the basket, they spoil tonight." Ush, with her tender heart yearning for others to believe as she has now believed—"But why are you weeping Ush?" (as she came out of church with tears streaming down her face)—"I want Dinoo should believe too." Can you picture her with her yellow hair pulled tightly back into a velvet ribbon, leaving only a fringe of bangs above her round face? . . . We have never met anyone quite like Ush and we praised the Lord that Priscilla had been given the opportunity of leading her to Himself. A week later we received a gift from Ush— four linen napkin rings, painstakingly embroidered with our names, "Mom," "Daddy," "Susan," and "Debby," in blue on the white cloth, bulkily sewn into round rings—accompanied by a letter of which this was the first paragraph: "My dear Schaeffer's family, I thank you once more for the nice days which I spent in your kindly family and in your pretty house. I will give you these things as a eternal remember." . . .

Remember Baroness von Dumreicher, whom we were able to help during our first summer in Champéry? Through her, we met a number of people to whom we were able to talk concerning the things of the Lord (Christian of Norway was one of them). Well, Betty and Gea are two more rings on the surface of that quiet pool that was disturbed by the splash of the pebble which was our meeting with Baroness von Dumreicher!! A letter out of the blue sky introduced Betty as the one whom Baroness D. had many times wished aloud we could meet. "Could I come to Chalet Bijou for a few days and bring my friend, Gea, along?" The girls took a reserved interest in family prayers and hymn singing, sunned themselves, walked a bit, read, played the piano (they are Conservatory of Music students), and seemed to us only to be listening politely to our conversation about Christian things as if we were discussing life on the moon. Friday they seemed reluctant to leave Champéry so we suggested that they stay in a pension over the weekend and come back to us after the beds were once more vacant!

That afternoon Priscilla arrived with her twin roommates, 17-year-olds from England. . . . Their father is a wealthy silk manufacturer and their life next year will be that of the debutante of London—being presented to the King and Queen, going to the races to watch their privately owned race horses compete, and attending all the usual whirl of social events that go with that life. Yet they are not snobbish but sweet girls who followed me around the kitchen helping to mix the birthday cakes, to pit the cherries for the jam I was making, and ironing Debby's "frock" for Sunday, while they entertained me with stories of their narrow escapes, and life, during the war and all the bombings. . . . We celebrated Priscilla's 14th birthday while the twins were here, though she was also to have a cake and celebration at the school on the actual day itself.

Monday morning our house was quite vacant! That afternoon we discovered that Betty and Gea had gone for a hike with Ange, an English Jewish girl who is secretary at a hotel in Champéry this summer and who was having her "day off," so we left word for them to return together for supper with us. . . . Gea adjourned with us to the kitchen while I began supper preparations and prepared things for canning rhubarb, and Fran search for places to put sticky paper to trap some of the hundreds of flies (no screens in Europe). Suddenly she began unfolding her life's history—the difficulties after her Dad left home—her mother's nervous breakdown—her own eager desire to be a famous musician, and perhaps a Hollywood star as well, keeping her tearing around in college determined not only to do well in studies but to be president of everything and head of the cheerleaders—her going into a beauty contest to prove the stature of her talent and beauty (a very hilarious story when told with Gea's own vivacious personality to color it), and her winning of it (Miss Wichita, Kansas!)—and then her meeting Betty and deciding to come with her for a year's study in the Conservatory of Lausanne while bringing "good will to Europe" at the same time!!

Betty is quite an opposite to Gea's animated dark beauty, being blond, Swedish in background, unusually intellectual and serious in her approach to things, not at all emotional, and with a variety of interests which extend from music and writing to flying (having her own pilot's license). She has her master's degree in education, excels in athletics, wrote a column during the war for a G.I. newspaper, and is one of those rare individuals who gives you the feeling that she could undertake any type of thing she wants to do and do it well. Betty has spent several years in Europe, going home to Illinois in between to visit her loving family. Gea brought us up to date in the autobiography by telling us that this past year in Lausanne had resulted in both of them deciding that there must be more worthwhile values in life than those upon which they had based their past ambitions. They disagreed a bit as to what was necessary to do, but did go in a searching attitude to the classes at the Scotch Church. "Now," they said, "we are not sure—we certainly have heard here in your home something we have never found before."

Just then the doctor arrived. I had had some pains in my legs for a time and was wondering what might be the explanation. The doctor prescribed rest—"Lie down at least two hours after dinner each day." I had a vague feeling that maybe I would try that, but regretted that he could not put the hours into a bottle to be swallowed with a small amount of water! Since the rolls had turned out so perfectly and dinner was ready to be served, I suggested that the doctor stay for supper, which he agreed to do. Hence it was that at our meal we were entertained with all sorts of stories about a Swiss mountain doctor's fascinating experiences. He also told the girls about the Bible studies—"Mr. Schaeffer has prepared them especially for *me* and now they're going to a lot of people—it makes me very proud!" So we were glad to hear that his interest keeps up. By the way, he is taking up flying as a hobby! It was after 11:00 when he left, remonstrating himself for prescribing rest and then keeping the "patient" up. . . .

During the last week of June the Lord gave us a few free days in which to get a bit caught up. We spent some time in the office, some time finishing the couch cover so that the sewing machine is now out of the living room; we welcomed Priscilla home for the summer after her grueling week of study and exams, and Susan also as she informed us at the top of her lungs from a block away that school was finished earlier than they had expected! Priscilla's marks haven't arrived yet, but Susan had an average of five and one-half when the highest possible mark is six, so she has earned her vacation! Nevertheless—out came the American School books—the summer work which we insist the girls do just to keep up!

The last day of June was a Saturday and we had invited Mr. Grandjean of Neuchâtel to spend the weekend with us as there were some things we needed to discuss with him. Saturday, evening brought not only Mr. Grandjean but his wife, daughter, and son-in-law—so once more our beds were full—and June went out having kept its reputation right up to the last moment as being a month of "open house." . . . Our beds had been consistently full with a flow of people from widely differing places and backgrounds.

Thank you for your faithfulness as we realize that it is your prayers which are being answered in results over here.

Love,

EDITH

August 15, 1951   Champéry, Switzerland

Dearest Family:

When I brought Priscilla home in the last letter I didn't have room to describe her arrival with, not only overflowing suitcases, but four cardboard boxes, someone else's airplane handbag, a canvas shopping bag full of sheets, and even her pocketbook full of last-minute things. *Voila!* The first attempt at packing a term's collection of stuff at boarding school! People helped her from one train to the other and all went well until she was sitting on the steps of the little mountain train and her pocketbook tumbled off into the dusty grass. Without hesitating, she jumped off the moving train, retrieved the bag, and caught the train again, jumping up on the last step of the last car as the conductor shook his finger at her out of the window. I often thought that train went about as slowly as walking, and now I am sure of it.

Speaking of Priscilla—you know we had wondered what would work out for next year's schooling, not daring to hope Mr. Fonjallaz would extend his generous invitation to cover another year. However, just a day before she was to leave school he called her into his office and said, "How have you gotten along this year? Do you think you have really learned something here?—Now, when you come back in the fall I think it would be nice if you took your music with us." And just that simply the problem of another year was settled, and Priscilla is to have that wonderful opportunity again. Her marks came along by mail showing that she had kept her honor standing throughout. Her English literature exam was one put out by Cambridge University, and according to that she has finished with honors her high school English! What grade she is in is a problem, as she takes subjects with girls much older than herself, and is not in any particular "grade." However, Miss Walker of Stevens School in Philadelphia has kindly sent cooperative tests in various high school subjects, which Priscilla is taking and sending back to her. Her school reports from here and her marks from those cooperative tests will be kept on file at Stevens, and they will give her the proper credits toward college entrance. This was an extremely thoughtful thing for Miss Walker to do and will mean a lot in the future when the time comes to count up credits for an American college. It is sometimes difficult to get young people to feel that education for the sake of *knowledge* is worth much if there is no credit attached to it. It makes me think of the Christian life—how many Christians there are who want to be sure to have all the credit that is due them for their work now, and Jesus so often reminds us (as in the sixth of Matthew) that if we do things to be seen of men, we already have our reward. How much sweeter will be the reward *He* is planning to give us for these things we have done unto Him "in secret." . . . A bit later Marlise called from

Aigle announcing, "I'm on my way back and I'm bringing an American girl, Toni, who needs to talk to you."

It was Fourth of July morning when Toni walked into our kitchen and followed me around as I made jam and prepared a festive dinner while trying to find out a bit about her background. "My folks are both Dutch, originally, but are American now—we live in Texas. Dad has a rice plantation, among other interests. He graduated from the University of Lausanne and wanted me to study there too. I'm taking the Art course there now—I'll be in Holland with relatives this summer and expect to be back in Lausanne in the fall. My folks believe nothing—they have no religion at all—" And so we got snatches of background which helped us to understand the mood of this slim, bronzed University student with the look of a little girl. We talked a long time around the dinner table and then she went off with the children to swim while we got down to office work. That evening we were invited to a Fourth of July celebration which took place in front of the chalet. A bench had been prepared with cushions and blanket for grownups, but it was a bit difficult to sit there long enough to get the benefit of the comfortable arrangement. "*Ohhhh*, there's the fountain—come closer so you can see it. Whee—isn't that pretty? Now for the pinwheel—we nailed it to the post. Don't *sit* there—come over here where you can see—oh Daddy, don't run way across the field—*Debby, come back!* Why, what was it—I didn't look at the right place—did anybody see it—? Oh, a ball of fire up there? These are green flares I think—no sparklers—well, Happy Fourth of July!!" The fireworks had been bought by the three girls by pooling their savings of a few weeks. The store people had opened up their "First of August" fireworks for the girls because it was the "American First of August." . . .

When the excitement quieted down—the youngsters were in bed and I was in the kitchen hovering over the boiling jam and sterile jars—Fran had a good talk with Toni about Jesus coming to make it possible for anyone who would believe in Him to have everlasting life, that Jesus Himself has made plain He is the *only* way—no matter what the world tries to say about the "good" in "all religions." . . . Before she left for the train a few hours later, Toni whispered, "I did believe—I do—but I'd rather pray alone." Who brought one girl from Texas to Champéry "seeking"? . . .

We have had rain and cold weather most of the summer, but those two days in Lausanne were hot and we were glad to get back to our mountain breezes. The following week was taken up by office work, gardening, classes, and visits from various folks in the village. Mme. Marclay came one afternoon and, as always, wanted to talk about the Bible. We have bought her a German Bible now, as she reads German better than French. The music teacher came one evening and a child's nurse from Les Poussins came another evening. Toward the end of the week we had to prepare for Fran's and Priscilla's departures. Priscilla left on Saturday on the early train, her box of stuff having been sent the day before by parcel post. She was headed for Isonfluh—the summer camp and conference place of Action Biblique, Mr. Alexander's work. There she spent a week sleeping on hay in a tent, eating from an aluminum bowl which she had to wash in cold water, doing her part of the daily work ("Oh, how awful it was to try to wash big soup pots with cold water, using sand to get them clean!"), taking some long mountain hikes with a pack on her back like all the rest, and following the camp schedule. They had private groups in the tents. It was a week of real spiritual growth as well as an education in how to "rough it." She came back full of enthusiasm and singing camp songs, much the same as the children and young people we have sent home from our camps in America. . . .

After saying goodbye to Fran, who had left that same Saturday for Holland, I turned back down the village street and, seeing some plums at a good price, bought a big box of them and spent that afternoon canning. Wonderful thing, to be able to put fruit at the summer price into jars to be opened on a snowy, blustery winter day. The colorful jars of fruit are lined up opposite the shelves of tracts, Bibles, and Children for Christ materials. All sorts of food stored in that room, you see! Sunday I had to turn our service into a Bible Class as Fran was not there to preach. I was really glad that there were not many there that day! Mlle. B., a Christian whom we had met our first year in Lausanne, greeted me before we began. She is the governess of a little Italian girl, whose parents want her to speak English, and she had brought the child to Champéry for the summer. She didn't know that we were here and was so thrilled to find Christian fellowship. . . .

During that week we had the girls from the "home," L'Aube Claire, come for a "treat." After 25 cups of hot chocolate were emptied, filled up, and emptied again, and a batch of cookies consumed as the girls crowded around the two rough wooden tables on the front porch, they all filed into the living room, squatted on the floor, and turned up their eager faces to watch and listen as Marlise gave them the "Door of Salvation," in French. We feel certain that several of them really accepted Christ as their Savior this summer, while others seemed uncertain about themselves. It has been the first time they have heard "the way" made plain. They attend the State Church Sunday School in the town where the "Home" is situated and they get little if anything there. As they presented Marlise with a bouquet of flowers and a Book of Remembrance with a page made by each girl, the teacher of the Home also gave an invitation to Marlise to come down and continue the lessons from time to time in their place near Lausanne.

Mr. Fonjallaz (Director of Priscilla's school) also called during that week and asked if we could spare a room for Miss Hughs and her mother. "Miss Hughs is to be sort of supervising a group of my girls who will be in Champéry for a time. There are two other teachers with them, but

Miss Hughs is having her vacation and I don't want her to work—just to be there in case of emergency." It was little enough to do after all he has done for us, so Priscilla's room was made ready for the Hughses.

When Fran returned on Saturday he found the Australian girls waiting to meet him, and his long talk with them that night about Bible-believing Christianity finished up the conversations I had had through the week with them. They left the next morning but will be in Europe some months longer. The morning train brought Carl Steinhauser in time to be our organist for the church service. He is a Faith Seminary graduate who has been studying this past year in Zürich. My, how he can play! The little rented piano in our living room filled our house with Bach, Chopin, Beethoven, and a multitude of hymns. Carl not only plays with excellent technique, but his interpretation of various of our favorites is more satisfying than anything we have heard. It was really restful to work to music during those days. Carl expects to teach German, but any college that has him as professor will also have an excellent source for piano concerts.

The first of August rolled around again. How many firsts of August have I described here? This was our third in Champéry, but our fourth in Europe. There were over 5,000 people in our wee village for the big Swiss National Holiday. People like to go to the mountains for this day and the hotels are always stuffed. In the afternoon we went up to the music teacher's chalet so that we might all hear Carl play on a good piano. Coming back to get supper I discovered that it was Carl's birthday so, along with the cooking of the meal, "whipped up" a birthday cake, using one of the new fast-method cake recipes that had arrived in a letter that very day! It really went quickly and was complete with green music notes decorating the white icing before supper was served. However, we left the cake for later, as the children were anxious to get up to the village before the lantern parade started. It seemed as though there were more people carrying lighted lanterns, more fireworks going up from overhanging balconies, more flares from chalets way up on the mountain, a larger bonfire in the field, brighter red and green flares on top of the highest peak of the Dents du Midi, and more children swinging sparklers right in the midst of the crowd listening to the patriotic speech—than ever before! When the speech was over and the Champéry Band had played its last patriotic piece, we made our way back down the village street, festive with flags, lanterns, bursts of fireworks, and crowds of people, and Susan remarked with a happy sigh—she says during the same occasion every year—"Oh, I hope I can *always* live in Champéry!" The Hughses shared our birthday party of cake, tea, and ice cream and we all went off to bed with the music still ringing in our ears. Carl had completed the week's concerts with some selections played by candlelight. The piano has two candleholders attached to it and you have a feeling you have stepped back a century as you sit in that flickering light. . . .

We have all arrangements made to go to Finland to speak at a number of churches—meetings arranged for every day—from September 23rd to October 5th. Then we are due to speak at a yearly conference of the Swedish Missionary Alliance in Jönköping, Sweden, October 7th and 8th, and we are to stay there a few days to help get Children for Christ started in Jönköping. Then Dr. Hedegard has arranged other meetings in southern Sweden, he himself planning to accompany us as interpreter. However, unless the money comes in for such a trip, and enough of the salary to care for the ordinary expenses plus care of the children in our absence, we will call it off in spite of the warm invitations and offers of hospitality that have been sent to us. Just pray with us that *if* He wants us to go, the money will come in time. . . .

Let me quickly bring you up to date, as I may not write again until the middle of September. We had two Sundays with rather big church services. One week there were over 50 schoolboys from London, with their professors; and the next week a lot of miscellaneous people, English, Scotch, Welsh, and Italian Waldensian. We never know ahead of time who will make up the congregation. I had laryngitis for a few days, which turned into some variety of flu. This kept me in bed for a number of days, and although I can type in bed, sew a bit, and study and read, it hindered me in the work. The doctor says this has left me with a bit of anemia, as I am so weak and wobbly, but a liquid form of iron and liver extract is helping that. During this time Susan contracted double bronchitis—"Terrible weather," the doctor proclaimed. "Everybody is sick." One night she coughed all night, though we even moved a bed into the bathroom to see if *steam* wouldn't stop it. (We have only one way of steaming anyone here—filling the tub with hot water.) However, she is much better now—though still coughing. She was so well last winter, but this rainy summer has seemed to have a bad effect on her health. The doctor insists a change of air is necessary for her, and a rest for me, and of course Fran needs it too. So we are going for a two-week vacation, the first of September. We saved up through the year for a vacation, and made reservations at a place in Alassio, a sunny spot on the seashore in northern Italy, a day's train trip from here, at the same place where Fran and I stayed alone last year. The prices are low after the season is over—really a cheaper place to stay than Champéry. We feel that since we saved the money for a vacation, and since the doctor says it is necessary to the health, the Lord would have us do that with it in spite of low funds. . . .

Do pray—we are as curious as you may be as to what the Lord will answer—and as to what news therefore there will be in the next "installment"!!!

Lovingly,

EDITH

September 21, 1951   Scandinavian Express, Basel to Copenhagen

Dearest Family:

We are on our way to Finland to speak, after which we will return to Sweden for further speaking engagements. The clear way in which the Lord led in this trip and the amazing way the money came in time to make all the arrangements will be unfolded as I go back over the past weeks. It can't possibly be more of a surprise to you than it was to us as we lived through it. It never ceases to be a thrill to watch the Lord work out all the details and see His perfect *timing* of letters, arrivals, departures, decisions, etc. . . .

As I left you in the middle of August, Susan was coughing away after an attack of bronchitis, I was feeling weak after the grippe, and the time for vacation was near. We were economizing because of lack of funds, but since we had saved up money for a vacation and the doctor insisted the change was needed especially for Susan and myself, we decided to use this special fund and trust the Lord to show us the next step—so plans were completed, tickets bought, and we determined to spend no money at all the two weeks before going! The garden provided an abundant variety of vegetables—in fact it is getting to be known as the prize garden of Champéry. Such a small handful of dry little seeds as we started with last May—how *could* such a crop come forth? The day we finished our last bit of breakfast cereal a box arrived from America with enough to last until we left! When the doctor decided the grippe had left me anemic he dropped in with a sample box of liver and iron capsules "to try"! A few personal gifts arrived in time to pay up to date the rent and electricity and to buy some fruit for canning. Thus the Lord met the immediate need.

As I was finishing up last month's letter the doorbell tinkled and this report burst into the office in the three children's voices: "It was the Bureau of Information man." "He said that 270 English people have arrived for a week." "They're all coming to church tomorrow and do we have enough place to hold them all at once?" "Daddy asked Marlise to go up to the church and count the places." "We don't have enough song books—what'll we do?" That night and early the next morning I was very glad for the energy the capsules were giving me! Marlise had gone to Lausanne to meet Hughette, and I kept the typewriter humming to get enough copies of three hymns and the order of service to go around to all that crowd. The last sheaf of copies went with me as I hurried through the village ten minutes behind the family—only to find there was no need of rushing—it was taking a long time for the number to file in and fill the downstairs and balcony. "Doesn't it seem peculiar to see all those strangers walking around with our yellow paper in their hands?" inquired Debby, while Susan was excitedly explaining. "This is how it looks when a church is *full*. This is the way church looked back home, Debby—why we used to have it all packed with kids for Summer Bible School." Debby sang so loudly that morning that people turned to see whose voice was carrying above all the others! The Lord gave Fran a wonderful gospel message which was received by intently listening ears. . . . Some stayed to talk with Fran afterwards and I overheard many remarking. "Never heard anything quite like it before—he seemed so *sincere."* . . .

Later that week Priscilla and Susan, Vic and I formed a sort of production line and managed to can tomatoes, plums, peaches, and pears, as well as some string beans and beets from the garden, so that over a hundred shining jars were stored away. Madame Marclay appeared one afternoon "to help you sew and mend while we talk together like family folks." She has so many questions to ask and always likes to hear more of the Bible explained. Fran and the children worked together in the garden cultivating and spraying DDT on the newest crop of bugs! During the last day Susan followed me around reading my list of things to be done. "Have you aired out the Thermos bottles? Have you packed a blanket for the beach? Have you put in the towels? Are the bathing suits washed and mended? Did you clean out the refrigerator?—" On and on she droned out the list, until I finally took it away from her. "Susan, it's bad enough to have to do all those things without your constant accompaniment." "But mother, I don't want you to forget anything."

At last the 5:00 A.M. alarm went off and Susan, who had been parading up and down the hall every 20 minutes since 3:00 A.M. "to see if it is five yet," burst into our room. "Better hurry—we'll miss the train." As we pulled out and pushed the *petit char* up the hill in a downpour of rain, we were glad the bulk of our luggage had been taken to the station the night before. We had lots of time to wait in the station and Marlise and Hughette came to see us off. . . .

With a sigh of relief that there was really nothing to do but "sit" we settled back to enjoy the quiet beauty of our mountains and their "music box" chalets in the early-morning light. We were quite loaded down with stuff to carry, since clothes for five for all kinds of weather, books for study and reading, and food for two days filled up backsacks, string bags, and suitcases; but the change at Aigle went off smoothly in spite of the rain. "Sit on this bag Debby, till Daddy comes back for it. Look for the first third-class car that seems to have some empty seats, Susan. Everything on? Oh—good—seats all together in the same compartment!" Now we had space enough to open up picnic bags and enjoy our breakfast of homemade sweet rolls, fruit, and milk. The skies cleared as we crossed into Italy, which seemed like a promise of good weather for the two weeks ahead. The children enjoyed their first glimpse of Italy and kept a constant watch for new things—"Oh, there's a palm tree—look at the pink house." And as we ate our lunch, Debby remarked contentedly while munching a sandwich, "The thing I like best of all is eating a picnic on a train."

"Milano! and the train is late—not much time to make connection. I'll push the big bags out of the window to that porter—you and the children gather up your stuff and go on out." "Genoa—Genoa—" The porter got the idea and trundled off his cart full of bags in the direction of the train to Genoa. Fran, Susan, and Debby ran along beside him while Priscilla and I fell a bit behind as we shifted bags and picked up some dropped things. "There they are, getting on there—hurry, Priscilla, get up behind Daddy—the porter hasn't put the bags on yet—I'll stand here beside him to make sure he puts them all on—" The train begins to move—"Mommy, mommy," shrieks Debby, and Susan and Priscilla shout, "Oh, look—we're going." Other passengers take up the shout in Italian—the porter stands helplessly looking at the four big bags he had expected to put on for us, then shrugs his shoulders at me. The train picks up speed and Fran shouts something to me about tickets—then the train disappears and I find myself alone with the heavy bags on one of the many platforms in that enormous Milan station. A few inquiries and I discover that no one near me speaks either English or French!!! The porter waves his arms in evident explanation of the situation to a nice-looking little lady with a small boy, then turns to me obviously wanting his money. I show him that I have no lira—only Swiss francs—so off he goes with the bags, leading me to the money exchange booth—it seems at *least* a mile away! With the francs now in lira, bulging out my purse with bills (it's all paper money—5-lira bills equal about 2 cents, and you have 10-lira bills, 50-lira bills, and 100-lira bills to contend with as well as the bigger ones—the larger the amount the bigger the actual piece of paper!). I am now led back to the platform where I am to wait about three hours for the next train to Genoa. Whether I can ride to Genoa or not, without a ticket, is the next question! It's *hot,* so I shed my suit jacket and sit down on the baggage. The lady with the little boy begins talking to me in Italian, none of which I understand.

An hour ticks by—trains coming and going—people, voices, whistles, rattles, hubbub—then suddenly the loud-speaker booms out. "Some train announcement I suppose, I don't hear Genoa mentioned." The loud-speaker persists in repeating the same thing and finally I catch "Sheffer"—could it be for me? "Evita Sheferrr, va a la beaureau de resignament—" It is French badly spoken and is telling me to go to the information desk. I turn to the lady and make sign language asking her to watch the bags and run down the long dingy platform into the station proper. It turns out to be a phone call—and wonder of wonders it is Fran's voice. "Hi Edith, are you OK? Poor Debby thought she'd never see you again! The kids were good though and people kind. We got off at the first station on the suggestion of the conductor and they fixed things so that I could call you from here. Now, you take the next train and watch out for us at the first station so that we can get on the same car with you—try to make the conductor understand that I have the tickets—goodbye—see you." My next anxious moments are as the train comes in and all porters ignore me! Only at the last do I have help with the bags and end up riding in the vestibule—all seats taken! An hour later four faces, intently searching the train windows from the platform, suddenly break into smiles—"Mommy, mommy, mommy—here we are!" Happy reunion! Fran, Susan, and I are squashed in the vestibule with all our bags and about 15 other people. Some woman has put her suitcase on our bag of sandwiches and is leaning on it! Amazingly, Debby wormed her way down the corridor from the other end of the car, where she and Priscilla had a seat. "I wanted to be with you—all the people in the care were undressing and dressing my dolly—isn't that funny? Old men and ladies and everyone acted like they had never seen such a little dolly with clothes—they said, 'Bella, bella' " (pretty, pretty). With her dolly safe in its little suitcase, Debby sat down on a small suitcase at my feet and went sound asleep in spite of noise, smoke, and heat. No air-conditioned trains over here, you know.

It was good to get out at Genoa knowing that we could stop for the night. We walked to an inexpensive hotel near the station—not far, but up flights and flights of steps—washed, rested, and ate a picnic supper in our room, complete with milk still cold from our refrigerator in Champéry! In the evening we walked a bit through the narrow streets of this old city, and the next morning Fran took the girls to see the wee house Columbus lived in before he sailed for America, an interesting old castle, and a museum, while I began my vacation by resting in the hotel room, actually feeling too exhausted to make any effort at all. We had food enough left to picnic again at noon, adding only a bottle of orangeade (very good in Italy). . . .

That afternoon we boarded the train again. The view from the train along the coast to Alassio thrilled us all. "How blue the water is." "Is our beach going to be like that—is it Daddy?" "Can we go in swimming as soon as we get there?" "Look at the big boat out there—wonder if it's going to America."

In less than three hours we were all piling into the horse-and-buggy taxi which took us to our pension hotel. Our rooms were bare with the usual stone floors that you find in Italy, but there wasn't to be much time spent in the rooms. Even as I was unpacking, the delighted squeals of Susan and Debby floated into the window from the beach across the street. What a lovely spot in which to rest. The soft air seemed relaxing from the first moment. Days spent in lovely warm sunshine on the white sand, interspersed with dips in the turquoise salt water, soon changed our color to shades of red and brown. Susan's cough stopped immediately and we all began to feel better. "It would be nice to live here all the time, except that the arithmetic would be terrible to do," remarked Susan. "Just think how many lira you would have to multiply and divide for problems! If a man went out to buy a pig at market with lira, that would be dreadful." When Grandmother Schaeffer's dollar was divided three ways for spending money into about 200 lira apiece, how-

*On our vacation to Italy we took a day
trip over the border for lunch in France.*

ever, it seemed like a lot more than 33 cents! A game of miniature golf
cost 50 lira apiece and a small ice-cream cone was 50 lira. You get about
520 lira for a dollar now, but when you think that before the war one
dollar was exchanged for about four lira, you get an idea what happened to the Italians' bank accounts. . . .

One night we decided to buy a few small things to send home for
Christmas. "I'll wrap and send them from here," I said innocently. "We
won't have time before leaving Champéry for Finland." I asked the hotelkeeper, Miss Prosipero, for a few boxes, explaining what I wanted to
do. "Few boxes? Oh no, you must send all in one box." "But they don't
live in one city," I answered. "Oh, but in Italy it is very difficult to send
packages—you must send only one." She was so insistent that I agreed,
"All right, I'll send one." Then I went out to comb the town for paper,
string, etc. In a dusty, dark stationer's I found paper, a ball of skinny
string, and some loose pieces of heavier string. I proudly showed Miss
Prosipero I had things with which to make a fairly secure package.
"Oh, no, you must not wrap here." "No? Where then?" "I will telephone to find out, but you cannot wrap a package at home." Three calls
and much Italian—then, "I will come with you—we go on bicycle—
come." My paper and string is dumped into the box along with the
gifts and the box given to the porter to carry. He leads the way on his
bicycle, box on his shoulder. I follow next on a borrowed one, and Miss

Prosipero brings up the rear. Up one street—ocean breezes in our hair; around a corner, bus exhaust and other smells now; on and on we go until we finally stop near the railroad station. In and out of several offices we pass, obediently, until we are finally pointed to a grey, dingy room back of the baggage room. "Here we must wait for the Customs Official." We wait! And wait! We telephone again, and wait! And finally almost at noon the Customs Official sweeps in with an air of great importance. Miss P. explains that this American wishes to send some few things to her family. He looks rigid and unimpressed. He states, "The American could carry the things home." She says, "But she is not going home; she is going to Switzerland—they are things for brothers, sisters, mothers". . . .

He bends to inspect everything in the box. He looks at them from all angles as if he had never seen such things before, when after all they are on every street stall in town. He shakes the box, solemnly shakes his head. "*Impossible* for the American to send these things by parcel to America," he states with arms folded impressively across his chest. A feeling of exasperation comes over me—it doesn't seem real—the dirty, dingy, old room—our poor little Christmas presents spread out over a marred old table, and this ridiculous man in a uniform telling me I can't send them to America. Miss P. waves her arms and argues. He argues back but finally, with a sweep of his arm, says, "This time, this *one* time, *I* will permit the American to send this box to America. It must be wrapped here while *I* am watching." Feverishly I begin to write tags—David, Jonathan, Lydia, Lucinda, Barney, Mother Schaeffer, etc., etc., and Miss P. starts to put paper on things. Half way through—just as the inside is done but the box is still open—our Customs Official holds up his hand. "It is time for my dinner now—I must go—come back at 3:00." We look a little dismayed and stop our work of wrapping. Nothing to do but go.

"We can't trust these things here," says Miss P., "we must carry the box over and leave it at the *bank* where I have a friend." The box safely under a table at the bank, we go bicycling back to the hotel. Dinner over, we mount the bikes again, and having gathered up the box we reappear in the musty old room, only to be told to wait—and wait. This time I decided to make use of my time and pulled out the Gospel Walnut; I gave the Gospel to Miss P. . . . Finally, the Customs man put in his appearance again. "Take *all* things out of the box." "But you looked at everything this morning." "Yes, but you might have put some other things in it. Show it *all* to me." Oh well—let him pinch and poke and pull out all the stuffing!! Now we repack, since he has nodded his approval, and put string around the box (enough I hope to hold it), then paper (too short, put two pieces overlapping), then heavy string. "Oh, those pieces are so short, I'll tie several of them together." I begin to do square knots when the Customs Official begins talking and waving his arms. "No, *no*—you must not tie knots—only one piece of string is allowed—that is the *law*. Such a stupid thing to tie knots." "But," I say pleadingly to Miss P., tell him the pieces are too short and I know that one piece of string will never hold that paper on for that long voyage." "He says he knows you have never sent a box anywhere before or you'd *know* there can only be *one* knot in the string and that is the knot to hold it all together. That is the *law*. I shrug my shoulders and put the longest piece of string around the box—it just reaches once around each way and makes a meager knot. With a final flourish of importance the Customs man puts a metal seal over the knot. With this seal, of course, the box is assured a safe arrival (no one would think of slipping the string off the side, of course!!) Now we are permitted to go a few blocks to the post office to stand in line with our box. Here a sheaf of forms have to be filled out and the boy in the post office must keep the whole line behind us waiting while he looks up in a big book the postage for America and while he fills out forms, cuts stamps with scissors, which he puts on the box and then puts *in duplicate* on a form which he carefully files away!!

After 6:00 P.M., Miss P. and I weakly wend our way home, feeling dizzy and scarcely believing that what we had just gone through was possible. "But do you go through this every time you send a box?" I inquire. "We never send a box. It is too impossible." How thankful we are that with boxes of Children for Christ materials to send out *every week*, we do not live in Italy. We'd need to hire one person just to take the boxes through customs and mail them! . . .

Champéry looked so good to us, and the three nights at home with the intervening days were filled to the brim with preparations. It was good to see Betty and Gea again, and to have Mlle. Bonnet and Alexandra with Susan and Debby when we left. Priscilla was due back at school in Lutry so she drove down with Betty and Gea. Her new roommate is a Turkish girl with whom she speaks French. We stopped to see Priscilla on our way to Lausanne and were glad to be able to leave knowing she was well and happy. Leaving her, we drove on to Lausanne, where we found we had time enough for me to dash to the store while Fran read and signed the letters he had picked up. He used a baggage cart for a desk! Hence, as we sank into the train seats (if you can "sink" into wood) we had the comfortable feeling of being as caught up as possible before starting out. We began this trip feeling very much that we were coming only because the Lord had provided in every way and down to the last detail.

Much love,

EDITH

September 20 to October 20, 1951   The Scandinavian Trip

Dear Family:

While I have been writing this letter we have received a threatening letter concerning our work here from someone in the village who has been antagonistic. We have known that sometime difficulties would arise because of the religious complexion of the Canton. Copies of this threat were sent to the village president and to another influential person. It is possible that the final outcome of this would be the curtailing of Priscilla's Children for Christ class in French, the loss of the chapel in which we have our English services every Sunday, and even possibly the revoking of our Police Permit to live here. So we do ask each of you to have special prayer that if it is His will, none of the above results may come to pass.

As the Express train between Lausanne and Basel slid along the rails, we found the light-colored, varnished pine seats of the third class a very appetizing background for our supper. There are convenient slide-in-the-wall tables which can be pulled out beside the seats in front of the windows and there we spread our sandwiches. At Basel the Scandinavian Express from Rome was an hour late. Schedules have been speeded up and the train we had taken last year, arriving in Stockholm at the same time, now leaves at 9:30 at night rather than 5:00 in the afternoon. Things are back to normal in Western Europe. It was after 10:30 when the train finally pulled into the chilly, dark and almost deserted Basel station, and the warmth of its well-lighted interior was a welcome change from our suitcase-seats. We hung up the suits from our suitcase and made ourselves at home. We went through German customs at midnight and so did not settle down for the night until after that. What a lot of value a bit of paper and ink has at a time like that. We slept our way through much of Germany and awakened as the train jerked to a stop in Hanover. After our beds were made up I tried to settle down to typing, but I must confess it didn't go very rapidly as the German countryside took up much of my attention. We were eating our sandwich lunch (by the way, we really enjoy carrying our own food—it means we can eat when we are hungry and be quite independent of dining cars) when the train stopped at the border town of Flensburg. Fran fished around in his wallet for some German marks he has had for ever so long, and I took them out to the platform to exchange them for two bottles or orangeade and a package of figs. Orangeade bottled in Berlin and figs from Algeria! This topped off our lunch very well. . . . We came to the Nyborg Ferry at about 6:00. This ferry takes the train right on it, which means quite a long time of shifting cars. When our car finally was shoved into its place, I had quite a stint of typing done and agreed it was time to leave "the office" and go up on the deck. . . .

Korsør to Copenhagen does not take long, but by the time our train had once more been shifted and pushed on to the boat to Malmö, it was 10:00 P.M. *This* water took about the same time to cross as the other stretch did, about an hour and 20 minutes. Since the other side of the water is Sweden, there are Danish and Swedish customs to go through, passport control men, "how-much-Swedish-money-do-you-have men," etc. We were glad when the parade ended and we could have our beds made up and settle down once more for a night's sleep. When we awakened in the morning we were passing little lakes, rocks, pine trees, and white birches which we recognized as some place close to Stockholm. . . . When we arrived at the docks where the boats leave for Finland, we found everything closed up except a little office, but they agreed to keep our baggage for us until it was time to "check in" for the boat at 4:00 P.M. . . . Everyone says, "If you haven't seen Skansen, you haven't seen Stockholm," so we decided to spend these in-between hours there. While we were waiting for the trolley the king's guards trotted past on horses, on their way for the morning changing of the guards. The band, playing a march, was also on horses and the brass trumpets were brilliant as they caught the sun's rays while the drum looked most out of place mounted, with its drummer banging away at it, on the horse's back. The trolley hissed to a stop behind the guards and we were soon on our way. . . .

Skansen is a sort of open-air museum. There is an entire village reconstructed—some of the buildings are actual old ones moved there—and in it you find a glass factory in full swing, with six or seven men making glass in the old manner. A little balcony of rough wooden benches enables you to watch this fascinating work as long as you want to stay. There is the old shoemaker shop, the bakery shop with its enormous brick ovens, the print shop, and the goldsmith's shop, and a variety of houses completely furnished, about which you may wander at will. As you leave this village you go on to various types of farm houses, manor houses, peasant cottages, etc., from all parts of Sweden, depicting various centuries. There is even a little Lapland house (something like a wigwam) in which a Lapp family lives every winter. The park also includes a zoo and restaurants and outdoor theaters. . . .

We got back to the boat dock in plenty of time to check our bags through Swedish customs and make out innumerable papers which are required in leaving and entering Scandinavian countries. . . . This time our night's sleep was undisturbed by any ice, and even our inside third-class cabin beside the noisy engine room did not keep us awake. It was Sunday morning when our boat slid in toward the Finnish wharf, and as Fran looked through his field glasses he saw two familiar faces. "Look, Edith, there's Miss Anderson and the pastor's daughter." As we came closer they waved vigorously and we waved back, and it was as if we were coming home. The very same porter carried our bags as had carried them last time. He gave us a big smile and welcomed us back to Finland! It was not long until we were in a taxi with Miss Anderson, and the girl, on our way to her apartment. There once more the small space was shared with us, and the folding beds, including the piano bench I described last year, were brought out at night. Things are better than they were last year, in that there is a greater variety of food (carrots were served often and small red tomatoes appeared at many meals), and clothing is more plentiful. The menace of Russia is always with them. Miss Anderson told of another Åbo family who disappeared this last summer when their sailboat drifted too close to the Russian-held shore, and the Finns who were formerly Russian live in constant fear. . . .

Early the next morning we were taken to the train and presented with tickets to take us on to Karis. . . . At our particular stop in the midst of a forest, we swung off with our bags, and moments later, who should gallop up to meet us but the same horse who had given me such a wild ride in the sleigh last year! This time his driver was standing on a two-wheeled flat cart without sides, and as the school director dropped off the cart to greet us, the student balanced the bags on the see-saw sort of wagon. "If there's anything breakable you'd better carry it," remarked the director, and then to me, "Want to ride or walk?" "I think I'd prefer walking." "Oh, get up right here," said the student, half pulling me up to a spot on the cart right next to the horse, and off we went! There was nothing to hang onto but the flat board I was sitting on—or the horse's tail—but I preferred the former! The reins of coarse rope went over my head, and my feet dangled over the sandy road. The horse went more slowly this time and seemed tamer than before, for which I was thankful. . . .

Between Fran's two lectures that day, we were taken to see Hangö, the seaport very near Santala, which is one of the favorite summer resorts of the Finns. There we walked about marveling at the beauty of the new buildings and fine streets of this town which had been just a heap of rubble after the war. There is a children's orphanage and school built as a gift from a Swedish town, but the rest the people have built for themselves. We went up to the top of the water tower to get a view of the town and its surrounding water and islands. It seems all water towers in Finland are equipped with an elevator and a fine lookout at the top. The water looks wonderfully inviting for boating, but if sailboats go out too far and are blown too close to the Russian section nearby, here too the people disappear! So the calm waves lapping against rocky islands are deceptive in their appearance of completely normal safety. . . .

As we got off in Kouvola, we were met by the pastor, who took us to his waiting bicycle upon which he balanced our luggage, with Fran carrying what remained. I walked along helping to hold the big suitcase on the bike as the pastor steered it. He told us that in Finland if a pastor has a car, the people think he is *very* rich and that he doesn't need a salary! This church building includes rooms for the pastor, some for the caretaker and his wife, and a room just off the auditorium for "visiting speakers." With our bags placed in this small room with its table, daybed, and corner stove, we went over to the pastor's apartment for dinner and a talk. We found that he and his wife had returned from China recently and had most interesting stories to tell. In case any of you have read the recent biography of Mrs. Howard Taylor, you will remember that it tells of a young man in Finland who gave his life to China as a result of reading Mrs. Taylor's book, *The Triumph of John and Betty Stam*. This pastor *is* that young man! But now his days in China are over, at least for a time, and he had just two weeks before he came to take up his work as pastor of the Free Church in this town so close to Russia. Both he and his wife had their home in Karjala formerly, and they told of the day when everyone shut his door upon his own home and turned to leave it forever—with most of his possessions left behind. They said that as everyone had the same sorrow, trudging along the road or riding in trucks or wagons, it was easier to smile together and make the same joys in the situation! All these folks are scattered over Finland along with the ones who later lost their homes in the section Russia took out of the coastline between Helsinki and Åbo, and you are constantly reminded that they are *not* in their own homes as you see pictures of what they left and of their own churches, on mantelpieces and in snapshot books. Now this couple had fled China and once more had lost many of their possessions—because of that same Russia. We couldn't help but wonder what might lie ahead of them in Kouvola. . . .

We worked on correspondence in the morning, and at 1:00 went to the railroad station to see the Russian train which comes through from Leningrad every other day on its way to the Russian-held "bite" of Finland on the coast. Fran got a picture of this as it came with its red star on the engine. It is supposed to be a "very fine train because they want us to see how fine their trains are," according to the people there, but it made us laugh as we compared it to our American trains, with its wooden coaches painted green, its little engine puffing away so importantly for all the world like a toy. Out of its windows peered curious faces, and we walked right beside them as the train stopped for a few minutes. There were pale-faced children and a few women, but mostly men in uniform—who had three hours ago been in Leningrad and now were going to live in their new homes—what thoughts were in *their* heads as we peered at each other so curiously? Fran went on after that, to go through the largest paper mill in Scandinavia, where among many things he saw great bundles of paper addressed to Philadelphia.

At four we were taken to dinner at the home of the mayor of the town, who also has the largest pocketbook and ladies' bag factory in Finland. His apartment is built right up over the factory, just as a butcher might live over his shop! It is pleasant, but extremely humble compared to what a man of his wealth and position would have in America. He has nine children, a private airplane, an automobile, and he travels extensively for his business as well as flying up to Lapland to hunt and fish. We had delicious fish for dinner which he had caught in a nearby lake, and we enjoyed a variety of subjects of conversation. At the 5:00 o'clock meeting, there were many children present who listened intently to the flannelgraph stories and object lessons, and then we found there was only a short recess during which we could prepare for the evening meeting. Although it had been announced for those who really wanted to begin classes, there were more people present than even the day before! As I finished my part of the message, I mentioned that if there were time I could give several interesting illustrations of how the Lord has used Children for Christ in various places. What happened was that the pastor (who speaks English perfectly, by the way, since his father was English) asked the people if they wouldn't like to stay and hear some of these stories, and they all nodded and made no move to go!! So I went on, and after one story paused, only to be told "Tell another," until it was 10:30 when I finally stopped telling stories.

We came out of that meeting to find that the sauna had been diligently heated up for us to refresh us for the night's sleep! After the sauna we were served "silver tea," which is what the Finnish restaurant menus called hot water during the war. The next morning we packed up and left, accompanied by the pastor who was coming with us to translate at the next place. . . . We talked our way through the miles and miles of woods broken only by occasional lakes, keeping our eyes turned towards the windows that we might not miss seeing this most eastern section of Finland. As we arrived in Mikkeli we were farther north than we had ever been before. Here the pastor had ordered a taxi for us and we were taken in a brand new, shiny blue Nash (nicest taxis in Finland are in this town, it seems!) to the church building. This barracks-like building is built on a lot right next to the jagged ruins of the foundation of their old church building. The foundations encircle a heap of earth with grass and bushes growing on it, while the old steps lead to a cluster of scrubby bushes. You see, during the war a fire bomb landed in the middle of the church and it burned in a matter of minutes. They hope to rebuild where the old foundations are. We left our bags at the church and went to the pastor's home for coffee (it seems we had missed "breakfast" that day) and for an afternoon of concentrated talking on the children's work. I disappeared into the bedroom where this whole family of five sleep—triple-decker bunks for the children— to do some typing. Then after supper we went off for the meeting. The building was really packed with the most enthusiastic and warm audience we had yet spoken to, and the translator kept me telling stories again—since he had heard them the night before and wanted them all repeated—until it was time to rush for the train. We had only a moment to swallow some tea and leave for the 11:00 P.M. train for Helsinki. The pastor had thoughtfully bought tickets for two and a half persons, which gave us a whole third-class sleeping section to ourselves. As he came on board with us to inspect the sleeper he said, "Oh, fine, they don't use the paper sheets anymore—you have real cloth" so we found there was something to be thankful for that we might not have appreciated otherwise! We were farewelled with real warmth and were sorry our time there had had to be so rushed. That night we slept fairly well in spite of the fact that the berths were wooden and the sheets scarcely made up for the lack of mattresses! A bit of stiffness the next morning was the only ill effect.

Morning found us in Helsinki with Kaleva there to meet us again and take us to the hostel where we read our mail, typed a bit, and ate our dinner before taking the train to Åbo. This time we were on the train that was to go straight through the Russian-held "bite" of Finland, 60-by-60 kilometers. As we approached the one kilometer of "no-man's land" the train stopped and our engine was shifted to a side track and a Russian engine with a Russian engineer was put in its place. All the sheets of iron on the outside of the train were slipped up into place over the windows and locked securely. The doors were all shut and we could hear the click, click of metal as the door handles were securely fastened with strips of wire and sealed with lead. Even the freight cars were sealed, and the Finnish conductors were sealed in with us. The train then moved ahead one kilometer when it stopped again at the Russian border. Here we were told that Russian soldiers mount the steps, one to each set of steps on the train, to ride there as "guards" with their guns ready! As far as we were concerned, it was black as a coal mine, with only the train's electric lights giving us any illumination. This is the way all Finnish trains must proceed through this section, which the Russians have supposedly "rented"—and incidentally, the trains must pay for the privilege of being thus "guarded" and taken through! It is not a pleasant experience as you ride along for an hour and a quarter this way, and the thought that the bright sunshine is shining on the other side of that piece of iron gives you a frustrated feeling. From a practical viewpoint, it becomes very "close"; in the summer it must be unbearable. And one shudders to think what would happen if there were an accident on this stretch. Of course, if the Russians wished an "accident" to happen, it could do so easily, as they have complete charge. We were told that it is known that Russian spies always ride this train, listening and watching. It was a relief when the other side was reached, the Russian engine shifted off, the Finnish engine put on, and the iron curtains dropped down to let the sun stream in. Ordinary farmlands are now seen from the windows, and as farmers go about their work, cows graze, the wind blows gently through the gay-colored leaves, red houses send forth grey wisps of smoke, and children bump their school bags against their knees coming home from school; it seems impossible to believe that less than a couple of miles away a powerful enemy is so strongly entrenched behind such a wall of secrecy. . . .

As we left for the boat Miss Anderson insisted on giving us gifts for the children—a wee copper kettle for Debby, Finnish knives (miniature ones) for the two older girls, and a book of pictures of Finland, as well as pinning a corsage of carnations on me. When we arrived at the dock we found there were two girls from the church and a boy with his father to say "goodbye." No delay this time—check in the bags, money control, time to go on board—warm handclasps, tears, "Goodbye—till we meet again here—or—up there." The boat begins to move and the strip of water widens when suddenly a big fat boy arrives, puffing and out of breath. He makes a motion as if to throw something, hesitates as Miss Anderson evidently tells him that is not allowed, dashes over to an officer to ask permission, receives it, and comes back to the now very wide strip of water and heaves the little bag—plop. It lands on the deck behind us—he grins a happy grin and waves goodbye. "Come again" he shouts, "thank you." We look in the bag and find a warm pair of knitted wool gloves, bright blue and red—for me! "Thank you, thank you," we shout. Were there ever warmer-hearted, more generous people than the Finns? They are so ready to give out of their little, when those who have much are often so selfish. It is a lesson to all of us who live in easier spots of the world. . . .

That night on the boat was not such a pleasant one. We ate in our cabin the lunch we had brought from Åbo. The people next to us were having some sort of a party and the noise continued until very late, after which we couldn't seem to sleep much. So we were feeling tired when we arrived in Stockholm the next day. We had hoped for a day's rest and a quiet night in a hotel there before going on, but a letter informed us we were expected early the next morning in Jönköping, that Fran was to be the main speaker at the quarterly conference of the Swedish Alliance Mission and his first message should be given at 11:00 A.M. So we needed to go on closer to Jönköping that same day. We had reservations to book for our trip home, and stopped first of all at Cook's travel bureau to get the tickets to Jönköping. Our breakfast consisted of rolls which we bought at a bakery and which we munched as we hurried along the street from the station to Cook's. After the nice clerk had everything else fixed up, he recommended a restaurant to us, "But I am not sure of your train time yet. If you return in half an hour I'll have all the information ready." We decided to walk around a bit in the sunshine, go back to Cook's and *then* go to the restaurant. We were looking forward to that nice hot meal in a place with a good view of Stockholm! When we stopped back at Cook's, he said, "I'm sorry but there is no hotel in Jönköping with a free room tonight and the later train would get you there after midnight. You'd better take the train leaving in 11 minutes—if you run, you can make it." So we tore around the corner, down the street—"Don't forget, they drive on the left here—" across some streets—"You get the baggage out of the check room, I'll look for a porter—" "Track 4—that's it." Whew! We made it! We pile our baggage in the vestibule, find two places where we can sit down, and the train starts.

It is with a good deal of regret we watch Stockholm go by from our windows. We had hoped to have more time there. "Oh, there's the restaurant where we were going." My tummy feels neglected as my mind concocts an imaginary dinner. "The Cook's agent said we could eat on this train. Let's look for the dining car." So we make our way through the lurching train, car after car. What a long one! At last we come to the dining car. Tables gleam with white lines and shining silver. The first course—bread and butter, pitchers of milk, plates of cold meat and salad—is already on the table and the menu promises good hot things to follow. The saliva begins to flow! And then the waiter comes up and says, "Ticket." "What ticket?" "Your pink reservation ticket." We have none and all seats are reserved! No possible chance of staying here and no way to get a meal until late afternoon when the first two sittings are over! Slowly we make our way back again—car after car. After reading for an hour or so we decide we might as well eat up what's left in the lunch box, and fish out a couple of apples, some stale pastry from Finland, a chocolate bar, and a piece of cheese.

At 7:00 P.M. we arrived in Nässjö, where we were to change trains for Jönköping. It is frosty cold and dark and we decided on the spur of the moment to stay right there and go on in the morning—if we can find a room. A hotel porter was on the platform and assured us of a room, and we shivered our way across the town square to the building he pointed out to us. There in the combination town hall and hotel we had a room way up in the tower, but the stairs didn't detract from the welcome sight of fresh comfortable beds and hot water. We hungrily ate the delicious-tasting dinner and went to bed, feeling much refreshed, after deciding to leave on the 7:30 train the next morning. In the middle of the night I awakened with the horrible knowledge that I was going to be sick. There is nothing more sudden and violent than the vomiting that comes from food poisoning, and this was clearly that. The rest of the night was disturbed frequently, and by morning, Fran knew that whatever it was had poisoned him too. Somehow we managed to get down the street to the train. Fran seemed to have a milder case than I, but he was definitely miserable. We arrived in Jönköping an hour before anyone expected us, and so came into a cold and cheerless station feeling most forlorn. We were without Swedish money—had spent it all at the hotel. As we sat on a bench asking the Lord to show us what to do, I saw a "Telefon" sign across the street. Over there we found a woman at the telegraph window who understood English and who, seeing our slightly green color and obvious illness, said she would do all she could to help us. In the providence of the Lord she knew the Secretary of the Swedish Alliance Mission and immediately called him up without charge. It seemed no time at all after that until we were in good hands. We were taken to the "Young People's home" of their mission and given hot tea and a place to rest. . . .

That evening we had to leave before 6:00 as our meeting was to be on the other side of the lake. The long evening drives were beautiful in the moonlight, though cold, and the windshield was frosty. We were served tea in the pastor's apartment and there we found that his own two children are deaf mutes, a sadness which casts a shadow over the home but doesn't affect his glowing testimony for the Lord. It was well after midnight when we arrived back at the school from Olmstad—and we were locked out! Banging at several of the doors, we aroused a tousle-headed student who rushed around the halls trying to find a key to let us in. After that the Director kept remarking to us that he must give us a key, but he never quite got around to it, so that each night—and they were all late ones—we had to go through the same process of banging around until we could get in!!

Our next day was spent in letter writing and washing clothes. As we went out to hang up clothes we met a very recent missionary arrival from China, also hanging up clothes, so as he and Fran talked I hung up both sets, which was a pleasant recreation! Their talk lasted much longer than my recreation did, though. He will not be taking a pastorate in the Swedish Alliance Mission there in Sweden. It was intensely interesting to hear the story of his recent experiences. That evening our meeting was at Huskvarna, a factory town up on a hill around the curve of the lake. The next day was a very full one, as we had to be at the office in Jönköping at 9:00 in the morning to give a Children for Christ demonstration to the Board members and office staff. It was a bit difficult as people kept coming and going in a most informal way, but it was a great success in the matter of capturing interest. "How can we have these materials and go ahead?" "We must have someone to translate—Mrs. E.?" (The very missionary lady who had offered to do it the first night!) After coffee at 11:00 Fran gave his lecture on Barthianism and the councils to this group of leaders. We had missed our large meal of the day when we got back out to the school and we had to rush through supper to leave for our evening service at Nässjö, far enough away to require our leaving at about 5:00. . . . It was after 1:00 A.M. when we got home that night, as they insisted we stop for tea, and the drive was a long one. The night seemed too short as the bell clanged for "morning milk" at 7:30. After the usual 10:30 "breakfast" we were driven through miles of lovely farm land with rolling hills and sparkling lakes, over bumpy dirt roads, narrow little lanes, until finally we swished up a hill to come to a standstill in a thick grove of trees where the buildings of the new "People's High School" stand. The students come to live here as they take the two-year course in a Christian atmosphere, and as they gathered in the assembly room I was asked to give them a Children for Christ demonstration. . . . The week before the King of Sweden had visited this school during war maneuvers which were held in that wooded territory, and as I wrote in the guest book, "It is wonderful to have had a visit from the King, but even more wonderful to know that the King of Kings is always in this place," the headmaster, reading over my shoulder, said, "Oh good—it will be fine to have the King read that—you see we are sending this book to him for his signature"! As we came back through the colorful countryside, we suddenly exclaimed over a beautiful little wooden church set in a trim garden-like graveyard with a separate wooden bell-tower some distance from the church building. "Would you like to stop and see it?" Scrunch went the wheels, and in no time the miniature auto stopped and we unfolded ourselves to get out. What a lovely old building to be set out in the middle of the country!

This church near Habo was built in 1682, and as we pushed on the heavy wooden door and found, to our joy, that it swung open, we expected to find a damp and musty interior. To our amazement the inner door opened to reveal a breathtaking surprise. Soft lights concentrated our first gaze upon the paintings which covered every inch of the heavy wooden beams, the wide board walls, the pillars, and even the pews. When a space was too small for a Bible scene, these Swedes of long past had put rough little designs, and many colors were muted by the years into a lovely soft effect. . . .

We scooted home rapidly as the car bounced over the hills, but Mr. Skoglund was already waiting for us when we arrived—a quick change of the flannelboard, the suitcase of materials from one little car to the other—grab a pair of wool gloves and a scarf for the evening drop in temperature—and we are off again. Mr. Skoglund is not a small man, and Mr. Svensen prides himself on being a really big Swede—"I'm bigger than either my father or grandfather," he states—and the effect of having two such men along with us other three in such a tiny car is that of being wrapped together in a blanket of steel, rather than being inside a car! We had no choice as to the shape of pretzel we wanted to imitate in the next two hours. Part of the time we drove over narrow dirt roads and part of the time we were on the "highway," which is a wider, smoother dirt road. We were taken to the home of the pastor next door to the church when we arrived in Gnosjö, and given a dinner in real Swedish home-style. This meant that the mother of the home did not sit down to eat with us, but hovered over the table passing things, replacing things, whipping up the next thing in the kitchen, etc. It is the custom for the mother and daughters of the family to wait upon the men and boys and then to eat later. Any of you men want to move to Sweden?

If you like herring in many different forms, then to Sweden you must go. There is herring that tastes like cloves, like onions, like mixed spices; there is salt herring and pickled herring—oh, more varieties than you can imagine, served to you at all times of the day. That night we had a variety of herring for the first course, accompanied by scalloped potatoes with flakes of herring through it! The main course consisted of meat balls made of elk meat. It was hunting season and people either shoot their own elk or buy the meat in the butcher shops. In Gnosjö there are over 150 "factories." I put that in quotes because some of them are so tiny they have only three or four workers. It is certainly a town of free enterprise as people have used their ingenuity to make all sorts of things which find a wide market. Many were formerly poor but went years ago to America to work for two or three years, to save up enough money to begin a little enterprise of their own—making everything from wee hooks and eyes to furniture, and so the town is today a thriving development. The church was packed that night, and the choir (in Sweden this also includes two or three violins, several guitars, and maybe a bass viol) filled the platform with fine-looking young people. It was an easy crowd to speak to as their interest was keen and their faces responsive. Afterwards two ladies came up with tears in their eyes and said, "We felt we really touched heaven tonight." After the meeting about 20 guests were invited to the pastor's house for coffee and cakes (and in Sweden you *must* take one of every kind as all eyes are upon you and it is insulting to the hostess to refuse one sort—the feeling is—"What could be the matter with that kind?"), during which time the other two men came back from their meeting and joined us. Many of the guests could speak some English as they had been in Chicago or Detroit for a year or two! Our drive that night seemed long and cold as we traveled back over the dark dirt roads which twist and turn sharply through black woods. At one sharp turn we skidded dangerously on little pebbles, thanking the Lord for His protection as the car righted itself again. Finally, at something before 2:00 A.M., we tumbled into bed— looking forward to three services the next day! . . .

Jogging back to Lund that night on the midnight train, we decided to rest the next morning, as we were getting a bit woozy with the constant speaking and in between conversations to say nothing of travel. Our hotel was a very cheap one across from the railroad station, but Dr. Hedegard recommended it as clean and reliable. I think it was quiet too, at least we slept like logs until 9:00 and then did some reading and card writing. You know we always try to send one card a day to our three girls, as well as writing to Swiss friends while we're away. Priscilla wrote regularly, and though much of her news concerned her school, she was home every weekend and in that way we heard her angle of how things were going. Debby seemed to have a lovely time with Alexandra as a constant companion. . . . Susan had kept on inviting children and Priscilla wrote with amazement, "You should see how my class has grown. I am having it on Saturdays now and Susan has brought a lot of new children. They are almost all village children now as no one from Home Eden is left who is coming. I'm using Bible School report cards to mark their attendance and the verses they're learning—hope you don't mind." We were thrilled, as you can well imagine, that the youngsters were going ahead on their own to continue their missionary work.

We were to meet Dr. Hedegard at noon in front of the historic and picturesque clock inside the Lund Cathedral. When 12:00 arrives, two horsemen in armor, who stand above the face of the clock, strike each other 12 times with their swords, after which figures appear at the doors at the bottom of the clock's face and slowly pass a figure of Mary. These are supposed to be the wise men visiting from the East bowing to the baby Jesus and presenting their gifts. During this, two trumpeters appear at the sides and blow the medieval hymn "In Dulci Jubilo." Every noon there is a solid group of people gathered about this clock, and that day was no exception. When the clock finished its performance, which it has repeated since medieval days, we went out with Dr. Hedegard to eat at a restaurant patronized by the students of the University. You buy a ticket at the door, and then proceed to serve yourself from a table spread with plain but good food, plenty of bread and butter, and great pitchers of milk. No student needs to go hungry if he can fill up even once a day here, for something like 38 cents! No restrictions on "seconds." . . .

The next night Fran was asked to give the same message to another E.F.S. provincial group at Malmö. This time I stayed home to pack for an early-morning departure and to rest a bit. This evening rounded out a month of speaking and traveling and Fran was looking forward to a break—as was I. We both felt that if we had been intending to go on to Norway, we would have needed a couple of days rest in between. In Finland and Sweden we had spoken (either one or *both* of us) 33 times, as well as having numerous private conferences and conversations. The next morning found us saying "goodbye" to our Swedish farewell party of one—the 12-year-old son of the electrical engineer who kept looking anxiously up the street for his father who didn't get there in time. The boat from Malmö lands in Copenhagen in an hour and a half and by noon we were settled in an obscure hotel in the Danish capital. Did you ever hear that one-fourth of all the Danes in Denmark live in Copenhagen? It is a tremendous city for the size of the country—tremendous and also very beautiful and interesting. . . .

We had a full day of rest in Copenhagen, which meant much to us at the time but even more to us after we got home, for it meant that we were ready to pitch right in to office work without the "letdown" feeling that usually comes when we first arrive home from a trip. We bought the makings of a picnic before we boarded the Scandinavian Express so that the trip home was just as cozy as the one up had been. Mlle. Bonnet had to leave three hours before we arrived in Champéry, so that when we got to our chalet it was to find we were all alone as a family for the first time since last April. Though we were sorry to miss seeing Mlle. B. and Sandra, it was perfectly lovely to have the family all together and completely alone. Priscilla stayed home an extra day so that we had a chance to get really talked out. Susan and Debby had a touch of epidemic grippe, their teacher had had it first—Priscilla had been having Bible reading times with her Turkish-Jewish roommate—Debby was doing second-grade arithmetic and learning to write rather than print—Mme. Fleischmann said they had all made progress in their music—the ski teacher's two girls were coming to the class and really learning the Bible verses—etc., etc.—until all the news was out. Of course, they had to stop to sleep! . . .

Keep praying—
Much love,

EDITH

December 22, 1951   Champéry, Switzerland

Dear Family:

We keep track of the number of days left before December 25th as each morning we are awakened by Susan shouting to Debby, "What did your calendar have today?" The answer comes, "It's the 15th, isn't it? Well, my door is in the head of a little girl and there's a lantern in it." The Swiss Christmas calendars give a lot of pleasure as youngsters open the little doors marked from 1 to 24, and discover the little picture inside. When door #24 is opened, the next day is Christmas. Today is so close to the final date that it is too late for this to arrive in time to send you greetings, but not too late to let you know that we are praying for each of you who read this letter, that the Lord may give you a real blessing at this time of year as you attend the special services and have your family times together. . . .

So many of you have been praying about the threatening letter of which I wrote last month that I know you are anxious to have news as to how the Lord has answered. To go back to what happened: When Priscilla left the boys' school here in Champéry, the Director was not very nice about it and was angry with us for some criticisms we made to him during our frank talk. It now appears that ever since then he has been trying to do something against us, although we hadn't heard of it. Just before we left for Finland six of the boys from that school appeared at our church service, which made us very happy. Of course we cordially invited them to come back when the services would start regularly again. After our return Fran saw one of the boys on the street. "Services start again tomorrow and, of course, we'd be glad to see you boys again." That was all. Sunday two boys turned up and seemed to enjoy the service, listening intently to the sermon. They were two American boys whose family comes from Seattle and whose father is in the Navy, now stationed in Italy. The next day we received the letter. Mr. N. was accusing Fran of waylaying his students on the street and almost forcing them to "assist" in his services. The students had been placed in *his* care, he bragged, and it was *his* business to look after their religious needs. He went on to threaten that if "Mr. Schaeffer" ever spoke to his boys on the street again he would bring a formal complaint against us to the authorities of the Commune. He was, he stated, sending copies of this letter to the President of the Commune and to the Pastor of the State Church down in Monthey. It happened that that very day Dr. Otten was in the village and he dropped in at the chalet. As he read the letter he grew incensed and stated that the way it was written made it sound as though we were very dangerous people. "I will talk to the pastor myself to explain it," said Dr. O.

We did nothing for a couple of weeks. One of our main concerns was for the two boys themselves who, we were sure, would be prevented from coming back—if only we could contact the *family* and at least have an opportunity of witness to them! Then we wondered how this would affect our Children for Christ class—it could easily direct unfavorable attention to it. As a matter of fact, the fire kindled by this little flame could be enough to drive us out of this village entirely. The doctor told us to talk to no one about it until he had a chance to talk to the pastor.

During this time the days marched along in a very ordered fashion. Each day began with the lighting of a fire in the dining room brown-tile stove. The crackling of the wood makes one feel warmer even before the stove heats up! After Susan and Debby trudged off over the fields to school, we would settle down to office work—correspondence (Fran dictating into the tape recorder mike while I did other work, then my typing from the rolls with the "split-a-word control")—articles—and lessons. After time out to cook, eat dinner, have prayers, and send the girls off to school again, we would light the fire in the living room stove. To do this we take a piece of metal out of a niche where it fits into the dining room wall, and build a fire in what seems to be a deep dark cave. When the fire has caught the wood in its flames, we replace the piece of metal in the dining room wall, and the living room stove has a fire in it! The living room stove is built right *into* that wall. It emerges from the wall over four feet high, two feet wide, and three feet deep, almost solid granite. A carving on the front informs us that the stove was built in 1900 and that the owner is C. O., and a carved picture of a rope, a pick, and other mountain climber's equipment informs us that the original owner was a guide.

This granite monument didn't impress us very much when we first took the chalet, but now it is a favorite of the whole family. It warms up gradually, but by evening it is really radiating heat. We gather round it for family prayers at night, and for the evening story we curl up cozily on the built-in couch which an Irishman put there 50 years ago so he might bask in warmth as he read! Then, before going to bed, I put a pot of oatmeal into a little cubbyhole at one side of the stove where it simmers away all night and is surprisingly warm in the morning, in spite of the fact that the fire has been out for hours and hours. The granite holds the heat. Not only do wood stoves have more personality than modern heating systems, but they have a lot of advantages. It's even fun to go down the outside steps to the "cave" and enter the soft sawdust-carpeted, pine-scented wood room and fill your arms with chunks of pine wood to replenish the various wood boxes. This house has a furnace by the way, but we have decided to do without it if possible, thus saving money, as coal is *much* too expensive, and now it seems as though we are going to get through the winter nicely. But to go back to our days—the afternoons were spent in more typing, etc., and the evenings very often in spreading out our flannelgraph board and working on lessons. Gradually we went down through mountains of work, but always another mountain loomed up in the place of the one just removed!

The picture of solitude and quiet work changed on weekends. Late Friday afternoons Priscilla arrived, full of conversation and laden down with homework—"Oh, I simply can't learn all this German—our German class is having a play and I have pages to memorize, to say nothing of being a doctor in the French play too! They changed me—I'm in a new room—I have an Italian roommate now, Carla. Carla is teaching me Italian and I'm teaching her English—listen to me talk Italian—" "Oh Priscilla," chorused Susan and Debby admiringly, "you sound just like the people in Alassio." There is always a scramble for the piano, each one wanting to show the others how much progress she is making. It was hard to get things quieted down Friday nights. . . . Saturday morning Fran left at 6 A.M. to go down the mountain for his day of work with the English secretary and Saturday afternoon we had the Children for Christ class here. Sunday morning was the church service and Priscilla needed to take the train that afternoon to get back to Lausanne.

Two evenings during those two weeks we had company—village folks. One night the trio of Obers—Rachel, Herman, and Robert—came to see slides and enjoyed immensely seeing themselves haying last summer! It was fun to see these hardworking folks relax. . . . Do you remember my mentioning the "electric man" who sat next to Fran on the train last summer and showed an interest in talking of Christian things? Fran stopped in to pay our electric bill, but it wasn't ready yet (they have ordered a meter for our hot-water heater and it has not come yet—so he had to figure out a fair rate), and he said he'd bring it down "some evening." Then and there Fran made it a definite evening and the man readily agreed. He, by the way, is not only owner of the only electric shop in town but is head of the community electrical committee, head of the village Swiss Ski School, and takes an active part in all the village improvement committees. When he arrived, his wife was with him, and we wondered if that might hinder us from getting around to Christian things. He speaks and understands English, though his wife knows only French. We started off by looking at slides, then had refreshments, and finally the way opened up. "What," he asked, "is the difference between Roman Catholicism and Protestantism anyway?" As the Bible was pointed to as *the* authority in our Protestant church, he asked, "But who can understand the Bible? It is very confusing, isn't it?" As Bibles were brought out—a French one apiece for each of them to look at—and questions multiplied, Fran started with Genesis and took them through a real Bible study, illustrating just how we study the Bible and what it means to us, and how clearly it points the way of salvation, and how wonderfully it gives assurance. He did this in English and I translated for the wife, though the man was eager to go straight on and often didn't wait for her to catch up. Never have we seen a more earnest interest or a greater eagerness. When we offered to let him take the Bible home with him, he almost snatched it and agreed to read it regularly "until we can talk again," he said. They left after midnight, and although he was clearly the one with the interest, she was not annoyed or impatient at all. . . . Please join us in praying for Mr. Exhenry that the Holy Spirit may open the eyes of his understanding as he reads the Bible.

I'm going to step out of the chronological order here to go on to what happened next with Mr. and Mrs. Ex. They invited us to come for an evening at their house. I should have written that in caps! It is the first time we have received an invitation to a village home for an evening. We arrived, after slipping and sliding our way up the hill to the village street (our path is a glaze of ice) to be greeted and ushered in to an evening of conversation. He had read Luke, John, and half of Acts and wanted to discuss some of it, but mostly complained because "nothing happened to me when I read it and lots of it means nothing to me." Fran had a long, long talk with him—the evening lasted until almost 1 A.M. and Mr. Ex. continued to be eager. He finally got to the point where he said he would like to believe, he would like to have the assurance that we have, and agreed to go on reading and asking God to show him. He said he would mark any places he did not understand and come with them the "next evening we are together."

Meantime his wife and I sat on the other side of the room and had our own conversation. She started out by telling me of how cute it was that her little girl believed still in the "Baby Jesus"!—and when I looked puzzled she said, "Pere Noel, you know." You see here the version of Santa Claus is a dreadful mixture of folklore, with Jesus and heaven. "Pere Noel" and the "Baby Jesus" are identical. A child is supposed to put salt on the window sill the eve of Christmas and the baby Jesus will come from heaven on a donkey. The donkey will stop to lick up the salt while the baby Jesus leaves an orange, some candy, and a small gift. "Do you do that for Deborah?" she asked. I explained to her then that we never tell the children things that are not true, since we want them to have confidence in that which we do teach them, and we want them never to confuse fairy stories with the true stories of the Bible. "Jesus does not come to the window sill—in fact He is no longer a baby at all. How terribly confused a child would be to think of Him as a baby, doing such things, and then to hear of what Jesus truly is later. What a wonderful thing it is to be able to tell a child of the true Son of God Who was born as a wee babe that He might live and die for us to prepare the one and only way for us to enter heaven. A child should know that Jesus died for his sins that he might be forgiven and made a child of God. A child should love Jesus because He has done so much for him. A child should have confidence that Jesus will hear and answer his prayers, and should know that He can do all things." She nodded her head vigorously and said, "I agree with you—I always hate to make up so many stories that aren't so. Like today, I had to tell Martine that Jesus had to take her doll to heaven to measure it for pajamas, and now she tells all her friends that her doll is in heaven so that is why she can't play with it." I can't report all the conversation, but the Lord led, and this mother, who last summer forbade her three children to come to our Children for Christ class (as did also several other mothers), astonished me by saying, "My children hear so much about the nice stories other children hear at your house—*could* they come too? Are you sure it wouldn't bother you?" Oh, what a break in the ice that is—I was afraid she would hear my heart singing! Only the Lord knows what He is doing in this village—we keep being amazed as things happen. . . .

The next week Mr. and Mrs. Wutrich came up from Geneva. Mrs. Wutrich and the baby stayed here, while he and Fran went down the mountain to Monthey to talk to the pastor concerning the letter we had received, and then Mr. Wutrich came back again for the evening, leaving the next morning for Vevey, and returning again in the evening. The talk with the pastor revealed that the school director, Mr. N., had a whole year ago (right after Priscilla left the school) stopped him in the street and asked *why* Mr. Schaeffer was allowed to use the church when he belonged to a sect!! The pastor who has heard good things about us did nothing about this, and he is now thoroughly disgusted with the school director. As long as our service is in English, he is pleased to have it going on and to make no move against it. Of course, the building has nothing to do with him anyway, as it is privately owned by a committee. It was built by an English woman as a gift to Champéry, as you remember my telling you a couple of years ago. However, you see how determined this man is to make trouble, and if he changes his attack to another direction it might do really great harm. Soon after this we saw the President of the Communes who also seemed to sympathize with us and reassured us very kindly. . . .

There was a long list of things we had to do in Lausanne—shopping, banking, clock to be mended, typewriter to be repaired, tape-recorder to be repaired, children's feet to be fitted for new heavy winter boots, Priscilla's eyes to be examined and frames to be selected for the new glasses, Susan to be taken to a doctor friend of our friends for consultation as to why she had been sleepless so much of the time lately, a young dentist to talk to (a Christian who has gone through some very difficult times and needs special help at the present moment), and a request from the Andres for an evening of conversation concerning the children's work, etc. We decided to accept the Andres' invitation to stay there with the children, and get everything done at once. We spent three very full days in Lausanne, leaving on the 6:00 A.M. train of the first day and returning on the 10:00 P.M. train the third day. The young dentist is coming up for a weekend at the end of January, welcoming the opportunity for Christian fellowship and a time in which to talk over his problems, as well as a complete change of scenery. His wife died tragically a short time ago leaving him with two little children, aged one and two.

The next day brought 15 youngsters to the Children for Christ class— a new high! Our hearts rejoiced as we heard them lustily singing "I Am the Door" and other choruses. They are village children almost entirely now, who come rushing down our path after school, mouths still full of black bread and cheese (their "gouter" or afternoon tea) and their coloring card clutched in their hands. We give them each a cardboard square with a verse to color each week, and these they bring back until they have an entire set, at which time they may keep them. They also memorize the verse very faithfully. It is thrilling! They are frequently calling Priscilla "ma soeur" (my sister) by mistake, as they have never had a teacher of *any* kind except a black-robed Catholic sister. Some come very much on their own, and with a heavy odor of the barn about them. Others come very obviously scrubbed, dressed in best aprons, and beribboned by mothers who feel it is a special occasion. . . .

When Priscilla came home next, it was with all her belongings, since it was time for Christmas vacation, after which the school will all be up here in Champéry until March. This past week has been full of office work and Christmas preparations. There has been the church to trim— Michel cut the branches from the pines down over the cliff below our chalet, Fran and the children dragged them up to the church in a little cart and arranged them artfully in contrast to the hundred red candles. There have been posters to make—19 of them, which Fran and the girls placed in 19 different places—hotel lobbies, pensions, store windows, and the *telepherique* station. There have been cookies to bake—hundreds of them which have been placed in 12 boxes (old boxes covered by Priscilla and decorated by Susan) to be taken Christmas Eve to schoolteachers, music teacher, old or especially poor folks, an invalid boy, etc.—others to be served at the Children for Christ special Christmas tea. And then there was the dining room to fix for the tea today. We had told the children to be sure not to eat their "gouter" before coming to class this time as they would be served something special. We had brought in the big old table from the porch and put white cloths on it and the dining room table. In the center of one table we put the plastic tree Mother Schaeffer sent us and in the center of the other a small pine tree in a flower pot. To the branches of these we tied tree ornaments made of chocolate and covered with bright paper (very convenient as they can be eaten—two were to go home as "favors" with each child), and at the base of each tree we placed a circle of pink popcorn balls—the corn is that which you folks have sent from America. Susan popped it while I made the pink syrup which was to coat it and make it into balls before it hardened. Such a sticky haste for a few minutes, but what a nice pile of pink balls finally emerged! The windows made up for the lack of snow outside as they were decorated with frosty white stars and snowflakes and other shapes which looked as if they were etched in real frost.

The children began arriving before we were ready for them, having gotten out of school early for the holidays. Most of them had never been to anything resembling a party before, so you can imagine the excitement. Such wide eyes as they passed the dining room and went into the living room to sing while preparations were being finished. We had to add a small table at the last moment, because the children kept coming until the final count reached 24. Now 24 may not sound enormous to you, but consider that in the village school (which has all the children of the village and the surrounding mountainside in it between the ages of six and 14) there are only a few more than 60 altogether. We have a few under school age, and a couple from Home Eden, but even so—it makes an amazing proportion of homes being touched through this class. When the electric man's three children entered the class that day the others cheered and clapped. Last summer they "sneaked" to the class twice. This time they came not only with permission but with a little gift for the Schaeffers for giving them the privilege (a small box of miniature chocolate bars). When the hot chocolate was finally ready ("Debby, run up to the village and get two cans of milk—we've run out of milk because there are so many") and the enormous platters of bread were spread with jam, we lighted the candles on the tables and ushered the children in. How excited they were with such a special tea party! The bread and jam disappeared, to be followed by cookies and then a slice of cake. The littlest boy there was so overcome he forgot to drink his chocolate and didn't even notice when his nearest neighbor changed cups and drained his forgotten one! Fran went around cleaning up sticky hands and sugary faces, and then they all disappeared into the living room for Priscilla's giving of the special Christmas story, which ended with the clear presentation of the way of salvation. Do pray that the Holy Spirit will open the eyes of these children that they might truly understand. Humanly looking at it, it seems difficult to think of their jumbled-up ideas straightening out into the Truth, but our God is able, and He can not only draw these children unto Him and open their minds now, but He can hold them fast for ever, long after our influence has been removed.

May the God of all peace keep you in the coming year and give you everything you need, materially and spiritually.

Much love,

EDITH

1952

February 13, 1952   Champéry, Switzerland

Dear Family

This is the January letter, but it starts with the end of December and I hope to bring it up to date—if the paper doesn't gobble up the words too fast! In fact I can't begin without telling you of the February weather. Snow—snow—snow! We have had snow every day except one—and that day it rained. We've had thick white flakes, fine misty flakes, gentle, silent powdery flakes, and wet flakes that stuck to everything. We've had snow that came straight down, snow that whirled in dizzy circles, and snow that seemed to go absolutely horizontally as the wind howled and blew it past our windows. It has piled up higher and higher on the roofs until yesterday a driving rain turned much of it into heavy sodden masses that groaned and creaked and thudded as it separated on our roof—and then slid and plopped down in frightening masses on the ground below. How thankful we were that no one happened to be under it to be crushed. We awoke this morning to find that the soggy deep slush (four-foot-deep snow that had been rained upon) had disappeared from sight and a new covering 20 inches deep was resting not only on the ground but on bushes, twigs, and roofs. Once more the children had to plough their way through to the distant village street above us—knee deep! The snow started in January—and even in January there were not more than six days of sunshine. The temperature has been unusually low too—which meant that our rooms without stoves froze water some days (ice four inches thick on water pitchers) and the other rooms found it difficult to overcome the temperature of 38°—where they started in the morning—to reach anything akin to comfort before late evening. The snow has been too constant for good skiing as the "pistes" never have time to become properly patted down, but Priscilla has had to continue practicing with the ski teacher who is working with her school this year. She was chosen as one of seven for the ski team which will represent Le Grand Verger at the ski concourse between the various Swiss girls' schools. Now the team has been narrowed down to three, as none of the others "shaped up" well enough. That has left Priscilla, an Italian girl, and a Swedish girl. The concourse will be on March 7th at some other ski resort, and the teams will go three days ahead for practice. You might be remembering her that day, as it is easy to get nervous and make foolish mistakes. Of course sports are not important in themselves but since Mr. Fonjallaz has done so much for her, it would be nice if she could "place" in the meet for the sake of the school. When Christians excel in some such sport it gives openings for speaking at times with those who otherwise might not listen. . . .

The weather isn't the only thing that I'm going to report backwards! There is something else that has just come up which I want you to read about before something interrupts you. You remember the wonderful growth of the Children for Christ class and what a large proportion of the village children were coming? Well, after Christmas first one family of children and then another began staying away. One of the most eager—who always knew her verse and sang vigorously with her short hair flopping as her head bobbed up and down over her funny little long-sleeved apron—came breathlessly in one Saturday and catching Priscilla in the storeroom began questioning her—"Can I have my report card to take home? Can I have the verse for today if I stay in the hall while you have the class?—(pause)—If I stayed in the hall I might as well come into the room where I could hear the story—yes I will (biting her lip). Are you a Catholic or a Protestant? I don't see what difference that makes"—then a *big* sigh as she determinedly went in and took her place among the others. That was the last time we have seen her here! Our suspicions were of course aroused—we know it wasn't the children who were deciding to stay away. Then just last week a child stopped Debby in the village street as she was coming home from school. "We can't come to the class on Saturdays anymore—the "sister" at school told us to stop—then they told us this week that if we put a foot inside Chalet Bijou again they will give us a big punishment." That same evening Rachel—one of the owners of our chalet—came down, and suddenly in the conversation she began to inquire about the Saturday class—"What is it you have for the children?" As I explained to her she said, "But the sisters are angry and they do not want the children coming anymore—you had better be careful." I told her we would never turn a child away and we would continue the class for anyone who wanted to come. I explained that we felt people should have liberty—for instance the parents should decide whether or not they wished their children to come to the little class. I told her we taught only the Bible—at present from the Gospel of Luke—and that she was free to read the lessons if she wanted to. She shrugged her shoulders and said she supposed the parents should have the say but that in a Catholic country it wasn't like that!

My next visitor came the next morning when I was alone in the house. It was not long until she rather nervously inquired what we had here for the children. I gave her a more full explanation and we had a rather long discussion on real freedom versus totalitarianism. She said she wished to "warn" me. I replied that we intended to do nothing different than we had been doing. We had never gone out and either forced or even urged children to come; in fact the class was entirely run by our own children and we couldn't understand the turmoil over the simple Bible teaching of a fourteen-year-old girl!!! We said we would not prohibit our children from inviting others to the gospel because this was exactly what we felt all believing Christians should always be doing no matter where they lived in the world. She seemed troubled that I was not "backing down" nor being apologetic—and she said that she was afraid the sisters were very *upset* and might therefore issue a complaint against us to the cantonal authorities. She didn't have to go on to explain that it would be an easy matter for our police permit to live here to be removed—we already knew that! She intimated that someone from Sion (the seat of the cantonal government) might soon make us a visit. . . .

They have, as Vic says, "only heard one bell"—in other words for many generations they have had all their teaching from the "sisters," all their commands from the priest, and all they know of any other religion—especially Protestantism—is that it is wicked and not to be touched. No Protestant testimony has ever reached them before and now 24 children have been in the classes for long enough to know a little bit and a number of homes were very happy about the teaching. Discussions and arguments are now widespread. The Lord can use it in His own way. Pray that if it be the Lord's will He may give us the victory in this and allow us to remain here—but that if He wants us somewhere else He will also make that very clear and that even in our being put out the issues would be kept clear and the Lord glorified. . . .

Now to go back: Christmas Eve was a rushed one full of "last-minute" preparations. I wish you could have seen the little procession going up the mountain to visit the boy who was hurt last July while cutting hay and has never been out of bed since. It consisted of the three girls and myself—carrying a tiny evergreen (pulled up by the roots and planted in a pot of earth) covered with bright foil-wrapped chocolates and tiny candles, and a box of homemade cookies, a bag of oranges, two gaily-wrapped games, and two nice sweaters that came out of a box of clothing sent from America. Vic met us part way up to guide us down the obscure little path which led to the typical peasant chalet perched on the steep mountain side. The view here was breathtaking—peaks, jagged rocks, smooth steep pasturelands, clusters of pines, cliffs—and no hint of a village in the distance or even another chalet. We were met at the door by an indescribably dirty woman with hair like an ancient grey floor mop. Her French was the broad "patois" of the mountain folk and even that was grunted more than spoken. She led us reluctantly inside, after Vic explained the purpose of the visit, and the odor was as breathtaking as the view—in an entirely *different* way!! I shuddered when I thought that milk comes from this place to the "laiterie" every morning—how thankful we are for our Sears and Roebuck's Home and Farm pasteurizer.

The boy was on a cot in a crowded little room, his leg stretched out with a weight holding it that way through the months. A cat was trying to finish the cafe au lait that was left in a cracked cup beside him, while his older brother watched us entering, a rather sullen and suspicious look on his face. When we unwrapped the tree and placed it on a table, arranging the oranges, cookie box, and gifts under it, the sick boy's face lit up like a candle in a dark place. From then on a happy grin never left his face. It was the very first Christmas tree the boy had ever had, and the mother had never seen one in the house before—she had been brought up sleeping with the cows. The girls sang some songs and choruses in French and by the time we left all of them were smiling. Not only were we glad to have brought a bit of sunshine into that dismal place, but we felt it to be a good testimony. People here have such distorted ideas of Protestants that little kindnesses help to give a different impression and to break down the walls of reserve.

That afternoon our dining room was full of paper, ribbons, glue, and tinsel powder. Priscilla and Susan covered and decorated old boxes while I lined them with tissue and filled them with cookies. We trimmed another wee tree in a flower pot to be placed as a surprise for the lonely music teacher to find on her return from the service in the evening—and by that time it was time to go. "Will you light the candles if we are the only ones, Daddy?" "No, we'll save them for next week." "But if ten people come will you light them?" "Oh yes", "And if only *one* comes? It says on *our* posters that we will have the service by candlelight." "We'll see." Oh would anyone be there? You can imagine the delight in Debby's heart, and the shine in her eyes, as the people began coming. Her job was to hand out the carols which had been mimeographed. Two by two—one—three—until finally there were over thirty-five. Susan went around lighting the lower candles—the glow lighting up her rosy cheeks and happy brown eyes, while Priscilla lit the higher ones fastened on the branches stuck up at the windows. The soft glow that filled the church made me sorry electricity had ever been invented! . . .

After the Christmas Eve Service Fran and the three girls took the dozen boxes of cookies and went caroling. In front of each house where they delivered cookies they stopped first to sing Christmas carols. Our own Christmas was a quiet one as the folks we had invited couldn't come, and we were happy to be just a family for the day. The packages from America were such fun to open and brought home so close, that our time together seemed to include family and friends from America too. . . .

Monsieur and Madame Marclay came one evening to help us fill out our tax forms. Foreigners in Switzerland must pay taxes just as the Swiss do—local taxes, cantonal taxes, and federal taxes for national defense. The Marclays are always ready and anxious to help us out in any way possible. She continues to read her Bible every day and likes to talk to me about various things she does not understand, although her husband is a very strong Roman Catholic and when he is here usually steers the conversation away from any such topics. . . .

The dentist left about 6:30 to drive back to Lausanne in a snow storm, the girls came about 7:30—it was not early when we got to bed—and Fran left at 5:30 A.M. to make his ways slowly through deep snow to the station for that early-morning train Monday. He had to dictate that day because the girl had Monday "off" instead of Saturday that week. After his work in Vevey he went straight on to Geneva to meet Mr. Bennet, who had come to Switzerland on his way back from his trip around the world for the I.C.C.C. . . . Wednesday was Fran's birthday and we called Geneva to discover that he was coming home that afternoon, so we had a cake made and decorated and in the ice-box before he arrived, a birthday dinner cooking, and the "celebration" planned. After we had finished our last crumb of the delicious chocolate cake, Debby went over to her daddy and patted him lovingly. "Grandfather"—she said. "What?" said Fran a bit startled. "Nice grandfather," answered Debby. "What are you talking about?" asked Fran. "Weeellll," sighed Debby, "now you're forty you're so *old* you *must* be a grandfather!" Of course, she thought she was bestowing a compliment something like big folks do when they say, "What a big girl you are now," to a little girl. The loud burst of laughter that followed almost reduced her to tears! . . .

The next two days were completely uninterrupted. We worked all day and evening each day and had the satisfaction of seeing another Luke lesson finished. Wednesday morning we got off the two new Luke lessons to the translators in the various countries. Sighing with relief we went to eat lunch and plan the afternoon. Two of the girls were coming to tea at four to bring some private questions they wanted to ask me, but until then we thought we had a couple of hours free!

The phone rang—it was Mr. Fonjallaz of Priscilla's school announcing the death of King George VI—"Would you be so kind as to have a special service for us? Both Mr. Juat and I think our English girls would appreciate some special church service because of this." "Why, yes," replied Fran, "eight o'clock tonight." "Oh thank you *so* much." Now ordinarily we get our news in *Newsweek* (and occasionally, when Fran is down in the valley, he gets a European edition of the *Herald Tribune*) about a week late—hence we would not have even heard of the King's death for some time. But here we were at two o'clock of the *same* day, calling all the hotels and schools to inform them of a special service for the English at the church! Fran called Mr. D., the Vice-Counsul, to ask him if "God Save the Queen" should be immediately substituted in the English National Anthem, and he told him that it *should*—"She becomes our Queen the moment the King dies." He also said he and his wife and a friend from the State Department in London were coming up for the service, and expressed appreciation for it. Vic ran across a snowy field to find Michel who was nearby and dispatched him with a load of wood from our woodpile with directions to make as hot a fire as possible in the church and to stay by it until 8 o'clock to see that it didn't die down. A message was sent to Madame Fleischmann concerning the music, and Fran shut himself up in his study to prepare a message for a most difficult type of service. . . .

There were well over sixty there, not only English folks, but the directors of the pensions (praise the Lord for an opportunity to have Mr. Fonjallaz himself in a service) and the Indian girls, Swedish girls, etc. Everyone who understood English seemed to want to come. Who would have dreamt that the death of King George would open an opportunity to preach to over sixty such people in a mountain village of the Swiss Alps?!! . . .

We get letters from so many—the girl in Brazil for one. And from the Pierces in England, people we met at the beach in September—such a nice family. He is reading the Bible studies and writes his questions. He is an agnostic. Now I've got to stop; I have taken three days to write this and have left lots unsaid.

Much love,

EDITH

April 7, 1952   Champéry, Switzerland

Dear Family:
. . . Before coming to the exciting middle of March I must take you back to the 14th of February where I left you last time. That was Valentine's Day and Susan entertained the family at one of her inimitable parties. She had not only sent us invitations, placed a decorated box in a conspicuous place, and urged everyone to drop their valentines in the "mail-box," but she "passed the hat" and everyone dropped in their extra centimes with which she bought the necessary things for decoration and refreshments. These family parties planned by Susan are always enjoyed in a room festooned with decorations, and are complete to the very end. Added to games Susan has now a new form of entertainment—puppets—most of which she has made herself and stuffed with sawdust. It gives her an incentive to do a bit of sewing, designing (for backgrounds), memorizing (for the dialogue), as well as the manipulating of the strings.

Starting with the middle of February we had the schoolgirls twice a week; Sunday nights, Priscilla's school as usual, and then Thursday nights, the girls from Jua. There were seven girls and one teacher from Jua—all English—who seemed so thrilled to come into a *home* after being always in school. They were all lovely girls, so appreciative of everything, so helpful in offering to pour tea, pass cakes, and clear up a bit afterwards, and so very quiet and attentive all through the evening of Bible teaching. Their questions were rather slow in coming and rather shyly spoken. We could see that they were hearing things very new to them and though surprise and wonder were on their faces at times, there seemed to be no stormy reactions, no great struggling doubts except on the face of the teacher. The two groups were *very* different. In the Sunday night group we had the Indian girls, Kit always full of questions and doubts, Swedish girls who were definitely agnostic and not afraid to say so, girls who wanted to argue for evolution, Roman Catholic girls who tried to show how right the Roman Catholic Church is in their eyes, Ush who has believed but who still can come out with remarks which are not always helpful! Shirley was the only one who listened and questioned as a new believer.

Then Carla began coming—Carla who is Italian (Priscilla's former roommate), an intellectual agnostic who is completely disillusioned with the Roman Catholic Church after spending some years in a Convent School, Carla who is the "clown" of the school, famous for her funny remarks and whose droll haircut gives her the appearance of an impish newly shorn lamb (blond hair cut about an inch short all over her head, curling into a wooly covering), Carla whose knowledge of English is limited to about a half a dozen words. She plopped herself on a rug in the center of the room—on her tummy with the Italian Testament Priscilla had given her open before her, and began to monopolize the question-asking time! Those who expected to laugh were rewarded at the beginning when as Fran was answering a question about a philosopher he said rather rapidly "as a thinker" and Carla's face lit up—"a stinker—a *stinker*" (one of her half a dozen words had been used, she thought!). When the laughter died down Priscilla straightened her out and Fran went on. I wish you could have been there that night. Priscilla translated into French almost as rapidly as Fran spoke (clearly through the help of the Holy Spirit because the rapidity with which she was able to transfer all that into French surprised not only the teacher and other girls but Priscilla herself)—and Carla continued to ask questions straight from the Testament as well as from the things that had troubled her in her past thinking. There were no more opportunities to laugh— Carla was not only serious—her face was full of an eager desire—a thirsty desire. She was reluctant to stop at the end of the evening—we had had to pass cake and tea *around* her, since there had been no pause even for refreshments. In spite of the disapproval of the Roman Catholic teacher at the school, Carla and two of her Italian friends kept coming after that, and Sunday nights became bilingual affairs. . . .

March began with a great excitement over the ski meet. Mr. Fonjallaz insisted that ski practice was more important than studies—so Priscilla's studies rather piled up—and she gave herself a handicap for later on. She was the only one from her school in the "meet" who is taking the "serious" studies. The night before the departure the whole family pitched in to help our skier prepare! Mommy checked on clothing, extra warm things "in case," and such mundane things as toothpaste and mittens while Daddy gave the skis several coats of quick-drying "ski-wax," a sort of shellac which gives a good hard surface on the bottoms—twenty minutes to dry between coats—"Don't step on them anybody"— Debby and Susan pranced around giving unwanted advice and wishing they could go too. Finally everything was ready—skis securely fastened together, *batons* (ski poles) beside them, and the blue rucksack ready to be hoisted to her back in the morning. Mr. Fonjallaz drove the girls to Chateau d'Oex the next morning, where all the teams spent a day in practice. I'm afraid there wasn't too much sleep that night as most of the schools were staying in the same hotel, and many awoke early in the morning from sheer excitement. There were eight schools taking part and 59 participants. The school which came in last last year had among several very good skiers the girl who had won the Swiss Junior championship, and other schools from other parts had also surprisingly good skiers—so the school which Priscilla had thought would give them the most competition didn't "count" among these others. Therefore, when she came home with a bronze medal—having come in 14th in her combined times for the "downhill race" and the "slalom"—we were very proud of her. The five first were given gold medals, the five second silver medals, and the five third bronze. Priscilla helped her school take fourth place. Since she has the cheapest skis we could buy and they are three years old, that is another point in her favor. Her teacher claims that with a pair of really good Swedish skis she could take off quite a few seconds from her time. The glories of doing so well soon faded as exams made their grim appearance. For some unexplainable reason Mr. Fonjallaz gave his girls no time in between and in a day or two the second "trimester" examinations began. Such a frantic feeling did this give Priscilla. However, they are over now, and she lived through them and has apparently done quite well—though reports haven't come yet. . . .

The day Priscilla left for Chateau d'Oex, I went down to Lausanne to shop, talk with the Andres, and visit the doctor for a check-up. Dr. Kousmine is very thorough and we like to get a check-up every once in a while with her. She found me to be in fine condition except for a rather low hemoglobin count for which I am taking iron now. On the way to Lausanne the Lord placed me in the same seat with the "smiley man"— the other one who runs the *telepherique*, who was in the avalanche last year, and did not die, though he was seriously injured. Almost immediately he began questioning me—"What are you, Protestant? Just plain Protestant? What do you Protestants believe?" etc. He was most eager to know, and it was obvious that his interest had been stirred by the talk that has occurred as a result of the "Sisters' edict." I was able to give him not only a bird's-eye view of Church history and the Reformation (dating from the book of Acts) but as question led to question we were able to get into the basic teaching of the Bible, and why the Bible was the most important thing in the world—the only "Word of God"—not to be added to! He really got the way of salvation clearly and that is a load off of my own soul because I had wanted to witness to him ever since that accident last year. Other people in the car turned to listen—and in spite of my bad French (I know I make loads of mistakes but it is understandable now anyhow) I went right on. At the end he leaned closer to close out other ears and whispered—"My children came to your class—it was the sisters who stopped them—they *liked* it—they liked it better than their school." I told him we knew the sisters had stopped the children but that we thought the parents should make up their own minds—that was what freedom meant! He shrugged his shoulders and said, "But what can you do—the sisters can make the children very miserable in school." . . .

We had a quiet Sunday—two more stages of *Pilgrim's Progress!* And now we are in the midst of a what-shall-we-do-first kind of a week. There is for me—sewing and mending for myself and children, washing and ironing for ditto, packing for ditto, and all the last-minute things. But this letter had to come first! We leave for Geneva on Friday, then return Monday—one day to finish up, get Debby and Susan settled at Home Eden, and then Wednesday we leave again for Geneva and the next morning for Barcelona, where we will be for nine days of meetings. Pray for us during this month in Spain and Portugal. I hope to write you one letter on each country as there will be too much to put in one letter. So my next letter should be partially written in Madrid and finished in Lisbon—D.V. We do need your prayers daily all during this trip—for safety, and for Holy Spirit power and wisdom in giving messages and in the many contacts.

Much love to you all,

EDITH

April 29, 1952   Madrid, Spain

Dear Family:

Greetings from old Madrid! It doesn't seem possible that we are in the middle of Franco's dictatorship, eating, sleeping, writing, speaking, and traveling in a Fascist land where freedom is an unknown thing. But even a Fascist dictatorship with its rules and its soldiers and police cannot keep out the power of the Holy Spirit. . . .

As I finished the last letter we were packing Priscilla's trunk for the spring trimester at school, getting odds and ends of office work caught up, preparing suitcases for the trip to Geneva, etc. There were people on our minds whom we felt we should see before going away but couldn't see how the time could be given to entertaining for even one evening— but the Lord brought each one to us without our having to prepare ahead or even stop for an entire evening. Each one just "dropped in" prompted by a desire on his or her own part. Madame Marclay came while I was sewing and just picked up something to hem while we were talking. She went away armed with the Bible Studies in French saying that she had *hoped* Mr. Schaeffer would get them translated! Madame D., from the hotel, stopped in to say "goodbye," her dog running in ahead to announce her arrival, and we sat beside the open trunk and piles of Priscilla's things to drink orange juice and chat for a few moments. Then—the phone rang and Mr. Exhenry said he would like to talk to Monsieur Schaeffer before we left. He came at five-thirty and stayed until about seven. As he and Fran talked in the living room the rest of us went on as quietly as possible, praying as we worked. . . . As he and Fran left the house to walk up the path toward the village I sent Priscilla out to suggest to her Dad that perhaps Mr. Exhenry would be interested in some of the meetings of the Easter Conference. It was a sudden inspiration. Fran told us the story afterwards. The conversation had started with a question from Mr. Exhenry, "Why did God accept the sacrifice of Abel and not that of Cain?"—and went on from there directly to his own need of coming to God in the way He has appointed—through the Lord Jesus. He was very evidently prepared by the Holy Spirit because he went so easily through all the steps until he was substituting his own name for the "whosoever." Fran asked him to pray, and he even did that without hesitation, and very simply, as a child—"I am a sinner, I believe in Jesus as my Savior. Thank you God for sending Jesus to die for me." It was hard for us to believe that it had happened! The first adult in this Roman Catholic village to make a profession of faith in such a definite way. . . .

At any rate we were both in Geneva at midnight—and ready to take off for Spain with nothing forgotten. Anticipating my very *first* plane ride caused me to waken several times through the night—some of the time wondering what it would be like to be up in the air, and some of the time wondering what it might be like to crash (hoping I'd never find out), but most of the time praying that the Lord would bring us safely back to the three girls and our work. There's nothing quite like a *first* time! Priscilla (who stayed on at the Bible School at Le Roc until her school started April 20th) and Mr. Wutrich were at the airfield to wave us off. "Passengers for Barcelona, Madrid, Lisbon"—and out we went— through the gate and across the field to the waiting Spanish Iberia plane. We waved to Priscilla and Mr. W. on the other side of the barrier and then up the steps and into the plane we stepped. A Douglas DC3 is not very big, and its 18 seats didn't impress me very much after all the pictures I'd seen of planes! And then we were moving like a strangely shaped bus with a most unusually noisy roar. It hardly seemed possible that the wheels had left the ground and that I was actually in the air for the first time looking down on trees and rooftops. The wheeling and constant climbing gave me a few dizzy moments but soon that was over and for two hours and a half we rode with very little sensation of speed. As for a mode of travel—it is like being borne along on a magic carpet out of contact with the world itself. . . . But it was not until we swooped down and flew low along the coast of Spain that I felt we were actually close enough to have a contact with things as they are! . . . I felt as if we had made a little map study and a distant city had suddenly come to life. Flying isn't travel as far as I'm concerned—it is in a different class all by itself.

We were met by Mr. Cignoni and guided to our hotel. . . . Later in the afternoon Mr. Cignoni and another man came to go over our schedule of meetings with us, and at eight o'clock that night we had our first meeting. This happened to be with a Brethren group, a very strong and alive work in Spain. We had our first experience that night of entering an unmarked door in the side of a building that might have been used for any purpose at all. No Protestant church or meeting place can place any kind of a sign or indication on the outside announcing its existence. This law of course excludes all Scripture texts being placed in any public place, as well as shutting off possibility of announcing meetings, or having Bible stores. However the meeting was well attended by regular members and by some outsiders invited by word of mouth, and we were told that the numbers had doubled during the last years when persecution began to increase. . . . Verses are prohibited on the outside—but they blossom forth on the inside, and this plain hall has its walls covered with painted Scripture verses giving the way of salvation clearly and exhorting to study the Scriptures. We found this the usual method of church decoration in Spain. . . .

Another result of our time in Barcelona was a definite beginning of the work of Children for Christ. Although it is against the law to do Christian work outside of the four walls of whatever meeting place has been designated, some courageous souls want to try gathering a small number of children in their homes. For these, and for the many small Sunday Schools meeting inside the various meeting halls, our Luke lessons are now being translated. Sunday School material is very scarce and the workers who do work with children were thrilled with the plan of our lessons and the other materials. They felt it would draw more children to the Sunday School in spite of regulations. . . .

In Seville Fran was met by the pastor whose church was burned, Mr. Molina, who showed Fran his church and demonstrated the manner in which the seven young men fought him, stood on him, poured gasoline on the hymn books and Bibles, and set fire to them. He told how the police had "searched" the town for the seven men but *couldn't* (!) find them. There are now two policemen sitting outside the church door "guarding" it! Fran spent an interesting day with Mr. Molina and spoke in the evening at a meeting in which the four Protestant churches of Seville participated. . . .*

Poverty makes it almost impossible to find a self-supporting church. Of course the Catholic Church is supported by taxes and it along with the government bleeds the population dry. We were at one meeting of over two hundred when the pastor thanked us for our message and said our coming had also helped them financially because they had such a "big offering"—it consisted of 200 pesetas—exactly five dollars! . . .

Pray for general needs and problems mentioned in this letter, for Fran's article on Barthianism as it is translated and circulated among Christians, and of course for the *masses* who know not Christ and are in a bondage truly pagan.

Money is needed for the beginning of Children for Christ work—the lessons and the pictures. As we go from country to country we note that works most widely advertised, works receiving the largest gifts from the outside, are *not* the ones doing the greatest work, nor the ones most deserving of help. Often groups struggling along financially, completely unknown in America, are winning far more souls to Christ and would make far more worthwhile use of gifts if they did receive them.

Now—on to Portugal—in the next installment!

Much love,

EDITH

July 21, 1952   Champéry, Switzerland

Dear Family:

Some of you have repeatedly said to me, "I don't see how you find time to write that long letter." This time I don't seem to have found that time! One thing after another has absorbed my time, so that Portugal has been laid aside. Now I am full of things to say concerning the last two months—but I must discipline myself and fly back to Portugal carrying you along with me that you too might have a glimpse of this colorful country with its needy people with hearts open to the gospel. . . .

We were glad to get away from the confusion of the Madrid Airport, where we had to wait two hours "in line," while money and passports were checked. . . .

Our first day in Portugal we awakened to the ring of the telephone,

*Fran traveled alone during part of this trip because I was six months pregnant with Franky at this time. This also added certain problems to finding the right food with Spain's concentration on olive oil causing discomfort!!

and from then on we had phone calls and appointments of various kinds. We met with a missionary and his wife for lunch, had a talk with all the Action Biblique workers at teatime, met later with a Baptist leader, and had a short time with a young TEAM worker who is Portuguese. We could not spend longer with him as he was on his way to the hospital to see his wife and brand-new baby. We had dinner at our own hotel with the American who is the president of the Presbyterian Seminary as our guest. This man has come from pastoral experience in the States, and is heading the seminary here at Lisbon. He stated that he did believe the Bible in a conservative way, but although he always clung to that claim, he also defended various well-known liberals and Barthians. A younger professor in that Seminary in Lisbon is reported to have made statements in sermons that would show conclusively that he is Barthian, and the Barthian we met in Spain is a friend of these men. These are active danger signals. Portugal, a Roman Catholic country in which Christian Protestants have a little more freedom than Spain but who know what persecution means nevertheless, is in a better condition as far as protestant churches go, than any place we have ever been. Not one church has thus far joined the World Council and liberalism has not made the progress it has made even in Spain. *But* there is danger very real and present. When poison is sprayed into the air, it is a sure thing that someone is going to breathe it to their own detriment. Barthianism is a sweet-smelling poison and when people do not know its odor they sense no danger.

A woman who worked at the seminary office has left because of the things preached by this younger professor which to her keen discernment denied the historicity of the Bible. She has now left the Presbyterian Church to join the Action Biblique group because she wishes to be free from this thing. She is translating Fran's booklet on Barthianism into Portuguese, and Action Biblique is putting it out. Our missionaries in Brazil are happy about this as they feel it is a very needed booklet there too.

Our meetings in Portugal were thrilling because of the eagerness and joy on the faces of the people, which reminded us of that described in books on the early days of missions in other countries. Many of the groups are new—twenty-five years, twenty years, ten years, six years or even one year or a few months old. This means that the Christians to whom you speak have taken a step in faith which has cost them something and makes them regard their new-birth into the family of the Lord as a precious thing. They do not follow in the footsteps of generations of Protestant church members.

We had four meetings in the two Action Biblique halls in Lisbon. Both these halls were brimming over with people for all the meetings. Every inch of space was full, right up to the platform and out to the doors. They are modest mission halls, but from the looks of these meetings the great need is to stretch the walls! We estimated over 130 each time at one place and 160 at the other—conservative estimates! Sunday afternoon I spoke on Children for Christ and the enthusiasm was great. It seems that in Portugal it is permitted to have 20 people (and this includes groups of children) gathered together in one place at a time without an official permit. Therefore although Portugal is a dictatorship, and is intolerant of Protestants, the door is quite open for small children's classes of 20 or under. The adults at that meeting were just as interested and delighted as the children themselves with the Door of Salvation, the Heart of Salvation, and one of the lessons from Luke illustrated on the flannelboard, and several spoke of wanting to begin classes in their homes. Of course the first step is translation of material, as always, but this is even now going on. . . .

There was little time for any special "sightseeing," though Fran did make use of some in-between time to see various points of historic and artistic interest, while I made use of the same time to rest!* The "sights" I enjoyed most in Lisbon were those which could be seen as we went from meeting to meeting and appointment to appointment—buildings, parks, flowers,—yes, those—but more than those I enjoyed the women walking barefoot and erect with enormous baskets of fruit or vegetables balanced on their heads, girls with huge bundles of washing balanced as easily as a straw hat, and fish-sellers with their wide trays of fish which stay on their heads while they called out their wares to hungry housewives. I never got over being amazed at the feat of balance, and of the strange mixture of women walking on high heels and in "chic" clothes on main streets with these barefoot, aproned women proudly carrying their daily loads among them.

We left Lisbon early Tuesday morning and I had my fill of watching the loads come into the market place on the heads of the farm women as we swished through the streets in our racing taxi to the boat dock. Our boat was a ferry which was to take us the half-hour trip across the bay that we might board the train for Faro in the south. Crossing that bay seemed like a trip through the pages of an old history book with pictures of Portuguese sailing vessels. Such a variety of sails we saw! Huge lumbering boats like outsized rowboats curving up in the front in some picturesque shape with sails like a Chinese junk, three-mast sailboats, enormous frigates, every variety of shape in sails and boats—except for the ordinary type you'd see in a summer yachting center. These were not sportsmen's boats—these were for carrying freight, or for fishermen, boats that have not changed in style for generations. As the sun came streaking through early-morning clouds and caught these sails in its light we couldn't help exclaiming over and over again, "What a picture!" An artist ought to have plenty of subject matter in Portugal. . . .

Our ticket said "delux" as it designated our sleeping compartment!

---

*I was then six months pregnant with Franky, our fourth child, so stayed behind at times to rest.

But the "delux" was all on the ticket! Now we know why everyone raved so about the "rapid" upon which we had come south; this one started and stopped at least every ten minutes—I'm sure that's no exaggeration, so with hard beds and short sheets there was not so much sleep that night. The ferry to Lisbon took us back to the hotel.

Fran had a meeting in a Baptist Church in Lisbon that night in which he carefully explained the need of a firm stand against apostasy and unbelief during this day in which we live. We do so hope that these people will not be "taken unawares."

The next morning found us again on a train, this time headed north in the company of the Baptist leader who was to be our translator. . . . His great desire is to get more missionaries into Portugal while he is still alive to help them get there. It is very difficult to obtain a visa which will permit one to live and work as a missionary in that country. This man has been successful in arranging visas for missionaries, and thinks he could get a few more in—but how long the door will remain even that much open, he does not know. Therefore he spent much time on that train trip urging us to come ourselves, or to get the Independent Board to send in others. He feels the Independent Board has a real work to do there which could not be duplicated by another mission, even his own. . . .

The next day Fran and I separated, he going on a strenuous trip, and I being sensible, going back to Lisbon to do a less tiring work of seeing some more individuals, taking our passports to the boat office, and packing for the trip home. . . .

That night Fran returned to Lisbon. We had a missionary guest for dinner and another time of talking concerning the need of Portugal. Morning found us preparing for the trip home. Our boat sailed in the late afternoon taking us away from a country that had stirred us deeply with its tremendous need, its deeply spiritual and humble Christians, its missionary challenge. Trains took us from Milan to Monthey and up our own mountain to Champéry, where we were greeted by two little girls to whom a month had seemed a long time! One more month of blessing in the Lord's business behind us.

Much love to all,

EDITH

End of July, 1952   Champéry, Switzerland

Dearest Family:
. . . It's always good to get back to Champéry from anywhere! There is no place quite so tucked away from the busy world as Chalet Bijou with its outlook on cliffs, pine forests sweeping upward, mountain peaks snow-covered, fields of flower-strewn hay gently blowing, and its "noise," consisting mostly of birds chattering and mountain streams rushing through rocks. Some wonder if we aren't terribly lonely—"You are so cut off"—but that is something we haven't had a chance to discover, because as you know we are seldom alone!

Our first days back I finished the letter on Spain, and then got busy helping as Fran and the children planted the gardens. Priscilla had a long weekend* and so the whole family worked on getting the seeds placed in orderly rows. The "unusual heat" has seemed to be a universal thing this year, and it reached even the Alps. It meant the peasants did their usual haying in broiling sun, the city folks sought the mountains for some relief, we knew for the first time in ages what it meant to be uncomfortably warm, and our garden flourished! We should have a fine crop of corn this year, in contrast to last year's tiny crop due to the rain and cold. Besides being in a hurry to get in the garden, I had the need of doing a mundane housecleaning—putting away winter things in mothballs, etc. Fran had many letters to write, including those back to Spain and Portugal, and packages of promised things to send off. By the way, we discovered that it costs just as much postage to send a box of clothing from here to Spain as it does to send from America here, so it would be cheaper if anyone wants to send clothing to send it directly to this address: Mario Cignoni, Pasajo, Marimon 19, pral 2a, Barcelona, Spain. If you do send boxes direct to Mr. Cignoni, please write us about it, as it will help us to be more help to Spain. Then came a few days spent in Geneva and Lausanne—one of those full-to-the-brim trips. My passport had run out and had to be renewed during a specified time (neither earlier nor later will do—and you *must* appear in person); Fran had been asked to speak on Spain and Portugal to the Bible School; there were things concerning Children for Christ we needed to attend to in both Geneva and Lausanne; necessary shopping to do; and a Bible class for Fran to teach. . . .

Fran also started another weekly Bible class with just one member in it! That is Mr. Exhenry; your prayers are really being answered. . . . Fran went to see him the first week we were home, but discovered that he was at military service. As you may know, every Swiss man is in the army: each boy must serve six months in military service at 20, and then every

*Priscilla was then studying at La Grande Verger, a preparatory school in Lausanne, to which she had been given a scholarship.

year after that for three weeks until he is about 40. This year older men have had to go back for the three weeks because they are intensifying their efforts on preparedness. This year each man has been given 30 rounds of ammunition to keep in his home along with the equipment that has been standard. There is no other nation quite like this little one for efficient and trustworthy organization. . . . Mr. Exhenry told of how right after we left for Portugal and Spain he had told the Lord he wanted to quit smoking (a thing we have never mentioned to him at all)—"and I haven't smoked since, not even in the military service"—which amazes us, as he was a chain smoker before. He agreed with Fran to come to the chalet for an hour's Bible study each week. Now his quick step down the path is familiar. . . .

For three weeks during the latter part of June and the beginning of July Vic, the peasant woman who helps me with housework, was able to come only for a couple of hours in the evenings because she was "haying." This meant an extra hurdle for me, because the housework had to be added to my regular work. Fran helped by organizing the "dishwashing squad," which pitched in effectively!

It was during this time that our family increased considerably. Remember the Miss P. who helped me get those Christmas boxes mailed in Italy last year? She is the owner of that hotel where we stayed in Alassio. . . . Well—she wrote in June asking if her two nephews might come to stay with us for a month. They live in Sardinia (a Mediterranean island) and have always lived by the sea, but have never seen the mountains. She felt the change of air would do them much good after a year of hard work in school, and suggested working out an exchange—"We will give time in the hotel in exchange for time at your home in the mountains." Now Susan has an allergy every summer up here in the Alps, and she benefited much by the sea air last year, but we simply didn't see how we could afford any such vacation this year. Since the third-class railroad fare to Alassio is very little, it means a vacation practically without cost for the girls. Fran will then be able to visit the Children for Christ work at Grasse (nearby in France), and to see some people in Genoa and perhaps other places in Italy from which we have received inquiries concerning Children for Christ. This all presents a reason for our saying "yes" to her proposition—but another reason was the fact that we'd have these two Sardinian boys (we call them "the Sardines") in our home, at family prayers, at the classes, to talk and to answer questions for, for a month.

On July 1st, Marco (13, extremely advanced in school studies but much younger in appearance and social interest than an American boy of 13) and Maurizio (10, ditto to the above, plus the fact that he is very little bigger than Deborah) arrived, accompanied by Miss P., their aunt. We had a wonderful time of conversation with her after the children were in bed. She was so appreciative of a few days in the mountains for herself and of our arrangements for her boys, that her letters keep com-

Marco and Mauritzio, from Sardinia, with Susan,
Priscilla, and Debby.

ing, written as from a close friend. Now the boys have been here four weeks and their mother wants them to stay in Champéry until she comes for them later. We have enjoyed having two such nice boys in our family. If you could peek in at mealtime you'd hear a conversation going on partly in French, partly in English, partly in very excited Italian or Sardinian. The French conversation is for the benefit of the boys, because that is the language in which we must communicate with them. They really speak it very well. The English is for the benefit of Miss Anderson, and for the rest of us when we forget to stick to French!

Miss Anderson is the dear Finnish lady who shared her tiny apartment with us and gave us the piano bench to sleep on. Each time we went to Finland she did more than she should have done to minister to our needs. The last time she bought some woolen stockings *before* we came, to be certain that I would not be cold. Naturally, when she wrote that she would be able to visit us for her vacation this summer if it would be convenient—were were *sure* it would be convenient!!! You see she has never been farther from Finland than Sweden and Estonia. To come to Switzerland was a tremendous treat and adventure for her. She is a person who quietly fits into the family, doing whatever she sees to be done in a helpful way. She arrived July 10th to stay until the 28th. But to go back to mealtimes—the Italian and Sardinian languages are spoken always in great excitement because the boys resort to their own two languages whenever they become excited about anything, such as the comparative merits of Italy and America, whether their doctor father is only a mental specialist or also a surgeon, or if the predominant number of old towers in Sardinia are Roman or Moorish! There interests are varied and their fund of information surprising. I do wish you could see the little one when he becomes intense about something—expressive face, eloquent dark eyes, and gesturing hands make his fiery arguments and opinions interesting even when they are in another language. The older one is calmer with a much more easygoing makeup. When something has been decided in Italian, they give us the result in a French translation. Our mealtimes lack nothing in entertainment. . . . I can't leave the boys without telling you what Maurizio said today. He came solemnly to us after dinner and said he didn't think there were any classes (Children for Christ) on Sardinia, and he thought there should be. He has, he said, twenty friends and he would like to start such a class with them. Could he have some Hearts of Salvation and other things to begin with and how much money would it cost, please? . . .

Last summer we had a Swiss Christian helper with us, who taught Children for Christ classes. This year Priscilla has taken over that work. She has also had an English class of four 12- and 13-year-old girls each morning for one hour. This, plus some other help, has made a busy summer for her. We invited the children's pension "Le Joli Nid" to send their children to the Saturday afternoon class, Susan invited another smaller pension of children and some summer visitors' children (earning 17 fish one day!), and the class has increased until it numbers about 40 as an average. Priscilla does remarkably in holding the attention of this assortment of children from two to 14 years of age throughout the lesson periods, and the sound of so many singing is a joy to our hearts. In addition to that, the Home for girls from undesirable home environments, called "L'Aube Claire," brought their group of girls up to Champéry for a mountain vacation again this year. The first thing the mistress did was to come to Chalet Bijou, along with all the girls, to inquire as to whether they might have some more of "those nice Bible classes" this year. Since their stay is comparatively short she wondered if they might have two or three classes a week. "You can't imagine how much good it did last year, and how they have remembered the lessons." . . .

Our church services this summer have been having an attendance of about 30 to 40 each Sunday. No larger busloads of English have arrived since Spring, and the individual visitors have come and gone staying short periods of time in various hotels and pensions. Besides these people, we have had some of the girls from schools which come for a few weeks in the summer. As a result of this summer attendance at Fran's preaching services, we have had a few guests for tea and further conversation, among whom was an Australian psychologist and his wife. As well as tea conversations around the Bible, Fran has been teaching a small Bible class at 6 P.M. Sundays. Besides Madame Fleishmann and our own girls, there have been an English nursemaid (working for a French family vacationing here) and a half-Czechoslovakian, half-American girl as regular attendants. . . .

August 5th—Chalet Bijou has been the scene of many "new births" this past year, births that have brought many into our eternal family. Since writing the above at the end of July, I have another birth to report—a first birth this time!

Very early in the morning of August 3rd, even while it was still dark and a storm was clattering the chalet shutters and howling through the pine tops, a new little voice added its wail to the wailing of the wind! It was the first cry of Francis August Schaeffer, Jr.—who entered Chalet Bijou at 2 A.M. Sunday morning with the help of Dr. Otten, nurse Helen Waridel, and his own daddy!! (Oh yes, his mommy had something to do too!!!) He weighed 9 pounds 6.2 ounces and was dressed in a "hairdo" of inch-long, black hair!

We do praise the Lord for this precious "bijou" (jewel) He has given us, and for answered prayer for us *both*. Because of the baby's size and poor position, it was only the skill of Dr. O. which saved both lives that might otherwise have ebbed out. The Lord is good! Please add little Franky to your prayer list.

The entire happy family send their greetings along with my love,

EDITH

November, 1952   Champéry, Switzerland

Dearest Family:

The scene from this window has changed considerably since my last letter. Winter began early this year—and we have been having a month of snow, sleet, grey fogs, and low temperatures. The wood pile has already "melted away" alarmingly as the sticks have been fed into the three wood stoves, and the whole family has been wearing winter clothing—even little Franky, who kicks around during his waking hours in a knitted Swiss baby garment with long stockings which continue into panties which in turn come all the way up under his chin and button on the shoulders. He needs to be covered with wool in the temperature of this house. His bath takes place near the granite living room stove in the evenings when that spot is really hot, but he doesn't care if the time and place has changed for the major events in his life—nor does the deep snow make any difference to him. The house has been filled with the mid-winter smell of liquid ski-wax as skis have been brought out and painted in readiness for a bit of late-afternoon exercise in the field the other side of our stream. The drying rack by the dining room stove is in constant use—filled with baby clothes in the daytime, and with wet mittens, ski socks, and jackets at night. Today seems like a day November has borrowed from February, a diamond tucked away among plain grey pebbles. The jagged stone peaks of the Dents du Midi are frosted with fresh sparkling snow, and as the sun outlines their brilliance against the bright blue sky it hurts our eyes to look up at them. We had a few days in October too when the sun flooded the village and its mountain walls with a beauty which seemed closer to heaven than earth. At that time the black pine forests above us were splashed with streaks of red and gold where hardwood trees remain hidden at other times of the year. I was ready to declare those October days the most beautiful of the year—because of the tremendous variety of color against a light snow-covered background, but nothing could surpass today!

The last time I wrote I ended the letter a bit abruptly as the baby had just arrived. As you remember, the summer was full, and we had visitors scheduled to be here right up to a day or so before August 5th, when we were expecting Franky to come. August 1st the nurse arrived from Geneva, and a carload of friends came with her for the drive. August 1st is the big Swiss National holiday, so we served a special tea for these folks in the afternoon, and had an evening of fireworks and refreshments—following the village celebration. Our two little Sardines (the boys from Sardinia) had stayed on to be with us for the holiday, and we had planned to take them over to "Le Joli Nid" the next day to wait the week or so before their parents were to come for them. Le Joli Nid is one of the children's pensions which was coming to Priscilla's class all summer. It was so full that we had to take Debby's double-decker bed over for the boys to sleep in (Debby slept on a mattress and spring placed on her floor!)

However the work I had planned to do during the next few days had to be done suddenly during the night of August 1st, as I received "notice" that Franky was on his way! Such a scurrying around to prepare Priscilla's room to be the hospital! We did not waken the boys—but let them go over to Le Joli Nid right after breakfast. Priscilla moved into their room after they left. So you see I had no wasted days of waiting! Before the boys left they signed in the guest book, and we were thrilled to read in Maurizio's writing, "I came to know of the love of Jesus in this house." The baby was about nine days old when the parents of Marco and Maurizio came to get them, and to visit me. The father is little and energetic—talking animatedly with much gesturing and many changes of facial expression. His pointed black beard gives him a pixie air—though he is a leading doctor on the Isle of Sardinia and has a very fine private hospital for nervous breakdown cases. Maurizio is very like him in looks, in his actions, and in intelligence too. The mother is a more placid Italian type—a bit on the heavy side, round face framed in dark hair, and a smiling quiet manner. Marco is almost exactly like her. The "hospital" room seemed full of people as we served them tea—and conversed in French (Marco translating from Italian when his parents were "stuck"). They had brought an elaborate silk-covered basket of sweets made of almond paste—a special gift from Sardinia which is always given to the parents of a new baby. They seemed happy and grateful to find that the boys had gained weight and were so rosy. . . .

Having the baby at home meant that his three happy sisters could come in and gaze at him when he was only a few hours old. I wish I had a photo of their awestruck look as they beheld him for the first time! For days Susan always preceded her entrance into my room with, "Oh, is he still there?" as if she expected he had been spirited away in the meantime, while Debby tiptoed in as if walking on eggs and never said a word—just glowed silently! The nurse gave the baby and me good care, Fran helped in many ways, Priscilla cooked the supper each night, and Vic came to do housework in the daytimes—but still there was a good bit of meal-planning, making of market lists, etc., that I had to do myself, and because of the difficult time I had had, I didn't have too much pep. My first day up had, of necessity, to be filled with canning beans—as the garden was producing them faster than we could eat them. Fran organized to help string them, wash them, and cut them up. As the end of August came near—it meant a time of sorting, washing, ironing, and packing for the vacation the girls were to have in Alassio in exchange. You remember we were to have free time in the hotel in exchange for keeping Marco and Maurizio here. Fran was to take the girls and get some work done in Italy at the same time. I was to have my vacation by being alone with the baby. I tried to pack so that all could easily find their own things—without mama on the trip! . . .

Fran and the girls left together on the early six o'clock train. They departed down in the valley, going straight by third-class train to Florence, where they arrived by six in the evening. Twelve hours from Champéry finds one well in the middle of several countries depending on the direction taken. They spent two days in the summer heat of Florence—covering the important places and museums and adding to their education of art and history, and then took a bus to Alassio—which went via Pisa, where they got slightly seasick climbing the leaning tower. Daddy did well traveling alone with three daughters—and all reported a fine trip! At Alassio they were welcomed like old friends by the hotel folks, storekeepers, and visitors who remembered them from last year. Fran was delighted to find that Mr. P. from England with his wife were not only there, but that Mr. P. was eager to begin conversation and Bible study with him. . . .

One day Fran took Priscilla with him to Genoa to talk with the Italian man who heads the House of Bible in Genoa. This is a part of the Action Biblique work. Priscilla acted as interpreter—since the man speaks only Italian and French. This man agreed to translate the Luke lessons into Italian, and to begin four classes there in Genoa. . . .

Fran left the three girls alone in Alassio as he went on to Rome and

Naples. They were under the supervision of Miss P., the hotelkeeper, but the English folks were good to them in taking them out to tea and to hear music in the evenings. In fact they wrote that they were being spoiled with Daddy away!

Meantime I was enjoying (?) the solitude of Chalet Bijou without a soul in it except a wee baby. I kept busy in the daytimes with the baby, correspondence, and canning. I did keep my promise to rest, by going to bed early nights—and wee Franky did his part by demanding only four meals a day. Some folks asked if I was not afraid to be down here, away from the village street and surrounded by dark, quiet, and towering mountains at night. No, I didn't feel a bit afraid—but I must confess that I was terribly lonely after being so accustomed to a full house—with family plus! There was one break in the aloneness when company arrived from Holland. The man and his wife who gave Fran a bed back in 1947 when hotels in Rotterdam were full and Fran was making his survey trip of Europe called up to find out if I could keep them overnight as they were trying to vacation in Switzerland as cheaply as possible. With so many empty beds in the house—I said "yes" of course, so I spent one evening talking to them. That one late night exhausted me so much that I appreciated my vacation more after they left.

Then one grey day when the rain was coming down in torrents, all four of them arrived home drenched, but joyous to be back again—and no one was gladder than I that the vacation was over! Of course the baby was the center of attention, "Hasn't he changed!" "Look how he smiles." "Isn't he a darling!"

Since there are only a few very small children at Home Eden this year, the mistress didn't start school until the middle of October. That meant that Susan and Debby were home all that time. We started them on a schedule of American schoolwork interspersed with music practice. We had wondered much through the summer about what to do with Priscilla for the winter. She has had two years at that Swiss boarding school due to the kindness of the director, but for several reasons we felt two years were enough. We had a desire, among other things, to have Priscilla home with us for a few months. She has missed being with the family—and now with the baby as an added attraction she looked forward to being in Champéry. Her school is going to another winter resort this year, and that would have meant that she would have been away more than ever. She has her credits from her school for her first and second years of high school and now a wonderful way has opened up for her to go on with her junior year here at home. Miss Walker of Stevens School in Philadelphia has made a lovely arrangement whereby Priscilla is studying at home the same course the juniors in Stevens are taking. Then when, Lord willing, we arrive home on furlough and settle in the Philadelphia area this spring, Priscilla will continue her junior year with the class at Stevens finishing with them in June. She then will be able to go on with them next fall as a Senior. We felt this was of the

Lord—one of His marvelous provisions for His children. In October each corner of the living room was a different class in school! Then as Susan and Debby went back to Home Eden to be two of five pupils there, Priscilla continued her own school in any cozy spot she wanted to choose for the day. In a way it is lonely for her, but letters help to keep contact with her old school friends, and later in the winter other schools will be coming up here for skiing. She is being a great help to us in addition to doing her schoolwork. Her help to me, in baby care, cooking, etc., might be considered a Home Ec. course! While her help to her Dad in translating and writing French letters, filing, and going daily to the Post Office is an education in itself. She is now playing the funny little pump organ at church, since Madame Fleischmann has moved to Neuchâtel. She remarked once that she was our "native" helper—and actually she does help us as much as another worker would in many ways . . . or more!

As the three girls settled into their winter schedule, Fran and I began our new writing project. We are writing a History of the Old Testament in lessons for the flannelgraph, and are trying to get as much as possible done during the quiet months before the winter visitors arrive in Champéry. We would like to get at least half of the lessons finished before it is time to leave for furlough. You know as we write these lessons to be used in so many different languages, and by so many different groups, we keep in mind the needs of the many different ones who will use them, which is quite different from writing for one country or one church group. Sometimes a lesson goes quickly—and other times we work over and over one before it satisfies us, so it is difficult to tell how long it will take to finish them. We need to write a long letter to the artist to accompany each lesson we send him as he is working on the lithograph illustrations. Since we need to conserve space on the stones,* it takes some time to decide about the number and size of the various illustrations. Altogether it is a long work and requires, more than anything else, quiet stretches of time. Do pray that the Lord may give us the needed quiet, the ideas, and the words to make these lessons ones that will be truly helpful in giving children a Biblical world-outlook, and an understanding of life from God's Word.

Of course fitting a baby's schedule into the other work makes an added hurdle to jump, but the Lord has certainly given us an easy baby to care for. He has eaten only four meals a day since the beginning, and now has spaced these meals to give us a good night's sleep. In between meals he sleeps soundly or plays contentedly with his cradle gym, gurgling and cooing at anyone who happens to stop to talk to him. He had two days of fever recently, which we think was a touch of the grippe—which Debby had first. But now he is fine again. Pray that he may keep well in spite of the uneven and often low temperature in this chalet.

*The lithograph stones.

In October we had a visit from a Brazilian pastor and his wife, who came to us as representatives of a Presbyterian church in Brazil to invite us to come to São Paulo to live and work. He urged us very strongly, speaking of the need of leadership for the Christians there and telling of his plan to build a seminary to train young pastors. Their desire is for Fran to head this seminary. We feel very touched by the need in Brazil and would love to be able to help—but—we can only be in one place at a time, and that place must be where the Lord wants us. . . .

Priscilla's class has been changed to Thursday afternoons now that she is here all the week. That means that an 11-year-old girl, Christine, whose parents are divorced, and who visits her father weekends, may now come regularly. Two little girls whose father is Protestant (mother Catholic) also come, as well as two small boys of two other families. Lillian Exhenry is now a regular attendant too. At present the other village children are still afraid to come, but the Lord can change that too. . . .

Our furlough is due this spring, and we made reservations many months ago on a French liner while there was still the "pick of cabins." We were glad to have two cabins, which would mean a comfortable arrangement with the baby. However, as we received no confirmation from the Board on time concerning our furlough to make these reservations binding, on the date the company fixed (the middle of October) we had to let them go. The travel company told us that to begin again will mean much less possibility of good accommodations. Now we received word that the Board has authorized the furlough. . . .

I rather shudder at the thought of packing for such a trip and being en route so long—but many missionaries have traipsed farther around the world with more children! The Lord has given us the possibility of keeping our chalet while we are in America without paying the rent ourselves. The Andres of Lausanne are going to rent it from us for their winter and summer vacations. They will use our things, as well as the furniture that belongs to the chalet—so we plan to leave the washing machine, the office equipment, the books in the bookcases, all right where they are. That should make things easier—though it is a bit difficult to know what things we will have need of in America, when we don't yet know what our living quarters are to be like! . . .

The Board has asked that missionaries speak concerning the needed finances for furlough travel—as it is too great a burden upon the Board's General Funds. Therefore I am mentioning this so that if any of you wish to contribute to the expenses of our probable trip to England or to the expense of our passage across the Atlantic you may. Incidentally, the fare of Franky on any transatlantic steamer is $10—same as is charged for a dog or a bicycle!—but unhappily Franky can't come without us, so pray that the money may come in for the whole family!!

As I close this letter the snow is over a *yard* deep—but a fine misty rain is coming down through the fog making heavy slippery stuff of the snow, and causing it to crash down from the sloping roofs dangerously to the paths below. Avalanches are coming down in places—a most unusual thing for November. We wonder what sort of a winter is ahead. However, the weather is not so much a cause for concern as the *people* the winter will bring. Remember to pray for the winter opportunities.

Much love,

EDITH

P.S. Letters are pouring in from England and other places as girls from the finishing schools write wanting to keep in touch. Increased correspondence adds to each day's work but is like caring for a garden—much tending, weeding, watering, are necessary to produce fruit.

1953

January 10, 1953   Champéry, Switzerland

Dear Family:

Today as I write, we are in the very middle of the winter. . . . It has been another of those times when we have had the wonderful thrill of watching the working of the Holy Spirit. My fingers want to plunge right in and tell you the most exciting of the news, but they must be obedient to my mind which says they have to type this news in its proper chronological order.

The lessons for our Old Testament History for children began to take shape, and Fran also prepared a booklet of articles—some reprints, and two additional articles which have been on his mind. During this time, among the encouragements that the postman brought down the path were continual requests from Spain for Children for Christ certificates. Something else came down our path late in November—two pairs of khaki-covered legs which brought two G.I.'s straight from Germany! We had decided to keep on writing until about 7 P.M. and then just stop for a quick supper of soup and bread and "spread" when about 6 P.M. the phone rang. It was a boy who had been told by a reader of the family letters to "look up the Schaeffers sometime." Late November finds Champéry hotels closed, and of course we invited them to "come right on down." The whole family went into action to clear up the living room (where everyone congregates for warmth), put away typewriter, papers, books, studies, games, etc., and set the table for a company dinner. I beat up a "prepared" chocolate cake one of you had sent from America, and used my imagination to enlarge that soup supper into something filling and tasty for two hungry G.I.'s. By the time it was on the table the baby needed to be fed and bathed and made ready for bed (all of which has to be done in the warm living room). So while the folks ate, I busied myself with the baby, behind that granite stove, and kept one eye open to see when it was time to serve the next course.

It all worked out very smoothly, so that the baby was ready to go upstairs to sleep in the cold, just when the folks were ready to come into the living room for the evening. As for my supper—I have rarely so thoroughly enjoyed missing a meal! It was a real joy to be able to do some small thing for two of our country's army boys, and to know that they were having a taste of home life for the first time in a year and a half. Fran showed them some of his slides in the evening and then had a talk with them about Biblical things. Of course we had family prayers as usual both in the evening and the next day at noon, and Dave thanked us for thus "helping" his buddy. He later wrote that it had awakened in him a new desire to testify to those around him, just to be in a home again where even the children were quite natural about speaking of the things of the Lord and praying aloud. We do need to follow all the boys we know in the army with our prayers and letters, it's the least we can do to make up for the homes and churches they are missing, and the believing boys are in a place of real opportunity but they need much encouragement and prayer backing. . . .

December was now well on its way and we were still finding time for writing. A "pause" which was always refreshing for Fran was the weekly evening with Mr. Exhenry. His understanding of spiritual things makes an evening of Bible Study with him one not only of "giving"—but of true Christian fellowship. What he needs most now is the courage and opportunity to speak to others about the Lord. . . .

As Christmas came nearer—there was less quiet time for writing. Priscilla planned the special party for her Children for Christ class, and though there were inquiries from village children as to when it would be, they were told that it was to be a reward for faithful attendance. There was nothing to be gained by an inrush of children simply for the party itself. We took pains however, to make it a memorable time for those who had come regularly through the year. Priscilla gave the Christmas Story stressing what Jesus means to us as Savior and as Mediator—having Lillian Exhenry read aloud the verse, "For there is One God and one Mediator between God and man, the man Christ Jesus."

After the classtime Fran showed the children slides for a treat—and it was a treat to us to hear the children's "oohs and ahs." One little boy—the grandchild of the concierge of our chapel—kept saying, "C'est pas villian ca," to all that he saw which was beautiful (that's not bad, that's not bad that) whether it was a picture of Holland's tulips or the ice cream! His blue eyes were shining with happiness throughout it all, as it was the very first party he had ever attended—and quite a contrast to the dingy smoke-darkened room which provides him with his daily environment. As the children were gathered around the gay dining room table which had red-and-green plaid place mats from my sister Elsa in Watertown, and a tiny tree bright with tinfoil-wrapped chocolates, pine branches, candlelight, and scripture verse place cards, and they were munching sandwiches, drinking hot chocolate, and anticipating the ice cream and cake—in walked the old grandmother of the little lad. She brought the odor of the barn in with her as she sat her black-garbed bulk down on a chair we quickly pulled up to the table for her, and her scarlet headscarf—the mark of a Champéry peasant—bobbed in the candlelight as she bent to make sure her child "minded his manners." Priscilla grasped this opportunity to witness to the old peasant by sending Debby for the "Heart of Salvation"—and had the children sing the song while various ones turned the pages. When the little boy shyly refused to turn the pages—the old grandmother turned them for him. I wish you could have seen her wrinkled mouth forming the words as her scarlet-covered head kept time with the music and her gnarled hands turned the pages of the heart. The way of salvation was made clear and a few more songs were sung before the children left with their "favors" clutched in their hands. One little boy said as the time drew near to go, "I brought a sack with me for whatever we have to take home!" And we were glad it wouldn't be empty! Our prayers followed the old grandmother—that her heart might one day be full of the joy of assurance of eternal life; this life has been so empty of joy for her.

We were not sure how many English would be coming for the holidays, but we filled the village with posters. We made them this year with a background of the red-and-green plaid paper place mats—and they were tacked upon the bulletin boards of hotels and pensions as well as in some of the stores. They announced that there would be Christmas Eve Service at 5 P.M. the 24th, a special Christmas service Sunday the 28th, and a New Year's Eve Service at 8:45 the 31st. This year we had a new victory in that for the first time our services were announced on the village printed program of activities. Fran and the girls made the church attractive, meantime I cut the stencils for song sheets, and Priscilla took them to the one man in the village who has a mimeograph machine. As we made these preparations, we prayed that the Lord would bring some prepared hearts.

The moon was growing full as Christmas approached, and Fran and I often went out to the field at midnight, and enjoyed a bit of sledding before going to bed. Did I say the mountains are at their best in the bright sunlight? I think I've changed my mind. The young moon casts a pale bluish light that turns the snow-covered peaks and glaciers into rhinestone-studded ornaments of gigantic size against the black velvet of pine forests and midnight sky—but as the moon grows full, the light changes and becomes amazingly brighter. The almost-full moon casts a dark shadow across the snow, each tree has its shadow, and our own shadows go skidding down the snow beside us. Debby and I went out and skied in our field just before supper one night—and had the beautiful experience of watching twilight change to moonlight. At first there was a faint rosy glow that colored the white peaks a pale pink—this changed to a cold white as the pink left the sky and a baby blue covered it instead. The blue constantly deepened as the minutes passed, deepened finally into a dark bright blue against which the stars, moon, and mountain peaks looked artificial—like a painted backdrop. We hated to miss a single evening of the changing moon, which reached its peak of beauty on New Year's Eve when it became full.

We are happy that the people arriving in the village were met with such lovely snow and beautiful weather—the nicest weather we've had for winter visitors since we've been here. Many were French-speaking—but bits of news came which made us hopeful—"The Jua girls have arrived and they have eight English with more coming after Christmas." "Madame D. just called and said a busload of Scotch girls arrived today." We prayed that they would be drawn to the little chapel—and that the Lord would prepare their hearts. Priscilla showed a lack of enthusiasm about the coming services—but prepared for them with much hard work! What was wrong? Well, you see Madame Fleischmann has moved to Neuchâtel and Priscilla is the sole organist. She practiced Christmas carols until I thought she'd wear out the pedals on our piano. Why-for the pedals? Well—she was "pumping" on them so as to train herself to pump the funny little organ. She was sure her playing would ruin everything—but it turned out to be a real victory for her as she mastered an I-can't-do-it sort of a thing.

The 24th dawned bright and clear. The morning was spent in caring for baby, cooking our meals for that day, plus cookie and pie baking, and cooking a special dinner for a poor old peasant woman with a withered arm. The children decorated a small pine tree for her while Fran gathered together some tracts, a Gospel of John in French, and a scripture calendar to take to her. By three-thirty the baby was fed and sleeping peacefully, the old lady's dinner was steaming in two cardboard boxes and some canned food and fruit was in another, the tree was ready, and all of us dressed for our church service. We made a strange parade across the deep-snow-covered fields as first Fran went, carrying the tree and a briefcase with the song-sheets, etc., for the church service, then Priscilla with a big box, Susan next with another box, then Debby empty-handed, while I brought up the rear with a box that mustn't be tipped! There was just enough crust on the snow that each step almost held—and then crashed through. Debby kept singing out—"Look at me, I'm walking on top—it doesn't break with me." We went downhill toward the little stream that tumbles down the narrow rushing mountain river below. Fran put his things down on the other side to help us across—slip—slide, "Watch out don't fall," now up the steep bank, and we are all on the other side. Across another field we made our way down toward the river, for her little chalet perches on its steep perpendicular garden as we round the house. "How can she ever garden there with only one good arm?" We had heard that she had never had a really good meal in her life—a miserable childhood followed by a life of hard work. For years she has lived in this lonely spot with only enough for an existence. Knock, Knock—an unkempt head appears from a slowly opening door on the balcony for all windows are shuttered tight to keep in the heat—"Oh?—" Surprise casts a softening light over the dirty wrinkled face—the door opens wider to let us into a room so dark we can see nothing for a few moments. Then gradually we see the black smoke-covered walls, the piles of wood and chopping block in the room's center, the littered table with its cracked dishes and its end of a loaf of black bread—a piece of dry cheese being the only other food in the room. "We've come in the name of the Lord Jesus to bring you a Christmas dinner. You know the Lord Jesus came into the world to give His life for sinners who would accept Him as Savior—Jesus died for us, and we would like to do a small thing for you at this time as we remember what Jesus came to do for us." We lift out steaming dishes of food—a casserole of potatoes scalloped with cheese, a small roast of beef—hot home-made rolls, a fresh pumpkin pie, fruit, cans of food—and she keeps exclaiming, "Mais—mais—c'est pour *moi?*"—"But—but is it for *me?*" Am I to *keep* it? When I have finished shall I bring back this dish? For me to keep? But I never have had food like this—why this is my *first* Christmas dinner." Now there are tears in her eyes. The children sing some gospel songs in French, and Priscilla gives her a clear testimony of the way of salvation. Then we give her the tracts, scripture calendar, and things, Fran prays, and Priscilla translates the prayer phrase by phrase—and we leave her. For the first time she has had some good meals, but you might pray that the gospel will speak to her heart, that she might understand and receive the Bread of Life, the eternal food!

Our arms are lighter, empty of boxes, and so are our hearts. "It isn't right to sit down and eat three meals a day without ever sharing with those around us who have nothing," we agree. We find the church filled with smoke but not much heat, and soon after we enter the seats begin to fill up with the entire "party" of Scotch girls, the Jua girls, and some other individuals. Debby, Susan, and I light the candles without mishap, Priscilla plays the organ without "ruining" anything, and Fran preaches the gospel clearly as he gives his Christmas message on the pre-existent Christ. What results there were inside the people who listened, we won't know until we get to heaven (except for a few instances perhaps)—but we know they have heard the most important message that human ears can hear, the message of salvation as God sets it forth in His Word.

After the service we hurried home in the early moonlight to eat supper and prepare cyclamen plants for delivery. Fran and the three girls started off after supper to deliver the red-flowering plants while I stayed home to feed Franky and begin my evening's work. They went to six homes, the old lady's whose garden we rent (opposite Chalet des Frênes), the Marclays', Home Eden, etc. At each place they stood outside and sang carols—an unknown thing here—and we later heard that many others, who were not being visited, listened to the singing.

With the plants went scripture calendars and everywhere that they were invited inside Fran closed the time of talking with prayer. We felt this was a real testimony, for as Fran and I visited the old lady of our garden the next day to show her little Franky, we found the calendar hanging in a prominent place on her living room wall and she said, "You know I thought it was the angels singing last night. I told my nephews today that I never heard anything so lovely, and all the things you left for me to read speak to my heart." Her nephews are storekeepers and ski teachers—and so little by little a testimony is being given in Champéry. Vic told us the next day that they had run out and listened as the four were singing at another place, and others must have done the same thing, as in the silence of the mountains songs, even the words, can be heard for great distances. We got ready for our family Christmas after they returned—the girls trimmed the tree and filled socks for mother and daddy, while I cleaned a turkey from France and handed out oranges and tangerines from Spain! We spent most of Christmas day quietly alone together as a family, except for the walk in the afternoon when we went to the old lady of our garden with Franky; and the girls delivered a Christmas gift to the lady who runs the children's pension called "Le Joli Nid.". . . .

Tuesday Doctor Otten was to come for dinner. I had saved a nice portion of turkey to slice cold, and prepared a dinner that could wait without spoiling—happily, because his "be there at eight o'clock at least" finally turned out to be about nine o'clock! We had a fine dinner together with conversation interesting enough to satisfy Debby and Susan, who hadn't wanted to eat first because "Doctor O. always tells such interesting things—like treating people who have been shot while smuggling on skis." After dinner he fixed himself comfortably on the couch behind the stove, to toast himself warmly as he drank his after-dinner coffee. Fran and he talked about many things, art, philosophy, and the chaos in the world—as contrasted with the certainty the Bible gives. As if the Lord wanted me out of there—the baby awakened for a late feeding (a most unusual thing) and from 11 P.M. on, I was busy behind the closed door of the dining room. I knew they had Bibles out and that Fran was progressing toward asking Doctor Otten for a decision, and as I spooned cereal into Franky's mouth I prayed fervently that this might be the night of salvation for dear Doctor Otten. I had a strange experience, because as the voices were low, I could not know what was being said, and during my fervent and earnest pleading with the Lord, I suddenly was filled with a peace—and even as I attempted to continue my praying—my mind was filled with the phrase, "It is finished." I became convinced that the Lord had answered and the need for that particular prayer was finished. As Doctor O. and Fran came out—the doctor simply wrung my hand and said, "Thank you so much for this evening"—and he and Fran were gone. I had to be patient for a few more minutes before I found out what had taken place.

Fran came back with the story. When Fran had asked him if he believed Jesus was God—and other questions concerning the facts surrounding salvation—he had said "yes"—but to "Have you really accepted Christ as your personal Savior" he said, "I don't know." Fran explained and gently led him–until Doctor Otten bowed his intelligent and educated head—and praying aloud for perhaps the first time in his life—he thanked the Lord for saving him, and for sending the "famille Schaeffer" to make this clear to him. He prayed as simply and earnestly as a little child and seemed to mean his decision from the bottom of his heart. We could have had no one person whose salvation could have given us more joy at the end of the year. Fran said that as he walked up the hill to his waiting car the doctor immediately began talking of others "who ought to be talked to" in this village and he agreed heartily to having Bible study with Mr. Exhenry and Fran. These two men would be good elder material anywhere in the world.

That was Tuesday the 30th—Wednesday was New Year's Eve. There was a hockey match scheduled for 5-7 P.M. and balls at two of the hotels for 10 P.M. to 3 A.M.—would anyone come to church service at quarter of nine? The Jua girls called in the late afternoon to say that they couldn't possibly come to church—"Please excuse us as we must dress for the ball!" This being a new group—all unsaved girls—it probably was surprising they even bothered to call—but we felt disappointed. On our way to the church we thrilled at the beauty of the full moon. The light was stupendous reflected on the white snow at our feet and all around us on our mountain walls. "It gives the same effect as sunlight when you are wearing the darkest of dark glasses," I remarked—glad to have hit on a way of describing it. We met "tailing" parties (sleds hooked together behind a horse) taking rides before the balls, we met English people walking in the wrong direction—and all of us began to feel that we would be having a family service! But we hadn't been in the church long when a school (we later learned from Wales) began to file in—all dressed in grey coats and grey berets—all girls from 8-18 years of age, plus two headmistresses. There must have been over forty of them. Then gradually individuals began to come and take their places too. One filled us with a special joy. *Mr. Exhenry came for the first time!* After lighting the candles Debby and Susan went to sit with him "so he won't feel lonely and strange." He had stopped to talk in the afternoon and had learned of Doctor O.'s decision, rejoicing with us over it. Now he had kept his promise and had come to the service. . . .

Our sailing is now definite; we leave Southampton on April 2nd on the SS *Liberte*. In connection with this we've had another answer to prayer, the President's office of the French Line has written that Fran is to have the Good Friday Service and the Easter Service on board the *Liberte* and that I am to have an Easter children's service—all of which will be placed by the Captain on the ship's program. The boat's capacity is about 1,200 so do pray that the Lord will use these services to reach many on board with the gospel at a time when they are in mid-ocean and will have time to think. . . .

Fran leaves for Denmark, Sweden, and Norway on February 1st and will return on the 15th. He will have meetings arranged for him by Dr. Hedegard in the first two countries and will be with our friends of the Free Church in Oslo after that. Please pray for this time. Since we are leaving for England about the 16th of March—this doesn't leave much time for all the work of the winter plus the preparations for the trip. There is much to pray about this time, but it is a time when you may have a special part in the work here—for when the Holy Spirit is working, the devil is sure to attempt to hinder and your prayers are needed.

Much love,

EDITH

April 10, 1953   Champéry, Switzerland

Dear Family:

This will be the first installment of the closing letter of our five years in Europe. My writing time has been completely gobbled up by other work for the last months (a thing you will understand better when you have finished this) and therefore it is being written from the American side of the Atlantic Ocean, where we all safely arrived two days ago.

The snows of early January prepared the fields and slopes for a perfect winter for the schools which had come to Champéry for sports. Day after day the sun shone hot enough to bronze the skin of the ski enthusiasts, while night after night the temperature dropped low enough to keep the snow hard and the skating rink glassy. It was the kind of a winter the alpine hotelkeepers dream about, but to us personally it did not spell recreation! True—the baby enjoyed his mornings kicking in the sun, shedding his wool stockings for a time, and the girls had some memorable hours skiing down the mountain, but it was the busiest winter we have had yet, and as a matter of fact I didn't leave the chalet itself for several weeks. The Jua girls came every Tuesday night, Angela and Deirdre came for their more advanced Bible study every Monday afternoon from 4:00 to 7:00, the girls from Florriss came for their Bible study every Wednesday night, Thursday afternoons Priscilla had her Children for Christ class, Friday afternoons two boys came for a Bible study time, and of course Sunday we had the usual service at the chapel. These were the "fixed" periods and in between we needed to find time to fit in the various visitors who found their way to Chalet Bijou, *and* to continue our correspondence and writing, baby care, and cooking.

It wasn't long after that that the Lord gave us a glimpse of a particularly interesting spot in that gigantic tapestry of His, in which each detail of the lives of His children is woven. Priscilla was biting her pencil in despair as she struck a snag in second-year Algebra, through which she was struggling along—"Oh I'll *never* be able to do this without a teacher—it's just hopeless." "Have you prayed about it?" Fran and I questioned, thinking that the Lord could help her to think the problems through without any help. We prayed that evening. The next day a professor who had been at church Sunday brought his wife to Chalet Bijou for tea. During the preliminary conversation he spoke of being a mathematics professor, and told us a bit about his background. He is a Czechoslovakian refugee now living in Switzerland, studying French at the University of Lausanne, teaching math in a boys' school, married to a Swiss-German wife, who had a religious experience when she was about 14, but for years had felt that she had "lost all that." "I have no faith now," she said. Once she began to ask questions, they just spilled out—one after another. Seven o'clock arrived, and they had to go back to their school for supper. "May we come back to finish up these things?" We felt that it wouldn't be wise to postpone the conclusion of this conversation so assured them that they could return that same evening. Such a mad scramble as we had during the next hour! Supper to prepare—tea things to clear away—baby to care for—no wonder we were still eating when they returned. Priscilla went into the living room to continue to translate for her father, as the Czech man understands English but his wife only French and German—and I continue to care for the baby and the two younger girls until all three were asleep for the night. Although I joined the others after ten, there was still plenty of time left since they stayed until after two A.M. As question after question was answered and many doubts and misunderstandings cleared up, Madame Czerny came to see that her early experience was not one of true salvation, but that she had merely confessed a sin—and had then gone on to try to live a good life in her own strength. After she realized that she had never been born again, she gradually came to see her need of Jesus as her Savior. Before praying with her, Fran turned to Mr. Czerny and asked, "Wouldn't you like to accept Christ as your Savior too?" The reply came so quickly—"Oh yes, I *would*. I never understood these things until this evening. I joined the Swiss Protestant church when I came to this country—but the pastor did not explain things as you have done tonight." Both of them prayed very sweetly and simply, thanking the Lord for dying for them, and thanking Him for bringing them in contact with someone who could make it clear to them.

As they stood to go, Mr. Czerny turned to Priscilla and said, "You are studying alone this year, can't I help you with your Algebra? Show me your book." As he looked over the book he speedily divided it up into sections and told her how many hours together they would need to spend to go over what he considered to be the proper amount. "I'll come over here to tutor you whenever I have free hours from my school." A little more than 24 hours since we had had special prayer concerning Priscilla's Algebra—and the Lord had answered by giving her a mathematics professor who would give her private lessons! Isn't it thrilling the way the Lord picks up threads and weaves them together in the pattern of His own design, and isn't it an ever-amazing mystery how our prayers can move His hand? His wife then asked if she couldn't help me out by doing some mending, knitting, or ironing as there was so much to be done in those last weeks before going away. What a wonderful Lord we have. A Swiss-German and a Czech refugee discouraged and in need of spiritual help are brought to Chalet Bijou where the Lord meets their need—and as they with grateful hearts seek to do something helpful, they find their particular talents are just the ones we needed. The Lord's solutions to our problems are not *our* solutions but when we come to difficult places we should never forget that "He is able—and we should pray earnestly, *believing*. . . .

By this time we were only four weeks away from the day we would have to leave Champéry. Trunks had to be packed and sent to Le Havre ahead of time, then suitcases had to be packed for the ones going by train by way of Paris, and finally the last-minute things had to be packed and taken by me along with Franky and Debby by plane to London. Of course the house needed to be prepared for the Andres who were to come into it after we left, and various personal things had to be prepared for storage and stored in a spare room—properly protected against moths and mice and possible leaks in the roof. It was a temptation to just close our doors against visitors for a time and get ahead with the packing—but it was a time to put into practice the putting of first things first. After all, souls are more precious than any material possessions could be, and the Lord Who gave us our possessions in the first place could provide duplicates if He so desired if it turned out that we had to leave much behind because of lack of time of packing. So we didn't turn anyone away—and although it seemed at the time an impossible task to get everything done—what actually happened was we didn't know the *half* of what was going to be added to our long list!

The dining room was filled with open trunks and the table with trunk drawers—and in between the usual housework, care of baby, correspondence, etc., we stopped and packed whenever we had a spare moment! but then came the deluge of unexpected things! Priscilla was skiing the next afternoon, and after I had the cakes finished for the Jua girls who were to come that evening Fran and I were working on some letters when we heard a wail coming in the front door—"Oh mother and daddy, I'm hurt and I've had the most horrible time"—and in came Pris supported by Madame A., who had a bottle of arnica in her hand. Priscilla had had a bad fall, and when one of the ski teachers (who lacks good sense) found that her leg was not broken, he gave her the choice of walking back up the mountain or skiing on down to the village—instead of getting the "Samaritan" to pull her down on the emergency "luge." He went on down with his class when she chose to try to go up. She had some bad moments when she was afraid she was going to faint and perhaps freeze to death in the snowy vastness and her ankle hurt so she could hardly keep making progress on what is a difficult feat when a person is feeling fit—climbing through the deep snow up terribly steep and lonely stretches of mountain.

However the Lord took care of her as the party of English folks from Chalet des Frênes came skiing down and saw her and set to work doing all the necessary things. One of them went for the "Samaritan" with his stretcher-like sled, and while that one undertook the hard climb to the rescue station, the others stayed to keep her spirits up. Her ride down strapped on that sled as it slid and swerved behind the skiing Samaritan was an experience not a little frightening—and she was *so* relieved to finally be back by the warmth of our old granite stove, that she didn't mind too much the swelling ankle. There is a village man with "sensitive hands" who is called upon to fix up displaced bones in cows, goats, and people—and since Madame A. sent him down that evening, we let him take care of Priscilla. He pronounced it displacement of some ligaments, and after maneuvering them into place ordered hot compresses and rest interspersed with exercise. This accident brought a stream of phone calls and visits from the Chalet des Frênes English folks—which gave us some new contacts as well as consuming time!

Priscilla sat with her foot up the next day and talked to her English callers—and I excused the disorder but went on getting slipcovers washed and put back on as Fran "packed" and sorted his files. The Florriss girls came for the last time that evening and were very quiet and prayerful at the end—though no one spoke out loud to say that she had accepted. . . . The following day Priscilla managed to hobble around enough to teach her children's class, which was growing so rapidly that she hated to think that she would have to leave them so soon. Since Madame A. had begun to bring the children from her pension, and Madame M. of Le Joli Nid was bringing hers—the class was having close to twenty again. This particular day both Madame A. and Madame M. stayed to talk with me and I served tea among the open trunks and talked of the things of the Lord. That was the day Madame A. expressed her desire for the Bible Studies and said she would be looking forward to more times of study with us "when you come back again."

When Bill came for his class the next afternoon Stevie arrived on the dot of time along with his brother Ricky, for not only had he persuaded his Dad to let him stay an extra week—but he had succeeded in getting Ricky to have a week in the mountains in spite of the cast on his leg. Stevie had told us before—"Ricky believes in a religion started by a big boy in our neighborhood. He believes that there is a god named George, and that to follow him you mustn't eat apples with red streaks in them— and there are all sorts of rules like that. We gotta get Ricky straightened out or he's going to be lost for sure." Terrible to think of such a blasphemous religion started by a youngster and taught to other youngsters in a University town in our own America—"You may choose your own religion," say many of the present-day parents, and the children are doing just that! Ricky was interested and full of questions, but time was short to give him all that he needed. He's a quiet pensive lad with deep dark eyes, so different from his blue-eyed bouncy brother, and harder to get to know. They both had to leave the next afternoon, but returned with their two parents before leaving, so we met the whole family except for the baby brother. We were having tea outdoors in a warm sunny spot with "Pookie,"* who had arrived for the weekend, when Stevie breathlessly appeared announcing that his mother and dad were coming. We served them in the living room while Priscilla and Pookie finished their tea and went off to the village—Priscilla limping slowly along. Do pray for Stevie and his whole family, and pray that the Lord may open the way for us to have some good talks with them while we are in America. . . .

Next installment will go on from here—

Love,

EDITH

May 19, 1953   Philadelphia, Pennsylvania

Dear Family:

Here is the second installment! By the way, the first installment and this one are being written a little at a time in between a variety of things necessary-to-be-done-on-a-furlough, which in case you have any misconceptions is not often a time of rest for a missionary! . . .

Tuesday, February 24th, and the packing only partly done! We did get a couple of hours of packing that afternoon before it was time to make cakes for the evening. I remember that by that time I was beginning to cook with an eye to coming out even by the end and not wasting anything. An applesauce cake full of nuts and raisins used up some winter apples and Christmas nuts and turned out to be a favorite to be repeated in the future. Doubled in two and baked in loaves it cuts easily for a crowd. . . .

The next day was fairly free for packing, and as we sat around a late supper Dr. Otten popped in. "Hello, folks. Ready to be vaccinated?"

---

*Pookie is the Siamese girl Priscilla met at the swimming pool last summer. Her father, a Lieutenant General in the Siamese army, wrote to us and to the strict convent school where Pookie has been a boarding pupil for several years, and gave permission for his daughter to spend the weekend with us. This vivacious girl from Bangkok had lots of her questions completely and thoroughly answered that weekend, and left with a French Bible.

Vaccination is a necessary part of getting ready for a furlough. No one can enter the U.S. unless he has been vaccinated within three years. Dr. Otten gave a quick glance at the serving dishes and finding food that suited his taste, accepted the invitation to join us. As he ate he spread out the tiny ampules of vaccine and the needles for the six of us on the table in front of his plate. That rather spoiled the appetites of the family, though it didn't bother the doc! Before dessert was finished, he whirled around in his chair so that he would have the proper light, fixed up the first needle, and asked for the first arm to scratch. Debby offered her bared arm and mentioned a pain in her side. "We'll look at that after we're through with these," the doctor remarked. Debby had been having an attack of pains, but since she has often had tummy aches during the past three or four years, we were waiting to get home to discover the cause. After each arm was duly scratched and the baby's tears were dried, Debby underwent a poking which ended in this pronouncement: "I think Debby has appendicitis, and since you are going on that long journey, I wouldn't waste any time getting the appendix out. Take her temperature, see how the pain progresses through the night, and I'll call back later." His midnight call settled it—he wanted her brought into the hospital at St. Maurice early in the morning. I packed her little suitcase, putting in the necessary pajamas, robe, slippers, her favorite doll, reading material, crayons, etc., with many tugs at my own heartstrings. It had been decided that Daddy should accompany her and stay until after the operation at least. He could take along some work to do and Mommy was needed by the baby. However, inside Mommy didn't feel like the smile that was on the outside of her face when the little girl went off in the morning tucked in on the sled behind her suitcase. A phone call from the hospital room a couple of hours later reported that the taxi had delivered Daddy and Debby safely at the hospital door, that Debby was tucked in bed in a cheerful room, that Daddy was to have a bed beside her, that there was a dial phone right there, and that they would keep in touch with us until the patient was safely out of the ether. Debby had Bible reading and prayer with her Daddy before going up to the operating room and was most cheerful and cooperative, for which we thanked the Lord. She had the usual nausea and gas pains, but her recovery was normal. That evening, after I talked with Fran again and learned that Debby was sleeping and that he would stay right there with her as her special nurse, and that he had a good table and light to work by while she slept, I was so relieved and calm that I felt quite ready to tackle a big piece of work that had been awaiting a "free stretch of time"—this was my "free" night! That, then, was the night that I wrote the American Council Children's Lay Program for this year, the one the Children for Christ Board had asked me to write. The house was quiet, the baby slept well, I felt wide awake and was sure that that which was finished before morning was what the Lord had helped me to write.

Saturday afternoon Susan had "off" from school and she delightedly betook herself on the train to the hospital to visit Debby. She had full instructions to catch the last train that would make connections back up the mountain that night. Debby called up and wept over the phone that night, homesick because she was all alone; but another call followed soon after we had comforted her. "Hello, Mommy—this is Susan—I ran and ran after the train all the way up the tracks to the second station in Monthey but I couldn't catch it."—"Yes, I know it was supposed to wait for me but I didn't think of telling the man at the station it was leaving me. When I got off the other train and saw this one leaving, I just ran and ran along the track to catch it. Oh, I'm so tired and what will I *dooooo?* The man told me to keep on running and maybe I'd catch it farther on!" She had run about eight blocks after the train, which stops at two little stations in Monthey and then goes slowly up the mountain. Of course she couldn't catch it even if it does go slowly for a train, and she had visions of having to hike home, poor child. "Listen to me, Susan. You go to the hotel a half a block up the street there—that little one that has a cafe on the first floor. Tell the lady there just what happened and ask for a room for the night, with breakfast. You can buy some *petit pain* to eat in your room before you go to sleep."—"Yes, you may buy a paper to read—yes, you can have a hot Ovaltine. Now be sure to call us back to let us know that you are safely there." Susan's next call was not at all dejected—she was elated to be having an adventure and felt most important to have signed up for a room in a hotel, even a modest little wooden hotel like that. She reported having had a fine sleep, when she came back early the next morning, and said the ladies were ever so nice to her. She only regretted that she couldn't have such an exciting adventure more often! It wasn't such an expensive adventure at that, as the whole thing cost less than two dollars. . . .

Monday, Priscilla went down to be with Debby, taking her Algebra along with her. Mr. Czerny, her teacher, was ill, and so as she had an especially large assignment to be finished for the next lesson, she decided to stay all night with Debby and profit by the quiet there. Our house had ceased to be a quiet place for any kind of study—people were coming and going all the time, the packing getting very little attention. Susan came screaming home that noon, blood gushing from her hand. "A dog bit me—I didn't do anything. No, I wasn't running, I just knocked at Christine's door and when her mother opened it the dog ran around her and bit my hand. Oooooww—what'll we do?" This wasn't such a funny adventure. Dr. Otten advised soaking it in camomile tea. It is always on our shelves because it is ordered for various kinds of compresses, for enemas, for drinking when anyone has a tummy ache, etc.! So into camomile tea went Susan's hand for the next hour or so! That was Angela and Deirdre's day for the tea–Bible study, and before their four o'clock arrival we were trying to sort out the French Luke lessons, putting them in "book" order, as they were in stacks just as they had come from the mimeograph machine. The dining room table had to be cleared of packing things to make way for the lessons, and just as this was under way Madame Czerny came to "talk a little bit" and Mr. Exhenry came to see Fran. Fran and Mr. Exhenry disappeared into the office for Bible study and prayer, and I enlisted Mme. Czerny to help me with my sorting job. It sounds hectic and it rather was; in fact, it continued to be for the next weeks. . . .

There was no hope of packing trunks the next day either, as that was the day all our Children for Christ bookroom supplies and any other materials we have in French, such as the Bible studies and Fran's articles, were to be packed and handed over to Mr. Wutrich to take to La Maison de la Bible in Geneva. They are going to handle these supplies for us while we are away. The morning was given to dismantling our bookroom, a very nice-sized room originally meant for keeping food supplies, which is shared by our trunks and jellies! Early afternoon brought Mr. Wutrich's smiling face, along with Helen, my nurse when Franky was born, and another girl from the Bible House in Geneva. We had general conversation, and Fran and Mr. W. toted the supplies up to the car, which had to be left on the village street above because of the snow. Then the girls took the "new girl" to "see Champéry," while Helen and I had a talk privately about some personal problems of hers. This had to be done while I was bathing and feeding the baby, so was somewhat of a strain as she speaks no English and when I'm talking French I need to concentrate! We finally served tea to the assembled family and visitors and waved off the visitors just as Debby was calling to bid us a tearful good night and ask, "When can I come home? I'm homesick down here." . . .

Time was rushing on and the first installment of packing had to be brought to a close. The trunks were to leave the house the next day at 7:00 P.M. The last things were being stuffed in when a weather-beaten old man with a decrepit old horse caused us to send across the field to Vic's for her husband. He is strong of arm and shoulder and could practically carry a trunk to the station alone! Vic is now owner of a heavily mortgaged chalet which she rents in the summer (four apartments!) and they have moved there, just across the field from us, for the winter. Vic later told us that the horse found it so difficult getting up the hill that her husband practically took all the load as he pushed the cart up the hill. We paid him the same price as the driver charged us for the horse!

Trunks off, it suddenly seemed empty in the chalet, but that didn't last long. Now it was time to pack suitcases for Fran and the girls as they were going to carry most of the weight by train through Paris to London, while I was to go with the baby and Debby by plane. The things the Andres would not want to use, such as the typewriter, office files, children's toys, personal belongings of various kinds, had to be packed away in a spare room. Bicycles had to be tied up to the beams of the attic (shared by us with a haystack!), and umpteen details needed attention. People didn't stop coming either. Rachel (the owner of our house along

with Robert and Herman) came one evening that last week to settle up—
we were paying for anything lost or broken during our time there, etc.
While I bathed Franky she waited patiently, mingling the odor of cows
and stable with the perfume of his bath creams and powder. As she
made clucking noises at him, enjoying his responses, I felt so sorry for
her hard and lonely life. She works like a man in the fields and with the
animals, and seems to have no softness at all in her grim features until
she begins to talk about roses or look at a kitten or a baby. Again I prayed
that the Lord might open a way. And that night the opening did come.
Rachel began to talk of the fact that "fate" was hard and all you could do
was just accept it. I tried as well as I could in French to explain the difference between having a ruling "fate" and a loving Heavenly Father to
care for you, and we talked on into the night. She eagerly accepted the
Bible I gave her as a parting gift, and just as eagerly her hard rough
hands grasped the mimeographed sheets of the Bible studies and she
promised to read a little every night. I prayed with her and there were
actually tears in her eyes as we parted. . . .

Mr. Exhenry came for his last time of Bible study and prayer, and he
was discouraged because he had failed to interest his wife but had only
stirred up antagonism in his family through his witnessing. He seemed
quieter in his mind and heart after the fellowship together with Fran.
How he needs your prayers in this time of his "aloneness"! He said that
he was going to come to our church service for the last Sunday. He kept
this promise and there he was for the first time at a Sunday service (he
had come to a New Year's service before). To walk past the Roman
Catholic Church at Mass time and continue on down to the Protestant
chapel farther down the little village main street is in itself an open confession of faith. It was hard for Fran to close the doors of that chapel and
to know that in all probability they would remain closed as far as regular
services are concerned until he came back to open them. Do pray for *this*
winter's crowds of English-speaking people. Travel agents in England
have already asked Fran if there are to be special holiday services. . . .

The next day was the day the first half of the family was to depart. The
old horse was able to manage the suitcases, projector, etc., and though it
didn't seem possible that it was true, the moment came when they were
gone and I was left all alone to finish up and remember not to lose my
tickets to London!—and to get there!

In planning we had thought those extra two days would be a good
"break" for me, but as it worked out it wasn't long enough to get everything done. Of course if doors had been locked to callers more could
have been accomplished, but there are spiritual things so much more
lasting than material things, that I therefore set my mind to the fact and
told the Lord I would do whatever He sent me to do if He would just
give me the strength. I did say "no" to one thing—Mme. Czerny asked if
I'd make a sponge cake for her husband as it reminded him of his home
in Czechoslovakia! That is a promise for when I come back. But when

Mme. Marclay came the last evening about 5:00 and said, "Oh, Mrs. Schaeffer, I want to go to the same place you people are going when I die. How must I do to do that?"—then I knew that rush must be put aside for a time. Carefully I went over the way of salvation, making it as clear as possible. "But do I have to leave the village church? My husband would not allow that. Can I believe without doing that?" Poor, frightened one—what a storm that *would* cause. But the Lord is able and the Holy Spirit will guide and direct you as to what you must do when He lives in you. "I want to believe, but now you are going away—I will study and read the Bible, and when you come back I will say 'yes'—then I will believe—" She asked if Mr. Exhenry was one who had believed. (Is there talk about him? Was it his going to church that made this more open? What are people saying?) She said she would talk to him if anything ever happened to keep us away. We had prayer together and she said she would be with me on the train.

That last night can't be fully described. Franky developed a cough and the only place that was warm was the bathroom with hot water in the tub and the electric heater, so when the cough wakened him, I couldn't leave him in the cold bedroom but had to take him into the bathroom. I took a couple of suitcases into the bathroom and did part of the packing there. When he went to sleep I went downstairs to prepare bottles, etc. Hour after hour went by, morning came, and I realized that I was paying the price for putting first things first.

You know it is foolish to say, "Yes, I'll give this up for the Lord," and then want both the blessing plus the thing you have handed over to Him. Slow, orderly packing was the thing I'd given up, and I found it hard to be perfectly content with having to push things in and really leave things behind I felt I wanted with me. Our "school"—the one of the Christian life—never ends and the "lessons" continue to need to be learned. Morning brought Vic to help us to the station and Christine to "help" too. We called the town "jeep," which was to meet us at the top of the first rocky uphill stretch, and for some reason Christine and Debby took part of the things up and Vic grabbed the baby and ran with him before I had a chance to check up. "Everything's gone from upstairs, Mme. Schaeffer," Christine called, and I, having my mind now on that baby's cough with the cold air outside and not properly wrapped in a blanket, just took her word for it and hurried out too, with what I thought to be the remaining suitcases. Mme. Marclay met us in the middle of the village street and climbed into the jeep too. She had another jeep ready at the station in case I had missed the train to take us to the valley!! The Czech professor was on the train ready to help too—bless his heart—and it wasn't long before we were waving a tearful farewell to Vic and an assortment of others. Mme. Marclay was in the little wooden compartment with us and she boohooed out loud along with Debby. I couldn't keep back the tears myself when I saw the dear familiar mountains moving away into the background, and all that the work and people have meant to us moving into history. I was glad it was only for a year. Mopping my eyes, I suddenly missed the grey bag with Franky's formula for the trip.

"Oh!" brought the attention of all and a search was made—no grey bag. At the first village the conductor phoned back to Champéry and when we reached Monthey, a jeep came to its clumsy stop and there was the bag. Paying the driver the two dollars for the trip, I thought, "Is there any place like Switzerland?" Mme. Marclay said, "Ah, see how God answers your prayers!" Mme. Marclay's son joined us for a way and they left the train together. At Lausanne, Voyage Kuoni, the travel agents, sent a representative to help me change trains and Franky chose that moment to lose his breakfast! It was soon cleaned up, however. On we went and when the train stopped in Geneva, three of the Action Biblique folks, led by Mr. Wutrich and Helen, the nurse, came to help us off and to "do what we can" to make the change easy to the airport. As the baggage was checked (what a queer assortment it is—nine pieces instead of two and including a string bag with forgotten rubbers and cameras!) a special letter was handed to me—Mme. Fleischmann's farewell letter, sent to the airport!

Finally the moment comes to actually leave Swiss soil—and with Debby running ahead, a plane hostess carrying Franky up the steps, I turn to wave to the last friends I see, the dear group representing Action Biblique—goodbye for a time.

The welcome in England and the trip home must wait to go in with the next letter, which will also cover a bit of our impressions and activities as missionaries on furlough. But please continue to pray for the ones we've left behind and ask that the Holy Spirit may continue the work there which He had begun.

Love,

EDITH

1954

S.S. ILE DE FRANCE

September 3, 1954   On Board the *Ile de France*

Dear Family:

... Saying "goodbye" is the hardest part of setting forth on a new missionary venture—yet the very emotions which choke us at that time are a reminder of just how important our going is—so that those to whom the Lord is sending us may have the opportunity to know Him—whom to know is life eternal—and that life eternal has *no* place for "goodbyes."

When our mothers and the loved ones who had come to New York to see us off became simply a part of the mass of backs moving quickly down the gangplank, we seven tore up the nearest stairway to find a place at the rail where we could catch the last glimpse of familiar faces and wave and shout our final farewells. ... The water between us widens—the faces become blurred—and yet so short a distance has cut off communication—but oh, how wonderful it is to know that faces don't become dim and far off to the Lord. The distance never changes with Him. "And lo, I am with you always." ...

The first few times we gathered together at our deck chairs, we read aloud the messages in the telegrams, cards, and letters which had formed such a nice fat pile on our cabin shelf. We had to stop to tell Betty Carlson a little bit about each person who had written, so it took quite a long time altogether. . . . Now Betty is right here with us, going back to Chalet Bijou to help in any way she can during this first part of our new term when there will be such a heavy load of work—and when Franky needs someone's eyes constantly on him. Betty looks forward to serving the Lord with her life wherever He leads her, and this will be a period of further preparation, as well as a time of actual service. Betty not only will be the help that any person of her willingness and ability would be, but she knows Lausanne and the student life there. . . .

This letter, by the way, is just to form a bridge—a bridge from the last letter I wrote (which ended with our leaving Switzerland), over our entire furlough period, to the beginning of the first letter you will get from Chalet Bijou. You know, I had hoped to write regularly during the furlough, but that resolution was dissoved in a torrent of furlough speaking and work and other time-consuming things.

The plane that flew out of Geneva almost 18 months ago carried Debby up in the nose, where she had the fun of watching the pilots "drive" and having tea with them, while Franky, then 8 months old, slept in a zipped-up traveling case on the floor at my feet. We had only a short struggle with the case containing the now-bobbing baby head, and the other baggage, when we were rescued by Joanell and her father, who met us at the airport and whisked us into their car. In a few minutes I was having a very satisfactory first impression of England as old stories came to life during our drive through Eton, where we saw the quaintly dressed schoolboys—either in their sport clothes of shorts and jerseys and an enormously long wool scarf wound around and flowing down, tossed out by breezes, or in their only other permitted clothing—striped trousers and formal coats with long tails, worn to classes as well as to meals!

No sooner had Fran and the girls arrived, and we were planning our schedule of Bible study groups, luncheons, and teas with various parents of girls eager to have us talk about the Lord more effectively than they could do in their own homes—when, bing! Debby came upstairs after having just won a quiet Bible game played happily on the hearth of the drawing room saying, "I feel dizzy—I think I'm sick." That was when we really saw the social medicine program swing into action. As her fever went up and up the doctor kept returning, until he decided he wanted consultation, at which time a specialist, a public health official, and a woman doctor from the children's section of a hospital arrived and began poking and questioning—adding a panicky feeling to Debby's severe headache and 104-degree fever. A few hours later an ambulance swung up the graveled driveway and out went Debby on a stretcher to be taken 30 miles away—feeling more as though she was

On our way to America aboard the Liberte. *Edith, Susan, Priscilla, Debby, Franky.*

being kidnapped than anything else. Soon she was tucked into a bed in a ward with about 25 other children in various stages of recovery. . . .

Meantime our schedule was completely upset. Fran had to carry on alone (he even had to visit Edinburgh to answer an SOS for spiritual help from that family saved the last New Year's in Chalet Bijou), as my time was taken with going back and forth to the hospital, calling for reports on X-rays, etc., finding out what steps would have to be taken to put off our sailing if necessary, etc., etc. It was not at all what we had expected our time in England would be like, and it was embarrassing to be causing our hosts extra trouble—but our ways are not the Lord's ways, and how can we experience His sufficiency in all things, His comfort in tribulation, if we never go through the times of tribulation? We need to experience all kinds of tribulation if we are to also experience His wonderful ways of bringing us through and supplying our every need.

Priscilla had thrust upon her the job of being Franky's nurse during the hours I had to spend away (my lunch these days was eaten from a paper sack on the bus), and Susan spent her time making elaborate "get-well" cards to send to Debby. . . .

Two cars were driving us and Joanell's family to Southampton through the pouring rain to get the boat, and we reflected that our English stay had certainly proved the need of saying "Lord willing" when we make plans. There had been Bible classes, contacts had been remade, much had been accomplished for the Lord it seemed—but Mr. P. had had his father die, one-fourth of his factory burned down during those short two weeks—so that a time with his family was impossible. And there had been other disappointments. But here we were: Debby with us and on the road to recovery, long conversations with the S.'s behind us, and it had been the Lord's plan.

Easter on the boat gave Fran the opportunity to preach of the resurrected Christ on the *Liberte*, and our days gave us other times when the door was open for witnessing to one or another of the passengers. We discovered that one man, a scientist from Canada, was the same one we had talked to five years before, when he had gone over on the *Nieuw Amsterdam* with us. The Lord must have had some reason for bringing us back together for another conversation, though as far as we could see he continued steadfast in his rejection of the revelation of God, the Bible.

And so our furlough began: happy reunions, family ties tied a little tighter again, new adjustments to make to being back in the homeland, all without a pause for breath, for speaking engagements began immediately and the schedule filled up before we had time to buy a date book! . . .

We lived in Philadelphia—Fran teaching weekly (except when he was away) at Faith Seminary, and speaking in various places, the children attending Stevens School made possible through the gift of a dear friend, and I keeping house, caring for Franky, and holding up my end of a variety of responsibilities. For the first time I understood why so many missionaries seem relieved to see the time arrive when they are to go back to the field—a furlough is really not a rest in any way, and I'm sure that friends and family feel it certainly isn't a time when they can truly catch up on the years of absence. When you've left a work that is calling you back, it is like being pulled in two directions at once during that year, at best!

We had had a taste of a certain kind of tribulation in Debby's illness, called "serious" by those doctors, and throughout our furlough we had various other kinds of tribulation. What child of God doesn't? The wonderful thing is to discover the startling fact that we have become truly thankful for tribulation. Not that we ask for it, not that we enjoy the times of physical pain, the loss of material property—whether by moth and rust or by thieves—not that we enjoy the illness of loved ones or the lack of understanding of friends—but we suddenly get a glimpse of what it means to be pressed to our knees and thrown completely upon the Lord, and to see Him working out the impossible in such a way that it takes it completely out of our hands.

"The baby was awake all night—oh what weariness, but thank you, Lord, for those hours of prayer I would never have taken time for otherwise, and for letting me find out that it's *true* that 'they that wait upon the Lord shall renew their strength'—what an exciting assurance of Thy sovereign power." "That new sweater eaten by moths—what a disappointment, but thank you, Lord, for the reminder I need so often—how easy it is to transfer affections to earthly things when they aren't worth it. Thank you for this needed lesson and the resulting peace." That sudden baffling misunderstanding, that situation—who but the Lord can help? And so with an urgency which nothing else in all the world could have given, we put aside the ordinary tasks and spend the hours we feel must be spent in prayer, and what do we find to our surprise? A heart that is singing—"Thank You, Lord, for this new closeness I find to Thee—thank You for this deep joy even before Thou hast shown the way ahead—what a gift *assurance* like this is—yes, thank You for this tribulation that You knew was needed to bring about this result in me." Oh, what a comfort to have a personal Heavenly Father who cares about our individual spiritual growth and works all things together to that end as well as for His work and His glory. He is the One who knows us so well—and He knows when we do need the tribulation!

When we left Champéry we had a longing in our hearts and a prayer on our lips that the chapel might not stand vacant during a holiday season of '53-'54, and that the winter sports visitors might not have a season without a witness—as well as for the isolated saved ones that they might have some fellowship during our months and months of absence. The Calvary Presbyterian Church of Willow Grove had this need presented to them by their pastor, and voted to buy the round-trip air ticket so that Fran might go back to Champéry and break the furlough with a six-week period of witness there in the village again, stopping to have another couple of Bible Classes in London on the way there and back. And so that which at first had seemed an unlikely dream became a reality as Fran went back and was warmly welcomed by Dr. Otten and Mr. Exhenry and Professor Czerny, each of whom had grown wonderfully in the Lord and seemed ready to talk about the possibility of establishing a church; and was able to have a Christmas and New Year's service attended by over 150 visitors from a number of countries. . . . Fran stayed in our own Chalet Bijou during those weeks—for, as you know, we rented it to Christian friends during our absence so we could keep it, and they in turn used it as a rest home for various Christian friends and workers. A South American family was there the weeks Fran stayed, and he slept in our office on a cot placed in there temporarily.

During the middle of our furlough Priscilla and Susan made a fat thermometer to put up on our kitchen wall—"To show how the money is coming in for our passage back." We contemplated sending out a letter informing people of this need, but kept deciding against it—"Let's just pray about it for the time being." And so it went on in this way. Very little red crayon was needed as the weeks and months went on, for the thermometer was very low! "What is the Lord saying to us? If He wants us to go, He will send it in; let's just keep praying." When Fran was in Switzerland in January he talked to Voyage Kuoni about our travel back, because they have handled all our travel arrangements through the years and have a personal interest in doing it economically and well for us. Therefore it seemed logical to put the trip back into their capable hands and to set the date for them as September 1st—as by that time we would have been home 17 months, which was more than long enough. To make these reservations definite, we determined that we would have to have a letter and check in the mail on July 29th. That was the date the children and I began "praying towards." "If you want us to keep these reservations and get back to the work then, dear Lord, please send in the needed passage money by that date."

At the end of June we left Philadelphia to spend four weeks in a Ventnor missionary furlough cottage. One of the girls remembered to untack the thermometer and tuck it in a suitcase to be taken out and tacked up on the dining room wall of the Janvier Cottage. "Mummy, only four more weeks—and there just isn't *anything* in it compared to what is needed." "We know that if the Lord wants us to go on that date, He'll provide the ticket money—and if He doesn't, we don't want to go—it's just as important to have the Lord shut the doors *He* wants shut as to have Him open the doors He would open for us."

Another week went by, times of prayer together as a family, times of prayer alone—and then came a night of being pressed down before the Lord in a way that can't be described, but can be understood by any of you who have gone through it too. You know those times a Christian comes to when he feels he is unworthy of the Lord—the times when we catch a glimpse of ourselves as we should see ourselves all the time, and cry out to have the hindrances taken away, the sins forgiven. "If it is presumption that makes us press on toward that date—oh, Lord, remove any wrong motives but show us Thy will—if it be thy good pleasure do give us a sign tomorrow in some way that we might know." And in the next morning's mail came a letter which had been mailed in Italy some time before—a letter asking us to speak at a missionary conference in southern Italy September 13-19. We would be arriving in Le Havre on September 7th, in Champéry on the 9th—that would just make it possible to leave again at 5:55 the 13th to get to the Italian city that same evening. Betty is coming with us, so the children would be cared for! Oh, how perfectly the Lord works the details. "Yes, yes, we're coming in time—Lord willing"—for if the Lord has shown us that is the date, He will also send the needed money. Is anything too hard for Him? This request was not only a thing the Lord used to give us guidance, it was an answer to prayer during our last few years in Europe—an opening to contact other missionaries working in Europe.

Do I mean I think the Lord sent a letter mailed some days before as an answer to a prayer of the night before? Ah, yes, "Before we call, He answers." Then why call? Because He has told us to and He has told us it is necessary. A mystery? Yes, but a wonderful one—the mystery of the reality of prayer and a prayer-hearing and answering God.

And then? Well, it was the *next* day the money began to come in. Yes, there were less than three weeks left before that date, the 29th, and every day the thermometer was added to! The Lord was sending money in as a direct answer to prayer, for those letters letting the need be known had never been written. The Lord touched hearts that were attuned to His speaking, and some who were not quite sure why sent in a sum "for a special need," others sent in some "for your passage," two had been led to pray way back in May—impressed with a special need for prayer for the Schaeffers, though they didn't at the time have any idea what that need was. These two began to save money to add to their prayers, and later sent that money just in time to help finish up the sum needed by the 29th. Money came from all over the United States, on *the last day the last amount needed* for the boat tickets themselves arrived, and the letter was sent off quite in time. It couldn't have been mere coincidence; the Lord so wonderfully proved that it was all of Him by not even allowing it to come from any of the sources I had had in my mind when praying. It was as though He were saying, "No, it is not necessary to bring it from those places you think are possibilities. I am able to make it *all* a surprise to you, my child." How wonderful He is to make His leading *sure* when we seek His will. . . . You can imagine what fun the girls had making that red shoot up to the top of the thermometer!

And so our time drew to a close. Priscilla had been graduated from high school (because the Lord had opened up a way for her to continue her studies in Switzerland through the help of Professor Czerny), so she was ready to come back with us. Susan, through with the seventh grade and not quite sure what the change back to French schooling would mean for her, was already certain of returning of course, and Debby, at the end of fifth grade, would have adjustments to make again too when it comes to doing schoolwork in French. But all three were thrilled that the Lord had opened the door so wide. Franky doesn't know what is ahead of him, but he is ready to follow the family wherever they go! And we know the Lord has a place for him in His plan for the next few years too.

Now the tiring weeks of packing and preparation are over—and here we all are, returning with much expectation to see what the Lord has in store for us. As I finish this it is the evening of September 6th. The Lord gave Fran a real message for the Sunday service on this boat, and a few other opportunities to witness, though most of his voyage time has been spent in catching up on correspondence. No one has been seasick, though we have had colds, sore throats, and a bit of intestinal trouble. We got into the edge of a hurricane for two rainy, blowy days—but there has been no other excitement. I have slept more than I have for a long time, but at queer hours, as Franky doesn't know when he should stay awake and when he should sleep, now that all six hours have been dropped!* Tomorrow we land at Plymouth at 6 A.M., and then at Le Havre, France, at 4 P.M. we are supposed to disembark and see to our baggage, and then board a train by something after five, and it will be about nine o'clock when we get into Paris. We will stay there over one day to get our breath before taking an early-morning train to Switzerland.

Think of us leaving for Italy on September 13th and pray for that conference there, and do pray too for the ease the Lord would have us have in obtaining our permits to live in Champéry again.

This ends the rather bumpy "bridge" closing the gap in time—and from now on you'll be hearing regularly. Thank you so much for all your help in getting us off.

Lovingly,

EDITH

October 22, 1954   Champéry, Switzerland

Dear Family:

The field directly in front of Chalet Bijou has been rented by 11 cows and seven goats for a dining room complete with a menu of extra-green grass and purple crocuses, and so as I write this, the tenants are munching their afternoon meal and clanging their 18 bells beneath my window. The old man guarding them (appearing with an enormous umbrella on rainy days) stands reading a wee book—ready with his stick to chase them out of the section we have rented for the children's play yard. Yes, only the house comes with the house rent and any ground for play or vegetable garden must be rented separately by the square meter or else it automatically belongs to the landlords to rent for munching purposes. The grass is especially green this fall because of a cold rainy summer, but a warm and rather sunny October has kept the snow from descending to our level, and the animals revel in being let out of their part of the chalet twice a day. They spend a long winter inside, in their room next to the chalet kitchen, and find the clear, sweet air outside a welcome relief.

Our kitchen, which was also originally made for the animals and always looked like a barn with its uneven plaster walls, dark paint, and rusty black wood stove, has been transformed this past week so that all resemblance to a barn has departed (unless the concrete floor might be a hint of its past). It has blossomed forth in a coat of yellow paint with white ceiliing and trim—painted by Fran himself. The amazing thing to all who see it is the *light*—in contrast to the previous dark. Those dark

*The difference between Eastern Standard Time, U.S., and that in Europe.

walls made night seem to come earlier and the electric light seemed always to be dim. Now the source of light hasn't changed—same electric bulb—same twilight or foggy days—same sunshine when it appears—but what a difference! Those lovely yellow walls and white ceiling and doors *reflect* the light with a true brilliance so that even when the sun cannot be seen outside, it appears to be still shining in the room, and we need to examine the light bulb to be sure it hasn't been changed to one twice as strong. No, the source hasn't changed—but the surface reflecting it has. I can't go into the room without thinking of how like our lives that room *is*, or *was*. Lives cluttered up and darkened with sin and self can't reflect the beauty of the *Light* with which we are to shine. After all, the source of light for the Christian is the same—we have the same glorious Lord—but what kind of reflection does our life permit? It's important because some will never see the source of the light unless they are impressed with the brilliant reflection coming from us—and are then led to the source.

My last letter was written in the cabin on the boat, and as I was finishing it, Franky was trying to climb up and help me type. The typewriter had to be shut up and put away in a hurry, as it was getting late and the stewardess had appeared with a tray of supper for Debby, Franky, and me. Debby wasn't feeling well and we two kept her company that evening. It wasn't long after supper when Franky began to shriek and scream—"Tummy hurts kiss it, tummy hurts kiss it"—and he seemed to be in such violent pain that I wondered if it could be appendicitis. Then he began to vomit and this alternated with shrieking until suddenly he was relieved and fell to sleep exhausted in my arms. Of course, the ship has a doctor, but at 11 P.M. the last night at sea, with a sick baby that has just gone to sleep, and three other children ready for the night, one hesitates to call in a strange doctor. Sleep seemed the best medicine, especially when we thought it might be seasickness or a touch of grippe. The morning came with the urgency for repacking and preparing ourselves to disembark. Franky seemed better—though he had a fever and slept a lot until it was time to dress and go out on deck. Le Havre was flooded with brilliant sunlight as we approached the docks, and stood out like a study in buff, cream, and tan against a bright blue backdrop of sky. When Franky, in my arms on the upper deck (right under the whistle), wanted to get down and walk, it seemed a natural thing to let him run around a bit in the warm sunshine away from the crowd before it came time to be lined up to await our turn to be checked through by the officers checking passports, etc. He was completely normal at that time—and as energetic as most healthy youngsters are even when they have a fever. . . .

The open windows in the long narrow corridors of the European trains let in dirt and the clackety-clack noise of the train wheels, but also bring the countryside almost into the train in a way that makes you feel you are walking through it all. However, darkness soon cut off our contact with the quiet fields, grazing cattle, and lines of poplar trees of rural France. Coming into the Paris station Fran busied himself with getting our many bags shoved through the window to be piled high on a station cart while I arranged a blanket around Franky so that he wouldn't get chilled as we walked to our nearby hotel. I noticed as I got out on the platform that Betty and our girls were being greeted by a slim young Swiss lad, a son of Betty's former pension landlady in Lausanne who had come to the train all on his own to help us. How thrilled Betty was as he evidenced such interest in the things of the Lord, for he had been such a worry to his mother formerly, and Betty had been praying for him through the years. Robert is studying now at the Sorbonne.

Franky looked around him and said solemnly, "This is Paris, Mommy, this is Paris," in the way he has of announcing obvious facts with the air of a great discovery. It took some time to get our baggage sorted out and get up to our rooms, only to discover that no meals were being served at that time of night; but still I knew Franky and I must satisfy ourselves with whatever we could find as there was no question about his needing to go to bed, in spite of his being apparently not too sick. He took none of the rolls and hot milk I found available—but did drink the Bib orange juice I had happily carted along with me from America. As I tucked him into the lumpy hotel crib and removed the enormous eiderdown, I thought, "One good day in bed and he'll probably be all right to go on." Betty and the girls and Fran went off the next morning to do a bit of sightseeing and to meet Pastor Guiton for tea. Franky was asleep when they left and I left the curtains pulled to darken the room until late afternoon when he awakened. I pulled back the heavy drapes to let a streak of sunshine make a path across the floor and turned to look at my view of Paris for this trip—a few restaurants across the street and a street full of people waiting for trams or to cross to the other side. Turning back again, my heart sank—a sick feeling swept over me—"Oh no, Lord—is it that? Could it be that? If it is that, please, Lord, give us the grace we need—" for in the streak of sunshine Franky was stumbling; his legs seemed to be crippled and for two or three steps they stuck strangely out from his hips until—crash—he went down in a heap! "I can't walk, Mommy, I *can't* walk!" he wailed with a question is his voice. I gathered him up in my arms and tried to be gay for his sake—"Let's string some beads, Franky—" and we began some quiet games on the big bed. I couldn't leave him to go anywhere—not even out of the room—and I couldn't take him anywhere—a little hotel room down near the Paris station—nearly four-thirty in the afternoon—reservations to leave at 7:30 the next morning by train—"Give us the needed wisdom, Lord; show us what to do."

When Fran and the girls burst in, I had to let him see what happened when Franky tried to walk. This time it was worse. Doctors and theories differ so from country to country, and it is so hard to know how to go about finding someone you would have confidence in, and so much easier *not* to get into the hands of wrong persons than to get away from them once you have put yourselves into their hands. This is one of the prices a missionary pays for being away from his home country and his trusted circle of medical help, no matter what country the missionary is in. "Let's try calling Doctor Otten in Switzerland and getting his advice." Several hours went by—no success—no one answered. We called the airport. "If they have places on a morning plane, you, Franky, and Debby will go by plane tomorrow. That will give you only one hour and ten minutes instead of the ten-hour train ride," said Fran. There were just the right number of places left, so it seemed of the Lord that we take the 11 A.M. plane. Calling the Maison de la Bible in Paris we found that Helen, the Christian nurse I had had when Franky was born, was visiting there—she would be so glad to come in the morning and help me to get to the airport. And so it was as though the Lord were giving us His dear hand to steady our feet as we passed through deep waters.

Drinking the orange juice and sleeping and waking to talk a blue streak were Franky's occupations that night and the next day as we went by taxi to the airport and then boarded the plane. "I'm 'cared of the noise—" "We're going above the clouds, Franky, just like birds, dear—see that wee little cloud all alone—we're way up above the trees—" And off he went to sleep again while I prayed into his soft hair and encouraged Debby to eat her nice tray lunch. At Geneva the warm sun (first warm day of summer, I was told) took away any chance of chilling, and Franky awakened to talk so brightly that Mr. Berthoud, who met us, felt he couldn't be very ill. We drove through almost-deserted streets, past peaceful, sleepy-looking villages and terraced grape vineyards, along the blue lake sparkling with a dancing brilliance in the sun. "Could anything be wrong?" It seemed like a figment of my imagination. Dr. Otten still did not answer and we went to Aigle before we decided that he must be away. There we called our old friend, Dr. Kousmine, in Lausanne (the one mentioned so frequently in my earlier letters) and she said, "Take your boy to Dr. S. in Aigle; it is not prudent to keep him out of bed. If Dr. S. says this is nothing serious, then go straight to Champéry and put him to bed. This is the clever thing to do." Following this advice put us in Dr. S.'s office, where he made a thorough examination, even tesing knee reflexes and taking a chest X-ray—final conclusion: "Just fatigue and a little grippe." "But, doctor, he cannot walk—look!" "No doubt a case of rickets." !! Where else *could* I go? I had a ride up the mountain if I went *right* way. The others would be halfway up the mountain in the train by now. "All right, Mr. Berthoud, we'll go on to Chalet Bijou."

It was not a very gay homecoming for me. The girls, Betty, and Fran met us as we rounded the bend to the railroad station, as their train had just come in. Nothing could dampen the girls' ardor at that moment. "Oh, doesn't it look good? Doesn't the air smell good? Isn't it *home?*" Franky caught the last word, and as he and I went down the path in the twilight (he in my arms) he began to whimper, "I'm scared of home, I'm scared of that noise, I'm scared of that—" The dark shadows cast by trees and the overhanging cliffs, the clang of the cowbells, and the cold mountain air, the darkness of wooden-walled rooms as we entered the chalet, all must have mingled in his baby mind with his sick feeling and inability to walk, for so often during the past month he has repeated, "I'm scared of home."

The next morning another doctor was recommended—a Monthey surgeon who has made a special study of polio ever since his son died with it years ago. Our call brought him up in a short time and his examination brought the immediate pronouncement—"It is polio—and the result which remains is in the lower back muscles and the left leg." He ordered hot baths and massage, and said he would come again soon—and he told us to watch for a second attack. The next few days found us living among half-unpacked suitcases as I spent all my waking hours caring for Franky, and that included some of the night hours, as he was awakening frequently with what we now know as muscle spasms, though then we did not know the cause of the screaming spells. During those days his baths were his only happy moments— and ignorant of this disease as I was, many were the worries that popped into my head. I was realizing more and more the *need* of learning a more complete trust in the Lord.

Of course, our plan for going together to the conference in Italy, while Betty stayed with the children, was completely finished. Fran wondered whether *he* should go or not, but I insisted that we would be all right. "You just go ahead and keep your promise, as you are needed there." So after working hard to get his part of the unpacking done, and the pasteurizer working again, etc., he left early Monday morning. It was Wednesday night that I discovered that Franky had a fever and seemed worse again. The agony of deciding to call the doctor might be hard for you to understand; again I was so unsure of what he might do. He came as fast as his car could drive up the mountain, and after a quick examination said, "It is a second attack—already the right leg is beginning to be affected. Quickly bundle him up and bring some things in a suitcase and come with me." I confess my mouth was dry with fear and my inward calm was gone. We drove down the mountainside with a picturesque moon peeping behind mountain peaks and Franky thought the valley stretched out below was the ocean. "Oh Heavenly Father, keep me calm, let me be a testimony to these people—but oh, please prevent mistakes."

Our footsteps echoed through the halls of the night quiet of the tiny hospital, and a nun all in white with a black cross and beads jangling pulled a lamp nearer to the operating table. "Hold him still," I was told, while an ether mask was clamped down over Franky's screaming and perspiring face—and lifted again moments later to pour on a fresh supply. When I left the room the doctor's daughter told me that after making a spinal puncture to remove fluid for examination, her father would give Franky an injection which is his own invention for preventing paralysis in polio. "Father has been working on this for years—but in this tiny canton he has very few cases. It is a pity; that is, we do not want the illness, but he desires the opportunity to prove his invention. Your boy will be the sixth one to receive it, except for the monkeys Father has experimented upon." This did *not* have a calming effect on me!! And you may be sure I prayed through the long night as I watched over Franky and rinsed his mouth when he awakened spluttering and objecting to the nasty taste.

I was allowed to do all the nursing as Franky was terrified at the nurses, all nuns in full habit. They did not insist upon doing anything, for which I was thankful. Another one of those injections to be given worried me for hours and I struggled for calm as I prayed and read the Bible through the night. The Lord gave me this: "The King's heart is in the hand of the Lord, as the rivers of water: he turneth it whithersoever he will."* I was suddenly struck with my own lack of faith, my worry. "Oh, Father in Heaven, I do believe that Thou hast complete power. Thou canst turn kings according to Thy will, and surely thou canst also cause this doctor to change his mind about another injection if it is not necessary this morning." In just a few minutes the doctor came in and standing at the foot of Franky's bed, he turned to the nun, "I've changed my mind; we won't give that injection after all." I praised the Lord that my peace had come ten minutes *before* when He had given me a new measure of trust.

Meantime, at home, Betty was holding the fort and being a real spiritual help and comfort to the girls. Priscilla called Italy so that her Dad would know of the second attack—and after thinking and praying about it, Fran felt he should come home, since at that time the outcome was so uncertain and the train trip was about 17 hours. It was a hard moment for him to face: *why* would the Lord take him away in the middle of the series of messages which seemed to be being used as a blessing; and, of course, the long train trip—from 2 A.M. until he arrived at the hospital at about 7:30 P.M.—was a time of real testing and heart searching before the Lord as he wrestled with the possibilities that lay ahead. But he, too, experienced a peace *before* he arrived to find that Franky was full of chatter, and seemingly even better than when he left. Later a letter came from the one having charge of the conference in Italy saying that the time of prayer and testimony they had after Fran's leaving was tremendously blessed, and showed in a marked way that the Holy Spirit had really used those first messages. Several of the men expressed a desire to have the series completed at a later date and the various mission stations in Italy invited us to come at any time. Thus we now see that instead of lessening the blessing, the Lord *used*

*Proverbs 21:1

Fran's having to leave to emphasize in a very special way the messages that had been given. How wonderful is our Lord!

The week at the hospital was not an easy one, but it did give me time during Franky's naps to have longer times of Bible reading and prayer than is possible with the household responsibilities—and I find that when our hearts have been touched with real aching and sorrow, we are hungrier and thirstier for spiritual food than ever before. The Lord's comfort is sweet—but how could we experience it without experiencing the deep *need* for comfort?

The day came when Franky, who hadn't been able to sit up, could stand alone, and the doctor thought he should come home. That second homecoming was happier than the first one and how much we appreciated being all together again. The Lord had been giving me strength to be able to go through sleepless nights and strain in the hospital on top of an already fatigued condition and He continues to supply the needed strength. But I do know I am not going ahead efficiently at present and it seems my work is moving *very* slowly. However, the Lord sent Betty to make these first weeks not impossible. She took over the two baths a day, the massage, and some "outings" for Franky to release me for small spurts of unpacking, cooking, typing, etc. Isn't it wonderful to have a heavenly Father who can see ahead and make all things fit together for our good and His glory? Franky has improved steadily, so that now he can walk—though with a limp and with one leg definitely thinner than the other. What a thrill it was to see him take his first steps alone!

Priscilla began her Children for Christ class as soon as possible—having it every Thursday afternoon. Children from Pension Joli Nid came, as well as some of the village children. One week there were 15 lustily singing and learning Bible verses. Mr. Exhenry's middle boy and girl are coming regularly, though his eldest girl is away at school, and Madame Avanthey immediately sent the only two boys she has at her pension during this in-between season. There were two little Egyptian girls, 12 and 10, who were at the Joli Nid until the middle of October and who came each week. After the first couple of weeks they began coming in between to hear a bit more and we invited them to play with Susan and Debby and then to stay for tea while Priscilla would talk further with them. One afternoon at tea Priscilla brought them to a place of understanding through the Door of Salvation—"All the doors lead to black," Rarvya remarked as several of the false doors were shown. "Oh yes," Chahiror explained quickly, "you'll see—they'll all lead to darkness, I think, until she comes to the last one, and I think that one will say, 'Accept Jesus as your Savior,' and *that* will be the *right* one." "Oh, I do want to accept Jesus and I want to begin studying the whole Bible right now," said Chahiror eagerly later. "Can I have a whole Bible to take with me today?" Betty offered to give her French Bible to the child and so now Betty's French Bible has gone off to Egypt to be studied in earnest by these two dear children. Black, black hair and distinctive Egyptian faces—these two girls could have stepped down from an Egyptian frieze. Two days later, when they came for tea again, their dark eyes were full of sparkle. "I've read 27 chapters of Matthew already," Rarvya said. "And *I* want to have you help me with the first Bible studies today," Chahiror broke in. They have Fran's Bible studies in French to take with them and we do believe they will earnestly go on unless someone puts a hindrance in their way. They came of their own accord to church that Sunday morning and Priscilla whispered a translation of the English sermon, translated it into French sentence by sentence. They expect to come back here all next summer and the next—if things go according to plan. Their father is an automobile dealer in Cairo and they spend each summer season in Switzerland. Won't you pray for them that the Holy Spirit will care for them and open their eyes of understanding day by day? . . .

Fran began a Bible class for Wednesday nights, in spite of the fact that the village is empty of visitors at present. Mr. Exhenry came regularly and then Madame Avanthey started coming. The wife of a very intelligent ski teacher and guide, she has had much interest ever since Stevie was saved while he was staying at her pension. . . .

Those of you who know this village from past letters are waiting to hear how Madame Marclay is. What a welcome she gave us! "Oh, Madame Schaeffer, I counted all the days—now you are here—I look down the mountain at the village below and think—*quelle chance!!*—Madame Schaeffer is back there—so I have a friend. No, I cannot come to a Bible class with the others—you and I study together, hah? We can do that— you can be my teacher *privé*—hah? My husband, he doesn't want to change, but I want to learn from you." Her French is spoken with a thick German accent letting all know that she comes originally from German Switzerland. This village "couturiere" makes dresses well, but has never felt at home in a place which rarely accepts outsiders in spite of their being married to villagers. She is now working in between her other sewing on making drapes to brighten our rooms as well as to keep the warmth in during icy winter evenings. Speaking of warmth—we have been given a special gift of coal to burn in the furnace, which has stood unused in past years. We always stuck to wood fires in the three stoves because coal was too expensive. Now we really have some warmth to keep in! It is marvelous to feel the always damp and icy upstairs rooms turn into places where you can actually stay and do something. Before, we made one wild leap into bed with a hot-water bottle, shivered into clothing in the morning, and stayed away from upstairs. How we praise God for this provision just when we have sickness which would be difficult to care for without heat. . . .

Now I must hasten to close before the paper comes to an end! A couple of ties with the past for you to pray about: Betty went for a few days to visit dear old Baroness von Dumreicher—the very one who was saved in Chalet Bijou years ago and urged Betty and Gea to visit us in the first place. Madame von Dumreicher is now back in Germany and living a lonely life in a Deaconess home in Düsseldorf. . . .

We need prayer for the Lord's guidance in planning our time to make it count where He would have it count; and for His guidance in our care of Franky in his need for another doctor's examination and opinion to make sure we are doing all that should be done. Susan has been having rheumatism, which Doctor Otten says is a type of rheumatic fever. The opinion of another doctor friend confirms his opinion that she should stay in bed for some weeks. . . .

Our joy in Him must come in an increased faith day by day—and faith is not *sight*. Did you ever think of that for some length of time? If we could *see* all the answers to our problems and know just how the Lord were going to work it all out, we would be deprived of our privilege of simply trusting Him, and in *faith* walking day by day. It is in the moment *before* the Lord turns for us a fresh page that we can show Him our love by faith *without sight*—oh that we might be found with love, belief, and joy at *that* time.

Love,

EDITH

December 17, 1954   Champéry, Switzerland

Dear Family:

. . . Betty left November 2nd and we trudged back from the little station where the train had tooted its farewell blast and disappeared around the curve to jog its way down the cogs to the Rhône valley below. Franky never has stopped asking, "Where *is* Betty?" as though we were hiding her—and he wasn't the only one who needed to make adjustments. . . . Priscilla had a couple of free weeks before beginning her course of study so she pitched in and helped by taking Franky each morning to see the flock of sheep and lambs that live under the hill below us, and Franky came home for lunch all full of wonder of the "baaaaing" of the dear little lambs—having exercised his own little lame leg by climbing the rocky paths. She also spent time reading to Susan and giving her some nursing care—like a daily back rub to break the monotony of staying quiet in bed. And she took our letters to the post office and did the daily shopping. So it was still possible to go on with a certain amount of office work, on my part.

One evening right after Betty's departure, Mr. Exhenry came to take a new stand as he desired to be baptized and take communion with us, and so in spite of handicaps we had a sweet private service in the living room where he had been born again, taking Christ as his Savior two years ago. The *handicaps* were to care for Franky and Susan so that the rest of us could be together. As we gathered in the quiet solemnity of that service, no one would know that Franky was in his hot bath, soaking in the hot water as usual, with Susan fixed up in a big lounge chair stuck in the bathroom by the tub to watch him! Nor would they realize that when Priscilla slipped out after playing a hymn, she quickly dressed Franky and popped him along with picture books into Susan's bed so that we could go on to the communion service without wails and frustrations from above, breaking into our serious moment below. It all worked out beautifully, and we thanked the Lord for helping with the details. I thought of each of you who have been so faithful in prayer for Mr. Exhenry as I watched the earnestness of his expression while he answered so clearly the questions concerning his own faith, making a public profession before us who represented God's people to him as much as though we were a large group. To watch him listening eagerly to the explanation of the communion, then taking of the bread and the cup, not only were eyes misty in emotion, but how misty were those things that so often seem important in this world! It is in a moment like that that eternal values take their proper place in our thoughts and feelings. After we shook hands and he thanked us huskily, Fran went up to take communion to Susan and I to tuck Franky in bed and pat him off to sleep—and Mr. Exhenry talked for awhile to Priscilla until we came down again. He told her that he had thought life wasn't much worth living before. He just couldn't see any reason for it all and nothing had much appeal to him—nothing satisfied his longings or gave him true happiness. "Now," he said, "everything is changed for me; now I have a purpose and for the first time in my life I am happy. . . .

A few days ago Mr. Wutrich, one of the three men who had just been with us, came back up to bring some Children for Christ work, and to do us a big favor by taking Susan down to Montreux for an electrocardiogram and blood test. He has a tiny French car, so her lying down on the back seat was a sitting-up position which left very little room for Debby, who went along for company as Fran and Mr. Wutrich would be talking in the front seat. The results at that time were good, although we are told another test must be taken after the proper lapse of time. Penicillin and rest seem to be helping Susan tremendously, though I know very little about rheumatic fever so have no knowledge as to what good signs might be. Certainly Susan thinks she should be just about ready to get up and have everyone else go to bed! She is doing the Calvert Course 8th grade and finding it a lot of fun—but the problem of who is going to mark her mounting pile of daily papers presents itself! We now have a polio therapy class in the bathroom, college going on in Pris's room, and 8th grade in Susan's bed—only Debby has an outside life at this moment, bringing us daily tales of the goings-on in Home Eden and her French 5th-grade work.

At that same time Fran and I had been talking and praying about the possibility of taking a short trip for the work. Several requests had come for speaking to young people, and openings for Children for Christ and an invitation to Fran to speak on the deeper spiritual life in another country, and we felt it would be a good time also to see some of the young people who had been saved in Champéry before—and might like to come back for deeper study. We roughly planned a trip—and asked the Lord to show us His will in it. The only problem seemed to be the one of the proper person to stay with the children, and Mr. Wutrich gave us a solution for that when he told us that Helen, that same Christian nurse who was here when Franky was born, and who helped me to get to the airport with Franky the day he was so ill, would be free for a few weeks at this time. She has become engaged to be married since she was last here in Champéry with us, and her fiancé, also a graduate of the Geneva Bible School and a member of Action Biblique, feels led to go to establish a testimony on the Island of Corsica. . . .

Helen agreed to come for a few weeks, until another "job" should open up for her. She feels the need of earning money to save up for their needs in getting started, so has applied for a couple of jobs. With her coming as an apparent solution to our "main" problem, we waited day by day for our trip plans to become complete. There was one little flaw— our *permis de séjour* had not yet come! But surely, I thought, that will be here in time, because didn't the Lord arrange Helen's coming so that we could go? How foolish we are to be so dogmatic about the pieces of this jigsaw puzzle of life, when we only *think* we know where a piece fits in!

We had heard that there was a little delay in the granting of our permit. The village *gendarme* (policeman) assured us however that the permit would be here in plenty of time to get our passports back for our projected trip. But days went by, and no permit arrived. Then one morning we had a visit from Mr. Marclay. He went into the living room, closing the hall door to the dining room and the door between the living room and the dining room, and began to whisper: Mr. ———, one of the leaders of the village, has put something against you on the papers sent to Sion. He doesn't know anyone knows this but I found out from my friend O., who is just an office boy but who is allowed to see certain papers that cross his boss's desk. I'm going to take a trip to Sion myself to see someone there about it and tell them good things about you." You can't imagine what an amazing providence of God this represents, for this Mr. Marclay himself is a leader politically in the village, and a strong Roman Catholic, but his wife dearly loves us, dear Madame Marclay. You see this Mr. ____, quite obviously expected to fix it so that our permit would be refused, we would have no reason given, and *no one* would *know* that he had done anything against us! But the Lord had his "butler in the prison"*—the young office boy was in a place, and had an interest in us, that made him usable to upset this well-laid plan! Without

*See Genesis 40 and 41.

our doing a thing, except to pray, the Lord had started an opposition rolling! Mr. Marclay made his trip down to Sion to "speak" in our behalf. But his word was *not* enough to completely stop that which was started by the "religious" complaint, for it had been said that we were a religious influence in the village! Our papers were sent back up here, and a whole sheaf of material was attached to them before they traveled back to the Sion office.

Days went past and during them we had some qualms. "What if we are put out? We lose all the work, time, money we have put into this house. Where would we find another place to live, and what about the contacts we have established! We are just too tired to face another big move and a starting all over again." But these worrisome, nagging thoughts were sin, for they were a denial of the power and wisdom of our Heavenly Father who makes *no* mistakes, and again we had lesons to learn *before* things would change outwardly!

You see the Lord had shut us *away* from a trip for the work—but He also had shut us up *to* Himself with a problem which drove us more to our knees and to His word. As time went on we found we were entering the most blessed and happy period we've ever had yet. It gave Fran time to take the series of messages he gave in America and develop them further, first for his own life and thinking, and then in a form which you will be reading along with my letters in the next few months. We have had an inward peace concerning the uncertainty of whether we are to remain here, to locate in another village out of this canton, or to work out some other arrangement where we would be residents elsewhere and return here as visitors (three months at a time allowed to any visitors). All this is only possible in Him, for in ourselves we have no such source of calmness with such an ax of uncertainty hanging over our heads. In ourselves we would be planning and fretting and figuring out all the possibilities, but the Holy Spirit is able to live through us in a way quite contrary to our natural selves.

The next word we had came from Sion—a summons for Fran to appear at one of the offices there. Priscilla went along to be sure everything was understood by both sides as far as the French was concerned—and Mr. Marclay accompanied them down on the little train, hoping to be a help. However, he had to stay outside the office when the moment came, and Fran and Priscilla were ushered in alone to the dark little crucifix-dominated office. An obviously prepared list of questions was asked, taking two hours for questions and answers! The church services, the Bible classes, the children's classes in French, the purpose of our trips in other countries, whether we ever did any speaking on politics, whether we were acceptable to other Protestants or whether we were a strange sect, all sorts of matters were gone into, as well as the obvious complaints of the school director and the nuns at the school. As far as Fran could tell, this official changed his tone toward the end of the conversation and indicated that he would do what he could to see that our papers received a good recommendation—however, he was handing the problem on to higher authorities in Bern. . . .

The only further news we have on the permit is that the opposition against us has been fanned to this large proportion by the whole family connection of Mr. Exhenry. He shook his curly head and looked like a troubled boy as he said, "This is terrible, your trouble coming because of me." But a smile of bright understanding came as Fran assured him we didn't mind suffering persecution because of his salvation—*that*, after all, is an eternal value, and can't be put on a balance with the troubles of this life. . . .

On Thanksgiving Day (we ourselves had a chicken dinner and a little Thanksgiving service the day before), Fran and Priscilla met Mr. Exhenry at the station and rode together down the mountains as the sun played its daily drama of changing the view moment by moment as it slid from one position to another behind the peaks. Their destination was Lausanne, where they were met by Professor Czerny and his wife. After a lunch together the five went to Madame Turrian's pension, and gathered together in the very "salon" where we spent our *first* evening in Switzerland learning the rules of the boarding house—mealtimes, how many baths a month we could have, etc.! Little Miss Massey, who with her canary used to eat breakfast with us that first year, and dear Madame Turrian herself, were appropriate ones to meet together with those who were saved in Chalet Bijou, and to pray together with them as they asked the Lord to show them His will in the forming of a wee International Church. Mr. Exhenry and Professor Czerny were most solemn as they were elected to the office of elder, and one tiny incident will give you a glimpse of the spirit in which all matters were decided. As Professor Czerny stood to make a motion, he bowed his head and first made it to the Lord, in a very natural way literally showing he truly considered the Lord to be the Head. How we pray that the Lord may always keep these men so close to him that they may go on, deeper and deeper spiritually—never losing the sweet naturalness with which they accept the Word and the leadership of their Lord and Master. . . .

We had the Christmas party for Priscilla's class this week, giving the New Testaments earned by faithful attendance and Scripture memorization to the ones who had kept on, and having the special Christmas story, followed by a big "gouter" or "four o'clock" or afternoon tea! Almost all of the village children had been forbidden to come, by parents scared once more by the nuns and priest—but there are four boys and a girl who have continued. Two of the boys are from Madame Av.'s pension and live in Geneva, one boy is the son of a Protestant hotelkeeper, and another is the son of the lady who has "Le Joli Nid," another children's pension, the one who is in that Apostolic Church which is sweeping through Switzerland, having begun as a sect in Germany. Debby and Franky swell the ranks, and no one could look forward to the class each week more than Franky! "Class is coming—going to sing hallelu—going to be a good boy." The Christmas party was interrupted for him though when the "rubbing lady" came, as he calls her. We have been having a woman who does massage professionally, having studied in a Swedish method school in Geneva, and who does quite a number of polio cases in hospitals. She comes three times a week and Franky hails her with, "Oh here's the rubbing lady"—as he trots off to the bathroom where he knows the "rubbing table" is! We are praying that she may not only be a help to his walking, but that we may be used to help her to come to the place where she can walk in newness of life. . . .

I'll bring this to a close as the village hotels and pensions are getting their halls scrubbed, their beds made up, their kitchens in order, their larders stocked, and decorations made—while weather reports are anxiously scanned with an eye to hopeful signs for more snow and better skiing conditions. It is the approaching "season" whose success depends on cold and snow, and is the only time some of these people have an opportunity to make money. For us it means the time will soon be here when visitors will be coming to services, to Chalet Bijou for tea, and when later schools will arrive for the rest of the winter full of students who need to know about what life can mean with Jesus Christ as their Savior. Pray with us for prepared hearts—our own and those of the unsaved who may come. Pray too that if it is the Lord's will, we may see some young people come to stay here for Bible Study daily.

May the Lord give you a happy season during the time when the name of Jesus is on the lips of so many of the people around you—happy because He is guiding your life and using you to show the difference between having Jesus on your lips and *in* your heart!

Love,

EDITH

1955

March 7–9, 1955   Champéry, Switzerland

Dear Family:

Probably this will be the last letter you will get with this heading—for Chalet Bijou where so many young and older people have heard of the love of the Lord Jesus Christ, Chalet Bijou surrounded by peaceful fields and chalet-studded slopes and enclosed by a circle of mountain peaks—is soon to be, "For rent"!!! . . .

The holidays, though busy, stand out in our memories as a period of "normal" time contrasted to all that has happened since. The denim curtains and bedspreads were finished by Madame Marclay and the bedrooms had a "furnished" and home-like air for the various guests. The kitchen not only looked cheerful in its new yellow glow, but the installations of the stove and so forth were completed so that cooking for special teas and company meals was speeded up. The children had their built-in desks, made by the local carpenter Mr. P. (out of the packing-box wood), for Christmas gifts ahead of time so that they were enjoying their studying more—Franky was walking a bit better and had learned to really ride the tricycle, and Susan was excited about coming downstairs for the entire day the 25th. We breathed deeply and felt the moment had come to get into a real routine for the winter's work.

The first guest to arrive was a young American lawyer who is studying for a year in Germany, whose family have been friends of ours for years. It was like having some of the family come "home for Christmas." He helped with decorating the little chapel for the special services, and with delivering some food and flowers to people in need of someone to express a little love. He helped the children to trim the huge tree Vic's husband had dragged down for us from the forest above—the top cut out of a big tree he had felled for wood—and joined in the general hilarity of the family day which followed the candlelight service of Christmas Eve. Franky was full of appreciation for each package he opened

Our last family picture in Chalet Bijou.

and for each item of food and decoration—and he even thanked the Lord for each of the people sitting there! His aspirations of what he is going to be when he grows up are guaranteed to cheer up anyone listening—"When I grow up I'm going to be a doctor and fix peoples with a saw and a hammer and screwdriver—oh no, I'm going to be a dog and bark—oh no, I'm going to be a man and say, 'Go home dog'—I'm going to be a cow—no, I'm going to be a man and hit the cow and wind it up to make milk come out." With Franky to make everything amusing, warmth and food which the Lord has given us—with loving remembrances of friends, and anticipation of interested visitors coming for teas during the week—with conversation about the things of the Lord, and fellowship in prayer and Bible reading—it was a day to be remembered as one of the relaxed and beautiful moments of life. . . .

L'Abri is what we feel the Lord would have us add to the work He had given us here in Switzerland. L'Abri means "shelter" in French, and our thought is to have a spiritual shelter for any who have spiritual need. There are a number of people who have been saved in Chalet Bijou who want to come *back* again for short or longer periods of Bible Study in a most informal way. We want them to feel free to come and in addition to these we want to open the doors for unsaved friends, for others who are Christians but who long for more reality and a deeper spiritual life, and for Christian workers who desire to dig deep into a spiritual study and have time for discussion and meditation. All this we feel can be wonderfully combined with skiing or walking in the mountains, as the beauty of the Alps is a perfect background for a time of forgetting and leaving behind the "world" and concentrating on the things of the Lord. We have no plans for something "big"—but we are praying that one by one people may be led to us whom the Holy Spirit will help *here*. If there are many at one time, we can easily have them stay in a pension and be with us for Bible Study periods, etc. Edward W.'s being here, our having family prayers twice a day and much discussion in the evenings was a sort of beginning of our idea, L'Abri— and when Caroline H. came from England on New Year's Eve to stay two weeks, she came expressly because we had told her of L'Abri. . . .

Early the next morning we awakened to the sounds of muffled talking coming from outside, excited voices from Priscilla's room, the steady roar of the torrent coming down the streambed, and rain on the roof. What could be going on? I slipped out of bed and into Priscilla's room to find her and Susan both peering intently out of the window— "Look, Mummy, the torrent is *full* because of all the rain and melting snow—and a lot of logs backed up against our bridge and the whole thing overflowed. Look out here—it looks like a lake—they've been here ever so long digging ditches to carry the water away from the house, and taking the bridge apart and fishing logs and stones out of the stream. Why doesn't Daddy go out and work too?" Well, Daddy didn't know this was going on as nothing had awakened us on that side of the house, but soon he had stuck on some old clothes and was out in the pouring rain with a shovel and rake. Susan looked like Eliza crossing the ice as she picked her way through the water with a tray full of cups of hot coffee from time to time through the morning, serving Rachel, Herman, and Robert as well as her daddy and a man from across the fields as they worked to direct the water back into the regular streambed. Fran came in at noon to change his drenched clothing, eat a hot dinner, and then to start off again. "They need help up in the village as several of the other torrents are in danger of jumping their beds, and new torrents are coming down where none have been before. I'm going to help."

Bridges were all down and only one plank laid across each place where something was needed. Fran found clusters of men at each place where a torrent crossed the street—all with shovels keeping the stones and mud cleared away so that the water would keep on going down. He helped first in one place and then another, having opportunity to get to know some of the men better by working side by side with them. At suppertime he came home again to change clothing and eat. Then he went back again for a night shift! That night avalanches began to make their way down the mountainside with frightening rushes. We could hear the roar at our house. As mud, stones, and branches swept everything along with them, suddenly the stability of man-made houses, the permanent appearance of an old village seemed as nothing more than a child's building of blocks. Sudden destruction seemed so possible with a shifting earth and we realized in a very real way that only our all-powerful God can be depended upon to take care of "all" our needs—for surely man's wealth, brains, and physical strength are as nothing in the face of the so-called "forces of nature."

Fran had gone to visit Madame Fleischmann at 2 A.M. to assure her that she could come to us if she felt afraid to stay there. Her wee chalet consists of two rooms—one upstairs and one down—and two torrents were rushing past it too near for comfort. No one was going to bed in the village that night—so a visit at two was not out of order! This new day was Friday, and the rain had been coming without a stop since Monday. In the afternoon Fran and I walked up to the village to see how things were coming. Two chalets had been hit and the foundations were sticking out beyond the houses. One barn had collapsed entirely just after the sheep and horses were removed. The street was full of mud and stones— six feet deep in some places. All the stores had a pitifully small protection of sandbags and planks across the windows and a small bulldozer was at work removing the deep mud from in front of Mr. Exhenry's store. We went up as far as the Marclays' house to see whether they were all right—crossing two torrents that had never been there before—and inspecting the avalanche that had just missed our church. As we arrived back home we saw Madame Fleischmann ahead of us, a village man helping her carry her belongings. She had a small suitcase full of important papers and valuables, a larger one with clothes, a bundle with her feather bed, and a bag full of food so that she could continue her special diet. She had been ordered to evacuate and was so thankful to have a safe place to come to. "No avalanche could ever reach here; there is so much field between you and the mountains." Supper over, Fran went back up to the village to continue shoveling, Madame Fleischmann was installed in the guest room to sleep, relaxing in the quiet safety of this chalet so far removed from the center of danger. Helen (who was back with us for a couple of weeks) and Priscilla, attracted by their curiosity to see what was going on up in the village, decided to take flashlights and cross the fields to see. Since our bridge was down they could not cross here. Enormous searchlights had been brought by the soldiers the state had sent to help out, so the whole mountainside was lit up in an attempt to see any beginning of an avalanche so that people might flee in time. Men were stationed at various places along the mountain to watch the torrents from above. They would signal with flashlights and it was hard not to stay by a window to watch the drama. We were doing just this, Susan, Debby, and I, when we saw the bobbing flashlights announcing Helen and Priscilla's return.

Suddenly, as they were nearing the house, a great shout went up from the darkness of the fields and road above: *"Attention! Attention! C'est ici! C'est ici!"* The girls stopped dead in their tracks, turning to see what it might be, and then they broke into a wild run for the house, screaming, "C'est ici! It's coming here, it's coming here!" Electric lights had been strung from our house to the torrent to facilitate work in case it flooded again, and in this light I could see an oozing, writhing mass of mud slithering toward us—as wide as the field, and in the middle of the mud there seemed to be a host of little streams. By the time I got downstairs and outside, Robert had arrived looking like a wild man. Fear seemed to have frozen his tongue and he just sort of grunted when I spoke to him. The only thing I could think of doing was to drag planks from the former bridge and try to protect the house's foundation with them—we had no sandbags. "Where do sandbags come from, anyway?" I wondered, thinking of all the newspaper reports of floods, but never remembering having read where they *got* those helpful sandbags! Priscilla was tugging away at planks too and we tried to make a barricade which would help turn the mass of mud in another direction. However, many of our boards just went floating merrily away! Rachel and Herman appeared on the scene with shovels and planks. Fran appeared too, seeming to drop from the skies, but later we found he had crossed the torrent in spite of protests from the men, endangering himself, because this was a real avalanche and enormous stones were coming down at a great rate right where he had crossed over. Helen was telephoning for more help and at the same time she called Ecole Biblique in Geneva to ask for special prayer.

Susan and Debby had been told to take some of the things from the first-floor store room (files, etc.) upstairs—out of danger of becoming wet—and I came in to find Susan dashing up with my best tea set—removing it from a top shelf to "save" it!!!! Many weird things were being dragged off upstairs by this army of two! Now the boards had given out, so someone went up to the attic and began passing our packing-case wood down, and poor Madame Fleischmann was up once more acting as a middle man to get that wood downstairs. What a night it was! Barricades were made and no water came in the house, though muddy boots brought enough of the mud in to cover the floors. We discovered later that the avalanche had started to come in the torrent bed, then it had all jumped the torrent way up above, spreading out over the fields and coming toward our house. However, a few hundred feet above us, the central force of the water and enormous stones crossed the torrent to the other side, and came straight down the path—the other side of our bridge. The field over there is full of enormous stones now, and the water cut a deep gully where our path formerly was—but our chalet was spared because of this. The Lord is good to us. We had deep mud and smaller stones all around us, but nothing big enough to break foundations.

The days that followed were one jumble of muddy floors, soaked clothing, meals served in between coffee being handed out to the outdoor workers, dark settling down too soon every day to make a nightmare out of the always-present dangers. Searchlights scanning the mountainside all night, men flashing lights (which Susan was constantly interpreting as a signal that a new avalanche was coming!) as they patrolled the heights above, the noise of the roaring torrents, the never-ending rain and winds, the need of keeping our torrent clear of stones and branches which might stop it up and cause another flood, and the straining of one's ears constantly for the village church bell (which was to announce further disaster) made it impossible to get any consecutive sleep. We kept dressed because it was "prudent" to do so in case of sudden evacuation. Fran and Priscilla spent one entire day cleaning the torrent, and making a new barricade, and Fran took his shift up on the village street too. The danger lasted over a week, and during that time an English family was at Hotel Swiss, and we had a dreadful time trying to have some time with them! It was a man and his wife and two children, and his mother, who had stopped for a skiing vacation on their way back to India, where he is managing an Indian branch of the J. P. Coates cotton thread company.

After the avalanches we began having the Jua girls come one evening a week for the usual Bible Study and tea combination. Ecole Monivert arrived too, and with them Professor and Madame Czerny (saved during our last year here); and an English professor with an Irish wife, both of whom have an interest. Deep snows followed the days of muck and rain, and the scene changed again inside as it seemed we were always getting *ready* for some to come, or *talking* to them. We had the girls one night a week, Professor Czerny came several times a week for a concentrated Bible Study with Fran, while his wife (who is "lighter" in her interest) would talk with me; the local Bible class continued to come Wednesday nights, and the Marclays' son came to take a walk and talk with Fran some afternoons, and Madame Marclay came from time to time and started the study of Romans, always asking, "Can we have that reading and some prayer, and can it be the same place we left off?" When the Monivert boys came we had two from South Africa, one of them a German Jew whose family had gone to South Africa during Hitler's regime. Our only concern was to work out a good schedule which would give us time to keep up on office work, write some of the lessons and articles which are on our hearts, talk to the ones the Lord was sending us, and keep enough open time each day for prayer and private devotions, without which our own spiritual health would suffer. Our greatest problems were the need for additional help, and for guidance as to how to use time.

Then February 14th arrived! We had a call from the village *gendarme* asking that Fran go to get some papers which had something to do with our permit. When Priscilla and Fran arrived at the *gendarme*'s he simply handed them two papers—an orange one and a white one. Such a shock they had when they began to read the typewritten entries! The white one said that the Schaeffers (and each one in the family was named) were to leave Champéry before the 31st of March, because of an ulterior motive! The orange one came from the federal officers in Bern and said that our eviction from Champéry was extended to all the territory of

Switzerland. We were to be out of Switzerland before the 31st of March and were not to come back (except for passing through) for two years; reason given—"ulterior motive"!

That was eleven o'clock in the morning. By noon we knew the "ulterior motive" was based on the fact that we were said to have "a religious influence in the community." We also began immediately to contact those who could give advice as to what to do, for an appeal had to be made within ten days to the Canton, and within thirty days to the country in order to have a reconsideration of the case—and the papers were dated in such a fashion that nine days had already passed! Our Christian friend Mr. Andre in Lausanne said he must have the papers immediately in order to have a proper appeal typed right away, so we dispatched Susan with a briefcase to the first train. She was to be met in Lausanne by the company's chauffeur, taken to the office to deliver the papers, and then to Andres' home to rest for the night so that the trip would not be too much for her. A call to the American Consulate advised us to come in person to Geneva to talk this over, and the writing of letters took up the rest of the afternoon. The Marclays came down to weep before the afternoon was over. Their reaction of complete shock and, "this can't happen to you—it isn't religious liberty and we are supposed to have liberty," is the reaction of *many* of the villagers. We didn't spend much time on supper that night, and I put together a chocolate cake mix and had it baking while I put Franky to bed. The Monivert boys were coming, along with the English professor, so I had to hurry to get refreshments ready. The seven-minute frosting turned out perfectly so that a thin, dry crust formed while the tea was brewing, and when I pushed the tea wagon into the living room, you'd never have known that the icing had only been put on minutes before! It was one of those thrilling evenings when we felt the Holy Spirit working and the interest was keen. Mr. Exhenry arrived at ten to talk over the "edict" that had just arrived, so he was with us for the closing prayer. After the boys left we had a precious time with Mr. Exhenry. He felt sick at heart about what had happened, but his fondest hope was that we could live somewhere close to here. "They talk about getting a lawyer in Sion and trying to fight the thing here in Valais," he said, "but they don't realize the power of the church—what has happened is that the Bishop has said you must go, and even a liberty-loving lawyer will fold up if enough pressure is brought to bear on him." We prayed together and he prayed not only for us, but for the help of the Holy Spirit in talking to all who would be coming to him with questions. "Now is the time I must try to go deeper with some of the men,"he said. There was no note of fear, nor of retreat! Though he well knew that all this had come about largely because of his clear stand

Fran and I left on the early train for Lausanne the next morning, leaving Priscilla in charge at home. Our first stop was to sign the appeals at Mr. Andre's office. He expressed shocked concern for us, and shame for his country that such a thing had happened. "*Voila*, this is the Roman

Catholic Church." We had lunch with the Andres and Madame Andre kept insisting that this *couldn't* be done; Switzerland just couldn't put people out for religious reasons. In Geneva an hour later we were met by Godfrey Wutrich of Action Biblique, who was anxious to be helpful and took us over to the American Consulate in his car. He, too, was shaking his head in shocked surprise—with that unbelieving air most people have when they hear of this edict. Our Consul in Geneva gave us an hour and a half of his time—"I'll give you a letter of introduction to our Consul of the Embassy in Bern, and I urge you to go to Bern to see him immediately." He called someone in an office somewhere else in the building and in a short time we were handed a list of trains to Bern, both for that night and early in the morning. We were going to Ecole Biblique for supper and the night, and so decided on a 6:00 A.M. train. We had a lovely time of fellowship that evening, though everyone was speechless at the news for a time! The faculty prayer meeting was turned over into a time of special prayer for our problem, and what a time of spontaneous, Holy Spirit–led prayer it was—for us, for Mr. Exhenry, and that the whole thing might be a testimony to all who hear about it. Five A.M. came before we could believe it, and we went out into the cold darkness to drive to the station with Mr. Wutrich. Fran led us in prayer as we drove through deserted streets and Mr. Wutrich prayed for a few minutes after we parked in front of the station. . . . It all seemed like a bad dream we were living. "Accused—accused—rejected—rejected" the train wheels seemed to clackety-clack over and over.

After our breakfast Fran and I found a seat and settled down to our individual quiet times. We have been carrying our Bibles along on these trips lately so that each moment on the train can be spent reading and praying. It is so important to stay very close to the Lord so that He can speak to us through His Word each step of the way. My first chapter that morning was Isaiah 30, and oh, how the Lord did use it with me for a spiritual experience! We were still on the train, but as I read on, it seemed as though my spirit was flying! "Oh Lord *Thou* art *able*—the thousands will flee at Thy word, when *thy* time comes—yes Lord thou *hast* heard our cry—" The 21st verse was a promise—yes, He *would* lead, and if *He* is leading, what does it matter if the way is thorny? And although no outward circumstances had changed, I stepped off the train with an inner excitement and expectancy and a "song" in my heart. A snow flurry stung our faces with cold spatters and it took some time to find the right autobus to take us to the Embassy. We were crowded in with a mass of children and skates—pushing and shoving and buzzing like bees in German—all going to a skating rink to spend the special "sport holiday." It was too early for offices to be ready for business, so we walked along, shivering, by the river, near the zoo, waiting for the polite hour to arrive at the Embassy.

We were shown into the office of the younger Consul, who quite evidently is to shield the Consul of Embassy from being bothered with everything, and he listened politely to our story, but assured us that there was little any Americans could do about it. "You see," he said, "Switzerland is one of the few countries which has no treaty agreement to cover this sort of thing with the U.S. and their law is such that they reserve the right to eject anyone they wish to without giving any explanation. The cantons are supreme and each canton may do what it wishes to about keeping or ejecting foreigners. It *is* strange that this has been made to apply to all of Switzerland, but as for the Canton of Valais, nothing could be said about their decision." However, we had a letter of introduction to the Consul of Embassy, and respecting that, he took us upstairs to his office. . . .

The Consul of Embassy rose to greet us, took the letter, and ripping it open began to read. "Oh," turning to Fran, "I see you were born in Philadelphia. So was I." "What part of Philadelphia?" asked Fran. "Germantown," replied the Consul. "So was I," said Fran. "What school did you go to?" "Germantown High School," replied the Consul. "Why, so did I," answered Fran. "What year did you graduate?" "A long time ago now—in fact, it was 1930." Fran's face broke into recognition as he exclaimed, "That was my year!" And the Consul looked again at the name in the letter and said, "Why, *Francis Schaeffer!*" slapping him on the back and pumping his hand heartily. "Roy Melburne—of all things." "Francis was the Secretary of our class—I went to school several years with him—think of it!" said Roy turning to the astonished-looking younger Consul. "Been twenty-five years since we met. Tell me, Fran, what you've been doing all these years—I've been all over the world myself. Just got into Switzerland a few months ago." And so they launched into a conversation about mutual acquaintances, old times, their lives since then—only stopping to exclaim from time to time, "Think of meeting this way—" And Roy said, "In all the countries I've been for my work, I have never met a classmate before." *Is the Lord able?* We must believe that He is, though Satan loves to thrust at us the temptation to depression even when we have such a Father as this to care for each detail of our lives. *He is able* to order lives in such a fashion that He can place the right man in the right place for His children, to do that which is His will to be done.

You can imagine that as he finally said, "Now what is all this thing about?" Roy Melburne opened a sympathetic ear to our case. The telling of the story is a wonderful opportunity to give the gospel, for of course, in telling of our life and work in Europe, and what has happened in Champéry, it is necessary to tell of the salvation of Mr. Exhenry and that entails a telling of how clearly he came to accept Christ as his Savior, and how marvelously he has grown since then in his understanding and courage to take a clear stand. . . . Roy listened with interest and with the feeling, "This is impossible in such a country as Switzerland," such as all who hear it feel. He took us home for lunch ("I must call my wife, excuse me a moment") and after lunch arranged an interview for us with the Ambassador. Madame the Ambassador, Miss Willis, was very gracious as she received us in her lovely office and exclaimed over the coincidence of two old friends meeting at such a time. She, too, heard the story of Mr. Exhenry's salvation and said, "Well surely it couldn't be that you would be ejected for a religious reason—there must be something else. Or it is a mistake." She said she would certainly take an interest in the case.

We praise the Lord that as the dossier in Sion and the dossier in Bern have been thoroughly gone over, they find there is *nothing* against us except that we have had a religious influence in the community, and several cases are stated to prove that. It is clearly persecution for the Gospel's sake, and nothing has been injected to make the issue fuzzy, and for that we are very thankful.

Roy Melburne promised that he would personally go to the high officials at Bern and talk the matter over with them, expressing personal interest in the case. He also said, as the younger consul had said, that from a legal viewpoint, Americans could do nothing for us, although he would use his influence to speak in our behalf. That, along with the Ambassador's interest, was more help than we could have had from the State Department in Washington, and it came within 48 hours from the moment we had the news ourselves! The *Lord* is the influential friend to have!!! His are the most rapid of all systems of communication.

We were able to get back in Lausanne that day in time to see a few folks before offices closed at 6:30. Our friend at the travel agency was absolutely incensed and said he was going to see the Chief of the Bureau of Strangers of the Police Department of the Canton of Vaud that night. The Chief's son works for him so he knows the Chief well. "This is a Roman Catholic move, but they just can't do that to you for all of Switzerland." Next we found that Mr. Andre had already seen this Chief of the Bureau of Strangers for us and had laid the case before him, with the influence of his large business making it more impressive. At a later time we "acidentally" bumped into Mr. Fonjallaz (the director of the school whose girls used to come to us for classes all the time) in the Post Office and as he expressed his shock and disgust at what has happened, he said, "I am going to call my very good friend the Chief of the Bureau of Strangers for the Canton of Vaud"!!! So you see this man heard a lot about us in a short time from people whom he respects—*and he is the man who must sign a paper eventually giving us the right to live in Vaud!*

The advice given us at that stage was that the next thing to do was to find a house in the canton of Vaud—then fill in a paper asking permission of the local Commune in which that house would be located to live there. Then the paper would go to the Chief in Vaud, and after his signature it would be automatically a request when it arrived in Bern for them to change their decision and let us live in another Canton of Switzerland, namely Vaud. Our job then was to find a house, and in this we were on our own as far as our Swiss friends were concerned. They could do nothing more until we had a definite address in Vaud. But we were not on our own either, for the Lord had gone on ahead.

We arrived home late that night and had to leave early the next morning again. Priscilla was beginning to wear down a bit under the strain of having full responsibility for the children and home, but our homecoming with some food from Lausanne shops which would be easy to prepare, and the encouragement of our story gave her fresh courage. The phone had been ringing a lot and she was beginning to get reactions from the village. Of course, the village was buzzing and all sorts of stories were going around. The one which disturbed Priscilla was a false report that we had already been "kicked" out of Lausanne before! Of course, one of the best ways to disprove that would be to go back to the Canton of Vaud to live!

The next morning we started off in a blinding blizzard in our ski clothes to go house-hunting in a country where we had been given notice to leave! It was a strange feeling. The train and autobus took us to the Huemoz, Chesières, Villars, Arveyes, and Gryon section. They are five villages fairly close together in a mountain section of the Canton of Vaud just across the Rhône valley and up on the mountains the other side—just opposite from the mountains upon which Champéry is built. Villars is a large resort where all sorts of the world's celebrities go to ski—and where there are several large hotels, boys' and girls' boarding schools, children's pensions, etc. There are seven ski lifts, skating rink, and all the facilities a Swiss resort offers. Chesières and Arveyes are almost one with Villars—just all running together—and Huemoz and Gryon are villages some distance on either side of the three, but within an hour's walking distance and with good transportation. We arrived first at Villars to make some inquiries, and within a very short half-hour we were talking with a gracious English woman who has owned a hotel there for years, and who was giving a most sympathetic hearing to our story. "Why, if you settle near here, maybe you can help me with a children's class I'd like to start. I went to England to attend the Billy Graham meetings and had quite an experience—I'm being followed up, you know." She invited us to tea to meet some ladies—insisted that we come back to spend the night, and had our suitcases whisked off to a room to await our return! How wonderfully He sends the ravens to provide for our needs!!*

Soon we were wading waist deep in snow to look at houses to rent—only a very few on the list—and we discovered that the rent for the smallest of summer chalets was more than twice as much as we have paid for Chalet Bijou. This we found is a much more expensive place to live. That night we went as far as Gryon, and though it was dark, tried to find a chalet that had been recommended to us. Gryon is a typical village

*See I Kings 17:1-5.

hugging the side of a steep mountain and full of children's pensions. We couldn't find the chalet for which we were searching, and selected a square of light to head for—to knock at someone's door to ask for directions. A few minutes later we were sitting in a warm room with a sensitive-looking artist and his wife—surrounded by oil paintings and soft noises of a children's pension being put to bed for the night! They were a Swiss couple who have run a children's pension for 30 years here, and of course, knew each house in the district. They had only one place to recommend, but we found it was not for rent, and later we found that the house was not too good a buy if it were to be bought. *But* the night's work had given us two new friends who had a real interest in our work, and who would be open to children's classes.

Back at the hotel we found that our "skipped supper" had been provided by the "ravens" once more, for Mrs. Davis had ordered hot soup and cold meat and rolls and tea to be served to us no matter what time we came in! How grateful we are for the Lord's tender care—though as yet we had no light at all as to what we could do about the needed "address." . . .

Our next trip to Villars was to meet Professor Czerny and his wife to help them look into a school there in which they had interest—then we were to stay for the night and house-hunt again. But we had been with the Czernys no more than five minutes when she began to feel ill, and I became convinced that her baby, due in April, was already on its way. A flurry of phone calls, the visit of the Villars doctor, and before I could think about it, I was tucking the borrowed blankets around her in the back of a taxi, and instead of going house-hunting, I was on my way to Lausanne in the capacity of a nurse!! The little hospital welcomed my help, and I stayed by this very nervous mother until her wee son was born—my first experience as a nurse in that capacity. There was only time for a few snatches of sleep during the night, but I was sure that the Lord had sent me to help this dear woman who is so young in the faith, and has had such a difficult life. Poor Professor and Madame Czerny, who have so little home life themselves, and have had such a stormy time as they look back—he on a slave labor camp, she on losing her father to the Hitler regime—were so looking forward to having a child and a normal home. The little one was a bit less than four pounds, and in the morning was taken to a special hospital for premature babies. I went off at ten the next morning praying that that little one might be given good care and live to bring joy to these two.

My sleepless night was not a good preparation for house-hunting, and I found myself feeling like a lost child gazing wistfully at other children safe in their homes. Walking along icy paths, hearing prices that made my head swim, I got to the place where tears were very close, and they spilled over at embarrassing moments. You see, we had received word that very day (I found out when I telephoned home from a booth during the afternoon) that although Bern had extended our time in Switzerland in answer to the appeal, the answer of Valais was, "No extension of time; you must leave Champéry by March 31."

Mr. Gabuz, the real-estate man I met on the Villars street at the end of the afternoon, drove me down to the village of Huemoz to see the house he had in mind. He stopped at a chalet on the main road which carries all who are driving to any one of five villages. It is on the upper side of the road, and looks out across a panorama which can't be equaled, but the view was blotted out by fog that day, and my exuberance was blotted out by fatigue. I looked through the three-story chalet and found it was completely furnished, including blankets. I found with interest that it is exactly one hour and twenty minutes by bus and train to Lausanne from the doorstep, and one hour and twenty minutes by bus and train from Champéry. That seemed amazing, for if we lived there, people could come from either place to see us and the distance would never be prohibitive. I thanked him, and told him I'd bring my husband back to see it the next day, and went wearily to take the bus back to the valley, and then the train back up to Champéry. . . .

But now time was getting short and a call from the lawyer made it imperative to get an address soon. That night I spread it before the Lord. "Oh, Lord, you know the police say we must choose a house and give an address right away now. You know we have not found a house to rent. Please show us Thy will tomorrow; if it is Thy will to keep us here, oh show us *Thy* choice in a house, and send us $1,000 tomorrow if we are to buy one." It was not a usual sort of prayer—I have never asked for what seemed such an impossible sign, and truthfully I was about ready to admit that the door to Switzerland was shut. But I did believe God was able to answer in a way that would be completely clear, and we know He knows when we really want His will. We went off on the 11:00 A.M. train the next day, but before we boarded the train, our mail was handed to us. The first letter was from a pastor in Belgium who assured us of the prayers of his people. The next letter so amazed us that we both were moved to tears very literally, and as we were alone in the *non-fumer* (non-smoking) compartment, it didn't matter. It was from dear friends in Ohio who have followed our work closely, and were blessed in Fran's meetings during the furlough. They wrote that three months ago the Lord unexpectedly put an amount of money into their hands and they had been praying as to how to use it. Finally, after discarding certain investments, they had decided to invest it "where moth and rust do not corrupt." On the day when the letter was written, the Lord, they felt, had led them to send it to the Schaeffers to start a fund to buy a house where young people would come to learn more about the Lord Jesus. Can you guess the amount? Yes, it was the Lord's answer, prepared three months ago—just exactly $1,000!! Can you wonder we wept?

We found the house to be roomy enough for our family needs and for guests. It had been prepared for apartments at one time, so has extra kitchens, and though it has no living room, there are two rooms at the front on the ground floor, having a door opening directly into them from the lawn, which are bedrooms now, but which could be thrown together to make a living room which would double for church services or young people's meetings. It appeared to be in good condition, and could be had for 68,000 francs, or a bit less than $17,000, including the furnishings. The bank will give 40,000 francs, interest on which can be paid as rent. We put the name of this place, Chalet les Mélèzes, down on the green form, and the first step was taken. The next bus took us to Lausanne, where we went to the lawyer, the police, the notary, etc., and found that we had put the chalet down just in time; there was no time wasted, they told us. The form was to be filled out completely (the Chief helped us with this) and then sent to the President of Ollon (who is President also of Huemoz, where Chalet les Mélèzes is), and guess what? *Fran had already met the President of Ollon,* as he is a friend of our dear Mr. Exhenry and so Mr. Exhenry personally sent the form to him to sign! . . .

Meantime all sorts of things were going on in the village. The lawyer had said that any Swiss friends we had ought to write letters for him to present at Bern, and many other people in the village also wrote letters. The carpenter (who is the village judge) came and had a long talk with us in which we were able to give the gospel clearly. He then talked to Mr. Exhenry until 2:00 A.M. and Mr. Exhenry's face glowed as he later told us about it. The judge has written a letter in our behalf, as did several other courageous ones, and Rachel, Robert, and Herman made a petition to keep us here, which has been signed by some. Several have come and wept their sorrow concerning our going, and a number declare they will come to see us if we move not too far away. The Lord could be answering our prayers for the village in this in a way nothing else would do! Keep praying. Mr. Exhenry does not waver, but he needs your prayers. . . .

The Lord has now sent us a helper for this month of extreme need before moving. An English girl, Eileen, was in Champéry for two months of skiing. She reminds us a bit of Betty Carlson before she was saved, going from one interesting thing to another. She was a Wren during the war and served in that capacity in India for two years, she is a graduate nurse, she was head of a children's home for two years, and has her "diploma in housekeeping." Right now she is a travel guide during the summer, spending her savings during the winter skiing. She had come to the end of her money and wandered down to ask us if we could use her help for a month, in exchange for room and board and some time to ski. We felt the Lord sent her. She is so good and calm with Franky and can take over much of his care while we are getting more and more rushed as things pile up to be done. Pray for her, for I feel the Lord has brought her to us for more than just our need for help.

Today, Wednesday, was the day set for a decision re the house. A decision to be made with the reservation that if we do not get our permit, the whole deal is canceled. We have an older Christian friend, Mr. D., an uncle of Mr. Andre, who is a notary and an expert in real estate; he felt we should not buy, and he declared his intention of going to see the chalet to give his "advice." We wondered what the outcome might be—but decided to put this into the hands of the Lord as the final fleece. Yesterday he went; last night he called us, and this morning his letter came, right on the *day* for the decision. His conclusion was, *this is a terrific bargain,* a most unusual buy which is a rare find in this day. It would be easy to sell at any time; there are two other buyers interested, it couldn't be rented, so says he, "My advise is to buy *immediately,* and you will need to put 8,000 francs down to seal the transaction. You may move in April 1st or a few days before, you may live in it rent free until May 31st, when the final payment must be made. Do you have 8,000 francs?" We counted our money: the $1,000 that came first, Christian's, and the rest that the Lord sent during the week, and the total was—? Yes, we can *just* pay the 8,000 francs, sir! To be completely exact, we had $3.52 over this amount! It is a step of faith, but it would be a denial of the Lord's leading to do anything else than step out. He can also accomplish that which He has begun, and we will be praying that we will see a final miracle before May 31st.

Just as I was writing this, the telephone rang, and it was a sad Professor Czerny. "My little son died—" Oh do pray for him and for his wife. They need comfort, and oh how we pray that the Lord will strengthen them through the Holy Spirit so that this may be used for their spiritual growth, and not to turn them aside. Pray for them. We have also just heard the news that Mr. Exhenry's wife has threatened to separate from him. We are convinced it is all a part of the spiritual struggle in which we are and feel we can see as never before the reality of the struggle between spiritual forces. We long for these three dear ones in the Lord, and pray you may have a deep compassion for them—a compassion which will cause you to speak much to the Lord in their behalf.

We all need your prayers. Fatigue is upon us; Debby is down today with a sore throat and high fever, the packing looms up as an impossible task; tearing apart this house we have just fixed up will "hurt" as well as take time. To get everything up to the road over fields (since our path is a gully from the avalanche) seems an insurmountable task. And remember we still do not have the permit to stay in Switzerland. The devil would beset us with torturing thoughts as to the impossibility of it all. Oh, but our God is soveriegn; He can remove mountains of every kind, and our prayer is that in this entire situation He will bring glory to Himself—that "they" may know that He is God indeed, the Ruler of the whole universe—and the tender Father of His blood-bought children. We do *love* Him and trust Him—and how certain we are that what He allows is necessary and good.

With love to you all—and thanks to you for your prayers,

EDITH

March 30, 1955   Champéry, Switzerland

Dear Family:

Here I sit with shredded paper thick on the floors, dishes partially in open barrels and partially piled on the table, trunks and boxes full, but other things still waiting to go in boxes—the kitchen looking as though a cyclone struck it. Susan has just flown out the front door to take a train for Huemoz with Madame Fleischmann, to open windows and make beds in the new chalet; dinner must be prepared in the midst of the disorder; the phone keeps ringing and people come to say good-bye—yet even if I have to stay up all night, I feel compelled to write this one last letter to you all from Chalet Bijou so that you may know of the amazing things that are taking place and join us in immediate prayer for the continued work of the Holy Spirit, Who will remain here when we must leave tomorrow.

It has only been two weeks since I mailed the last letter—but what a two weeks it has been! Even today we do not yet have the definite permit to live in Switzerland, but the Lord is showing us one step at a time very literally. We went through some days when we thought we were going to have to leave Champéry with only suitcases in our hands, to go to some intermediate place until a permit arrived, for the lawyer told us we must *not* move to Huemoz unless we had a permit. It gave us a strange and most strained feeling to be packing without knowing whether we were packing for Switzerland, for storage, or to move elsewhere! Just two days ago we got final word that we have permission to *move* into the Huemoz chalet to *await* the final permit. What a great relief *that* was! Mr. B. of Voyage Kuoni called a few days ago and said, "Listen Madame Schaeffer, I know what it must be like to be so uncertain and with a family that large waiting to move. I am going to talk to my friend the Police Chief and I'll call you back." He started the ball rolling to get us this permission by telephone to go ahead and move. The actual state of things now is this: the official word has come by lawyer that "Bern" has said that they will OK things as soon as the Canton of Vaud makes it official and as far as they are concerned, we may move to await the decision in our new chalet. Then the Police in Vaud have said that they now have every reason to believe we will be issued a permit, and that therefore they give us permission to move into Vaud to await the decision. There were several moments during these various phone conversations when we stopped to have prayer—for that verbal permission to move was hanging by a thread so to speak, and could have just as easily dropped on the other side (that is, to a "No, go to a hotel for a while") as on this one! How we praise the Lord that we may make one big move rather than having to store things, etc., which would have been so much more difficult. . . .

What you cannot imagine is what the Lord has been doing during the last two weeks in the hearts of some people among the villagers in answer to your prayers. It is for this reason I am stopping everything else to write to you. I think it is only fair that you have the thrill of knowing how the Holy Spirit is working, as well as having the added impetus to pray even more fervently during the next weeks. . . .

Madame Fleischmann is another answer to prayer. Through the years, as she has taught the children piano, and as she has played our organ at church and has been with us in our home, we have grown to love her dearly, but we have been distressed at her frequent display of a lack of understanding at the difference between salvation by grace and salvation by works. So often she would say she did not think it mattered whether people were getting to heaven in their own way, or whether they were trusting in Jesus alone. *Our being put out has been used to completely open her eyes.* She not only understands now, but she is praying for the village in a wonderful way. She also has a new love for the Bible and is reading six chapters a day, and following a German Bible Study course we have given her. She comes frequently for study with us, and suddenly the slippery paths did not bother her any longer, and she came to church no matter how deep the snow. (Previously, she never came on very bad days.) She said the other day, "It is like the reformation days; I must carry my Bible in the streets like this—" and she held her Bible in front of her a bit like a flag! She says she must study the Bible well now for after we are gone, she *must* know how to answer people and give them the gospel clearly! . . .

This *is* revival—it is a *small* reformation—it is so clearly *all of Him*, to whom be praise and honor and glory forever and ever. The "Hallelujah Chorus" seems to fill the air—oh, and dear praying family (all of you *are* one family in the Lord) this is *our* Father—never be shaken as to His reality and His power—nothing matters except staying close to Him! . . .

The truck cannot get near our chalet because the avalanches and floods ruined our path. Therefore they will have to come with a jeep straight across the fields and make many trips to take our things by the jeep to the waiting truck on the road above. Since we have had rain (even another small avalanche last Sunday) the fields are a sea of mud, so it will be no easy task. The moving man is one recommended by the same practical Mr. B. who knows this man. Mr. Schneider, the moving man, not only talked with much efficiency about the moving, but he showed a real interest in Christian things and we feel the Lord has brought him to us. Rachel also wants to come with us and stay four days to help out in getting settled—and to study the Bible at the same time! The jeep and truck will make two trips—loading up and taking one-half of the family in the morning, and taking the second load at the end of the afternoon. Franky is excited at the prospect of a jeep ride! We will have a houseful as we settle in that first night, for

Madame Fleischmann is staying for a few days—Rachel also, and Eileen, the English girl who is with us, is going to stay until next Monday. We feel that first night is a picture of what we hope Chalet les Mélèzes will *always* be—a chalet full of people interested in hearing what God has to say!

But I'm not through yet with the wonder of the work of the Holy Spirit in this place at this time. Yesterday afternoon Madame Marclay came for a final Bible study together before we leave. She is so sad about our going and weeps almost constantly—that is, between excitedly telling us of the wonderful things that are happening. "Listen, listen," she said yesterday, "my husband is changing. He always liked you people but he would not think about what you teach at all, but ever since you have been told you must leave, he has *loved* you and he *thinks a lot*. He will listen to me now. . . .

And then, after telling us that her own post-office-worker son, Norbert, is also very interested and intends to come to us some weekends (!) she went on—lowering her voice to a whisper at this time—"My husband talked to Marc D. (husband of the blond, worldly Madame D. and owner of the big hotel of Champéry, a man who drinks heavily and has no interest that we have ever known of in any kind of religion), and he said Marc said, 'I have been intending to talk to the Schaeffers myself because I see that Georges Exhenry has something I would like to know about—I have a need—but my sisters are of course very against the Schaeffers' teaching.' " . . .

And so we approach the last evening of our sojourn at Chalet Bijou— and we know that we had to be put out that the Holy Spirit could use it to open some blinded eyes. We do not know what the remaining hours will bring forth—we pray another soul may be saved before we turn the key in the lock and leave this place to strangers to use for holidays. We go with mixed feelings: sadness, of course, for it has been our beloved home and the place of Franky's birth, as well as of many spiritual births, but surely without any shred of rebellion in thinking of being put out, for the Lord has not only assured us that His will is perfect, but in this particular instance He has allowed us to see so soon some of His reasons. As we go, we look forward to an entirely new chapter in our lives. We know this time of testing has been a preparation for the next chapter, but the Lord has not revealed what the next chapter is to contain. We ask only that we may be filled with the Spirit so that His plan may in no wise be hindered by our flesh. Thank you for praying each step with us—for what has happened could only be a result of answered prayer. In praying for the blessing of the Lord in Chalet les Mélèzes (and that is the name of the larch tree), you will never forget to pray for Champéry—and for the ones who will find their way over to us. Pray too for the *permit* and please pray that the Lord who promises that He will care for the material needs of His children will send just what is needed to meet the payment on Chalet les Mélèzes by the deadline of May 31st. He does *time* things perfectly, and we need to keep our minds stayed on Him so that we will not be "anxious" in any-thing—but truly bring to Him the needs both material and spiritual with *thankgsgiving*.

With much love,

EDITH

April 30, 1955   Huemoz sur Ollon, Switzerland

Dear Family:

Just a month ago today I sat writing to you in Champéry—and now from this sunny balcony spot in Chalet les Mélèzes I can look right across the Rhône valley, seeing fourteen villages and towns hugging the mountainsides or dotted on one side or another of the Rhône River be-low, and then looking up and beyond the inhabited parts of the moun-tainsides to the rocky, snow-covered tops of the Dents du Midi (our old friends!) and many, many other peaks as well. . . .

After a week of rain, moving day dawned with a partially clear sky, and not a drop of rain fell all day. Two trips were made by the stubby little jeep carrying boxes and furniture across the bumpy fields to the truck on the road above, before the men stopped for their breakfast of coffee, bread, butter, cheese, and jelly I served in an assortment of left-over dishes and glasses spread out on a table in the middle of the living room—a kind of ludicrous finale to the entertaining that has taken place in that room! The four puffing men, with the addition of Herman, Fran, and Norbert Marclay, carried things back and forth, with dogged deter-mination to do away with the obstacles the avalanche had placed in our way! Franky was the blissful front-seat guest for each trip the jeep made, and he took on a new swagger with the importance of his position, lean-ing against a wall to drink a glass of milk in perfect imitation of the workmen drinking coffee! The first truckload went before noon to Hue-moz—Fran, Franky, Debby, Norbert, and a couple of the men filling up the jeep as it followed close behind. The top of the jeep was down and they waved to people on the village street and the ones who are "for" us waved energetically back. That left Priscilla, Eileen, Rachel, and me to go on with the last-minute packing and clearing up, making a few last phone calls and visits before the jeep and truck returned. Dark had fall-en before we were finally ready to leave, and this time the jeep had its canvas top up to keep us a bit warmer on the drive down and across the valley and up the mountain again. As we passed the humble little chalet of Madame G. she ran out to say goodbye with tear-filled eyes. Then we came to a second stop by Rachel's chalet and she jumped in the jeep with

Our little village, Huemoz—population 200!

a little bag of nightclothing, sacrificing precious time and courageously riding off with us as we left a few hours before the "deadline" of our eviction. The village street was almost empty as it was the supper hour (almost 8 o'clock). Crossing the Rhône River in the valley below a half-hour later, we were out of Valais and in Vaud, and our being put out for the gospel's sake became a physical reality.

The next few days were a blur and confusion of unpacking and trying to find places for things which cannot be put into order until some changes are made in the house, and of trying to find out just how and where to get a supply of food, etc., as well as to prepare meals in a tiny, crowded kitchen. But in spite of all that which could so easily have seemed like a nightmare, we found oases of peace when we gathered around the Bible twice a day and had the joy of having family prayers and study with Madame Fleischmann with her new interest, Rachel with her intense desire to hear more, and Eileen with her freshly awakened determination to consider the Bible which for so long she has pushed aside as not true. And so literally L'Abri began in Chalet les Mélèzes immediately upon our arrival—with a German musician, a Swiss peasant, and an English ex-Wren and ex-nurse for our first guests. By dint of much hard labor on Saturday night, Fran had the multitude of trunks and boxes carried out into the hall and back room of the basement, and by hiding the wash basin with an old wooden panel propped up against it, and taking out the bed, hanging a few pictures, and arranging some chairs and tables, he managed to make it look pleasant as a little church. There are a dozen plain wooden chairs in the house that are

This is it! Chalet les Mélèzes (can you see Fran on the balcony?)

all alike, not needed anywhere else, which can be lined up to form our first two rows of seats for Sunday services. This was Rachel's first Protestant service, which made it more thrilling for all the rest of us. She sobbed uncontrollably that evening as she waited for the bus, for she had found a satisfaction in the studies of the Bible, but felt it was almost impossible to return for more for a long time. Her two brothers—and several cows—depend upon her to have meals always ready as well as to do much of the hard work in the fields, and to find a substitute to take her place seems like an impossibility. Won't you pray that the Lord may open up opportunities to her to come oftener than she could now expect?

Eileen expected to leave on the 8 o'clock bus Monday morning, but she and I sat up until the wee hours talking, so she put off going until the noon bus! Her agnosticism has taken a different form. "I just tingle up and down my spine at all the wonderful things in the Bible we study at family prayers. I always thought Christians were dull, unhappy people, but you all seem to be so excited about it—and your life is anything but dull! Heaven and eternal life sound so real when you tell about them, and I think, 'Why don't I jump to accept?' and then something holds me back. I can feel a *struggle* going on inside me which I don't really understand. You see, I am not desperate about anything; I like life as it is and I haven't been unhappy or felt a need—and—well—I guess I like my independence. I don't want someone else's will instead of my own. I keep thinking, if I accept, perhaps God will want me to go off to the heart of Africa like Doris who was here last week, and I wouldn't want to be without enough water!" We all like Eileen tremendously and we feel that she would be a person who would "go all the way" if she were born again. She is very honest. . . .

With no one but the family left—no telephone—no electrical equipment—no help—everything we seemed to want still packed or hidden (!), we suddenly began to feel the tremendousness of the hindrance to our day-by-day work this being put out of home and village was, and we *still* had no word concerning our permit. Debby fell off her bicycle (just trying it out on the gravel terrace) the same day that it began to rain and freeze and we discovered that in addition to the central furnace being out of commission the wood stoves in the halls smoked too much to use! Debby was in bed four days with bruised intestines, hot-water bottles were our only heat, trekking off to get milk at the dairy or some food at the tiny grocery (no refrigerator to depend on) and washing by hand seemed to take up all of our time, and we were driven to His Word for comfort in the midst of these small nagging difficulties as well as for peace concerning the bigger problems. . . .

Monday the girls and I were terribly sick with a food poisoning we must have gotten from the little cream-filled *patisseries* we had bought for a "treat" to take the place of my usual home-made cakes. (Baking is one hurdle that is too high for me at present in the inconvenient little kitchen.) Poor Susan slept little that night and felt life was not much worth living for a few hours! She asked us to please have her eyes sent to the New York hospital to be used for someone waiting for a cornea—if she died!!!! Fran seemed fine—until the middle of Monday night and then he discovered it had affected him too. Franky had not eaten any of the sweet things so he was hale and hearty. In spite of being so "seasick" Fran decided to take the 8 A.M. bus Tuesday because there was no way to get word to Priscilla, who would be waiting for him. And later he was so glad he did—for *in addition* to going with Priscilla to the University of Lausanne, where they found that everything would work out fine for Priscilla to enter the "Faculty of Letters" as a foreign student for one year—and then (passing some exams in Philosophy, History, and the various French literature and grammar courses) she would become a full-fledged student along with all those who have passed their "gymnasium" exams (she is not in "gymnasium" classes however—but in the regular University classes); he *also* went to see Mr. Ramuz, who is the chief of the Bureau of Strangers in the police department, where he found that surely the Lord had led him that day! Fran discovered in the police bureau that our entire permit affair had been placed in the hands of the Committee of Education and Religion, and that they would have to make a recommendation to the police department concerning our case! Another place where it would be easy to meet with a complete lack of understanding and found ourselves *out* altogether. The department would never have telephoned to tell us, but with Fran there in person they advised us to go to meet the president of a Committee dealing with the affair.

The appointment was made for Saturday afternoon, and then Fran bumped into Mr. Andre and he insisted that someone would accompany us Saturday! Isn't the Lord wonderful the way He times the goings and comings of His family?

Meantime at home on Tuesday I opened a letter from Madame Fleischmann. She told of how on Easter morning she felt an urgency— "I must go to the little church and play the organ and pray for the Schaeffers"—so she got dressed and then sat down to study a Bible study in German we had given her on the Resurrection. The feeling of "now it is time" came upon her when she finished, and she took her Bible, hymn book, and for some reason the sheets of Bible study and hurried off down her steep little path in the direction of the church in order to "be on time"! Alone in the church she went into the little room we used in the winter when the big season was over, and "lit" the two electric stoves and sat down to play hymns. Suddenly the door opened and people began to enter—people and more people until there were forty! They were English visitors to Champéry for Easter—we had forgotten to take down our church notices from the hotels! Dear, timid Madame Fleischmann, who had never even taught Sunday School class, and who so recently was not clear herself concerning the importance of the gospel message, thought—"They must have something—I will ask the Holy Spirit to tell me what to do and say"—and she stood up to *explain* to them *why* there was no pastor! After giving this startling information, she told them that she would help them to have a service in spite of the fact that her English is far from perfect. "I prayed in English and in French for I found that there was one French family present too—then we sang together—and then I asked a nice-looking English lady to read from John as I thought the Word of God should be pronounced properly. She read it with such feeling, I was glad I had chosen her. Then I took the two sheets of Bible study and translated them into English and French—and then we sang again and had prayer. I spoke of how it is necessary to take this risen Jesus as one's Savior—and then I sang a little German benediction for closing as we had no pastor to give the benediction." Debby and Susan and I were overwhelmed as we read this letter—what a tremendous thing the Lord had done within Madame Fleischmann, and her story not only thrilled us but her request for fifty testaments or gospels of John and some hymn books—"just in case something happens again." Fran went to Aigle later in the week and met Madame Fleischmann and Mr. Exhenry and had a wonderful time of fellowship and prayer with them—talking over many problems with which they are both faced, and giving her some of the things for which she asked (though we do not have a full supply of gospels or testaments or hymn books either). They planned to come for Sunday Service here in Mélèzes two Sundays after that to have a day of fellowship here. Later Madame Fleischmann told us that the following week she had twenty-eight Irish schoolgirls between the ages of eight and sixteen coming much in the same way as the first group! It is such a heartening example of how the Lord can care for the lambs left behind when shepherds are driven away. . . .

Priscilla went off to Lausanne the following Monday to begin classes with the new term, which lasts until the middle of July. She has a nice room right across the street from Madame Turrian's pension and she will eat most of her meals at Madame Turrian's. Students must find their own rooms, as the University has no dormitories. The way her classes are arranged, she may come home every Friday night and stay until the first bus Monday morning, and students may travel for one-fourth fare on railroads and buses. So it will cost her only 50 cents to come home! You see our dear Heavenly Father can plan for the good of each of His children at the same time. He knew that the University would be the place for Priscilla and chose a house convenient to transportation. For Susan, who needs much rest and a place to study alone, this place always looks out on a view which takes her to distant villages and towns along the Rhône without any need to walk! For Debby the village school with its one room, its young, imaginative man teacher who thinks up the most interesting things for his pupils to do, children who accept her into their midst, and one little girl who even comes to play with her here, life is more normal and happy, and for Franky, the hedged-in property becomes a place where he can play unsupervised, and the flattened section in the front (made that way by leveling off—something we couldn't afford to do, but which the builder of this place did years ago) gives him the first outdoor opportunity to ride his tricycle. . . .

Priscilla came home to hear the exciting news yesterday—with so much to tell of her own wonderful week. "Guess what—L'Abri is beginning right away—I'm bringing a girl home next weekend. Oh, Mother, it is amazing. Grace is a beautiful, American girl who never speaks to any of the American girls and always speaks French and keeps to herself. But this afternoon she came to me and began talking. 'Your father is a pastor, isn't he?' she said, and I don't know who could have told her that. 'I'm so mixed up myself I don't have any religion—and no one in my family has any stability. I *wish* I could talk to your father.' Then she invited me to her room, and we had an hour or so together before my train left. Mother, she is *interested* in hearing about the Bible, thinks L'Abri is a wonderful idea, and can't wait to come up here to see us. She is coming next weekend. Of course, I don't know what she'll think about the house the way it is now, but I don't think she'll mind. I *like* her ever so much and she was so friendly. She *needs* the Lord so badly because she really hasn't had any happiness in spite of her money. She's going to be here for years—she expects to come *often*." The description went on for a much longer time, and we heard about another interested group—a student group headed by a boy who had been saved only a year. "Oh how excited they were when they

Fran, me, and Franky—a rare moment alone before the Saturday
night hot dog roast and discussion began.

heard about L'Abri! They *all* want to come. Where are we going to put them? We're going to need more room, lots to eat, and that unfinished living room to sit in!"

Saturday night we built a fire outside on the bit of gravel terrace tucked under a rise of ground. There is a natural bank of grass in a semi-circle around this gravel—just perfect for crouching to toast hot dogs, and later to sit and listen to the Bible. We were just the family and Ingrid, but it seemed almost a "practice" for L'Abri to see how it would go! An old wooden table stands on the cobblestone open-porch affair that is on ground level at that side of the house, and there the food can be spread out to be served in buffet style. In clear weather this is the answer (when it is warm enough) for the need of a good place to give the cozy campfire atmosphere for talking about spiritual things. For this summer the outdoor "campfire" will solve the difficulty of at least *one* weekend meal to be cooked without my big stove (for the stove cannot be hooked up until electrical installation is put in)—as well as a memorable background for a hymn sing and Bible study. What a wonderful combination the Lord has given us in this place.

Next week also we will be having two other American girls with us, as Dorothy Jamison and her University friend will be stopping for a few days on their way around Europe. We are glad to have the Chalet used for L'Abri even before it is "fixed up." . . .

But the month ahead is one during which I would ask you, the "family," to pray with us very specially again. We need prayer ourselves that we might be kept in perfect peace with our eyes, our minds, and hearts on *Him* alone—for there is another "impossibility" ahead in the next 30 days. Now our permit is a sure thing, our promise to pay for this house on May 31st holds! Pray that the way the money comes in may be another proof to watching ones that He Who guided us so clearly to make this promise is the One Who doeth all things well. Pray that the 31st may be a date that will bring special glory to His name among those many people who are watching and waiting to hear the next chapter to this story. May we be willing to have it done in *His* way—and may we *trust* Him before we see how that staggering prayer is to be answered.

With much love,

EDITH

June 17, 1955

Huemoz sur Ollon, Switzerland

Dear Family:

Just a year ago today Priscilla was graduating from high school in Philadelphia, Franky was running around on two strong legs, Susan was just recovering from a strep throat, Debby was eagerly looking forward to returning to her beloved Champéry—and we had begun to pray as a family for specific guidance as to whether we should return to Europe— "Anything, Lord, that we might be completely in *Thy* will—take away any desire except that Thy name be glorified." His promises to lead have been wonderfully fufilled. He does not promise that the way will be easy. The polio, the rheumatic fever, the withholding of Swiss permits, the cancelled trips, the edict putting us out of Switzerland, the loss of time and money spent on making Chalet Bijou home—these were not easy, but they were every bit necessary as the final annulling in our passports of the edict against us, giving complete victory over that thrust of the devil, the choosing by the Lord of this chalet in Huemoz, and all the wonderful answers to prayer that have come since.

The Christian life is not an easy life, but it is full of a quiet confidence and an exhilarating joy when lived in the light of the fact that the infinitely powerful Creator of the Universe, who "spoke and it was," is now our loving Father who bends His ear to our slightest whisper—and who promises us not only to answer our requests, but to plan our lives according to *His wisdom*. Who else can tell us what is for our good and for His glory except He Himself? We would never choose the tragic illnesses, the heavy disappointments, the deep hurts—but can we dare to plan the sensible, logical, reasonable plan our own finite intellect would map out? Never does the peace of God so pass *all* understanding as when we put our "times" completely in His hands and step back to watch Him work. . . .

You know, I had often wondered in past years how the Lord would work out the education of the children financially, and the way still seemed fuzzy when we arrived back here in September so far as college for Priscilla was concerned. You all know the story of how she studied for six months—and then how she discovered right after our move to Huemoz that there was a way, scholastically, for her to immediately enter the University of Lausanne. But I haven't told you the amazing discovery we have made concerning the cost of this school. Previously the Olive Branch Church in St. Louis gave a personal gift to the four children of $100. A confab was held, and the three younger ones (Franky without knowing what he was doing, we suppose) voted to give most of their share to Priscilla so that she might have almost the entire $100 "for her education." The trip to the secretariat's office of the University revealed that *tuition for a whole year is less than the $100!!* So, the Olive Branch folks have (without knowing it) paid for one year at the University of Lausanne! The other expenses are: room, $15 a month; food—breakfast consisting of tea, bread, margarine, and jam in her upper-dormer-window room; lunch—often invited to friends, sometimes consisting of rolls, tea, and fruit in her room, and other times at Madame Turrian's; and supper in the evening almost always at Madame Turrian's. Madame Turrian is the one in whose "pension" we lived during our first year in Lausanne. She is like a member of the family and has given us a low rate for Priscilla's meals. She is delighted to have Priscilla there so often, and Priscilla is happy to have time to talk about the things of the Lord to Madame Turrian. Any of you young people who could understand French well enough to begin taking courses taught in French could save practically enough on college expenses to pay your passage over here to study! It was Priscilla's Heavenly Father and not her earthly parents who did the perfect planning in this.

Dorothy Jamison of California and her University of Minnesota friend, Anne, who are traveling around Europe in a most inexpensive way, and staying at youth hostels, came to see us that first week in May and the result of that was that Dorothy asked if she might come back in July to do what she could to help here in L'Abri, delaying her sailing for a time. So we are looking forward to her return as it promises to be a very busy summer. . . .

The following weekend we had Rosalee, a Swiss Christian who has a Children for Christ class in a home and one in the hospital, but who had some questions and problems raised by her studies. The Lord brought Rachel from Champéry for that Sunday, and Rosalee's Christian parents and sister came Sunday afternoon for tea and supper to drive Rosalee back to Lausanne. It was good for Rachel to hear these Christians speaking of spiritual matters in French together. But I took Rachel aside during the afternoon for a long time of Bible study on the square corner balcony, and toward the end she began to weep. "I can never become a Christian, Madame Schaeffer, for I have been reading the Bible you gave me, and I find that Christians must love one another, and show forth love to the world, and I *can't ever do that* because I *hate* some of my brothers, and I will never forgive them." Now her mouth was set in a hard line and the tear-filled eyes had taken on a fierce look. I explained that she had it backwards. She did not need to wait to be able to love her brothers (not the ones she lives with, but two others whom she feels treated her badly and who have an easier life than hers), but that this hate was one of the sins Jesus would wash away if she would but come to Him acknowledging her sin and accepting Him as her Savior. "The love will follow, Rachel, if you are truly born into His family, for when the Holy Spirit comes to dwell in your heart and you begin to let Him live through you, then the *fruits* of the Spirit will *follow*. Love is one of the fruits of the Spirit, but you must be a branch before you bear fruit." A wistful look passed her face, and then it was set again—for the struggle seems to be a real one against the *preference* to continue to hate. . . .

All too soon they had to leave. By Monday morning we were all alone again! Nothing left to do then but washing, etc. Please do pray that it may not be too long before the Lord will open up the way to install the washing machine and other electrical helps as at present the ordinary tasks of washing and ironing with no equipment consume such quantities of precious time. That is the "Marthaish"* side of things, but I have been impressed lately that I must *not* just shoulder this burden as something it is up to me to "do or die," but that the Lord can take care of this need too. It's so easy to "save out" some worrying to do on the side while one is rejoicing in big victories! At least that is my weakness!! . . .

And so we face a busy summer as L'Abri Fellowship begins, and such a thing as a vacation must be put off again. But the Lord is sending those who need a time in L'Abri, and He can just as easily provide an opening for a vacation when He knows it is necessary.

There are a few things that you should know concerning L'Abri Fellowship. The material needs of the work, and of ourselves, will be met as the Lord sends in gifts in answer to prayer. We believe that if He sends the people to us who need to be here for study and asking questions and prayer, He will also send in the means to feed them. There is the garden for instance. A big crop of vegetables will make a difference in feeding the summer guests of L'Abri and the Lord who controls the weather also can send in the needed support for workers and open the way to repair the furnace, put in electrical installations, etc. Each need will be prayed about and we will wait for guidance to proceed according to His specific answers in sending the means. . . .

Finally, and most important—L'Abri Fellowship may seem very small—but we know there are many who are having a daily part in the work here through their faithful prayers. The ones who are working here through prayer we wish to speak of as the Praying Family of

*See Luke 10:38–42.

*I am holding the thrilling first bean
from our garden!*

L'Abri. You yourself know whether you are one whom the Lord has joined to us in this way or not. May L'Abri truly be a shelter in a weary land for those who will find Christ their shelter here. May the early months of its existence once more be a demonstration of the existence and power of our infinite Father, in His care and leading of His children.

Much love in Him whose name is Wonderful, Counselor—

EDITH

August 18, 1955   Huemoz sur Ollon, Switzerland

Dear Family:

Remember the first day you went to school, the first time you ever dove from a diving board, the first time you ever spoke in public, rode in an airplane—or on a horse? We each have "firsts" we'll never forget so you can sympathize with me as I approached the moment when I had to give Susan an injection! I had practiced thrusting that hypo needle into a pillow hundreds of times, but what was flesh going to feel like? And could I *do* it, or would my hand stop short? Susan, who used to break out in a rash at the sight of a hypodermic needle, has changed tremendously since she began to dream of being a nurse herself, and so as we went to

Dr. Kousmine's that morning, I think I was far more nervous than Susan! I was still practicing when the doctor came into her office and laughingly got me started on the first part of my test, assembling the sterilized parts. Finally *the* moment arrived. One two three! And my hand stopped short! One two three again, and it was over, with the doctor's praises ringing in my ears—"Well done, you are a good pupil, next time it will go more easily." The experience had left me rather shaky. Since I have to give her an injection once a week, it is to be hoped that I'll improve—and relax! Susan herself had a "first" too recently, as she was invited to see an operation by the surgeon father of her Champéry friend, Christine. She went off to Montreux the night before in order to be on hand at 7:30. The delicate ear operation lasted for three hours, and Susan stayed beside the table the whole time without even a wave of faintness! She excitedly reported all the details, and her desire to become a nurse has tripled since that time. Christine's father took Susan on his rounds through the hospital after that, and then home for lunch with him. "He was so appreciative of all the help we've been to Christine, and I think he has a real spiritual hunger himself," remarked Susan as she came home. Christine lives with her mother in Champéry, for her parents are divorced.

July was a "first" for all of us, the first month during which we were L'Abri Fellowship, praying day by day for the supply of our needs, praying that the Lord would send those of His choice to our chalet and give us the power of the Holy Spirit in meeting their spiritual needs. We asked Him to show us clearly whether the step we had taken was His leading or not, and as the days of the month went by He gave us assurance with both material and spiritual evidence that this was His plan and not ours. As the days went on we had an increasing conviction that Someone had just gone before us preparing the way; for only He could have prepared us spiritually for the storms as well as the sunshine, and only He could have touched hearts so that the financial needs of the first month were met completely, and a special gift was given so that the electricians could be called in to begin their work. The powerful God of the Universe *does* give His children guidance in answer to prayer, and *does* work miracles in lives handed over to Him.

The last weekend in June brought the yellow bus to our gate with two passengers for L'Abri. Karl Woodson had discovered at Aigle that he had no Swiss money to buy his ticket, and a young fellow stepped up to him and said, "I can buy it for you, I have the francs." They went on to the train together and discovered that they were both headed for Chalet les Mélèzes in Huemoz! Karl is one of the St. Louis Church young people who is serving his two years in the Army in Germany, after having graduated from Northwestern University. John Sandri,* who arrived

---

*John Sandri is now, of course, our son-in-law, daughter Priscilla's husband. But that comes much later in the story!

with him, is an American citizen whose parents are Swiss. His parents lived in America as his dad worked for a Swiss company there, but now the dad is back in Switzerland as president of that company. Grace has known John for some time and had invited him to come to Huemoz with her, but when he met her at the station she breezily said, "Dick is bringing me up later on the motorcycle, so you go on alone. The Schaeffers are an American family and you'll love it there." So with that much information John came on alone. You can imagine the confusion aroused in this 19-year-old's mind, with a background of skiing and mountain climbing in Switzerland, school in America, and a fashionable modernistic church, when he started off on an afternoon hike (with Fran and Karl) innocently remarking, "I don't think Christianity has a leg to stand on intellectually, do you Mr. Schaeffer?" and then spent the next two hours listening to the reply!

Franky is usually the "life of the party" during the hot dog roast—as he waves his hot dog dizzily over the fire and pulls it out every two seconds to inspect it as to its readiness for the roll. "This is the men's place—only mens can sit here, all the other peoples have to sit someplace else," he announces as he seats himself on the bench nearby. That night we were half through our supper, munching away on salad and hot dogs, when a motorcycle roared up to the big gate separating our place from the Roman Catholic children's home next door, and there were Grace and her atheistic friend, Dick. They told us of the motor troubles they had had along the way, and joined the group around the fire. The questions that night were mostly the atheist's. I had put Franky in bed and was waiting to see that he went off to sleep as I stood on the balcony looking down on the heads of that little group sitting on the old quilts spread out around the campfire. An old oil lantern gave just enough light for the open Bible to be read in answering questions—but as I looked down on the heads below I prayed that the One who was looking from a greater height right into their hearts would send His light to illumine His Word so that each one might have what he or she needed that night. The next day Dick and Grace were the first to leave. After they had gone, we sat talking around the dinner table. John then said, "I'll admit right now that during the first hours here I was embarrassed, because I had never been with people who talked about God so openly. But after last night around the campfire, and this morning's sermon, and now all you have been telling me, I feel as if I were looking at a new world—one I never knew existed before. Why, you know, I have never once even heard the word "sin" in my church, though I went every Sunday. I thought Christianity was a sort of a rosy glow that didn't make any sense." Oh please do pray that this may be true for John, that those serious blue eyes may *soon* light up with complete understanding and acceptance of the gospel as true, and that he may personally accept Jesus as his Savior. . . .

By the way, Susan went back to Champéry for a week's visit, for she had been invited by the Marclays, and people greeted her with varying degrees of amazement, warmth, joy, icy chill, and downright fury! She made the rounds in her visits and we feel the Lord used it. The rest of the children went for one day as there was a specially priced trip by bus from Villars, and now this week Debby is visiting the Marclays. So the contact with Champéry is being kept alive. Keep praying.

Then came the first of August, the Swiss National Holiday. The village celebration was called for 8:30 and when just as 8 P.M. a hail storm began to rage, we decided that *that* was probably that. Alice called the schoolteacher, while some of us began a search for all the proper raincoats, boots, etc. "It's to be at the church with just singing and speeches." Great disappointment—"No fireworks? No bonfire? I want to carry a lantern!" But before we could even get the rainboots on, the phone rang, and it was the teacher again. "Come ahead, it's clearing up and we're going to the hill." So off we went, and sure enough the hail had stopped, the sky was clearing, and before we reached the "hill," the stars were out and a moon had appeared. Franky proudly stood with his funny-faced paper lantern bobbing precariously close to people's coats. It is not a large crowd that gathers from a village with only 70 households, but the band has twenty pieces, and the twenty schoolchildren manage to hold lanterns so that the band can see its music. The combined voices sing the national anthem, while the village president fumbles his speech papers, and the pastor finishes with a talk that seems too long to the impatient young people waiting for the bonfire. Kerosene makes the piled-up bonfire burn in spite of the wet wood—and in the heat and light of the huge flames, the schoolchildren gather to sing, with Debby as the soloist. Debby's clear voice rings out in the hush of the moment, the humming accompaniment making a lovely harmony. Other bonfires burst forth on other parts of the surrounding mountains marking other village celebrations. The hissing of sparklers takes the place of music as the villagers set off the fireworks they have brought with them. Lanterns are seen going back down to the little street below and gradually everyone follows until once again the group is together setting off more fireworks, singing, and listening to band music, moving only to let inconsiderate tourists drive past. Debby is called upon to sing again, Franky joins the older boys in trying to see who can swing a sparkler with the greatest gusto, and the community has celebrated—liberty!

Franky's third birthday was the event we celebrated on the third of August. He had asked for "a blue cake." Franky was the only one who didn't taste the cake; he just enjoyed looking at it and opening presents. His only request had been "a swhale." "I want a swhale for my birthday." Not being able to find a whale, we had substituted a red fish for his bath. "Is this a swhale?" he asked with curiosity. But he was satisfied, and the horn Susan gave him was soon filling his entire time, as well as our ears! . . . Late that afternoon the yellow bus dropped at the foot of our wooden steps a Buddhist girl who came searching again, still longing to know the truth. . . .

Won't you continue to pray that the existence of God may be demonstrated here in every possible way—materially, spiritually—with His plan bringing the right ones here at just the right time for the need of each heart? Nothing is impossible with Him whose strength is made perfect in our weakness.

Lovingly yours in Him in whom we are one family,

EDITH

November 2, 1955   Huemoz sur Ollon, Switzerland

Dear Family:

No, you didn't miss a letter because there hasn't been one since August 18th!! When I was mentally planning a "bowl" full of work for September I was sure that I could mix in a half a cup of time to write the long letter, but as the month wore on, the mixture of work in the "bowl" had risen like dough in a too-small container, and seemed to be spilling over the edges. At the end of the month there was a measure of chopped-up vacation that I thought could be partially removed so that the "family letter" could go in in its place, but Fran, who was dictating the recipe at that moment, said firmly that just wasn't allowed! Then October slid by, and now it is November 2nd and I have asked the Lord to give me quiet and speed so that I may get this finished before I am a year older, as tomorrow marks the beginning of another year of my life.

I wish every one of you in the "family" could join me this afternoon for tea out on this square place at the end of the first-floor balcony; then I could tell you about the last three months without measuring the words, and at the same time you could enjoy this rare Indian Summer day which has surprised us at the beginning of a usually gloomy month. Fran's out there now in the golden sun among the brown leaves, digging up a new patch of garden for next spring, and uncovering some big rocks at one end which will give that square of vegetables a "landscaped" air. He can go back into the office after dark (which comes by 5:30 these days). The snow is sticking to the jagged spires and crevices of wave after wave of mountains in the panorama surrounding us, snow coming down to 7,000 feet (from a height of about 10,000 feet), vying with the white clouds to form striking outlines against the contrasting blue sky. The dark green sweeps of pine forest below the snow form a background for the varied shades of colored leaves on the hardwood trees, and then, as though the artist were exaggerating the scene, the fields are still a bright green, full of pale lavender fall crocuses and deep blue-purple gentians. There's movement in the picture as animals wander in the fields or plod down the roads; trucks, buses, tractors, and jeeps wind in and out of the many curved roads spread out in the view, and trains twist through the valley below while a glint of the sun catches the movement of the Rhône River dividing Vaud from Valais. The whole scene is accompanied by its own symphony—a symphony of deep-voiced cowbells donging, goatbells dinging, and sheepbells tinkling while some small boy driving his animals cries out "ho." Occasionally a thunderous blast and a rumbling rat-a-tat-tat remind one that the "service militaire" (yearly three-weeks' army service, compulsory for Swiss men) is having a mock war nearby. . . .

The yellow bus soon brought another passenger to L'Abri as out stepped Deirdre at the end of her journey from London that morning. The flight from London to Geneva had not taken her as long as she had to wait at Ollon for a bus (!) but her wait had given her time to do a lovely pen-and-ink sketch of the quaint Ollon station. Yes, Deirdre is an artist with one more year's study at London Art School—and you've heard about her before as the one who accepted Christ in Chalet Bijou four years ago. It was good to hear her tell of the way the Lord had kept her close to Himself in spite of discouraging cold disinterest at home (hard on an only child) and hindrances which were placed in the way of her going to a place where she could worship and be fed on Sunday mornings, and we rejoiced over instances of her witnessing to others and seeking the Lord's will for her own life.

The eleven days she spent here were not exactly "quiet" ones in Chalet les Mélèzes. The little carpenter arrived at 7 A.M. the day after Deirdre came and began to make a "niche" in the wall of our tiny kitchen to hold the refrigerator, which otherwise would have had no place to stand. The "niche" consists of a hole cut in the kitchen wall into the bathroom adjoining the kitchen. The refrigerator really stands in the bathroom, with a wooden "box-like" structure all around it shutting it away from view. That morning Deirdre was brushing her teeth when the annoying sawing noise nearby grew louder and she turned to see a saw rhythmically moving in and out of the wall! She fled upstairs to finish her "morning toilet" in the upstairs bathroom! We have two bathrooms (which makes it very convenient with so many guests), one on the floor with the three guest bedrooms, the office, the dining room, and the kitchen, and one on the floor with our family bedrooms. Deirdre needn't have worried about a hole appearing in the wall that morning, for the carpenter discovered that the inside walls in this house were make of wood over three inches thick, under the thinner pine paneling, so sawing by hand it took him about three days to get that hole properly made, and another couple of days to make the "boxed-in" effect. . . .

August came to a close with the exciting noises of the washing machine washing the clothes all by itself, the refrigerator humming cold air into the milk, and smiling electric plugs ready to pour heat into the iron, toaster, etc., once again! The first step of "getting settled" was at last over and one of the big hurdles thrown up by our "ejection" was down. . . .

Just at this point Priscilla picked up some kind of a grippe germ combined with general fatigue, which gave her a few days of fever—and then a long time of dizziness and a complete lack of energy. We not only missed her help, but her addition to the mealtime conversations, and her note of light-heartedness in the family life. This cloud hovered over us the whole month of September and beginning of October, for we were never quite sure we had the "seat" of the trouble.

We were making good use of our new "convenience," the washing machine. The kitchen was cluttered because of the various stages of plumbing and cupboard making. We were bringing down the sink from the upstairs kitchen (to make room for the washer) and it was installed beside the downstairs one, giving us a place to drain dishes, so that we could throw away the stack of crates that had held a wobbly wooden drain before!! The Lord brought Mr. Exhenry over a few days later. We divided his time into three precious parts: A long walk, Bible study, talk and prayer time with Fran; a time during which he gave his testimony to Mrs. J. and her teenage son Jon from Georgia; and a communion service for our little International Church. . . .

I was picking peas in the pouring rain—Thomas Laxton peas had matured at last by the 9th of September! (the other varieties never did fill out)—when a very American "Hi" caused me to look up, startled, with water running down my face. "I'm Bill and I didn't wait for the bus— just hitchhiked up from Ollon." He had written a few weeks before, "I understand you have a place where people come, and I'd like to come for a few days." Bill was installed in the bunk bedroom and his fair, curly-topped head and big blue eyes added variety to our family which now numbers an even twelve!! You can imagine how thankful I was that the big stove was now working, as I tucked away the cakes in that oven. Saturday it was still pouring and the snows were coming down too close for comfort, as Fran talked to Bill and another in the dismal ground-floor room closed in from all the views; he had a vivid illustration of our need of a fireplace and a cheerful room before winter. That afternoon a man from Ollon stopped to ask if we would go with him to see his chalet his grandfather and grandmother had built years ago, Chalet les Sapins.* We donned raincoats and went dripping up the back road with him to hear the story of his grandfather's preaching in this local church during his holidays here, and of his prayers for a work of the Lord in this vicinity. Now their bodies lie in the village cemetery above us. "I wanted you to look through the chalet because it is for sale, and my hope is that you will buy it for your work among young people. I imagine you are going to need more room for your work. Then, another thing, I want to give

*Chalet les Sapins is now owned by L'Abri Fellowship.

you, as a gift, my grandfather's library—that is, if it interests you." The chalet is about three minutes up the back road from us with a wooded property that stretches straight up behind it. Well-built and with heavily beamed ceilings in all the rooms, "The Pines" has a large dining room and good-sized kitchen with a sun porch and balconies, closets, and built-in nooks galore. It must have sleeping space for twelve people (with room for at least eight more with proper beds), as well as a complete third-floor apartment, where the grandfather and grandmother were able to live apart from the houseful of grandchildren during the ski season!! It was in the third-floor living room that we discovered the library. The underlinings and careful notes penned in the margins of the old Bible revealed a deep understanding of spiritual things, and the 200 or so books we have received contain many by E. Hopkins, McCheyne, Bonar, and others of like spiritual understanding—what a feast for our own souls as well as for the young people who come for L'Abri! And how thrilling that the Lord should prepare a library for us right here in Huemoz. . . .

One thing our American guests wanted to see in Switzerland was Champéry, the place where we had been put out "for Jesus' sake." There is a little round old man named Aimé Ischi who owns a Volkswagen station-wagon holding about ten people. For a fixed price, he will take as many as can pile in, drive to the prearranged place, and come back later in the day. We figured that the price of his driving us to Champéry was actually cheaper than train for so many people, and he agreed to take us over early in the afternoon and bring us home about 6 P.M., giving us about four hours there. It was raining when we started, and we feared the view would be curtained off, but the Lord gave us a wonderful day, for the fogs disappeared as the little red, stubby-nosed car hurried down the mountain, and Champéry was at its best! The snows had come all the way down to Planachaux, so the peaks that tower above the village were a sparkling white against the sky. Jon, who, coming from the south had never played in snow, was anxious to get immediately up to Planachaux and so we took the first *telepherique* of the afternoon. Franky was delighted to be back in his favorite swinging boxcar, the *telepherique*, and the snows at Planachaux were deep enough to satisfy everyone. The "smiley man" was taking tickets, and I talked to him all the way up—"Stupid, absolutely stupid—putting you out of here—" he muttered as he tore tickets from the pad of white ones (half price for *residents* of Champéry!)—"I hope you are happy over there in Huemoz." I explained to him the reason we had been put out, retelling the story of Mr. Exhenry's salvation, and then explained also a bit about Children for Christ and just what our L'Abri was doing for young people who needed a "spiritual shelter" to come to with all the questions stirred up in the storm of life. The shorter curly-haired fellow was on duty our descending trip, and he expressed himself strongly too. (Amazingly enough the Lord gave me an opportunity to talk to him and his wife a week later for an hour and a half on a train to Lausanne—both listened avidly to the details of what had happened and of how God had answered prayer, then he remarked, "They're crazy if they think putting you out is going to change the faith of Georges Exhenry.")

While we were in Champéry we did some shopping at Mr. Exhenry's store, and his wife waited on us, so she had to be civil, but that was all; the president turned on his heel and snubbed us; Marclays rushed out and greeted us and she kissed all the children right in the street; the vegetable man waved and called out heartily; Madame D. at the hotel greeted us politely and then went to find Eileen. Eileen, by the way, has since written that she is coming to stay with us early in December before she goes to Chalet Bijou for the rest of the winter. Yes, she has *rented* Chalet Bijou, and wishes we would visit her there! Wouldn't that be something? Less than a year after being put out? We went to visit Chalet Bijou and that sort of tugged at the heartstrings and made us sigh—it was so much home to us, and the rooms were so big and rambling—and there they all were, those improvements we had worked so hard to make! Rachel came out of her chalet, wiping her rough hands on her apron to give us each a kiss on each cheek, and to unlock Chalet Bijou for us. She had been cleaning up after the summer people and had the old floors waxed to a yellow glow. *"Mais* what a work"—how she wishes we were still there. It suddenly seemed as though we should be putting sheets on the beds in those familiar rooms—the house where Franky was born—and serving tea in our cozy living room—was it just a dream that it was just an empty house?

We arrived back at Chalet les Mélèzes to find that the workmen had torn out the old kitchen cupboard, with a promise to bring the new divided cupboard with a work-surface and put it in within a few days—as soon as they could make it! Meantime the dining room table and floor were piled high with all the miscellaneous contents of kitchen cupboards—from pots and pans, graters and sieves, to cocoa and sugar. The kitchen was now in its most impossible stage, and there was no place left to serve a meal in the dining room. We ate on the balcony for the next few days. . . . [The way then opened for a vacation back in Alassio, Italy, with the "Sardines" and their Aunt for two weeks.] We arrived back in Huemoz feeling very thankful that the Lord had given us a time of refreshing before the fall and winter's work. Aimé Ischi told us coming up the mountain that the snow had come all the way down to Huemoz a few days before, and the icy air that evening was a shock after the "summer" we had just had. However a "spell" of sunny weather warmed up the house in the afternoons, and with wood fires in the hall stove, the heating hasn't become a problem yet, although it is now November and there has been no sign of the men appearing with the furnace! There was a variety of work to plunge into—40 letters needed immediate attention, and 60 others couldn't be put off too much longer, attic and "caves" (dirt-floored rooms at back of ground floor for keeping vegetables and fruit for the winter) and the little bedroom which will soon be a part of the living room all needed long, hard hours of cleaning, sorting, and straightening. The first weekend filled all the beds and formed a circle two deep around the campfire (which was needed for warmth as well as for cooking hot dogs), with fourteen Swiss young people from the French-speaking section of the G.B.U. This Bible study group had been brought by Jean and Andre, who wanted Fran to give them an introduction to their winter study, and to talk with them about spiritual things. Their Swiss-German professor-leader came for one night and Fran had a good time of fellowship with him.

Naturally cooking and serving meals to this crowd (plus eight in our basic family group) took almost all of Dorothy's and my time—and how did we "sleep" them? Some had brought sleeping bags. The four girls slept in the bunk bedroom, two boys in Dorothy's bedroom (one on the floor), the professor in the single bedroom, and the rest of the boys were strung out in a row on mattresses on the living room floor. The service that Sunday was conducted by Jean in French and the walls rang with French hymns. Fran's sermon was translated phrase by phrase by Priscilla, and went very smoothly and well.

Madame Marclay puffed up to the door with her overnight bag and a string bag full of wilty plants from her garden—"I've got rock-garden plants that will bloom all next summer for you—better set them out today!" she said, and, "What do you want me to sew first? Can we sew together? Ohhhh—" and she hugged me. "I'm so glad to be here. We're going to have three whole days together and nice Bible studies, won't we, hah? Listen, listen, I talked to a man who was in our chalet for the summer and he didn't believe anything—I told him that wasn't right, and tried to tell him the things you've told me. Listen, he believed in Jesus after that when he went back to Germany—was it the Holy Spirit helping me? Isn't that exciting—the Holy Spirit helping *me!*" Madame Marclay had come from Champéry to help get a start on drapes and slipcovers. She is quick in her movements and tries to do everything with all of us. She walked all the way to school with Debby, ran out to the fish truck with me, went to the post office with Susan, and played around with Franky. She hung on every word at our Bible study at family prayers, and she also got the drapes made for the dining room (out of sturdy handwoven linen sheets that were in this house when we bought it), and some covers for trunks to transform them into seats in some of the bedrooms. Naturally I needed to sew with her, and so used the time to make a slipcover for the dining room couch, which brought much more light into that room and seemed to make it bigger! Fran used those three days to work with the girls, in shifts, to clear out and straighten the yard, attic, "caves"—and workmen were banging a sliding door into existence to give the dining room a way to be shut off from the kitchen noises. The only time we've seen the workmen since then was the day two of them arrived and knocked out the partition between those two ground-floor rooms. Franky loved "helping" to pick up hunks of broken cement—and we all enjoyed our first glimpse of the size of our new room, but nothing has taken place since, and we now have *no* place for church! We *think* the workmen will reappear this week.

The Lord has marvelously answered prayer in supplying the money specifically sent for fixing up that room, and the furnace—and now we are praying that the *work* may be done before a sudden streak of bitter weather overtakes us. You'll thrill with us over the account book and wall chart, to learn that now one-third of a year has passed with every expense for the home and the entertaining of L'Abri guests directly met through answered prayer. Exciting to picture God, our Father, who knows we have "need of all these things," putting into the minds of other of His children amounts He would have them write on checks, at the time He would have them write them—amounts which when all added together meet the needs He knew about all the time. Keep praying that the work may go forward at His pace and that we may neither hold back nor run ahead, and that those to whom He speaks may have their ears attuned to hear. . . .

As you know by now, Dorothy didn't go back for the fall term at the University of Minnesota and now she has come to the decision not to go back for the mid-winter term either—for she feels the Lord is leading her to stay here longer as a worker in L'Abri. We praise the Lord for His choice of a helper at this time, and for all that her help is meaning to us. . . .

Brief snatches of news—Pris is back at school and reports that "millions of Americans are here this year" and that her energy is returning after strong doses of vitamin D; Karl Woodson writes that he and an unsaved G.I. friend plan to come for Christmas—New Year's week; Fran goes to Lausanne tomorrow for appointments with five of the University students; and my space has run out! Ooooo look at my watch, it's really morning, and I have a soft-spoken little visitor who whispers, "Mommy why aren't you in your bed? I woke up and 'cided I wants a 'yohourt' in the middle of the night."

I'd better sign off with much love to each of you in the "family"—in Him,

EDITH

1956

February 14, 1956   Huemoz sur Ollon, Switzerland

Dear Family:

Our emotions a year ago today will never be forgotten, for this was the day that Fran and Priscilla were handed the two pieces of paper informing us that we had been ordered to leave the village of Champéry and the entire country of Switzerland with our family and all of our belongings within six weeks! Our passports had been stamped to this effect, and the edict was final: cast out, with charges against us of having had "a religious influence on the village of Champéry." The shock of being plunged into such a hopeless and "impossible" situation with neither the physical strength nor the human wisdom to know what to do next was a feeling that will not be forgotten. . . .

Here I sit today one year later, just an hour and twenty minutes' drive from the village home from which we were ejected, in a house which without a doubt the Lord had chosen for us long ago. The Lord has given us Chalet les Mélèzes on a lovely piece of ground right by the bus stop. He showed us clearly that He wanted us to buy it, and week by week He has shown us that it was His will that it be prepared for this *first* winter as L'Abri. We prayed for electrical installation—by September all the appliances were humming; we prayed for a new furnace—by December the old one was torn out and a new one hooked up and warming the radiators; we prayed for a living room with a fireplace, and before Christmas the wall between the two ground-floor bedrooms was torn out, a new floor was laid, the ceiling was redone, and a lovely rustic stone fireplace with a raised hearth and a low stone bench stretched across one side of this "new" living room; we prayed for a piano, and a reconditioned piano now stands at the opposite end of the room from the fireplace; and the Lord has added more: material to cover couches, shelves to hold all our books, draperies from Chalet Bijou fitted to these windows. . . .

Yes, it seems like a year of miracles as we look back, rather than a year of difficulty. It has now been seven and a half months since we took another step of faith as the Lord led us to form L'Abri Fellowship, continuing our work with dependence upon him only to supply the material needs, and to show us day by day what He would have us do. Seven and a half months of thrilling realization that when the Lord plans a thing, He can plan all the details perfectly. When it is the Lord's plan to build a fireplace, He can touch the heart of the ones whom He would use to give the money for it to give exactly that which is needed, even before the Swiss workmen send an estimate of its cost. He can direct in the number and amount of gifts so that the total is always enough for the regular expenses and to feed the extra "mouths" around the table. He can touch hearts to send a box of food to make the budget stretch at *just* the moment when it needs stretching, because *He* is sending the people here, and knows who and how many are coming, long, long before we do! He is the Infinite Unchanging, All-powerful One for whom nothing is too hard.

Let met tell you what He did in relation to Champéry. One day in November as Madame Marclay was sewing with me to lengthen the drapes and so on, the doorbell announced the arrival of the Postmistress (who is our mailman). "Look here, Madame Marclay, a letter from England from a travel agency, asking us whether or not we are going to have the usual holiday services in Champéry. They say they will be conducting a large group to Champéry during the holidays and would appreciate service in English!" "Oh, Madame Schaeffer, you *must* come! I'm going to ask my husband about it—surely you must come." We would never have thought of trying to go back for services so soon, but this was an unsought-for request from a completely innocent source, an English travel bureau which did not know we had been put out of the village, and which was seeking simply something they considered as a favor! We spread it before the Lord and asked Him to open the door completely for this service if He wanted us to go back.

The next brush stroke in this picture was the arrival on Sunday afternoon of little, bent Pastor Spiros, the retired Swiss pastor who is our neighbor. "A little bird told me that you were working too hard, Madame Schaeffer, and I have come to scold you," he began. Later he asked, "What do you hear from Champéry these days—anything new?" I told him of the request from England and he became even more excited than Madame Marclay. "Ah, you must go! You have every right to go, for all that was attempted against you has been annulled. It is in the interest of liberty that you must be allowed to go. I feel so strongly about this, that I propose to write a letter to the authorities at Sion telling them of this request, and reminding them of the liberty the Roman Catholics enjoy in our Protestant cantons. They know me in Sion!" He winked and nodded his head, eager to get back home and begin composing the letter.

Meantime, in Champéry, Mr. Marclay was seeing some of the men of the village and discussing our coming for these services, and they all seemed agreed that it was the thing to do, though they knew others would be "mad" about it. While at the same time we wrote to another city entirely, asking permission to once more use the church building as before. The President of the "Committee" who has charge of this building was sick in bed when he received our letter, hence his wife just sent it on to the man in Champéry who has the key and takes care of the repair work, etc. When this man received our request, he became afraid to send us the key, and went instead to the village President asking, "Do you want the Schaeffers to come back for a service?" To which the President replied, "No—no, I would consider it an act of revenge if they came back." He, you see, is the man who instigated the action against us, and who also circulated the story that we were "spies" and so on! He is the one most furious about our being permitted to remain in Switzerland. Certainly he did not want us to have the complete victory of having services once more in that church.

But the Lord's plan kept unfolding. The president next received a letter from Sion enclosing Pastor Spiros's well-written letter. Sion was advising that we be allowed to have the services! The president took these things to the village priest trying to stir up a strong protest against our being allowed to come. The priest shrugged his black-robed shoulders and said, "I wash my hands of the Schaeffers. I have had enough trouble because of them. Too many people like them here—I'll do nothing about it." He then took it to the village Council of Seven and argued his cause. Mr. Exhenry is on the Council of Seven, and naturally he was eager for us to come for the service, but he knew his own salvation was the root of all feeling against us, so he left the room when a discussion started. With him *out* of the room, some of the conversation was reported to us to have gone like this: "The Schaeffers shouldn't have been put out in the first place." President: "Oh you men! Why don't you buy a chalet for them and move them back here?" (with great sarcasm). The village judge replied, "It's too late for that, though it is a good idea; they already have bought a very nice chalet in Huemoz and are established there." The final result was that the Council voted almost unanimously to have us come back for services New Year's Eve, New Year's Sunday, and to live in the village for a week if we cared to. The Lord has done the "impossible" in an "impossibly" short time, and the chapel was not to be dark and closed a single season! The services started in 1949 were not to skip a single "season" in spite of our being "thrown out"!—such a dancing around, hugging each other, and pinching each other to be sure we were awake, as took place in our family! You can imagine the children's excitement. The only cloud over it all was the fact that Susan could not come with us—she was back in bed again with another attack of rheumatic fever.

The morning of the 31st of December, we all piled into the VW station-wagon taxi (which is the cheapest way for a group of more than four people to go from here to Champéry), full of excitement as we contemplated the absolute wonder of what God had done in opening the way to go back. We arrived to find the church full of smoke (familiar sight in winter) and the janitress madly rushing around opening windows to let out smoke and let in icy air, kicking the draft open and shut by turns, and stuffing briquettes in the stove to see whether they might not make less smoke! Karl Woodson was with us, and we enjoyed the opportunity of showing him Champéry. Madame Marclay excitedly met us at the church and showed us the pile of evergreen branches and trees ready for decoration, and assured us she was coming back in the afternoon to bring us a "four o'clock" (a pail of tea and a loaf of bread), kissed us all around twice, and hastened us on our way to Tea Room Berra for a soup and bread and cheese lunch, guiding us importantly down the village street! We met Mr. K. (proprietor of one of the hotels) on our way and he was very cordial, telling us that he expected a group of 42 English the following week and was going to write Sion himself requesting that we have a service for them! He backed off down the snowy street bowing his goodbye and saying that our being put out had been Champéry's loss. . . .

By five o'clock the church was trimmed, the smoke was almost all out, and the fire was burning without making much impression on the cold air, though the candle flames gave an illusion of warmth. Karl stood at the back to give out hymn sheets, Debby and Dorothy lighted candles, and Priscilla sat ready to play the pump organ as people began filing in. You can imagine what a deeply emotional time it was for us to watch these English high-school-age young people come in groups, professors with them; some families coming as units; and some French-speaking people scattered among them. By the time the last person had slipped in during the first carol, there were about 175 people there, much to Madame Marclay's satisfaction as she poked her head in and out of the curtains at the back, peering around to see everyone. "I want to see Mr. Schaeffer standing and preaching in that pulpit again, but I won't sit down; I can stay back here." Although she has studied the Bible with us at family prayers for a long time, she had never been in a Protestant service before. Some of the amazed wonder at what God had done in giving this victory could be seen in the expression on Mr. Exhenry's face, and could be heard in Fran's voice as he preached the gospel that hour. Truly it was a Red Sea experience for us all.* This God is our tender Father— why should any of us fear what man or circumstances can do to us. . . .

The "in-between-days" when no one but the family is here, and when we can "catch up" on housework and correspondence, are becoming very few and far between, but we must not complain, for the Lord is sending them! The weekends are full with University students and the

*See Exodus 14.

*Fran always gives full attention to each individual in the
constant flow.*

American [military] fellows stationed in Germany come at any time their "leaves" or "passes" permit them to come—we never know just when one will be standing on our doorstep. Some of these boys are Christians seeking a spiritual shelter for some refreshing days, and some are unsaved brought by a Christian friend—with a hope that the Lord will use it to one day draw them to Himself. . . .

December 26th we had our traditional family day of gift opening and being together around the tree, before a blazing fire. Fran carried Susan down and enthroned her upon a couch so that it was almost as good as being up. Franky added much hilarity to the occasion by his reactions and remarks—"Just what I've been waiting for all my life," he said feelingly as he opened some overalls and shirts. "That's just what I needed," he declared loudly as he opened woolen stockings and pants knitted in one piece. We all had to stop to be jabbed and have our hearts listened to when he discovered that he was the owner of a doctor's set, and there were many intermissions—one every time a toy emerged from its wrappings. Packages from America brought us close to those who had sent them, and started a flow of reminiscences. We were just ourselves, and Dorothy. Dorothy is just four years older than Priscilla so fits in as an older sister—since the other girls are also four years apart! The day went all too quickly and it was time to go upstairs to the kitchen and dining room to begin dinner preparations. Karl Woodson and his friend Jack arrived in time to sit down to an eight o'clock dinner (Franky had had his earlier and was fast asleep), and naturally our conversation took us back to St. Louis! After family prayers and dishes were done, we relaxed and worshiped as we listened to the full "Messiah" which Karl had brought us. . . .

February blew in with the coldest weather most of Europe has had for this century. In spite of the furnace, it was impossible to keep the chalet warm—except for the area around the fireplace. I say "was"—it should be "is"—because the "cold spell" is still here. Finding enough covers to keep people warm at night—and hot-water bottles enough to go around, becomes a problem with our large "family." Without the fireplace it would be too uncomfortable to sit and talk—so we do praise the Lord that we have it—and of course the furnace! We have suffered one "casualty" from the cold—some pipes froze on one side of the house, meaning that for present the water has had to be shut off on that side. We discovered it when we heard the noise of running water one afternoon when the sun came out. It seems the sun had thawed out the frozen pipe enough to let the water run through the break that had appeared in it—and water was pouring through a wall—partly going outside the house, and partly running through a bookcase and out over the living room floor! I'm afraid that means a repair job of some considerable size in the summer, but the house is the Lord's and He knows all about that too! Many houses have had frozen pipes in this unusual cold.

One blustery night in January the doorbell rang and when we opened the door, in stepped two strangers who said they had been sent by a young Swiss Christian who knows us. They turned out to be professors at a private boarding school in Villars, and they are both Christian. Some time ago they started a Bible class on Tuesday nights in the apartment of one of them. Another professor attends and a handful of other people connected with other schools in that section. They had come to invite us. Our first evening with them proved to be one of sweet fellowship for us, and we felt they needed encouragement and help. Hence we invited them to meet in our home the next Tuesday. Now it is a regular thing—every other Tuesday they meet here, and in between time, up in Villars. They look to Fran to help with the teaching, and all have expressed their appreciation of what that means to them. . . .

The first week in February we had Byram, a Christian from Virginia, and Howie, an atheist from Baltimore, with the addition of Evelyn for the weekend. Then on Friday, the 10th, the weekend "crowd" arrived. We really didn't have enough blankets to keep everyone warm that time because it was unusually cold—and there were so many! There were John, Murray, Dan, Peter, and Alex, as well as Margaret, one of our English girls. At the same time M. and Madame Czerny came for the first time in some months—and they were thrilled to be able to be a part of one of the University weekends at L'Abri for which they had been praying. There was quite a bit of German spoken around the table, for Madame Czerny is German-Swiss, and as a Czechoslovakian, M. Czerny speaks German also. I say "table" but, with 17 in our family to feed that weekend, it took two tables. The big table holds ten, a smaller table can squeeze five in without much elbow space, and Franky and Alice ate in Franky's bedroom.

Space becomes a bit of a problem—but thus far we have managed—and if the Lord wants to send more than there is room for in Chalet les

Mélèzes—He will add either another chalet, or a small guest house on this property—do pray, for He alone knows what is His will for L'Abri. We dare not have plans of our own.

Can you wonder that as we look back to last February, and then look around us these days, it seems like a miracle? These are young people He is bringing, to a place He chose and prepared, to be taught His Word by servants He has placed here, fed physically and spiritually by His supply of "manna." His promises are enough, for He is real.

Thank you dear family, for your intercession for us over the past year. Oh that we might know more oneness, we who are really one in Christ, as we commune more and more with Him, "without ceasing" in these short years He has given us before we see Him face to face.

With much love,

EDITH

March 22, 1956   Huemoz sur Ollon, Switzerland

Dear Family:

Here I sit writing to you beside a side window overlooking the lake— and giving a good view of the French Savoyan Alps as well as our own beloved range of Swiss Alps beyond the end of the Lake. Well, the Lord (in answer to prayer for some needed extra hours of sleep and quiet to do office work) provided us with the use of an apartment in Lausanne equipped with a maid to cook for us for a few days this week! How marvelous are the plans of our loving Father as He bends to answer the requests we make known unto Him. Fran and I have been able to get about 80 letters out, and this afternoon, as he goes to Geneva to teach, I hope to tell you the story of the past amazing month. Dorothy and Priscilla are holding the fort at L'Abri caring for the household and the one girl who will be there for three weeks. Tomorrow we will return.

Early in November L'Abri had begun to go down the mountain to Lausanne once a week, for the saved young people there became hungry for more spiritual food, and everyone could not be invited here every weekend. A back room in a restaurant, windowless because it is built into the hill upon which the cathedral and university are built, becomes the scene of an unusual Bible class from 11 A.M. to 2 P.M. every Thursday. A nucleus of five young people, born again at L'Abri, met the first week to study the Word together and to ask all the questions that had piled up in their minds during their personal Bible reading. Today fifteen young people sat munching their sandwich lunch in that back room, and among them were unsaved friends and new acquaintances of the original five plus some newly born-again ones. Amazing! In the shadow of a

European University with all its swirling intellectual currents of modern thought, in such a *brief* time, a Bible class—studying and asking questions for three whole hours with no singing, no entertainment, nothing except a live consideration of what the Bible has to say—has really more than tripled (for several were not able to attend today though they wanted to). From what country do they come? United States, Holland, Germany, England, Canada, Greece, Portugal—amazing? No more amazing than the power of the Holy Spirit Who has drawn them. It is a Bible class in which the Bible is given the opportunity to give the answers in all fields of human thought, as Fran sets no limits upon the asking of questions.

There was no lull at the finish of my last letter because even while I was writing it, two American fellows stationed at an Army headquarters in Baumholder, Germany, arrived for a part of their leave. A third one joined them Thursday of that week as they met in Lausanne and went together to the Bible class in the back room of Cafe Vieux Lausanne. Dorothy burst into the kitchen that evening with, "Oh, it was wonderful, I wish you could have been there." And then went on to describe the questions and trend of the study, and the quiet hush that came at the end when John Sandri closed in prayer—John, saved in November but already growing deep in understanding, who now feels the Lord has called him into full-time service. All twenty-two young heads remained bowed for some minutes after that prayer—one agnostic girl remarked, "Why, it seemed as though we were standing right in the presence of God—I never have seen anything like it in my life before."

The next day Barbara came home with Priscilla for the weekend. Barbara, who is living in Lausanne in *this* apartment with her mother, came to Switzerland for her health. Her brother is in a boarding school in Switzerland; her sister in college in the States. Her father's business takes him constantly around the world, so it makes little difference where Barbara and her mother live. Barbara's difficulty is physical—but one weekend at L'Abri made her come to a decision which she declared to her mother upon return: "I'm not going to that psychiatrist to see why I don't eat any longer. I'm going back to L'Abri to study the Bible. I think God can help me." She is there right now, staying for three weeks. Her mother insisted that we use their apartment for a few days' rest while she was in London with her husband. And that is the story of how we happen to be here! But do pray for this girl—she is looking longingly at Christianity. "I want to believe soon," she says. But she has not yet accepted Christ, for "I do not understand how He can be God—and I know I cannot be saved until I believe that as a fact." The Holy Spirit can direct our words as we talk with her—and more wonderful even—He can open the eyes of her understanding. Pray for her, and for her family to be touched through her. . . .

March 8th was the last Thursday class at the University of Lausanne until after the long spring vacation. Some of the young people have gone on the University trip to Egypt, and others have gone home, but they will be coming back at various times, and some will start to arrive at L'Abri early in April. That last Thursday Evelyn came home with me for the weekend, and on Friday four others arrived. Jürgen, a German boy sent to us from Germany by Bob Rayburn, arrived that same weekend—so we had quite a variety of nations once more!

Two were Dutch girls who have been friends for years. Justine is an agnostic, with a wide variety of interests. Art is one of the interests of her family, and she very matter-of-factly told us of her uncle's large collection containing several Rembrandt originals. In spite of all the interests and the material means to follow them so thoroughly, Justine doesn't see any *"purpose"* in life and is most anxious to listen to just what we do believe that makes the difference. Annette and she have shared ideas for years, but Annette was in the church as a "liberal"—which didn't separate them too much in their conclusions. The long walk on the Pannex road brought no decision; the talks in the evenings ended without the needed understanding, but as the other young people gathered to pray together for these two, a sweet fellowship resulted for them. Then Sunday after the morning church service, Fran saw Annette standing, waiting, and went to speak to her. Very simply she sat down, folded her hands in an attitude of prayer, and said, "Mr. Schaeffer, I am ready to trust Jesus now," and closing her eyes she thanked Jesus for what He had done for her. Again we thrilled to see the work of the Holy Spirit—as the wind blowing through the trees bends the branches, so hearts are bent by Him.

We had quite a lot of "overlapping visits" that week. Jürgen stayed until Tuesday; Madame Marclay came to sew with me from Monday till Wednesday (that meant I had to sew and stay with her to talk while we sewed). A lot was accomplished, though office work suffered. Bill from Tacoma arrived Wednesday morning, full of many questions which have arisen in his faithful witnessing at the Army headquarters. Barbara arrived on Tuesday to stay three weeks. Then Saturday, Liselotte, a Swiss-German girl who has been attending the class, arrived for the weekend. In the midst of this came Thursday, when we had to go to Geneva to talk with one of the mistresses at the boarding school there, and to have the usual time in Geneva with the young people. This mistress was disturbed because of Anne's decision to stop going to church and so on. She told us that each young person must obtain special permission in a letter written by their parents before they can come to L'Abri for a weekend.

As we met with the young people, we found an intense interest. A new boy, Roger, was incredulous about L'Abri—"You mean you have a place where young people can just come and *stay* and ask questions? Boy, I always thought there should be a place like that, and it seems wonderful to know that there *is!* I can get a cable (parental permission) back from my home in 24 hours. I'm sure I can come; I've got so many questions." He is agnostic, but has such a wistful yearning as he tells you he is "searching for the answers to life" that you want him on your prayer list. Then Anne told the amazing story that two other girls had come separately to her room at the school and said, "I believe Mr. Schaeffer is telling us the truth," and after reading John 3, each one accepted Christ there in Anne's room. No space to describe these other young people, but pray for these 16-, 17-, and 18-year-olds who come from a variety of backgrounds as Americans living in other countries. The Spirit is doing a work there. . . .

Before I close, I want to answer one question some of you have been asking: "What is the charge for board and room at L'Abri?" L'Abri makes no charge whatsoever, and accepts no money from anyone for board and room. People are invited as to our family—and no mention is made of money. WE PRAY VERY SPECIFICALLY THAT THE LORD WILL BRING THE ONES *HE* WANTS, AND ALSO THAT HE WILL KEEP ANYONE AWAY WHOM HE WOULD *NOT* HAVE. We are trusting the Lord to bring only the ones He wants to send us, and trusting Him to send in enough money to feed them and enough strength to do the necessary work to make them comfortable. It is an experiment and demonstration of the *reality* of the leading of the Holy Spirit both in the choosing and sending of the souls He would have us deal with, and in touching hearts to give toward the material needs. L'Abri is committed in faith to the belief that the Holy Spirit will lead in practical matters. Will you pray with us in all this?

Thank you for your loving concern and prayer for this portion of the Lord's work.

Much love in Him in Whom we are one family,

EDITH

June 15, 1956   Huemoz sur Ollon, Switzerland

Dear Family:

How infinite and powerful is our Father as He weaves the pattern of lives which are to be a part of the Body of Christ. . . . How finite we are, and how we fail to accomplish that which we should like to do day by day as the hours speed by. Against this background, what can there be more important than intercessory prayer, which is not only commanded by the Lord, but given as a way of breaking through the limits of our finite *limitedness.* . . .

To catch up, I must go back to March when Barbara was still with us. Saturday night by the fireplace, Roger, with sparkling dark eyes and sensitive expressive face, brought many questions from the gospel of

John he had been reading. As the Word of God was unfolded, the Holy Spirit made it crystal clear to Roger, and as excitedly as any explorer finding a new country, he cried out late that night: "Oh I understand it all! It fits together like a jigsaw puzzle! Oh it's wonderful!" Howie was a sad contrast, for at the end of the evening he said, "I feel *almost* as though I could believe all this—but I don't." The next morning as we were sitting in the living room waiting for the church service to begin, Roger and Fran did not appear for a time—then came in with glowing faces. Roger had sought out Fran upstairs, saying, "You know this morning I settled it with the Lord in my bedroom. At first I asked Him for a sign that it was all true—then suddenly I thought, 'Why should He give me any special sign? He *has* given me the Bible,' and I thanked Him right then for sending Jesus to die for me." . . .

Two days later when we banged on the cowbells to announce that supper was served, Barbara called out, "Go on without me—I'll be there in a minute." When Barbara came in, it was almost time for dessert and a nicely iced cake was on the table. Just at that moment Franky padded in in his plastic-footed pajamas saying, "Let's sing happy birthday to somebody for that cake—let's sing happy birthday Barbara." We started the song for Franky, and for fun, heartily singing "Happy Birthday, dear Barbara"—but noticed a quality in Barbara's smile and pleasure that seemed all out of proportion to the little "fun" song. Barbara said, "You see, it *is* my birthday—I was born again today—Franky was right." Barbara's problem had been a desire to *understand* the Trinity before she could accept Christ as her Savior. But that evening the Holy Spirit had convinced her, and she suddenly saw that she did not need to wait to *understand* the Trinity, she needed to accept in faith what the Bible teaches. . . .

A telegram signed "Jane" informed us that two friends of a missionary in Italy would be arriving to stay over Easter weekend. I took Debby for a walk to Villars that Saturday afternoon to go marketing in order to give her a bit of an outing. When we stepped into the house out of a thick fog, Priscilla met us in the hall whispering, "They're here—and guess what? They're *opera* singers—go on down and meet them." Big, tall Jane, a dramatic soprano with a good-natured, hearty enthusiasm about many things, sat by the fireplace warming up. "This is Anita," she said, pointing to a tiny person. "She's a coloraturo soprano." Fran began conversations with them that afternoon while I was cooking, and in the evening I sat by the fire telling the whole story of our being put out of Switzerland, the Lord's victory over that edict, the miracle of our being provided this house, and the beginning of L'Abri. We all loved Jane, whose energy and interest knew no bounds. She helped wash dishes, read to Franky, talked with Susan, and enthused over the village and the woods. Her optimism had evidently made her feel that all religions were good and that the world was really on its way to getting better. However, she listened with increasing soberness to the teaching of the

Priscilla visiting Susan during her life in bed. Priscilla's room is across the hall.

Word, and the exclusiveness of the message of Jesus—"I am *the* door—I am *the* way, *the* truth, and *the* life; no man cometh to the Father but by me."

Easter Sunday we had a lovely service and a nice family dinner together with the table decorated with spring wildflowers. Susan had been going outdoors a little bit every day, and that afternoon she was in the garden taking some snapshots of Franky when she felt suddenly "all in" and felt a pressure on her chest, and a breathlessness. She went to bed directly and said she also felt some slight joint pains. The doctor was "busy" and did not come for two days, but when he came, he stated that Susan had had another attack of rheumatic fever, and that this time she had leaky valves in her heart. He carefully explained what that meant, and then said that she would have to live a very quiet life—in bed half of every day for at *least* three years, with *no* activity! It was a blow to receive just at springtime, when the outdoors was so inviting, and the thought of three whole years was a heartache to the whole family. How did Susan take it? So calmly it seemed she was a bit deaf! She began to live a full life in bed, as soon as she got over about a week of real fatigue which called for just lying there and resting. Not only did she do her Calvert Course on the new adjustable bed-table we got her, but she went ahead by leaps and bounds with her new hobby, Braille. She had sent for a Braille copy of a children's magazine and by comparing the Braille with the written page of the same magazine, she taught herself to read. Next she sent for a Braille copy of Luke and John, and Christian leaflets. After learning to read, she wrote to several places until she located a Braille slate and the special paper and punch that you write with. The next thing we found was that Susan was actually transcribing my articles on L'Abri into Braille! Then she found a Braille "pen-pal" by writing to the Philadelphia School of the Blind! It was all very exciting to Susan, and anyone who went up expecting to visit a depressed girl came down amazed at the enthusiasm they had found, plus having been helped in conversation, for the Lord used Susan to be helpful to the young people who visited her.

*Debby in her tiny room just around the
corner from Susan.*

Jane and Anita were going to leave Monday afternoon, but Jane went for a walk with Fran to talk over spiritual things, and something happened on that walk that made her put aside her plans to go back until the next day. We did not know what had happened to Jane until we received a letter from her from Milan a few days later. "You must have been somewhat taken aback when you received my telegram on Wednesday, but not nearly so amazed as myself! When Georgia spoke of you in our Bible class and mentioned a possibility of a visit, I was the *least* interested and later said quite flatly that I'd never find the time for such a thing. Now I am perfectly certain I was led to L'Abri by a power quite outside myself which now I am able to believe was the Holy Spirit leading me forward in God's plan for my life, just as it was right that I miss the bus and have the few remaining hours necessary for me to accept Jesus Christ as my Savior. Indeed I feel that the power of Christ's Spirit has opened my blinded eyes to the true light. You, dear Dr. and Mrs. Schaeffer, have quietly and simply shown me the pathway I have been searching for for so long. I regretted to leave without signing the guest book, but I had such a deep spiritual experience that it was not possible to find my own words to thank you. Luke 18:41–43."

John Sandri arrived Monday night for two weeks of Easter vacation Bible study, just in time to help pull up the old linoleum from the hall and to scrape and scrape the floor in preparation for the new to be put down the next day! That was a hilarious evening as we had to put the hall wood stove into Dorothy's room, a cabinet into the bathroom, and walk on boards stretched from doorsill to doorsill. Three army men arrived from the base in Baumholder the next day, and that was the day

Jane and Anita missed the bus, so we had to shift Dorothy upstairs into Priscilla's room and put Jane and Anita in the double-decker beds in Dorothy's room, with the four boys filling the four-bed room. All four boys were Christian and Fran started a study on the Holy Spirit with them, sitting at the table after breakfast and continuing the study until lunchtime! The afternoons were spent in the garden as the four boys divided the work—digging the vegetable garden and "turning under" the manure, raking and cleaning up the rest of the garden, and chopping old branches trimmed from our trees. It was fun to watch from the kitchen window while we were cooking or washing dishes (Dorothy and I) to see the boys working away while their voices rang out in harmony on hymns and choruses. . . .

Rachel, the owner of Chalet Bijou, our old chalet in Champéry, came over during the Bible study time. It was a bit difficult to fit in her housecleaning with all the cooking, but there never is a "free stretch" of time (by the way, in three months we have had only *one day* without visitors!), so it was necessary not to put it off. Rachel still has an interest in the Bible study.

Bill left one day, Roger a couple of days later—then three more students arrived. They got in for some of the studies on prayer, and Fran gave them a complete study on the Bible—that is, what the Old Testament claims for itself and what the New claims for the Old—as well as the devotional times at family prayers, and a study on "Guidance." John had to leave (after over two weeks here), then three others arrived to join the first group. Do you see what the Lord did? Instead of sending sixteen young people for ten days, as we had at first expected, He spread them out over three weeks, so that we never had more than seven at a time, which made it easier to cook, provide beds, and serve meals. How foolish we are to worry ahead of time when we place our "times" in His hands! . . .

You know that for a long time we have been having a class Tuesday evenings for Bible study in French and English with some teachers in various nearby boarding schools. The sister of the director of Beau Soleil, one of these schools, comes to these evening classes. The result was that the director called us to propose that we teach the Bible to her English-speaking children—this is a wonderful opportunity. Each Tuesday afternoon now, at 2:30, a station-wagon pulls into the driveway emptying out a group of English and American children for a Children for Christ class in the living room of Chalet les Mélèzes. It is a joy to be teaching children once more, and what a thrill to be giving the gospel to such a *variety* of children. We have an English boy whose father is the biggest movie producer in England, a Jewish boy from New York City, two sweet youngsters from Atlanta, Georgia, a girl whose father is in the American Air Force in Morocco, a boy from Main Line Philadelphia whose mother is a writer, a boy from London—and so on. Just this afternoon as I was writing, the movie producer's son,

Shawn, came to see me privately. I made a fire—for it is a rainy cold day—and talked to him for over two hours, trying to make clear to him the answer to his question: "Why did Jesus have to die—why couldn't He have just kept on living and living and teaching everyone through all the years?" After we went through much of the Bible together, Shawn said he understood—and he accepted Christ as his Savior right then and there. Pray for him as he leaves in two weeks. . . .

A lovely, clear, sunny Sunday brought two girls from Aldan, Pennsylvania, for a brief overnight visit. We had a beautiful afternoon walk above Chalet les Sapins winding up the tiny path that zig-zags up the sharp hill behind it. High in the woods is a place where the Christians who built that place made a deep grass bench which they called their "tea spot," climbing up with a Thermos bottle and cups for their daily tea on nice days! There we sat, gazing at the breathtaking view of mountain peaks and wide Rhône valley—dreaming of all the possibilities of Chalet les Sapins if the Lord has it in His plan for L'Abri. Please do pray with us about this place. The present owner, the daughter of those dear Christian people whose library we are now sharing with the young people, has just arrived for the month of June, to take out personal possessions and to try to "really sell it and get things settled this time." She wistfully talks of her parents' love of the Lord and their desire to have the chalet used for Him. "I don't even know what to do with my Father's Bible—he spent 30 years putting careful notes in it on pages he had bound in between the printed pages—you see, no one in our family would appreciate it." The one offer she has for the house is from a Roman Catholic family who want to make it into a Roman Catholic children's home. It will be sold with all its furnishings, dishes, sheets and towels, and kitchen utensils—ready for use—for about $17,000, which means a payment in cash of $7,000 with $10,000 mortgage being given from the bank. "Can't you use it for your work of L'Abri? That seems so appropriate for my father and mother's beloved chalet." "We can't make decisions ourselves," I replied. "We are praying about it, and if the Lord wants it for L'Abri—if He knows that we need it to expand and to bring more people here for Bible study, then He will give us a clear sign." "How?"—I then told her the story of how He led us to buy Chalet les Mélèzes, and finally said, "He will put a burden on some one person's heart—or a number of people's hearts— to supply the down payment; then we will know that He is speaking. Otherwise, we don't want it, you see? We couldn't take the responsibility of borrowing or doing it in another way." We can see her as we pass by, shaking out rugs, preparing the place to leave it forever, and we know she is wondering. Won't you pray that the Lord will make clear His guidance and *time* His leading so that it will bring glory to Himself? He *is* pleased to have us *trust* Him, and to pray *believing* that He can "remove mountains."

Hours whizzed by during the weekend of May 11th to 13th, and it was tantalizing to have Betty Carlson here without enough time to really talk together for a long period. She is traveling through Europe with two Christian friends. . . .

Karl Woodson arrived a bit later and that night we had the Tuesday night Bible class. Wednesday Karl went with us to Lausanne where we stayed overnight so he could go to the Thursday Bible class at the Cafe. Friday Anita came from Milan bringing an atheistic English opera singer, an Italian building contractor, and his English wife. This opening among these people is really fantastic. That weekend the four asked questions and studied the Bible with scarcely a break. Fran was exhausted at the end, but we stand amazed at the letters we have had from each of these as they *continue* studying the Bible and want to return with friends! On June 26th we are to go to Milan to have an evening with them again, and they say, "This time the room won't hold them, for everyone intends to bring a friend and come back." Keep praying—the Lord's way of bringing the good news to lost souls in various walks of life is astounding!

Monday, June 4th, I had to go to Geneva to renew my passport. At 2 P.M. I met Susan in the heart specialist's office in Lausanne, where she had been brought by a hired car, Alice and Franky accompanying her. Dr. Rivier listened intently to the whole story and gave Susan a thorough examination—fluoroscope, electrocardiogram, and a thorough "listening," with blood pressure, etc. "I have good news for you, Madame Schaeffer. I cannot find any leakage in the valves which the other doctor has reported. I find Susan's heart small (good sign) and the valves are closing properly. She has a functional murmur, and signs of a "nervous heart," but these are only minor things and should *not* restrict her in any way. Susan may now gradually return to full activity—don't try to climb the Dents du Midi tomorrow, Susan," he said laughingly, "but you *will* be doing it again, and skiing too!" Is it a miracle? or did the first doctor make a mistake? From the way Susan was feeling until just a few days *before* Dr. Rivier examined her, when suddenly she said, "I feel like climbing mountains," we are inclined to think it *was* a miracle. *But* whether a miracle of healing in answer to prayer, or a doctor's mistake, we think the Lord has answered prayer in a wonderful way. The experience of the last months is a spiritual one we would not exchange for ourselves, nor for Susan. The Lord has been "trying" us in that special "fire"—and we thank Him for it. Susan still needs prayer that she may be kept from further attacks. Another answer to prayer has come for Franky in that a way has opened up for Priscilla to take him to the beach at Alassio to live with an Italian doctor's family in exchange for our having the doctor's son with us for a month. Pray that we may all join them in Alassio in September. Pray too for Franky as we are soon to take him to an American orthopedic specialist in Frankfurt, Germany, to see whether he needs a leg brace.

I must stop short of my story this time as it will not all fit in. Next letter will follow in a month, Lord willing, and I will begin with the weekend we had two Jewish atheistic medical school students in Lausanne, a Buddhist Japanese boy from Hawaii, and six others in one weekend! Do keep praying for spiritual and physical strength and for the Lord's supply of all material needs. We must keep our eyes on Him as our own strength is only weakness—and our own faith would fill in the accomplishing of all that is before us. *Only He is able to do all things.*

Much love from us all,

EDITH

July 31, 1956   Huemoz sur Ollon, Switzerland

Dear Family:

So many of you ask, "How do you find the time to write the Family Letters?" The answer would be different for each letter written—as the Lord provides the time. Today Susan and Debby took Franky to the doctor in Villars (Franky slipped and fell from a counter in the kitchen where he was foraging for something to eat—the gash in the back of his head required doctor's care, but *this* time the doctor simply has to change the bandage), saving me a couple of hours, and then they are taking him on up to Bretaye for a day similar to Heidi's in the high Alps—eating a picnic lunch in the fields where goats graze. Priscilla is preparing lunch for the Dutch family and the others here at this time—and I am free to stay in my room until this account of the past weeks has been written—they'll bring me a tray! Fran is in Milan for three days teaching the Bible class, and having a steady stream of private conversations. Brigetta is hanging out sheets in the sunshine and getting ready for the next batch of visitors, and Alice is sweeping and scrubbing the garden dirt out of the rooms and halls! Everyone cooperates in a special way the day the "long letter" is being written, so everyone here has a part in getting it off to you. Brigetta is a German schoolteacher who escaped from the Russian zone, and who is now waiting for the Lord's leading as to His choice for her future work. Anne and Mary invited her to stay with them in Chalet Argentine for a time so that she could help us, and the Lord timed her coming to be immediately after Dr. Jennifer had to leave. Isn't the Lord wonderful?

With 187 guests in July—and the last half of June to tell you about—it would be easier to have you drop in so that I could just *talk* to you about all the new plants springing forth from the sown seed, some buds opening up more rapidly than others, as they grow in the light of His presence....

Going back to the weekend of June 10th—the group that circled the fireplace munching on hot dogs in firelight and candlelight (it was too cold to be outdoors) came from many parts of the States. . . . All were Americans that weekend—all from different backgrounds, but all brought here by the Lord to consider the Word of God together. Roy left saying that he had been faced with things he had never considered before, and would like to come back. Two others left armed with the Bible studies promising to study them in New York this summer and to come back to L'Abri in the fall with further questions. One of them said that he hoped that in the future everything he had heard was going to *mean* something very personal to *him*. Do pray that both of them may know Christ as the Messiah before the next school year ends. Alvin is a concert pianist—so during in-between moments, he filled the house with beautiful music.

That Monday, the visitors' sheets flapping on the clothesline numbered 18—and the family sheets had to be washed another day! Ten sheets had to be dry and back on the beds for the family of four who came for a time of fellowship on their way home from India, and for a college boy on his way home from an archaeological expedition in Palestine. Our times for conversation were brief—for during those two full days we had an afternoon Bible class for children, the usual Tuesday evening Bible class in French and English—and other pressing work to attend to. . . .

Friday afternoon an Italian Vespa putt-putted up to the gate, paused while its rider dismounted, opened the gate, and then got back on, and finally putt-putted up to the living room door. Lucca had arrived! He pulled off his grey motorcycle helmet, his big driving gloves, and stuck out a hand to shake, his white teeth gleaming in a wide smile, his crew-cut hair bobbing with a polite Italian bow. He then presented us with two jars of honey "make by my mother's bzzzzz" he said—not knowing the word for bees. Our graphic conversations had started as for the next month we would both listen to, and use, all sorts of picturesque speech, trying to make ourselves understood by Lucca! He came in an answer to prayer for a way to have Franky get a long time on the beach, and to swim in warm, salt water. Lucca's father is the doctor in Alassio whom we called for Priscilla's illness there five years ago, and Lucca's family have asked to have Franky and Pris stay with them in exchange for the opportunity for Lucca to spend a month in the Alps, and learn to speak some English. He really was no trouble at all, and very polite and considerate during the whole month. When he was here, he tried to understand the spiritual conversations, and during the weekends when we had Italian-speaking guests, much was translated for him. "It is so nice here—so full of nice happiness and friendliness and love—I think your religion must be better than other ones." At first he refused to read a Bible! "It is a sin for us to read the Bible." But later, he began to read, very curious and anxious to know just what was so interesting to the other young people. As Murray, John, and others talked to him of what the Lord Jesus means to them, and of the difference of being just a "Protestant" (which they told him they were before)—and a "born-again Christian"—his interest grew. . . .

Fran and I planned to meet Priscilla in Lausanne Monday evening for a birthday dinner. The peas had to be tied up that afternoon, so after searching in the woods for proper sticks, poking them in the ground, and tying the pea vines to them, we had only 15 minutes to wash off the mud and run for the bus! It was a treat to have a quiet supper in a restaurant with no dishes to think about, so *I* celebrated that momentous moment 19 years ago too! We also were able to say "goodbye" to Dorothy in Lausanne as that was the day she left for her summer trip around Europe with her mother. Dorothy didn't say goodbye for long though, as she feels led to come back in late August for another year at L'Abri.

We returned the next morning giving me just a few hours to get myself and Franky ready for our trip to Germany. It was exciting to Franky to think of having Mommy all to himself for three days, and I must say I enjoyed being able to spend that time with him. We rode to Basel by train (a five-hour ride) and arrived at Anne and Mary's apartment for supper that night. Then at 6:00 A.M. the next day, we started out for Frankfurt. Anne and Mary had the day "off" from their hospital work, and had planned to drive us. It was so thoughtful of them and made the trip so much nicer for us. The doctor was very nice and very skilled. He said that we could not have done anything any sooner, which was most comforting. It takes time to know just what is needed in Franky's type of case. Right now Franky's left leg, which has no calf muscles at all, is one-fourth inch shorter than the right one, and the bones in the foot and ankle are somewhat deformed. If he continued to walk without a brace there would be danger of curvature of the spine, for he was walking more and more on the inside of the ankle. The brace, the doctor said, will cause him to turn his foot the other way and the raised shoe will keep his back in a straight position.

On our way home the next day we had a few hours in the Basel Zoo, which made whole the trip "fun." The making of a cast of his leg worried him for a few moments but the sharp-looking knife that cut it off simply fascinated him, and he loved seeing the other "legs" hanging on the wall there. "Will he hang my leg up too?" It's a good thing he liked the whole experience, because he will have to return regularly for check-ups. The Lord's hand was seen in arranging this trip at a time when Lucca was the *only* L'Abri guest, and Susan was well enough to cook meals!

Fran met us in Lausanne, coming from his last class for the University group. Since exams had begun, only the Christians had made the effort to come, so they ended the meeting with a real prayer time, praying straight around the circle. When the class started in the fall, there were only three Christians. This last class consisted of 15 young people leading in prayer and not all the Christians were there. . . .

It's fun to wait for the 8 o'clock morning bus, especially on a sunny spring or summer day. Everything seems so fresh in the clear mountain air, and there is something special about the flowers in the early-morning light. I always like an excuse to go out, as I can examine my little rose garden to see if there are any new buds! This Tuesday morning (June 26th) Franky and I waved goodbye to Fran as he started off for Milan. He arrived in Milan a little after one in the afternoon, giving time for conversations before the class that evening. . . .

Five of the Milan students then made an arrangement to come up for the weekend. . . . They took an early-morning train (getting up at 5:00 A.M.) and then a taxi from Aigle up here, so that they could have as long a time to study the Bible as possible. . . . We served them a late breakfast out on the balcony and the conversation and Bible study started right then. When it was over, one girl followed Fran to the office and began to ask questions. The questions continued as he went out in the garden, and the others gathered around, sitting on the benches by the hot dog pit. I had some hoeing to do, and listened in praying and rejoicing as I hoed, first the rows of cabbages, and then the beans. The conversation continued through lunch, and family prayers just led to more questions and study. It seemed unbelievable, but the whole afternoon was spent in study, and Barbara only left it once to run in for pencils and paper to take notes!

At the hot dog roast that Saturday night, out under a starry sky, the family, the five from Milan, and Dr. Jennifer, Lucca, and John Sandri (from Lausanne) composed those staying at L'Abri, but we were also joined by the ones staying at Chalet Argentine (rented by Anne and Mary for the summer). The Lord gave a real blessing at the Bible study around the dying embers. And afterwards English John, an opera singer, and Dino went for a walk with Fran, while John Sandri, Priscilla, Jennifer, and I did dishes. . . .

We heard wonderful reports from Milan right after that weekend— truly there is a little revival going on there. Such changed lives have brought about much notice, and have stirred curiosity as to what has happened. John is so changed his friends are amazed—in things little and big. Old interests and old temptations have lost their attraction, and one is brought face to face with the reality of the new *birth*. Jane has told her friends, "You know, I feel so differently about things since I accepted Christ. For instance, I could always push and shove (and she is a tall, strong girl) as well as anyone in the Italian streetcars, but now, I find I don't want to push and shove anymore. I *want* to stand back and let someone else go first, and I'm just so *happy*." . . .

But I must hurry on—so *many* wonderful things happened these last weeks! The very day Doris and Anita left, Grace and her mother arrived for a few days. It was wonderful to have Grace back again and to know of her real interest. . . . While they were here, Madame Marclay came, after having long put it off, for two days of sewing and fellowship. "I need

*Lunch is served! You'll notice I managed to stop and eat for
a few moments while this picture was taken.*

help," she says, striking her chest. You can imagine the rush, trying to
cut out dresses, cook good meals, and serve them properly, talk to Madame Marclay on one hand, and have a few times of quiet talk with
Grace's mother on the other. Oh yes, Dan was with us too. He came at
that same time, and he stayed for two weeks. Dan became like one of the
family—making tea and entertaining people while we were busy, typing some letters, transplanting dozens of broccoli plants, spraying the
rose bushes, cutting the lawn. And with Dr. Jennifer to work on ironing,
dishwashing, peeling potatoes, we got lots of work done, but even then
we never finished all there was to do in a day! . . .

That afternoon Jennifer's three weeks came to an end, and after a farewell tea and the singing of her favorite hymn ("I Know Whom I Have
Believed") and prayer, Anne and Mary drove her down to Aigle for the
train, and Dan, Susan, Debby, and Franky went along. Franky wailed as
soon as the train pulled off, "I've got a scratch! Who's going to fix me
now that Dr. Jennifer's gone? Bring her back." We would all have liked
to have her come back.

The day after Jennifer left to return to Oxford, Hans Rookmaaker, the
Dutch art critic, and his family arrived with three children, six, three,
and two. They are staying for three weeks, as the distance was so great
and they do desire the spiritual help. That weekend we had 21 for meals!
It became almost impossible for me to do anything more than cooking—
though I longed to spend time in conversations. The folks at Chalet Argentine had three nurses for the weekend, and two lovely English missionary sisters had met for their furlough and were spending three
weeks next door! Hence, we had really a full room for church on Sundays, and for the evening Mr. Rookmaaker gave his lecture on Modern
Art and Christianity, and the next evening when the two ladies showed

slides of their work. One is from the Dohnavur Fellowship in India (Amy Carmichael's work) and the other is from Syria.

Are you feeling a little dizzy? My space is getting small and I want to crowd in the next few days! Friedrich and his sister left Sunday night, but Monday four others arrived to take their places!! And at 9 P.M. when we were *just* getting to the main course of dinner (I thought I'd never get the chiffon pies finished, having stopped too long to type letters in the afternoon), the front doorbell rang and Joe walked in. He hails from St. Louis, Missouri, and a girl he met on the boat told him about L'Abri and he had written asking if he could come!! Joe is also a towering 6'4", and big besides, and Dan is over 6' himself, so we had a problem deciding who was going to sleep on the short couch in the living room. Dorothy slept on a mattress on a bedroom floor those nights, and Evelyn bunked in with Priscilla. Every inch of L'Abri was used up. (We fed the four small children before other people ate—two sittings!)

Yes, it almost seemed like too many, but the Lord had His purpose, for us, and for each one who came. After having had Dorothy with us for a year, it was good to have her mother here to see the place, even though about the only time I was able to talk with her was the night she was packing, when we talked to each other until the wee hours. . . .

Yesterday was Monday, the 30th, our 2nd Annual Day of Fasting and Prayer for L'Abri Fellowship. Many of you were joining us in prayer yesterday. Fran prayed on the train, for he was on his way again to Milan for three days, and here at the chalet, Susan made a chart with the half-hours on it from 7 A.M. to 11 P.M. We each went and checked the half-hours we would take for prayer, placing our initials beside the time. The work of the day had to be carried on, but a continuous chain of prayer went on for those 16 hours. Priscilla, Susan, Debby, Evelyn, Mr. and Mrs. Rookmaaker, Justine, Anne, Mary, Brigitta, and I took part and the lady from Dohnavur took the first hour in the morning. We all felt that the day spent in the spirit of prayer, plus the uninterrupted half-hours we each took from time to time, helped us personally just as much as it could have helped the work of L'Abri—and we agree that we want to do it again soon.

Many of you have wanted to know about Franky's brace. It arrived after the Dutch children had come which, humanly looking at it, was too bad, for it meant too many adjustments all at one time. However, the Lord makes no mistakes, and He can show us how to care for the "frustrations." Franky opened it in our bedroom with just the family gathered. When the brown Dr. Posner shoe came out, followed by one for the left foot with a shiny chromium brace fastened into the sole extending up to below the knee with a thick leather strap to hold it in place, Franky's face fell. "I don't like the new brace"—and then as if to down the disappointment, he shouted, "Let's put it on—oh, isn't it shiny—let me see how it works!" and so on. He determinedly sticks it out to show people and acts proud of it before others, but whispers to me at times that he wishes he didn't have to wear it. It does make him fall more easily, and turning his foot the opposite way makes the bones ache. But he does not complain directly—it just at times comes out in rebellion in other ways. Pray that the time in Italy with Priscilla may be helpful to him, and that he may not be homesick. They will leave, Lord willing, in the middle of August, and we will all join them in September for a vacation which will be much needed by that time. . . .

Much love to you all and may He keep you in the hollow of His hand,

EDITH

October 11, 1956   Huemoz sur Ollon, Switzerland

Dear Family:

What a contrast met us as we stepped out of the taxi—"home again" after the vacation! We had summer clothes on, for we had just the day before left a sunny seaside where bathing was still a comfortable recreation, and here we stepped into *snow!* "It's winter, Mommy, it's winter here, isn't it?" shrilled Franky gleefully. We hoped it was just a freak storm, for under the various white mounds in the garden we still hoped to reap beans and cabbages, etc. The "weather" kept on for three days of intermittent storming, blowing, and just being grey. Then some gorgeously clear days came and we have had a contrast of scenes—winter sparkle of snow not far above us, reaching all the way up to the solid white peaks, and bright green all around us extending down into the mist-covered valley below. We have salvaged beans and cucumbers from frost-blackened plants, while Hurvey has been putting the garden, wood piles, and "caves" in order for the winter. . . .

You remember how lovely Chalet les Sapins seemed, and what a well-built, fine place it is—just five minutes up the road above us. It was so easy to walk around that place, and climb the lovely woodsy paths on the property and visualize it full of L'Abri guests, the Lord having provided a worker to help with all that would mean. We began to pray that the Lord would give this to L'Abri if it were His will. As the weeks went on a few gifts came designated "for providing more space," but not nearly enough came in to give an assurance that the Lord was leading us to make any move toward getting the chalet. Late in July we were told by the owner that a couple of people were interested in buying it, and that one person hoped to be able to buy it by August 15th. If the Lord wants it for L'Abri, we thought, He can bring in the needed money to show us that is His will; if not, we don't want it. It's so easy in human enthusiasm and with our own imaginations to think we "see" how things are going to shape up. It would have been so easy to simply think over this area, and knowing that the carpenter was right when he said it was the best buy in a chalet he knew of, to try to do something ourselves—to make promises on a "hope" that money would come in later. But, right there the *reality* of the Lord's ability to lead would have been put aside. Do we believe the Lord means it when He says in Scripture that He has a plan for His people? Do we trust Him to work all things together, to *know* ahead of time how long we have to make decisions on purchases and to bring the money in, in *time?* If we believe He can lead us today, in 1956, then we must let Him do it. There must be a little place where it shows up in a practical fashion that there is a difference between how we would act on our own wisdom and in "waiting upon the Lord" in prayer for His leading. All this we reminded ourselves of during those days in August when nothing came in to give us any leading to speak to the house owner, and on that day when she said to us, "Chalet les Sapins is sold, and the owners will be moving in on Friday." The answer had been "No." We were satisfied that it was *His* answer.

The sun was streaming into the cobblestone patio on the west side of the Chalet les Mélèzes one summer afternoon when Fran and I were walking around thinking of the need of extra sleeping space. "If that patio were enclosed you could put a double-decker bed in there," Fran said. "Maybe there'd be room for a sort of built-in daybed at one end, too," I added. "It would be more like a ship's cabin than a room, but let's measure the space." Fran ran off to get a piece of chalk and the measuring tape along with some big pieces of wrapping paper. Soon the floor was marked off into "space for the bed," "allowance for door into what would be the hall," and the paper was cut into "windows" which Lydia (my niece, Lydia Van Buskirk) and Debby obligingly held up while we squinted from across the garden—"It won't hurt the looks of the house, in fact, it might add to it." And so the idea of adding three more beds to this house took shape. Soon Mr. Dubi (the builder nearby) came to give an estimate of what this new room would cost. He brought a mason with him, who would be doing the foundation, cement block walls, a flagstone terrace (to replace the patio, giving a place for serving outdoor meals), and so on. A letter came just at that time—a letter from a member of the Praying Family who had already given a gift for providing more space in L'Abri, and the essence of the letter was that in praying a thought had come to her that a *room* might be *added* to Chalet les Mélèzes keeping all the young people under the same roof until the Lord would show that the time had come to increase the capacity in another way! We felt it was a seal of the Lord.

All this happened before Chalet les Sapins was sold. Before we went away for our vacation in September we talked with the mason, and as there was now enough money in the "enlarging L'Abri" fund to build a foundation, walls, etc., we ordered that much and told him he could begin work about October 9th. The Lord had sent us two new members for the L'Abri family, Hurvey and Lydia, and three extra beds would give us *just* enough space for one more at a time than we had when we had "full house" last winter. We knew we needed it, and it did seem the Lord was opening the way.

During vacation time we prayed very especially that the money would come in to finish the room, furnish it, fix up the old cellar kitchen as an attractive "wash room," make the flagstone terrace, repair some other things, and provide blankets and hot-water bottles (needed even last winter!) enough for keeping all 20 people warm at one time! We prayed that if this were the Lord's will for providing for those whom He would bring to us this winter, He would send the funds in *time* to get it done.

The mason and his helper were hard at work on the frosty morning of October 8th. Franky had a delightful time digging in the piles of dirt which were thrown up as the foundation work began, and at 10 A.M. we found him joining the other workmen for a cup of coffee (which they had brought from home). "Mr. Schaeffer," the boss said late the next afternoon, "if I can order all the stone for the whole job at one time, I can get a reduced price—have you decided yet?" We explained to him that L'Abri looked to the Lord for all the provision of its needs and that we could not order material until the money was in our hands to pay for it. At present there was enough for the foundation and the room, and that seemed the most important—the stone for the terrace and walk *could* wait. "But, monsieur—if freezing weather continues, the work outside will have to be put off until spring, and in a few days I must go to another outside job, *unless* you want the whole job done now." "We will pray about it, and let you know in a short time." That night Hurvey made a suggestion: "Why not order the stone to get the reduced price, and then let it stay in a pile until spring if the Lord does not send in the money before the decision has to be made, and let the workmen go on to their other job." As we thought and prayed over that, it was agreed that we should do this, *and* that we should call a day of prayer for the next day. . . .

Dorothy was in the prayer room praying for the needed funds when the mailgirl came. There was such a feeling of expectancy that there was quite a rush for the mail and—when the first paragraph of one letter was read, Fran gave a general call, "Come to the dining room everyone, we have something to tell you." A scraping of chairs, a hush, and everyone waited—Fran and I, the three girls, Lydia, Dorothy, Hurvey, two English boys from the R.A.F. Headquarters in Holland, little Franky, and Alice the mailgirl—and then Fran explained a bit of our need for this new room, the gifts that had made the beginning possible, and the reasons for our special day of prayer. He then asked me to read the letter, which told this story:

Some weeks before, the Lord had touched the heart of one of His children who knows L'Abri with a *desire* to provide money for enlarging. This one expected to have a certain amount of money in the fall. However, various legal matters were going so slowly that the money would not be in possession until sometime *after* the first of the year. A feeling of urgency came, a long-distance phone call was made to her lawyer, a sum was advanced, *and once again the Lord had worked details together to do the impossible,* for during the very day of prayer this word reached us and the workmen could be told to "go ahead, do the whole job." Enough was on hand to *finish* it all for *this winter.* When this information was read from the letter, we were all silent with awe when suddenly little Franky broke forth, "You know what *I* think? We should *all* clap!" So it was that Franky led us in clapping our praise to the Living God, the praise a little four-year-old could understand and mean in a very real way; and then Dorothy led us in a prayer of praise. . . .

The Lord blended some other prayer answers together when He brought Dr. Koop [Dr. C. Everett Koop, now Surgeon General of the United States] and his wife and two of his boys here for a time. That visit provided our children with an American "checkup" on their physical health, confirmed the thought that Franky was getting good care in Germany, shoes ordered for him to be made especially for his brace (for of course Franky's brace has to be changed as his shoes wear out and his feet grow), gave Debby a chance to play and hike with some children her own age, gave the Koops a glimpse of L'Abri "first-hand" and also a visit to Champéry, and gave Mr. Exhenry in Champéry an opportunity to have a time of fellowship and encouragement as the Koops drove us there for a visit. The Lord timed that visit for a time when Mr. Exhenry needed it in a special way, and used Dr. Koop's remark, "You may feel alone here, but you have many friends in America. I have prayed for you for a long time," to be a real "lift" to Mr. Exhenry in his isolated place. . . .

Another one of the Lord's lovely plans unfolded itself as Lydia Van Buskirk, my sister Elsa's daughter, came to live with us for a year. She is a tall, slim, red-haired girl of 16, whom we have prayed for daily since her birth, along with the other "cousins," so you can imagine the children's excitement when she became a part of the family. "Why, it's just like a storybook, like having a *real* family living close by," said one of our girls. It has made the rest of the family seem closer to have her with us. She is a junior in high school and is going to take a correspondence course from the same school in which Susan is studying. Debby was really under such a strain walking uphill that long three-mile walk to school each day, with heavy books often, and long hours of homework, that we are letting her take Calvert Course this year. So we have "school" in the home now with a real school spirit!! Dorothy is the supervisor, though each one will be studying alone much of the time. Until Lydia's books arrive, she is taking a "course in Home Economics," helping with the cooking and housework, and all three of them are going to have "cooking notebooks" and keep track of recipes, for they all take turns cooking something for our many guests. Susan has made highly successful apple pies; Debby, lovely oatmeal cookies; Lydia, some feathery lemon-cream scones.

The days when Dino and Lorna from Milan were going to be here were the very days when Betty and Mary Jo (two American college students from Christian backgrounds) were coming. The Lord gave us some days of perfectly beautiful weather, and the opportunity to take a trip to Champéry on one of the most perfect days. . . . We had a memorable trip on the 31st of August, and several things made it wonderful. For one thing we trailed up the mountain path and visited Vic, giving everyone the opportunity to see a peasant home, and giving me an opportunity to talk a bit with Vic. Then as we sat up at Planachaux eating our picnic lunch, who should come walking across to take his place with us at the outdoor tables, but Mr. Exhenry himself! He was to have met us a bit later in the village, but this was so much better. He suggested that the men walk down to the village 1,700 feet below while the rest of us took the *telepherique* down. . . . This walk gave a time of fellowship which was good for them. When they all stopped for prayer on the mountainside, Fran said it was a beautiful moment, with Dino praying in Italian, Mr. Exhenry praying in French, and Hurvey praying in English. . . .

We gave sighs of relief as the taxi wound its way down around the curves to take us to an early-morning train. "We're really on our way for a rest." Then suddenly a thud and a plop, a quick stop, and we discovered that two suitcases had fallen off from the top of the taxi, and at the same moment, someone called out, "Where's the lunch?" The suitcases were recovered unhurt, but the lunch was back in Huemoz sitting primly on the kitchen counter! . . . But here we all were, going to meet Priscilla and Franky at Alassio. The end of a day's train ride brought a happy reunion, with Franky excitedly talking a blue streak—"I can say tomato in Italian! It's 'pomodorrrrrrro,' " he said with a roll of his "r" which pleases Italians. "And I have a surprise for you in the water." This surprise turned out to be that he can swim! Walking out to the depth of his neck, he throws himself in the water, does a dead-man's float, swims a dog paddle, and floats on his back—but all this takes place about six inches *under* water, so he has to stand up frequently to take a breath! Prayer has been answered in that Franky has adjusted very well to his brace, and can now walk, run, climb, and slide down banisters just as well with it as without. I am to take him to Germany again for a checkup.

The University of Lausanne will be starting classes on about October 25th. That day Fran will be in Lausanne to gather the "nucleus" for the "Cafe Bible Class." Pray for the contacts each of these has already had, especially for the Jewish medical students who have said they are going to come to the class. The Lord can prepare hearts even before the class begins.

Much love from us all,

EDITH

December 29, 1956   Huemoz sur Ollon, Switzerland

Dear Family:

The Christmas season is so often one full of familiar smells, tastes, sights, and sounds that give a comfortable feeling of continuity to our lives, stringing the years together on a thread, like evenly matched pearls: fruitcake baking, turkey roasting, the cranberry sauce that is "just like Mother's," gaily decked streets, spiky bunches of holly, fresh pine branches, carols, the swelling notes of the "Hallelujah Chorus," the tinkle of sleighbells—whatever the family, town, country, customs are that blend together our childhood, growing-up, and from-then-on life and make memories combine with today to give us a warm glow. Then comes the first Christmas away from home, the first Christmas without a dear loved one, and memories *hurt*. It takes a *jolt* sometimes to awaken us to the fact that after all, life is a very temporary thing—that the world is a place full of sin and tragedy, and things are not *secure* and rosy.

If you walked down Lausanne's streets to shop and go to the Bible class with us this week, you'd receive a jolt, for the familiar, gay Christmas decorations are *missing*. The streets look almost as if it were October or February instead of the week before Christmas. Why? Because the Lausanne merchants decided to pool the money they would ordinarily spend on street decorations, and give it to help the Hungarians who have been taken in by Switzerland. This tiny country, the size of one of our smallest states, has taken 10,000 Hungarians who have fled from the terror of Russian rule, seeking freedom. To do this means that Swiss people are making sacrifices to help those who have landed penniless in their midst. My train was waiting to leave the Lausanne station when I looked across the tracks and saw another train standing there full of people who were gazing out the windows, smiling, waving, but oddly unlike any ordinary group traveling. There were no suitcases in sight, no racks full of parcels, just people! Yes, people: doctors, professors, grocerymen, bakers, factory workers—Hungarians who had had houses, furniture, and probably trunks full of possessions, but now they are just people, bare of possessions, glad to be free from an oppression. What a *jolt* it takes to get a different set of values sometimes. What is important after all? For those of us who believe the Bible, the Lord has told us to set our affections on things that are above—to store our treasures up in heaven. Whatever else the turmoil in the world right now does to us all, it should do one thing—it should jolt us into a feeling that our opportunities are *temporary*. . . .

The weekend began the "fall term" in Lausanne, and L'Abri filled up with seven students and a visiting pastor. Don't forget the "new room," and various alterations were only in the stages of being an added burden to us—of "mess" and workmen, and necessary phone calls for material, etc.—all through October, November, and part of December. So the house was *never* in a completed state during the weeks described in this letter! . . .

Franky and I got back home from his orthopedic checkup in Frankfurt in time to celebrate my birthday at the Saturday night hot dog roast in front of the fireplace. Lydia and Debby had festooned the room with balloons, and the birthday cake was festive with candles, a little pile of gifts beside it. That time will always be mingled in my mind with the Hungarian revolt, for the voices of the Hungarian intellectuals pleading with the "intellectual world" to help them began coming over the radio. The contrast of warmth, light, a happy celebration, with suffering, cold, people battling for freedom not so far away, seemed almost too much to bear. . . .

Monday we left for Milan. We went a day early in order to have time to look for a new meeting place. We had prayed that if the Lord wanted Fran to continue to teach there regularly, He would open up a permanent place for the class. We had suggested that perhaps a room could be found at the back of a cafe, as in Lausanne, or in a hotel, but all the experienced ones who had lived long in Italy, or who were Italian, said—*"Impossible*—in Italy it would be impossible to make such an arrangement for a Protestant Bible study class. No one would let you have it." As we left Huemoz Monday, a prayer chart had been made for a day of prayer. Each of us had signed up for our half-hour periods, and Fran and I had taken several periods for our train trip. The special need that topped the list was the need for guidance concerning Milan—that the Lord might show us His will in it—and that the opening up of a room might be the sign that we should continue to go down there. We arrived at 5:30 P.M. in a drizzling rain and with the streets so dark that it "felt" like midnight. As we walked away from the staion, we saw "Hotel Florida" in the first block. "This is the place we noticed this summer; let's stop in here for the night. I've thought of it often as a convenient place to get to from the station," said Fran. And we turned to the lobby. A room was vacant. We went up to it, deposited our things, and knelt down for prayer. "Oh Lord, we have prayed concerning Milan; now we shall begin our search. If it is Thy will for us to come here regularly, and if Thou wilt open up a place, please show it to us soon, as we are both *so* tired we would so appreciate having a free evening." Praying thus, aloud and in our hearts, we went down to the lobby again. Said Fran, "Before we go out, let's speak to the desk man here." Immediately I found myself explaining in French that my husband was an American pastor and that we lived in Switzerland. I told him a bit about L'Abri, and then said that in Milan there were some people who also would like to study the Bible and ask questions, "but we have no home in which to receive them. Could you suggest a place?" "I will call the director of the hotel," came the reply. In two minutes, a large, smiling man came in the front door, and the story was repeated to him in Italian by the desk man. The director turned to us and said in English, "How would you like to have your conferences here?" (waving his hand in the direction of a nice lounge). "Would it be big enough? How many people would there be?" To our questions, "How much would that cost an evening?" he said, "Nothing (a shrug of the shoulders), but if your friends would buy a cup of coffee or tea, that would be nice."

The Lord had answered—and in five minutes!! We had a sort of helpless feeling for a time, for it had come so quickly it truly amazed us. Can the Lord guide? Can He work in answer to prayer *now*—in definite things? How often He has shown us He can and does!

At the class the next evening each one was awestruck with the "impossible" thing which the Lord had done, and each one felt encouraged that truly it was the Lord who had made Himself real to them in a new way. Our next meeting was announced that night to be held in the Hotel Florida, and to be held every other Tuesday night from then on (Lord willing), and cards were handed out giving the address. The hotel supplied us with free cards to distribute! As we returned to Switzerland, we were praying about the finances. We had promised to go every other week, but what about the added cost? When the Lord truly leads, He will supply the needs. And, as if in token of this fact, we found mail when we returned with a check in it which amply took care of the Milan expenses for *that* month. It's so exciting to have the all-powerful Creator planning the work!

The weekends were full. We celebrated Thanksgiving on a Saturday for the University young people. . . . Meantime, all sorts of workmen continued to be "under foot"—so you can imagine the general "busyness." Finally, Fran and I got so far behind in correspondence that during the week of the 9th of December we stayed an extra day and a half in Milan, and an extra two days in Lausanne, just to "hibernate" in a hotel room and write letters, uninterrupted! . . .

Those of you who pray each day for L'Abri might like to have this regular schedule: *Sunday:* 11:30 A.M. church service; late afternoon, high tea and conversation*; *Monday* night: 8:30 P.M. Bible class for people nearby, translated into French by Mr. J.; *Tuesday:* one week the Bible class in Milan, Italy, 8:45 P.M. to 11:45 P.M.—the in-between week, informal time of Bible study in Madame Avanthey's home in Champéry; *Wednesday:* Children for Christ class *here* for the English-speaking children in Ecole Beau Soleil; *Thursday:* Lausanne Cafe Bible class, 11 A.M. to 2 P.M.; *Friday:* weekend "crowd" arrives in time for dinner, evening of conversation and Bible study; *Saturday:* walks and conversations with weekend crowd, evening "hot dog" roast by fireplace, with family prayers and conversation throughout the evening.

During this period Hurvey was painting the cellar, hall, kitchen, and bathroom, while workmen were building the small new room. Never was there a "settled time" for the schedule to work easily!

---

*Each time the world *conversation* occurs, it refers to intensive asking of honest questions and the attempt to give honest answers, on a wide variety of subjects.

The Lord opened up the way for us to have the Christmas Eve service in Champéry for English visitors again. Mr. Exhenry was there, of course, having helped to heat the church ahead of time, and Madame Marclay brought us tea as we decorated! Jewish Nurite went with us to her first Christmas service. She has not yet come to believe, but she hopes she will—do pray for her. . . .

When you get this, the new year will have already begun. It's so good to know that the Lord knows what is ahead of us, and that He has all the answers to the problems we will face, which we can't even guess! But it's also wonderful to know that there are things which will happen in answer to prayer, things *He* will do in answer to our requests. What a mystery—but wonderful it is true, for you and for me.

Much love in Him to whom we can trust the New Year,

EDITH

1957

Huemoz sur Ollon, Switzerland

Dear Family:

Two years ago today at *just this moment* (about noon) Fran and Priscilla were ploughing through the snow to bring the two pieces of paper to Chalet Bijou with the news which was to so shock us all, the edict saying we had to leave Switzerland within six weeks. In the turmoil of emotion that followed, and in the hurry of caring for the immediate "steps" that had to be taken, the Lord gave some quiet hours of Bible reading and prayer during the necessary train trips taken that day and the following days. My reading was in the book of Isaiah at that time, and this morning as sort of "anniversary" I have been reading those well-marked passages again. The Lord gave a marvelous succession of promises that day, and on the days that followed—promises that were wonderfully *real* in the midst of that heavy "fog," promises that have been fulfilled in the two years and which *are* being fulfilled from day to day now. Isaiah 26:3, 4, "Thou wilt keep him in perfect peace whose mind is stayed on thee: because he *trusteth* in thee. *Trust* ye in the Lord forever: for in the Lord Jehovah is everlasting strength." Isaiah 30:21, "And thine ears shall hear a word behind thee, saying, This is the way, walk ye in it, when ye turn to the right hand, and when ye turn to the left." . . .

That first week in January, as we came back from our fortnightly class in Milan, Claudia and Doris came with us. [The train ride] gave me time to have a five-hour talk with some L'Abri guests—which is almost impossible when I am here at the chalet with the other claims on my time. As you remember, Jane brought Doris (who is a singer from New York) and Doris was saved. Now Doris brought her friend, Claudia, to the class in Milan—and then up here. Claudia is a singer from California, an Episcopalian—who thought she *was* a "Christian." During her five days here, Claudia's eyes of understanding were opened, and she realized that she had never been a real Christian because she had never believed on the Lord Jesus Christ. It was during a conversation which started at breakfast—and kept the dining room occupied until it was time to set the table for lunch—that Claudia stepped out of darkness into the glorious light,* and that night she wrote in the guest book that this was the most important moment of her life—"but I know it is only the *beginning*." Claudia is full of a burning desire to "make Christ known" to all those with whom she comes into contact. Claudia was almost asphyxiated with a faulty gas hot-water heater in her boarding house, and just before she fainted, she asked the Lord to please let her live so that she could go home to tell her parents the truth which she now knows! The Lord has used the story of this to make an opening for some of the others to invite friends. And so the circle of those who hear widens. . . .

Then there is Champéry—the classes have been going on every other Tuesday night with real blessing. Hurvey went over to teach it one time, and Madame Avanthey asked him to have a Bible class for two English children for an hour before the adults! Hurvey also stayed and took a ski lesson from Mr. Exhenry the next morning, getting to know Mr. Exhenry better and having a bit of fellowship with him. This last week Dorothy went to Champéry to spend a couple of days at Eileen's at Chalet Bijou (to rest a bit away from this place for a while) and had wonderful openings to talk to Eileen and an English lady who is also agnostic. Hurvey went over with Fran this time too, and taught the children again. A wonderful thing happened—Madame Avanthey's husband, Fabien, the ski teacher, came to the class for the first time, and Mr. Exhenry translated it all into French and gave a wonderful testimony himself. What a thrilling answer to prayer that was! And the Lord has opened up the way for us all to go back to Champéry for five days, from February 26th to March 2nd, to stay at Chalet Bijou. Mr. and Mrs. Czerny (the Czech professor and his wife) will be in Champéry during that time, and he has a new deep sorrow—his mother died just this week—and she had *just* received permission from the government to visit them here in Switzerland for Easter! It seems to be another crushing blow. Do pray for them. We hope the five days there will give us opportunity to renew many contacts, as well as to spend a bit of time outdoors with the children. Please pray for us especially during those five days. . . .

Everything always seems too short—this paper for instance! And the time to do all there is to do—and time to pray for all the needs—but the Lord's love is not too short—nor His time.

Much love from us all in Him in whom we have eternity together.

EDITH

---

*See I Peter 2:9.

April 1, 1957   Huemoz sur Ollon, Switzerland

Dear Family:

"Wake up Mommy, it's another beautiful day! Come read your Bible in my room." It was Franky who had padded into our room to get me. As I came out into the hall he gleefully shouted, "You're stepping on a snake, mommy. April Fool's Day!!

April first is *another* special day for *us*, for we'll always remember that the first morning we awakened in Chalet les Mélèzes was April first, now two years ago. We'll never forget the thrill we had when we saw the sun-drenched view with mountains and valleys showing forth all their details as though the air were a magnifying glass. "Just look at the place the Lord has chosen for us." And now, two years later, the view is the same, filling us with the same wonder, but the chalet and the garden show some transformations. Come out to the garden with Franky and me. "Look, look—they're pink and blue and white now—" said Franky as we leaned over the circle of hyacinths planted around the apple tree. The daffodil buds are getting fat, and the tiny crocuses and miniature spring flowers are already in full bloom down by the gate, while sturdy tulip leaves are standing in clusters around the rose bushes. Yes, flowers have transformed the garden, which had grown wild before, but these spring flowers speak to us of a beauty deeper than their own, for they were sent to us by a Dutch couple in memory of their three weeks at L'Abri last summer, during which time they felt there had been a real transformation in their own lives. . .

Tuesday Bill (on a week's leave from his Army base) went with us to Milan once more, giving him an opportunity to meet the Christians down there and to see how the class was going in the hotel, and giving us time to discuss questions that had arisen in Bill's own study and witnessing. . . . We got home to find Anne fixed up on the dining room couch with her leg in a cast. Yes, she had broken it skiing on her second day here, so her time at L'Abri was slightly different from that to which she had been looking forward. Susan went with Anne to the doctor a day later, and he found that Susan's blood pressure was too high and her heart was beating too fast—so he ordered her to stay in bed and pronounced it "another attack of the same thing." We felt it important that the Lausanne heart specialist give his opinion immediately, and arranged to take Susan that same evening, taking John D. to the train at the same time, and giving us three hours to talk to him on the way to his train. The specialist felt sure that it was not Susan's heart, nor did he think it to be rheumatic fever, but he did feel that she should go to a hospital for a very thorough checkup. He gave Susan some medicine as a temporary thing, and she came back to stay in bed. She lost weight and had other symptoms which make us feel we really must try to get to the bottom of the trouble.

We have prayed much about Susan's need of a checkup, and have written some letters to doctor friends asking advice, asking the Lord to clearly guide us in the answers. We feel the Lord did answer prayer in this, and now we are in contact with an English specialist at the Great Ormond Street Hospital for Children. Plans are not yet completed, but the Lord has given us quite a number of encouragements that this is the right thing to do, and D.V. we expect to be on our way within a few days. By "we" I mean Susan and I, as it would seem that this is the way it must be done. Fran will carry on in our absence, and of course there are the other helpers here—Dorothy, Hurvey, and Anne, and others. Do pray with us that the time in London may show just what is wrong with Susan, and that the Lord may use the trip in some special way for His glory as well as for Susan's good. . . .

The Tuesdays when we go to Champéry for Bible Study, Hurvey now goes to Milan, so that the Milan class can continue to meet *every* week. The week Hurvey goes, they meet in one of the apartments of the Christians, and they invite the Christians to come, or the ones who are deeply interested. Then the in-between Tuesdays, Fran and I go and the meeting is in the Hotel, with a variety of unsaved ones, often new ones who come only once. It is wonderful the way some of them invite everyone they meet and talk with, to come to the class. The reason for the big "turn-over" is the fact that some invite everyone they can—from the hairdresser to the man who takes tickets. We laughingly say that you can follow Claudia through the week by seeing who comes to the class! . . .

And now, dear family, instead of using the remaining space to tell you more of the past six weeks' happenings, Fran and I want to make a very special announcement, and that is concerning the engagement of our daughter Janet Priscilla to John Paolo Sandri. John is the one who was introduced to you two summers ago, when he first came to L'Abri and wrote, "'my eyes have been opened to a new world in which I hope to dwell with a coming faith." You will remember that John accepted Christ as his Savior a year ago last November, and he grew rapidly in his Christian life. This year he has been a L'Abri Worker, making contacts at the University of Lausanne, where he is a student, and helping in other ways. Of course, you saw his picture in the last letter, standing behind Priscilla. John has both Swiss and American citizenship, as his parents were Swiss, but lived in Scarsdale, New York, for 17 years—most of John's life. His knowledge of French and English, and love of America and Switzerland, make him an understanding companion for Priscilla, who also has a background of love for the two countries, and the two languages. They do seem very well suited to each other, and we feel that the Lord has brought them together. Both of them have given themselves to the Lord for His use, and we do pray that He will use them in a special way together. They have been praying concerning the time of their marriage, and now feel that, unless the Lord shows them in some way that it should be another time, they will be married this August.

They would go away for a short honeymoon, and then plan to live at the chalet during September, while we go away for our vacation. Then, when school begins in October, they would live in a small apartment in the same house where Priscilla has been living. It is a house in La Rosiaz, just across from Madame Turrian's pension, where we lived our first year in Lausanne. It has lovely trees around it, and a wonderful view of the lake, with memories which stretch back to our family walks of 1948's fall. They have another year at the University, and then, Lord willing, they plan to go back to America, where after visiting the grandparents and friends, they will go to St. Louis, where John expects to enter Covenant Seminary, for he feels the Lord has called him into Christian work. We wish all you "family" folks could come to the wedding, but perhaps many of you will meet the bride and groom a year later!

We all send our love to you in Him in whom we are truly one family—for eternity!

EDITH

May 31, 1957   Huemoz sur Ollon, Switzerland

Dear Family

. . . You want to know about the London trip [I was taking Susan to London to have an extensive physical examination], so I'll plunge into that account first. Dinny was here when the final word came from the doctor, and she reminded us, "Nurite wants you to stay at her parents' flat while you are in London, you know." "But Dinny, how can we be sure they really want us? It doesn't seem possible that Jewish parents would be happy about their daughter becoming Christian. I think we had better plan to visit Nurite's parents, but to *stay* somewhere else." However, at the last moment, a telephone call came from Nurite—"Oh, Mrs. Schaeffer, I just talked with Mummy in London, and she said to tell you that she will be away for a few days and Daddy is coming to Paris to meet me, but you and Susan are to go to our flat. The porter at the door will be expecting you, and will give you the key. Everything is in order, and you are just to ask the maid about ordering milk and everything. Oh, I'm so glad it is all right." Nurite has a way of saying things in a kind of soft, breathless voice when she is excited—and it didn't seem right to disappoint her in this, which was an answer to *her* prayers, she felt. "All right then, Nurite, we'll go to your flat right from the air terminal."

We left Huemoz, Debby and Lydia going along to have a day's outing taking Susan and me to Geneva. Susan needed a new passport, which meant staying overnight there and calling again at the Consulate before taking our plane the next morning. . . . A grey sky and drifts of clouds brought a frequent flash of red-lighted words, "Fasten seat belts, please," and made Susan's first air trip a bumpy one. However, it was not long before I knew that my dizzy feeling and the chills going up my spine were *not* due to the roller-coaster effect, but to a rapidly developing fever! I had caught my one big cold and cough of the winter. By the time we had gone through the lines waiting for customs control, etc., had shivered through the Waterloo Station to find a Post Office where we could send a telegram, had tugged our suitcases out to a taxi, and had finally arrived in front of a very lovely apartment house, we were very grateful to have a dignified, uniformed Mr. M. open the taxi door to say, "Are you the Schaeffers? Mr. _____ (Nurite's father) told me to take you to their flat. Did you have a good flight?" I found that my fever was 102 degrees so you can imagine how glad I was not to have to go out to a restaurant, but to have a kitchen where Susan and I could prepare hot bouillon and toast. It seemed like a dream to find ourselves in the middle of London in a warmly heated, beautifully furnished apartment, fixing supper, washing dishes, reading, and praying together as if this were our home. The telephone rang after a short time, and it was Nurite calling from Paris to see if we were all right, and to welcome us! Susan was very tired from the trip, but I fear I was the patient that night and the next day, as my fever and cough developed by leaps and bounds—but oh, how grateful we both were to the Lord for giving us a place where we could be so comfortable, and where I could stay in bed all day Sunday to "get rid" of that cold.

"Ravens"* came the next day in the form of Jennifer and her sister, Jane, to bring us some food, and Deirdre also came with fruit and vegetables for dinner. That was the beginning of our many contacts in London with those who have been at L'Abri, or who came to Chalet Bijou during the years we were in Champéry. . . .

Susan spent about five days in the Great Ormond Street Hospital for Children and enjoyed the opportunity to observe a children's hospital from the inside, for this was her first hospital experience! It wasn't all just a lark, of course. She had a good many tests made, and among other things her heart was tested after she had sedatives, and the sedatives made her break out in a *very* itchy rash. However, the final news was wonderful. The conclusions were that regardless of what it had been before, this last "attack" was mistakenly diagnosed by the local doctor here, and that it was therefore probably simply a virus grippe like the rest of us had. In fact, the one before that might have been the same thing. At any rate, of this he was certain: Susan's heart is *perfectly fine*, and she is in a *good healthy state*. He explained the faster heart beat and

See I Kings 17:1–5.

the higher blood pressure as simply reactions to being kept in bed and, *told* that she had "the same thing" again. So he wrote to the local doctor here, and told Susan to go ahead and go into full activity again. We are thankful to have this matter cleared up, though we know that the Lord has reasons for even the "mistakes" that are made. Susan has gained so much spiritually through it all, that she wouldn't exchange the total results of the experience for extra hours of activity in the past—though now she is making up for it with bicycle trips, teaching Franky's kindergarten, cooking, and helping with housework and so on, in addition to her studies.

The blow fell at the end! Nurite and her father returned on Sunday night. Susan and I were to leave on Tuesday morning. The father was cordial and polite to us on the night of his arrival. The next morning he and I had quite a talk, but he did make it very plain that he was proud of being Jewish and wanted his daughter to be too. The conversation ended rather abruptly as I had a very important appointment with the doctor who was to talk with me about Susan, and Mr. _____ said firmly, "By the way, Nurite will not be here tonight; she will go with me to the home of Jewish friends. This is a Jewish holiday."

Late that night Deirdre was still with us, hating to say goodbye as it was our last time together; and the door opened—Nurite and her father had come home. Nurite was delighted to meet Deirdre, but the father was quite evidently angry, and dismissed Deirdre with a curt good night. Sensing that something had happened to stir up a real animosity, I spent much time in prayer through the night, and got up very early, not being able to sleep. Our suitcases were all packed and I was fully dressed by about 7 o'clock, though we had not planned to get a taxi until 9. I was startled when soon after 7 the bedroom door opened and Mr. _____ said in a coldly furious voice, "I have ordered a taxi to be here in *10 minutes*." The door shut. Susan quickly got out of bed and flew about dressing, so that in the specified 10 minutes, we were at the front door of the flat. Nurite kissed us goodbye and began to talk, but the father stopped her, sent her off to her room, and standing at the open door, with the taxi driver coming up the hall, dismissed us with this threat, "Mrs. Schaeffer, you have overstepped your bounds and I am informing the Swiss Legation." The taxi driver picked up our bags and started off with them to the elevator. Susan and I bid goodbye to the porter who had welcomed us so nicely, and he looked surprised. "My, you are leaving very early this morning!"

Is it pleasant to be glared at and threatened? No. Is it comfortable to be persecuted in any way? There was a struggle to be gone through in our emotions that day. Had we done the right thing in staying there? Would L'Abri be harmed? But there were lessons to be learned, too. And one of the first things the Lord showed me in it all was the fact that we must not take lightly the persecution and difficulties these babes in Christ face when they return to unbelieving parents. . . . I felt the Lord was giving me a new understanding of the need of *prayer*, the responsibility we have to pray for new-born Christians. Yes, it is thrilling to see them come to the Lord; marvelous to know that they are certain of eternal life; comforting to know that the Holy Spirit dwells within them—but surely we who are older in the Lord should *not* neglect to pray for them, for the battle *can* be very hot and the way weary and hard. I Samuel 12:23, "God forbid that I should sin [against the Lord] in ceasing to pray for you."

Just before we went out to the plane, a telegram was handed to me—"Terribly sorry stop writing, bon voyage love Nurite." So direct contact was to be cut off. But the Lord's direct contact with His own can never be cut off! . . .

We arrived home to find that they had had a full time during our absence; six students had been there for the first weekend. Dot had been taking charge of the cooking with Lydia's help; Debby had been "mommy" to Franky, putting him to bed and caring for him in the night; Fran and Hurvey had been taking all the usual classes and conversations, and there were many things to tell. The news that shocked us was that Fran and Priscilla had gone to Geneva one day to attend Mr. Alexander's funeral. Yes, Mr. Alexander had gone home to be with the Lord very suddenly. He had slipped and fallen while he was in their mountain chalet and a head injury resulted. An operation had been successfully performed in Geneva, but during his time of recovery, pneumonia set in, and he entered into the presence of his beloved Lord. And so, the earthly work of this faithful servant of the Lord, used to begin and lead the work of Action Biblique and the Geneva Bible Society with its far-reaching work, has drawn to a close. . . .

The possibility of some real difficulty arising from the "threat" in London was naturally in our thinking those first days after coming back, but the work of the Holy Spirit in our midst during the same period seemed like a voice speaking to us of the power of the Lord to use L'Abri according to His own plan. He who could so use it, could certainly protect it. . . .

In the letter written April 1st, I could have announced another engagement here at L'Abri, but then I thought I could wait until the first of May for that. However, things have moved along quickly, and I have been slow in writing, so that that engagement announcement has turned into a wedding announcement. Yes, it's Dorothy and Hurvey! But let me tell you a little of the history of their romance. When Hurvey came here last August, he met Dorothy for the first time, though his brother, Karl, had met her during his time in the Army when he visited L'Abri. All through the fall and winter Dorothy and Hurvey have been an integral part of L'Abri—Dot in the cooking, ironing, table setting, conversations, piano playing, and helping with the account books (among other things—supervising the children's schoolwork), and Hurvey in the care of the furnace, making the fires in the fireplace, scrubbing and waxing floors, painting walls, gardening, taking the trash to the dump, playing big brother to Franky, teaching classes (every other week in Milan, occasionally in Villars, and every week the boys from a school nearby), as well as conversations and walks with the L'Abri guests. In the busier-than-busy life here, there was never time for these two to be alone together and though (we later discovered, and they themselves later discovered) they were growing very fond of each other, neither one knew that the other one cared in the least! Hurvey felt that as a L'Abri worker his task here was to be as helpful as possible, and that a budding romance wouldn't be helpful—even if he might have a "chance"—so he gave no indication of his feelings, and Dorothy wondered, as girls wonder sometimes, what might be going on in his head, but decided that there was certainly no "interest" so she was a bit cooler than she might have been otherwise. Let me say right here to any young people who might be reading this, that both of these two learned a hard lesson at one point during these months, of putting it all into the Lord's hands, and trusting *Him*. And then facing the *fact* that the Lord's choice for us is really truly the best thing for our good and His glory in the very moment when we cannot *see* what that choice is going to be.

One Sunday night after the 7 o'clock bus had carried away the weekend group back to Lausanne, and the Sunday School for Franky was finished, and the fire had burned low, and the candles had been blown out, and the dishes were done, Hurvey and Dorothy went out for a walk during which a happy discovery was made. After their return, Fran went to the living room in his round of checking windows and doors, and was the first to receive the big news. Susan was halfway down and got it next, and her rush to the top floor was a speedy race with an excited, astonished shriek: "Guess what, guess what! Hurvey and Dorothy are engaged to be married—they really are." Everything is a family affair here at L'Abri. Lydia, Debby, and Susan were so happy they couldn't go to sleep, and before they even settled down to trying, they had written little surprise notes of congratulations and strung them up with ribbon, "so Hurvey and Dorothy will walk into them when they walk up the stairs." Their happiness was shared by everyone but Franky, who when informed by Hurvey the next morning remarked, "Well, what did you do *that* for, Hurvey?" At first, plans were made by them to be married in the United States. Dorothy's home in California would be so much more fun together as a honeymoon trip than as a trip going back to be married that they came to the conclusion that the "perfect thing" would be to be married right here at L'Abri. Of course, there were other factors that entered in—the time element, being ready for Seminary in the fall, and so on.

What has been written previously in this letter—the full weekends, the trips, the classes away from here—all took place as wedding plans were being made, so you know that Dorothy and Hurvey kept up on all their L'Abri work at the same time. It was while Susan and I were in

*The first wedding at Chalet les Mélèzes. Left to right: Lydia,
Dorothy, Fran, Hurvey, and Dan.*

London that Dorothy got time to make her wedding dress, and as time
went on, everything was ready. May 18th dawned bright and clear, as
perfect as could be. If you had dropped in that morning, you would
have found a hive of busy bees. Hurvey was cutting the lawn and trimming it, and John was helping him, while Dan, the best man, having
not brought any working clothes, gave bits of advice! Jo was starching
and ironing the damask tablecloth while Rosemary washed lettuce for
lunch and Lydia finished hemming her dress. Debby polished away at
the living room furniture while Susan polished candlesticks. I was
busy fixing 500 daisies into various arrangements so that the living
room looked like a veritable garden, while Franky and Priscilla ran
down together to the village store to get some satin ribbon to make an
"aisle" for the bridal party!

The bride herself just finished making her own and her bridesmaid's
bouquets before she had to go to get dressed, and I just finished decorating the tables set outdoors for the reception ten minutes before the
wedding was to start. The guests from Basel arrived just as the little
mademoiselle from the village and Monsieur Jean Richard arrived
from Villars. John ushered us formally to our seats, arranged with the
aisle in the middle (furniture had been moved out), and we sat in a
hush, until suddenly the wedding march broke forth from the record
player as though the organ were right in the room, and the men
stepped in the door arranging themselves at the front, waiting for the

bridesmaid and bride to come in down that aisle. Lydia in a pale green taffeta dress, carrying purple iris, yellow roses, and daisies looked like some wood fairy with her shiny copper hair caught back with an arrangement of daisies and dark green ribbon at the back. The short walk brought her to the front, where she solemnly waited for Dorothy in her white taffeta dress, lace trimmed at the neck and wrists with seed pearls, and a lovely delicate frame for her dark hair and glowing face, in the lace veil, carrying white roses, carnations, and sweet peas. The service was sweet and solemn, the first wedding at L'Abri, and the first wedding of our little International Church. After pictures were taken, the tea and conversation served outdoors, the gifts opened, Dot and Hurvey went off on a short honeymoon in the higher Alps above us, where they had rented a little chalet for a week. They had wonderful mountain climbing up there—a splendid place for a last good look at Switzerland. Then they returned for a brief day and a half to pack up and leave, and once more the "goodbyes" which are always hard were said and now they are somewhere on the seas, in a freighter bound for America and visits to their two homes. They expect to be living in St. Louis soon, where Hurvey will be attending Covenant Seminary this fall. . . .

When the owner of Beau Site died at Christmas time, and his sons agreed to rent the chalet at a very low price, it coincided with a request from the Williams family from Tennessee to rent a chalet for the summer near L'Abri. We took this as guidance to sign a lease for one year.

Meantime Chalet Beau Site has been torn up, a new furnace put in. We have chosen wallpaper and paint, and have watched it be transformed from day to day. The last two days, a small army of cleaning women have swarmed over it and have scrubbed every window, floor, door, and so on, in the place. It amazes us to see how the Lord has given these people a desire to put it in such fine order before handing us the key. All it lacks is furniture (though there are enough beds, tables and chairs, and general equipment to make it suitable for summer). Early in July our neighbors, the Williamses, will arrive and L'Abri will immediately be spread out into two houses! And then in the fall we expect Joyce and Jim Hughes and their boys, Jimmy, four, and Jon, two, to come, Lord willing. . . .

So much I haven't time to include like my visit to Neuchatel to talk with John's mother, Mrs. Sandri—nor of Fran's dizziness and feeling of exhaustion these last weeks. Also I have *not* the energy I *used* to have!! Never is the need for prayer lessened.

Much love in Him who has given us a love for each other and placed us together in His work,

EDITH

July 4, 1957   Huemoz sur Ollon, Switzerland

Dear Family

It's the Fourth of July—I wonder what you're doing? Franky started the day with a vomiting stomach-upset at 6 A.M.—slowly the intermittent calls of "Mommy, come quick" brought the rest of the household to life. After Fran's mad dash for the yellow bus which Lydia had stopped by the front gate, and his departure for his cafe Bible class in Lausanne, Susan hung out our large American flag and read parts of the Declaration of Independence to Franky, Debby, and me as we sat in our bedroom, and then Lydia was called from her studies out in the shade of the big blue spruce to salute the flag and sing, "My Country 'tis of Thee" along with the rest! Thus our Fourth of July began with much patriotism and ceremony, in the midst of an unusual heat wave in Switzerland— along with the rest of Europe. It was 102 degrees in the shade in Lausanne, even 98 degrees up here at 3,500 feet. . . .

It has been a busier than busy month, as we have missed the help of Hurvey and Dorothy. One person cannot take the place of two, especially two who worked long and hard, and jobs have had to be divided in a way that added new tasks to everyone's day. Fran took over the grass cutting and trimming (there's lots of it), and the teaching of Hurvey's class of boys from Ecole Beau Soleil. . . . Lydia has now been playing the piano for these children's classes (as well as the Sunday Services when Priscilla can't be home), and Susan has been teaching the younger children. All three girls have taken over more of the cooking and dishwashing, especially as I have had to be away more. I took Hurvey's place the "in-between weeks" when the Milan class meets in the apartment of one of the believers, which meant a weekly trip taking the better part of two days (one night in Milan).

As we traveled to Milan these summer days we found it hard to find two seats. 100,000 Italians arrived the 1st of July to work in Switzerland for July and August—each feeling he must bring a wine supply as well as odd bits of possessions! The heat is terrific as we go through the Simplon tunnel but if we were artists we'd have fantastic faces to paint in our crowded compartments!

Then I have inherited the care of the vegetable gardens, which sometimes means continuing transplanting and so on by flashlight! However, much of the summer supply of vegetables is grown in these gardens so weed-pulling and hoeing are a necessary part of the menu-planning!! I am eagerly awaiting the moment "fresh green peas" can be added to meals on the weekly menus we post on the kitchen bulletin board. Jo has been doing a variety of things, ironing, cleaning, pulling apart the "weekend beds" and making them up fresh for the next batch of guests, teaching the children's class over in Champéry on Tuesday nights, and typing some of the carbon copies. . . .

Susan, Debby, and Lydia took a bicycle trip (long, long planned for on winter nights around a map) from Huemoz along the lake to Geneva (60 kilometers), stopping in youth hostels for the nights. They found opportunity to give out gospel portions, and to talk to a variety of young people about coming to L'Abri, so felt it a good missionary opportunity as well as fun! In addition to such things as reading *Winnie The Pooh* in the twilight sitting on rocks along the lake shore, and reading Byron's *Prisoner* right in the dungeon of Castle Chillon, they visited Angelina in the kitchen of the big estate along the lake where she is now cook. Cocky little Angelina trotted off to ask the "Madame" if she would like guests for dinner. "They speak your language." But the American owner of this gorgeous estate, 70 years old, but with nothing stored up in heaven in spite of all the treasures here, naturally did not want the cook's guests for her dinner companions! However, Angelina has not given up trying to get her mistress to listen to the gospel. You can imagine the girls returned after five days with enough memories to last them a lifetime of "remember whens." And, Angelina herself trotted up here for a weekend two weeks later to "study some more—I need it," but she forgot to bring the notebook full of questions she has been making during her Bible study times alone. . . .

And what of the next seven weeks ending in the wedding of Priscilla and John? We do need prayer. The schedule is full with L'Abri visitors coming constantly. By the way, not only is Jennifer bringing Tim from Oxford in August, but in July Jane, Jennifer's *other* sister, also a doctor, is coming with another girl doctor! Pray that this may mean a trio of "like-minded" born-again sisters. If you just stop to add up all there will be to do you can imagine the dismay that sometimes fills our minds as to the accomplishing of all the summer seems to hold. August 23rd is the date for Priscilla's wedding. Dr. Martyn Lloyd-Jones, of London, is to perform the ceremony. He and his wife and daughter are coming through Switzerland on their vacation, and will be staying with us from the 22nd until the 24th. The wedding will be held in the Ollon church building, the place where Farel preached 450 years ago beginning the Reformation in this part of the country. Weddings take time for preparation, but the work cannot let up for a moment! Madame Marclay will help with the sewing, but needs Bible teaching as much as we need her help, so every step of the preparations even must be led of *Him*. How wonderful that in each detail of life, we can "wait upon His will." . . .

Joyce and Jim are preparing to come in September. Lydia is expecting to go back to the states at the end of August and the Schaeffer family (minus Priscilla this time) are praying for a vacation in September.

As we pray together on July 30th, our annual day of prayer and fasting, as well as through the weeks, let us thank Him for His answers, and for giving us the privileged place of intercessors.

Much love in Him in whom we are bound together from every tongue and kindred and nation,

EDITH

September 30, 1957   Alassio, Italy

Dear Family:

The fact that this summer was completed without a breakdown of some sort on the part of one of us, and that no one was turned away from L'Abri, nor any part of the work stopped, and that now this is being written during this first real rest we have had in years, is to me a tremendous proof of the *reality* of the truth of the promise, "My grace is sufficient for thee, my strength is made perfect in weakness," and of the power of prayer. Humanly looking at it, we felt too tired to keep up through June, but day by day, hour by hour, the Lord *did* give strength for all He had placed before us to do, and then He gave us a "rest," which we can be sure He knew was needed for whatever He has ahead of us this fall and winter. Words are so inadequate for praising Him who is the Mighty God, the Everlasting Father, and who has ordained that we, weak human creatures, are to be used for His eternal purposes when we are born into His household. . . .

The summer is definitely over, even here in Alassio, where a sudden rain has changed the weather completely. The hot sun seems to have departed, grey skies hang over the darkened sea, and a wild wind tosses the palm trees' feathery branches back and forth in rhythm with the waves. Fran has gone with Susan, Debby, and Franky to see some ancient villages with Roman ruins (situated on hills surrounding Alassio), leaving me free to "talk" with you! The Lord sent in enough money designated for a vacation to cover the expenses, and also caused Miss P. (the owner of this little hotel, whom we have known for years—she is the aunt of the Sardinian boys) to write and suggest a quieter room with a view of the sea, and the freedom to buy our own food and picnic on the beach. So every day we have divided care of Franky. Debby and I have had marketing trips back in the old village streets searching for the freshest tomatoes and lettuce, carrots, and other things that can be prepared without cooking, have stopped at the *latteria* for pasteurized milk, a pint apiece, and at fruit stalls for fresh fruit, and have come back to prepare our picnic to be spread out on the sand when "dinnertime" caused the beach to be deserted by others for a couple of hours. We've read out loud together, taken walks as a whole family together, and Fran has taken the girls on some longer hikes, as well as taking Franky for a "just men's walk" from five to seven each evening before Franky's supper and bed. It's the sort of thing we can't do at L'Abri—be alone with the children—and that, plus the rest and the change of air, has done us all a tremendous amount of good. It is such a joy to know that the Lord meant us to have this rest.

Fran, Susan, Debby, and I went off on the early-morning bus for Lausanne on the day of the last class in the Cafe for the summer. The University was over, and that evening we would be having our first Bible class in a hotel in Montreux (on the lake, between Lausanne and Ollon). Priscilla met us at the station, looking white and tired from exam study but excited and happy because she had received her Certificate, the exams were over, and the first bit of shopping which she had done for her trousseau, and had "lost" a few minutes later, had been "found," for a lady had discovered that she had taken the wrong package home with her, and had returned it to the store in the morning! The family went off to the class, and I spent a couple of hours shopping—foodstuffs for L'Abri, and various materials, threads, and buttons, etc., for the dressmaking ahead of us. I met Mrs. Sandri (Priscilla's mother-in-law) that afternoon to go over wedding plans and then later we all met to go on to Montreux, where Fran and I were to have dinner at Claudie's home before the class. The 19 gathered in that hotel room (a rather nicely furnished sort of living room on the first floor, quite shut off and private) were an interesting group. Mr. Conrad, the professor who used to attend the Villars class and accepted the Lord in Milan, was there, as he is now teaching in Montreux! And a variety of young people—friends and relations of Claudie's—had been invited and had come, as well as some Swiss-German young people invited by a nurse who has been at L'Abri. Claudie translated the message phrase by phrase into French, and there was some whispered translating going on in Swiss-German too! There's a wee island that you can't miss as you pass Montreux—just big enough for one big white house to stand on, leaving very little space around it. We've often remarked on that island and wondered who might live in that house, and that night we met the daughter of the family, for she came to the class! We were to see her again, for she was so deeply touched that the very next Sunday, she and another girl came to our Sunday morning church service at the chalet. . . .

This has brought us right up to the first of August, Franky's favorite day in the year, for it is the Swiss National Holiday and the Huemoz Band plays on the crest of the hill above the village, with Franky standing right beside the Milkman (who is band-leader) getting pointers (for Franky fondly supposes that when he gets a bit older, he'll be the leader, or at *least* the drummer), the village leaders make patriotic speeches while children set off fireworks under their noses, and the firemen end it all by importantly pouring kerosene on a huge pile of sticks for a bonfire that can be seen for miles, while all over the mountains other bonfires dot the darkness with flaming spots, and high above it all, on the dot of 9:30, green and red flares appear on the seven peaks of the Dents du Midi, and we know that the flare on *"that* peak," the most difficult one to ascend, means that Monsieur Avanthey, the guide from our Bible class in Champéry, has made it up all right with a lantern in his teeth, and we pray that he'll get back down safely in the dark!! . . .

Fran scribbles the names of people staying at L'Abri on a calendar that has a square of empty white space by each date. Here we are at the weekend before Priscilla's wedding, and in Fran's handwriting we have 15 names besides our family! . . . Most of the guests stayed until Thursday morning; of course, Thursday afternoon others were arriving, and Friday was the wedding!!

Wednesday morning the combination of hot sparkling sun, and the urgency of "we can't wait a minute longer," awakened me with a feeling of intense energy. "Today we *stop* all this canning business and clean the house from top to bottom." For our "spare time" *after midnight* for some weeks had been spent in grinding up quantities of green tomatoes, cabbage, peppers, onions, and soaking them in salt for "hot dog relish" which the next day we had rinsed, boiled, and bottled. Tomatoes had been canned too and now quarts and quarts of green and yellow bottles had to be lined up in neat rows on shelves in the "caves," and all the canning equipment put away. Everyone took a section of the house that day—Claudie and Jo did the living room, the girls each their own room plus something else, Anna the bathrooms, Mrs. Caldwell came over and helped Claudie with the dining room in the afternoon, I took one bedroom, the halls, and the laundry, *and* we got ten loads of washing out to dry in that lovely sun. By "cleaning" I mean window washing, rug washing, furniture waxing, and so on, so that not only were we ready for the wedding and a new batch of guests, but to leave the chalet later on in a fairly good condition when we left for our vacation.

Thursday, of course, there were still a few cleaning jobs left, the outside to get in good order (John pulled out pea plants and dug that section up, for spinach seed was to go in there before the vacation), and Lydia and Susan began a "cooking spree" to have a few things ready ahead, when suddenly it was 10:00 A.M., the taxi would soon be there, and it was time to go to the Civil Wedding in Villars!! Everyone in Switzerland must have two ceremonies, and usually the civil ceremony is the day before the religious one. The girls and Franky went along, but we didn't all go. "Back so soon?" We all crowded around to see the little booklet that stated officially that Pris was now Madame Sandri and went on to give pages of helpful advice about health, housekeeping, and baby care. "Mommy, guess what—he said that John is the 'chef de famille' and Pris the 'chef de menage,' " so the wife is the head of household affairs, and the husband head of all family affairs!! Now the coming wedding seemed a bit more real.

By dinnertime that evening the "wedding party" was gathered around the table, eating the meal which had somehow gotten cooked on time in spite of everything! And it was a thrill to look around and see how the Lord had brought this group together by His planning. There was Dr. Martyn Lloyd-Jones, who was to perform the ceremony (he had told me in London when Susan and I visited his church, pulling out a little notebook from his pocket, "Will you be home August 23rd, as I intend visiting your home with my wife and daughter then for a good long conversation with your husband?"). Later we had written that that would be the date of our daughter's wedding and it all worked out perfectly to fit in with their trip. Mrs. Lloyd-Jones and their 20-year-old daughter, Anne, an Oxford student, sat next, and then came Dan, the best man who was saved in L'Abri last year. Francois, Claudie's 15-year-old brother, sat on the other side of the table, listening eagerly to every word of serious conversation. He was to be the usher who would walk back down the aisle with Debby. Max was to be another usher, and we are praying that this year in Lausanne and at L'Abri may be used of the Lord to bring him to a full acceptance of the "truth." Jane Stuart Smith had come from Milan to sing "Ruth" for Priscilla. "I'd love to sing as my gift to them." We wouldn't have dreamed of asking her to do this, any more than we would ask a painter to paint a picture for us, but now we were excited at the prospect of hearing her voice for the first time. Jane accepted Christ at L'Abri over a year ago now. Then John, the bridegroom himself, is another "miracle of grace," having given his life to the Lord, about whom he first heard the truth two years ago at L'Abri. There was much that touched the emotions that night!

"I want to go to the pretend wedding, I want to go to the pretend wedding too"—so Franky went along for the practice, and thrilled with the rest of us over the wonder of that evening. The church was built in 1100, a tiny miniature of a cathedral, with double-arched ceiling painted in soft tans and terra cottas, like a series of cones held up by the fat curved stone pillars. The 17 pews are in a center block between the pillars, so the uneven old stone-paved aisles are on the two sides of the pews, no center aisle to come up. It is like stepping into the past to go into it. Across the front are the pipes of the organ, and at one side wall, in the front section, is a painting of "The Sower" done years ago by a Huemoz man, and on the wall opposite that is a plaque stating that Farel preached here 450 years ago, *starting* the Reformation in this part of Switzerland.

How are you supposed to walk on this bumpy stone?" Debby and Susan and I started trying to practice steps. "Mother, come up and talk to the organist; he says our traditional wedding march *isn't* written for the organ. They play Bach in Switzerland, oh, do make him play the right one." So after he understood more of our American tradition and custom this difficulty was ironed out, and it was time for Jane to practice. A hush fell over the place as Jane took her place at the front and waited for the first strains of her music. "And Ruth said—" Her voice filled the place; we were full of awe as we lost ourselves in the beauty of the music. It was a terrific experience, and we all just sighed as she finished— what a wedding gift! Priscilla came over to me. "Oh, Mother, I couldn't be nervous after hearing that—it just lifts you out of yourself." We went through the whole wedding once, warmed by Dr. Lloyd-Jones's service and interest in both John and Priscilla, thrilled that the organist's choice for a prelude was Fran's favorite of Bach's Toccata and Fugue, but forgetting many of the details we should have thought of, such as where to have a reception line stand to meet people, and so on! The funny old janitor was turning out the lights, limping around, and muttering to himself as we left. . . .

The wedding day itself was sunny only in the morning. By noon a light rain had started and a cloudy sky with showers added a few problems to the afternoon. "Hey, Mom, when is Madame Marclay coming with *my* suit she's making, can I go down and wait for the bus?" This was my "alarm clock" at six as Franky awakened worried about his "wedding suit." That bus was to come at 10 o'clock, but there was much to do, so it didn't matter! Madame Marclay was all excited as she came upstairs to help give a last pressing to the organdy dresses. Perhaps you ladies in the family will want to peek at Priscilla's dress as it comes off the ironing board to be hung at the window from a curtain rod. The bodice of embroidered white organdy dips into a point below the waistline back and front, with long sleeves pointed over the hand, and a high neck and sort of Elizabethan wing collar (starched to stand up properly) and with a very full gathered skirt. Debby's and Susan's dresses got pressed next—very simple pink organdy with Peter Pan collars, little puffed sleeves, and covered buttons on the bodices, and also very full gathered skirts. . . .

Ollon was full of Swiss soldiers that day, for they were having some sort of "tactics" there, so the only available room we could find for a dressing room was the "civil marriage room" on the third floor of the city hall up flights of steep stone steps. So it was down these steps the girls came, Lydia holding up Priscilla's dress, the others holding their own, out past the grinning soldiers and quickly across the courtyard to the low church door. Max ushered me to my seat, Franky waiting good as gold on the front seat. A hush, and then I remembered Lydia still helping Priscilla outside. After five minutes, Max solemnly walked up with Lydia, so after all it was Lydia, sole representative of the bride's relatives, who was seated last, with much formality! As the organist started to play Bach, the church bells began to ring, for it is the Swiss custom to ring the church bells for 15 minutes at the beginning of a wedding! Then it was time for Jane to sing, "Thy people shall be my people, and thy God shall be my God."

The men took their places at the front, the wedding march started, and little Debby started up the aisle looking so solemn and serious, with her pink rosebud crown and pink bouquet, fresh and woodsy with fern with a narrow black-velvet ribbon tying the rosebuds and matching the narrow black-velvet sashes. Susan followed with the rosebud crown and bouquet, pink cheeks bringing out those almost-black eyes, an even more serious expression on her face. And lastly came Priscilla with her daddy. She looked a bit white, but lovely, so slim and dainty in the billows of organdy and the fairy tulle veil; it all seemed to fit into the 12th-century building. John's voice rang out firm and clear as he repeated the

The Schaeffer family, the Sandri family, and Dr. and
Mrs. Martin Lloyd Jones at John and Priscilla's wedding.

vows, Priscilla's soft and low; and then Dr. Lloyd-Jones gave a splendid little talk on Christian marriage. No one knew until later that when John said, "With this ring I thee wed," the ring was his own and almost fell off of Priscilla's finger, for Dan had been given the wrong ring! So when Pris came to putting his on, she slipped it off her own finger and then put on the one Susan had handed her! Such radiant smiles John and Pris had as they turned to walk down the aisle to that happy "going out music." (For days after the wedding Franky and Margaret played "marry," which consisted of Franky being the "organist" and "playing" on the fence with much gusto "da da da" and Margaret walking slowly around the garden with a bunch of field flowers!)

When we reached the outside of the church, there was a triple confusion—we hadn't practiced a "lining up," the place was packed with all the "small fry" of Ollon accompanied by their parents, and it was sprinkling rain! It became impossible to form a reception line, for it is the Swiss custom to throw candy to children after a wedding, and the Ollon children were waiting expectantly. Lydia, Patsy, and Anne scurried to the car to get our six pounds of caramels to "throw," guests crowded around meeting each other and various members of the wedding party, the bride and groom decided to go in out of the rain, and the photographer wanted to take pictures. We had quite a time speaking to people in the crowd, but were glad to see the group from Champéry, Mr. Exhenry, Madame Avanthey, Madame Fleischmann, M. and Madame Marclay, and the ones from the University, and to meet various members of

John's family. The reception was a tea in Villars, and after that we went back to the chalet, Mr. and Mrs. Sandri, Yolanda (John's married sister), his maternal grandmother, and a few aunts accompanying us. Priscilla changed her dress, the gifts the folks brought were opened, and the Sandris had to leave, as they had a long drive ahead of them. Then suddenly the moment had come for Pris and John to leave. There'd been smiles all day, but in the garden, on the way to the taxi, Susan threw her arms around Priscilla and wept, and then Debby and Franky followed suit. "Oh, I don't want you to go away—" The moment of "break" had come! So Pris herself went off with a red nose and streaming eyes saying, "Oh do be nice to each other when I'm gone—" However about 40 minutes later she and John reappeared. "Hi, Mom, nice trip we had!" They had forgotten one suitcase! And something had gone wrong with the taxi so the driver had wanted to come back for another one. It helped the girls for it didn't seem as though the break was so final. That night each of us found a little note from Pris, pinned to our pillows, and we each felt delighted at this thoughtful message.

But the evening was a real L'Abri evening: a late supper served around the fire, flowers, candlelight, and a time of intensely interesting conversation with Dr. Lloyd-Jones telling what it meant to him to get a "call" into the ministry, for to obey this "call" from the Lord meant leaving a *very* successful medical career. We discussed the real meaning of wanting the Lord's will no matter what it means, and of how faithful the Lord is to show us His definite will, when this desire is complete and honest. So the day ended in a time of real spiritual blessing, and people went off to bed in a most thoughtful mood. . . .

Another very hard parting took place when Susan, Debby, and Franky were left waving goodbye to Lydia as we accompanied her down the hill and around the last curve leaving Huemoz behind on her first lap of the long trip to America. Could it be possible that a year was over? How strange a thing time is. A "long year," a "long life," yet suddenly it is as a vapor. And how precious are the eternal *everlasting* things that can't end! Our own hard moment of saying goodbye to our niece who had been such a real part of the family and of L'Abri came the next morning at the boat train, where the greatest comfort of all was the knowledge that the Heavenly Father always *goes* and *stays* at the same time, with no need of choosing! . . .

We step into October once again stepping out in faith. We have been certain that the Lord has led Jim and Joyce Hughes to sail on the *Liberte* on October 4th—for the very day the company which owns a freighter had removed their passage on that freighter, deciding that they did not want to carry small children, the Lord put it into the heart of one of His children on this side of the water to pay the difference in passage for them to come on a passenger liner, and another one of His children several thousand miles away gave the Hugheses a gift which covers the freight expenses coming on the passenger ship. We were sure even before this that the Lord was in their coming, but this remarkable answer to prayer and working together of "all things" seems to underline the assurance. However, their coming is a step of faith for the future, for it means that instead of one household, there will now be two in L'Abri, with an increased space for guests, increased help for the classes, and the possibility of being able to start the new classes people have been asking for. Do pray now with us that He who has led us will supply every need.

Much love in Him who has bound us together as one family in His love,

EDITH

November 28, 1957   Huemoz sur Ollon, Switzerland

Dear Family:

. . . We had come to Milan on our way home from Alassio and the Saturday night had been used to call together the usual Tuesday class. . . . What a happy ending the Lord had given us for our vacation—and beginning for the fall's work. Our homecoming was quite a new experience, for now we had a married daughter and son-in-law to greet us, and to usher us into a well-cleaned house, and to a steaming dinner! They had come back to take care of the chalet and continue their honeymoon vacation here after their trip to Venice and their time with John's invalid grandmother in Turin. But before Franky even came into the chalet, he tore across the path to Beau Site. "I want to see Anna's baby." Yes, Greek Anna who had been with us waiting for the birth for months, was now back from Aigle hospital with little Brand Constantine. I wondered what might be ahead for this baby boy and his single mother, but at the moment all Anna wanted was the advice of an experienced mother to a new one!!

The next two days were all too short for what had to be done. The first day was all used up in unpacking, washing the collection of soiled clothes, inspecting the garden—"Oh, look at the celery—it really looks like something you'd buy in a store." "There *is* some corn this year—we can taste it again." "Look—19 cucumbers—that's the crop. We'll have a few jars of pickles anyway." Reading the correspondence that had collected in the few days after it had stopped being forwarded, answering the most urgent letters, talking with Madame Fleischmann, and packing a small suitcase for our next trip took all of the second day. And then, we were on a train again, and it all seemed rather unreal as we sped through the night to Paris. . . .

Ooooo—the deep-throated whistle of the boat sent shivers up my spine and a choky feeling into my throat. A boat majestically gliding through the water toward a dock is one of the most emotional scenes I know, and this was no exception. The officials had come, had passed out the coveted green cards giving the holders admittance on the boat to meet friends, and we were out near the gangplank waiting for the rope to be lowered so that we could run out. "There's Joyce with the little boy in her arms, and isn't that *Lucinda* next to her?" "Now I see Jim behind them." We waved violently and they waved back. All seemed well. Soon we were running down wide stairs looking for the proper deck, and the cabins, and then, "Oh, hello, hello! Why, what's the matter? You have the grippe? The Asiatic flu* do you think? Oh, I'm so sorry." Everyone looked pale and sick, though the boys were still quite bouncy in spite of it all. "Where is Franky? I'm going to play with him. I've got my red wagon." This was Jimmy. There was no way of hurrying up the procedure of going through the various lines, getting the baggage taken out, going through customs, and so on. We began to be very glad that Paris hotels were full for the auto show, and that we had had to take rooms at a Le Havre hotel. At least everyone could go to bed that night immediately instead of going through a three-hour train trip.

The next morning, we missed the early train and Fran sat by the piles of baggage while the rest went back to the hotel to wait in, or on, their beds. Lucinda had a high fever, and Joyce's was beginning to rise, and Jim and the boys were in various stages of flu and fever. By that night we were once again sure that the Lord had worked it all out so that we had taken berths on a sleeper instead of staying and going by day coach. Joyce was having trouble breathing, and Lucinda's fever was 104°! How good that red bus-taxi looked, waiting for us at Aigle. I ran over to a phone booth and called up, "Get beds ready with hot-water bottles in them; we're bringing home some Asiatic flu cases!" That was quite a different beginning of our having two houses and two families at L'Abri, than either we or the Hugheses had expected! It's a comfort to know that our heavenly Father, who is planning our lives, knew that what He wanted us to do those next days was to glorify Him in whatever state we were to be!

The next week each of us came down with it. I was so thankful to the Lord that my case only made me miserable for two days and I didn't have to stay in bed at all. The rest had very high fevers and terrific coughs and all the other symptoms. We had to cancel the first Villars class, and the next Milan class, but Fran got up out of bed to go down and take the Montreux clas. Our first weekend of the fall at L'Abri saw us carrying trays for all meals, upstairs and next door, with only half the people in the house at the table and in the living room. But the Lord blessed in conversations with two Dutch girls, Magda (the spiritualist) and Mayja. Magda came to a point close to believing and wanted to return the next week, as she expected to leave for Holland soon.

*This was the time of the world-wide epidemic!

And the second weekend? If you had peeked in on Friday afternoon—you would have guessed that we'd have to "close up" for the weekend. Who was in bed? Priscilla, John, Susan, Debby, Franky, Lucinda, and Fran (yes, back up went the fever after he taught that class) in this house, and Joyce and Johnny next door. We had more people in bed that night, more trays to be carried around, than places to be set at the table. How could the weekend *ever* be lived through?

Hilary arrived from Basel Friday evening, and assured us that the other girls *had* had the flu. Then Saturday Anne, Mary, Rosemary, and Karen came to join Hilary, and they brought Brigitta with them. . . .

The "impossible" was made possible, for the sick were cared for somehow, meals were prepared somehow, Fran felt well enough again to go down for discussion Saturday evening, and except for the absence of all our children, Saturday night the living room looked as it looks any other Saturday night: a blazing fire, and hot dogs, relish, rolls, and salad making the rounds! That was a pretty terrific weekend. It almost seemed as if the battle between Satan and the Lord could be seen before our eyes. . . .

Before going on with the account of the past weeks—I must report a phone call that came this morning. "Madame Schaeffer—I'm sorry to tell you but the "permis de séjour" for the Hugheses has been refused, as the Committee 'official' does not think that Mr. Schaeffer needs help in the work he is permitted to do here." !!! Once again we are all thrust to our knees, and we ask you to join us. The Lord is able to work in order to change this decision in His own way, but the refusal is very real and serious at the moment. . . .

Perhaps I'd better give you a schedule of the classes, before they get squeezed off the last page! On Monday evening (every other week) Fran teaches a Bible class in Champéry at the home of Fabien Avanthey (ski teacher and guide—a real man of the mountains), with Mr. Exhenry translating into French, and giving answers himself at times. He is like a pastor himself, he's grown so in the knowledge of the Word. On the alternate Mondays, there is the Villars class, held alternately in Villars at the Jean Richards' and here at the chalet. Both these classes last from about 8:15 P.M. until 11:30 P.M. On Tuesday, every other week, Fran and I go down to Milan, Italy. We talk with individuals in the early evening, and the class is held from 9:15 until midnight. There are some new University-age Italian girls coming, who seem deeply interested. Jim Hughes goes to Milan the alternate Tuesdays when the class is held in Lorna and Dino's apartment. Every other Wednesday, Fran goes to Basel, in Switzerland, but the same distance as Milan from here, five hours by train. The girls there have found a private room in a restaurant in which to hold the class. There is an even dozen in the Basel class now, but the new ones are eagerly inviting friends. The hours are 8:15 to about 11:45 P.M. Early the next morning, Fran must take the train from Basel to Lausanne, for the Lausanne class is still held every Thursday noon (until 2 P.M.) in the Cafe Vieux Lausanne, near the University. Fran has the rest of the afternoon open for individual conversations, and then every other Thursday evening he stops in Montreux (halfway between Lausanne and Aigle, on the lake) for a Bible class there from 8:00 to 10:45 P.M. On Friday we have to be sure that lunch is over early for everyone has to get ready to make the 1:50 bus to Chesières. That is the day that Susan teaches five-to twelve-year-olds, and Fran thirteen- to fifteen-year-olds at the Swiss boarding school, Ecole Beau Soleil, in Villars. There are twenty in two classes from various parts of America and England, some from very prominent families. What a tremendous opportunity it is to have them for a solid hour and a half, in two quiet classrooms. Susan has started a course of study of the Old Testament, with report cards for marking memory verses and catechism learned with stars! The classes are held from 2:30 to 4:00 P.M. Jim will be teaching the older boys part of the time to relieve Fran. Debby, Lucinda, and Franky go along to attend the classes. We expect to have the children come to the chalet sometimes for Sunday dinner, or afternoon tea, to talk with them personally. Sometimes the "weekend" begins as students arrive on the 7 o'clock bus Friday night from the University. However, some weekends begin on Saturday morning, giving us Friday evening to catch up on office work. Saturday afternoons are taken with individual conversations, usually during walks, and Saturday night is the "hot dog roast" in the living room, during the winter, with long fireside "question-and-answer" time that goes on till the wee hours of the morning. Sunday morning church service in the living room (chairs lined up, and a table-pulpit at front giving quite a changed look to the room) begins at 11:30 A.M. and lasts until 12:45 P.M. Dinner-table discussions may last half the afternoon, Handel's *Messiah* is put on the record player after that, and some take walks, while others sit by the fire. Conversations are always going on, with each L'Abri family member feeling responsibility to keep these steered toward the most important things, for time is always too short to be wasted. Sunday high tea–supper ends the week, as usually guests have to leave right after that.

That is the "fixed schedule," and then, of course, there are all the "exceptions" that pop up and are cared for in addition to this! Fran especially needs your prayers, as dealing so constantly in classes and with individuals with intellectual and personal questions, so often from unbelievers, is exhausting. . . .

No time to tell the "so much more" there is to tell—of Joyce and Jim settling in, of the difference it made to be able to send Ingrid over there for tea yesterday, so I could go on typing, of Arnie's arrival and portion of the work, of Jimmy and Franky's hilarious ideas: "We need blood to examine" (as they stand with pins poised) and can't get any." "Debby, you prick us and start on Jimmy first"—exit Jimmy yelling. Franky in a resigned voice: "If anyone around here cuts themselves, *please* save the blood for Jimmy and me to examine, we're doctors." But perhaps it has been enough to give you another peek at the busy life of L'Abri, and the wonder of watching the Lord work when plans are handed over to Him. Those of you who pray and give have shared just as much as we who have scrubbed floors, cooked meals, taken the garbage to the dump, and let the Holy Spirit speak through us. We are "one body" and He has put us together in this portion of His work.

Much love in Him whom we love,

EDITH

1958

Dear Family:

Just three years ago today we were given six weeks to get out of Switzerland! . . . Today we can only thank God for everything that happened which gave us the opportunity of *stepping out literally upon His promises. . . .*

The yellow bus let out one lone passenger who puffed up the steps to the house. "Please excuse my shoes; I had no time to polish them—there was so much to do before I left I had to *run* to get the train." It was Madame Avanthey, who had come from Champéry that early December Monday, running from her chalet tucked into the woods on the other side of her village, leaving the dozen children in her "pension pour les enfants" in her helper's care for a most important event in her life! She had come for a special service at which she and Joyce were going to join our International Church, and have communion with us. The Bible class we continue to have in Champéry is held at her home, along with her husband, Fabien, a rugged man of the mountains, ski and hiking guide. It was Stevie, a "child" in her pension, son of a Yale professor, whose avid reading of the Bible and excitement about Priscilla's classes first interested Madame A. in truth.

Pop . . . rattle . . . pop. I was busily popping corn while Aly was stirring cocoa as we discussed how we would serve the refreshments to the children gathered in the living room for the Beau Soleil Bible Class Christmas party. "The cake isn't done yet . . . run over and see if Joyce's is out of the oven. If we put the ice cream and hot-fudge sauce on top, we won't need to make icing. We didn't start soon enough I'm afraid! . . . but the Christmas story is finished, the children are singing carols, and Susan is talking to that pretty 12-year-old Jewish Judy from Beverly Hills. We *must* serve refreshments right away, but we'd better serve Susan and Judy there in the dining room so's not to disturb their conversation."

Rrrrring! . . . Oh—the phone . . . but never mind, we'll have a free evening tonight for the family alone. "Hello—hello? oh yes, *Jay*—how many of you? Three others and you? Oh of course come, just anytime. For supper tonight and to stay the weekend? We'll be glad to have you." "Well Aly, I spoke too soon about tonight; just as soon as these 21 dishes of ice cream and cake are served, I must start the stew for supper!" That night instead of putting up his old electric train set for Franky, as he had planned (Fran's boyhood electric train set), Fran was answering the rapid-fire questions of three Jewish medical students from New York studying at the University of Lausanne, and one Swiss girl medical student. A different plan for the day had been "unfolded," and the next morning the other "weekend guests" arrived—including an English Naval officer, strongly atheistic, a Buddhist Oxford student, a theological student from Edinburgh. It added up to twenty-two people creating a hubbub of questions and challenges to answers . . . but ending with growing respect and interest. We had not planned, nor had we sat on a planning committee to organize such diverse and brief "contacts." It would seem to me that the Lord Himself made it clear that at this moment this is what He wants.

Our own family Christmas gave us a brief interlude in the busy time. This year Alice's brother had cut us a tree far too tall in the woods above Villars. Fran's bright idea was to cut the *top* off, fasten the tree so that it touched the living room ceiling, then to take the top up to the office above the living room, and fasten that top to the floor. "Look, our tree grows right through the ceiling!" And the effect of the decorations on the top—upstairs—was convincing. Fresh woodsy pine odor filled the house along with wonderful food odors, and we rejoiced in the Lord's gifts. . . .

A busy two weeks commenced the day after Christmas, and it seemed as if there was scarcely time to breathe! Beds were all full at Chalet Mélèzes, and the five-bed room became a boy's dorm at Beau Site. Conversations and questions and answers continued mealtime after mealtime but of course meals had to be cooked, dishes washed, marketing done, floors scrubbed, clothes washed, accounts cared for . . . without pause!

On New Year's Eve, after the two cars had returned from the Champéry Service (over eighty there that night; fifty had come to the Champéry Christmas Eve service), when supper was over and guests were gathered in the living room listening to classical records, Joyce came over with the L'Abri financial books. She had been eager to find out what had happened during the month. November had been "low"— and I had been praying for a full amount of $2,000.00 to meet the total need, including our having added Beau Site's rent and expenses for a second family. As Joyce read her totals from the listed gifts, she said, "We have just $109 short of the $2,000 you prayed for." Then suddenly she asked, "Did you want me to count the designated gifts in the total?" "Oh, yes." As her arithmetic was finished, her discovery once more assured us the Lord is able in this generation to answer prayer and give direct guidance. The total was exactly $2,000.35!!!

Tuesday January 7th the large number of guests dispersed, Fran left for the Milan class, and Susan packed me a large "lunch" in an insulated bag Dad and Mother Seville had given us for Christmas. I was going off to hibernate for two days in a room in an almost deserted hotel in Montreux to work on letters. We had 127 letters that had to be answered, and I had typed, on airmail paper with airmail carbon paper (Joyce put together 20 at a time for me, and I hit the keys very hard), 140 two-page letters to give news, and use with personal notes, to answer these letters—away from interruptions. It was when Fran had joined me (back from Milan) and we were deep in the work, that a telegram was phoned to us from Lausanne. "A cable from America, sir, 'Tax exemption granted Hallelujah Dad' " What a joyous piece of news from my father. A prayer answer, but this time something we had prayed for for two years, not just one month. *Now* L'Abri's receipts to people sending in gifts are tax deductible for the first time! "Let's call the two chalets so that all the L'Abri family can join in a prayer of thanksgiving!" said Fran.

Lucinda and Debby (each fourteen years old, cousins) were going to take care of Beau Site, and of Jimmy and Jonny for Jim and Joyce as they were going to Milan for the class. One thing was uppermost in all of our minds. What about passports? Their passports were in Lausanne waiting to see whether the Swiss authorities would issue the *permis de séjour* for them. Would their permits arrive in time for them to go? Again the Lord timed His answer to a long time of intercession perfectly. Two days before the trip to Milan, a tall, trim Swiss policeman stood on our doorstep talking to Alice, the postmistress. Alice was excitedly waving the permit book in our faces. "Look, look, it's come—they have a permit for a whole year, with Jim listed as a pastor officially permitted to help Mr. Schaeffer in the work." It was the "over-and-above" answer the Lord is so able to give—a complete victory, with the knowledge that in the process of explaining L'Abri to the authorities, a complete picture of our work as it is is now on the official files, and the permit has been granted on the basis of that. . . .

Fran's recent dizziness has caused him to take some time resting, and in the course of that he has invited little Franky to come up to his room to have supper, and a story with his daddy. They have both enjoyed that! This was made possible by Arnie's teaching two of the Champéry classes, releasing Fran for two evenings, and by Joyce's doing of accounts and letter lists. Mr. Exhenry has translated for Arnie and he is also able now to answer many questions by himself. . . . Susan came home glowing after teaching the younger children at last Friday's weekly classes at Beau Soleil. "Guess what? Four of the children asked to thank Jesus for dying for them, and said they wanted to be born again. They sat there looking at me so eagerly. I tried to make it very clear that they might be sure to understand." Susan is writing her own lessons now as she wanted to give them a whole bird's-eye view of the Bible, and not just parts—so she is making her own illustrations too. It is quite a work but very satisfying to her. She has two hours a week with the children. . . .

Letters keep coming from people, like Greek Anna, and Aly from Holland, and Mary in Basel, and others, which reassure us that the Holy Spirit continues to work in His own way, and not by any pattern we would have pictured—but surely in a way in which we can be sure it is *His* work, and not in any respect ours.

. . . Please pray as the battle continues! With love in Him in Whom we are One Family,

EDITH

April 14, 1958   Huemoz sur Ollon, Switzerland

Dear Family:

. . . You may remember my account of the Asian flu which seemed so designed to discourage us and hinder the work. As February went on, the picture grew darker. Joyce's illness continued, keeping her in bed for three weeks; Susan had a low fever which continued daily, developing a pain in her side with it, which took her to Aigle hospital March 3rd for an appendectomy! I stayed with her all night after the operation. Priscilla became well just in time to nurse her husband as he came down with a high fever which was later discovered to be infectious hepatitis (which, of course, will continue to need injections, a special diet, and a restricted life for a *long* time). Aly had a few attacks of chronic appendicitis which made her feel ill and without energy. Franky had bronchitis at the same time as Susan was having appendicitis (he said to someone who came up to see him, "Did you know I have appendicitis? Oh no, that isn't right, I have bronchitis. I'm always getting mixed up around here. We have so *many* things, I can't remember which one I have"). Surely Satan was trying to tempt us to succumb to the temptation of "self-pity," and to sink into the feeling of "I'm too tired to go on—it is *impossible* to talk to people, or to continue classes in the midst of all this." Surely he was trying to prevent the possibility of any more of his "children" leaving the kingdom of darkness for the kingdom of light.

Let me go back to the weekend of February 15–16 to give you the picture of what was *also* going on. That weekend an English girl, daughter of a former concert pianist, student of music and French, and a Portuguese student also in Lausanne University, son of a titled Portuguese gentleman and a Norwegian mother, came for the first time. A group of seven from Basel also came. It was a weekend filled with a succession of questions and answers—questions from *such* an assortment of backgrounds! On Sunday afternoon, just before time for the Basel group to leave, one girl came up to our little bed–sitting room with me, and said that she had come to a clear understanding of Christianity this weekend, and that the Lord Jesus Christ had become real to her for the first time.

Hilary stayed on for a week, reading Christian study books, biographies of missionaries, but spending most of her time in Bible study and prayer and in asking questions as they arose in her study. That Monday, the Army Sergeant Franky and I met in Frankfurt came bringing his wife and boys, aged three, four, and seven! Debby and Lucinda had almost full-time jobs some days—conducting a kind of "play school" for these three and Franky. It was the week when Fran and I usually go to Milan, but he went alone, and he also had to be gone that Thursday for the Lausanne class and the Montreux class. As the sergeant's wife was an ardent Roman Catholic and the husband a rather weak Protestant, it was not an easy week for those of us here seeking to say and do all that the Lord would have us do for those whom He brings here. However, Fran came home from Milan with wonderfully encouraging news. . . . Emma, an Italian stenographer, had accepted Christ as her Savior.

The snow storm that Saturday would have caused anyone with a lesser interest to stay home by a safe fireside, but in spite of deep drifts and driving snow, the doorbell rang at about 3 o'clock, and there stood a beaming Janet with her landlady, having driven safely the five-hour drive from Basel to Huemoz. Just a few moments before, a Christian teacher who teaches in a private school above us had come with her father, a pastor, and Fran was having tea with them in the living room, so I had retired to our bedroom to rest an hour or so. Frau H., the landlady from Basel, came up to be with me, being eager to talk to one of us *immediately!* During the next four hours, she told me the story of her life, and I went over many chapters with her, trying to make clear the message of the *whole* Bible, and the way of salvation. At about 6:30 P.M. she felt she had clearly seen "the way," and bowed her head to pray in German, telling the Lord Jesus that she did believe, and wanted to accept Him as her personal Savior, thanking Him for all He had done for her. She looked up with tears streaming down her face, clearly tears of joy, and then went on down to join the group having their hot-dog-roast supper around the fireplace, followed by a Bible study and discussion which lasted until midnight; and I went down to the kitchen, to wash dishes and prepare the vegetable soup and dessert for Sunday dinner. . . .

The weekend of March 9–10 Susan was still in the hospital, and no one could visit her, as we had a full chalet—four from Milan, a Jewish medical student from Geneva, and two from Lausanne. One boy was a concert pianist as well as a medical student, so he filled the house with classical music—"played as fast as a jet" according to Franky! It was a "long weekend," for Monday was an Italian holiday. Tuesday, Jane Stuart Smith came bringing an Italian friend for two days. Jane translated several long "conversations" which were really Bible studies into Italian. . . .

The 11th, as we were having our first day of prayer, a letter arrived from Ann Bent, now in Oxford. She said she had received a gift for L'Abri designated to be used in England, to be banked in an English bank under L'Abri Fellowship. The gift had come from dear Hilary, who had felt led to give what she had saved up to go to America, praying that the Lord would use it to reach some in England among her friends and family, and it amounted to 250 English pounds. It was just a year before on almost the same date, we had bowed in prayer with Deirdre and Jean in an apartment in London and prayed that the Lord would open up the way for us to in some way reach the friends and families of ones saved in L'Abri, and that He would do it in His own time. You can imagine the thrill of seeing *His* answer begin to unfold.

That same day Susan arrived home from the hospital. The next day, we continued our day of prayer, remembering not only Susan's need, but the great financial need of the month, increased by medical expenses, and though we had had that tremendous answer to prayer and glimpse of a coming work for L'Abri in England the day before, *nothing* had come for the needs right *here*. No "answer" came on the 12th, nothing arrived the 13th, and by this time Joyce was in bed sick with an earache, swollen glands, and fever, and Jimmy and Jonny were sick too. The morning of the 14th, Jane said, "Let's continue in prayer this morning; I'll take two hours," and others filled up the rest of the time. Lucinda was in the prayer room when the mail came. None of us will ever forget that long thin notepaper bordered in blue, and short little note, and then the check clipped to the second page. It was five hundred dollars! And we had had almost *nothing* for the month five minutes before! It came from a person we had not heard from before. "Oh, isn't it exciting," said Jane. "You know, that is just the amount I pled for this morning as I prayed." It *was* exciting, because once more the Lord was speaking: "Nothing is impossible to Me." . . . Before March was over, He had sent in the full amount needed for the month, and for the lack in February.

Sunday morning constant blizzard-like snow with thick fog blotted out the view completely. Jeremy (the English professor) called from Villars saying that he would be bringing twelve students between the ages of twelve and seventeen for church, and a bunch of daffodils to make it seem more spring-like! Breakfast over, dishes done, the dining room chairs were carried down to the living room to supplement the chairs Jim had arranged earlier in the morning. We soon were seated in a quiet hush, waiting for the opening prayer—*thirty-four people* waiting for a message from God's Word. That afternoon, conversations continued, and we knew the Holy Spirit was working. After the supper-tea (for which Jeremy stayed) a deep discussion was going on, and the doorbell rang. It was the pastor from the Swiss church in Villars, with an Italian girl who has been working there. "Am I disturbing you so late in the evening?" "No, we are still having Bible study. Come in." So he came, staying for the Bible study with an interest in hearing the various questions and Fran's answers. The girl he brought is an Italian agnostic from—*Milan!* A miracle. For she wanted to learn what the Bible teaches, and the pastor, who had heard of our work, thought this was the place for her! She stayed until Tuesday, eagerly, hungrily listening and asking questions. She has gone back to Milan promising to come to the Milan class.

Monday the conversations continued—Fran with some, I with others. It was as if the whole place were turned into an "inquiry room," not a man-made one, but one opened up by the Lord. . . .

Thursday of that same week, Aly Meester's sister, Marry, arrived, having had a free ride from Amsterdam with some Dutch people coming to Geneva. Marry is eighteen, and has been most eager to talk to Aly, as well as to be in L'Abri for a time. Aly began to translate all the discussions and family prayers to Marry, as well as to continue conversation in their room. By Saturday afternoon, the Holy Spirit had completed His work in Marry's heart to open *her* understanding, and Aly came into the kitchen to tell me, "Marry has just accepted Christ as her Savior—she said she *never* really understood it before. I have just gone through the whole Bible's teaching with her, and suddenly she said she saw it. She is crying now she is so happy." Marry is using her time here to discuss the Word, and also to discuss and pray with her sister over the need among the Dutch young people of her own age.

That Sunday . . . just as another Christian went down to the last bus of the day, Jose walked into the garden. Jose is an engineering student at the University of Lausanne, who came there from El Salvador. The contact was made through Marco (who came to L'Abri at Christmas time, from the University of Zürich) . . . also from El Salvador. Though Fran was expecting to relax Sunday evening, it couldn't be denied that God had brought this fellow and had also prepared for him, for the questions just *flowed* and then continued again through the next morning. He expects to come to the Bible class at the Cafe Vieux Lausanne.

We all stand amazed, and as Jim said, "It is almost frightening to watch such a real work of the Spirit in our midst." We feel we are seeing something very, very special—something so *real* we all know it is supernatural. But as the victory and work of the Spirit is real, so is the attack of the evil one. We need special prayer, every one of us here. Time goes by quickly, life is so short—not only our lives, but the lives of the lost all around us. Oh for a victory over all the hindrances in ourselves, and over those sent from without, that the flow of living waters might gush forth to the needy ones the Lord brings into our lives day by day.

Much love,

EDITH

June 21, 1958   Huemoz sur Ollon, Switzerland

Dear Family:

"Commit thy way unto the Lord; trust also in Him; and He shall bring it to pass." What shall He bring to pass? His will in your life?—in my life?—an exhilarating thought in itself! Just to have God guide us day by day, truly guide us, is enough to make one burst with excitement *if* we consider who it is who is doing the guiding. But—the Psalms go on to say, "But it is good for me to draw near to God: I have put my trust in the Lord God, that I may *declare* all thy works." When we trust Him, really trust Him, there will be something to declare of His works. "I will remember the works of the Lord; surely I will remember thy wonders of old. I will meditate also on all thy work, and *talk* of thy doings." We have a solemn reason for telling others of Him who "doest wonders." Listen—"For He established a testimony in Jacob, . . . that they should make them (the laws) known to their children; who should arise and declare them to their children; that they might set their hope in God. . . . " Each generation of children should be hearing from the lips of those who love the Lord, what has happened in their lives when they *trusted* in Him, a year ago, a month ago, a week ago!

The last letter left you in the middle of April, and if you remember all it contained, you will not be surprised to hear that at the Lausanne class on Thursday the 19th, Priscilla felt troubled by her Dad's apparent tiredness and suggested, "If you and Mother will go away this weekend to rest, John and I will come up on Friday, and take over the chalet. I can cook, you know, and if Mother's not there, I can manage. The girls will help me, and we'll promise to do our best to keep the L'Abri atmosphere as it should be. We discovered that the weekend had gone very well in our absence. Priscilla had recounted the story of L'Abri on Saturday night at the fireplace, Jim had preached a helpful sermon, Jeremy had brought down the La Villan young people, everyone had shared the work.

It was hot and steamy when we arrived in Milan Tuesday evening. The weather had been so cool in Huemoz that we weren't prepared for sudden "summer." Italian Luciana was waiting for us, and depositing our suitcase in the hotel we quickly followed her to a tram stop. Arriving at her apartment house, we climbed up long steep cement steps with open archways on the landings looking out over a dingy courtyard and strings of drying wash forming a zigzag pattern at various heights. We puffed to a stop on the 6th floor and entered a room with a sewing machine, a dining table, couch, and chairs—a tiny kitchenette on one side. Soon we were surrounded by tiny, slim Italian girls, dark haired, trimly dressed, full of questions about "religion," the Bible, the afterlife. Three of them, secretaries, understood and spoke English, the fourth, a dressmaker (sitting at her sewing machine), waited for them to translate an

Franky and Jane Bowman helping me plant a garden.

swers into Italian for her. They served us a truly Italian meal in the next room, surprisingly long with a glass door leading out on a tiny balcony over the street, large oil paintings and heavy carved furniture, tapestry-hung walls and a huge wrought-iron chandelier. When coffee was served we were joined by two more girls, and Luciana's parents. After dinner the six girls went back to the hotel with us for the evening Bible class and discussion. A vivid class that night—with intent listening.

I cannot give you an account of the whole month, as I know you are waiting to hear about the trip to England at the end of May. . . . But do look in at Fran, Jim, and Arnie digging gardens for days, as we have seven gardens to dig (vegetable gardens that is, with two small rose and flower gardens and some strips of hyacinths and tulips around trees and bordering walks). Arnie stood on his good leg, and used the one that had been broken to step on the spade! At times Franky or Debby helped to carry manure up to the proper spot. Time digging was not wasted! If you had perched yourself on the ground with me, planting seed in the prepared ground, you would have heard many discussions about the Bible, Christian life, and work, for men digging together can discuss just as well as men walking together!

On Saturday night the phone rang when the weekend group was gathered around the fireplace, and I was making Sunday desserts in the kitchen. It was the owner of one of Champéry's hotels with an amazing request. "Would it be possible for Mr. Schaeffer to preach in the Protestant Chapel for a group of English schoolgirls at my hotel? I will get the chapel ready for you for tomorrow afternoon." . . . It seemed unreal to step out of the car, greet the beaming Marclay family, step into the church with 22 having come with us, to watch 30 English schoolgirls in navy skirts, white blouses, green ties, navy berets, and white gloves to file in two by two with three teachers behind them! It is such a surprise so many times to discover what the Lord has prepared as a part of the "day's work" in affecting history. That same morning we had had 38 in our own church service in the living room of Mélèzes. . . . Then—"Happy birthday, dear Susan, Happy birthday to you." The cake with its 17 candles, and the little pile of gifts, were a part of the very late supper–high tea we were serving in the living room after coming back from the Champéry service. Priscilla and John had a ride with Pierre back to Lausanne late that evening so they could stay for the family birthday celebration. The glow of excitement over the whole surprising day gave the birthday tea an air of a very special occasion!!

When Thursday morning came, I had a whole box of petunias to transplant before getting dressed to go. Somehow planting petunias in the Alps in the morning and having afternoon tea in London seemed to make air travel more fantastic than ever. Fran started the class in Lausanne at noon that day and then John took it over. He and Prisca took the responsibility for the Lausanne class in our absence. Susan took charge of the chalet, planning a "Camp Mélèzes" with sleeve badges, schedule, and so on, so that Franky would not miss us too much, though others enjoyed it too!

As we left on May 29th the month's funds were not yet all in. In fact over $400 was still needed. We felt that what was designated for going to England (by Hilary) was for *that* one purpose only. You can imagine the excitement as well as relief we felt when we heard that everyone we had left back at the chalet had had a special burden to pray for funds. Each one wrote us their account of how their prayer was answered as several gifts had come from thousands of miles away, timed to arrive just when they would strengthen the faith of those left with new responsibilities.

As Deirdre met us at Heathrow airport, she had in her hand a little book with a page for each morning, afternoon, and evening of our stay, empty and waiting to see how the Lord would fill it! The pages no longer empty are before me now. I'll give you a glimpse of some of the days:

Sat. noon: Lunch with Jane (a doctor, also Jennifer's sister) and her fiancé Jack, who is doing research work on a special grant in Oxford on the magnetic field of the sun. They will live in Oxford after their wedding, and hope we may come there to meet with interested science students in their home.

Sat. afternoon: We continued talking to Jane and Jack on our way to visit friends of Hilary's—a Yugoslavian violinist, Igor, and a Hungarian Jewish professor and his psychiatrist wife. A *most* interesting trio of people in a charmingly artistic apartment overlooking a green square. We left there to be rather late for tea in another apartment some blocks away, where we had a wonderful two hours with Hilary's grandmother, a most cultured intellectual Jewish lady in her eighties, whose personality shines through vividly in spite of painful arthritis and also weakness after a case of pneumonia. We spent most of our time in Bible study there, but found it all-too short. Please pray for her.

Sat. evening: We returned so late from our afternoon that people were already gathering in the hotel rooms. There were 19 there that night. Deirdre had brought three atheistic Jewish fellows, a Roman Catholic boy and girl; Ann Bent had brought friends; Lorna's mother and cousin had come a long distance to be there (that is Lorna of the Milan class); and Nina the teacher from South Africa had brought friends. The questions and arguments against the Bible were very hot at times, but we felt it to be a most worthwhile time though we went to bed exhausted in the "wee hours" of the morning.

Sunday morning we went to Martyn Lloyd-Jones's church and found a whole pew of L'Abri young people in the pew ahead of us! That afternoon we went directly from church to Surrey, where we visited the home of Wendy (saved in Mélèzes at Easter time). Her home is set in an apple orchard, with a charming rambling garden surrounding it, and a fenced-in field where her sister's horse lives (rescued by her sister who bought him in a scraggly condition for $15 and loved and nursed him back to health!). In the living room Fran talked to Wendy's atheistic father at one end of the room, while I told the story of L'Abri to her equally agnostic mother, and to a wistful ballet dancer (Linette) at the other end of the room.

Sunday evening we had supper with Susan, Hilary's actress sister, who wanted to ask questions as she has longed to find . . . "a satisfactory religion." While we were there Hilary's mother and father "happened to drop in," and invited us for lunch the next day!!

There are so many other days, people, incidents, conversations, such as Hans Rookmaaker's coming to our hotel rooms with some of his Dutch art students (on a tour of the British Art Museum, etc., etc.) for the discussion, and of the Jewish singer who came to talk to me alone about her own needs (she is studying at the Royal Academy with John Dobson, who came to Chalet les Mélèzes from the Milan class), . . . but there isn't space to let you have a copy of that whole notebook. You must know about this however:

Wednesday: In the morning Fran had an elderly lady who wanted to talk with him at the hotel, while I went to be with Hilary's grandmother once more, to give her another Bible study and have lunch with her. We were to meet at the train! I caught the train for Cambridge by a "hair" literally, as the conductor pushed me on after it had started, and then anxiously peered at my face—and finding a dirty spot, proceeded to help me wipe the spot off! (Who says the English are stiff and unfriendly?) Fran was already on the train having come straight from the hotel. We were met by Mike C., a South African student (saved after he was in Cambridge for a few months, now a senior and expecting to go into Christian work). After a time of tea and discussion with him in his room, we went to another student's room, where ten or more fellows were gathered for tea and to hear Fran's message and have a time of questions and answers afterwards. I wish I had time to describe Cambridge's beautiful quadrangles, quiet river, and fields with placid cows grazing, within sight of the University buildings. Perhaps another time! We got back to London after midnight. (Incidentally, some of these boys hope to come to the chalet, and we have been asked to return another time.)* . . .

As we returned, we went straight from Geneva to the Lausanne class, found John teaching it, then Fran went on to Montreux in the afternoon to teach the Bible class there that night, and I continued home. You will have to imagine the happy reunion with the children, and the rapid wagging of tongues as they wanted to report, and also to listen to our report!

With much love, and thanksgiving for your prayer support, which is so evident day by day—

EDITH

August 5, 1958   Huemoz sur Ollon, Switzerland

Dear Family:

One evening in July Susan rushed to the dinner table to tell us excitedly the news that had come over the telephone (in Switzerland you dial a number and get news), "American troops are landing in Lebanon. Perhaps we are going to have another world war!" Details followed and were added to, as everyone around the table gave an opinion or idea sparked by vivid imaginations. "And ye shall hear of wars and rumors of wars: see that ye be not troubled: for all these things must come to pass, but the end is not yet."** Are we afraid? We need not be as God's children—but—He would have us watch for His coming. Does He want us sitting outdoors looking up? No—to watch as He has commanded us is praying without ceasing, rejoicing in our salvation (a bubbling over that others see), giving ourselves, our money, our time, our energy to *Him*— and asking Him to guide us in the use of it all for His glory. "And again I say, Watch."

. . . The last letter brought you to the middle of June, as we returned from the first English trip. When we returned the "summer" began with a rush. Karl Woodson arrived to help at L'Abri, having given out his pupils' report cards in Michigan one afternoon, eaten lunch in New York the next noon, and the noon meal the following day in Huemoz! Karl is Hurvey's brother, and you may remember that he painted the

---

*When I wrote this letter in 1958, I had no idea that among those "boys" who "hoped to come to the chalet" were my own son-in-law-to-be, Ranald Macaulay, and also my nephew-in-law-to-be, Jeremy Jackson. They were simply lumped into the four words—"some of these boys!" Life's important "first meetings" are so often not announced as a "happening" to be noted at the moment!
**See Matthew 24:6.

Les Mélèzes kitchen yellow during an Army leave when he was stationed in Germany; now he heads a high school music department. The Lord has led him back to L'Abri to give the kitchen a second coat—and to help out in many other ways! We received Karl's letter inquiring about our need of a summer helper just a day before Arnie received a letter saying that he was required to finish his master's work at Wheaton this summer. Again we marveled at the Lord's planning things we couldn't have had the foreknowledge to plan.

During the first week we were home, the boarding schools finished their year's schoolwork. . . . At our "farewell" hot dog roast, which brought almost all of the students from La Villan to the chalet for some hours, six of them made a profession of faith, either personally to us, or through writing in the guest book. . . . One has returned to spend most of his vacation time getting questions answered. "I feel that if this is all true, and I believe that it *is*—there is nothing in life worth doing except telling others—so perhaps I should be a missionary." This from a 15-year-old boy who had been in a group known as "wild"! We are invited to have tea with his parents in Paris on our way to take Lucinda to the boat. . . .

We have a calendar stuck up on the office bulletin board which has an empty square of space for each day—so that the month is spread out before us with space to jot in the visitors at the chalet as they come. Weekends have been full, with several Sunday teas and dinners numbering from twenty-two to twenty-six at the chalet, and on the first of August, everyone in the two chalets gathered for refreshments after the village liberty celebration. There were thirty-two of us altogether, counting the Italian family of four from Milan here to spend their vacation near L'Abri for the month of August. . . .

Among the many visitors during the past six weeks were Monsieur and Madame Turrian, the Swiss couple with whom we lived in Lausanne our first year in Switzerland. Liselotte, the Swiss girl from Zürich, came for a week and unburdened her heart concerning her desire for a class in Zürich. Result: we agreed to go once, and see how the Lord will lead from there on, so there'll be a Bible class in Zürich in the back of a furniture store on August 15th. . . . Madame Marclay also came for a few days of sewing and Bible study. . . .

Now it is August 7th and we have gone through the difficult "goodbyes" to John and Priscilla.* We went to Lausanne to see them off, the whole family alone together for a goodbye luncheon at the station restaurant. Even then, we weren't alone for the entire time—Jose from El Salvador caught sight of us, and drew up a chair to talk a few minutes! It was hard not to feel selfish about these precious minutes, but again, we were glad because we had prayed that he would come to us before leaving, and now the arrangements are made for him to come this weekend

*John and Priscilla were journeying to Covenant Seminary in St. Louis.

Off to St. Louis—our last moments together.
Goodbye Priscilla and John!

when a group of eight will be with us from Milan. As Jose knows Italian and also comes from Roman Catholicism, it seems a special blending of the Lord's planning. Crying and laughing we said the last not-so-important things, but precious all the same, to each other, and the train pulled out of the station with Franky leading the family running beside it waving. Ten years ago we had arrived in that same station, Priscilla only an 11-year-old! Changes and separation are always difficult, but how wonderful to be able to commit each other into the Lord's keeping, knowing that He will plan our futures, and one day bring us all together for eternity—so *much* longer than "time." Our children are His children, our work is His work—we must ask for quietness and patience to truly "wait upon Him," and not to rush ahead in either our emotions or our plans for the future. He who has used us as a family unit, now has His plans as the changes take place.

Brief notes for prayer for the next weeks: We feel the following to be what He has led us to arrange: August 25th, we will take Lucinda to Paris to the boat train. August 27th, we will arrive in London for our second week of London L'Abri in the same hotel. September 3rd, we plan to arrive in Belfast, Ireland, for some days of similar "L'Abri" there, in a home opened up to us for that specific purpose. Already various ones are invited to talk with us there. Susan, Debby, and Franky will be alone in the chalet while we are in England. September 8th, we will arrive back in Huemoz to "catch up loose ends" and prepare for going on a *family* vacation. We expect, Lord willing, to be on vacation until early October.

Aly will probably remain at the chalet. The chalet will be having all sorts of visitors right up to the time of our leaving.

With much love to you all—and our prayer for you is that He may supply all your needs, both spiritual and physical—whatever they be as He sees them, according to His riches in Glory,

EDITH

November 4, 1958   Huemoz sur Ollon, Switzerland

Dear Family

. . . For three weeks I have been trying to get time to write this letter and now at last the time has come! It is so much easier for me to write six pages to cover a month than it is to write six pages to cover three months, for as you know, I am not much good at condensing. I'd rather tell it all in detail, for the details are so exciting when we relate the "working together" of the Lord's plans. As I was reading in Exodus to-day concerning the purpose of the signs God was showing Pharaoh: "That thou mayest tell in the ears of thy son, and of thy son's son, what things I have wrought; that ye may *know* how that I am the Lord," it spurred me on to write to you, for I think that today when we have clear instances of answered prayer, and the Lord's power manifested in changed lives, we also should tell for the encouragement of others in the family of God and for a witness to those who are yet outside.

All through August, just before mealtime, if you were near the kitchen you'd hear a conversation something like this: "How many places shall I set for lunch?" "Let me see now—I forget how many there are. Linette just left, Pris and John have gone, soooo, there'll be five Schaeffers, one Aly, one Lucinda, one Alice, one Karl, four from Basel, one Annie, one Marcia, three McManuses—that'll be 18. Put ten at the big table, four at the other two tables, or shall we put eight outside?" "Say, when is Jose coming back? Do you think he'll be in time for lunch?" "Might as well put 19 places just to be safe." "By the way, you realize, don't you, that Lorna and Mrs. Dugamore are arriving from Milan tomorrow, and Anita is coming tomorrow too?" (Anita was in Europe singing with the Moody Institute Choir). "Yes, I *do* realize that, and I also realize that though the four from Basel will be going on tomorrow to the Conference of Therapists in Denmark, the rest will all be staying on for some days, *and* others will be coming from Milan too, the next day—that is Dino, Ezio, and Emma." "When it comes to ordering hot dogs for Saturday, don't forget that Karl's friends from Princeton will be coming, and Miss Kopman from Wheaton, who heard about L'Abri in Belgium, plus Claudie from Montreux—oh *yes*, that isn't all either, because there's Miss Stephen, the governess of the Sheik of Kuwait's children, who is staying in Villars for her vacation, and she'll be down for the hot dog roast, and so will Vera and Mario and their two boys. Those boys brought up in Milan have never *seen* a hot dog roast—neither have the parents, so they'll have to come." "Well it's a good thing we have lots of lettuce and radishes and tiny onions in the garden, they'll add a lot to the supper without making it cost too much. It kind of makes you dizzy just keeping up with the cooking, dishes, table setting, and washing and ironing these days. Good thing there are two guest rooms at Beau Site, and that Joyce keeps the five beds in one of them all ready for overflow—they're going to be *full* next weekend all right!"

That's not an exaggeration of conversations frequently held in the kitchen as we decided such weighty problems as "how many pounds, or kilos, of hamburger shall we order?" or "Do you think it will take four or five packages of Jello for supper tonight?" For before an answer could be given, we had to discuss the comings and goings of guests! Occasionally during August we also added guests just for a meal—that is, people who came specifically to talk for a few hours, but who were not staying overnight.

However, the preparation, serving, and eating of the physical food is only incidental in L'Abri to the spiritual food, so everything must revolve around the hours of conversation concerning the truths of the Word of God, the answering of questions born out of philosophical struggles, religious doubts, a searching for truth, and a desire to find out whether there is any purpose to life at all or not. Naturally *some* who come have accepted Christ previously here, or were Christians before they came, and so their questions are on deeper truths concerning their continued relationship with the Lord day by day, the possibility of knowing the reality of the Holy Spirit in their lives, how to have a more satisfying prayer life—or perhaps questions which they have had "thrown at them" when they were speaking concerning Christianity to others, and which questions they could not answer. Of course, there is nothing more helpful for Christians who desire to talk to others about Christ, than to listen to the atheists, liberals, and those enmeshed in the Eastern religions *ask* their questions or set forth their arguments, and to hear them answered from the Word of God, or to hear their arguments crumble to pieces in the light of the marvelously clear explanations of the universe which the Bible gives. The Bible's answers are not true *because* they are logical, but logical because they are *true!* But no matter how clearly the answers are given, the new birth remains a complete miracle, for the final "I see, I *see*" cried by one who is ready to accept comes from a supernatural "opening of the eyes" which can only be done by the Holy Spirit. And the newborn babe's growth of understanding day by day, and his deepening life of communion with the Lord, must come from being committed to the work of the indwelling Holy Spirit in his everyday life. Hence, as hours are being spent in conversations here, in answering questions and teaching the word of God, those who are praying, whether in the next room, next door, across the road, or halfway 'round the world, are the ones who can call upon God, who hears and answers prayer, to work *within* hearts, while the ears are receiving the answers! . . .

Five days later at the supper table, Emma, a blond, blue-eyed, slim, and meticulously tidy-looking little Italian office clerk, began to weep and to have a chill. We put her to bed; Joyce came over to feel her pulse; Emma took some medicine the doctor had given her for her "nerves"; we gave her a hot-water bottle, a tray of tea and toast, and then we sat down to talk to her and to hear her life story. My heart was torn with the picture she gave—living in one room with a father who is drunk most of the time, and a mother who constantly fights with him. We wondered among other things how she ever could come to Bible class looking as though she had come out of a "band-box" when there is not even a bathroom connected with that one room! As she talked on, a curtain was drawn back for me to show the misery in the lives of so many Italians who have such a low standard of living, and as in her case, when they become Christians, have *no* place to be alone even to read the Bible, and find daily life so crushing. I talked to her of the power of the Lord, and our possibility of being in direct contact with Him, and the many, many different kinds of circumstances in which His children are living all over the world—some in prisons of stone, others in prisons of pain, some under terrible persecution, others in luxury but in danger of being drawn into sin through the temptations of their surroundings—and how that in every single circumstance of life the Lord is *able* to give us the strength needed to praise Him in the *midst* of that circumstance, and that though we cannot see the "whys," He had in His infinite purposes a reason for the great variety of circumstances in which His children can bring glory to His name in *this* life (even in the midst of a drunken brawl, when a chair is flying past one's head in the only room one can call home!). It is *possible* to demonstrate that His grace is sufficient for us, and that His strength is made perfect in weakness, and that His peace that passeth all understanding has nothing to do with a peaceful atmosphere.

Meantime, while I was talking with Emma, Ezio was talking with Dino and when Lorna and I came out, Ezio asked, "Can't we pray for Emma? We can help her in that way." And so we sat around the dining room table again—it was now almost midnight—and each one took part. Although I do not really understand Italian, I understand enough so that it was quite clear to me that Ezio was praying as an understanding Christian. What had happened? Dino and Fran took Ezio aside and discovered that he had come to a very real understanding and had accepted Christ as his Savior that *day*. Ezio stayed on for another week and read great sections of the Bible, listened in to all the conversations he could be present for, and talked much with Jose. I wish you could see Ezio's

Bible—for in three months it has become heavily underlined, and he turns directly to a reference, showing a great familiarity with all the books. Pray for him, as his stand before his parents, friends, at work, and so on is going to be a series of difficult times for him. The schedule of his night school conflicts with our Tuesday night classes now, so disappointing for him. His growth in the things of the Lord is a great joy and encouragement to Dino and Lorna and they have him come for times of fellowship and study with them and others.

As August flew by, the 22nd came all too quickly and it was time to say "goodbye" to Karl, who had become so much a part of the work during the summer that we felt we couldn't get along without him. However, there was no time to have any kind of a farewell celebration, for though some visitors had left, others were arriving; the trip to England was almost upon us, and when we weren't rushing around working at a furious pace, we were taking time out to gather for prayer, for we were feeling the need of a special strengthening by the Holy Spirit for what seemed like an "impossible" section of time once more.

The 22nd was a Friday and we had with us Ezio and Jose, a Dutch art professor sent here by Mr. Rookmaaker, and an Oxford graduate in History, who came last year. We thought this would be the sum total for the weekend, and we still wondered how we could be ready to leave for the two-week English trip by Monday noon! Fran had been sick with a cold and fever for a couple of days in the middle of the week, and both of us were feeling exhausted from the summer's concentrated work. Just as we had more or less planned in our minds the amount of time we could spend with the various ones needing personal conversation, and had set apart Monday morning for packing and preparing to leave, five "unexpected" guests arrived, unexpected by us that is, but planned by the Lord! . . . It was at *that* breakfast Minna believed!

By noon I was madly throwing things into the suitcases—"typewriter, letter material, letters to answer, warm clothes, clothes for hot weather, shoes, stockings—" so I listed to myself trying to forget nothing in the rush. . . .

Then Fran blew in with a whoosh to pack *his* things, and we ran to the taxi feeling utterly "messy" physically, for we hadn't even had time to wash properly. Would we *choose* to go off in this undignified and uncomfortable manner?? No, *never*—but over and over again as our train sped through the Swiss and then the French countryside, we said, "Well, it is worth it. Isn't it amazing—*just* before the last English trip, Ronnie was saved, and now just before *this* trip, Minna, her friend, was saved. What difference does it make how *we* look or feel!!"

The next morning I was able to stay in bed to write letters, while Fran took Lucinda to see something of Paris. Lucinda is our 14-year-old niece, sister of Lydia who was with us last year. Lucinda had spent a year with us during which she not only grew by leaps and bounds in her Christian life, but also helped tremendously by cooking, serving, caring for

Franky, etc., to say nothing of being a companion to Debby as they did the 8th-grade Calvert Course together. Lucinda is now back in Watertown, and Debby is attending Ecole Beau Soleil and going back into the French education—that is, she takes all her subjects, including mathematics and Latin, taught in French. We have been thrilled by the answered prayer of this school opening up to Debby at no cost to us. Franky is also going to Beau Soleil for two hours every afternoon and is learning to read and do arithmetic with French-speaking children, and teacher. John Boice and Priscilla Russell are giving reading lessons in English to Franky and Jimmy respectively.

As Lucinda was steaming out into the ocean, we were landing at the London airport. Time and space have very fuzzy definitions when such great stretches of space are covered so quickly, and so many things happen in such a short space of time. That whole English trip gave us such a sense of being caught up in the supernatural that we felt we could almost understand Philip's feelings as he was transported to a desert spot to be used to deal with *one* soul. And why should we not expect it? Our Triune God is made up of three Persons. We who are such varied personalities are being dealt with by a personal God—and it is an individual with whom God deals, not a mass; each individual must come to Christ *personally,* and each child of God receives *His personal* plan for his life, if he desires God's plan instead of his own. Therefore, why should we not expect God to have very, very different plans for each of us? His thoughts and imaginations are certainly full of variety. We only need to glance about us at His creation to know that.

Linette met us at the hotel, and from then on, she was our constant companion, taking phone calls, making arrangements, writing dates in the little notebook. Deirdre, who had done all this for the first English trip, was in the hospital, but the Lord had raised up a substitute in bringing Linette. . . . Michael and Tom, two of the boys we had met in Cambridge, came to talk with us one morning, and urged us to include Cambridge in the next trip. Two of them, and the sister of one, will be coming during the Christmas holidays to the chalet. The sister is not yet a Christian. The afternoon of that same day Linette took us to Guildford, where both she and Wendy were brought up. Linette's home was for sale, the furniture to be put up for auction, and it was a time she had dreaded, but the Lord has given her a tremendous sense of peace and joy which shines from her face. Neighbors and friends have been so curious as to "whatever happened to Linette???—she looks like a bride; she looks so happy" that quite a few wanted to meet us at the tea which an old friend of her family gave for us. So it was that we found ourselves telling "the story of L'Abri," how God raised it up so amazingly, and what the work is, to a group of people gathered in the charming, heavy-beamed living room of a 400-year-old English country house. After the story was finished, questions started "popping" and we barely got away in time to be taken to Wendy's home for dinner that night. Fran spent much of the evening talking with an electronics engineer and an inventor—an atheist, who did become somewhat interested and wants to meet Fran again; and I found that Wendy's younger sister is very close to accepting the Lord. This was the house where we had met Linette the first time on our last trip, and it was an amazing experience to see her sitting on that same couch telling two or three grouped around her what had happened to her in Switzerland to so change her life—and the next day we were en route to Ireland. . . .

We're coming down fast—wish I could see something through this fog. Oooooh, look at that green, green grass and all those hedges. "*This* looks really different, Fran. What *are* they?" Bump—bob-bob-bob—we were on the runway now, and the hundreds of brown things scattering in leaps and bounds in all directions like gigantic splashes of mud flying out from the wheels of a car were "rabbits, Edith—that's what they are—rabbits." "So this is Northern Ireland; I *really* like it. I didn't know I was going to be excited, but I am. It suddenly is very, very special to be visiting the place where my father's ancestors came from."

During the next few days, we felt the power of the Holy Spirit, and also the reality of the "battle" in which Satan's power is known to be real, in a more vivid way than we ever have before anywhere. We felt that the Lord had brought us there to deal with us personally, and also to open up a door of witness among individuals of His own choice. . . . There were moments when we felt engulfed in a feeling of unreality—sitting in a Belfast living room in a country that always before seemed to me to be only in books and on maps, talking away earnestly, answering questions, with various small gatherings of people who seemed to be prepared in a special way to listen. More than once we had a rush of feeling, "What are we doing here?" followed by the equally strong feeling of having been brought not in any way by our own wisdom, but in His plan. . . .

For the greater part, these people are Unitarian in background and in church affiliation, who therefore have always been taught that Jesus is merely a good man, not the Son of God.

Leaving Belfast in a driving rain, on an 8-o'clock-in-the-morning plane, we walked up our own front steps in the bright sunshine of late afternoon. After the first hugs and greetings were over, Susan informed us that she had been corresponding with Betty Carlson—"and I've just sent a telegram—hope I did the right thing!"

You see, before we left for England, we had felt led to tell Betty that the lovely chalet across the road from us was for sale. We thought she might like to come over to see it, as she has spoken coming over here again. Her answer was a thrilling surprise—"Your letter brought me a bright streak of lightning: 'This is it'—I was certain. I am asking you to *buy* Le Chesalet for me; please let me know all the details." We had had an exchange of letters, the Lord had amazingly arranged for us to be able to go to Basel together on our way to Zürich for a Bible class, to see the owners of Le Chesalet, and everything was under way before we left for England. Now the owners had come to stay for a few days to clean and fix up the place for sale, and were hoping to close the deal within a short time. Susan had taken care of much of the business end of it, and now we needed to see the *notaire*, go over the furniture (to be left in it) with an official appraising it for insurance, etc. And within a week, Chalet le Chesalet became the property of Betty Carlson, and she wrote: "Now I want it used by L'Abri immediately, not so much to enlarge, but to 'ease things' a bit. Go over there to type, or to get a place to rest, or for any needed quiet." She said much more, but this gives you the gist of the "investment" Betty has made for the Lord's work as she has invested in a house. She also expects to come over here to do some writing, and we look forward to the day she will be living there. The chalet has already been a blessing to us. It is in perfect condition, completely furnished—beds even made up and waiting with clean sheets. The Lord is *marvelous* in the way He surprises us—this opens up the possibility of a place for prayer, for a Bible class, for a private conversation with someone in need, when the house is full; for so many, many things. He alone knows all that He has planned for its use. It will be exciting to find out! Thus, we now have the use of three chalets—Les Mélèzes, Beau Site, and Le Chesalet.

Our vacation was postponed some days as we found too much to do at home—correspondence, gardening, canning, washing, and ironing—and then we were off: first to Milan for the Bible class, and then on to be alone as a family and get a rest. Ah, but it did not turn out as we had dreamed—one difficulty followed another: people visited us to get help (followed us there), sickness came as one after another of the family had intestinal grippe, Fran had an infected jaw, and so on, small accidents: we counted 19 things in 20 days which tempted us to discouragement or frustration. The temptation was to feel, "How can we go on this winter without a proper restful rest now?" But victory was given, and we also look back on wonderful times as a family, reading *In the Arena* aloud even when we were all sick, and taking some walks in the olive-grove-covered hills. Franky took some real climbing hikes with his Daddy, up over rocks, even for four hours at a time, without seeming too tired, which encouraged us about his leg. We came home to begin work with a rush, and to have even more illness, as I had quite an attack of some gastric trouble, Fran the grippe, Debby a sore throat; so it was a hard beginning. We have felt ourselves in the center of "the battle" at times, which though not easy, has given us the opportunity of rejoicing in victories. This past weekend began in a most discouraging fashion as it seemed Fran might be too ill even to have conversations, but in the end, the Lord gave very special strength, and the climax came when Barbara, a Smith College student studying in Geneva, brought to L'Abri by Minna, marvelously came to an assurance of her salvation Sunday afternoon! Two others, students of Albert Schweitzer College in another part of

Switzerland, went back to school very thoughtful, and promising to do the Bible studies and then to come back again. We have also had many other encouraging things as the fall has begun. . . .

Hurvey and Dot Woodson, who have worked previously at L'Abri, and then went back to Covenant Seminary, after much prayer and waiting on the Lord came to the conclusion that He was leading them to come back to Europe, and to apply to L'Abri as Workers. They are on the sea right now, and will be arriving here at the end of the week to be warmly welcomed by us all. We shall be praying and waiting together for the Lord to show us just what He would have them do as L'Abri workers. They do want to learn one European language. We are certain that the Lord will clearly lead both them and us in the steps ahead as we pray and wait upon Him for guidance.

Hurvey and Dot will be staying here during our next English trip, which will take us away less than a week after they arrive. Both Franky and Debby are greatly relieved to know that they will be taking our place here, as the upstairs would seem pretty empty in the morning, especially after Debby leaves at 6:45 for school. Most of the classes will continue, there are the Sunday services, and of course there are sure to be "unexpected" people coming. Jim is doing some part-time teaching in a private school in Villars, where he is in contact with another group of boys we have never contacted before, as well as in a Jewish school in Bex, but he will take over one Sunday service and John Boice and Hurvey will divide the others. We leave, Lord willing, for England on November 14th and will be gone about two weeks. Pray for us in London, Oxford, Guildford, Kent, Cambridge, Belfast. Linette is moving out so that her flat can be used by us as our center in London while we are there, and many letters have come from various ones wanting to bring friends with questions, but I'll wait until we have been there to tell you about it—better not say what *may* happen: the future is in the Lord's hands, and *His* alone, for all His children. How wonderful to know we can *trust* it to Him.

With much love in Him in Whom there is no uncertainty,

EDITH

1959

Dear Family,

. . . Minna met us in Geneva, and had questions to ask, so that our time was efficiently used at the station there. Linette met us at the taxi in London, with a rush of description concerning the people "who are coming in a half-hour for the evening." So with only time for a bite to eat at a little restaurant on Sloane Square, we plunged into the long conversations with the people the Lord brought there to Linette's "Flat 4," which she has given for the use of L'Abri in London in two ways. First, she moves out when we come, so that we can sleep there as well as have people come there by twos or threes or in groups (giving us a home-like atmosphere, and a kitchen to prepare tea for them), and she wants the L'Abri young people to use the flat for prayer in between our visits. . . .

Sunday afternoon, if you'd peeked into a red plush second-class coach on the London-Guildford line, you'd have seen us talking to Linette while the train was moving, and writing a "picture-letter" to Franky, as the train stopped at each station. We were on our way to Wendy's home, where we had been invited for dinner, and where a group of about 20 family friends, plus the Vicar and his wife, would be gathered to hear the story of L'Abri, and to ask questions. After the telling of the story, the Vicar came over to me and made it plain that he is a Barthian, and others among the older people argued violently against the first three chapters of Genesis. Several nights later in Belfast, Ireland, we had a group of older people, almost all of whom are liberals of the "old-fashioned variety," or neo-orthodox (that is, Barthian). It was one of the most difficult evenings we have ever had. Fran was not able to round out or finish *one* idea—at times not able to finish a sentence! Someone always was breaking in to refute and argue before anything could be said, and no one seemed interested even in *listening* to a logi-

424

cal presentation of the other "side"—that is, the Biblical side—nor did anyone want to hear the logical conclusion of *their* position. They were quite satisfied to quote a few slogans based on no authority at all, and to hang their intellects on a nail while they have "faith" in an abstract something quite divorced from time, space, or history, the important thing being "faith" not *truth* nor the One in whom one's faith is placed. After this group left, Malcolm, the atheist son of the Mrs. C. who had invited some of her old friends to hear a presentation of what she now believes, said, "Mr. Schaeffer, I'm not ready to make a decision yet, but if I do become a Christian, it will surely be the Christianity you teach that I will believe, that makes *sense*. Just listening to these people talk tonight has made me think that all this liberal stuff is ridiculous. Either the Bible is *true*, or it's not."

Fran and I felt that we had learned something ourselves that evening, and that was to thank and praise the Lord for His work through the power of the Holy Spirit, in the many, many other evenings, and the classes, and conversations at the chalet, when people ask questions with a desire to really *listen* to what the Bible has to say, and who *think* as they argue, whether from the viewpoint of atheism, Hinduism, Judaism, etc., seeming sincere in their search for truth. We felt this—*we must not take for granted the seeming ease of bringing people to a place of honest consideration of the Biblical teaching versus the logical end of their own belief.* It is not a "natural" kind of thing at all; it is clearly an answer to prayer, and one of the "results" I spoke about on the first page. Just as startling a "result" to prayer, as is the money coming in to meet the month's needs, as we pray for it. Naturally we have always counted it as a work of the Spirit when people have been "born again," but we felt we had not been realizing what a real work of the Spirit has been going on in answer to prayer, in the *interest* on the part of the majority who come to the chalet, and many who are in the classes. We were glad for what the contrast of that night showed us.

However, that evening was not typical of the rest of our time in Ireland. The Lord did take us there we are sure, and we had some lovely times with other people, gathered for a "class" or talking to us as individuals. . . .

Susan surprised us by meeting our train in Aigle, with a small frozen turkey under each arm, which she had bought for Thanksgiving. Yes, it was Friday the 28th, and we had said we would celebrate Thanksgiving on Saturday, the 29th. "Oh, Mommy and Daddy—there are two girls coming up on the 7 o'clock bus for the weekend. I've had such a terrific conversation with them, and with others at tea the other day, and told them the 'story' and gave them a quick, bird's-eye view of the Bible from beginning to end. *Do* pray for the weekend. I hope you're not too tired." You'll have to imagine the glad reunion upon our arrival, and the recounting of what had happened here, and what had happened in London. It was hard to get cooking done with so much to talk about! . . .

December flew by with a rush and a jumble of people, discussions, meals, classes. And on the first day of the New Year, Dot and Hurvey began a new phase of their lives, and L'Abri a new phase of its work, led by the Lord, to whom we had looked together for guidance. With a pile of luggage and boxes, topped by a "surprise picnic lunch" for their New Year's dinner on the train, Hurvey and Dot waited for the yellow bus, with all of us there to wave them off. The next morning, just mid-morning, the phone rang. It was Hurvey giving us the exciting news of another tremendous answer to prayer. "The impossible has happened again: we found an apartment, furnished and well located, the first one we looked at. Dino said it couldn't be found and now we have actually signed for it." The excited shrieks of joy and surprise must simply be imagined. What a wonderful seal of the Lord's upon the opening of the Italian L'Abri center. The Woodsons will be studying Italian, having people in their home for tea and conversations, having Sunday services and the weekly Bible class (though Fran will continue to go down twice a month, when it is possible). And after our first time down there after Hurvey and Dot had gone, an additional "seal" was given by the Lord for this new step in the Milan work, as Ezio told Fran after class that when we next go down (that will be in February after the next English trip), he would like to be baptized and join the church. Hurvey and Dot have been there only two weeks now, but so much has already happened in that time to further encourage them. Jane Stuart Smith was able to be in Milan for a few days after her singing in Bari, and her earnest prayers for and keen interest in the work there, plus bringing someone with her for the class, pointed out more definitely that this is all of the Lord's planning, and *timing*.

As we came out of the Milan Railroad Station and hurried across the street to go around that corner to the Hotel Florida where the Bible classes are held every other week, guess who came with us to meet Hurvey and Dot for supper together before the Class?? Anne and Mary, who were the ones whom the Lord used to begin the Basel class a couple of years ago, and who brought so many other occupational therapists to the chalet, talked with them about the Lord, and prayed for them, and who since leaving Basel have been going along one step at a time (though for a time it looked as though Vienna would be the next place the Lord had for them), had felt led of the Lord to come to L'Abri to pray with us concerning the immediate future. They were going to Milan with us because of a "possible opening" in their field of occupational therapy there. However, three days later they came back to the chalet, for what they found was a "shut door" for the moment. What did the Lord have? As they offered to stay on as L'Abri Workers for the present, we rejoiced at what once more was a marvelous "timing" of the Lord, for *never* have things been more "behind." The laundry was piled high with sheets, etc., the house was full of guests, the correspondence was 200 letters behind, and another English trip was "coming up," for we are to leave, D.V., on the 19th for London. How marvelous is the planning of our Heavenly Father; here were two capable people who *know* and love L'Abri, and who could fit right in in any "department" of the work. Anne started right in on the discouraging stack of laundry, and Mary teamed up with me to dig into the correspondence, and we decided to go to Le Chesalet so that we could spread out the work on the big table in the living room over there. . . .

We had had a postcard saying that a group from Cambridge and London Universities would arrive at 3:23 and a half P.M. on January 2nd!! We knew they were coming in a 1938 lumbering old London taxi, so laughed heartily at the joke, but not as hard as when at exactly 3:23 (and a half, depending on how one's watch was set) the old taxi dubbed "Theodoric" chugged up the driveway, and I mean chugged! How it ever made it from London to Huemoz, I don't know. The Lord brought these six, already having accepted Christ as Savior (though not from Christian homes) to us for deeper teaching on the Christian life, and also to help them see the terrific dangers of neo-orthodoxy and other false teaching which had confused them, but which they had never heard explained. Also the three from South Africa feel a great burden for their country, and coming from very prominent families, they have a unique responsibility and opportunity. Do pray for the clear leading of the Lord in their lives. . . .

That weekend in addition to the "Cambridge group" we had two missionaries studying French in Paris before going to French Africa, and seven others. Yes, an overflowing house! And Sunday afternoon the "television-writer mother" of a schoolmate of Debby's came to talk with me. . . . It was a time of endless "conversations" which were like classes. Never have we had such a "solid succession" of people coming. One day Fran was sick with a cold, but that was the only day it seemed possible to see the Cambridge fellows separately, so one followed another to talk to him for personal counsel. Meantime "tons" of food needed to be prepared and served, and so on, and in between, the correspondence needed to be "squeezed in." All of us at L'Abri have marveled at the way the Lord is working, but are very conscious of Satan's way of attacking even on the basis of the very busyness, for it is so easy to find it almost impossible to have quiet for prayer, and to allow irritations to spoil a work of the Spirit, when one is tired. We did have a Day of Prayer in the midst of this time in which the Cambridge group took part. . . .

Hurvey and Dot have asked that they be allowed to have the privilege of looking directly to the Lord for the work in Milan, praying that the money the Lord means them to have for their needs, and the needs of the work there, would come designated for "the Woodsons," rather than taking anything out of the "undesignated fund." We have agreed to this, and have rejoiced with them as the needs of their first months with us have been fully met. We did feel, however, that those who are especially praying for them should know this fact.

You should also know that once more, as Joyce worked long and hard on the "books," not only did they show a marvelous picture of the Lord's care as the year closed with every need met, but also she got them ready in time for Susan to take off to Lausanne on last Monday to the Swiss C.P.A., who will officially check them for the year 1958.

Do pray for us now as we leave for England, January 19th, to be in Oxford until the 22nd, in Cambridge the 24th and 25th, and again in London from the 26th to the 30th. Back to Switzerland the 30th, to be in Milan the 3rd of February to have the baptismal service for Ezio that night, *and* (Fran just came in from his trip to Zürich and Basel to give me this last-minute piece of news for you) Jose is expecting to go with us, Lord willing, so that *he* can be baptized at that same time. One Italian, one Central American, both saved in the Alps last summer in one week, now to be baptized the same evening in Dot and Hurvey's apartment in Milan! What a thrilling thing to see something of the "working together" of the Lord's infinite plans—a tiny, tiny sample of the tremendous "whole."

Love in Him,

EDITH

March 11, 1959

Cambridge, England

Dear Family:

It's *time* for a letter to you again! If it gets finished it will be surprising. We're right in the midst of another "English trip," and I have an earlier one to tell you about—and weeks in between. A sandwich, so to speak, with two English trips for the bread!

We usually stay together during all the sessions of conversation with groups, or are talking to separate individuals. If Fran is alone for intense answering of questions, literally from morning until after midnight, it is exhausting—it is tiring enough if I am along to take over for part of the time. (If anyone asks, "What is your work?" Fran can relax and have a breathing spell, while I give "the Story of L'Abri." The hearing of this story of answered prayer and living by faith in this present time always provokes more questions.) However, this morning, our third day in Cambridge, Fran went off alone with red-haird Ran,* a third-year man from South Africa at whose invitation we came this time, to commence the day talking with a student now here who had polio at the same time Jennifer did, and whose occupational therapist in that Oxford hospital was Hilary! At the time he knew Jennifer as a fellow patient, and Hilary

*This was Ranald Macaulay, later to be our son-in-law, Susan's husband.

as a therapist, neither of them was a Christian. Both of them asked if we would look him up, and our first evening here one of his friends was in the group asking questions. The Lord constantly surprises us in the way He brings things together in His plan. Now as Fran is talking with him and a couple of other men at the same time, I am staying in the hotel room. I've finished our "drip-dry" wash for the day (so necessary when living in suitcases) and have had a time of reading and prayer, and have tried to sort out the events of the past two months in my own mind, and am now ready to talk with you. We carry the typewriter along for "office work."

Three weeks from now, Cambridge will be a blaze of color as the lawns (so they say) are then covered with gay crocuses and daffodils; but right now, the slashing rain and grey skies are only relieved by green grass and a faint green coming on the willow trees by the river. We are not here to sightsee and so catch only glimpses of the magnificent buildings of the 15 colleges of this University on our way to Ran's room, where the students are coming to ask questions (mostly unbelieving students, atheists, agnostics, or those who are Anglo-Catholic, or taking Roman Catholic instruction, although some Christians are coming too with questions that trouble them, or to hear the answers given to others). Tom is having some come for tea, both yesterday and again today, and the evening is to be spent in Tom's living room tonight. We eat at the Copper Kettle Dive, a tiny restaurant under the street level, with black tablecloths, and cheap food students can afford! There we usually have lunch with one, supper with another, and so on. Yesterday we had lunch in Ran's room, as he wanted us to talk in a quieter place to Peter, an adult student, married, with three children, who, having taught school for some years is taking a degree in English here at Cambridge. Peter is troubled about having no belief, now that his little boy is asking him questions about God, and finds that he is not satisfied to hand down his agnostic position to the little boy. How we pray for the power of God which alone can open blind eyes, to be poured out by the Holy Spirit, so that such as this Peter may see, and believe. . . .

We had two full evenings in London—one night 19 people were literally squashed into that tiny living room, and I had to wash the teacups in the middle of serving tea, serving only half the people at a time! . . .

Back in London again after a weekend in Cambridge we had two very fine evenings. During one evening Jerry, a fellow from South Africa who, while studying with the Vicar for confirmation threw up everything and became agnostic, came back to the Lord, or came to Him for the first time—whichever it was; he *now* sees clearly and believes.

In praying for these young people from South Africa, remember that they do not come from Christian families and that they are going to meet with parental opposition unless the Lord intervenes. Humanly looking at it, the way will not be easy.

Our last two days in London were depressing. One of the worst

*At last, a quiet moment to rest and
enjoy the beauty of God's creation.*

London fogs for the past ten years settled down upon the city and oozed into the houses. To walk outside was a choking sort of experience and traffic almost stopped, making the few muffled sounds of cars and buses sound like ghostly affairs. We visited a woman (friend of Tom's from South Africa) and her husband—she is dying of cancer—and as we went in out of the fog and saw her lying there in the midst of all that this world could give her for comfort: dusty pink sheets and satin pillowcases bordered with lace, exotic flowers, but with nothing of the stable inner comfort the Lord gives His children, it was a most disturbing experience. Oh, how short an hour seemed, in which to try to open up the message of the Word of Life to one so close to death, and already in a "fog of pain" so to speak. The fog outside blurring reality and the fog of pain and closeness to eternity seemed somehow to merge together to give a desperate feeling of inadequacy. How could she be made to see that she needed to be born again? How can a life based on false beliefs, or none at all, be brought into focus with the truth at this fuzzy moment? I can't describe what this experience did to both Fran and me. I was alone with her for an hour while Fran and Tom talked with her husband, and then he came up for a short time before she was given her white medicine, which sent her into oblivion for the next few hours. I felt like crying, "Please don't take the pain killer until you hear a little more—" but I politely said "goodbye" after our prayer, and went down the soft carpeted stairs, into the fog outside. That night the heedless pleasure-seeking of the world kept me awake. Oh, do we pray enough for

My beloved Fran absorbed in thought.

people? What about all our contacts—our neighbors, our shopkeepers, our bus drivers. Do we *pray* as faithful intercessors?

That night Hilary came to the flat. She had little cakes and cookies—enough for twenty people, for that number was expected for the evening. But the telephone began to ring, and one after another said how sorry they were they could not get through the fog to come. "It took me two hours to get home from work, and I'd be scared to start out again tonight"—so the messages came. We were using our time for an unexpected prayer meeting when a knock came on the door and the man across the hall said, "Telephone for you." How Jerry had gotten the wrong number and the number of such a near neighbor we don't know, but Fran disappeared and was gone for two hours, for he had an extended conversation with the man in the neighboring flat. The man works with the British Museum, his special study being the tsetse fly, taking him to Africa six months of the year! It was a strange evening.

As morning came, and the fog kept us sitting at the airport talking to Hilary—while reports came out, "Planes delayed for another half-hour"—we finally decided to take a train, and spent the next two days going by way of Paris to Switzerland and finally to Huemoz. I must confess I arrived home tired and blue, and hoping that we wouldn't have to go to England for a long time. And Fran felt just about the same. . . .

Although we felt exhausted from the English trip and the weeks even before that, there was another week of work ahead of us before we could even think of taking a "break"—and that week included a time in Milan as well as other classes for Fran to teach. The Milan evening was a very happy one. . . . We have agreed together with the Christians in Milan that now with Hurvey teaching and their apartment open as a "L'Abri" in a very real way, we do not need to go to Milan so often and from now on will only plan to go once a month.

Following that week came a "high spot" of our family life, as the Lord opened up to us the opportunity to have six days away together in a high mountain spot. It seemed to make up in every way for the disappointments in the vacation last fall. The five full days we had there were really perfect. High above Zermatt—right up in the ski fields at 8,000 feet— is a mountain hotel. Not many people do more than eat lunch there, as people say it is too high for good sleeping, but the altitude did not bother us and we reveled in the quiet, for after 4 P.M. when the skiers went back to the village below, we were almost alone. The days were brilliant with sunshine, and we skied together as a family, Franky keeping up with us, as he went up the T-bar ski lift between his daddy's knees, and we took the easier ways down, enjoying the clear air and being alone among rocks and snow as we seemed to be away from all civilization. We had two books to read aloud together—*Mimosa* (one of Amy Carmichael's stories of an Indian girl), and a book about American pioneer life, *The Little House on the Prairie*. It was wonderful to be able to enjoy everything together as a family, to rest, and to have such a complete change. It was an answer to prayer, we were certain, and really refreshed us at a time when we were feeling too exhausted to go on. Thank you all for praying for this rest for us. It is a matter that needs to be held before the Lord, for each of the L'Abri Workers goes on day after day—often without a break, and frequently just as a "day off" is anticipated an unexpected visitor arrives, or some urgent work arises. This too can be put into the Lord's hands, however, for surely He knows far better than we how to care for our physical needs.

Fran and Susan went straight to Lausanne for the Bible class the Thursday morning we came home from this vacation, and they found a large group waiting at the Cafe to begin. That class has been growing and the weekends throughout February and the beginning of March were "tremendous"—that is, in our way of expressing it—many came to the chalet and the conversations progressed well, with questions leading right into the heart of Christianity. . . .

I am finishing this letter in Belfast on Friday, the 13th of March. We left Switzerland on March 6th after a series of things pointed to the fact that the Lord was leading a return to England again, even though all our own desire was to "stay put" for a longer time! . . .

We expect to be in Belfast until Monday morning. Lord willing, we'll have a group discussion time at Oxford Monday night, another three days in London, and then go to Amsterdam on Friday to stay until Monday, when we hope to arrive once more at the chalet! Yes, Amsterdam! You see, Aly could not get a visa to go to America as an engaged girl, finding that she must be married in Holland before the American authorities will allow her to enter the States. Therefore, Karl is coming over, Lord willing, on March 25th, and they expect to be married the 26th. She very much wanted us to come to the wedding. This seemed impossible, but we found we could stop in Amsterdam on our way home at very little extra cost. Hence, it has worked out this way, so that we can have a time of conversation and prayer with Aly and her family. Also, an evening of questions and answers.

Meantime at home, Workers are carrying on. Joyce is caring for the "books" and "receipts," etc.; Mary and Anne and Priscilla for the house, meals, children, and visitors who do come even while we are away; John is teaching classes and so on; Mary and Anne are helping with the children's classes; Jim and John are sharing the preaching on Sundays; Susan is taking exams; Debby has not been well following the grippe, and she and Franky share a special part in the trip as they "give" their parents as a gift in a real way, and follow a daily prayer list prepared specially to allow them to feel close to us in each step of the days. (Incidentally, for any of you other missionary parents who may be reading this, I have found it helpful to prepare a short note to be read at bedtime—one for each day we are away—so that the children have a message from Mother *every* evening. A tiny treat is usually attached to this note. Perhaps you'd find this helpful in times of separation too.)

With much love to you all, in Him who is the Author of Salvation, and who is willing to weave the pattern of the lives and work of each of us to fit into His tapestry of perfection—

EDITH

June 9, 1959   Huemoz sur Ollon, Switzerland

Dear Family,

... As it is impossible to go diary fashion through three months such as these months have been, I'm going to simply flash various "scenes" on an imaginary screen to give you glimpses of certain outstanding moments during these months. ...

The scene: Holland, Leiden—a big, light room lined with books, literally reaching to the ceiling, had two enormous windows overlooking a park with a little lake, the windows were framed in white drapes with a modern design in grey, a round low table in the center was being used to hold the white coffee cups of 22 or 23 people seated in a circle. Questions had been continuing for some time, as people drifted in from two to three o'clock in the afternoon (and stayed until midnight), and it was nearly suppertime. Mrs. Rookmaaker nodded her head to me and we slipped out into the hall, while Fran continued answering questions. In the dining room where there was a stack of bread to be buttered and made into sandwiches, Mrs. Rookmaaker introduced me to Cox, a secretary at the University of Leiden, and we pitched in to make sandwiches along with Aly (now Mrs. Karl Woodson). . . . The sandwiches were finished, and an hour later Cox raised her head after praying for five minutes aloud in Dutch, "Oh thank you; I am so happy. Thank you for showing me how to become a child of God." She told Aly and Mrs. Rookmaaker of her salvation—and a radiant group of "waitresses" went in to pass around the sandwiches!

Scene in Amsterdam: "Isn't it a little like the Chalet? Like at Les Mélèzes eh?" Mr. and Ms. Van der Weiden were eagerly showing us how they had arranged a living room with modern Danish and Dutch teakwood furniture and an enormous round coffee table in sections, soft white-shaded lamps with wooden bases placed around, all against a background of wood-paneled walls. It was a furniture store, and this "living room" was flanked by dining rooms and other furniture arrangements. There was a soft buzz of conversation as people came in and waited for the evening to begin. The Van der Weiden's children passed around lovely, dainty, open-faced sandwiches and tiny cheese biscuits to go with the coffee. . . . Then came a time of asking all the difficult questions they might have stored in their minds and hearts. "Do come back to Holland whenever you go to England again—we should always be glad to have this store used for a L'Abri class." This was an echo of what the Rookmaakers had said the night before in Leiden.

The scene: the living room of Chalet les Mélèzes, freshly cleaned so that the green cotton rugs looked like grass. Only two people were sitting there—Peter and myself—though Fran came in for a few minutes with us, and then left again. "My questions are all answered—and I don't think I have any particular doubt left." English Peter has been coming to the Lausanne Bible classes, and has been one of the *most* eager to ask questions during his various weekends at the chalet. "This will be it"—I thought to myself, and prayed for wisdom. Five long minutes went by as Peter looked at the floor—then he gravely shook his fair head and looked up with sober blue eyes. "No"—with an in-drawn breath—"It's no—I—it would mean a break with everything I have ever known—my family, my friends, the business—*no* one would understand if God became the center of my life—it—" and he just shook his head. There was no time for much more conversation; we prayed with him—and—"bus, bus, *bus*—the *bus* is *here*," Franky popped his head in at the door, and Peter went sorrowfully away. We could only think of the rich young ruler.

The scene: our bedroom—two fifteen-year-old girls sitting on the couch, I on the little rocking chair that belonged to my Great-aunt Rachel! Susan appeared at the door, "I'm sorry to interrupt, but it's time for the bus, Mother. John has finished with the Bible class and all the La

Villan kids are outside waiting for the bus." "Oh—" this was Pam, *"please* could we just stay on—I don't want to stop; this is so exciting, and we don't mind skipping supper. We can walk up." So I plunged back into the bird's-eye view of the Bible as the two girls hung on every word, and made little exclamations or remarks like, "Isn't it wonderful what God's done for us—and all that He promises us—it's *terrific!"* Jackie was at La Villan last year, and is with her mother in Munich this year, but came back to visit Pam, hoping she could get things "cleared up." "I thought I really believed last year, but I haven't had any joy, and I want to know what's wrong." The Holy Spirit worked in that next hour, to make things really clear to *both* girls, and as Susan reappeared to bring plates of scrambled eggs and sliced tomatoes ("so they won't have to go hungry") both Pam and Jackie bowed to pray and to accept Christ as their Savior in that time of prayer. They didn't have to walk up, for Anne drove them, and Anne came back saying that they were just bubbling over. That night they gathered other girls around them, and tried to explain the wonderful thing that had happened to them to others in that boarding school for children from eight to eighteen. . . .

The scene: the living room of Chalet le Chesalet, a fire in the stone fireplace filled the room with the odor of pine and a crackling sound of burning logs, while a huge bunch of yellow tulips reminded us of all the preparations made to welcome Betty that very morning. It was evening, and gathered together in a circle of chairs and the couch were Betty Carlson, the Schaeffers, and six worker-students. The occasion of this gathering was a communion service at the beginning of the month Betty was to spend in her new "home in the Alps," which she so generously shares with L'Abri.

Scene: a Sunday afternoon at the chalet. . . . Susan was talking to Gloria, Pam's 12-year-old sister, to answer the questions so urgent to her understanding, as they looked at the new kittens. In the next room, our Debby was talking to her dear friend, another Debby, a 13-year-old school friend whose daddy is a very well known Jewish writer, and whose mother is a television writer in Paris. Debby was filled with great joy as her friend Debby became convinced of truth. They had been reading and discussing French philosophers as well as Biblical teaching. I was in the next room talking in French to Annelise, whom Jose had brought up from Lausanne, Fran behind another shut door was talking to a Hungarian Engineering student, the kitchen was bustling with people cutting bread and spreading sandwiches for high tea—while John Sandri* was leading a serious discussion with all the others gathered in the living room. This scene was like a Chinese theater with several scenes happening simultaneously.

The scene: the garden of Chalet les Mélèzes on a warm, sunny spring day. Anne drove up in her car, and almost simultaneously I am bursting

---

*John and Priscilla had come from Covenant Seminary in St. Louis to help in L'Abri Switzerland for the summer.

out of the door waving a letter: "Wonderful answer to prayer! The Lord has given us our next worker, Anne. You'll never guess who! It's from Linette! Listen—'May I come to L'Abri as a Worker? Funny, but I used to say years ago I would never give up dancing unless I found someone or something I loved more, never thinking there ever could be anyone or anything. Little did I know!' " The letter went on to say that after prayer and waiting upon the Lord, she had decided that it was His will for her to apply as a L'Abri Worker. "The future is a question mark; but I cannot go on in the theater." Anne thrilled with me over the news, and then went on to pop her own big news. "And guess what! The Lord has sent in now all we need to make the promissory payment on Belle-vue and we can move in as soon as we sign the papers, to await the six-month period before we have to make the down payment. Isn't it terrific that this news from Linette came *just* at this moment, because we have been praying that the Lord would give you another Worker before Mary and I left the work."

For some months, even before they came to be L'Abri Workers for a time, Anne and Mary had been praying for guidance as to what the Lord's next step for their lives should be. The school of occupational therapy they had commenced in Basel in connection with the hospital there had come to the place where it could be placed in Swiss hands; the opening in Vienna proved not to be of the Lord; an offer of a top occupational therapy position in Sweden was put aside for a time for prayer and waiting upon the Lord. Gradually, it seemed clear to them that the next step should be a rehabilitation center which would be a real "home" for cerebral palsy people. There is a great need for help in Switzerland from a purely medical point of view, and in addition, they had a burden for the spiritual needs of these people (children especially) and their families.

An offer came to them with the possibility of government help to buy a sanitarium that is vacant. But, in the same time, Bellevue, the big 40-bed chalet next door to us, was put up for sale and the information reached us before this fact was made public. As the girls prayed about this, we continued praying as we had been praying ever since L'Abri began, that the Lord would remove the drawback that had been a "thorn" in our situation. For four years we have dreaded the summer day when a bus brings 40 or more children, several nuns, and priests, and our quiet becomes penetrated not only with shouts of children, but with masses being chanted and catechisms recited. The Roman Catholic group that had bought that chalet right after we bought Les Mélèzes intended to make a year-round home for children eventually, and to build a chapel on the vacant field behind us!—but thus far they had used it only for summers. Now, what seemed like a miracle to us, it was for sale! A Hindu-type of vegetarian cult had rented it for spring and we feared they were interested in buying it, so we prayed on for a complete victory, that this Bellevue which has a common entrance road with ours, and is so very close to us, would be used by the Lord. The girls prayed that *if* this were the Lord's choice for them, He would send them a sign. One thing after another seemed to indicate that the Lord was leading them to step out on faith, and rather than asking any government help, to pray that the Lord would send the money in direct answer to prayer to buy the chalet, so that they could have an independent place where the gospel could be freely given along with the therapy!

When they looked over the place they thrilled at the various indications that the Lord had prepared it for their use—even showers that were suitable for children who must be bathed in a wheelchair, and dining room tables that are round and have no hindering ledges or legs to prevent wheelchairs from being rolled up to them. What a marvelous God we have! Yes, Anne and Mary are in there now and we have a little Christian community. No organizational tie-up with L'Abri, but a common purpose of being used as a demonstration that the Lord exists and is *able* to hear and answer prayer. They will be joined soon by Rosemary Sperry, who has turned away from a prestigious O.T. job on the West Coast, to join them in this venture of faith. Rosemary was born again here at our chalet when she worked in Basel with Anne and Mary. Ursula, a Swiss nurse who also came to an assurance at L'Abri, is expecting to come as their nurse. Right now they are painting, making curtains, shifting furniture, filling out numerous government forms to apply for the permit to have such a "center," and Fran and Fritz and others have helped to clear away some of the undergrowth and wilderness look of the hedges and gardens. . . .

With so little space left, I must stop giving you "scenes" and try to summarize what is left to tell you. We have felt ever since the last weekend in April that we have been experiencing something very special here in the way the Holy Spirit has been working. We would appreciate your prayer for His continued work, and that Satan may not hinder these young people who are now interested from coming to a decision. . . . The weekends have been lasting from Friday to Monday, so there is little left of the week in between, but of course, the Universities will soon be finished for the summer, and then the work will change somewhat. . . . Paper's up! No space to even mention missionary friends who visited here or other guests.

Much love—in Him Whose time, and space—are limitless,

EDITH

September 1, 1959   Huemoz sur Ollon, Switzerland

Dear Family,

There's a dried-up pea pod—open, with dried-up peas still clinging to it—pinned up over my desk. A funny decoration? Ah—but there is a story connected with it. Some months ago we began to pray for a freezer for L'Abri. On January 13th, I see from our special book for recording prayer requests, Joyce made an entry to pray for a freezer. We especially remembered this before the Lord as the gardens were planted, watered, weeded, and as the pea blossoms began to bloom. The plea—"Oh Lord, if it be Thy will that we put aside some of this crop for winter use, please send us a freezer by the time the peas are full in the pods"—began to become a specific request in at least one private "prayer closet," as each one prayed in his or her own way for this which would be such a great help in the problem of feeding so many "guests of the Lord" here! There is never any warning before an answer comes—the Lord gives us constant opportunities to *trust* Him as to His ability and His perfect wisdom in timing His answers. When His answer is "no" we should rejoice in His wisdom just as thoroughly as when His answer is "yes." How many, many times He speaks to us in this in our prayer lives, and how tenderly He shows us in these smaller things of life that one day at the perfect moment all the tremendous promises of the future are going to be just as completely fulfilled with just as much reality as the individual answers to our individual prayers.

The day arrived when the Lord chose to fulfill this particular need by answering the volume of prayer in His own wonderful way. He put it into the hearts of two of His own dear children to give a freezer to L'Abri. He led them through considering sending one from the United States at some later date, to a feeling of greater urgency, so that one midnight they made a telephone call. "We want you to order a freezer *tomorrow*, sent up from Lausanne. Is that possible? The check will follow." The company in Lausanne, when they were called in the morning, found they had a truck passing here that *day*, and two men carried the freezer into the downstairs kitchen where the old gas stove came out to make room. . . . As soon as the freezer had entered the house, I dashed into the garden to see what condition the peas were in—and found the first full pod of the season! . . .

We praise God for the strengthening of our faith as we see those whom He touches in answer to prayer step out in faith in their giving and in seeing His care for their needs.

Somehow the advance of the garden through the summer and the extent of it, and the impossibility of sharing by description all the hard work of caring for it, and the excitement of seeing it grow illustrates vividly to me the entire life and work of L'Abri this summer. You can't really appreciate it unless you have lived through it with us. It can't be captured in words. Cold statistics of how many pounds of this and that can't capture the sunshine, rain, fear of hail, fragrance of blooms of a crop, yet each plant cannot be described in a large garden. So it is with L'Abri as the numbers increase of those whom the Lord sends here. *Since* writing you on June 9th, 185 different people of 16 different nationalities have been here (some of them several times over, of course, as students have returned several times—and in addition to the 16 nationalities, there have been missionaries from five other countries. Would it be dull to list the countries? There have been: Argentinean, Dutch, Swiss, American, South African, English, Malaysian, French, Greek, Italian, El Salvadoran, New Zealander, Australian, Belgian, Hungarian, German, and missionaries from Japan, India, Africa, Belgium, and the Congo.

In spite of your not being able to spend the summer with us, let's "walk" back through the months stopping to look at some of the most amazing spots. . . . Looking over the 20 days of June, you see the fat yellow postal bus stopping day after day and spilling out people and bags at the road in front of the dirt-and-log steps leading up to the chalet garden. One Thursday Liselotte stepped off the bus to come as a Worker, having left her secretarial job in Zürich to obey what she felt was the Lord's leading to join the L'Abri Family as a Worker, to take over the work of bookkeeper among other things, learning the books from Joyce. A week later, Jane Stuart Smith came laughing up the same steps, having left her singing behind for a two-month period, also to become a L'Abri Worker, pitching into everything from gardening to dishes, but being especially helpful in Bible teaching as day after day she gathered young peole around her to dig into a study on the Tabernacle, or Old Testament History, or some other favorite study of hers. Her enthusiasm, and her ability to speak German and Italian, made this talent of Bible teaching a means of often providing for more study for the L'Abri guests than they would otherwise have had.

A glance at the dining room on any one of the June Sundays would show you a crowded room, with a variety of people, always some unbelieving ones with questions, some newly born-again ones, some soon leaving and needing preparation to go back into unbelieving circles, some missionaries, then as your glance went on through the days, it would look as though the weekends were spreading all through the weeks. . . .

Excited squeals greeted the next arrival as Priscilla was engulfed in the hugs of her sisters, Susan and Debby, and little brother, Franky. Having been away for a year in St. Louis, and having to substitute letters for the former stream of chatter had been the first break in the family, but now came the thrill of reunion. . . .

To look over the days of July was to become confused. Susan began a Summer Bible School which was held in the living room and sun porch of Beau Site, with opening exercises, and two general classes; a children's class, and a young adult class. Jane taught the adult class and I almost forgot the two- and three-year-old class which Linette taught outdoors in the garden. The Hughes children, Franky, Debby, the Winston children (staying in Huemoz for their family summer vacation), formed the nucleus of the school, but as guests came and went, the Bible School had a large turnover of attendance. . . .

After high tea one July Sunday evening there were 5 who had come to believe and were soon going to leave (their request was for baptism arranged ahead of time). After the simple service by the fireplace and Fran had prayed, Susan put Handel's "Hallelujah Chorus" on the record player and everyone stood still and burst into song with their own joyous Hallelujas, as I explained to Debby's mother, Mrs. D., how these young people had come to believe.

July ended with the yearly special day of prayer and fasting marking the beginning of L'Abri's fifth year. There was much to bring with thanksgiving, as well as with requests. . . .

The Sunday before the Hugheses left there were 29 for dinner, but poor Jimmy could not join Jon Jon and Franky around the balcony table as he, Jimmy, had broken his wrist badly two days before, falling out of a plum tree, and was still under the effects of an anesthesia at dinnertime, having gone through a *second* setting of the bones! The Hugheses managed to get off almost on schedule in spite of the added difficulty of the broken arm and all the packing on top of Joyce's last-minute work in handing over "the books" to Liselotte. But as they went off on the first lap of their journey to Glasgow, where Jim will work on his Ph.D., the Schaeffer family had the unique experience of being all together, and all alone for a farewell family dinner over at Beau Site while the others cared for themselves! Pris and John were waving goodbye on the next day! . . .

We look ahead to further changes as Susan sits sewing on endless name tags as she prepares to pack her trunk for going to Oxford, where she'll be entering the Dorset House School of Occupational Therapy on September 9th. Changes—things hidden to us—a turn in the road ahead—but no surprises to the Lord. Nothing in the future is hidden to Him. . . .

One more change to tell you about before I stop to prepare to go on the vacation the Lord opened up to us for the next two weeks. Dr. George Seville* has been Treasurer of L'Abri since its commencement four and one-half years ago. However, the work of caring for the books in America, and so on, is more than he should be doing without help, as he progresses on into his "mid-eighties"!! Now we feel the Lord has raised up Karl Woodson to be Assistant Treasurer and to receive funds for L'Abri, which will remove the burden from Dr. Seville, although

*My father.

we will have the joy of having him still continue to be one with us in the work, as Treasurer. Mrs. Seville will continue to send out the Family Letters and the slides. . . . Karl and his wife, Aly, together will be American Representatives of L'Abri, and are now listed as "Workers" once again. You will find their address listed below. We thank God for His leading in this matter, and His evident preparation in it all.

With much love in Him who changes not,

EDITH

November 18, 1959   Cambridge, England

Dearest Family:

Once again the Lord has given me a day during which I am free to review for you His work among us during the past two and a half months—and again the day has been given *in Cambridge!* Fran is busy with a schedule of talking to individual fellows and groups—and I am sitting by a window overlooking the famous river which looks from here like a liquid street, bordered by a neat footpath, rows of trees, clipped lawns, and gardens. . . .

It all looks so *normal*, so peaceful, so beautiful a background for the pursuit of intellectual quests by students uncovering the secrets of the universe, until one begins to examine what is being taught the brilliant young minds of today and to realize that the *base* of it all, the underlying philosophy of it all, gives them no purpose in life whatsoever, no explanation that satisfies where human personality came from, or where it is going to end. Some are satisfied to go on living in the present, living for temporary, momentary, sensual pleasures; others are seeking, seeking, seeking. In October there were two successful suicides in Oxford. One girl student put a "Don't disturb" sign on her door, and turned on the gas jet; another young "don" (instructor) hung himself. Peaceful scene? Oh, the turmoil of the human soul trying to live in a world for which he has accepted Satan's lies as explanation, rather than the truth revealed by God, and in which he tries to construct a purpose for life based on the shifting sand of false "facts," which in reality are no facts at all, but simply men's theories. . . .

"You've turned into a fanatic," "gone off the deep end." "This is just a phase and you'll soon be normal again"—a few of the phrases those saved at L'Abri have told us their parents have said to them when they try to tell them of the God of the full Bible, and their relationship to Him through their new birth by Jesus Christ. "I know how it is," said Mario from El Salvador one day at the dinner table. "The whole world is so abnormal, that when anyone comes into a *normal relationship* with God, and into a real purpose for life, it seems *abnormal* to them." Yes, it is true enough. Students can come to Europe for a year with no restrictions whatsoever in their lives, all kinds of moral and physical dangers face them, and their parents are quite quiet in their minds. But let them write home of having come to believe the Bible as *true*, and having taken the step of accepting Christ as Savior, and in the majority of cases the parents become sincerely upset and worried as to the normalcy and sanity of their children. When someone comes to believe in the full supernatural teaching of the Bible, and to place his life into the hands of this truly existent God, he or she steps out of the whole stream of thinking of the 20th century and must be prepared to be considered "the oddball," or the abnormal one.

The autumn commenced with a series of "difficulties" that seemed designed to pull our eyes "down to the waves,"* and it was a battle to keep them looking steadfastly, with trust, at the Lord.

Our short vacation was really restful, and ended with the happy task of meeting Barney, 14, my sister's son (brother of Lydia and Lucinda, who each spent a year with us), who arrived for a year, having earned his own transportation and so on by cutting grass, carrying papers, and shoveling snow for a good many months! We came back to the chalet to find Linette recovering from an appendectomy and Liselotte preparing to leave to help her sister for a month when her new baby was born. At the same time, in addition to facing the work without enough help (and remember Susan had already left for Oxford some weeks before, so we were missing her), the mail each day for some time brought in only bills and papers and *no* gifts. When we say we pray, looking directly to the Lord to supply funds and workers, we really mean it. That means recurrent periods of times when our "meaning it" is tested, and tempted! During October we had to double up on office work, and the way was opened up only by strength, or special help, coming one day at a time. Financially the same thing was true. We could not see ahead one week, and we marveled that though there was nothing "ahead," yet each time when a bill came due the Lord answered prayer with enough to meet *that* particular bill. It was not a "comfortable" month during which we could forget the needs, but one during which our extra days of prayer gave us all spiritual growth in our individual lives, for which we are grateful. It is always the same story—it is during times of special need, of one kind or another, when we are pressed with urgency to our knees, that spiritual growth comes. . . .

The last of September and the early part of October went on, one day at a time, with this urgency of prayer for the various needs, Fran getting the gardens ready for winter, three chalets now to prepare for winter— Mélèzes, Beau Site, and Chesalet—and I picking and freezing vegetables with Linette's help, and working away on the typewriter (to say nothing

*See Matthew 14:25-31.

of regular meals, etc.). At times it seemed impossible to begin the big weekends and many classes, but the Lord sent in momentary encouragements as reminders to keep on praying. Jeremy, the Englishman who teaches at La Villan, returned for the winter, and finding he had some free time, came down and chopped wood for the fireplaces. The day arrived when the coal bill had to be paid, and there was enough to meet that. The first weekend brought Dino from Milan with a business friend of his—one of the first new Italians Dino had been able to bring for some time. Later we had a letter from Dot telling a glorious story of the salvation of the English wife of an Italian man in Milan, which news, as you can imagine, carried us to a spot of joy during a day of "darkness." It was as much of an encouragement to us, as it was to them and to all the Milan group. . . .

The very next weekend the chalet was practically bursting at the seams with the seven of us who live there, plus sixteen others from the Universities of Lausanne and Geneva! . . . With so many backgrounds, and such a strong atheist present, the conversations were very strenuous to say the least, but a wonderfully touching service on Sunday afternoon for which the Bellevue family joined us was the baptism service in which Mario* from El Salvador, and Judy from Florida were baptized, and joined the little International Church. After the service was over, and some dispersed for walks, the rest of us stayed and had a most glorious prayer meeting together with our two new members. It would be impossible to capture in words the very real and deep joy and oneness-in-Christ that filled all of us who were Christians, that day. . . .

Not only was there another full and wonderful weekend before we left for England, but the classes have been specially blessed. The Lausanne class is larger than ever, with 28 and 30 there each time. Fran sits on a table to teach to be able to see them all in that little room with the juke box competition. He has had so many new people, including a math professor from New Mexico, various Jewish students, all sorts and varieties of existentialists and atheists from such a variety of countries. . . . Our whole work continues to be committed to be a "demonstration" that God exists, that He acts TODAY in the material realm, and the spiritual realm, hence we continue to look to Him in prayer asking Him to send those of His choice to the chalet, to keep away any who would not be His choice for us to talk to, to lead us in going or staying. For seven months we did not go to England then very, very clearly the Lord led in this trip. We have had three full days in Oxford, with Janet Waters and our Susan inviting hospital people and university students for evening discussions. Then some days in London, also full to the brim, and now with

---

*Mario, an engineering student, Marco, now from Zürich, and Jose are all from El Salvador and each came to Europe because of outstanding scholastic work in his own country—and, although they lived about 400 yards from each other *there*, they met *here!!* All three, Marco, Mario, and Jose, are true Christians now!

Ran in Cambridge, Fran has not had a minute in between a series of group discussions and personal conversation literally from morning till night. At one time eight atheists were among twelve gathered in one fellow's room; another time eighteen "uncertain ones" gathered to ask questions, another time twenty-five professing Christians came together, but found to their surprise one atheist had come at that time too!! We feel the Spirit is working, but the results are not yet to be seen by us! We leave soon to go back to London for another few days with the time full again, and then Monday we fly to Amsterdam, where both groups and individuals will be talked with in Amsterdam and in Leiden. . . .

Are we in the minority? Yes—but not when we consider humanity as a *whole* through time and space—with the living God as the reality—the true center of the Universe—when we are *His,* and He is with us, the majority cannot be numbered!!

Lovingly yours in *Him* in whom we become normal as we find the real purpose for life!

EDITH

1960

Dear Family:

"If in this life only we have hope in Christ, we are of all men most miserable."—"The last enemy that shall be destroyed is death."

Death *is* an enemy—separating soul from body, separating loved ones from loved ones. If Christianity were only a "way of life" that made people happier until their death—and that was all—the "hope" would be just a "misery" in the end. It is far too short a life and death is terrifically *real* separation—the person who was there only moments before is out of reach—no more communication possible, in either direction.

This came home to me with a sudden bang of reality Sunday morning January 3rd when I was dressing for our church service, and Susan came into the little upstairs office, where I was, carrying a big white sheet of paper. "Mother—" Her tone of voice and that piece of paper gave me a sudden feeling of dread to hear the rest of the sentence. "Susan—is it bad news?" "Yes, Mother I am afraid it is—" "Susan—is it my mother?" "Yes"—"Ohh!" and I read the paper, with its message that had been phoned from the telegraph office in Lausanne and written in Liselotte's handwriting, "Wilmington—2nd—9:17 P.M.—Mother fell asleep in Jesus about 6 funeral Dr. Laird, love Father." The tears flowed, and my heart's first cry was, "Oh, but I wanted to tell her all about—. I wanted to write to her tomorrow—." And there is was. That wall of separation that death puts up against communication! The *enemy* death.

How can they stand it, those who have "no hope"? With what words do they "comfort one another"? And what *is* the hope? Why, the hope is that the dead will rise again, that Christ truly was the "first fruit," and that everyone, every single one who has died having believed in Christ, will one day *rise* again. The dear body and the soul will be reunited, never again to be separated—the loved ones will be reunited, never again to be separated, and we shall be together with the Lord *in our bodies*. If this is not true, says Paul in Corinthians, "let us eat and drink," for there is no use continuing to preach. Ah, but it *is* true and the moment is coming when death will be swallowed up in victory. A moment is coming when the enemy death will be defeated as the dead bodies will rise, *eternally alive!!* Thanks be to God which giveth us the victory through our Lord Jesus Christ. What a complete victory is this, our *hope*.

Dear Mother had prepared the last Family Letter envelopes (1,300 of them) and had folded the letters and "stuffed" many *many* envelopes that Friday, January 1st. Her note at the bottom was her last message to you all, and in some envelopes a tiny handwritten answer to some of your letters was added by her. She had no idea that it was her last set of the series of letters she has faithfully sent out in the past years. So many have written of the help her notes were to them, for you see the task was one which she loved, and saw *not* as a "secretarial job" but as a personal contact with those who composed the "L'Abri Family in the States" in the sense of praying for and being keenly interested in all the developments of the work here. Mother not only prayed for the needs brought out in the letter going into the envelopes, but for the individuals whose address she was writing on the outside of each envelope! She went to bed that night, praying for the Lord's use of the letter as it went out, expecting to get up and finish the job the next day. In the night a cough kept her awake, and she had difficulty getting her breath at times. The next morning she seemed better. It was afternoon before the doctor came, and at about 5 P.M. when the doctor made a decision to take her to the hospital. Before anything could be done for her in the hospital, in fact five minutes after she entered her room there, she had left her body, and was with the Lord! With the Lord she had loved and served for so many, many years but absent from her body, and from the rest of us who are still here. Heaven seems closer, and our eagerness to hear "the trumpet sound" is more keen.

Forty minutes after that telegram arrived, the usual Sunday morning church service in our living room was commencing. In that interval, Fran had changed his message to preach on the resurrection and eternal life. The Holy Spirit used this to touch each one present in a special way, on the background of the news received so shortly before. The Lord had given me strength to prepare Sunday dinner and hurry down for the church service in the living room, with Franky anxiously patting my hand from time to time during the service, but with no "break" to hide away and weep. The big crises in life not only are not announced ahead—so often there is no adequate time to adjust. . . . For me, no possibility of going to the funeral.

The last letter left you in the midst of our trip to England and Holland, written, as you will remember, from Cambridge! How I would love to tell you all the details of that journey and the work of the Holy Spirit during those days. . . .

We spent four days in Holland. Met at airport by Dr. Rookmaaker, we were taken to his home and welcomed. Twenty-two people were there that evening for a regular L'Abri question and answer time, students, a dentist and his wife from Aigle! We stayed in Leiden until next afternoon late, with people coming and going all day.

In Amsterdam there were 34 at the furniture store that first night, with questions flying thick and fast. Next days there was a constant stream of personal "conversations" with people coming to talk seriously to us, with *no* time to get even "fresh air" except late at night after the evening meeting. . . .

Home again, we plunged directly into Thanksgiving weekend. American students from Lausanne University were with us and we had Thanksgiving dinner Saturday evening with testimonies around the dinner table of things for which each of us were thankful.

Thanksgiving Sunday afternoon the scene was Chalet le Chesalet living room by the fireplace, where sat Fran Scheaffer and a young man from Cornell University. As he told us later, "I had had all my intellectual questions satisfied, but as Mr. Scheaffer was bringing me to the question of my *own* decision concerning all this, it seemed I could *not* either accept it or reject it. We talked for a long time—then suddenly my attention was caught by a spider, trying to crawl up a table leg nearby. I watched it fascinated, as it crawled a few steps, and then slipped back, crawled a few more, and slipped again. Suddenly the spider became myself, the table top, Christianity, the floor, the morass of the 20th Century. Would I make it? or would I slip back into the morass? The spider made progress but kept slipping. Then, I turned to Mr. Schaeffer, engrossed in what he was saying, and a few minutes later I had made the decision, and had prayed, thanking God for bringing me to this understanding, and for sending Christ to die for me. I looked up after I opened my eyes, anxious to see what had happened to the spider. It was *still* struggling! But why? I wondered. I had made it to the table top—it seemed the spider should be there too. I reached out and lifted it up with my fingers to place it on top, and suddenly it became clear to me. He couldn't make it without my help, but I hadn't made it alone either; the Lord had lifted me up. It was through His help that I had been able to take that last step!" What wonderful variety in the things the Spirit uses to open understanding!

That Monday a TIME reporter came and interviewed us for four hours and we couldn't seem to convince him not to write a story. Tuesday and Wednesday we went to Milan. Ran Macaulay arrived December 5th from Cambridge to be a Worker for six weeks. . . .

The TIME photographer arrived the next day and took much time taking pictures, but also became interested in what was being taught!

Next weekend many from Lausanne came up and a special work of the Spirit came among us, strongly felt. Linette during the next week came *twice* weeping with joy to the kitchen after her Bible classes as a total of *six* 11- to 13-year-old children accepted the Lord (from two boarding schools)!!

December 20th was a huge weekend! During that time Susan arrived home from Oxford; with a grueling trip across the Channel, and the trains *so* crowded, she was glad to be home and safe!

The 24th we all went to Champéry in the station-wagon taxi with Christmas posters painted by artist Allan, and beautifully lettered by Mario, to cover the village. Madame Marclay brought her usual pail of tea, a basket of cups and saucers, and a tray of bread. We had tea on the pews, cleaned up and decorated the church. A new electric heating system has done away with the smoky stove! Our 11th (!) Christmas Eve service there had about 75 present. The sermon was terrific and cut a sharp line. Two English students got mad and walked out in the middle of it! Others were deeply affected—in a positive way.

Christmas Day was a family day "alone" with only five Schaeffers, one Cousin (Barney Van Buskirk), Workers—Ran, Mario, Linette, and Olave, lovely family sort of Christmas. . . .

On January 5th came the funeral in Wilmington with a memorial service in Le Chesalet during the same hour here!

The weekend of 10th was again a large one. Susan left for Oxford Monday, Ran left for Cambridge, and the holidays were over!!!

The TIME article came out; letters came to us as a result, most of them seriously interested ones. . . .

The doctor pronounced Fran in real need of exercise and rest by the end of January. The Lord provided for two weeks away and sent a gift designated for a winter vacation from an amazing source, and also brought Jane Stuart Smith at *just the right time* to teach the classes in our absence, and help at the chalet with weekends continuing as usual. Jeremy Rutland, the La Villan teacher, who is a London Bible College graduate, preached the two Sundays.

Dominie and Mrs. Meester (Aly's parents) came from Holland during our absence and acted as a "mother and father" in the home! This was great blessing for the Workers, and the spiritual growth of these young converts was a blessing to the Meesters too.

A decision was brought through the Lord's leading for the Rookmaakers to become the Dutch Representatives of L'Abri. We praise God once again for His obvious preparation through the years for this new step.

Ran now feels led to leave Ridley College altogether (he has already graduated in Law, and is at present in the liberal theological college) and come back as a L'Abri Worker at end of March. *Praise God!* Jane faces a momentous decisions as she returns to Vienna. . . .

There are many open doors, *much* to pray about in every direction!! *He is the God of the impossible,* and in His wisdom we can expect *leading* superior to any plan or solution we might imagine.

Forgive the scribblings, but I hope they have given you a quick impression of the weeks.

So much love in Him who has brought it all about,

EDITH

May 10, 1960   Mid-Atlantic, Aboard the *Corviglia*

Dear Family:

Here we are—closer to America than Switzerland as this little freighter ploughs through the sea at a steady 16 knots an hour this lovely sunny day!

My last letter left you in the middle of February, and since then some rather tremendous things have happened—as far as the L'Abri family is concerned—as usual, my problem is condensing it into the space allowed!

You will remember that Jane Stuart Smith had returned from America, stopping at L'Abri on her way to Vienna, just at the time when the doctor ordered Fran to take an imperative rest. Jane had had a remarkable experience with the Lord on her air trip, as she has been struggling over her future, desiring the Lord's will above all else, yet agonizing in prayer as to just what His will was. When a lifetime of preparation for a career such as opera is behind one, and one is close to the very top rung of the ladder, it is not a simple thing to jump off, give the ladder a kick, and walk down along the dusty ground honestly saying, "Wherever *You* lead me, Lord, I'll follow." Such things are easy to sing in our hymns, but another thing to live through. And when one has a voice which is a gift, and a love of using it in the way it has been trained, to "die" to this is a vividly excruciating experience. I have told something before of Jane's growth since her salvation four years ago at Easter, at L'Abri, of her reading the Bible through three or four times a year, of her perusal of correspondence courses in Bible study (taking exams even in her dressing room at the opera sometimes), of her throwing aside, temporarily, other books to read well-written Christian biographies and then such works as F. B. Meyer, Andrew Murray, etc., as well as her deep prayer life, and her witness among others. But I haven't told of how as time went on she began to feel the gentle leading of the Lord out of opera altogether. As hints of what was going on within her were told as she asked us for prayer, we prayed for her and committed her to the Lord's direct leading. . . . In the end, it all comes back to this: Do we *really* believe He exists? And do we *live* on the basis of His existence?

On the air trip from Paris to Geneva, one motor suddenly stopped on the two-motor plane in which Jane was riding. Soon after that something went wrong with the *other* motor. Everyone was told to remove their glasses, etc., and directions were phoned in to the Geneva airport to prepare the field for a crash landing. Ambulances were ready, and fire-fighting equipment, and all other planes were moved to clear the field. Meantime Jane prayed, as her whole life suddenly seemed to slide past her eyes as a film, and there was nothing in life more important than *doing* the Lord's will. "Oh, Lord, if it be Thy will, please give me a longer time; please bring this plane in safely, and the rest of my life belongs to You in a very real way." . . .

Thus it was that when Jane arrived at the chalet, and found that we were needing to go away to carry out the doctor's orders, she offered to stay and teach classes. But when we returned, she went on her way to Vienna, praying for the Lord's strength for the next step on the "way" she had taken, the "way" where He was leading. Her manager, one of the leading opera managers in the world, was aghast at her decision to leave opera, but as she talked on for hours, telling him of all she believed and of the reality she had found in her life with the Lord, and of His definite leading in recent months, he became wistful, and admitted that *he* was a most unhappy person himself, finishing by saying that perhaps he would visit L'Abri someday to find out more! As she prayed there in Vienna for clear guidance, Jane became convinced that the Lord was leading her back to the chalet to be a L'Abri Worker.

"But what about her singing?" I can hear some of you say. I feel that all too often we Christians feel that the Lord *must* use the talents we think are important, hence we feel a talented pianist, when born again, *must* be used in some outstanding way to play the piano for Christian gatherings; a talented surgeon *must* become a medical missionary, if he feels called to the mission field; a talented singer *must* sing in some outstanding Christian meeting so that the largest number of people can hear that voice singing Christian hymns. Perhaps the Lord will use the most outstanding, or all of a person's talents, but perhaps not, also. The only possible way for a person to *truly* trust Him and His wisdom, it seems to us, is to let *Him* choose that which is His will for us to do. If we are going to say, "Anything Lord, within this realm"—then we have set our own limits! Who are we to say what will bring the most glory to God? Our lives are to glorify *Him*. Glorify Him before whom? Before men? Yes, but also before demons who are watching us so avidly for sin and self to taunt our Lord about us (as in the book of Job), and before the watching heavenly hosts of angels. Who is to say whether the *using* of a talent—or the willingness to *not* use the talent, is to glorify the Lord the most? Only He can know.

So Jane became a Worker, living at Chesalet, where she can take people for Bible study, have some for coffee and conversation and so on, helping with the teaching of classes, and all the spiritual work of L'Abri. She helps with the writing of the monthly prayer lists, takes great sections of time for prayer, but also makes beds, helps clean Chesalet, digs in the garden, washes dishes, pitching into the family life and work of L'Abri just as all the Workers do. One March Monday prayer day, while Jane was taking her prayer time in the living room of Chesalet (which we now set aside on Mondays as the prayer room) the thought of her costumes, lying folded away in trunks under the eaves of a dusty apartment house attic in Milan came constantly to her. And in her prayer time, she gave them to the Lord. It was another part of the "death" I have been speaking of, death to something which had meant so much to her in the past. A singer's costumes (in her case costumes for the lead part of several operas, as she has always sung the lead dramatic soprano parts) are more than just garments, for woven into them are hours of designing, and they seem to be a blend of the individual's personality and ability, as well as being full of memories of the past. In addition, these costumes of hers are elaborate and gorgeous, museum pieces of brocades and gold-embroidered velvets, satins, hand-painted trains, with matching accessories including fabulous headpieces and wigs, which represent much money. "Lord, take them—I give them to Thee." It can be quickly said, but to say that about anything that means as much to you as these did to Jane is to come to another place of reality in your life before the Lord. As Jane looked out over the field below Betty's chalet (the one Betty bought last fall), she prayed that the Lord would use the costumes to help begin a chapel building there for L'Abri's Sunday services.

So it was that on April 6th Jane, Rosalind, and I sat in a Milan apartment living room, surrounded by a dazzling display of costumes spread out on every available chair and couch and overlapping each other, and prayed together, asking the Lord to find a buyer for them, if it were His will, that they might turn into stone and wood to be placed in that field for a chapel. . . .

The rest of the three months' happenings had better be condensed into a kind of "Ship's Log" account, but first, perhaps you are curious as to how we happen to be on this freighter with its prow pointed straight toward New York—taking us mile by mile farther away from those who are caring for the L'Abri work the Lord has given them to do during our absence.

After the news of Mother's death reached us at the beginning of January, we began to pray specifically for the Lord's will to be clearly shown as to when and how we might visit the States, to see my father, Fran's mother, and to make arrangements for the sending out of this Family Letter in the future, and other L'Abri business. It has been *six* years since we have been in the States—L'Abri will be *five* years old this July—and it seemed a logical time to go, yet we didn't feel we should suddenly take the reins into our own hands and make plans for this piece of our lives, as though the Lord's will didn't matter in this. *If it was His will for us to go,* then He could give unmistakable direction to us in this as in any other part of the work. Hence we continued in prayer, and went on with the busy work of the moment, making one or two inquiries as to the cost of transportation. One Monday in February, the mail brought several letters which together gave us an indication of the direction in which the Lord was leading. One letter was from our friend, M. Jean Andre of Andre et Cie, in Lausanne, whose business includes shipping; he was answering an inquiry we had made about freighters, with an offer of a place for Fran and myself, Debby, and

Franky on a particular freighter leaving for New York sometime in April and returning sometime in July on the same ship. He quoted a very low price, making the trip a partial gift. Three other letters arriving in the same mail had checks in them, coming from widely separated places in the United States and each designated for "going home to see your father." The *total* amount of the checks was exactly to the penny the cost given for the round-trip voyage on the ship for the four of us. Needless to say, the prayer list in the day of prayer that day had added to it an item for praise!! It seemed almost unbelievable that the Lord had sent such a combination of things in *one* mail! As you will see when I tell you of some of the things which were going on in L'Abri over that same period of time, we had little time to think about going to America, or to make specific plans as to living arrangements, etc., there, but one thing after another worked out, and fit together so that as we go, details seem to be falling into place in a way which assures us further that *He is* planning those days ahead. As it is all in His plan, we wait with interest to see how He will work out the time, to accomplish whatever He is taking us there to do. We do not look upon these short three months as a "furlough" or as a "speaking trip." We believe that Lord is taking us to be with our parents for some time, and to do the needed L'Abri business. As someone in St. Louis has offered to take Mother's place in getting out the Family letter, we felt it to be necessary to talk with her and pray with her, asking the Lord to show us His will in the matter. (There is a dear one who has faithfully prayed for years for L'Abri, in Canada, who also offered to do this Family letter work). In going to St. Louis, it seemed right that Fran should accept a speaking engagement there at the time of the Baccalaureate of Covenant Seminary. Also as you realize, we shall be seeing Priscilla and John there. . . . Now to go back—

On February 16th Jane returned from Vienna as a Worker, bag and baggage, no longer temporary, amid much rejoicing!! . . . Then on February 22nd, in our talk and prayer with Deirdre before her going back to England, she asked us when we could come again to England, and in a very short time, a calendar was studied together, a 10-day period was found which seemed possible from every angle and which fit in perfectly with several widely separated factors that needed to be considered. We looked at the condition of the "English Fund" and discovered that there was just enough for one more trip, as we dispatched three telegrams: one to Oxford to Sue, one to Cambridge to Ran, and one to Holland to Rookmaakers. By the next morning the answers had arrived in the affirmative from all three places, agreeing on the time. Deirdre was called by telephone in Zermatt, where she was spending a day or two with her mother, and everything fell into place for another English trip. As we were marveling over the rapidity of it all (at a time when we had been too busy to even think of another English-Dutch trip), we realized that with our going to America, we could not possibly have gone to England again until next October, which would have made almost a year between trips!! . . .

Linette has felt led of the Lord not only to give up her dancing career to become a L'Abri Worker at the chalet, but to put her apartment in London at the disposal of L'Abri just as Betty has done with Chalet Chesalet. . . .

On March 8th we arrived in England, to be met by Hugh at the air station in London's West End. We went by taxi to Liverpool Street Station, where we took a train for Cambridge, with rapid-fire conversation all the way across the city! Ran came to talk to us that evening as we arrived in Cambridge, to give us the schedule for our time there. The Lord marvelously worked in those short days of concentrated conversation. Fran talked to individuals and groups of fellows from ten-thirty in the morning until midnight each day. One night thirteen atheists gathered to ask questions, another night there were over twenty Christians who felt the Lord had given a message especially meant for them through a work of the Holy Spirit. One afternoon in the pouring rain, sitting by the river Cam on a bench after a walk, the atheist who asked the most questions during the last Cambridge trip come to a decision that God *does* exist, the God of the Bible; that this Word *is* His Word, the truth; and he accepted the Savior as his own Savior. Another afternoon we were sitting by one of the gas fireplaces in a room overlooking a series of majestic spires, and a man from Kenya Colony also came "out of darkness into the light"—he too had been an atheist! March 12th found us traveling on to Oxford to be met by Susan, who told us of how the Lord had worked in answer to prayer there. Susan has been joined in her early-morning prayer times in the tower room of her girls' dormitory by Veronica, who has been growing in her understanding and Christian life. They prayed together for the "impossible" matter of a room for our L'Abri evening, and found a splendid private living room in a hotel, which Veronica said she would like to rent with her own spending money as her gift to the Lord (a real sacrifice for her). Then they were amazingly led into contact with students, conversations opened up, leading to a number wanting to come. Twenty were there that night, ten fellows from the University, ten girls from Susan's school. An atheist from Australia led the questioning time and the Lord used it to "shake" several into much thinking over their own position. The girls rushed off at 11 P.M. to make their deadline in the dorm while Sue and Veronica stayed up till the wee hours talking to one girl who made a profession of faith that night. The fellows were loath to end the evening and asked if we would stay over Sunday afternoon. Twenty-four gathered in an Oxford student's room for "coffee at two," which ended up in an all-afternoon question-and-answer session! The whole time was amazing in its working out so smoothly, yet without human planning. On to London, Monday, March 14th, to stay two days with our time completely full of people coming one after another to the flat, with groups in the evenings. . . . One afternoon Fran spoke to a group of men at Oak Hill Theological College.

March 16th found us in Holland met at the airport by Sue S., so recently saved! We were driven to Rookmaakers, where people were invited for a simple buffet supper, twenty-two for the evening; again the questions continued until after midnight. (We were locked out of our hotel coming in too late, and had quite a time arousing someone to let us in!) On to Amsterdam the next day for a very worthwhile evening with a group coming to ask questions, etc., at Dominie Meester's home. The next day we went quite a distance by train to Harold's home, where we had lunch and the afternoon talking with his parents, who have become interested through the change in his life. They expect to visit L'Abri in August. That night we were back in Amsterdam in time for the gathering in "Arty/Home" (the furniture store of Van der Weidens'), where another intensive evening of questions and answers was spent. March 19th we were back from England and Holland exhausted from a bumpy air trip on top of the intensive ten days—to find not a "free evening" *before* the weekend, but a weekend *starting* with some very difficult conversation ahead of us, as among others there was an outspoken Irishman with Hindu leanings, and a superior sort of atheistic Jewish fellow, formerly a newspaperman, now studying medicine. It was one of those moments Fran and I face when it is a great temptation to simply run away into the woods! Only by the grace of God can we face the difficult type of conversations we must plunge into when rest is longed for. It surely is *not* possible in our own strength, not at any time, and most *impossible* when we are exhausted. There are times at the chalet when all of us feel the "spiritual battle" most vividly, as if a heavy darkness of Satan's power were closing in upon us, and this was one of them. How thankful we are that there are faithful prayer helpers engaging in the fight too!

March 23rd was the L'Abri Annual Members' Meeting with Georges Exhenry coming for the meeting. At our special tea Jane remarked, looking around at the room full of those born again at L'Abri, "Not one of us would be here if it hadn't been for Mr. Exhenry and his salvation, leading to the Schaeffers' being put out." . . .

March 28th Anne Bent and Ron Clarke were married at 2 P.M. in the Chalet les Mélèzes living room with the reception at the Central Hotel in Villars. A general housecleaning of the living room was undertaken by all of us in the morning, and it was transformed into a veritable garden with 200 daffodils, one bouquet of yellow tulips, and much ivy, forsythia, and woodsy bark arranged around and in the fireplace. Barney played the wedding march, Linette was the bridesmaid in the turquoise dress she managed to make herself "in between," the bride was dressed in a lovely white lace wedding gown, and everything went off beautifully, with "substitutes" having arrived to help out at Bellevue, freeing the three girls to come to the wedding, and two patients who are less handicapped being brought in their wheelchairs for their first time at a wedding! . . .

On March 29th, Ran Macaulay arrived as a L'Abri Worker, after a time which would take as long as Jane's story to tell about, during which the Holy Spirit has clearly led him in spite of a variety of opposition. We rejoice at his safe arrival as thought his coming had been through "dangerous waters" physically. March 31st Madame Marclay came to help me sew in preparation for coming to America, with some new summer clothing not often needed in the mountains. . . .

After a wildly busy two weeks, April 11th the church held a morning communion service with Franky joining church, Georges Exhenry having come from Champéry especially for it, to "examine" Franky for membership. That same afternoon there were three more arrivals. One was Rupert from England.

I won't even try to list Easter Sunday and the very full time we had! Then came Olave's return from England, where she had had an operation, and Tuesday's birthday dinner for Susan (a month early as we will be in America and she in Oxford on that birthday) nor will I describe Sue's leaving amid Franky and Debby's tearful farewells on Wednesday—for three months of being separated by ocean!

Nor will I try to list the *log entries* for our last weekend at the chalet, with a wonderful evening communion service with twenty-seven there. I won't try to go into all the phone calls and delays of the ship's leaving, changes of plans, etc., . . . so that as we sat in a Paris hotel lounge at one A.M. having a most intense L'Abri conversation, both Fran and I felt as though we were in a dream—and hadn't left home after all!!

We left Europe with a great prayer burden for the work in each place, but with thankful hearts for the Workers the Lord has placed there to care for His work. In Huemoz and Lausanne there are six Workers from six countries whom the Lord led and brought together in that Swiss spot on the earth's map, in His own marvelous way

With much love to you each one, in this letter I am bringing to America, instead of sending—in the name of Him who stays, comes with us, and goes before each of you—our *omnipresent* Heavenly Father,

EDITH

AFTERWORD

The end of this book is not in any way the end of a story, nor is it the last letter in the pile of letters. As I told you in the Foreword, the letters have been "cut" or "amputated" or "pruned," whichever word you prefer. They have covered a period of thirteen years—but there are twenty-six to come!

Please remember as you put the book down that month by month, year by year, as these letters were written, there was *no* way of knowing what was ahead—no way of knowing there would be a growing, developing, changing L'Abri, tapes, films, books written, conferences, and so on—not a single *thing* of what might be ahead was given to us. We lived in the *present*.

Reading the letters for the first time in many, many years has been for me an experience of amazement, as well as of sharp, vivid memory. I feel an awe of increased realization of what *God* has done, without fanfare. He has constantly answered prayer to show us that we were not doing it on our own energy. Part of the recognition of the reality of God's Word being true and dependable is the reality of "the battle," as well as the reality of the provision of needs. Job's history is in some measure the history of each of God's people.

This is a "part one," a "first volume" of a continuing story. As you put this volume down, you do not know what to expect when you travel to L'Abri. Fran is in Heaven, so you won't find him in the Swiss Alps. That sentence is too obvious, perhaps, but it is important not to expect history to be frozen, to have waited for you to find out what it was like twenty-five years ago! You must read on to get the story, and to have an understanding of how God unfolded further plans, or branches, or diversity on an unchangeable base of presenting true truth—in a changing world.

You need to know that up to this point, when the word *guests* is used, it is valid and truthful as a description of people invited to a home. We did not "charge" anything in those early days, or ask anyone to contribute. People helped with dishes, gardening, and so forth, because that is what we were doing when they wanted to ask questions! We did not have any "servants" to clean toilets, dig manure, chop onions, or cut grass. We shared our food and electricity, and washed clothing and bedding and hung it up, often talking to someone as we hung up sheets. We prayed for sufficient money so that we might have no need to turn people away, but we prayed for the Lord's people to come, and for the Lord to keep us from having too many. We still do diverse work, but there are differences.

Just in case you do not have the second book yet, you need to know that present-day L'Abri does have a study opportunity called "Farel House" and that there is a daily fee of ten or twelve dollars (depending on the exchange rate of money) for someone coming to study at any branch. That in no way meets the cost of rents, mortgages, electricity, food, Workers' salaries, insurance, taxes, etc., so the work still continues with the need of praying for the material needs to be met with gifts; but people can no longer all be cared for as "guests" in the early sense of that word, and many of them come as "students" for something closer to a period of three months.

I have written this P.S. to avoid confusion until you read the second volume. Now that I have "relived" the first twelve years in Switzerland, which represent only the first six years of L'Abri, I am eager to go on and relive the next twenty-six—and invite you to walk through those years with me this time!

With love,

EDITH